RUGBY COLLEGE OF F.E
624653

POL MARTIN

A GUIDE TO MODERN AMERICAN COOKING

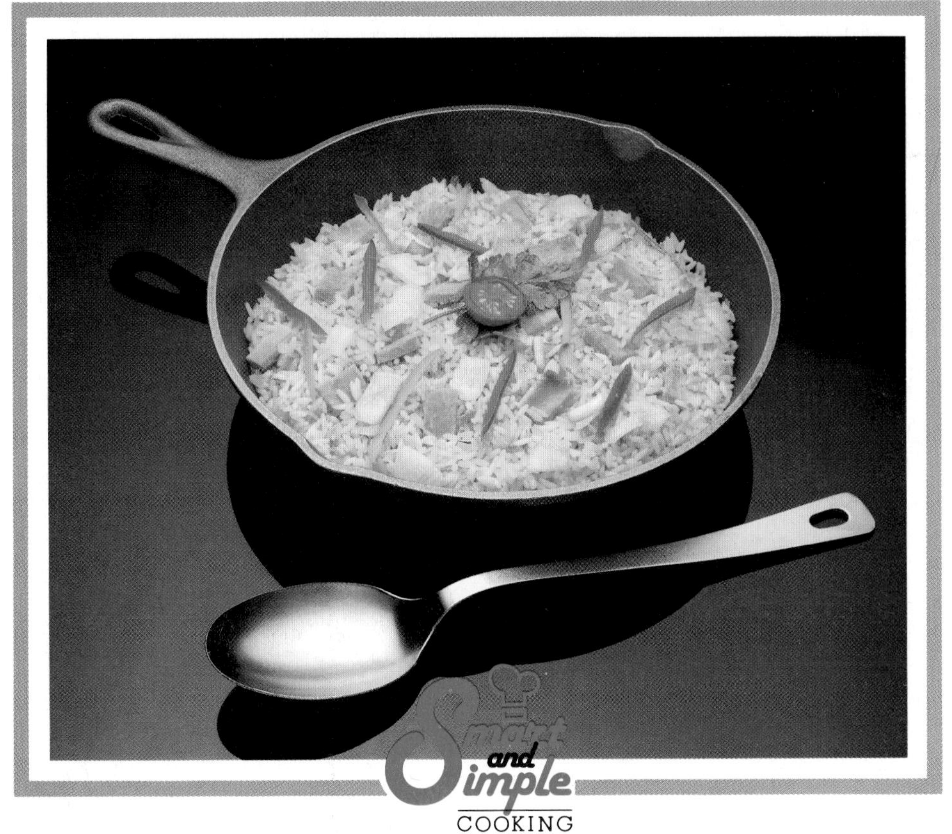

OVER 620 PHOTOGRAPHS IN FULL COLOR
EASY STEP-BY-STEP TECHNIQUES
A SPECIAL MICROWAVE SECTION
SMART AND SIMPLE RECIPES
NUTRITIONAL DATA FOR EACH RECIPE
CALORIE, CARBOHYDRATE, PROTEIN, FAT AND FIBER CONTENT

CRESCENT BOOKS
New York • Avenel, New Jersey

The author wishes to thank Melissa du Fretay for her invaluable assistance.

Cover Design
Zapp Studio

Graphic Design
Barsalo & Associés

Photographs by
Pol Martin (Ontario) Ltd Studio

This 1993 edition published by
Crescent Books, distributed by
Outlet Book Company, Inc.,
a Random House Company,
40 Engelhard Avenue, Avenel, New Jersey 07001

Random House
New York • Toronto • London • Sydney • Auckland

The information in this book is true and complete to the best of our knowledge. All recommendations are made without any guarantees on the part of the author and the publisher. They disclaim all liability in connection with the use of this information.

ISBN: 0-517-10327-3

Printed and bound in Canada

CONTENTS

INDEX

†: Microwave Recipe

T

V

W

Y

Z

KEBAB IT!

KEBAB IT!

It seems to me that shish kebabs have been getting the short end of the stick because the rare time you do come across a kebab dinner is usually in a restaurant and with only a selection of two on the menu! Now don't you agree that it would be far more interesting (and less expensive) to experience the delight of scallop kebabs nestled on a bed of fried parsley? I thought you would and that is the reason for this book which is just brimming with innovative and exciting kebab recipes for the home. For those of you who have yet to make kebabs before, be assured that it is easy and little effort is needed for success especially if you have these utensils: a selection of skewers in metal and wood, a large ovenproof platter and a very sharp knife for accurate trimming and shaping. I urge you to be creative with these recipes and by all means serve them for lunch as well as dinner. Besides fantastic meat and fish kebabs you will find some super vegetable kebabs that are ideal for spicing up an otherwise routine meal and a selection of fun desserts that can add the finishing touch. So with your skewers in hand, off we go to the kitchen — let's prepare something different tonight!

Mustard Marinade for Meat or Fish

1 SERVING	207 CALORIES	0g CARBOHYDRATE
0g PROTEIN	23g FAT	0g FIBER

1¼ cups	(300 ml) olive oil
5 tbsp	(75 ml) Dijon mustard
2	garlic cloves, smashed and chopped
1 tsp	(5 ml) tarragon
	juice 1 lemon
	few drops Tabasco sauce
	salt and pepper

Mix all ingredients together in small bowl. Pour marinade over chosen meat or fish and refrigerate 30 minutes.

In preparation for cooking, drain marinade and reserve for basting.

This marinade is strong enough to use just as flavouring without marinating 30 minutes. Keep this in mind if you are short of time.

Marinade for Lamb or Fish

1 SERVING	175 CALORIES	1g CARBOHYDRATE
0g PROTEIN	19g FAT	0g FIBER

1 cup	(250 ml) olive oil
3	garlic cloves, smashed and chopped
3	shallots, finely chopped
½ cup	(125 ml) lemon juice
½ tsp	(2 ml) crushed rosemary
½ tsp	(2 ml) oregano
	salt and pepper

Mix all ingredients together in small bowl. Pour marinade over chosen lamb or fish and refrigerate overnight.

In preparation for cooking, drain marinade and reserve for basting.

Pineapple Chicken Kebabs

(serves 4)

1 SERVING	321 CALORIES	12g CARBOHYDRATE
21g PROTEIN	21g FAT	0.4g FIBER

2	chicken breasts, skinned, halved and boned
½	pineapple, cut in 1 in (2.5 cm) pieces
5	slices cooked bacon, cut in half
3 tbsp	(45 ml) butter
2	garlic cloves, smashed and chopped
2 tbsp	(30 ml) chopped parsley
	few drops Worcestershire sauce
	salt and pepper

Preheat oven to 450°F (240°C).

Cut chicken in 1 in (2.5 cm) pieces. Alternate along with pineapple and bacon on skewers; set aside.

Melt butter in small saucepan over medium heat. Stir in garlic, parsley and Worcestershire sauce.

Set skewers on ovenproof platter and baste with melted butter mixture. Season well with pepper.

Cook 12 minutes in oven, turning skewers over once or twice. Baste again if desired.

These kebabs serve well with sautéed apples and pine nuts.

1 The first step in making kebabs is to prepare the ingredients as directed in the recipe.

3 A simple mixture of butter, garlic, parsley and Worcestershire sauce will give a delicious flavour to kebabs.

2 Alternate chicken, pineapple and bacon on skewers.

4 It is important to baste the ingredients evenly before cooking.

Marinated Drumsticks

(serves 4)

1 SERVING	277 CALORIES	13g CARBOHYDRATE
27g PROTEIN	13g FAT	1.4g FIBER

2 lb	(900 g) chicken drumsticks
1 tbsp	(15 ml) Trinidad-style hot sauce
1 tsp	(5 ml) Worcestershire sauce
2 tbsp	(30 ml) oil
1	green pepper, in bite-size pieces
2	bananas (not too ripe) peeled and sliced thick
	salt and pepper

Preheat oven to 450°F (240°C).

Score drumsticks with knife and place on plate.

Sprinkle hot sauce, Worcestershire, oil, salt and pepper over chicken.

Place chicken on skewers and cook 10 minutes in oven. Turn skewers over and cook another 10 minutes.

Remove drumsticks from skewers and let cool.

Alternate chicken, green pepper and banana on skewers; place on ovenproof platter. Cook 8 minutes in oven.

Serve with a spicy sauce.

1 Score drumsticks with knife and place on plate.

3 Place chicken on skewers and cook 20 minutes in oven.

2 Sprinkle hot sauce, Worcestershire, oil, salt and pepper over chicken.

4 Add green pepper and banana to skewers with chicken; finish cooking 8 minutes.

Indonesian Chicken

(serves 4)

1 SERVING	381 CALORIES	7g CARBOHYDRATE
23g PROTEIN	29g FAT	1.0g FIBER

2	chicken breasts, skinned, halved and boned
½ cup	(125 ml) chopped walnuts
½ cup	(125 ml) lime juice
1 cup	(250 ml) hot chicken stock
2	garlic cloves, smashed and chopped
1 tbsp	(15 ml) olive oil
1 cup	(250 ml) sour cream
2 tbsp	(30 ml) chopped chives
	salt and pepper

Cut chicken into ½ in (1.2 cm) pieces. Place in bowl along with walnuts, lime juice, chicken stock, garlic, salt and pepper; marinate 2 hours in refrigerator.

Thread chicken on skewers and place on ovenproof platter. Reserve ⅓ of marinade.

Baste skewers with oil and broil 6 to 7 minutes each side in oven 6 in (15 cm) from top element.

Before kebabs are done, mix reserved marinade with sour cream and chives. Serve with chicken.

Spicy Chicken Breasts

(serves 4)

1 SERVING	290 CALORIES	23g CARBOHYDRATE
27g PROTEIN	10g FAT	1.2g FIBER

¾ lb	(375 g) mushroom caps, cleaned
¼ tsp	(1 ml) lemon juice
1 lb	(500 g) chicken breasts, skinned, halved and boned
1 tbsp	(15 ml) Worcestershire sauce
2	beaten eggs
1 cup	(250 ml) breadcrumbs
1	red pepper, in bite-size pieces
	Mexican hot sauce to taste
	few drops melted butter

Preheat oven to 450°F (240°C).

Place mushroom caps in bowl and sprinkle with lemon juice; set aside.

Cut chicken in 1 in (2.5 cm) pieces and place in another bowl; add Worcestershire sauce and hot sauce. Marinate 15 minutes on countertop.

Pour beaten eggs into large bowl. Using tongs add chicken pieces; mix until coated.

Roll chicken in breadcrumbs and alternate along with mushroom caps and red pepper on skewers.

Place skewers on ovenproof platter and sprinkle with melted butter. Cook 15 minutes in oven, turning skewers over once or twice.

1 Marinate chicken pieces in Worcestershire and hot sauces. Place bowl on counter for 15 minutes.

3 Roll chicken in breadcrumbs.

2 Coat marinated chicken in beaten eggs.

4 Alternate chicken, mushroom caps and red pepper on skewers.

Garlic Wing Kebabs

(serves 4)

1 SERVING	251 CALORIES	14g CARBOHYDRATE
15g PROTEIN	15g FAT	0.9g FIBER

32	chicken wings, middle section only
3	garlic cloves, smashed and chopped
½ cup	(125 ml) barbecue sauce
2 tbsp	(30 ml) honey
1 tbsp	(15 ml) lemon juice
2 tbsp	(30 ml) oil
1 tbsp	(15 ml) wine vinegar
½ tsp	(2 ml) brown sugar
16	green onion sticks, 1½ in (4 cm) long
16	zucchini sticks, 1½ in (4 cm) long
	salt and pepper

Place wings, garlic, barbecue sauce, honey, lemon juice, oil, vinegar and brown sugar in bowl; marinate 30 minutes in refrigerator.

Drain and reserve marinade.

Alternate onion, chicken and zucchini on skewers; place in ovenproof dish. Baste with marinade and season well. Broil 12 minutes 6 in (15 cm) from top element; turn over twice.

Change oven setting to 450°F (240°C) and finish cooking 7 minutes close to bottom of oven. Season during cooking.

Serve kebabs in baskets if available.

1 Note that the middle section of the wings should be used for the kebabs. Use remaining wing parts for other recipes.

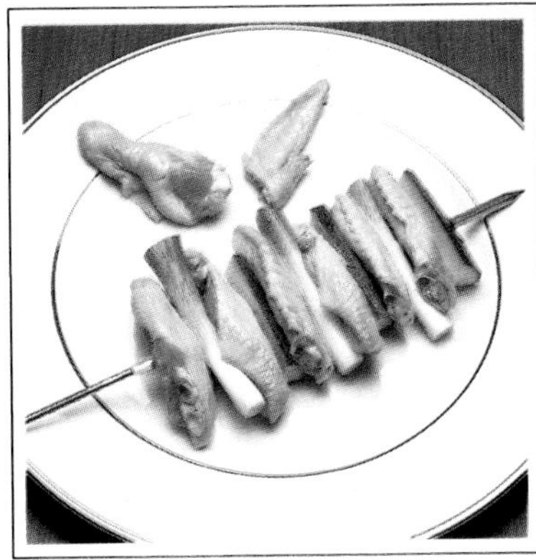

2 Marinate wings in garlic, barbecue sauce, honey, lemon juice, oil, vinegar and brown sugar.

Mid-Wing Skewers

(serves 4)

1 SERVING	153 CALORIES	4g CARBOHYDRATE
14g PROTEIN	9g FAT	0g FIBER

32	chicken wings, middle section only
12 oz	(355 ml) can beer
2	green onions, thinly sliced
½ cup	(125 ml) catsup
2 tbsp	(30 ml) HP sauce
1 tbsp	(15 ml) soya sauce
1 tbsp	(15 ml) finely chopped fresh ginger
1 tbsp	(15 ml) wine vinegar
¼ tsp	(1 ml) Tabasco sauce
1 tbsp	(15 ml) honey
1 tbsp	(15 ml) oil
	salt and pepper

Preheat oven to 450°F (240°C).

Reserve leftover parts of wings for other recipes. Place the middle sections in bowl; add beer and green onions. Marinate 1 hour in refrigerator.

Meanwhile, mix catsup, HP sauce, soya sauce, ginger, vinegar, Tabasco and honey together; set aside.

Drain chicken and discard marinade. Fill skewers with chicken and place in ovenproof dish; season well and baste with oil.

Cook skewers 18 minutes in middle of oven; turn over twice.

Remove from oven and baste with catsup mixture. Change oven setting to Grill (Broil) and place dish on rack 4 in (10 cm) from top element; broil 5 to 6 minutes.

Turn skewers over, baste again and finish broiling 5 to 6 minutes.

Remove chicken from skewers and accompany with baked potatoes.

1 Marinate chicken in beer and onions for 1 hour in refrigerator.

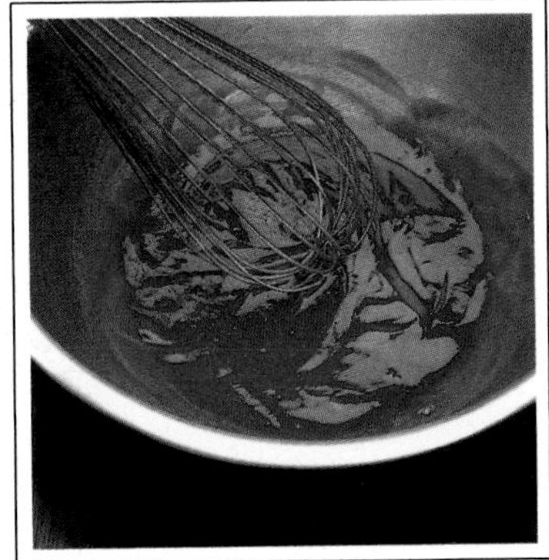

2 Mix catsup, HP sauce, soya sauce, ginger, vinegar, Tabasco and honey together; set aside. This mixture will give chicken lots of flavour.

Chicken, Onions and Zucchini

(serves 4)

1 SERVING	166 CALORIES	8g CARBOHYDRATE
20g PROTEIN	6g FAT	1.4g FIBER

1 lb	(500 g) chicken breasts, skinned, halved and boned
1 tbsp	(15 ml) chopped fresh ginger
3 tbsp	(45 ml) soya sauce
1	garlic clove, smashed and chopped
8	pearl onions, blanched
1	yellow pepper, in bite-size pieces
8	small pieces zucchini
1	red pepper, in bite-size pieces
4	lemon wedges
1 tbsp	(15 ml) oil
	salt and pepper

Cut chicken into $\frac{1}{2}$ in (1.2 cm) cubes. Place in bowl along with ginger, soya sauce and garlic; marinate 30 minutes in refrigerator.

Drain chicken and reserve marinade.

Alternate chicken, vegetables and lemon wedges on skewers. Place in ovenproof dish and season well. Baste with marinade and sprinkle with oil.

Broil 8 minutes in oven 6 in (15 cm) from top element. Turn skewers over once and baste with marinade twice.

1 Marinate chicken in ginger, soya sauce and garlic for 30 minutes in refrigerator.

2 Alternate chicken, vegetables and lemon wedges on skewers. The lemon will give a special flavour.

Stuffed Turkey on Skewers

(serves 4)

1 SERVING	321 CALORIES	4g CARBOHYDRATE
29g PROTEIN	21g FAT	0.7g FIBER

3 tbsp	(45 ml) butter
2	shallots, finely chopped
¼ tsp	(1 ml) tarragon
¼ lb	(125 g) mushrooms, finely chopped
1 tbsp	(15 ml) chopped parsley
3 tbsp	(45 ml) heavy cream
16	thin slices raw turkey breast, flattened
¼	red onion, in pieces
1	green pepper, in bite-size pieces
1 tbsp	(15 ml) lemon juice
	salt and pepper

Preheat oven to 400°F (200°C).

Heat 2 tbsp (30 ml) butter in frying pan. Cook shallots and tarragon 2 minutes.

Add mushrooms and parsley; continue cooking 4 minutes over medium-high heat. Season generously.

Pour in cream, mix and cook 2 to 3 minutes over high heat. Remove from heat and cool slightly.

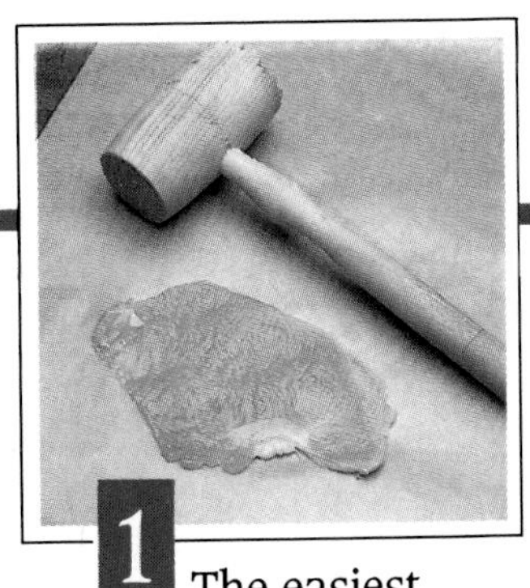

1 The easiest way to flatten the turkey slices is with a mallet on waxed paper.

2 After shallots and tarragon have cooked for 2 minutes, add mushrooms and parsley; continue cooking 4 minutes over medium-high heat.

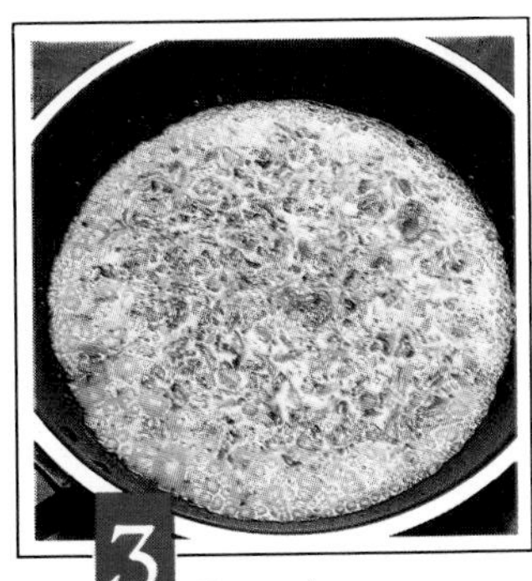

3 Pour in cream; mix and cook 2 to 3 minutes over high heat. Remove and cool slightly.

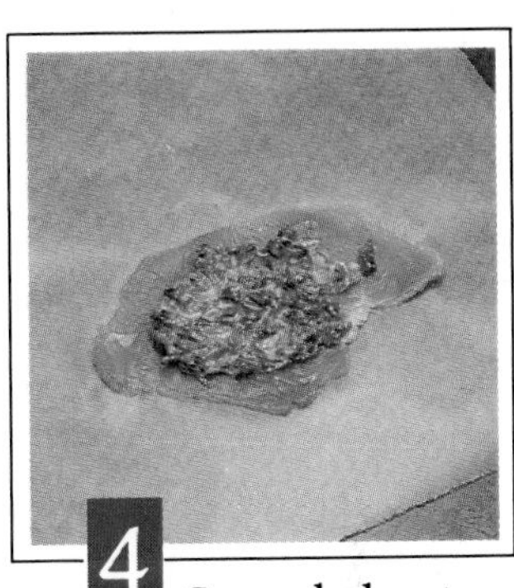

4 Spread about 1 tbsp (15 ml) of mushroom mixture over meat. Fold sides and roll.

Lay turkey slices flat on counter; spread about 1 tbsp (15 ml) of mushroom mixture over meat. Fold one side over and then the other side so that they overlap slightly. Start at one end and roll.

Alternate turkey rolls with onion and green pepper on skewers. Set aside in ovenproof platter.

Mix remaining butter with lemon juice; brush this over kebabs and season well.

Change oven setting to Grill (Broil) and cook 12 minutes 6 in (15 cm) from top element. Turn skewers over once and baste occasionally.

Strips of Beef and Vegetables

(serves 4)

1 SERVING	389 CALORIES	12g CARBOHYDRATE
47g PROTEIN	17g FAT	3.7g FIBER

2 tbsp	(30 ml) olive oil
$1\frac{1}{2}$ lb	(750 g) sirloin tip
3	garlic cloves, smashed and chopped
1	head broccoli (in flowerets), blanched 4 minutes
16	large cherry tomatoes
$\frac{1}{2}$	red onion, cut in 2 and sectioned
	juice 1 lemon
	salt and pepper

Heat 1 tsp (5 ml) oil in frying pan. When very hot, add whole piece of meat and sear on all sides. Season well.

Slice beef into $\frac{1}{2}$ in (1.25 cm) strips. Place in bowl along with remaining oil, garlic and lemon juice. Marinate 15 minutes.

Drain beef and reserve marinade. Fold pieces in half and alternate on skewers along with vegetables.

Place on ovenproof platter and broil 6 minutes 6 in (15 cm) from top element. Turn skewers over once and baste several times with marinade.

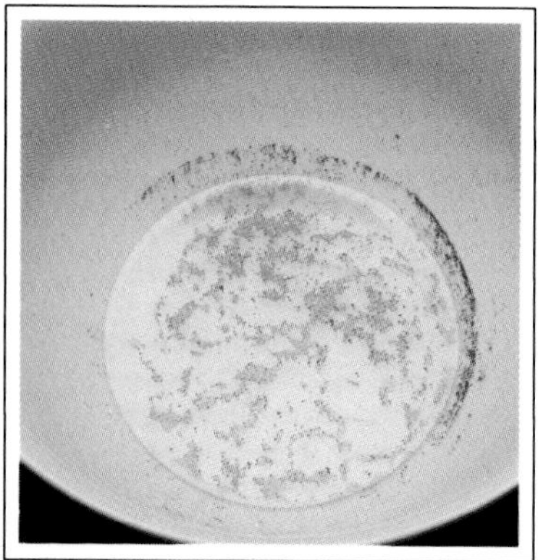

1 Place remaining oil, garlic and lemon juice in bowl.

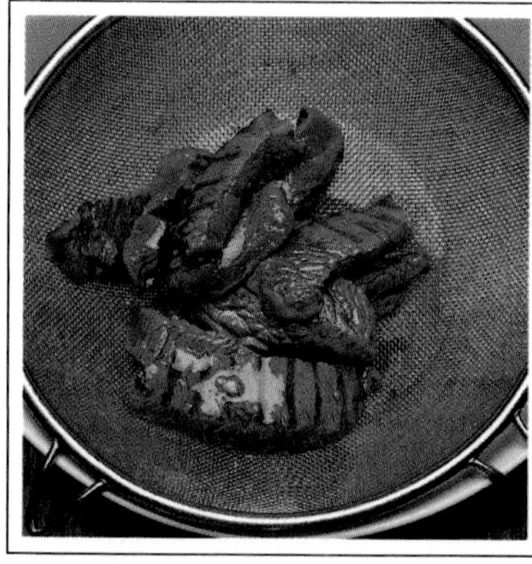

3 Drain beef and reserve marinade.

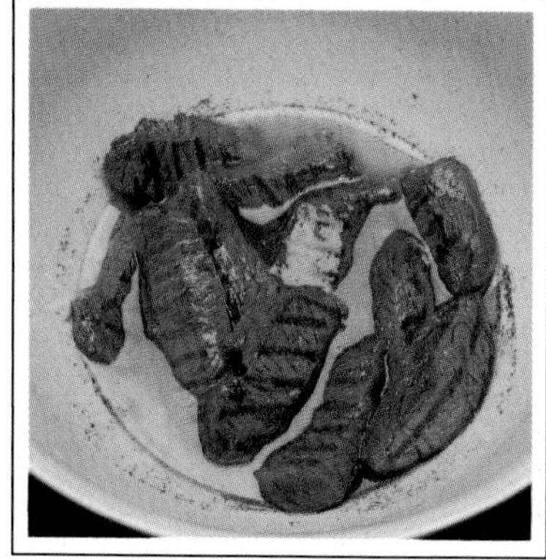

2 Add strips of beef and marinate 15 minutes.

4 Fold pieces of meat in half and alternate on skewers along with vegetables.

Meat and Potato Kebabs

(serves 4)

1 SERVING	441 CALORIES	27g CARBOHYDRATE
45g PROTEIN	17g FAT	4.8g FIBER

1 ½ lb	(750 g) sirloin steak, in 1 in (2.5 cm) long strips about ¾ in (2 cm) thick
3 tbsp	(45 ml) soya sauce
2	garlic cloves, smashed and chopped
2 tbsp	(30 ml) vegetable oil
16	small new round potatoes, peeled and cooked
2 tbsp	(30 ml) catsup
1 tbsp	(15 ml) honey
	salt and pepper

Preheat oven to 400°F (200°C).

Place beef, soya sauce, garlic and oil in bowl; marinate 15 minutes.

Alternate beef and potatoes on skewers; place on ovenproof platter.

Mix catsup with honey and brush over skewers; season generously. Broil 7 minutes in oven 6 in (15 cm) from top element. Turn skewers over once.

Serve with salad.

Beef Marinated in Bourbon

(serves 4)

1 SERVING	435 CALORIES	13g CARBOHYDRATE
53g PROTEIN	19g FAT	1.5g FIBER

2 lb	(900 g) sirloin tip, in 1 ¼ in (3 cm) cubes
¼ cup	(50 ml) bourbon
2 tbsp	(30 ml) soya sauce
1 tsp	(5 ml) Dijon mustard
¼ tsp	(1 ml) Worcestershire sauce
12	blanched mushroom caps
12	bite-size pieces bok choy (stem only)
2	white onions, cut in 4, blanched and sectioned
2	large carrots, cut in ½ in (1.2 cm) lengths and blanched
2 tbsp	(30 ml) vegetable oil
	salt and pepper

Marinate sirloin in mixture of bourbon, soya sauce, mustard and Worcestershire sauce for 1 hour.

Drain beef and reserve marinade. Alternate beef and vegetables on skewers and place on ovenproof platter; brush with oil.

Season skewers generously and broil 4 minutes in oven 4 in (10 cm) from top element. Turn skewers over once.

Move skewers 6 in (15 cm) from top element; finish broiling another 4 minutes turning skewers once. Baste with a bit of marinade.

Veal in Beer Marinade

(serves 4)

1 SERVING	186 CALORIES	11g CARBOHYDRATE
13g PROTEIN	10g FAT	1.4g FIBER

½ lb	(250 g) veal tenderloin, sliced in ¼ in (0.65 cm) thick rounds
1 cup	(250 ml) beer
1 tbsp	(15 ml) chopped fresh ginger
¼ tsp	(1 ml) Tabasco sauce
¼ tsp	(1 ml) Trinidad-style hot sauce
12	green onions, in 1¼ in (3 cm) long sticks
1	small zucchini, sliced ½ in (1.2 cm) thick
1	red pepper, in bite-size pieces
1 tbsp	(15 ml) vegetable oil
1 tbsp	(15 ml) honey
	salt and pepper

Marinate veal in mixture of beer, ginger, Tabasco, hot sauce and salt and pepper. Refrigerate 1 hour.

Drain veal and reserve marinade.

Alternate veal (fold each piece in two) along with onion sticks, zucchini and red pepper on skewers. Place in ovenproof dish and baste with marinade; sprinkle with oil and honey.

Broil 16 minutes in oven 6 in (15 cm) from top element. Turn skewers over twice.

Serve on rice.

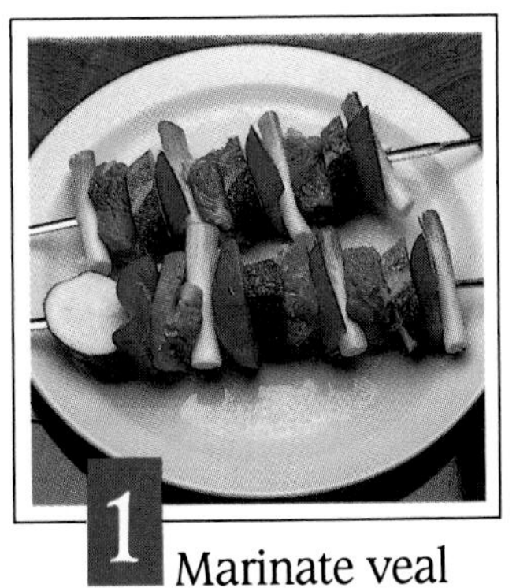

1 Marinate veal in mixture of beer, ginger, Tabasco, hot sauce and salt and pepper. Refrigerate 1 hour.

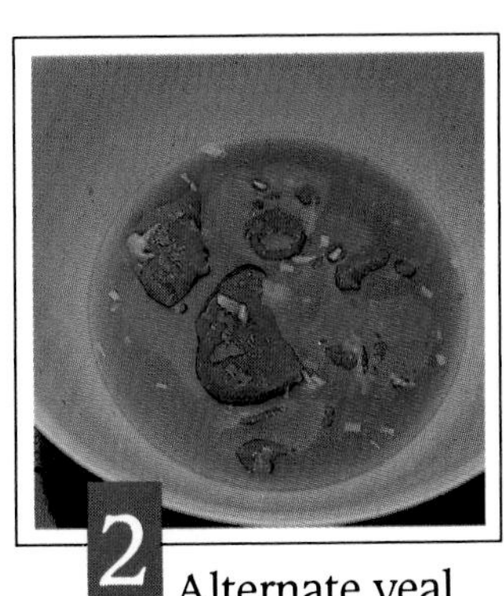

2 Alternate veal pieces folded in two along with vegetables on skewers.

Veal Scallopini on Skewers

(serves 4)

1 SERVING	216 CALORIES	6g CARBOHYDRATE
12g PROTEIN	16g FAT	0g FIBER

4	veal scallopini from leg
3 tbsp	(45 ml) olive oil
2 tbsp	(30 ml) maple syrup
¼ tsp	(1 ml) tarragon
1 tbsp	(15 ml) wine vinegar
	few drops Trinidad-style hot sauce
	salt and pepper
	lemon juice to taste
	paprika to taste

If butcher has not already pounded veal, place pieces between two sheets of waxed paper. Flatten with mallet until very thin. Trim away fat and season generously.

Roll scallopini lengthwise keeping meat fairly taut. Secure each roll on very long skewer. Refer to Photo 2 for visual help.

Place skewers on ovenproof platter and set aside.

Mix oil, maple syrup, tarragon, vinegar, hot sauce, salt, pepper and lemon juice together.

Brush mixture over skewers and broil 7 minutes in oven 6 in (15 cm) from top element.

Turn skewers over and season with paprika; baste with maple syrup mixture. Continue broiling 7 minutes.

Remove veal from skewers.

Serve with green vegetables and garnish with broiled tomatoes.

1 If butcher has not already pounded veal, place pieces between two sheets of waxed paper. Flatten with mallet until very thin.

2 Depending on the length of your veal rolls the skewer need only be inserted twice in order to keep meat in place.

Veal and Mushroom Caps

(serves 4)

1 SERVING	285 CALORIES	4g CARBOHYDRATE
20g PROTEIN	21g FAT	0.6g FIBER

½ lb	(250 g) veal tenderloin, in bite-size pieces
12	mushroom caps, cleaned
12	bite-size chunks of celery
8	slices red onion
¼ cup	(50 ml) wine vinegar
2	garlic cloves, smashed and chopped
3 tbsp	(45 ml) olive oil
¼ tsp	(1 ml) fresh ground pepper
1 tsp	(5 ml) chopped parsley
9	bay leaves
3	½ in (1.2 cm) thick slices cooked back bacon, cubed and sautéed in butter

Place veal, mushrooms, celery and onion in bowl; set aside.

Place vinegar, garlic, oil, pepper, parsley and 1 bay leaf in small saucepan; bring to boil and cook 5 minutes over medium heat.

Pour hot liquid over veal and vegetables in bowl; marinate 1 hour on countertop. Drain and reserve marinade.

Alternate bacon, veal, mushrooms, celery, remaining bay leaves and onion on skewers. Place in ovenproof platter and broil 12 minutes 6 in (15 cm) from top element. Turn skewers over once and baste occasionally with marinade.

1 Place veal, mushrooms, celery and onion in bowl; set aside.

2 Pour hot marinade into bowl and leave on countertop for 1 hour.

BOCQUET
Product of France
Ingrédients: Mustard seeds-Vinegar-Salt
Graines de Moutarde -Vinaigre dilué-Sel
POIDS NET: 500 G. – NET WEIGHT

Lemon Veal Kebabs

(serves 4)

1 SERVING	265 CALORIES	11g CARBOHYDRATE
17g PROTEIN	17g FAT	2.0g FIBER

½ lb	(250 g) veal tenderloin, sliced in ¼ in (0.65 cm) thick rounds
16	mushroom caps, cleaned
1	yellow pepper, in large pieces
¼ cup	(50 ml) olive oil
¼ cup	(50 ml) wine vinegar
1 tbsp	(15 ml) chopped fresh tarragon
2	broccoli stalks, cubed and cooked
½	red onion, in large pieces
	juice 1 lemon

Place veal, mushrooms and pepper in bowl. Sprinkle in oil, vinegar, tarragon and lemon juice. Refrigerate 35 minutes.

Drain and reserve marinade. Alternate veal (fold each piece in 2), mushrooms, yellow pepper, broccoli and onion on skewers.

Place in ovenproof dish and pour marinade over skewers. Broil 12 minutes in oven 6 in (15 cm) from top element. Turn skewers over once.

Serve with baked potatoes or other vegetables.

1 Marinate veal, mushrooms and pepper in a mixture of oil, vinegar, tarragon and lemon juice. Refrigerate for 35 minutes.

2 Alternate veal and vegetables on skewers. It is important to fold each piece of veal in two as you add them to the skewers.

Veal and Prune Kebabs

(serves 4)

1 SERVING	480 CALORIES	44g CARBOHYDRATE
40g PROTEIN	16g FAT	8.8g FIBER

1½ lb	(750 g) veal sirloin, cut in strips
½ cup	(125 ml) rice wine
2 tbsp	(30 ml) oil
1 tsp	(5 ml) lemon juice
24	pitted prunes
1½	green peppers, diced large
24	¾ in (2 cm) celery pieces, blanched
12	fresh mint leaves
	pinch thyme
	salt and freshly ground pepper

Place meat in wine, oil, lemon juice and thyme; marinate 15 minutes on countertop.

Drain meat and reserve marinade. Alternate veal, prunes, green peppers, celery and mint leaves on skewers; place on ovenproof platter.

Generously brush with marinade and broil 10 minutes 6 in (15 cm) from top element. Turn skewers over once and season during cooking.

Spicy Meatballs

(serves 4)

1 SERVING	490 CALORIES	21g CARBOHYDRATE
52g PROTEIN	22g FAT	0.5g FIBER

¾ lb	(375 g) lean ground pork
¾ lb	(375 g) lean ground veal
2 tbsp	(30 ml) chili sauce
3 tbsp	(45 ml) breadcrumbs
¼ tsp	(1 ml) chili powder
1	egg
1 tsp	(5 ml) Worcestershire sauce
¼ tsp	(1 ml) paprika
½ cup	(125 ml) chili sauce
½ cup	(125 ml) catsup
2 tbsp	(30 ml) oil
2 tbsp	(30 ml) sherry
	salt and pepper

Preheat oven to 400°F (200°C).

Place pork, veal, 2 tbsp (30 ml) chili sauce, breadcrumbs, chili powder, egg, Worcestershire sauce and paprika in mixer; process until meat forms a ball and sticks to sides of bowl.

Cover with waxed paper and chill 1 hour.

Dust hands with flour and shape mixture into small meatballs; thread on skewers. Place on ovenproof platter.

Mix remaining ingredients together. Cook skewers 8 minutes 6 in (15 cm) from top element; turn over once and baste often with sauce.

Dinner Party Skewers

(serves 4)

1 SERVING	215 CALORIES	21g CARBOHYDRATE
17g PROTEIN	7g FAT	1.1g FIBER

¼ cup	(50 ml) molasses
¼ cup	(50 ml) vinegar
1 tbsp	(15 ml) tomato paste
3	anchovy filets, chopped and mashed
1	large pork tenderloin, sliced thick
2	large celery stalks, in 1 in (2.5 cm) lengths
1	large green pepper, in bite-size pieces
1	seedless orange
	juice ½ lemon
	juice 1 orange

Preheat oven to 500°F (260°C).

Mix molasses, vinegar and tomato paste together in large bowl. Add lemon and orange juices, anchovies and mix very well.

Place pork, celery and green pepper in marinade; set aside 1 hour on countertop.

Slice other orange in two; cut each half into ¼ in (0.65 cm) thick slices. Do not peel.

Alternate double slices of orange along with ingredients in bowl on skewers; place on ovenproof platter.

Cook 14 minutes, turning skewers over once.

1 Mix molasses, vinegar and tomato paste together in large bowl. Add anchovies, lemon and orange juices; mix very well.

2 Place pork, celery and green pepper in marinade; set aside 1 hour on countertop.

Ribs and Tomatoes

(serves 4)

1 SERVING	383 CALORIES	16g CARBOHYDRATE
19g PROTEIN	27g FAT	0.9g FIBER

2½ lb	(1.2 kg) pork back ribs
3 tbsp	(45 ml) maple syrup
¼ cup	(50 ml) catsup
2	garlic cloves, smashed and chopped
1	large yellow pepper, in large pieces
6	slices precooked bacon, cut in half and rolled
1	tomato, in thin wedges
	juice ½ lemon
	few drops Tabasco sauce
	salt and pepper

Place ribs in large saucepan and cover with water; bring to boil. Skim and continue cooking 1 hour over medium heat.

Remove ribs from water and cool; cut into 1 in (2.5 cm) pieces.

Mix maple syrup, catsup, garlic, lemon juice, Tabasco, salt and pepper together in bowl. Stir in ribs and let stand 15 minutes on countertop.

Alternate rib pieces, yellow pepper, rolled bacon and tomato on skewers. Place in ovenproof platter and broil 8 minutes 6 in (15 cm) from top element. Turn skewers once and baste with leftover catsup mixture.

1 After ribs have been cooked in hot water, remove and cool. Then cut into 1 in (2.5 cm) pieces.

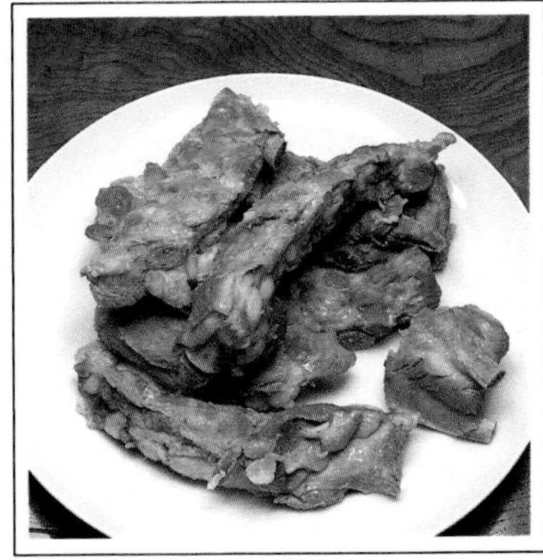

2 Alternate rib pieces, yellow pepper, rolled bacon and tomato on skewers.

Pork and Vegetable Kebabs

(serves 4)

1 SERVING	224 CALORIES	12g CARBOHYDRATE
17g PROTEIN	12g FAT	1.6g FIBER

5 oz	(142 g) piece Polish sausage
1	pork tenderloin, fat trimmed
1	small zucchini, in ½ in (1.2 cm) thick slices
1	yellow pepper, in bite-size pieces
8	green onions, in 1½ in (4 cm) long sticks
¼ tsp	(1 ml) Worcestershire sauce
½ cup	(125 ml) catsup
1 tsp	(5 ml) horseradish
	few drops Tabasco sauce
	salt and pepper

Preheat oven to 500°F (260°C).

Remove skin from sausage and slice in 1½ in (4 cm) rings. Cube pork tenderloin and place in bowl along with sausage, zucchini, yellow pepper and onion sticks.

Add Worcestershire sauce, catsup, horseradish, Tabasco sauce, salt and pepper to bowl; mix until everything is evenly coated. Marinate 15 minutes on countertop.

Alternate ingredients on skewers and place on ovenproof platter. Cook 15 minutes 6 in (15 cm) from top element turning skewers over twice.

Serve with potatoes if desired.

1 Prepare ingredients as directed in recipe then place them in a bowl.

2 Add Worcestershire sauce, catsup, horseradish, Tabasco sauce, salt and pepper to bowl; mix until everything is evenly coated. Marinate 15 minutes on countertop.

Pork Kebabs with Sweet-Sour Sauce

(serves 4)

1 SERVING	388 CALORIES	27g CARBOHYDRATE
34g PROTEIN	16g FAT	2.8g FIBER

1 tbsp	(15 ml) vegetable oil
1	garlic clove, smashed and chopped
1	small onion, thinly sliced
1	small carrot, thinly sliced
2	pineapple rings, cubed
2 tbsp	(30 ml) soya sauce
2 tbsp	(30 ml) wine vinegar
1 tbsp	(15 ml) sugar
3 tbsp	(45 ml) catsup
1 cup	(250 ml) hot chicken stock
1 tbsp	(15 ml) cornstarch
3 tbsp	(45 ml) cold water
1 lb	(500 g) pork tenderloin, in strips
16	baby carrots, blanched
1 ½	yellow peppers, diced large
	salt and pepper

To prepare sauce, heat oil in frying pan. When hot, cook garlic, onion and carrot 3 minutes over medium heat.

Stir in pineapple, soya sauce and vinegar; cook 2 minutes.

Add sugar and catsup; mix well. Pour in chicken stock, season and bring to boil.

Mix cornstarch with water; stir into sauce and cook 2 minutes. Remove from heat.

Fold pork strips in half and alternate along with baby carrots and pepper pieces on skewers. Season well and place on ovenproof platter.

Generously brush sweet-sour sauce over skewers; broil 4 to 5 minutes each side 6 in (15 cm) from top element. Baste frequently.

Ham and Apple on Skewers

(serves 4)

1 SERVING	355 CALORIES	37g CARBOHYDRATE
36g PROTEIN	7g FAT	2.5g FIBER

2	slices Virginia ham, ¾ in (2 cm) thick and in ¾ in (2 cm) cubes
3	apples, in wedges with skin
3 tbsp	(45 ml) maple syrup
2 tsp	(10 ml) soya sauce
½ cup	(125 ml) catsup
¼ cup	(50 ml) apple juice
	pinch cinnamon
	pinch ground clove

Place all ingredients in bowl, mix and marinate 15 minutes.

Drain and reserve marinade. Alternate ham and apples on skewers; place on ovenproof platter.

Broil 8 to 10 minutes 6 in (15 cm) from top element. Turn skewers over once and baste with marinade.

These kebabs are very tasty for brunch.

Cabbage Rolls on Skewers

(serves 4)

1 SERVING	334 CALORIES	5g CARBOHYDRATE
38g PROTEIN	18g FAT	0.6g FIBER

1 tbsp	(15 ml) butter
½ lb	(250 g) ground pork
½ lb	(250 g) ground veal
¼ tsp	(1 ml) paprika
¼ tsp	(1 ml) ground clove
½ cup	(125 ml) grated cheddar cheese
½ cup	(125 ml) cooked chopped onion
1 tbsp	(15 ml) chopped parsley
1 tbsp	(15 ml) sour cream
1	egg, lightly beaten
8	large cabbage leaves, blanched
	salt and pepper

Heat butter in frying pan. When hot, brown pork and veal 4 to 5 minutes over medium heat; season with paprika and clove.

Transfer meat to bowl and add remaining ingredients except cabbage leaves. Mix until well combined, cover and chill 1 hour.

Lay cabbage leaves flat and spread about 3 tbsp (45 ml) of meat mixture over each leaf. Roll fairly tight and tuck in ends. Place tube-like rolls on plate and weight down with another plate; chill 15 minutes.

Cut each cabbage roll into 3 pieces and carefully thread on skewers. Broil 6 to 8 minutes in oven 6 in (15 cm) from top element; turn skewers over once.

This unusual kebab dish also serves well topped with a hint of tomato sauce.

Italian Sausage and Beef Kebabs

(serves 4)

1 SERVING	611 CALORIES	17g CARBOHYDRATE
39g PROTEIN	43g FAT	1.3g FIBER

1 lb	(500 g) sirloin tip, in bite-size pieces
1 lb	(500 g) Italian sausage, in ¾ in (2 cm) pieces
2	onions, cut in 4 and sectioned
1½	red peppers, in bite-size pieces
8	garlic cloves, peeled
½ cup	(125 ml) olive oil
¼ cup	(50 ml) chili sauce
	juice 1 lemon
	freshly ground pepper
	dash paprika

Alternate beef, sausage, onion, pepper and garlic on skewers. Place on ovenproof platter.

Mix oil, chili sauce, lemon juice, pepper and paprika together; brush over skewers.

Broil about 6 minutes on each side (depending on size) 6 in (15 cm) from top element. Baste once or twice.

Accompany with a spicy rice.

Polish Sausages and Bacon

(serves 4)

1 SERVING	169 CALORIES	10g CARBOHYDRATE
12g PROTEIN	9g FAT	0.8g FIBER

2	¾ in (2 cm) thick slices back bacon, diced large
½	red onion, cut in 3
4 oz	(115 g) Polish sausage, peeled and diced large
½	cucumber, peeled, seeded and cut in ¾ in (2 cm) thick slices
½ cup	(125 ml) catsup
1 tbsp	(15 ml) horseradish
	juice 1 lime
	few drops Tabasco sauce
	pepper

Preheat oven to 500°F (260°C).

Alternate bacon, onion, sausage and cucumber on skewers; place on ovenproof platter.

Mix remaining ingredients together and brush over skewers.

Cook 14 minutes 8 in (20 cm) from top element. Turn skewers over once and baste with leftover catsup mixture if desired.

Cocktail Sausages on Skewers

(serves 4)

1 SERVING	320 CALORIES	7g CARBOHYDRATE
10g PROTEIN	28g FAT	0.5g FIBER

8	slices bacon, precooked 2 minutes
8 oz	(230 g) can cocktail sausages
10 oz	(284 ml) can mandarin sections, drained
	barbecue sauce for basting

Cut bacon slices in two and roll; alternate along with sausages and mandarins on thin wooden skewers.

Place in ovenproof dish and baste with barbecue sauce. Broil 5 minutes in oven 6 in (15 cm) from top element.

Serve as an appetizer or snack.

Tasty Lamb Kebabs

(serves 4)

1 SERVING	266 CALORIES	10g CARBOHYDRATE
16g PROTEIN	18g FAT	0.4g FIBER

½ cup	(125 ml) mint sauce
1 tbsp	(15 ml) olive oil
2	garlic cloves, smashed and chopped
8	small lamb chops, ½ in (1.2 cm) thick, boned and fat removed
2	small onions, cut in 4 and sectioned
10	bay leaves
1½	celery stalks, cut in 1 in (2.5 cm) lengths and blanched
	salt and pepper
	juice ¼ lemon

Preheat oven to 400°F (200°C).

Place mint sauce, oil, garlic, pepper and lemon juice in bowl. Add lamb and mix thoroughly; marinate 15 minutes on countertop.

Alternate lamb, onion sections, bay leaves and celery pieces on skewers; season generously. Place on ovenproof platter.

Change oven setting to broil. Cook skewers 3 minutes each side 6 in (15 cm) from top element. Leave door ajar and baste with leftover mint marinade.

Serve with hot mustard if desired.

Hearty Lamb Kebabs

(serves 4)

1 SERVING	733 CALORIES	20g CARBOHYDRATE
44g PROTEIN	53g FAT	2.9g FIBER

2 lb	(900 g) boneless leg of lamb, in ¾ in (2 cm) pieces
2	onions, finely chopped
1 tbsp	(15 ml) crushed rosemary
½ cup	(125 ml) olive oil
2	bay leaves
1	large Spanish onion, cut in 8 and sectioned
1 tbsp	(15 ml) olive oil
2	garlic cloves, smashed and chopped
3	tomatoes, peeled and chopped
4	slices Italian bread, toasted
¼ cup	(50 ml) grated Parmesan cheese
	salt and pepper

Place lamb, chopped onions, rosemary, ¼ cup (125 ml) oil and bay leaves in bowl; mix and marinate 1 hour on countertop.

Alternate pieces of lamb and Spanish onion on skewers; place on ovenproof platter and set aside.

Heat remaining measure of oil in frying pan. Cook garlic and tomatoes 7 to 9 minutes over medium heat; season well. Reduce heat and simmer.

Place skewers in oven and broil 5 to 6 minutes 6 in (15 cm) from top element.

Spread tomato mixture over toasted bread slices and top with cheese; place in ovenproof dish.

Turn skewers over; broil another 5 to 6 minutes. Place bread beside skewers and broil, but for only 3 to 4 minutes.

To serve place one skewer on each slice of bread.

Salmon and Cucumber Kebabs

(serves 4)

1 SERVING	171 CALORIES	1g CARBOHYDRATE
26g PROTEIN	7g FAT	0.6g FIBER

2 tbsp	(30 ml) grated lemon rind
½ cup	(125 ml) dry white wine
1 tsp	(5 ml) tarragon
3	salmon steaks
½	English cucumber, peeled and diced large
8	fresh mint leaves
	juice 1 lemon
	salt and pepper

Mix lemon rind, wine, tarragon and lemon juice together in large bowl.

Remove middle bone from salmon steaks, leave on skin and cut in 2. Cut each half into 3 pieces. Add to bowl along with cucumber; marinate 15 minutes.

Drain and reserve marinade.

Alternate salmon, cucumber and mint leaves on skewers; place on ovenproof platter and season.

Broil 4 minutes 6 in (15 cm) from top element; baste once with marinade.

Turn skewers over and broil about 3 minutes, depending on size. Baste once more.

Perch Kebabs

(serves 4)

1 SERVING	392 CALORIES	8g CARBOHYDRATE
45g PROTEIN	20g FAT	1.1g FIBER

2	garlic cloves, smashed and chopped
1 tbsp	(15 ml) oyster sauce
2 lb	(900 g) perch filets, cut in half then in 1 in (2.5 cm) pieces
8	cherry tomatoes
4	small onions, blanched and cut in 4
3 tbsp	(45 ml) olive oil
2 tbsp	(30 ml) sherry
	juice 1 lemon
	salt and pepper

Preheat oven to 400°F (200°C).

Mix garlic, oyster sauce and lemon juice in bowl. Add fish and marinate 15 minutes.

Roll fish pieces and alternate along with tomatoes and onions on skewers. Place on ovenproof platter.

Mix oil and sherry together; brush over skewers. Season to taste.

Change oven setting to broil. Cook skewers 3 minutes each side 6 in (15 cm) from top element.

1 Mix garlic, oyster sauce and lemon in bowl.

2 Add fish and marinate 15 minutes.

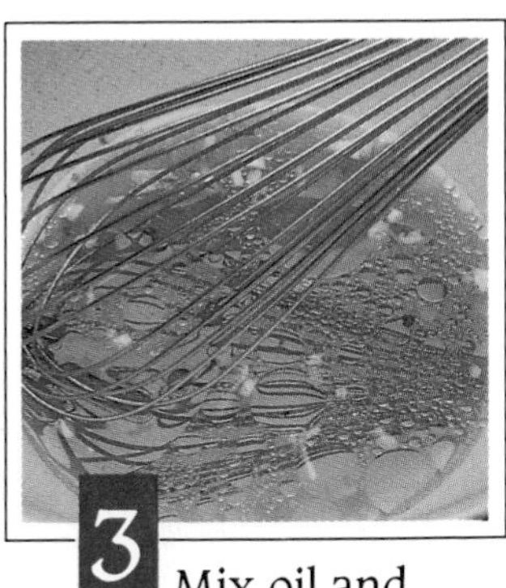

3 Mix oil and sherry together.

4 Brush sherry mixture over skewers before broiling.

Sturgeon, Brussels Sprouts and Carrots

(serves 4)

1 SERVING	254 CALORIES	18g CARBOHYDRATE
23g PROTEIN	10g FAT	4.8g FIBER

2	sturgeon steaks, ¾ in (2 cm) thick and in ¾ in (2 cm) cubes
24	cooked Brussels sprouts
24	cooked baby carrots
½ cup	(125 ml) sake
2 tbsp	(30 ml) oil
1	garlic clove, smashed and chopped
8	oyster mushrooms
	salt and pepper

Place fish, sprouts, carrots, sake, oil, garlic, salt and pepper in bowl; marinate 15 minutes.

Drain and reserve marinade. Alternate fish and vegetables on skewers. Note: It is best to fold mushrooms in half.

Place skewers on ovenproof platter and broil 8 to 10 minutes 6 in (15 cm) from top element. Turn skewers over once and baste with marinade.

Fish Lover's Kebabs

(serves 4)

1 SERVING	385 CALORIES	10g CARBOHYDRATE
48g PROTEIN	17g FAT	1.0g FIBER

2 lb	(900 g) halibut steaks, ¾ in (2 cm) thick and in 1 in (2.5 cm) pieces
1	onion, finely chopped
4 tbsp	(60 ml) oil
2 tbsp	(30 ml) lime juice
¼ tsp	(1 ml) Tabasco sauce
¼ cup	(50 ml) dry white wine
6	green onions, in 1 in (2.5 cm) sticks
7 oz	(199 ml) can water chestnuts, drained
12	lime slices
12	apple wedges with skin

Marinate halibut 15 minutes in chopped onion, oil, lime juice, Tabasco sauce and wine.

Drain and reserve marinade.

Alternate fish, green onions, water chestnuts, lime slices and apple wedges on skewers. Place on ovenproof platter.

Broil 8 to 10 minutes in oven 6 in (15 cm) from top element. Turn skewers over once and baste occasionally with marinade.

Clam Kebabs

(serves 4)

1 SERVING	406 CALORIES	33g CARBOHYDRATE
28g PROTEIN	18g FAT	0.2g FIBER

24	large clams, scrubbed
1 tsp	(5 ml) lemon juice
1 tbsp	(15 ml) teriyaki sauce
1 cup	(250 ml) seasoned flour
2	beaten eggs
1 ½ cups	(375 ml) crushed Corn Flakes
	melted garlic butter
	pepper

Preheat oven to 450°F (240°C).

Spread clams in one layer in large roasting pan. Place in oven for 4 to 5 minutes or until shells open.

Shuck and discard shells. Place clams in bowl with lemon juice and teriyaki sauce; mix well and season with pepper.

Dredge clams in flour, dip in eggs and coat with corn flakes. Put on skewers with skewer going through each clam twice. Set all on ovenproof platter.

Change oven setting to broil. Baste skewers with garlic butter, leave oven door ajar, and broil 6 minutes 6 in (15 cm) from top element. Turn skewers over once and baste again if necessary.

Oyster Kebabs

(serves 4)

1 SERVING	681 CALORIES	50g CARBOHYDRATE
55g PROTEIN	29g FAT	0g FIBER

36	large shucked oysters
8	slices cooked bacon, cut in half
1 cup	(250 ml) flour
¼ tsp	(1 ml) paprika
1 tsp	(5 ml) chopped parsley
4 tbsp	(60 ml) butter, melted
¼ tsp	(1 ml) teriyaki sauce
	salt
	juice 1 lemon

Preheat oven to 400°F (200°C).

Alternate oysters and rolled pieces of bacon on skewers.

Mix flour with paprika and parsley. Roll skewers in this and place in ovenproof platter.

Mix butter, teriyaki sauce, salt and lemon juice together; pour over skewers. Change oven setting to broil and cook skewers 3 minutes each side 6 in (15 cm) from top element.

Serve with garlic bread.

Brandy Jumbo Shrimp

(serves 4)

1 SERVING	164 CALORIES	6g CARBOHYDRATE
17g PROTEIN	8g FAT	0.8g FIBER

20	raw jumbo shrimp, shelled and deveined
2	garlic cloves, smashed and chopped
½ cup	(125 ml) brandy
2 tbsp	(30 ml) olive oil
4	stems bok choy, in ¾ in (2 cm) pieces
	juice 1 lemon
	salt and pepper

Place all ingredients in bowl and marinate 30 minutes on countertop.

Alternate shrimp and bok choy on skewers. Place on ovenproof platter.

Broil 12 to 14 minutes in oven 6 in (15 cm) from top element. Turn skewers over once and season during cooking. Baste with marinade if desired.

Serve with tartare sauce.

Breaded Mussels on Skewers

(serves 4)

1 SERVING	610 CALORIES	60g CARBOHYDRATE
43g PROTEIN	22g FAT	0.2g FIBER

6½ lb	(3 kg) mussels, scrubbed and bearded
½ cup	(125 ml) dry white wine
4 tbsp	(60 ml) butter
1 tbsp	(15 ml) lemon juice
1 cup	(250 ml) seasoned flour
2	beaten eggs
2 cups	(500 ml) breadcrumbs
	few drops Tabasco sauce
	few drops lemon juice
	salt and pepper

Place mussels, wine, 2 tbsp (30 ml) butter, lemon juice and pepper in saucepan. Cover and bring to boil; continue cooking over medium heat until shells open.

Drain liquid into small bowl. Shuck mussels and pour any juices from shells into the small bowl. Set aside.

Dredge mussels in flour. Dip several at a time in eggs then coat with breadcrumbs.

Thread on wooden skewers and place on ovenproof platter. Broil 4 minutes very close to top element; turn skewers once.

Meanwhile, prepare sauce by transferring reserved mussel liquid in bowl to saucepan. Reduce by ⅔ over medium-high heat.

Stir in remaining butter, Tabasco sauce and few drops lemon juice; cook 1 minute.

Serve with kebabs.

Chinese Shrimp Kebabs

(serves 4)

1 SERVING	237 CALORIES	21g CARBOHYDRATE
27g PROTEIN	5g FAT	0g FIBER

16	chunks fresh pineapple
2 lb	(900 g) raw shrimp, shelled and deveined
24	fresh snow peas, blanched
½ cup	(125 ml) rice wine
2 tbsp	(30 ml) sesame sauce
1 tbsp	(15 ml) oil
1 tsp	(5 ml) lime juice
	salt and pepper

Preheat oven to 400°F (200°C).

Place pineapple, shrimp, pea pods, wine and sesame sauce in bowl; marinate 15 minutes.

Alternate ingredients on skewers and place on ovenproof platter. Mix oil with lime juice; set aside.

Cook skewers 6 to 8 minutes in oven 6 in (15 cm) from top element. Baste occasionally with oil mixture and turn skewers over once. Season to taste.

Serve with steamed rice and chopsticks.

Escargot Appetizer

(serves 4)

1 SERVING	462 CALORIES	20g CARBOHYDRATE
19g PROTEIN	34g FAT	0.2g FIBER

24	canned snails, drained
8	slices bacon, precooked and in 2 in (5 cm) pieces
16	cooked pearl onions
½ cup	(125 ml) melted garlic butter
1 ½ cups	(375 ml) seasoned breadcrumbs

Alternate snails, rolled pieces of bacon and pearl onions on short skewers. Place on ovenproof platter and baste generously with garlic butter.

Roll skewers in breadcrumbs until well coated. Broil 4 to 6 minutes in oven 4 in (10 cm) from top element. Turn skewers over once.

Serve with extra garlic butter and lemon wedges.

Scallop Kebabs with Fried Parsley

(serves 4)

1 SERVING	434 CALORIES	10g CARBOHYDRATE
31g PROTEIN	30g FAT	0.8g FIBER

½ cup	(125 ml) olive oil
3 tbsp	(45 ml) wine vinegar
½ tsp	(2 ml) crushed rosemary
2 tbsp	(30 ml) lemon juice
1 ½ lb	(750 g) large scallops
12	bay leaves
1	large lemon, sliced (remove seeds)
1	bunch fresh parsley
	freshly ground pepper

Reserve 3 tbsp (45 ml) oil. Place remaining oil in bowl along with vinegar, rosemary, lemon juice, scallops and pepper. Toss and marinate 1 hour on countertop.

Drain scallops and set marinade aside.

Alternate scallops, bay leaves and lemon slices on skewers; place on ovenproof platter.

Broil 3 minutes each side in oven 6 in (15 cm) from top element. Baste occasionally with marinade.

Before kebabs are done, heat reserved oil in frying pan. When hot, sauté parsley (as is, in bunch) about 2 minutes.

Serve as an unusual garnish with kebabs.

Stuffed Mushroom Caps

(serves 4)

1 SERVING	552 CALORIES	43g CARBOHYDRATE
32g PROTEIN	28g FAT	1.3g FIBER

1 lb	(500 g) ricotta cheese
¼ lb	(125 g) grated mozzarella cheese
1 tbsp	(15 ml) chopped parsley
¼ tsp	(1 ml) basil
32	blanched mushroom caps
2	beaten eggs
2 cups	(500 ml) seasoned breadcrumbs
	dash paprika
	salt and pepper
	Tabasco sauce to taste

Mix both cheeses, parsley, basil, paprika, salt, pepper and Tabasco together. Stuff mushroom caps.

Press two mushroom caps together (to keep stuffing in place) and thread 4 sets on each skewer.

Roll skewers in beaten eggs, then in breadcrumbs. Place on ovenproof platter and broil 6 minutes in oven 6 in (15 cm) from top element. Turn skewers over once.

Serve as an appetizer or with a main dish.

Mushroom Garnish

(serves 4)

1 SERVING	208 CALORIES	10g CARBOHYDRATE
24g PROTEIN	8g FAT	1.0g FIBER

1 tbsp	(15 ml) butter
1	onion, finely chopped
½ lb	(250 g) lean ground beef
1 tbsp	(15 ml) chopped parsley
¼ cup	(50 ml) grated Gruyère cheese
16	large mushrooms caps, blanched 3 minutes
3 tbsp	(45 ml) seasoned breadcrumbs
	salt and pepper

Heat butter in frying pan. Sauté onion 2 to 3 minutes over medium-low heat.

Add beef and parsley; season to taste. Continue cooking 3 to 4 minutes.

Mix in cheese and cook 1 minute. Remove from heat and stuff mushroom caps.

Thread mushroom caps on skewers with stuffing side up. Place on ovenproof platter and sprinkle breadcrumbs over stuffing.

Broil 3 to 4 minutes in oven 6 in (15 cm) from top element. Do not turn skewers over!

Serve as a vegetable garnish.

Assorted Pepper Kebabs

(serves 4)

1 SERVING	155 CALORIES	12g CARBOHYDRATE
2g PROTEIN	11g FAT	2.1g FIBER

4 tbsp	(60 ml) olive oil
¼ tsp	(1 ml) Tabasco sauce
½ tsp	(2 ml) lemon juice
2	garlic cloves, smashed and finely chopped
2	green peppers, seeded and halved
2	yellow peppers, seeded and halved
2	red peppers, seeded and halved
	freshly ground pepper

Preheat oven to 450°F (240°C).

Mix oil, Tabasco, lemon juice, garlic and pepper together. Place peppers in ovenproof dish and pour in mixture. Cook 10 minutes in middle of oven.

Remove and let cool slightly.

Cut pepper halves into 3 and alternate colours on skewers; brush with oil mixture. Broil 6 minutes 6 in (15 cm) from top element; turn over once.

Serve.

Eggplant and Bacon Skewers

(serves 4)

1 SERVING	88 CALORIES	9g CARBOHYDRATE
4g PROTEIN	4g FAT	0.8g FIBER

2	eggplant slices, ¾ in (2 cm) thick
1	back bacon slice, ¾ in (2 cm) thick
8	pieces of red onion
8	cherry tomatoes
¼ tsp	(1 ml) Worcestershire sauce
1 tbsp	(15 ml) oil
3 tbsp	(45 ml) plum sauce
	salt and pepper

Cut eggplant and bacon into ½ in (1.2 cm) cubes. Alternate along with onion and tomatoes on thin wooden skewers.

Place in ovenproof dish and season generously. Sprinkle on Worcestershire sauce, oil and plum sauce.

Broil 10 minutes in oven 6 in (15 cm) from top element. Turn skewers over once.

1 Cut eggplant and bacon into ½ in (1.2 cm) cubes.

2 Alternate along with onion and tomatoes on thin wooden skewers. Place in ovenproof dish and season generously. Sprinkle in Worcestershire sauce, oil and plum sauce.

New Potatoes

(serves 4)

1 SERVING	548 CALORIES	34g CARBOHYDRATE
22g PROTEIN	36g FAT	7.1g FIBER

24	new round potatoes, cooked in jackets
24	slices bacon, medium cooked
1 cup	(250 ml) finely grated cheddar cheese
	dash paprika
	freshly ground pepper

Wrap potatoes with bacon slices and place on skewers. Set on ovenproof platter.

Broil 3 minutes in oven 6 in (15 cm) from top element. Turn skewers over; sprinkle with cheese, paprika and pepper. Finish broiling another 3 minutes.

Serve with meat or fish.

Mixed Vegetable Kebabs

(serves 4)

1 SERVING	74 CALORIES	12g CARBOHYDRATE
2g PROTEIN	2g FAT	2.1g FIBER

2	red peppers, in bite-size pieces
1	zucchini, cut in two and sliced thick
1	red onion, in large pieces
2 tbsp	(30 ml) soya sauce
1 tsp	(5 ml) Worcestershire sauce
1 tsp	(5 ml) oil
2	garlic cloves, smashed and chopped
½ tsp	(2 ml) tarragon
½ cup	(125 ml) barbecue sauce

Preheat oven to 450°F (240°C).

Place vegetables in bowl. Add soya sauce, Worcestershire sauce, oil, garlic and tarragon. Marinate 30 minutes at room temperature.

Drain vegetables and reserve marinade.

Alternate vegetables on skewers and place on ovenproof platter; baste with barbecue sauce.

Cook 8 minutes in oven 4 in (10 cm) from top element. Baste several times with marinade and turn skewers twice.

Serve with barbecue sauce for dipping.

1 Place red peppers, zucchini and onion in bowl.

2 Add soya sauce, Worcestershire sauce, oil, garlic and tarragon; marinate 30 minutes at room temperature.

Tomato Fruit Kebabs

(serves 4)

1 SERVING	140 CALORIES	34g CARBOHYDRATE
1g PROTEIN	0g FAT	2.7g FIBER

2	small bananas, sliced thick
¼	pineapple, in large chunks
1	apple, peeled and sliced in wedges
1	large tomato, cored and sliced in wedges
1 tbsp	(15 ml) brown sugar
1 tsp	(5 ml) cinnamon
2 tbsp	(30 ml) maple syrup

Place fruit, tomato, brown sugar, cinnamon and maple syrup in bowl; toss gently. Set aside 15 minutes on countertop.

Alternate pineapple, tomato, banana and apple on thin wooden skewers; repeat until ingredients are used.

Place on ovenproof platter and pour juices from bowl over kebabs. Broil 6 minutes in oven 6 in (15 cm) from top element. Turn skewers over once.

Serve as an interesting dessert or with a meat dish.

Pineapple Chunks and Water Chestnuts

(serves 4)

1 SERVING	143 CALORIES	15g CARBOHYDRATE
5g PROTEIN	7g FAT	0.4g FIBER

16	chunks fresh pineapple
8	slices bacon, medium cooked and cut in half
12	canned water chestnuts
2 tbsp	(30 ml) maple syrup
1 tsp	(5 ml) lemon juice

Wrap pineapple chunks with bacon. Alternate with water chestnuts on skewers and place on ovenproof platter.

Mix maple syrup with lemon juice; brush over skewers. Broil 3 minutes each side in oven 6 in (15 cm) from top element.

Serve as an appetizer or as a snack.

Apricot Dessert

(serves 4)

1 SERVING	259 CALORIES	47g CARBOHYDRATE
2g PROTEIN	7g FAT	2.9g FIBER

24	apricots, pitted
½ cup	(125 ml) Tia Maria
2 tbsp	(30 ml) butter
2 tbsp	(30 ml) sugar
	juice 1 orange
	juice ½ lemon
	whipped cream for topping

Marinate apricots in Tia Maria for 30 minutes.

Drain and reserve liquid; thread apricots on skewers.

Heat butter in frying pan. Stir in sugar and cook until golden brown; stir constantly!

Pour in reserved marinade and flambé. Add orange and lemon juices; cook 2 minutes.

Pour sauce into fairly deep baking dish and place skewers on top. Broil 6 minutes in oven.

Top with whipped cream if desired.

Double Orange Skewer Dessert

(serves 4)

1 SERVING	400 CALORIES	70g CARBOHYDRATE
3g PROTEIN	12g FAT	2.4g FIBER

2	mandarins, peeled and sectioned
1	seedless orange, peeled and sectioned
½	orange honeydew melon, cut in bite-size pieces
2 tbsp	(30 ml) granulated sugar
2 tbsp	(30 ml) orange liqueur
2 oz	(60 g) unsweetened chocolate
¼ cup	(50 ml) heavy cream
1 cup	(250 ml) icing sugar
	few drops vanilla

Place fruit in bowl with granulated sugar and liqueur. Toss and let stand while you make the sauce.

Place chocolate, cream, icing sugar and vanilla in double boiler. Cook until mixture is completely melted; stir constantly.

Alternate fruit on wooden skewers and place on individual dessert plates. Drizzle chocolate sauce over kebabs and serve.

Passion Fruit Kebabs

(serves 4)

1 SERVING	141 CALORIES	29g CARBOHYDRATE
4g PROTEIN	1g FAT	0g FIBER

4	passion fruit*, cut in half
2 tbsp	(30 ml) orange liqueur
2	egg whites
2 tbsp	(30 ml) sugar

Carefully thread fruit halves on short skewers. Sprinkle liqueur over each and place on ovenproof platter.

Beat egg whites until fairly stiff. Slowly incorporate sugar and continue beating 1½ minutes.

Spoon a large dollop of egg whites on each fruit half. Broil 2 minutes in oven 6 in (15 cm) from top element.

Serve immediately. Diners should eat passion fruit with a spoon.

* Choose your passion fruit carefully. Look for dark purple skin with a lumpy texture that is fairly firm.

Strawberry and Kiwi Kebabs

(serves 4)

1 SERVING	104 CALORIES	23g CARBOHYDRATE
3g PROTEIN	0g FAT	1.2g FIBER

24	ripe strawberries, hulled
4	ripe kiwis, peeled and cut in 4
3 tbsp	(45 ml) sugar
¼ cup	(50 ml) Lamb's Caribbean Cream
1 tbsp	(15 ml) grated lemon rind
2	egg whites

Preheat oven to 400°F (200°C).

Place strawberries and kiwis in bowl; add 1 tbsp (15 ml) sugar, Caribbean Cream and lemon rind. Toss and marinate 1 hour.

Alternate fruit on wooden skewers and place on ovenproof platter.

Beat egg whites until fairly stiff. Slowly incorporate remaining sugar and continue beating 1½ minutes.

Carefully arrange dollops of egg whites on top portion of skewers. Change oven setting to broil and brown 2 to 3 minutes 6 in (15 cm) from top element.

Serve immediately.

Skewer Sundae

(serves 4)

1 SERVING	429 CALORIES	54g CARBOHYDRATE
6g PROTEIN	21g FAT	1.6g FIBER

1	banana, sliced
12	strawberries, cut in half
12	chunks fresh pineapple
8	scoops French vanilla ice cream
2 tbsp	(30 ml) butter
2 tbsp	(30 ml) sugar
½ cup	(125 ml) orange juice
	grated rind ½ lemon
	grated rind ½ orange

Alternate fruit on short wooden skewers. Divide ice cream scoops between four sundae dishes and set skewers on top; refrigerate.

Heat butter in frying pan. Stir in sugar and cook until golden brown; mix constantly!

Add orange juice and rinds; continue cooking to reduce by half.

Cool slightly then pour over kebabs and serve.

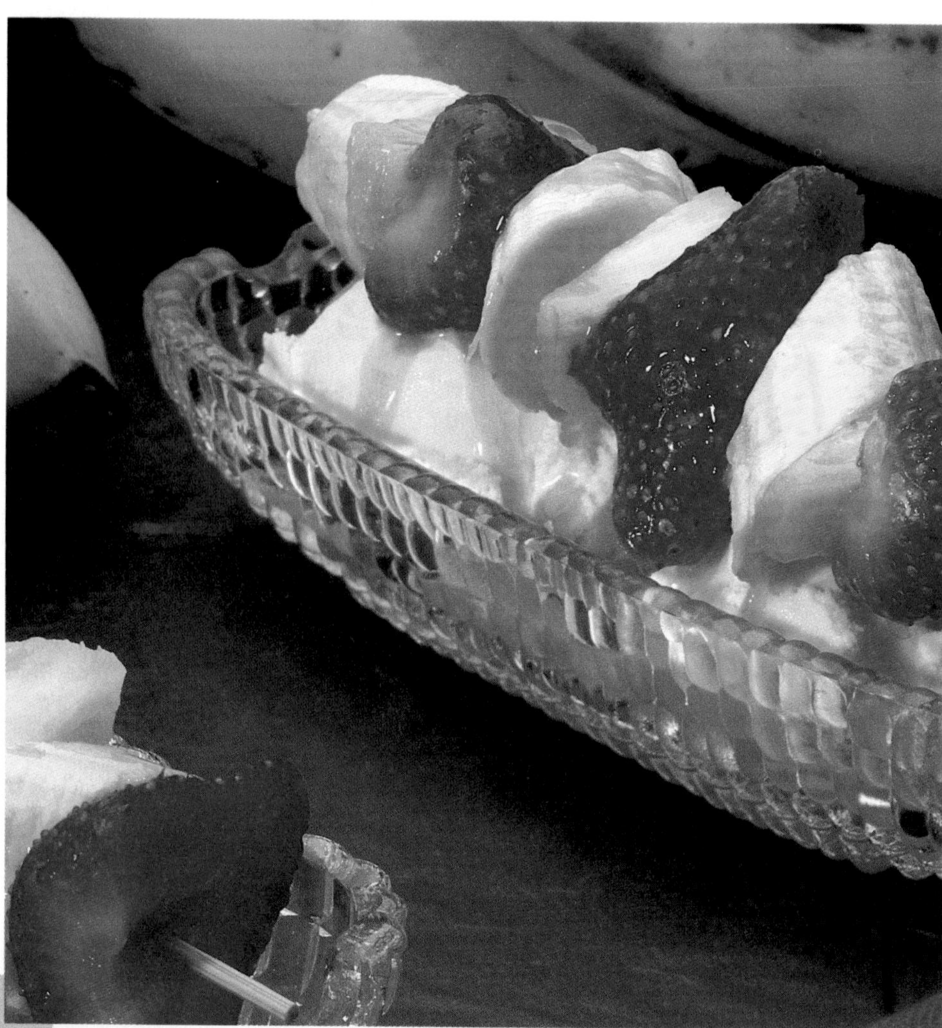

Plums with Jubilee Sauce

(serves 4)

1 SERVING	175 CALORIES	36g CARBOHYDRATE
1g PROTEIN	3g FAT	2.9g FIBER

8	ripe plums, pitted and cut in half
¼ cup	(50 ml) kirsch
1 tbsp	(15 ml) butter
2 tbsp	(30 ml) sugar
¾ cup	(175 ml) cherry juice
½ cup	(125 ml) canned cherries
1 tsp	(5 ml) cornstarch
2 tbsp	(30 ml) cold water
	juice 1 orange

Marinate plums in half of kirsch for 10 minutes. Drain and reserve marinade; thread plum halves on short wooden skewers.

Heat butter with sugar in frying pan. Stir constantly and cook 1 minute.

Add cherry juice, cherries and orange juice; mix well. Add remaining kirsch and marinade; bring to boil.

Set skewers in sauce and cook 2 to 3 minutes over medium heat. Transfer skewers to dessert dishes and continue cooking sauce 2 to 3 minutes.

Mix cornstarch with water; stir into sauce and cook 1 minute.

Pour over kebabs and serve.

Onion Mustard Sauce

1 SERVING	17 CALORIES	2g CARBOHYDRATE
0g PROTEIN	1g FAT	0.1g FIBER

1 tbsp	(15 ml) olive oil
1	onion, chopped
¼ cup	(50 ml) wine vinegar
2 tbsp	(30 ml) capers
1 tsp	(5 ml) chopped parsley
¼ tsp	(1 ml) freshly ground pepper
1 cup	(250 ml) dry red wine
1½ cups	(375 ml) brown sauce, heated
2 tbsp	(30 ml) Dijon mustard

Heat oil in deep frying pan. When hot, add onion and cook 3 minutes over medium heat.

Stir in vinegar, capers, parsley and pepper; cook 3 minutes.

Pour in wine and cook 6 to 7 minutes over high heat.

Mix in brown sauce, correct seasoning and simmer 6 to 7 minutes over low heat.

Remove pan from stove, stir in mustard and serve sauce with beef or veal.

1 After onion has cooked 3 minutes, stir in vinegar, capers, parsley and pepper; continue cooking 3 minutes.

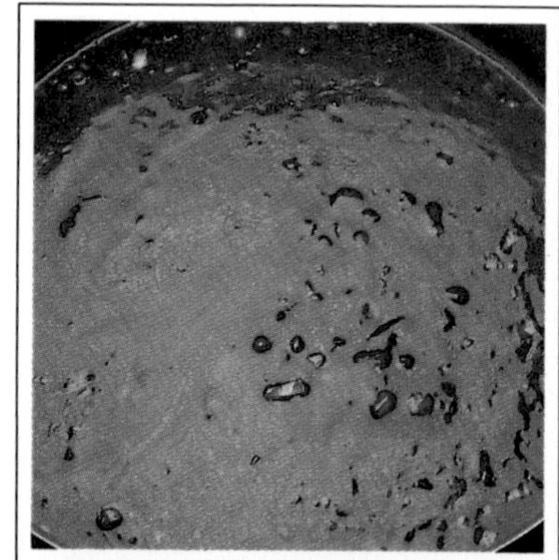

3 Mix in brown sauce, correct seasoning and simmer 6 to 7 minutes over low heat.

2 Pour in wine and cook 6 to 7 minutes over high heat.

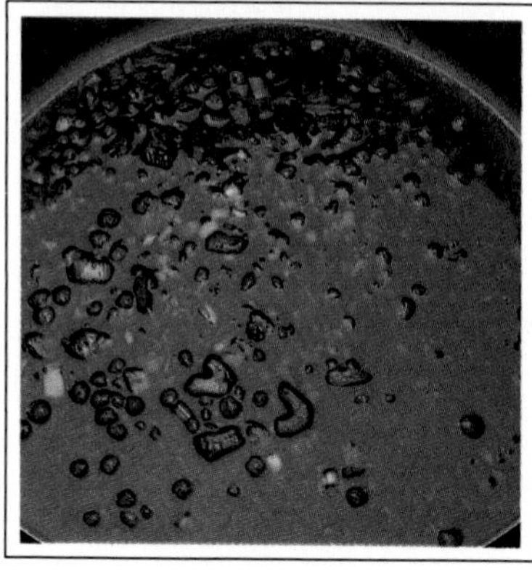

4 Remove pan from stove and stir in mustard before serving.

Parsley Sauce

1 SERVING	13 CALORIES	1g CARBOHYDRATE
0g PROTEIN	1g FAT	0g FIBER

1 tbsp	(15 ml) butter
2 tbsp	(30 ml) chopped parsley
1 tsp	(5 ml) oregano
1 tbsp	(15 ml) tarragon
2	shallots, chopped
2 tbsp	(30 ml) wine vinegar
½ cup	(125 ml) dry white wine
1 ½ cups	(375 ml) hot chicken stock
1 tbsp	(15 ml) cornstarch
3 tbsp	(45 ml) cold water
	salt and pepper

Heat butter in deep frying pan. Cook parsley, oregano, tarragon and shallots 2 minutes over medium heat; season well.

Pour in vinegar and cook 1 minute over high heat.

Add wine; cook 3 to 4 minutes over high heat.

Pour in chicken stock, bring to boil and continue cooking 3 to 4 minutes. Correct seasoning.

Mix cornstarch with water; stir into sauce and cook 2 to 3 minutes.

Serve this sauce with chicken or veal.

1 Cook parsley, oregano, tarragon and shallots 2 minutes in hot butter over medium heat; season well.

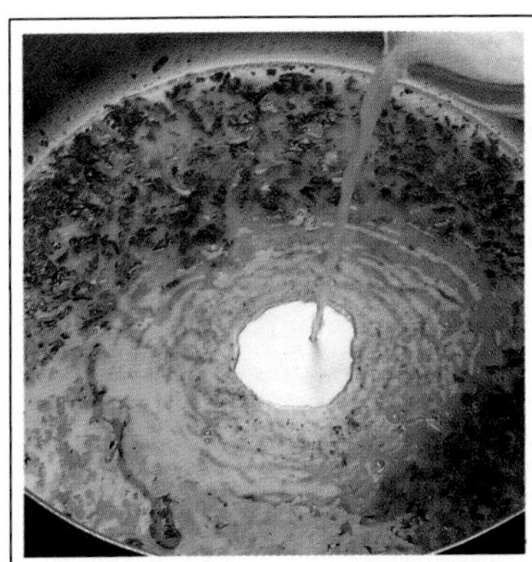

3 Pour in chicken stock, bring to boil and continue cooking 3 to 4 minutes. Correct seasoning.

2 Pour in vinegar, cook 1 minute, then add wine. Cook another 3 to 4 minutes over high heat.

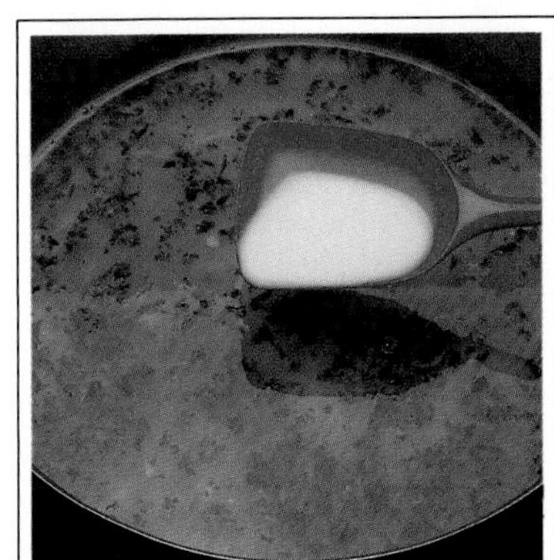

4 Stir diluted cornstarch into sauce and cook 2 to 3 minutes to thicken.

Curry Sauce

1 SERVING	48 CALORIES	3g CARBOHYDRATE
0g PROTEIN	4g FAT	0.1g FIBER

2 tbsp	(30 ml) butter
2	large onions, finely chopped
3 tbsp	(45 ml) curry powder
2 cups	(500 ml) hot chicken stock
1½ tbsp	(25 ml) cornstarch
3 tbsp	(45 ml) cold water
¼ cup	(50 ml) heavy cream
	dash paprika
	salt and pepper

Heat butter in deep frying pan. When hot, add onions and season with paprika; cook 4 to 5 minutes over medium heat.

Mix in curry powder and cook 3 to 4 minutes over very low heat.

Pour in stock and season well; mix and cook 4 to 5 minutes over medium heat.

Mix cornstarch with water; stir into sauce along with cream. Cook 4 to 5 minutes over low heat.

Serve with a variety of kebabs.

1 Cook onions seasoned with paprika 4 to 5 minutes over medium heat.

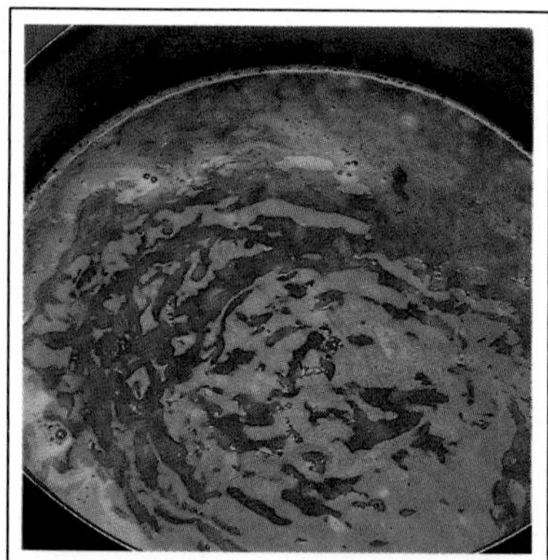

3 Pour in stock and season well; mix and cook 4 to 5 minutes over medium heat.

2 Mix in curry powder and cook 3 to 4 minutes over very low heat.

4 Stir diluted cornstarch and cream into sauce; cook 4 to 5 minutes over low heat.

Bourguignonne Sauce

1 SERVING	43 CALORIES	3g CARBOHYDRATE
1g PROTEIN	3g FAT	0.2g FIBER

1 tbsp	(15 ml) vegetable oil
2	shallots, chopped
2	garlic cloves, smashed and chopped
1 tbsp	(15 ml) chopped parsley
1 tbsp	(15 ml) tarragon
1 cup	(250 ml) dry red wine
1	bay leaf
1½ cups	(375 ml) brown sauce, heated
1 cup	(250 ml) diced mushrooms, sautéed
	salt and pepper

Heat oil in deep frying pan. When hot, add shallots, garlic, parsley and tarragon; cook 2 minutes over medium heat.

Add wine, bay leaf and season with pepper; cook 6 to 7 minutes over high heat.

Mix in brown sauce; cook 4 to 5 minutes over medium heat.

Add mushrooms, correct seasoning and cook 2 to 3 minutes.

Serve with beef kebabs. Remember to discard bay leaf before serving.

1 Cook shallots, garlic, parsley and tarragon in hot oil 2 minutes over medium heat.

3 Mix in brown sauce; cook 4 to 5 minutes over medium heat.

2 Pour in wine, bay leaf and season with pepper; cook 6 to 7 minutes over high heat.

4 Add mushrooms, correct seasoning and cook 2 to 3 minutes.

Orange Honey Sauce

1 SERVING	70 CALORIES	13g CARBOHYDRATE
0g PROTEIN	2g FAT	0.2g FIBER

1	onion, finely chopped
1 tbsp	(15 ml) oil
1 cup	(250 ml) orange juice
4 tbsp	(60 ml) honey
1 tbsp	(15 ml) finely chopped fresh ginger
2 tbsp	(30 ml) wine vinegar
	few drops Tabasco sauce

Mix all ingredients together in small saucepan. Bring to boil and continue cooking 2 minutes.

Cool slightly and baste over chicken or pork before broiling.

Peppercorn Sauce

1 SERVING	82 CALORIES	5g CARBOHYDRATE
2g PROTEIN	6g FAT	0.1g FIBER

1 tbsp	(15 ml) butter
1	onion, finely chopped
1 tbsp	(15 ml) chopped parsley
3 tbsp	(45 ml) green peppercorns
½ cup	(125 ml) dry white wine
1 ½ cups	(375 ml) hot white sauce
1 tsp	(5 ml) cumin
	salt and pepper
	dash paprika

Heat butter in saucepan. When hot, add onion and parsley; cook 2 minutes.

Stir in peppercorns and wine; cook 5 minutes over high heat.

Mix in white sauce, cumin and remaining spices; cook 6 to 7 minutes over low heat.

Correct seasoning and serve with almost any kebab.

Tartare Sauce

1 SERVING	99 CALORIES	0g CARBOHYDRATE
0g PROTEIN	11g FAT	0.2g FIBER

1 cup	(250 ml) mayonnaise
3	pickles, finely chopped
24	stuffed green olives, finely chopped
1 tsp	(5 ml) chopped fresh parsley
1 tbsp	(15 ml) capers
¼ tsp	(1 ml) paprika
1 tsp	(5 ml) lemon juice
	salt and pepper

Mix all ingredients together in bowl until well combined. Correct seasoning and chill until serving time.

Stroganoff Sauce

1 SERVING	43 CALORIES	3g CARBOHYDRATE
1g PROTEIN	3g FAT	0.2g FIBER

1 tbsp	(15 ml) olive oil
1	medium onion, finely chopped
¼ lb	(125 g) mushrooms, finely chopped
1 tsp	(5 ml) chopped parsley
½ cup	(125 ml) dry red wine
1 ½ cups	(375 ml) brown sauce, heated
¼ cup	(50 ml) heavy cream
	salt and pepper

Heat oil in deep frying pan. Cook onion 3 minutes over medium heat.

Mix in mushrooms and parsley; cook 2 to 3 minutes.

Pour in wine; cook 4 to 5 minutes over high heat.

Mix in brown sauce, correct seasoning and cook 6 to 7 minutes over medium-low heat.

Stir in cream and finish cooking 2 minutes.

Serve sauce with either beef or chicken.

1 After onion has cooked 3 minutes, mix in mushrooms and parsley; cook 2 to 3 minutes.

3 Mix in brown sauce, correct seasoning and cook 6 to 7 minutes over medium-low heat.

2 Pour in wine; cook 4 to 5 minutes over high heat.

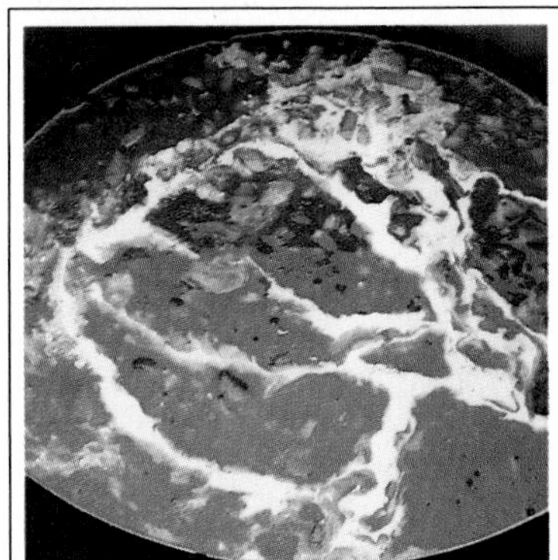

4 Stir in cream and finish cooking 2 minutes.

Spicy Kebab Sauce

1 SERVING	61 CALORIES	12g CARBOHYDRATE
1g PROTEIN	1g FAT	0.3g FIBER

2 tbsp	(30 ml) horseradish
1 ½ cups	(375 ml) catsup
½ cup	(125 ml) chili sauce
1 tsp	(5 ml) Worcestershire sauce
	few drops Tabasco sauce
	few drops lime juice
	dash salt

Mix all ingredients together in bowl until well combined. Spread over kebabs and broil as directed in recipe.

Paprika Sauce

1 SERVING	74 CALORIES	4g CARBOHYDRATE
1g PROTEIN	6g FAT	0.2g FIBER

1 cup	(250 ml) chopped onions
2 tbsp	(30 ml) butter
2 tbsp	(30 ml) paprika
½ cup	(125 ml) dry white wine
1 ½ cups	(375 ml) hot white sauce
	few drops Tabasco sauce
	dash salt
	few drops lemon juice

Place onions in small saucepan and pour in water to cover. Bring to boil and continue cooking 2 minutes; drain and set aside.

Heat butter in saucepan. Cook drained onion and paprika 5 to 6 minutes over low heat.

Pour in wine; cook 5 minutes over high heat to reduce liquid by ⅔.

Mix in white sauce and remaining ingredients; cook 6 to 7 minutes over low heat.

Serve sauce with a variety of kebabs.

PASTA

How To Cook Perfect Pasta

We have allowed ¼ lb (125 g) or less of dry pasta per serving, depending on the recipe.

Allow 16 cups (4 l) of water per 1 lb (500 g) of pasta as the water must be able to circulate easily.

To help keep pasta from sticking, add about 1 tbsp (15 ml) of oil or vinegar to the water before adding pasta.

To draw out the pasta's flavor you can add about 1 tsp (5 ml) of salt.

Be sure to bring the water to a full boil before adding pasta and when you do so, stir the noodles well.

During cooking keep the water boiling and stir several times or as often as needed to prevent the pasta from sticking.

One way to check if the pasta is cooked is by biting into a strand or piece and deciding by your preference. The package directions will give you a guideline for cooking times.

When pasta is 'al dente', stop the cooking process by draining pasta into a colander or large sieve and rinsing with cold water. Shake off excess water and set aside until ready to use. If you need to heat pasta quickly simply rinse with hot water.

For your convenience we have given these measurements in cups, which are equivalent to ¼ lb (125 g) of the pasta listed. All measurements are for dry pasta.

Rotini	1 cup	250 ml
Conch Shells (medium)	1⅓ cups	325 ml
Penne	1¾ cups	425 ml
Fusilli	1¾ cups	425 ml
Macaroni	1 cup	250 ml
Broad Egg Noodles	2¼ cups	550 ml

Last Minute White Spaghetti

(serves 4)

1 SERVING	579 CALORIES	94g CARBOHYDRATE
17g PROTEIN	15g FAT	0.3g FIBER

1 tbsp	(15 ml) white vinegar
1 tsp	(5 ml) salt
1 lb	(500 g) spaghetti
3 tbsp	(45 ml) butter
¼ cup	(50 ml) grated Parmesan cheese
¼ cup	(50 ml) grated mozzarella cheese
¼ cup	(50 ml) grated Gruyère cheese
¼ tsp	(1 ml) celery seed
	white pepper
	dash paprika

Bring 16 cups (4 L) water, vinegar and salt to full boil in large saucepan. Add pasta and stir; cook at full boil uncovered, stirring occasionally. Using package directions as a guideline, test pasta several times by biting into strand. When 'al dente', drain into colander reserving ¼ cup (50 ml) of cooking liquid. Rinse pasta with cold water and set aside.

Melt butter in same saucepan. Mix in cheeses and reserved cooking liquid; blend together well.

Add pasta and seasonings; mix well but gently and cook about 2 minutes over medium heat. Stir constantly!

Sprinkle with more paprika and serve immediately.

Four Cheese Sauce and Noodles

(serves 4)

1 SERVING	882 CALORIES	111g CARBOHYDRATE
33g PROTEIN	34g FAT	0.5g FIBER

4 tbsp	(60 ml) butter
4½ tbsp	(65 ml) flour
4 cups	(1 L) hot milk
½ tsp	(2 ml) nutmeg
¼ tsp	(1 ml) ground clove
¼ cup	(50 ml) grated Fontina cheese
¼ cup	(50 ml) crumbled Gorgonzola cheese
¼ cup	(50 ml) diced mozzarella cheese
¼ cup	(50 ml) grated Parmesan cheese
1 lb	(500 g) broad egg noodles, cooked
	salt and pepper

Heat butter in saucepan. Mix in flour and cook 2 to 3 minutes over low heat.

Add half of milk, whisk well and pour in remaining milk. Add seasonings and cook sauce 8 to 10 minutes over low heat.

Stir in cheeses and cook 4 to 5 minutes over low heat. Stir as required.

Serve with noodles.

Basic Tomato Sauce

1 SERVING	154 CALORIES	21g CARBOHYDRATE
4g PROTEIN	6g FAT	2.2g FIBER

2 tbsp	(30 ml) vegetable oil
1 tbsp	(15 ml) melted butter
2	onions, finely chopped
2	garlic cloves, smashed and chopped
12	large tomatoes, peeled and chopped
3	parsley sprigs
1 tsp	(5 ml) oregano
½ tsp	(2 ml) thyme
1	bay leaf
¼ tsp	(1 ml) crushed chillies
5½ oz	(156 ml) can tomato paste
	salt and pepper
	pinch sugar

Heat oil and butter in skillet. Add onions and garlic; mix well, cover and cook 4 to 5 minutes over low heat.

Stir in tomatoes, seasonings, parsley and sugar; continue cooking covered 15 minutes over low heat. Stir occasionally.

Remove cover and stir in tomato paste. Finish cooking 10 to 15 minutes over low heat uncovered.

Force sauce through sieve. This recipe will yield about 4 cups (1 L).

Meat Sauce for Spaghetti

(serves 6 to 8)

1 SERVING	265 CALORIES	15g CARBOHYDRATE
22g PROTEIN	13g FAT	1.7g FIBER

2 tbsp	(30 ml) olive oil
1	onion, chopped
1	carrot, diced small
1	celery stalk, diced small
3	garlic cloves, smashed and chopped
½ lb	(250 g) lean ground pork
½ lb	(250 g) ground beef
¼ lb	(125 g) sausage meat
¼ tsp	(1 ml) crushed chillies
½ tsp	(2 ml) thyme
½ tsp	(2 ml) oregano
¼ tsp	(1 ml) chili powder
¼ tsp	(1 ml) sugar
1	bay leaf
1 cup	(250 ml) dry white wine Chardonnay
2	28 oz (796 ml) cans tomatoes, drained and chopped
5 ½ oz	(156 ml) can tomato paste
	salt and pepper

Heat oil in deep skillet. Add onion, carrot, celery and garlic; cover and cook 3 minutes over medium heat.

Add pork, beef and sausage meat; mix well and continue cooking 4 minutes. Do not cover.

Add seasonings, sugar and wine; cook 3 minutes over high heat.

Stir in tomatoes, tomato paste and correct seasoning; bring to boil. Cook sauce, partially covered, about 1 hour over low heat; stir occasionally.

Serve this sauce with spaghetti or use it in a variety of pasta dishes as it is versatile.

1 Cook vegetables and garlic 3 minutes over medium heat. Cover pan.

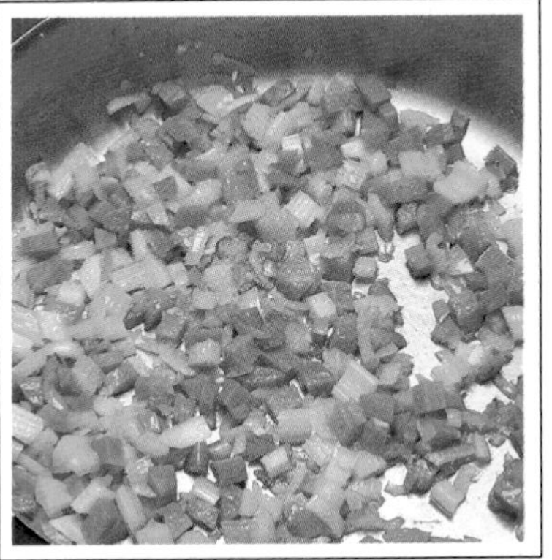

3 Add seasonings, sugar and wine; cook 3 minutes over high heat.

2 Add pork, beef and sausage meat; mix well and continue cooking 4 minutes uncovered.

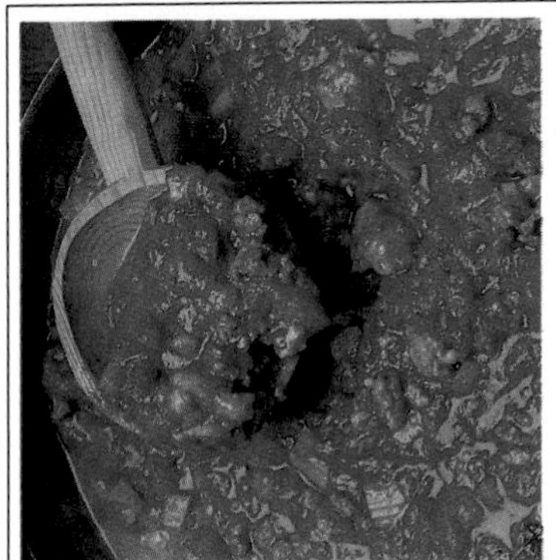

4 Stir in tomatoes, tomato paste and correct seasoning; bring to boil. Cook sauce, partially covered, about 1 hour over low heat.

White Sauce

1 SERVING	60 CALORIES	4g CARBOHYDRATE
2g PROTEIN	4g FAT	0g FIBER

4 tbsp	(60 ml) butter
5 tbsp	(75 ml) flour
5 cups	(1.2 L) hot milk
1	onion, studded with 1 clove
¼ tsp	(1 ml) nutmeg
	salt and white pepper

Heat butter in large saucepan. When melted, add flour and mix well. Cook 2 minutes over low heat stirring constantly.

Whisk in half of milk. Incorporate remaining milk and season. Drop in onion, stir in nutmeg and bring to boil.

Cook sauce 8 to 10 minutes over low heat, stirring occasionally. Use this sauce in a variety of pasta recipes.

Spicy Tomato Sauce

1 SERVING	182 CALORIES	15g CARBOHYDRATE
8g PROTEIN	10g FAT	1.5g FIBER

1 tbsp	(15 ml) olive oil
4	slices bacon, diced
1	large onion, finely chopped
2	garlic cloves, smashed and chopped
6	large tomatoes, peeled, seeded and chopped
1	fresh jalapeno pepper, finely chopped
1 tbsp	(15 ml) basil
1 tsp	(5 ml) chili powder
¼ tsp	(1 ml) sugar
¼ cup	(50 ml) grated Parmesan cheese
	salt and pepper

Heat oil in skillet. Cook bacon until crisp then remove, leaving fat in pan. Set bacon aside.

Add onion and garlic to pan; cook 3 to 4 minutes over low heat.

Stir in tomatoes, jalapeno pepper, seasonings and sugar. Cover and cook 20 minutes over low heat; stir occasionally.

Remove cover and continue cooking 15 minutes.

Mix in cheese and bacon. This recipe will yield about 2 cups (500 ml).

Perogies in Sauce

(serves 4)

1 SERVING	465 CALORIES	48g CARBOHYDRATE
21g PROTEIN	21g FAT	2.9g FIBER

2 tbsp	(30 ml) olive oil
1	onion, chopped
½	medium eggplant, cubed
1	zucchini, sliced
½ tsp	(2 ml) oregano
1 lb	(500 g) package perogies, cooked
2 tbsp	(30 ml) butter
28 oz	(796 ml) can tomatoes, drained and chopped
1	garlic clove, smashed and chopped
1 cup	(250 ml) chicken stock, heated
4 tbsp	(60 ml) tomato paste
3 tbsp	(45 ml) ricotta cheese
	salt and pepper

Heat oil in skillet and cook onion 2 minutes over medium heat.

Add eggplant, zucchini, oregano, salt and pepper. Cover and cook 10 to 12 minutes over medium heat stirring occasionally.

Meanwhile brown cooked perogies in 2 tbsp (30 ml) butter. When lightly browned on both sides remove from pan and set aside.

Add tomatoes and garlic to eggplant in skillet; mix very well and pour in chicken stock. Correct seasoning and stir in tomato paste; bring to boil and continue cooking uncovered 8 to 10 minutes.

Mix in cheese and perogies; simmer 2 to 3 minutes or until heated.

1 After onions have cooked 3 minutes, mix in curry and continue cooking another 3 minutes. Do not cover.

3 Pour in chicken stock and season; bring to boil and cook 15 to 18 minutes over medium heat.

2 Add mushrooms and cook another 3 to 4 minutes.

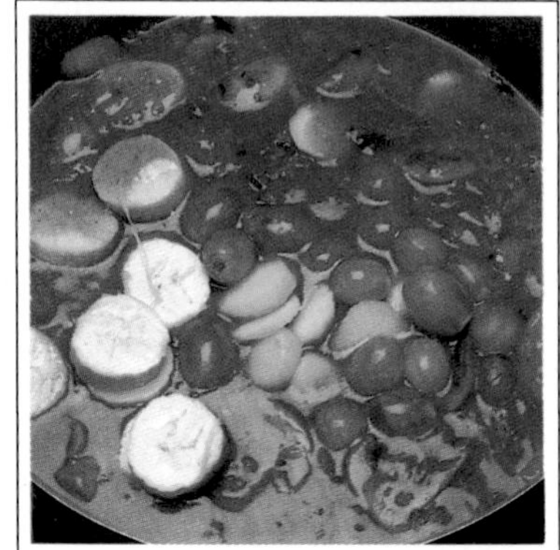

4 After sauce has thickened, add grapes, banana and water chestnuts and cook 1 minute.

Tortellini with Curry Sauce

(serves 4)

1 SERVING	325 CALORIES	43g CARBOHYDRATE
9g PROTEIN	13g FAT	2.6g FIBER

2 tbsp	(30 ml) oil
2	onions, chopped
2 tbsp	(30 ml) curry powder
½ lb	(250 g) mushrooms, sliced
3 cups	(750 ml) chicken stock, heated
2 tbsp	(30 ml) cornstarch
3 tbsp	(45 ml) cold water
1 cup	(250 ml) seedless green grapes
1	banana, sliced thick
10 oz	(284 ml) can water chestnuts, drained and sliced
½ lb	(250 g) cheese tortellini, cooked
	salt and pepper

Heat oil in skillet. Add onions and cook 3 minutes over medium heat covered.

Mix in curry; continue cooking 3 minutes uncovered.

Add mushrooms and cook another 3 to 4 minutes. Pour in chicken stock and season; bring to boil and cook 15 to 18 minutes over medium heat.

Mix cornstarch with water; stir into sauce and cook 1 minute.

Stir grapes, banana and water chestnuts into mixture; cook 1 minute.

Add tortellini and simmer 3 to 4 minutes.

Yellow Peppers Stuffed with Spaghetti

(serves 4)

1 SERVING	417 CALORIES	70g CARBOHYDRATE
14g PROTEIN	9g FAT	3.6g FIBER

2½ cups	(375 ml) spaghetti, broken into 1 in (2.5 cm) lengths
4	large yellow peppers, blanched 4 minutes
1 tbsp	(15 ml) butter
½ lb	(250 g) mushrooms, diced
2 tbsp	(30 ml) chopped pimento
1¼ cups	(300 ml) tomato sauce, heated
½ cup	(125 ml) ricotta cheese
	salt and pepper

Cook spaghetti al dente. Drain well and set aside.

Using small knife cut tops off peppers and remove white fibers and seeds; set aside on ovenproof platter.

Heat butter in saucepan. Cook mushrooms 3 minutes over medium heat; season well.

Add pimento and spaghetti; mix well and cook 2 minutes.

Stir in tomato sauce and cheese; correct seasoning. Pour into peppers and broil 4 to 5 minutes in oven.

Tortellini in Sauce

(serves 4)

1 SERVING	320 CALORIES	24g CARBOHYDRATE
11g PROTEIN	20g FAT	0.9g FIBER

3 tbsp	(45 ml) butter
1	onion, chopped
1 tbsp	(15 ml) chopped parsley
1	garlic clove, smashed and chopped
¼ lb	(125 g) mushrooms, diced
1 cup	(250 ml) dry red wine
2 cups	(500 ml) beef stock, heated
2 tbsp	(30 ml) cornstarch
3 tbsp	(45 ml) cold water
½ lb	(250 g) tortellini, cooked
¼ cup	(50 ml) crumbled cooked bacon
½ cup	(125 ml) grated Parmesan cheese
	salt and pepper

Heat butter in skillet. Add onion, parsley and garlic; cook 3 minutes over low heat.

Mix in mushrooms and season; cook 3 to 4 minutes over medium heat.

Pour in wine and cook 4 minutes over high heat. Add beef stock and cook 3 to 4 minutes over medium heat; correct seasoning.

Mix cornstarch with water; stir into sauce and cook 2 minutes.

Add tortellini, simmer 3 to 4 minutes then serve with bacon and cheese.

Fettuccine and Mussels

(serves 4)

1 SERVING	828 CALORIES	113g CARBOHYDRATE
58g PROTEIN	16g FAT	0.7g FIBER

8½ lb	(4 kg) fresh mussels, scrubbed and bearded
3	shallots, finely chopped
1 tbsp	(15 ml) chopped parsley
2 tbsp	(30 ml) butter
1 cup	(250 ml) dry white wine
2 cups	(500 ml) tomato sauce, heated
1 lb	(500 g) fettuccine, cooked
½ cup	(125 ml) grated Parmesan cheese
	salt and pepper

Place mussels in large pan with shallots, parsley, butter and wine. Cover and bring to boil; cook about 4 to 5 minutes or until shells open.

Remove shells, pouring liquid back into pan. Discard shells and set mussels aside.

Strain cooking liquid through cheesecloth into saucepan. Bring to boil and continue cooking 2 to 3 minutes.

Mix in tomato sauce, season and cook 4 to 5 minutes over medium heat.

Stir mussels and fettuccine into sauce. Cook 3 to 4 minutes over low heat or until heated through.

Serve with cheese.

Fettuccine with Peas

(serves 4)

1 SERVING	737 CALORIES	103g CARBOHYDRATE
25g PROTEIN	25g FAT	1.0g FIBER

3 tbsp	(45 ml) butter
2 tbsp	(30 ml) grated onion
3 tbsp	(45 ml) flour
2¼ cups	(550 ml) hot milk
¼ tsp	(1 ml) nutmeg
¼ tsp	(1 ml) white pepper
1 lb	(500 g) white fettuccine, cooked
1 cup	(250 ml) snow peas*, blanched
4	slices crisp bacon, finely chopped
½ cup	(125 ml) grated Parmesan cheese
	salt
	few drops Tabasco sauce

Heat butter with onion in saucepan. Mix in flour and cook 2 minutes over low heat, stirring only once.

Pour in half of milk, whisk well and add remaining milk along with seasonings; cook sauce 10 minutes over low heat. Stir at least 2 to 3 times.

Add pasta and peas to sauce; stir and cook 2 to 3 minutes more.

Correct seasoning and garnish portions with bacon and cheese.

* Snow peas are available fresh in the pod. Be careful not to accidently choose the green garden peas which are also sold fresh. After shelling the peas you can save the pods for another recipe such as a stir-fry.

Stuffed Cold Tomatoes

(serves 4)

1 SERVING	216 CALORIES	23g CARBOHYDRATE
4g PROTEIN	12g FAT	3.4g FIBER

8	large tomatoes
3	mint leaves, chopped
2 tbsp	(30 ml) olive oil
1 tsp	(5 ml) wine vinegar
1½ cups	(375 ml) cooked ready-cut macaroni
3 tbsp	(45 ml) mustard vinaigrette or substitute
1 tbsp	(15 ml) chopped parsley
1	green pepper, finely chopped
2 tbsp	(30 ml) pickled sweet pimento
	salt and pepper

Using sharp knife and spoon, hollow tomatoes. Discard insides and set shells aside.

Mix chopped mint, oil and vinegar together. Season well and sprinkle in tomatoes; let stand 15 minutes.

Mix macaroni with remaining ingredients; let stand 15 minutes.

Fill tomatoes with macaroni mixture, chill 15 minutes, and serve.

Meaty Macaroni and Cheese

(serves 4)

1 SERVING	826 CALORIES	88g CARBOHYDRATE
60g PROTEIN	26g FAT	2.0g FIBER

2 tbsp	(30 ml) olive oil
1	onion, finely chopped
1	garlic clove, smashed and chopped
½ tsp	(2 ml) oregano
1 tbsp	(15 ml) chopped parsley
½ lb	(250 g) ground beef
½ lb	(250 g) lean ground pork
1½	28 oz (796 ml) cans tomatoes, drained and chopped
¾ lb	(375 g) macaroni, cooked
¾ lb	(375 g) ricotta cheese
	salt and pepper

Heat oil in skillet. Add onion and cook 3 minutes over low heat.

Stir in garlic, seasonings and meats; cook 5 to 6 minutes over medium heat stirring often.

Mix in tomatoes and correct seasoning. Continue cooking 10 to 12 minutes over low heat.

Add macaroni and cheese; cook 4 to 5 minutes over low heat and serve.

Seafood Macaroni

(serves 4)

1 SERVING	795 CALORIES	112g CARBOHYDRATE
53g PROTEIN	15g FAT	5.1g FIBER

5	large tomatoes, cut in 2 and seeded
1 tbsp	(15 ml) olive oil
1	large onion, finely chopped
½ tsp	(2 ml) basil
½ tsp	(2 ml) tarragon
½ tsp	(2 ml) chopped parsley
1 lb	(500 g) small cooked shrimp
1 lb	(500 g) macaroni, cooked
1 cup	(250 ml) ricotta cheese
	pinch sugar
	salt and pepper

Purée tomatoes in blender for 3 minutes.

Heat oil in large frying pan. Cook onion 3 minutes over low heat.

Add basil, tarragon, parsley, sugar and tomatoes; season well. Cook 25 to 30 minutes over low heat.

Stir in shrimp, macaroni and cheese; cook 3 minutes or until heated through.

Serve.

Garnished Penne

(serves 4)

1 SERVING	623 CALORIES	90g CARBOHYDRATE
23g PROTEIN	19g FAT	0.5g FIBER

2 tbsp	(30 ml) butter
¼ cup	(50 ml) Monterey Jack or cheddar, crumbled or grated
½ cup	(125 ml) grated Parmesan cheese
1 lb	(500 g) penne, cooked and still hot
12	thin slices salami, in julienne
	salt and pepper
	chopped parsley

Heat butter in large saucepan over medium-low heat. Stir in cheeses and cook 2 minutes over low heat. Mix to avoid sticking.

Add hot penne and season generously. Mix well and continue cooking 2 to 3 minutes over low heat.

Stir in salami, garnish with chopped parsley and serve.

Penne Vegetable Salad

(serves 4)

1 SERVING	591 CALORIES	95g CARBOHYDRATE
31g PROTEIN	43g FAT	1.7g FIBER

1 lb	(500 g) penne, cooked
1	yellow pepper, in julienne
½	zucchini, in julienne and blanched
4	slices cooked ham, in julienne
1	large tomato, cored and in wedges
½ cup	(125 ml) pitted black olives
1 tbsp	(15 ml) chopped parsley
½ tsp	(2 ml) chopped fresh oregano
3	mint leaves, chopped
1	egg yolk
2 tbsp	(30 ml) catsup
3 tbsp	(45 ml) wine vinegar
½ cup	(125 ml) olive oil
½ cup	(125 ml) grated Parmesan cheese
1 tbsp	(15 ml) chopped jalapeno peppers
	salt and pepper

In large serving bowl, toss together penne, yellow pepper, zucchini, ham, tomato, olives, parsley, oregano and mint.

In another bowl mix egg yolk with catsup. Incorporate vinegar then slowly add oil while mixing constantly.

Add remaining ingredients and poor over salad. Toss and serve.

Linguine with Artichoke Hearts

(serves 4)

1 SERVING	707 CALORIES	195g CARBOHYDRATE
20g PROTEIN	23g FAT	1.3g FIBER

5 tbsp	(75 ml) butter
4½ tbsp	(65 ml) flour
2 cups	(500 ml) hot chicken stock
8	artichoke hearts, quartered
1	garlic clove, smashed and chopped
½ cup	(125 ml) stuffed green olives, halved
1 tbsp	(15 ml) chopped parsley
¼ cup	(50 ml) dry white wine Chardonnay
1 lb	(500 g) linguine, cooked
½ cup	(125 ml) grated Parmesan cheese
	salt and pepper
	dash paprika

Heat 4 tbsp (60 ml) butter in saucepan. Mix in flour and cook 2 minutes over low heat while stirring.

Pour in chicken stock, mix very well and season generously. Cook 8 to 10 minutes over low heat.

Meanwhile, heat remaining butter in frying pan. Cook artichoke hearts, garlic, olives and parsley 2 to 3 minutes over medium heat. Season well.

Incorporate white wine and continue cooking mixture 2 to 3 minutes.

Add artichoke mixture to sauce and mix well. Pour over pasta and sprinkle with cheese and paprika before serving.

1985
PRODUCT OF ITALY
FOLONAR
CHARDON
ALTO ADIGE
DENOMINAZIONE DI ORIGINE CONTROLL
White wine
0 mL
BOTTLED IN THE CELLARS OF
MIS EN BOUTEILLE DANS LES CAVES DE
FOLONARI S.p.A. LAZISE

Meaty Lasagne

(serves 6)

1 SERVING	785 CALORIES	85g CARBOHYDRATE
64g PROTEIN	21g FAT	2.4g FIBER

1½ cups	(375 ml) cottage cheese
¼ tsp	(1 ml) allspice
½ tsp	(2 ml) oregano
1 tbsp	(15 ml) chopped lemon rind
½ cup	(125 ml) grated Parmesan cheese
2 tbsp	(30 ml) vegetable oil
2	onions, chopped
1	celery stalk, chopped
2	garlic cloves, smashed and chopped
1 lb	(500 g) ground beef
½ lb	(250 g) ground veal
1 lb	(500 g) mushrooms, chopped
1 lb	(500 g) lasagne, cooked
1¼ cups	(300 ml) grated mozzarella cheese
4 cups	(1 L) hot tomato sauce
	salt and pepper

Preheat oven to 375°F (190°C). Grease lasagne dish.

Mix cottage cheese, allspice, oregano, lemon rind and Parmesan cheese together in bowl; set aside.

Heat oil in large skillet; cook onions, celery and garlic 3 to 4 minutes over medium heat.

Add meats, mix well and brown 5 to 6 minutes; season well. Mix in mushrooms and finish cooking 3 to 4 minutes over high heat. Correct seasoning and remove from stove.

Dividing ingredients equally build lasagne with layers of pasta, meat, cottage cheese, mozzarella and tomato sauce. End with a layer of pasta then cover with sauce and remaining mozzarella.

Bake 50 minutes in oven.

Lasagne Rolls

(serves 4)

1 SERVING	949 CALORIES	57g CARBOHYDRATE
70g PROTEIN	49g FAT	0.9g FIBER

2 tbsp	(30 ml) vegetable oil
1	small onion, finely chopped
¼ tsp	(1 ml) thyme
1 tsp	(5 ml) oregano
1 tbsp	(15 ml) chopped parsley
¼ tsp	(1 ml) ground clove
1 lb	(500 g) ground veal
3	slices ham, finely chopped
¼ cup	(50 ml) hot chicken stock
1 cup	(250 ml) cooked spinach, chopped
3 oz	(90 g) diced mozzarella cheese
1	beaten egg
8	strips lasagne, cooked
4 cups	(1 L) hot white sauce
1 cup	(250 ml) grated Gruyère cheese
	salt and pepper
	paprika to taste

Preheat oven to 375°F (190°C).

Heat oil in large frying pan. Add onion, thyme, oregano, parsley and clove; cover and cook 3 minutes.

Stir in veal and ham; season and cook 3 minutes uncovered.

Add chicken stock and spinach; cook 3 to 4 minutes. Stir in mozzarella and cook 2 to 3 minutes while mixing. Remove pan from heat and cool.

Add egg to bind stuffing. Lay lasagne strips flat and sprinkle with paprika. Spread stuffing over full length of strips and roll.

Place rolls in baking dish and cover with white sauce; top with cheese. Bake 20 minutes in oven. Serve with a vegetable garnish or salad.

1 Lay lasagne strips flat and sprinkle with paprika for extra taste.

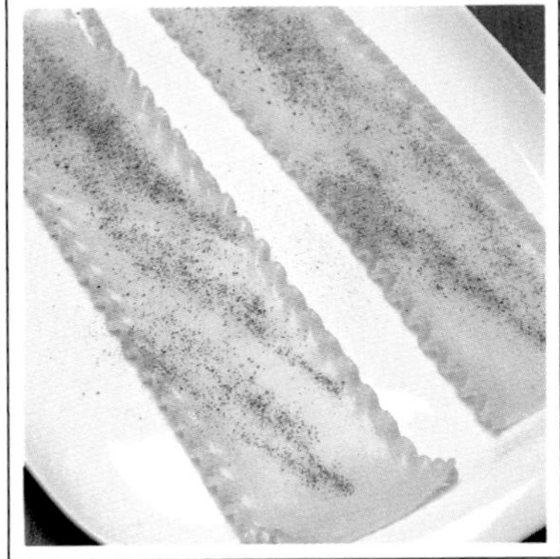

3 Place rolls in baking dish and cover with white sauce.

2 Spread stuffing over full length of each strip then roll.

4 Top with cheese and bake 20 minutes in oven.

Vegetable Lasagne

(serves 6)

1 SERVING	666 CALORIES	81g CARBOHYDRATE
27g PROTEIN	26g FAT	4.7g FIBER

½ cup	(125 ml) grated Parmesan cheese
½ cup	(125 ml) grated Gruyère cheese
½ cup	(125 ml) grated Romano cheese
3 tbsp	(45 ml) butter
1	red onion, finely diced
1	celery stalk, finely diced
1	small zucchini, diced
½	small cauliflower, diced
1	yellow pepper, diced
1	small eggplant, finely diced
1 tbsp	(15 ml) chopped parsley
1 tbsp	(15 ml) grated lemon rind
½ tsp	(2 ml) nutmeg and ground clove
2	garlic cloves, smashed and chopped
¼ cup	(50 ml) chicken stock, heated
1 lb	(500 g) lasagne, cooked
6	tomatoes, thinly sliced
3 cups	(750 ml) thin white sauce, heated
½ cup	(125 ml) tomato sauce, heated
	salt and pepper
	sliced mozzarella for topping
	paprika to taste

Preheat oven to 375°F (190°C). Grease lasagne dish.

Mix grated cheeses together; set aside.

Heat butter in large skillet; cook onion and celery 4 minutes over low heat.

Add remaining vegetables (except tomatoes), parsley, lemon rind, seasonings, garlic and chicken stock. Mix well, cover and cook 10 to 12 minutes over low heat.

Dividing ingredients equally, build lasagne with layers of pasta, vegetables, tomatoes, grated cheeses and white sauce. End with a layer of pasta then cover with tomato sauce and mozzarella cheese; sprinkle with paprika.

Place lasagne dish on cookie sheet and bake about 50 minutes.

1 Cook vegetables (except tomatoes), seasonings, garlic and chicken stock in large skillet for 10 to 12 minutes. Be sure to cover pan and keep heat low.

2 When building the lasagne try to spread layers evenly.

3 After the layers of lasagne, vegetables, tomatoes and grated cheeses, top with white sauce.

4 End with a layer of pasta then cover with tomato sauce and mozzarella cheese; sprinkle with paprika.

Fusilli, Broccoli and Cheese

(serves 4)

1 SERVING	892 CALORIES	101g CARBOHYDRATE
32g PROTEIN	40g FAT	1.1g FIBER

2	small heads broccoli, in flowerets
1½ cups	(375 ml) cold light cream
½ lb	(250 g) Gorgonzola cheese, crumbled
1 tbsp	(15 ml) butter
1 tbsp	(15 ml) chopped parsley
1 lb	(500 g) fusilli, cooked
	few drops lemon juice
	salt and pepper

Cook broccoli in boiling salted water for 3 to 4 minutes. Drain and set aside. Sprinkle with lemon juice.

Pour cream into saucepan and bring to boiling point. Add cheese and butter; mix very well and season.

Cook 4 to 5 minutes over low heat to melt cheese. Stir occasionally.

Stir in broccoli, parsley and lemon juice; simmer 1 to 2 minutes then serve with pasta.

Fusilli and Chicken Livers

(serves 4)

1 SERVING	648 CALORIES	87g CARBOHYDRATE
39g PROTEIN	16g FAT	1.8g FIBER

1 tbsp	(15 ml) oil
1 lb	(500 g) chicken livers, cut in 2
2 tbsp	(30 ml) butter
1	onion, finely chopped
½ lb	(250 g) mushrooms, diced
1	red pepper, diced
½ cup	(125 ml) dry red wine
1 cup	(250 ml) tomato sauce, heated
1 cup	(250 ml) beef stock, heated
¼ tsp	(1 ml) thyme
½ tsp	(2 ml) basil
1 tsp	(5 ml) cornstarch
2 tbsp	(30 ml) cold water
¾ lb	(375 g) fusilli, cooked and still hot
	salt and pepper

Heat oil in frying pan and cook livers 3 minutes each side; season well. Remove and set aside.

Add butter, onion and mushrooms to pan; cook 3 minutes over medium heat. Add red pepper and cook 2 minutes; season well.

Pour in wine and cook 3 minutes over high heat. Mix in tomato sauce, beef stock and seasonings; cook 2 minutes.

Mix cornstarch with water; stir into sauce and cook 1 minute. Add livers, simmer 5 minutes then pour over hot fusilli.

Eggplant and Conch Shells

(serves 4)

1 SERVING	567 CALORIES	92g CARBOHYDRATE
16g PROTEIN	15g FAT	2.8g FIBER

2	medium eggplants
3 tbsp	(45 ml) olive oil
1	garlic clove, smashed and chopped
1 tbsp	(15 ml) chopped parsley
1 tsp	(5 ml) marjoram
2 cups	(500 ml) spicy tomato sauce, heated
¾ lb	(375 g) medium conch shells, cooked
½ cup	(125 ml) marinated pitted black olives, sliced
	salt and pepper

Preheat oven to 375°F (190°C).

Cut eggplants in half lengthwise. Score flesh and brush with 2 tbsp (30 ml) oil. Bake 50 minutes in oven.

When cooked, remove and chop flesh.

Heat remaining oil in skillet and cook garlic 1 minute. Add eggplant and seasonings; mix and cook 3 to 4 minutes over high heat.

Pour in tomato sauce, mix well and simmer 5 minutes over low heat.

Stir in conch shells and olives; simmer 2 to 3 minutes over low heat.

Rotini with Mushrooms

(serves 4)

1 SERVING	623 CALORIES	77g CARBOHYDRATE
18g PROTEIN	27g FAT	0.8g FIBER

2 tbsp	(30 ml) olive oil
2 cups	(500 ml) quartered mushrooms
2 tbsp	(30 ml) capers
1 tsp	(5 ml) chopped fresh parsley
½ tsp	(2 ml) oregano
½ cup	(125 ml) dry red wine Valpolicella
1½ cups	(375 ml) hot light cream
2 tbsp	(30 ml) tomato paste
2	green onions, chopped
¾ lb	(375 g) rotini, cooked
¼ cup	(375 g) grated Parmesan cheese
	salt and pepper

Heat oil in saucepan. Add mushrooms, capers, parsley, oregano, salt and pepper; cook 3 to 4 minutes over medium heat.

Pour in red wine and cook 3 to 4 minutes over high heat.

Add cream and mix well. Stir in tomato paste and onions; cook 3 to 4 minutes over low heat.

Correct seasoning and serve sauce with pasta. Sprinkle with cheese before serving.

Egg Noodles and Anchovies

(serves 4)

1 SERVING	677 CALORIES	80g CARBOHYDRATE
24g PROTEIN	29g FAT	2.3g FIBER

5	large tomatoes, peeled
2 tbsp	(30 ml) olive oil
1	garlic clove, smashed and chopped
3	fresh basil leaves, chopped
1	small jalapeno pepper, in 2 pieces
4	anchovy filets, chopped
1 cup	(250 ml) marinated black olives, pitted
3 tbsp	(45 ml) capers
1 cup	(250 ml) grated Emmentaler cheese
¾ lb	(375 g) extra-broad egg noodles, cooked
	salt and pepper

Purée tomatoes in blender; set aside.

Heat oil in skillet and cook garlic and basil 1 minute over medium heat.

Add tomatoes and pieces of jalapeno; mix well and stir in anchovies. Bring to boil and cook 18 to 20 minutes over low heat. During cooking, taste sauce occasionally; remove jalapeno pieces when they have imparted enough flavour.

Add remaining ingredients and mix well. Cook 3 to 4 minutes before serving.

1 Purée tomatoes in blender.

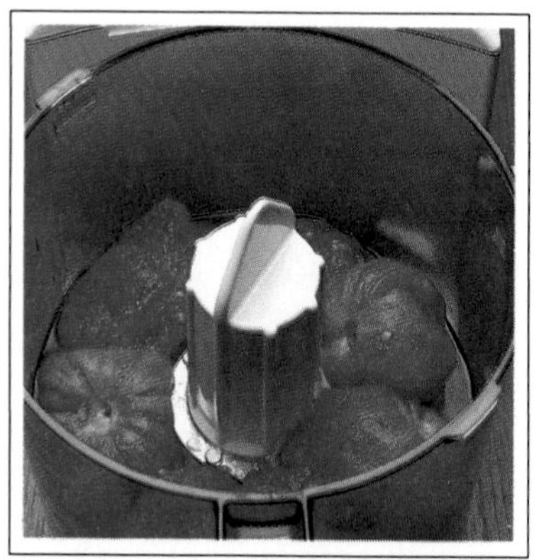

3 Mix well and stir in anchovies. Bring sauce to boil and cook 18 to 20 minutes over low heat.

2 Add tomatoes and pieces of jalapeno to cooking garlic and basil leaves.

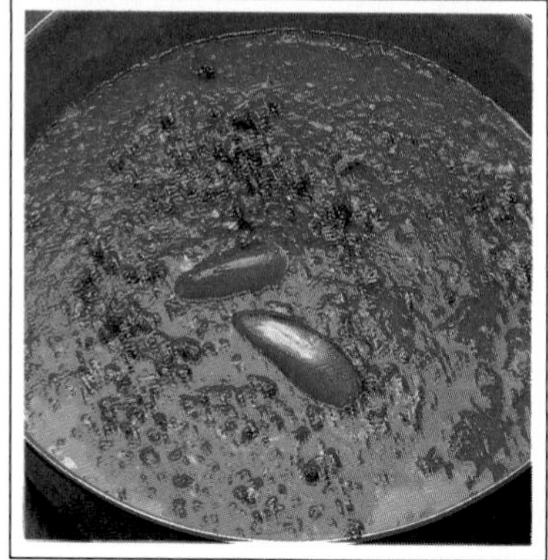

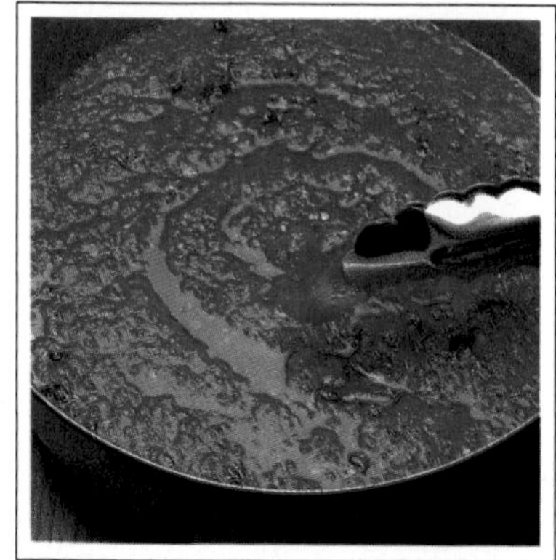

4 During cooking, taste sauce occasionally and when pleased with taste remove jalapeno pieces.

Spinach Egg Noodles Stroganoff

(serves 4)

1 SERVING	781 CALORIES	80g CARBOHYDRATE
59g PROTEIN	25g FAT	1.3g FIBER

1 tbsp	(15 ml) vegetable oil
1½ lb	(750 g) sirloin steak, cut in 1 in (2.5 cm) strips
2 tbsp	(30 ml) melted butter
2	shallots, chopped
1	onion, thinly sliced
½ lb	(250 g) mushrooms, diced
1 tbsp	(15 ml) chopped parsley
¼ tsp	(1 ml) thyme
1 cup	(250 ml) dry red wine Valpolicella
2 cups	(500 ml) beef stock, heated
1½ tbsp	(25 ml) cornstarch
3 tbsp	(45 ml) cold water
¾ lb	(375 g) broad spinach egg noodles, cooked
½ cup	(125 ml) ricotta cheese
	salt and pepper

Heat oil in frying pan. Add meat and cook 2 minutes over medium-high heat. Turn over, season and cook 1 more minute. Remove meat from pan.

Add butter, shallots and onion; cook 3 minutes over low heat.

Add mushrooms, parsley and thyme; cook 3 minutes over medium heat.

Correct seasoning and add wine; cook 3 minutes over high heat. Stir in beef stock; cook 3 minutes over low heat.

Mix cornstarch with water; stir into sauce and cook about 2 minutes.

Replace meat in sauce, fold in noodles and simmer 2 minutes. Stir in cheese and serve.

Continental Egg Noodles

(serves 4)

1 SERVING	765 CALORIES	128g CARBOHYDRATE
16g PROTEIN	21g FAT	1.7g FIBER

3 tbsp	(45 ml) butter
2	onions, finely chopped
2	green onions, finely chopped
3 tbsp	(45 ml) curry powder
1 tsp	(5 ml) cumin
3 cups	(750 ml) chicken stock, heated
2 tbsp	(30 ml) cornstarch
3 tbsp	(45 ml) cold water
½ cup	(125 ml) golden raisins
½ cup	(125 ml) grated coconut
1 lb	(500 g) broad egg noodles, cooked
½ cup	(125 ml) plain yogurt
	salt and pepper
	sesame seeds

Heat butter in large skillet. Add both onions and cook 3 to 4 minutes over low heat. Stir in curry and cumin; continue cooking 3 to 4 minutes.

Add chicken stock, season and bring to boil. Cook 15 minutes over low heat.

Mix cornstarch with water; stir into sauce and cook 1 minute.

Add raisins, coconut and noodles; simmer 2 to 3 minutes.

Stir in yogurt and top with sesame seeds.

Vermicelli and Spinach

(serves 4)

1 SERVING	701 CALORIES	110g CARBOHYDRATE
27g PROTEIN	17g FAT	1.9g FIBER

1 lb	(500 g) spinach leaves
2 tbsp	(30 ml) olive oil
2	garlic cloves, smashed and chopped
3 cups	(750 ml) tomato sauce, heated
1 lb	(500 g) vermicelli, cooked
1 cup	(250 ml) grated Parmesan cheese
	salt and pepper

Wash spinach very well. Cool about 3 to 4 minutes in salted boiling water; cover pan.

Drain spinach, shape into balls and squeeze out all excess water. Chop and set aside.

Heat oil in skillet. When hot, add garlic and spinach; cook 3 minutes over high heat.

Add tomato sauce, vermicelli, salt and pepper; simmer 2 to 3 minutes over medium-low heat.

Serve with cheese.

Vermicelli, Bacon and Peas

(serves 4)

1 SERVING	489 CALORIES	83g CARBOHYDRATE
19g PROTEIN	9g FAT	5.8g FIBER

2 tbsp	(30 ml) butter
1	Spanish onion, chopped
½ tsp	(2 ml) oregano
½ tsp	(2 ml) paprika
4	slices back bacon, in strips
¼ cup	(50 ml) dry red wine
1½ cups	(375 ml) beef stock, heated
1½ tbsp	(25 ml) cornstarch
3 tbsp	(45 ml) cold water
1½ cups	(375 ml) frozen green peas, cooked
¾ lb	(375 g) vermicelli, cooked
¼ cup	(125 ml) grated Parmesan cheese
	salt and pepper

Heat butter in skillet; cook onion and seasonings 8 to 10 minutes over low heat.

Add bacon and cook 3 to 4 minutes. Stir in wine and cook 3 minutes over high heat.

Mix in beef stock and cook 5 to 6 minutes over medium heat. Mix cornstarch with water; stir into sauce and cook 1 minute.

Add peas and vermicelli; mix well and simmer 3 minutes. Stir in cheese and serve.

1 Cook onion and seasonings 8 to 10 minutes over low heat.

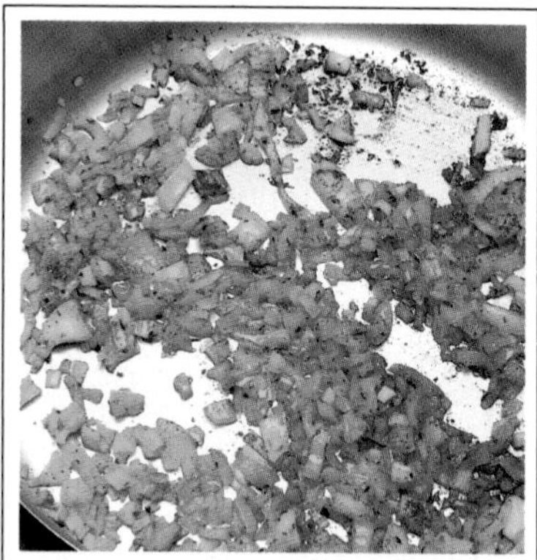

3 Stir diluted cornstarch into sauce and cook 1 minute to thicken.

2 Add bacon and cook 3 to 4 minutes. Pour in wine, stir and cook 3 minutes over high heat.

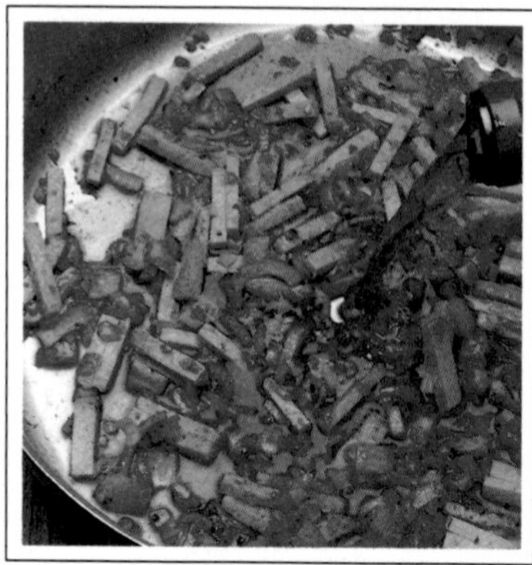

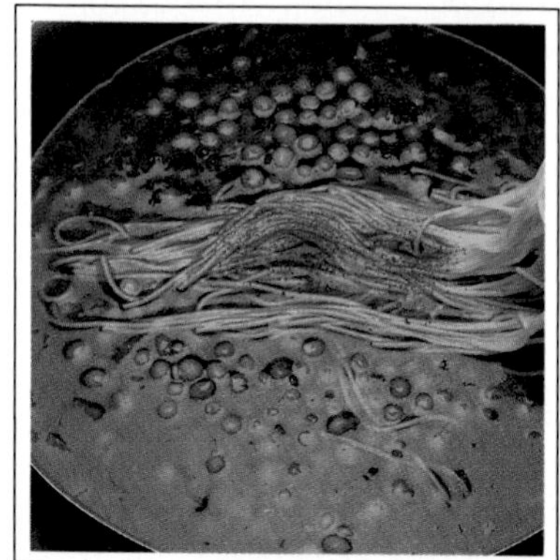

4 Add peas and vermicelli; mix well and simmer 3 minutes. Stir in cheese before serving.

Layered Gnocchi

(serves 4)

1 SERVING	488 CALORIES	42g CARBOHYDRATE
26g PROTEIN	24g FAT	0.3g FIBER

½ cup	(125 ml) ricotta cheese
2	eggs
1 cup	(250 ml) grated Parmesan cheese
1½ cups	(375 ml) sifted flour
1 cup	(250 ml) grated Gruyère cheese
1½ cups	(375 ml) thin white sauce, heated
1 cup	(250 ml) tomato sauce, heated
1 tbsp	(15 ml) chopped parsley
	salt and pepper
	paprika

Preheat oven to 375°F (190°C).

Place ricotta, eggs, Parmesan, salt and pepper in blender; mix 1 minute.

Add flour and mix 1 minute; transfer dough to bowl, cover and refrigerate 1 hour.

Bring plenty of salted water to boiling point. Drop in small pieces of dough and cook 8 minutes. Keep water at boiling point and when cooked, remove with slotted spoon and drain on paper towels. Depending on the size of pan you may have to cook gnocchi in two batches.

Place half of gnocchi in lightly greased baking dish. Add half of Gruyère, half of white sauce and paprika.

Pour in half of tomato sauce and finish with remaining gnocchi, cheese, parsley and sauces.

Bake 30 to 35 minutes in oven.

1 After dough has been chilled, drop small pieces into hot water and cook 8 minutes. Do not crowd.

3 Pour in half of tomato sauce.

2 Place half of gnocchi in lightly greased baking dish. Add half of Gruyère, half of white sauce and paprika.

4 Finish with remaining gnocchi, cheese, parsley and sauces.

Potato Gnocchi

(serves 4)

1 SERVING	400 CALORIES	42g CARBOHYDRATE
13g PROTEIN	20g FAT	1.0g FIBER

1 cup	(250 ml) flour
2 cups	(500 ml) cooked riced potatoes
4 tbsp	(60 ml) butter
½ cup	(125 ml) grated mozzarella cheese
1½ cups	(375 ml) tomato sauce, heated
½ cup	(125 ml) ricotta cheese
	salt and white pepper
	pinch nutmeg

Place flour in bowl and form well in center. Add potatoes, nutmeg and 3 tbsp (45 ml) butter; pinch dough to incorporate.

Season and remove dough from bowl. Place on counter and knead with the heel of your hand until smooth.

Shape dough into ball and cut into 4 quarters. Roll each quarter into a cylindrical shape with a diameter of about 1 in (2.5 cm). Slice into ½ in (1.2 cm) pieces.

Cook in salted simmering water for about 5 minutes. Monitor heat to keep water simmering without breaking into a boil.

When cooked, gnocchi should rise to the surface. Remove with slotted spoon and set aside to drain on paper towel.

Preheat oven to 375°F (190°C).

With remaining butter grease large baking dish.

Season mozzarella with salt and pepper. Mix ricotta cheese with tomato sauce over low heat for 1 minute.

Layer gnocchi, mozzarella and sauce in baking dish. Bake 12 minutes.

Change oven setting to broil and continue cooking 4 minutes. Serve.

BUDGET COOKING

BUDGET COOKING

Economical cooking should not imply that you're getting the bottom of the barrel nor should it be an indication of a meal with little taste, variety or nutrition. But rather, inexpensive eating should simply mean that you're getting your money's worth and making the most of what you buy. As you are probably well aware, there are many ways of literally saving cash such as using coupons, taking advantage of in-store sales or just generally 'shopping around'. But the best rule of thumb I can offer you is to never settle for poor quality and pay for it! Treat food shopping as you would any other — if the goods are damaged or not up to par, the price should be adjusted accordingly. If on Tuesday the red peppers are a sorry lot then substitute them for another vegetable that is fresh and worth your money — in other words be ready to compromise! Aside from being flexible, be prepared to spend a little extra time in the kitchen as some foods like inexpensive cuts of meat may need marinating or longer cooking times to bring out the best flavor and tenderness. And lastly, think of your freezer as you would your best friend. Let's get started...

Corned Beef and Cabbage

(serves 4)

1 SERVING	1777 CALORIES	54g CARBOHYDRATE
73g PROTEIN	141g FAT	6.3g FIBER

4 lb	(1.8 kg) corned beef brisket
3	cloves
1	bay leaf
3	parsley sprigs
½ tsp	(2 ml) thyme
1	large cabbage, cut in 4
8	carrots, pared
4	large potatoes, peeled and cut in half
2	leeks, cut in 4 lengthwise to within 1 in (2.5 cm) of base, washed
	salt and pepper

Place brisket in large saucepan and pour in enough cold water to cover beef by 3 in (7.5 cm). Bring to boil, then skim.

Add cloves, bay leaf, parsley and thyme; partially cover and cook 3 hours over low heat. Skim if necessary.

Meanwhile, blanch cabbage and carrots in salted boiling water about 10 minutes. Drain well.

Add blanched vegetables, potatoes and leeks to beef. Continue cooking 1 hour partially covered.

To serve, remove beef and vegetables from liquid and arrange on serving platter. Moisten beef with a little bit of cooking liquid, slice and serve.

Boiled Beef

(serves 4)

1 SERVING	486 CALORIES	7g CARBOHYDRATE
56g PROTEIN	26g FAT	1.5g FIBER

4 lb	(1.8 kg) cross-rib roast, tied
2	celery stalks, cut in ½
2	leeks, cut in 4 lengthwise to within 1 in (2.5 cm) of base, washed
1	Spanish onion, cut in 4
2	garlic cloves, peeled and whole
4	cloves
½ tsp	(2 ml) allspice
4	parsley sprigs
2	bay leaves
	salt and pepper

Place all ingredients in large saucepan and pour in enough cold water to cover; bring to boil.

Skim then continue cooking 4 hours over low heat; partially cover. Serve with horseradish sauce.

Horseradish Sauce

1 SERVING	51 CALORIES	5g CARBOHYDRATE
1g PROTEIN	3g FAT	0.5g FIBER

4 tbsp	(60 ml) horseradish
2 tbsp	(30 ml) sour cream
1 tbsp	(15 ml) breadcrumbs
⅓ cup	(75 ml) whipped heavy cream
	few drops Tabasco sauce
	fresh ground pepper

Mix horseradish, sour cream and breadcrumbs together.

Add remaining ingredients and season generously. Serve with boiled beef.

Pot Roast

(serves 4)

1 SERVING	488 CALORIES	21g CARBOHYDRATE
56g PROTEIN	20g FAT	3.0g FIBER

2 tbsp	(30 ml) vegetable oil
3 lb	(1.4 kg) sirloin tip roast
5	onions, peeled, cut in 4
2 cups	(500 ml) dry red wine
2 cups	(500 ml) tomato sauce, heated
1	garlic clove, smashed and chopped
½ tsp	(2 ml) thyme
½ tsp	(2 ml) basil
½ tsp	(2 ml) allspice
	salt and pepper

Preheat oven to 350°F (180°C).

Heat oil in large ovenproof casserole. Sear beef 6 to 8 minutes over medium-high heat on all sides; season well.

Add onions and continue cooking 6 to 8 minutes over medium heat.

Pour in wine and tomato sauce. Add garlic, seasonings and bring to boil.

Cover and cook 2½ hours in oven.

Serve with additional vegetables if desired.

1 Sear beef 6 to 8 minutes over medium-high heat on all sides; season well.

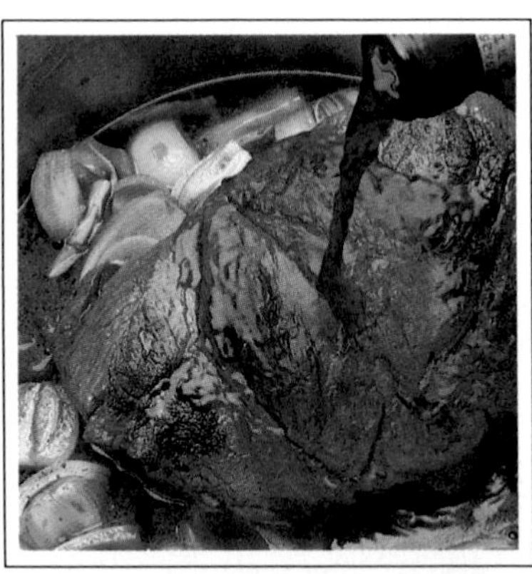

3 Pour in wine.

2 Add onions and continue cooking 6 to 8 minutes over medium heat.

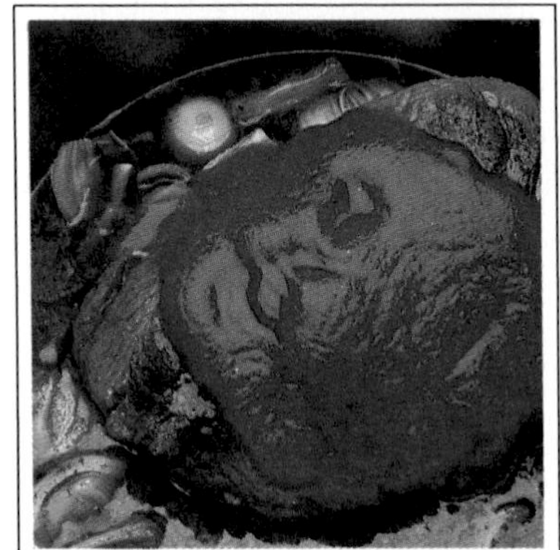

4 Pour in tomato sauce. Add garlic, seasonings and bring to boil. Finish cooking 2½ hours in oven.

Beef Stew

(serves 4)

1 SERVING	513 CALORIES	36g CARBOHYDRATE
36g PROTEIN	25g FAT	3.0g FIBER

2 tbsp	(30 ml) vegetable oil
2 lb	(900 g) stewing beef, cubed
½ tsp	(2 ml) chili powder
4 tbsp	(60 ml) flour
1 tbsp	(15 ml) butter
1	garlic clove, smashed and chopped
1	onion, coarsely chopped
1	celery stalk, diced
¼ tsp	(1 ml) thyme
1	clove
½ tsp	(2 ml) tarragon
½ tsp	(2 ml) basil
28 oz	(796 ml) can tomatoes
2½ cups	(625 ml) beef stock, heated
2 tbsp	(30 ml) tomato paste
2	large potatoes, peeled and cubed
2	large carrots, pared and cubed
	salt and pepper

Preheat oven to 350°F (180°C).

Heat oil in ovenproof casserole. Sear meat (in two batches) 3 minutes over medium-high heat. Turn pieces over and add chili powder, salt and pepper; finish searing 3 minutes.

With all meat in casserole sprinkle in flour. Mix well and cook 2 to 3 minutes over medium heat.

Remove meat and set aside.

Add butter to casserole. Cook garlic, onion, celery and seasonings 3 to 4 minutes over medium heat.

Pour in tomatoes with juice and correct seasoning. Replace meat and mix well.

Add beef stock, mix and stir in tomato paste; cover and bring to boil. Finish cooking 2 hours in oven.

1 hour before beef is cooked, add vegetables to casserole, forty minutes later, remove cover.

Serve stew with garlic bread.

1 Sear meat (in two batches) 3 minutes over medium-high heat. Turn pieces over and add chili powder, salt and pepper; finish searing 3 minutes.

2 With all meat in casserole sprinkle in flour. Mix well and cook 2 to 3 minutes over medium heat.

3 Cook garlic, onion, celery and seasonings 3 to 4 minutes over medium heat.

4 Pour in tomatoes with juice and correct seasoning.

1 Stir-fry meat and garlic for 2 minutes then pour in soya sauce. Mix well to coat meat strips then remove.

2 Add onions and cucumbers to pan; cook 2 minutes over high heat. Season with pepper.

3 Add yellow pepper and pea pods; continue cooking 2 to 3 minutes over high heat stirring frequently.

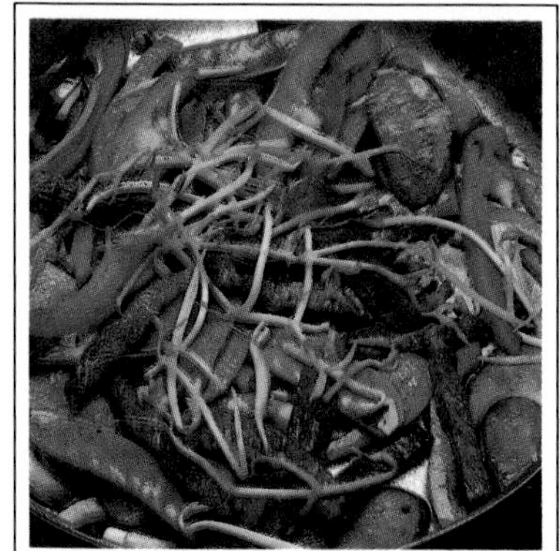

4 Replace meat in pan along with sprouts; simmer 2 to 3 minutes over medium-low heat before serving.

Beef Stir-Fry

(serves 4)

1 SERVING	410 CALORIES	11g CARBOHYDRATE
51g PROTEIN	18g FAT	2.2g FIBER

2 tbsp	(30 ml) vegetable oil
2 lb	(900 g) strip loin steak, cut in strips
1	garlic clove, smashed and chopped
2 tbsp	(30 ml) soya sauce
4	green onions, in 2.5 cm lengths
1	red onion, cut in half and sliced
2	dill cucumbers, sliced
1	yellow pepper, sliced
7 oz	(200 g) snow peas, ends trimmed
1 cup	(250 ml) bean sprouts
	salt and pepper

Heat oil in large frying pan. When hot, add meat and garlic; stir-fry 2 minutes.

Season and pour in soya sauce; mix well and remove meat from pan.

Add onions and cucumbers to pan; cook 2 minutes over high heat. Season with pepper.

Add yellow pepper and snow peas; continue cooking 2 to 3 minutes over high heat stirring frequently.

Replace meat in pan along with sprouts; simmer 2 to 3 minutes over medium-low heat before serving.

Chuck Roast with Vegetables

(serves 4)

1 SERVING	749 CALORIES	24g CARBOHYDRATE
71g PROTEIN	41g FAT	3.7g FIBER

2 tbsp	(30 ml) vegetable oil
4-5 lb	(1.8-2.3 kg) chuck short rib roast, tied
3	onions, peeled, cut in 4
1	bay leaf
¼ tsp	(1 ml) thyme
¼ tsp	(1 ml) basil
1½ cups	(375 ml) beer
1½ cups	(375 ml) brown sauce
4	carrots, pared
4	leeks, cut in 4 lengthwise to within 1 in (2.5 cm) of base, washed
1 tbsp	(15 ml) cornstarch
3 tbsp	(45 ml) cold water
	salt and pepper

Preheat oven to 350°F (180°C).

Heat oil in ovenproof casserole. Sear meat 8 to 10 minutes on all sides.

Add onions, bay leaf and seasonings; continue cooking 4 to 5 minutes.

Pour in beer and bring to boil. Add brown sauce and bring to boil again.

Cover and cook 2½ hours in oven.

About 1 hour before roast is cooked, add carrots to casserole. And 20 minutes later, add leeks.

Arrange beef and vegetables on serving platter.

Place casserole over medium-high heat and bring liquid to boil. Mix cornstarch with water; stir into sauce and cook 3 to 4 minutes over medium heat to thicken.

Correct seasoning and serve sauce with beef and vegetables.

Mock Pepper Steak

(serves 4)

1 SERVING	387 CALORIES	12g CARBOHYDRATE
51g PROTEIN	15g FAT	1.5g FIBER

1½lb	(750 g) ground beef
1	egg
2 tbsp	(30 ml) breadcrumbs
1 tbsp	(15 ml) chopped parsley
½ tsp	(2 ml) Worcestershire sauce
2 tbsp	(30 ml) vegetable oil
1	onion, chopped
1 lb	(500 g) mushrooms, sliced
2 tbsp	(30 ml) green peppercorns
1½ cups	(375 ml) beef stock, heated
1 tbsp	(15 ml) cornstarch
3 tbsp	(45 ml) cold water
	salt

Mix meat, egg, breadcrumbs, parsley and Worcestershire sauce in mixer for 2 minutes at high speed; season to taste. Shape into steaks.

Heat oil in large frying pan. Cook steaks 8 to 10 minutes over medium heat turning over 4 times. When cooked, remove and keep hot in oven.

Add onion to frying pan and cook 2 minutes. Add mushrooms and peppercorns, season and continue cooking 3 to 4 minutes over medium heat.

Pour in beef stock, mix and bring to boil. Mix cornstarch with water and stir into sauce. Cook 2 minutes more to thicken.

Remove steaks from oven and serve with sauce.

Salisbury Steak

(serves 4)

1 SERVING	436 CALORIES	16g CARBOHYDRATE
57g PROTEIN	16g FAT	2.1g FIBER

2 lb	(900 g) ground beef
2 tbsp	(30 ml) breadcrumbs
1	egg
1 tbsp	(15 ml) chopped parsley
½ tsp	(2 ml) chili powder
2 tbsp	(30 ml) vegetable oil
4	onions, thinly sliced
2 tbsp	(30 ml) tomato paste
½ tsp	(2 ml) basil
2 cups	(500 ml) beef stock, heated
1½ tbsp	(25 ml) cornstarch
3 tbsp	(45 ml) cold water
	salt and pepper

Preheat oven to 150°F (70°C).

Mix meat, breadcrumbs, egg, parsley, chili powder, salt and pepper together until well incorporated. Shape into steaks.

Heat oil in large frying pan. Cook 8 to 10 minutes over medium heat. Turn over 4 times and season twice. When cooked, remove from pan and keep hot in oven.

Add onions to pan; cook 4 minutes over medium heat.

Add tomato paste and mix well. Stir in basil and beef stock; bring to boil. Correct seasoning.

Mix cornstarch with water; stir into sauce and cook 3 to 4 minutes.

Pour onion sauce over steaks and serve.

Braised Beef Brisket

(serves 4)

1 SERVING	558 CALORIES	5g CARBOHYDRATE
22g PROTEIN	50g FAT	0.5g FIBER

2 tbsp	(30 ml) vegetable oil
4 lb	(1.8 kg) beef brisket, tied
2	large onions, thinly sliced
1	clove
2 tbsp	(30 ml) paprika
¼ tsp	(1 ml) thyme
1 tsp	(5 ml) chopped parsley
1 cup	(250 ml) beer
2 cups	(500 ml) light beef stock, heated
2 tbsp	(30 ml) cornstarch
4 tbsp	(60 ml) cold water
¼ cup	(50 ml) sour cream
	salt and pepper

Preheat oven to 350°F (180°C).

Heat oil in ovenproof casserole. Sear beef 8 minutes on all sides over medium heat. Remove and season well.

Add onions to casserole and cook 4 minutes.

Stir in seasonings and parsley; cook 2 minutes.

Pour in beer, bring to boil and cook 3 minutes over medium heat. Replace meat in casserole and add beef stock; correct seasoning and bring to boil again.

Cover casserole and finish cooking 2-2½ hours in oven. Meat should be very tender when served.

When done, remove meat from casserole and set aside.

Place casserole over medium heat and bring liquid to boil. Mix cornstarch with water; stir into sauce and continue cooking 3 minutes.

Remove from heat, stir in sour cream and serve sauce with meat.

Italian Sausages and Vegetables

(serves 4)

1 SERVING	276 CALORIES	31g CARBOHYDRATE
11g PROTEIN	12g FAT	3.6g FIBER

2	carrots, pared and sliced on the bias 1 in (2.5 cm) thick
24	fresh pearl onions
1	small zucchini, sliced on the bias 1 in (2.5 cm) thick
2 tbsp	(30 ml) vegetable oil
2	apples, peeled, cored and in wedges
4	Italian sausages, sliced on the bias 1 in (2.5 cm) thick
2	garlic cloves, smashed and chopped
1½ cups	(375 ml) chicken stock, heated
1 tbsp	(15 ml) tomato paste
1 tbsp	(15 ml) cornstarch
3 tbsp	(45 ml) cold water
	salt and pepper

Place carrots in saucepan, cover with water and boil 6 minutes uncovered.

Add onions and zucchini; season and cook 3 minutes. Drain vegetables and let cool slightly.

Heat oil in large frying pan. Cook vegetables, apples, sausages and garlic 4 to 5 minutes over high heat; season well.

Pour in chicken stock and bring to boil.

Stir in tomato paste and cook 1 minute over medium-low heat. Mix cornstarch with water; stir into sauce and finish cooking 1 minute.

Serve with rice.

Creamy Chicken Stew

(serves 4)

1 SERVING	333 CALORIES	29g CARBOHYDRATE
25g PROTEIN	13g FAT	2.7g FIBER

3½ lb	(1.6 kg) chicken, cut in 10 pieces and skinned
1	small onion, coarsely chopped
1	celery stalk, diced
1	bay leaf
1	parsley sprig
¼ tsp	(1 ml) celery salt
½ tsp	(2 ml) basil
3 tbsp	(45 ml) butter
4 tbsp	(60 ml) flour
2	large cooked carrots, diced large
1	large cooked potato, diced large
1	cooked parsnip, diced large
	salt and pepper
	paprika

Season chicken pieces with salt, pepper and paprika. Place leg and thigh pieces in large skillet and cover with cold water.

Add onion, celery, bay leaf, parsley and seasonings. Cover and bring to boil. Continue cooking 16 minutes over medium heat.

Add remaining chicken pieces and continue cooking 20 minutes covered.

Transfer chicken pieces to bowl and strain cooking liquid through fine sieve into second bowl.

Heat butter in skillet. Mix in flour and cook 2 to 3 minutes over low heat, stirring occasionally.

Pour in half of strained cooking liquid and whisk well. Incorporate remaining and season. Cook sauce 3 to 4 minutes over medium heat.

Place cooked vegetables in sauce and cook 3 to 4 minutes over medium-low heat.

Add chicken and finish cooking 8 to 10 minutes over low heat. Do not cover.

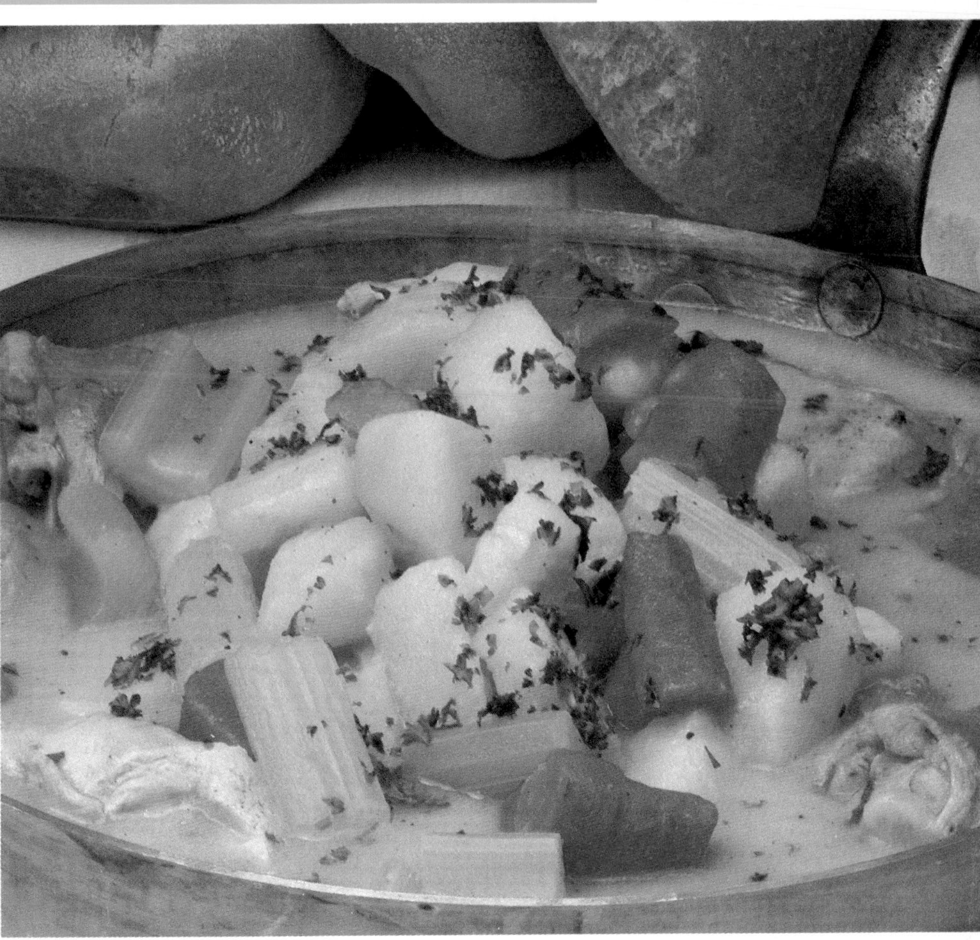

1 Cut chicken in 10 pieces and skin. Season with salt, pepper and paprika.

3 Cover with cold water. Add onion, celery, bay leaf, parsley and seasonings. Cover pan and bring to boil.

2 Place leg and thigh pieces in large skillet.

4 After all chicken has been cooked and removed, add vegetables to sauce.

Roast Chicken

(serves 4)

1 SERVING	321 CALORIES	12g CARBOHYDRATE
30g PROTEIN	17g FAT	1.9g FIBER

4-5 lb	(1.8 - 2.3 kg) chicken, cleaned
1	large carrot
2	celery stalks
1	onion, cut in half
2-3	parsley sprigs
1	bay leaf
3 tbsp	(45 ml) melted butter
1	onion, diced
½ tsp	(2 ml) tarragon
1½ cups	(375 ml) hot chicken stock
1½ tbsp	(25 ml) cornstarch
3 tbsp	(45 ml) cold water
	salt and pepper

Preheat oven to 425°F (220°C).

Stuff cleaned chicken with carrot, celery, halved onion, parsley and bay leaf. Force inside and dribble in 1 tsp (5 ml) melted butter.

Secure legs with string and baste with remaining butter. Place in roasting pan, season generously and sear about 15 minutes in oven.

Reduce heat to 350°F (180°C) and finish cooking chicken 25 to 30 minutes per 1 lb (500 g).

When cooked, remove chicken and set aside.

Place roasting pan over high heat; add diced onion and tarragon and cook 4 minutes.

Pour in chicken stock and bring to boil. Season and continue cooking 3 to 4 minutes.

Mix cornstarch with water; stir into sauce and cook 1 to 2 minutes or until thickened.

Serve onion gravy with chicken.

1 Stuff cleaned chicken with vegetables, parsley and bay leaf. Force inside and dribble in 1 tsp (5 ml) melted butter.

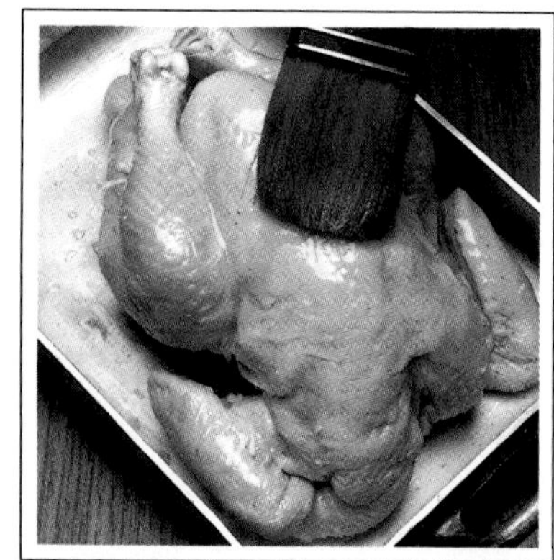

3 Place in roasting pan, season generously and baste with remaining butter. Sear about 15 minutes in oven.

2 Secure chicken by drawing a string threaded on a trussing needle through the legs twice. Knot string between legs.

4 After chicken is cooked, prepare gravy by using juices that have collected in roasting pan.

Pineapple Chicken

(serves 4)

1 SERVING	252 CALORIES	14g CARBOHYDRATE
22g PROTEIN	12g FAT	0.5g FIBER

2 tbsp	(30 ml) vegetable oil
2	chicken breasts, skinned, halved and cubed
1 tbsp	(15 ml) chopped ginger
3 tbsp	(45 ml) pine nuts
14 oz	(398 ml) can pineapple chunks
3 tbsp	(45 ml) wine vinegar
1½ cups	(375 ml) chicken stock, heated
1 tsp	(5 ml) soya sauce
1 tbsp	(15 ml) cornstarch
3 tbsp	(45 ml) cold water
	salt and pepper

Heat oil in large frying pan. Add chicken, ginger and pine nuts; season and cook 4 to 5 minutes. Stir once.

Drain pineapple and reserve ½ cup (125 ml) of juice. Add pineapple chunks to pan and continue cooking 3 to 4 minutes over low heat.

Remove chicken pieces and set aside.

Add vinegar to sauce and boil 1 minute. Stir in pineapple juice, chicken stock and soya sauce; season well and bring to boil. Cook 3 minutes.

Mix cornstarch with water; stir into sauce and bring to boil. Cook 1 more minute.

Replace chicken in pan, correct seasoning and simmer over low heat until heated through.

Chicken Livers Marsala

(serves 4)

1 SERVING	397 CALORIES	21g CARBOHYDRATE
40g PROTEIN	17g FAT	0.8g FIBER

1½ lb	(750 g) chicken livers, cleaned, fat trimmed and halved
½ cup	(125 ml) seasoned flour
2 tbsp	(30 ml) vegetable oil
1 tbsp	(15 ml) butter
1	small onion, finely chopped
½ lb	(250 g) mushrooms, sliced
1 tbsp	(15 ml) chopped parsley
½ cup	(125 ml) Marsala wine
1 cup	(250 ml) chicken stock, heated
1 tsp	(5 ml) cornstarch
2 tbsp	(30 ml) cold water
	salt and pepper

Dredge livers in flour. Heat oil and butter in large frying pan. Cook livers 4 minutes over high heat, stirring once.

Add onion, mushrooms and parsley; season and continue cooking 4 to 5 minutes over medium heat.

Pour in wine and chicken stock; mix and cook 4 minutes over low heat.

Mix cornstarch with water; stir into sauce and bring to boil. Simmer 2 minutes over low heat and serve with noodles.

Pork Tenderloin Sauté

(serves 4)

1 SERVING	357 CALORIES	12g CARBOHYDRATE
30g PROTEIN	21g FAT	1.5g FIBER

2	pork tenderloins
2 tbsp	(30 ml) soya sauce
¼ cup	(50 ml) dry sherry
3 tbsp	(45 ml) vegetable oil
1	leek, (white part only) thinly sliced
½ lb	(250 g) mushrooms, sliced
3	green onions, in sticks
1	green pepper, thinly sliced
½ cup	(125 ml) frozen peas, cooked
2 cups	(500 ml) chicken stock, heated
2 tbsp	(30 ml) cornstarch
4 tbsp	(60 ml) cold water
	salt and pepper

Trim meat of fat and slice on the bias ¾ in (2 cm) thick. Place in bowl with soya sauce and sherry; marinate 30 minutes.

Remove meat from bowl; reserve marinade.

Heat 1½ tbsp (25 ml) oil in frying pan. Cook half of meat for 3 to 4 minutes over medium heat; turn pieces over once and season well.

Remove cooked meat, set aside and repeat for remaining meat but avoid adding any more oil.

When all meat is cooked and removed, add rest of oil to pan. Cook vegetables 3 to 4 minutes over high heat; season well.

Pour in chicken stock and reserved marinade; bring to boil.

Mix cornstarch with water; stir into sauce and cook 1 to 2 minutes over medium heat.

Replace meat in sauce, simmer 3 to 4 minutes and serve.

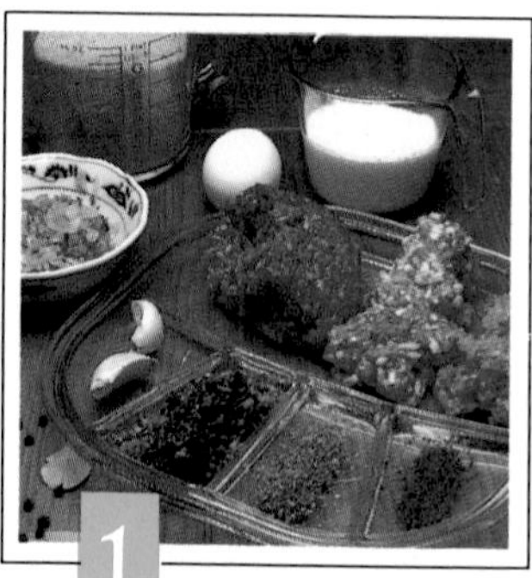

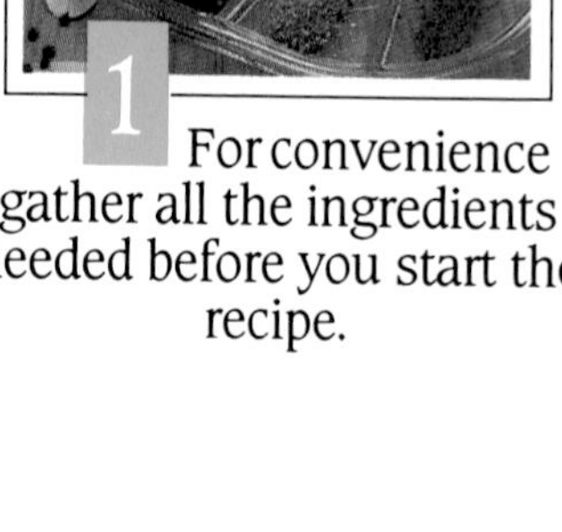

1 For convenience gather all the ingredients needed before you start the recipe.

2 Place all meat, parsley and seasonings in large bowl. Add onion and garlic; mix well.

The Best Meatloaf

(serves 6 to 8)

1 SERVING	317 CALORIES	14g CARBOHYDRATE
36g PROTEIN	13g FAT	0.3g FIBER

1 lb	(500 g) ground beef
½ lb	(250 g) ground pork
½ lb	(250 g) ground veal
1 tbsp	(15 ml) chopped parsley
¼ tsp	(1 ml) thyme
¼ tsp	(1 ml) chili powder
¼ tsp	(1 ml) basil
1	onion, chopped and cooked
2	garlic cloves, smashed and chopped
1½ cups	(375 ml) breadcrumbs
2	eggs
1 cup	(250 ml) light cream
	salt and pepper
	several bay leaves

Preheat oven to 350°F (180°C).

Set aside 10 × 4 in (25 × 10 cm) mold.

Place all meat, parsley and seasonings in large bowl. Add onion and garlic; mix well.

Add breadcrumbs and eggs; mix, then stir in cream.

To double-check seasoning, cook a tiny patty of mixture in hot oil. Taste and adjust remaining mixture if necessary.

Press mixture into loaf pan, place bay leaves on top and set in roasting pan with hot water. Cook 1½ hours in oven.

Serve plain or with mushroom sauce.

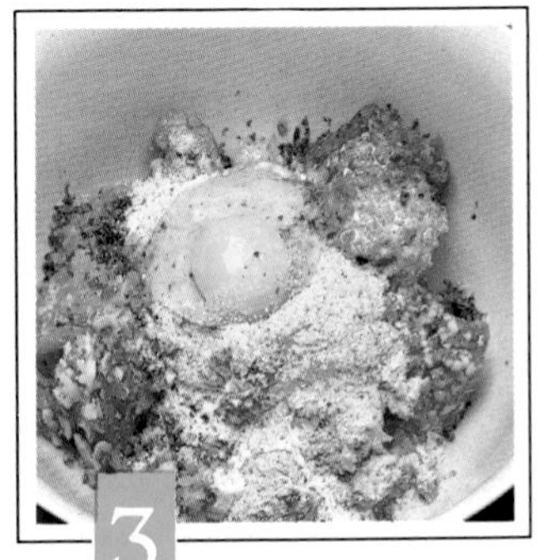

3 Add breadcrumbs and eggs, mix then stir in cream.

4 Press mixture into loaf pan, place bay leaves on top and set in roasting pan with hot water.

Mushroom Sauce for Meatloaf

1 SERVING	30 CALORIES	2g CARBOHYDRATE
1g PROTEIN	2g FAT	0.2g FIBER

2 tbsp	(30 ml) vegetable oil
½ lb	(250 g) mushrooms, sliced
2 tbsp	(30 ml) chopped onion
1 cup	(250 ml) peeled diced eggplant
2 cups	(500 ml) beef stock, heated
1 tbsp	(15 ml) chopped chives
2 tbsp	(30 ml) cornstarch
4 tbsp	(60 ml) cold water
	salt and pepper

Heat oil in frying pan. Add mushrooms, onion and eggplant; cover and cook 10 minutes over low heat. Season well.

Add beef stock, chives and season well; bring to boil.

Mix cornstarch with water; stir into sauce and cook 4 to 5 minutes over low heat.

Pour sauce over meatloaf or serve with burgers.

Meatballs and Garlic Spinach

(serves 4)

1 SERVING	446 CALORIES	14g CARBOHYDRATE
57g PROTEIN	18g FAT	1.9g FIBER

1½ lb	(750 g) lean ground pork
1	onion, chopped and cooked
¼ tsp	(1 ml) chili powder
1 tsp	(5 ml) Worcestershire sauce
1	egg
2 tbsp	(30 ml) vegetable oil
1½ cups	(375 ml) chicken stock, heated
1 tbsp	(15 ml) soya sauce
1 tbsp	(15 ml) cornstarch
3 tbsp	(45 ml) cold water
2	garlic cloves, smashed and chopped
2 lb	(900 g) spinach, cooked and chopped
	salt and pepper

In mixer blend together pork, onion, chili powder, Worcestershire sauce, egg, salt and pepper. When mixture is smooth, shape into small meatballs.

Heat half of oil in large frying pan. Add meatballs and cook 3 to 4 minutes on all sides; season generously.

Using small spoon remove most of fat from pan and discard. Add chicken stock and soya sauce to meatballs. Cover and cook 6 minutes over low heat.

Mix cornstarch with water; stir into meatball mixture and continue cooking 3 minutes.

Meanwhile, heat remaining oil in second frying pan. When hot, cook garlic and spinach 3 minutes over medium heat; season well.

Serve spinach with meatballs.

Pork Shoulder Roast with Cider

(serves 4)

1 SERVING	1107 CALORIES	32g CARBOHYDRATE
112g PROTEIN	59g FAT	2.2g FIBER

2 tbsp	(30 ml) vegetable oil
5 lb	(2.3 kg) pork shoulder, fat trimmed and tied
2	onions, thinly sliced
2	apples, peeled, cored and in wedges
2 cups	(500 ml) apple cider
1 cup	(250 ml) chicken stock, heated
¼ tsp	(1 ml) thyme
½ tsp	(2 ml) basil
½ cup	(125 ml) sultana raisins
1 tbsp	(15 ml) cornstarch
2 tbsp	(30 ml) cold water
	salt and pepper

Preheat oven to 300°F (150°C).

Heat oil in ovenproof casserole. Sear meat 8 minutes on all sides over medium heat. Remove and season well; set aside.

Add onions and apple to casserole; cook 5 to 6 minutes.

Add cider and bring to boil; cook 2 minutes.

Add chicken stock, mix well and replace meat in sauce. Add seasonings and bring to boil with cover.

Finish cooking meat 2 to 2½ hours in oven with cover.

When done, transfer meat to serving platter. Place casserole over medium heat; bring liquid to boil and skim.

Stir in raisins. Mix cornstarch with water; stir into sauce and cook 1 minute. Correct seasoning.

Serve sauce with pork.

Rice Hash Pancakes

(serves 4)

1 SERVING	396 CALORIES	28g CARBOHYDRATE
17g PROTEIN	24g FAT	1.0g FIBER

3 tbsp	(45 ml) oil
1	onion, finely chopped
¾ cup	(175 ml) ground beef
1 tbsp	(15 ml) chopped parsley
¼ tsp	(1 ml) ground clove
2 tbsp	(30 ml) flour
1½ cups	(375 ml) leftover cooked rice
½ cup	(125 ml) grated Gruyère cheese
1	egg
2 tbsp	(30 ml) butter
2 cups	(500 ml) spicy tomato sauce, heated
	salt and pepper
	Parmesan cheese to taste

Heat oil in frying pan. Cook onion 3 minutes over low heat.

Add beef, season. Add parsley and clove; mix and cook 3 to 4 minutes over medium heat.

Mix in flour and rice. Add Gruyère cheese and mix again; cook 3 minutes.

Cool, then add egg. Transfer to mixer; blend 2 minutes.

Dust hands with flour and shape mixture into pancakes. Cook 4 minutes each side in hot butter.

Serve with tomato sauce and Parmesan cheese.

Tomato Rice

(serves 4)

1 SERVING	209 CALORIES	35g CARBOHYDRATE
6g PROTEIN	5g FAT	1.5g FIBER

1 tbsp	(15 ml) olive oil
1	onion, chopped
1	garlic clove, smashed and chopped
1 tbsp	(15 ml) chopped parsley
1½ cups	(375 ml) canned tomatoes, drained and chopped
1 cup	(250 ml) long grain rice, rinsed
1 tbsp	(15 ml) tomato paste
1¼ cups	(300 ml) tomato juice
½ cup	(125 ml) grated Parmesan cheese
	salt and pepper

Preheat oven to 350°F (180°C).

Heat oil in ovenproof casserole. Cook onion, garlic and parsley 2 minutes over medium heat.

Stir in tomatoes and cook 3 minutes over high heat; season.

Mix in rice, tomato paste and juice; bring to boil.

Cover and cook 18 minutes in oven.

About 5 minutes before rice is cooked, stir in cheese with fork.

Vegetable Baked Rice

(serves 4)

1 SERVING	242 CALORIES	33g CARBOHYDRATE
5g PROTEIN	10g FAT	3.7g FIBER

1 tbsp	(15 ml) olive oil
3	green onions, finely chopped
1 cup	(250 ml) long grain rice, rinsed
¼ tsp	(1 ml) thyme
1	bay leaf
1½ cups	(375 ml) chicken stock, heated
2 tbsp	(30 ml) butter
¼	celery stalk, diced
½ cup	(125 ml) cooked green peas
½ cup	(125 ml) cooked diced carrots
½ cup	(125 ml) diced zucchini
½ cup	(125 ml) diced mushrooms
	salt and pepper

Preheat oven to 350°F (180°C).

Heat oil in ovenproof casserole and cook onions 3 minutes over low heat.

Stir in rice; cook 2 minutes over medium heat. Season and mix in thyme and bay leaf.

Pour in chicken stock; cover and bring to boil. Finish cooking 18 minutes in oven.

Meanwhile, heat butter in frying pan. When hot, add all vegetables and cook about 3 to 4 minutes. Season generously. Add these vegetables to casserole about 5 minutes before rice is done.

Celeriac Pancakes

(serves 4)

1 SERVING	409 CALORIES	37g CARBOHYDRATE
18g PROTEIN	21g FAT	1.6g FIBER

1 lb	(500 g) celeriac, peeled and in lemony water
4	large potatoes, peeled and blanched 15 minutes
1½ cups	(375 ml) grated Gruyère cheese
2 tbsp	(30 ml) vegetable oil
	salt and pepper

Preheat oven to 425°F (220°C).

Dry celeriac and cut into very fine julienne; place in bowl. Cut potatoes in fine julienne and add to bowl along with cheese; season everything well and mix. Chill 1 hour.

Heat oil in large frying pan. When hot, place celeriac mixture in pan and press down with spatula. Cook 15 minutes over medium heat.

Wrap frying pan handle in foil and finish cooking pancake in oven for 15 minutes.

Slice as you would a pizza and serve.

Potato Pancakes

(serves 4)

1 SERVING	408 CALORIES	34g CARBOHYDRATE
5g PROTEIN	28g FAT	2.0g FIBER

8	potatoes, peeled and boiled
3 tbsp	(45 ml) butter
2	egg yolks
½ tsp	(2 ml) ginger
½ tsp	(2 ml) savory
1 tsp	(5 ml) sesame seeds
¼ cup	(50 ml) heavy cream
3 tbsp	(45 ml) peanut oil
	salt and white pepper

Mash potatoes through food mill. Add remaining ingredients (except oil) and mix until thoroughly blended. Set aside to cool.

Dust hands with flour and shape mixture into small pancakes. Heat oil in large frying pan and cook 3 minutes each side over medium-high heat.

Serve immediately.

Shepherd's Pie

(serves 4 to 6)

1 SERVING	587 CALORIES	44g CARBOHYDRATE
42g PROTEIN	27g FAT	3.9g FIBER

2 tbsp	(30 ml) oil
½	red onion, chopped
1 tbsp	(15 ml) chopped parsley
½ lb	(250 g) mushrooms, coarsely chopped
¼ tsp	(1 ml) ground clove
¼ tsp	(1 ml) allspice
1 lb	(500 g) ground beef
½ lb	(250 g) ground pork
½ tsp	(2 ml) basil
¼ tsp	(1 ml) thyme
12 oz	(341 ml) can whole kernel corn, drained
1½ cups	(375 ml) hot tomato sauce
½ cup	(125 ml) grated Romano cheese
3-3½ cups	(750-875 ml)) mashed potatoes
2 tbsp	(30 ml) melted butter
	salt and pepper
	dash paprika

Preheat oven to 375°F (190°C).

Heat oil in skillet and cook onion and parsley 2 minutes. Add mushrooms, clove and allspice; continue cooking 3 minutes over medium heat.

Stir in beef and pork, add basil and thyme; cook 5 to 6 minutes over medium-high heat.

Mix in corn, season and cook 3 to 4 minutes. Add tomato sauce, cheese and continue cooking 2 to 3 minutes over medium heat.

Spoon mixture into large baking dish and completely cover with mashed potatoes. Use a pastry bag for a fancy top as shown in the picture.

Sprinkle potatoes with paprika and moisten slightly with melted butter. Bake 45 minutes in oven.

1 Cook mushrooms, clove and allspice 3 minutes over medium heat.

3 Mix in corn, season and cook 3 to 4 minutes. Then add tomato sauce, cheese and continue cooking 2 to 3 minutes.

2 Add beef, pork, basil and thyme; cook 5 to 6 minutes over medium-high heat.

4 Spoon mixture into large baking dish and cover with mashed potatoes. If you desire a fancy top, use a pastry bag.

Pita Pizza

(serves 4)

1 SERVING	553 CALORIES	57g CARBOHYDRATE
25g PROTEIN	25g FAT	3.9g FIBER

4	small whole wheat pita bread
1-1½ cups	tomato sauce, heated
12	mushrooms, sliced
½	green pepper, in rings
½	red pepper, in rings
12	pitted black olives, sliced
2	raw sausages
1 cup	(250 ml) grated mozzarella cheese
1¼ cups	(300 ml) grated cheddar cheese
	chopped parsley to taste
	salt and pepper

Preheat oven to 425°F (220°C).

Place pita bread on cookie sheet and cover with tomato sauce. Add mushrooms, peppers and olives.

Remove sausage meat from casing and arrange on pizzas in tiny clumps. Top with a mixture of grated cheeses and season with parsley, salt and pepper.

Cook pizzas in the middle of the oven for 10 minutes.

Pita pizzas are a great way to use leftover vegetables — be creative with what's in your fridge.

Hot Potato Salad

(serves 4)

1 SERVING	180 CALORIES	27g CARBOHYDRATE
9g PROTEIN	4g FAT	1.4g FIBER

4	large potatoes, boiled with skin and still hot
4	slices bacon, diced
3	green onions, chopped
1	stalk celery heart, finely chopped
1	garlic clove, smashed and chopped
½ cup	(125 ml) red wine vinegar
¾ cup	(175 ml) chicken stock, heated
1 tbsp	(15 ml) chopped chives
	salt and pepper

Peel and cut potatoes in thick slices. Place in oven at 150°F (70°C) to keep hot.

Cook bacon in frying pan for 4 minutes or until crisp. Remove bacon leaving fat in pan and set aside.

Add onions, celery and garlic to pan; cook 3 minutes over medium heat.

Mix in vinegar; cook 1 minute over high heat. Add chicken stock and continue cooking 2 minutes.

Stir in chives and season generously. Pour over hot potatoes and let stand 10 minutes on counter.

Serve on lettuce leaves and sprinkle portions with reserved bacon.

Sole Croquettes

(serves 4)

1 SERVING	543 CALORIES	42g CARBOHYDRATE
33g PROTEIN	27g FAT	0.2g FIBER

4 tbsp	(60 ml) butter
3½ tbsp	(50 ml) flour
1 cup	(250 ml) hot milk
3	sole filets, cooked and chopped
1	small envelope unflavored gelatine, softened in water
1	egg yolk
¼ cup	(50 ml) heavy cream
1 tbsp	(15 ml) chopped parsley
3	egg whites
1 tbsp	(15 ml) oil
2 cups	(500 ml) breadcrumbs
	salt and pepper
	juice ¼ lemon

Heat butter in saucepan. Add flour and mix; cook 2 minutes over low heat.

Whisk in milk and season; continue cooking 5 minutes.

Remove saucepan from heat. Stir in fish and gelatine. Mix egg yolk with cream and incorporate.

Stir in parsley, lemon juice and correct seasoning. Spread mixture on large dinner plate, cover with plastic wrap and chill 2 minutes.

Beat egg whites with oil just until slightly foamy.

Shape croquette mixture into tubes; roll in breadcrumbs then dip in egg whites and finish by rolling in breadcrumbs again.

Deep-fry sole croquettes in hot oil until evenly browned.

Cheese Stuffed Tomatoes

(serves 4)

1 SERVING	180 CALORIES	18g CARBOHYDRATE
9g PROTEIN	8g FAT	3.2g FIBER

4	large tomatoes
1 tbsp	(15 ml) vegetable oil
1	small onion, finely chopped
1	garlic clove, smashed and chopped
½ tsp	(2 ml) oregano
15	mushrooms, sliced
1 tbsp	(15 ml) chopped parsley
½ cup	(125 ml) ricotta cheese
⅓ cup	(75 ml) breadcrumbs
	salt and pepper

Preheat oven to 375°F (190°C).

Core tomatoes, turn them upside-down and cut away a top. Scoop out most of flesh but leave a sturdy shell. Place shells in baking dish, season insides and moisten with a sprinkle of oil. Set tomato flesh aside.

Heat oil in frying pan and cook onion and garlic 3 to 4 minutes.

Add tomato flesh, oregano, mushrooms and parsley. Season well and cook 4 to 5 minutes over medium heat.

Mix in cheese and breadcrumbs; cook 2 to 3 minutes over medium heat.

Fill tomato shells with mixture and bake 30 to 35 minutes in oven.

1 Core tomatoes, turn them upside-down and cut away a top. You can keep the tops for decoration at serving time.

3 After onion and garlic have cooked, add tomato flesh, oregano, mushrooms and parsley. Season well and cook 4 to 5 minutes over medium heat.

2 Scoop out most of flesh but leave a sturdy shell. Season insides and set shells aside.

4 Mix in cheese and breadcrumbs; cook 2 to 3 minutes then fill tomato shells with mixture. Bake 30 to 35 minutes in oven.

Potato Salad with Lemon Dressing

(serves 4)

1 SERVING	291 CALORIES	18g CARBOHYDRATE
3g PROTEIN	23g FAT	1.4g FIBER

½ cup	(125 ml) mayonnaise
1 tbsp	(15 ml) chopped parsley
2 tbsp	(30 ml) grated lemon rind
4	boiled potatoes, peeled and diced large
2	celery stalks, diced
¼ cup	(50 ml) chopped red onion
	juice ½ lemon
	salt and pepper

Mix mayonnaise, parsley, lemon rind and juice together; season to taste.

Place potatoes, celery and onion in bowl; toss together.

Pour in lemon dressing, toss again and serve.

Beef Tongue Salad

(serves 4)

1 SERVING	232 CALORIES	10g CARBOHYDRATE
12g PROTEIN	16g FAT	

1	large cucumber, peeled, seeded and in julienne
1	apple, peeled, cored and in wedges
1 cup	(250 ml) cooked beets, in julienne
2 cups	(500 ml) cooked beef tongue, in julienne
3 tbsp	(45 ml) capers
¼ cup	(50 ml) mayonnaise
1 tbsp	(15 ml) strong mustard
1 tbsp	(15 ml) anchovy paste
	few drops lemon juice
	salt and pepper

Place cucumber in bowl, sprinkle with salt and marinate 30 minutes on counter.

Drain liquid and transfer cucumber to clean bowl. Add apple, beets, tongue and capers; mix.

Stir mayonnaise, mustard, anchovy paste, lemon juice and salt and pepper together. Pour over salad ingredients and mix until well coated.

Serve on lettuce leaves.

Delicious Turkey Salad

(serves 4)

1 SERVING	262 CALORIES	11g CARBOHYDRATE
23g PROTEIN	14g FAT	2.3g FIBER

2 cups	(500 ml) leftover cooked turkey, diced
2	carrots, pared and grated
½ cup	(125 ml) finely chopped onion
2	green onions, finely chopped
1	celery stalk, diced
1	cucumber, peeled, seeded and sliced
24	mushrooms, sliced
¼ cup	(50 ml) lime juice
2	mint leaves, chopped
3 oz	(90 g) cream cheese, soft
1 tbsp	(15 ml) oil
1 tsp	(5 ml) wine vinegar
	few drops Worcestershire sauce
	salt and pepper

Place all vegetables in large salad bowl.

In blender, mix together remaining ingredients until smooth. Pour dressing over salad, chill and serve.

Leftover Vegetable Soup

(serves 6 to 8)

1 SERVING	140 CALORIES	22g CARBOHYDRATE
4g PROTEIN	4g FAT	2.4g FIBER

2 tbsp	(30 ml) melted butter
2	onions, chopped
2	green onions, sliced
2	carrots, pared and sliced
2	potatoes, peeled and diced
1	small turnip, peeled and sliced
1	parsnip, pared and sliced
1	bay leaf
3	parsley sprigs
½ tsp	(2 ml) basil
¼ tsp	(1 ml) rosemary
½ tsp	(2 ml) chervil
¼ tsp	(1 ml) marjoram
¼	cabbage, in leaves
8 cups	(2 L) chicken stock, heated
1	yellow pepper, diced
1	red pepper, diced
1½ cups	(375 ml) large croutons
¼ cup	(50 ml) grated Gruyère cheese
	salt and pepper

Heat butter in very large saucepan. Add both onions and cook 3 minutes covered over medium heat.

Add carrots, potatoes, turnip and parsnip; mix well. Cover and continue cooking 5 minutes.

Add all seasonings including bay leaf and parsley; mix well and stir in cabbage. Pour in chicken stock and bring to boil uncovered over high heat.

Cook soup 35 minutes uncovered over medium-low heat.

About 5 minutes before soup is done, add peppers. Serve with croutons and garnish portions with grated cheese.

Scrambled Eggs with Vegetables

(serves 4)

1 SERVING	251 CALORIES	5g CARBOHYDRATE
15g PROTEIN	19g FAT	1.3g FIBER

2 tbsp	(30 ml) butter
12	cherry tomatoes
¼	cucumber, diced small
4	green onions, in 1 in (2.5 cm) sticks
8	beaten eggs, seasoned
6	slices salami, in strips
	salt and pepper

Heat butter in nonstick pan. When hot, add vegetables and cook 3 to 4 minutes over medium-high heat. Season well and stir once.

Reduce heat to medium and pour in eggs. Mix rapidly and continue cooking 1 to 2 minutes while stirring.

Add salami strips, mix and serve immediately. Accompany with bacon if desired.

Flat Spinach and Cheese Omelet

(serves 2)

1 SERVING	441 CALORIES	5g CARBOHYDRATE
31g PROTEIN	33g FAT	0.8g FIBER

2 tbsp	(30 ml) butter
1½ cups	(375 ml) cooked chopped spinach
6	eggs
½ cup	(125 ml) grated Gruyère cheese
	salt and pepper

Heat 1 tbsp (15 ml) butter in nonstick frying pan. When hot, add spinach and season well. Cook 3 minutes over high heat.

Break eggs into bowl and beat with fork; season well.

Remove spinach from pan and pour into eggs; mix well.

Heat remaining butter in nonstick pan. When hot, pour in egg mixture and cook 3 minutes over medium heat.

Sprinkle top with cheese; cover and cook 2 to 3 minutes over medium-low heat.

Slide omelet out of pan and serve.

Potato Omelet

(serves 2)

1 SERVING	441 CALORIES	18g CARBOHYDRATE
18g PROTEIN	33g FAT	1.1g FIBER

2 tbsp	(30 ml) butter
1 tsp	(5 ml) vegetable oil
2	potatoes, peeled and sliced
2 tbsp	(30 ml) chopped onion
1 tbsp	(15 ml) chopped fresh parsley
5	eggs
	pinch nutmeg
	salt and pepper

Heat 1 tbsp (15 ml) butter and oil in small frying pan.

When hot, add potatoes and season well. Cook 2 to 3 minutes on each side over medium heat. Stir once during cooking process.

Sprinkle nutmeg over potatoes and mix; cover and continue cooking 8 to 10 minutes.

Mix well; add onion and parsley. Cook, uncovered, 3 to 4 minutes. Meanwhile, break eggs into bowl and beat with fork; season well.

Heat remaining butter in nonstick frying pan or omelet pan.

When hot, pour in eggs and cook 1 minute over high heat.

Stir eggs rapidly and add potatoes. Roll omelet (see technique) and continue cooking 1 minute.

Serve with cooked broccoli and decorate with several cooked potatoes.

Stuffed Egg Halves with Mustard

(serves 4 to 6)

1 SERVING	241 CALORIES	0g CARBOHYDRATE
13g PROTEIN	21g FAT	0.2g FIBER

12	hard-boiled eggs, cut in half lengthwise
2 tbsp	(30 ml) Dijon mustard
4 tbsp	(60 ml) mayonnaise
	several drops Tabasco sauce
	lemon juice to taste
	salt and white pepper
	chopped fresh parsley
	several lettuce leaves, washed and dried

Force egg yolks through sieve using back of wooden spoon. Place in mixing bowl.

Add mustard, mayonnaise, Tabasco sauce, lemon juice, salt and pepper. Mix until well combined and correct seasoning.

Spoon mixture into pastry bag fitted with star nozzle. Stuff egg whites; sprinkle with some parsley.

Place stuffed eggs on lettuce leaves and serve.

If desired, refrigerate until serving time. Cover with plastic wrap.

Poached Eggs with Bacon

(serves 2)

1 SERVING	288 CALORIES	1g CARBOHYDRATE
17g PROTEIN	24g FAT	0g FIBER

6 cups	(1.5 L) water
1 tsp	(5 ml) white vinegar
4	eggs
6	slices bacon, cooked crisp
	salt
	buttered toast

Place water, vinegar and salt in large saucepan; bring to boil.

Reduce heat so that water simmers. Carefully slide eggs, one at a time, into water. Cook 3 minutes over medium heat.

Remove eggs with slotted spoon and drain.

Serve on buttered toast and with bacon. Decorate with tomato slices.

OUTDOOR COOKING

Tips for Barbecuing

Whether you are barbecuing with gas or over coals or an open fire, make a habit of preheating your barbecue.

After the barbecue has warmed up a bit, oil the grill; it will help prevent foods from sticking.

Keep an eye on foods being barbecued and turn as needed to avoid charring.

Because of the variety of barbecues available, treat our cooking times as guidelines and use your own judgement; taste when in doubt.

Remove fat from meats to prevent it from dropping on the coals and creating flames which will tend to increase charring.

If you are using charcoal be sure the coals have turned grey before adding any food.

If you do not use a marinade always oil meat before placing on the hot grill. This will not only give the meat taste but will also speed up and improve searing.

Barbecuing fish takes some patience because it tends to stick to the grill more than other foods. You can eliminate this by using a stainless-steel fish grill equipped with a long handle for easy turning.

Barbecued Steak Diane

(serves 2)

1 SERVING	445 CALORIES	1g CARBOHYDRATE
35g PROTEIN	26g FAT	trace FIBER

4 tbsp	(60 ml) melted butter
4 tbsp	(60 ml) cognac
4 tbsp	(60 ml) sherry
2 tbsp	(30 ml) chopped chives
2	strip loin steaks, 8-10 oz (250-300 g) each
	salt and pepper

Preheat barbecue at HIGH.

Place butter, cognac, sherry and chives in small saucepan; bring to boil.

Meanwhile, trim all excess fat from steaks.

Pour hot liquid over meat and let stand 15 minutes.

Place steaks on hot grill. Cook 8 to 10 minutes depending on taste. Season well and turn 3 to 4 times.

Fabulous Flank Steak

(serves 4)

1 SERVING	1064 CALORIES	11g CARBOHYDRATE
46g PROTEIN	94g FAT	trace FIBER

Marinade

1 ½ cups	(375 ml) vegetable oil
½ cup	(125 ml) soya sauce
¼ cup	(50 ml) Worcestershire sauce
½ cup	(125 ml) wine vinegar
½ cup	(125 ml) lemon juice
2 tbsp	(30 ml) dry mustard
1 tsp	(5 ml) salt
1 tbsp	(15 ml) pepper
1 tbsp	(15 ml) chopped parsley
2	garlic cloves, smashed and chopped

Recipe

2	large flank steaks, excess fat trimmed

Preheat barbecue at HIGH.

Mix marinade ingredients together, pour over meat and refrigerate 4 hours.

Drain meat and slice on an angle into large pieces. Set on hot grill and cook 3 to 4 minutes each side. Season and baste once with leftover marinade.

Serve with potatoes.

Strip Loin Steaks

(serves 4)

1 SERVING	314 CALORIES	13g CARBOHYDRATE
33g PROTEIN	14g FAT	trace FIBER

4	strip loin steaks, 8-10 oz (250-300 g) each
2 tbsp	(30 ml) butter
3	medium onions, chopped
1	garlic clove, smashed and chopped
1 tbsp	(15 ml) chopped parsley
¼ cup	(50 ml) raspberry wine vinegar
½ cup	(125 ml) taco sauce
	oil
	salt and pepper

Preheat barbecue at HIGH.

Brush steaks with oil and place on hot grill. Cook 8 to 10 minutes depending on taste. Turn 3 to 4 times and season after searing.

Meanwhile, heat butter in saucepan. Cook onions, garlic and parsley 3 to 4 minutes over low heat.

Add vinegar; cook 3 to 4 minutes over medium-high heat.

Season and stir in taco sauce; cook 2 to 3 minutes over low heat.

Serve with steaks.

1 When not using a marinade it is important to brush steaks with oil.

3 Add vinegar and increase heat to medium-high. Cook 3 to 4 minutes to reduce liquid.

2 Cook onions, garlic and parsley in hot butter for 3 to 4 minutes over low heat.

4 Season and stir in taco sauce; finish cooking 2 to 3 minutes over low heat.

Tangy T-Bone Steaks

(serves 4)

1 SERVING	319 CALORIES	18g CARBOHYDRATE
24g PROTEIN	17g FAT	trace FIBER

4	T-bone steaks, 1-1¼ in (2.5-3 cm) thick
½ cup	(125 ml) catsup
2 tbsp	(30 ml) melted butter
1 tbsp	(15 ml) Worcestershire sauce
½ tsp	(2 ml) chopped ginger
2 tbsp	(30 ml) wine vinegar
2 tbsp	(30 ml) honey
1 tbsp	(15 ml) lemon juice
1 tbsp	(15 ml) strong mustard
	salt and pepper
	oil

Preheat barbecue at HIGH.

Trim most of fat from steaks and slash remaining fat with knife to prevent curling. Moisten meat with a bit of oil then set aside.

Cook catsup, butter and Worcestershire sauce 2 to 3 minutes over low heat in saucepan.

Add ginger, vinegar and honey; continue cooking 2 to 3 minutes.

Remove from heat and stir in lemon juice and mustard.

Spread mixture over steaks and place on hot grill. Cook 12 to 14 minutes depending on taste. Turn 4 times, baste occasionally and season well.

1 Trim most of fat from steaks and slash remaining fat with knife to prevent curling. Moisten meat with a bit of oil.

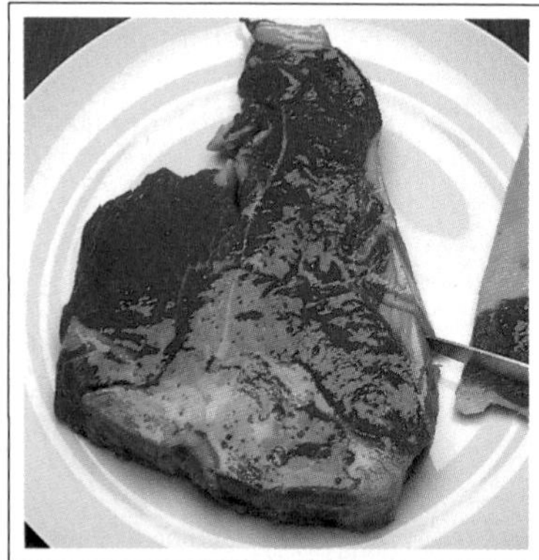

3 Add ginger, vinegar and honey; continue cooking 2 to 3 minutes. Remove from heat and stir in lemon juice and mustard.

2 Cook catsup, butter and Worcestershire sauce 2 to 3 minutes over low heat.

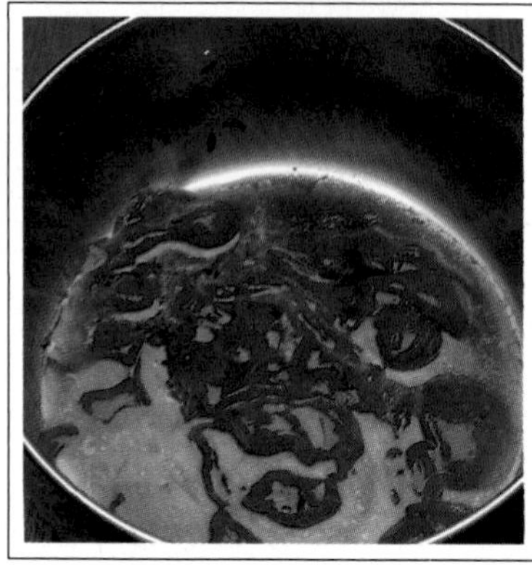

4 Spread mixture over steaks before cooking.

MOUTARDE A L'ANCIENNE
GRAIN MUSTARD
BOCQUET
Product of France

Juicy Burgers

(serves 4)

1 SERVING	437 CALORIES	7g CARBOHYDRATE
70g PROTEIN	13g FAT	trace FIBER

2 lb	(900 g) lean ground beef
1	medium onion, chopped and cooked
½ tsp	(2 ml) chili powder
2 tbsp	(30 ml) tomato paste
3 tbsp	(45 ml) breadcrumbs
1	egg
	dash paprika
	salt and pepper
	oil for basting

Preheat barbecue at MEDIUM.

Place all ingredients, except oil, in mixer; blend until well incorporated and meat forms ball.

Shape into patties and brush with oil. Place on hot grill and season well. Cover and cook 8 to 10 minutes depending on taste. Turn patties 2 to 3 times and season once again.

Serve burgers with the usual condiments and a side order of onion rings.

Onion Rings

(serves 4)

1 SERVING	259 CALORIES	31g CARBOHYDRATE
8g PROTEIN	11g FAT	trace FIBER

2	medium onions, in rings
1½ cups	(375 ml) milk
2	beaten eggs
1½ cups	(375 ml) crushed soda crackers, well seasoned
	dash paprika

Place onion rings in milk and let stand about 15 minutes.

Drain onion rings, dip in beaten eggs and coat with crushed crackers; season with paprika.

Cook onion rings in hot oil for 3 minutes or until golden brown. Serve with burgers.

Rib-Eye Steaks

(serves 4)

1 SERVING	426 CALORIES	11g CARBOHYDRATE
40g PROTEIN	24g FAT	0.5g FIBER

Marinade

3	green onions, finely chopped
¼ cup	(50 ml) soya sauce
¼ cup	(50 ml) sesame oil
1 tbsp	(15 ml) sugar
2 tbsp	(30 ml) sesame seeds
	fresh ground pepper

Recipe

4	rib-eye steaks

Preheat barbecue at HIGH.

Mix marinade ingredients together and pour over steaks. Set aside in refrigerator for 1 hour.

Place steaks on hot grill and cook 5 to 6 minutes each side depending on taste. Baste occasionally and season with pepper.

Steaks with Vegetable Sauce

(serves 4)

1 SERVING	328 CALORIES	19g CARBOHYDRATE
34g PROTEIN	13g FAT	1.0g FIBER

2 tbsp	(30 ml) oil
3	fresh jalapeno peppers, very finely chopped
2	onions, chopped
1	yellow pepper, chopped
2	tomatoes, peeled and diced
1	zucchini, diced small
1 cup	(250 ml) diced pineapple
½ tsp	(2 ml) cumin
½ tsp	(2 ml) oregano
½ tsp	(2 ml) basil
3 tbsp	(45 ml) tomato paste
4	strip loin steaks, 8-10 oz (250-300 g) each
	salt and pepper

Preheat barbecue at HIGH.

Heat half of oil in saucepan. Cook jalapeno peppers, onions and yellow pepper 3 to 4 minutes over medium heat.

Mix in tomatoes and zucchini; cover and cook 5 to 6 minutes.

Mix in pineapple, season and add cumin, oregano and basil. Cover and cook 13 minutes over medium heat. About 3 minutes before end, stir in tomato paste.

While vegetables are cooking you might want to start steaks.

Brush meat with remaining oil and place on hot grill. Cook 8 to 10 minutes depending on taste. Turn 3 to 4 times and season well after searing.

Serve vegetable sauce with steaks.

1 Cook jalapeno peppers, onions and yellow pepper 3 to 4 minutes over medium heat.

3 Add pineapple and all seasonings. Cover and cook 13 minutes over medium heat.

2 Mix in tomatoes and zucchini; continue cooking 5 to 6 minutes with cover.

4 About 3 minutes before end of cooking time, stir in tomato paste.

Marinated Pork Back Ribs

(serves 4)

1 SERVING	1014 CALORIES	15g CARBOHYDRATE
47g PROTEIN	84g FAT	trace FIBER

Marinade

¾ cup	(175 ml) pineapple juice
3 tbsp	(45 ml) soya sauce
2	garlic cloves, smashed and chopped
¼ cup	(50 ml) catsup
1 tbsp	(15 ml) honey

Recipe

3 lb	(1.4 kg) pork back ribs
	salt and pepper

Preheat barbecue at LOW.

Place pineapple juice, soya sauce and garlic in large bowl.

Mix well, add remaining marinade ingredients and season to taste. Add ribs and let stand 15 minutes.

Place ribs on hot grill. Partially cover and cook 40 to 45 minutes, turning frequently and basting as needed. Season well.

New York Steaks

(serves 4)

1 SERVING	341 CALORIES	2g CARBOHYDRATE
41g PROTEIN	15g FAT	trace FIBER

2	garlic cloves, smashed and chopped
2	bay leaves, finely chopped
1 tsp	(5 ml) green peppercorns
½ cup	(125 ml) dry white wine
2 tbsp	(30 ml) wine vinegar
1 tbsp	(15 ml) oil
4	New York steaks, 8-10 oz (250-300 g) each
	salt and pepper

Preheat barbecue at HIGH.

Place all ingredients in deep plate; let stand 15 minutes.

Place steaks on hot grill and cook 8 to 10 minutes depending on taste. Turn at least three times, baste and season.

Veal Chops with Tomato Hollandaise

(serves 4)

1 SERVING	665 CALORIES	3.2g CARBOHYDRATE
52g PROTEIN	49g FAT	0.3g FIBER

3 tbsp	(45 ml) oil
1 tsp	(5 ml) Worcestershire sauce
1 tsp	(5 ml) curry powder
1 tsp	(5 ml) chili powder
4	large veal chops
1 tbsp	(15 ml) hot water
2 tbsp	(30 ml) horseradish
3	egg yolks
1 tbsp	(15 ml) tomato paste
½ tsp	(2 ml) cumin powder
½ cup	(125 ml) melted butter
	juice 1 lime
	salt and pepper

Preheat barbecue at HIGH.

Mix oil, Worcestershire sauce, curry, chili powder and lime juice together; brush over chops and season well.

Place chops on hot grill. Cook 5 to 6 minutes each side depending on thickness. Baste occasionally and season.

Meanwhile, mix water, horseradish, egg yolks, tomato paste and seasonings in blender for 30 seconds at high speed.

Reduce blender speed to low; very slowly incorporate butter. Keep mixing until butter is well blended. Season and serve with veal.

Juicy Veal Chops

(serves 4)

1 SERVING	576 CALORIES	18g CARBOHYDRATE
52g PROTEIN	30g FAT	0.6g FIBER

2 tbsp	(30 ml) butter
2	green onions, chopped
1	garlic clove, smashed and chopped
1	large tomato, peeled and diced
1½ cups	(375 ml) brown sauce, heated
2 tbsp	(30 ml) chili sauce
1 tbsp	(15 ml) teriyaki sauce
1 tsp	(5 ml) chopped ginger
4	large veal chops
	salt and pepper

Preheat barbecue at HIGH.

Heat butter in saucepan. Cook onions, garlic and tomato 3 to 4 minutes over high heat; season well.

Mix in brown sauce, chili sauce, teriyaki sauce and ginger; continue cooking 3 to 4 minutes over low heat.

Brush mixture over chops and set on hot grill. Cook 5 to 6 minutes on each side depending on thickness. Season well and baste several times.

If desired serve with baked potatoes.

Tomato Veal Chops

(serves 4)

1 SERVING	402 CALORIES	11g CARBOHYDRATE
50g PROTEIN	16g FAT	trace FIBER

4	loin veal chops, ¾ in (2 cm) thick
1 cup	(250 ml) tomato juice
2 tbsp	(30 ml) corn syrup
2 tbsp	(30 ml) vegetable oil
½ tsp	(2 ml) tarragon
½ tsp	(2 ml) chervil
1 tbsp	(15 ml) green peppercorns, mashed
1 tbsp	(15 ml) lime juice
	salt and pepper

Preheat barbecue at HIGH.

Trim excess fat from chops and place them in deep dish; set aside.

Mix tomato juice, corn syrup and oil together in bowl.

Add seasonings, peppercorns and lime juice; mix well and pour over veal. Marinate 30 minutes.

Place chops on hot grill. Partly cover and cook 15 minutes. Turn 4 times, baste often and season once or twice.

1 Trim excess fat from chops and place them in deep dish; set aside.

2 Mix tomato juice, corn syrup and oil together in bowl.

3 Add seasonings, peppercorns and lime juice; mix well.

4 Pour over veal and marinate 30 minutes.

Veal Scallopini

(serves 4)

1 SERVING	279 CALORIES	2g CARBOHYDRATE
33g PROTEIN	15g FAT	trace FIBER

Marinade

¼ cup	(50 ml) oil
1 tbsp	(15 ml) tarragon
1 tbsp	(15 ml) soya sauce
1	garlic clove, smashed and chopped
1 tbsp	(15 ml) lemon juice

Recipe

4	veal scallopini, ¼ in (0.65 cm) thick
	salt and pepper

Preheat barbecue at HIGH.

Mix marinade ingredients together in large bowl. Add veal and let stand 30 minutes.

Place veal on hot grill. Cook 8 minutes turning once and basting occasionally. Season generously.

Serve with grilled eggplant.

Stuffed Veal Scallopini

(serves 4)

1 SERVING	292 CALORIES	13g CARBOHYDRATE
34g PROTEIN	14g FAT	0.7g FIBER

1 tbsp	(15 ml) butter
1	onion, finely chopped
1 cup	(250 ml) finely diced eggplant
1 tbsp	(15 ml) chopped parsley
1 tbsp	(15 ml) tomato paste
4	large veal scallopini
8	vine leaves
2 tbsp	(30 ml) vegetable oil
1 tbsp	(15 ml) lemon juice
	salt and pepper

Preheat barbecue at MEDIUM.

Heat butter in small saucepan. Add onion, eggplant and parsley; cover and cook 7 to 8 minutes over low heat.

Mix in tomato paste and continue cooking 2 to 3 minutes.

Spread stuffing over scallopini, roll tightly and wrap in double vine leaves. Secure with toothpicks.

Place rolls on hot grill and baste with mixture of oil and lemon juice. Partially cover and cook 12 to 14 minutes, turning often.

Serve with hot barbecue sauce.

Stuffed Veal Loin

(serves 4)

1 SERVING	462 CALORIES	20g CARBOHYDRATE
55g PROTEIN	17g FAT	0.5g FIBER

2	¾ lb (375 g) veal loins
10 oz	(284 ml) can mandarin segments
2 tbsp	(30 ml) honey
2 tbsp	(30 ml) butter
1	onion, finely chopped
⅓ lb	(150 g) mushrooms, finely chopped
½ tsp	(2 ml) tarragon
2 tbsp	(30 ml) ricotta cheese
1 tbsp	(15 ml) breadcrumbs
	salt and pepper

Preheat barbecue at HIGH.

Trim excess fat from veal. Slice both loins open lengthwise so that they can be stuffed. See Technique for visual help.

Drain mandarins and pour juice into small saucepan. Set fruit aside. Add honey and cook 15 minutes on high to thicken. Remove from stove and let cool.

Heat butter in second saucepan. Cook onion 2 minutes over medium heat.

Add mushrooms and seasonings; cook 4 minutes over high heat. Remove from stove; stir in cheese and breadcrumbs.

Spread stuffing on both sides of meat. Add a row of mandarin segments (save some for decoration) and close; secure with kitchen string.

Brush loins with mandarin/honey mixture. Place on hot grill and partially cover. Cook 30 minutes turning often; baste occasionally with mandarin mixture.

Heat reserved mandarin segments with leftover basting mixture in small saucepan. Pour over loins before serving.

1 Trim excess fat from veal.

3 Spread cooked stuffing on both sides of meat and add a row of mandarin segments.

2 Slice loins open as shown so they can be stuffed.

4 Close and secure with kitchen string.

Curried Veal Scallopini

(serves 4)

1 SERVING	337 CALORIES	8g CARBOHYDRATE
34g PROTEIN	14g FAT	0.7g FIBER

1 cup	(250 ml) dry white wine
3 tbsp	(45 ml) olive oil
1 cup	(250 ml) tomato sauce
½ tsp	(2 ml) caraway seed
1 tbsp	(15 ml) curry powder
1	garlic clove, smashed and chopped
4	large veal scallopini
	salt and pepper

Preheat barbecue at HIGH.

Bring wine to boil in small saucepan; continue cooking 3 minutes over medium heat.

Mix in oil, tomato sauce, seasonings and garlic; simmer 3 to 4 minutes.

Brush mixture generously over veal. Roll tightly and secure with toothpicks; brush again with sauce.

Place veal rolls on hot grill. Cook 8 to 10 minutes, turning often and basting occasionally. Season to taste.

Garlic Veal Chops

(serves 4)

1 SERVING	370 CALORIES	1g CARBOHYDRATE
37g PROTEIN	23g FAT	trace FIBER

½ lb	(250 g) soft butter
2	garlic cloves, smashed and chopped
1 tbsp	(15 ml) finely chopped parsley
1 tbsp	(15 ml) smashed green peppercorns
¼ tsp	(1 ml) lemon juice
4	veal chops, ½ in (1.2 cm) thick
	salt and pepper

Preheat barbecue at HIGH.

Place butter, garlic, parsley, peppercorns, lemon juice and some salt in mixer or food processor; blend until well incorporated and smooth.

Melt ⅓ cup (75 ml) of butter mixture in small saucepan. Wrap remaining in foil and store in refrigerator for further uses.

Place chops on hot grill and generously brush with garlic butter. Partially cover and cook 8 minutes, turning 2 to 3 times. Baste often and season once.

Veal Bites

(serves 4)

1 SERVING	556 CALORIES	1g CARBOHYDRATE
68g PROTEIN	29g FAT	--g FIBER

12	bite-size cubes Gruyère cheese
12	4 in (10 cm) squares veal scallopini, seasoned
3 tbsp	(45 ml) melted butter
	salt and pepper

Preheat barbecue at HIGH.

Wrap cheese cubes in scallopini squares; secure with toothpicks.

Baste with butter and place on hot grill. Cook 3 minutes each side depending on thickness. Season generously.

If desired serve with caper sauce or other dipping sauce.

Caper Sauce for Veal

1 SERVING	172 CALORIES	12g CARBOHYDRATE
4g PROTEIN	13g FAT	0.8g FIBER

1 tbsp	(15 ml) butter
2	shallots, chopped
3 tbsp	(45 ml) capers
2 tbsp	(30 ml) vinegar
1¼ cups	(300 ml) white sauce, heated
1 tbsp	(15 ml) tomato paste
	salt and pepper

Heat butter in saucepan over medium heat. Add shallots, capers and vinegar; cook 2 minutes over high heat.

Stir in white sauce and tomato paste; correct seasoning. Cook 5 to 6 minutes over low heat.

Serve with barbecued veal.

Best Veal Burgers

(serves 4)

1 SERVING	593 CALORIES	34g CARBOHYDRATE
51g PROTEIN	27g FAT	0.6g FIBER

¼ cup	(50 ml) melted butter
8	small medallions veal, about ¼ in (0.65 cm) thick
4	kaiser buns
4	slices fresh tomato
4	slices mozzarella cheese
	salt and pepper

Preheat barbecue at LOW.

Brush butter over veal medallions. Place on hot grill and cook 2 to 3 minutes each side; season very well.

Remove and transfer medallions to bottom parts of buns. Top with slices of tomato and cheese; close buns.

Squeeze buns slightly to help them hold; place on hot grill. Barbecue 2 minutes each side for added taste.

Serve with decorative fries.

Club Steak Bahamas

(serves 4)

1 SERVING	348 CALORIES	22g CARBOHYDRATE
36g PROTEIN	13g FAT	trace FIBER

1 cup	(250 ml) catsup
½ cup	(125 ml) wine vinegar
2	garlic cloves, smashed and chopped
1	onion, grated
4 tbsp	(60 ml) butter
1 tsp	(5 ml) Tabasco sauce
1 tbsp	(15 ml) dry mustard
4	club steaks, fat trimmed
	salt and pepper
	juice 3 limes

Preheat barbecue at HIGH.

Place catsup, vinegar, garlic and onion in saucepan; mix together.

Stir in butter, Tabasco, mustard, salt, pepper and lime juice. Bring to boil over medium-high heat. Continue cooking 4 to 5 minutes.

Remove saucepan from stove and spread mixture over steaks. Place meat on hot grill and cook 8 to 10 minutes depending on taste. Turn meat 3 to 4 times, season and baste occasionally.

Lamb Surprise

(serves 4)

1 SERVING	533 CALORIES	11g CARBOHYDRATE
58g PROTEIN	27g FAT	0.6g FIBER

12	pieces of lamb, 1½ in (4 cm) long and 1½ in (4 cm) thick
12	pieces of mozzarella, sized to fit over lamb
1 cup	(250 ml) hot barbecue sauce
¼ tsp	(1 ml) paprika
¼ tsp	(1 ml) sage
12	vine leaves
	salt and pepper

Preheat barbecue at HIGH.

Season lamb and place pieces of cheese on top. Brush with barbecue sauce and sprinkle with seasonings.

Wrap in vine leaves and secure with toothpicks. Place bundles on hot grill and cook 10 to 12 minutes. Turn several times and season vine leaves once.

Serve as appetizer.

Lamb Steaks with Sweet Marinade

(serves 4)

1 SERVING	318 CALORIES	11g CARBOHYDRATE
35g PROTEIN	14g FAT	trace FIBER

Marinade

2 tbsp	(30 ml) maple syrup
2 tbsp	(30 ml) wine vinegar
1 tsp	(5 ml) chopped parsley
¼ tsp	(1 ml) aniseed
¼ tsp	(1 ml) celery seed
¼ tsp	(1 ml) marjoram
2	garlic cloves, smashed and chopped
	juice 1 orange

Recipe

4	lamb steaks, (from leg), ½ in (1.2 cm) thick
2 tbsp	(30 ml) oil
	salt and pepper

Preheat barbecue at HIGH.

Mix marinade ingredients together; pour over lamb and marinate 2 hours in refrigerator.

Place lamb steaks on hot grill and brush with oil. Cook 10 to 12 minutes depending on taste. Turn 3 times, season well and baste occasionally with leftover marinade.

Serve with vegetables.

1 Your butcher will prepare the lamb steaks for you as it is necessary to use a saw to cut through the middle bone.

3 Add seasonings and garlic.

2 Prepare marinade by mixing maple syrup, vinegar, parsley and orange juice together.

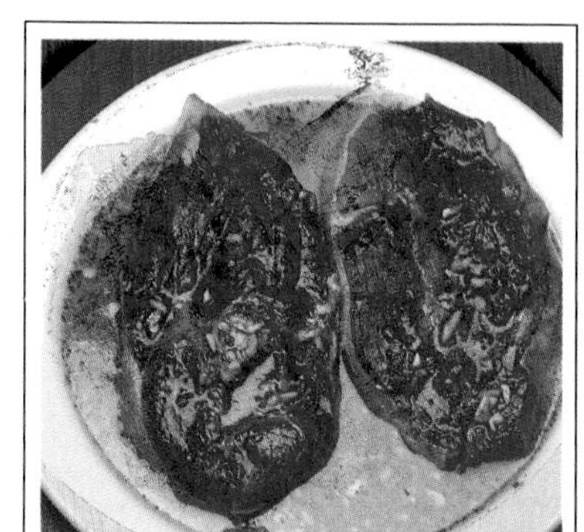

4 Pour over lamb and marinate 2 hours in refrigerator.

Lamb Roulade

(serves 4)

1 SERVING	287 CALORIES	5g CARBOHYDRATE
38g PROTEIN	12g FAT	1.0g FIBER

8	lamb cutlets (from leg)
1	onion, chopped and cooked
2 tbsp	(30 ml) green peppercorns
1 tbsp	(15 ml) coriander
	salt and pepper
	oil for basting

Preheat barbecue at MEDIUM.

Trim excess fat from cutlets. Place between waxed paper and flatten with mallet; season lightly.

Divide chopped onion, peppercorns and coriander between flattened cutlets. Roll and wrap in foil as shown in Technique; refrigerate 12 hours.

Unwrap lamb rolls and baste with oil. Place on hot grill and cook 14 to 16 minutes with cover. Turn at least 4 times.

1 Trim execss fat from cutlets.

3 Divide chopped onion, peppercorns and coriander between flattened cultlets.

2 Place between waxed paper and flatten with mallet; season lightly.

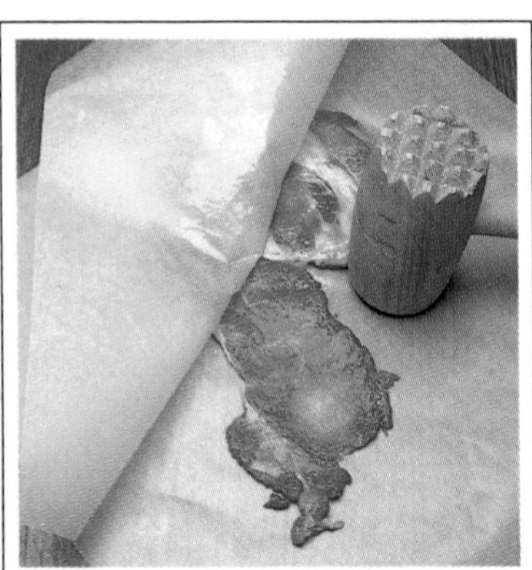

4 Roll and wrap each in foil; refrigerate 12 hours.

Fancy Lamb Rolls

(serves 4)

1 SERVING	380 CALORIES	5g CARBOHYDRATE
46g PROTEIN	18g FAT	trace FIBER

4	lamb kidneys, fat removed, well rinsed and ground
4 tbsp	(60 ml) breadcrumbs
1 tbsp	(15 ml) chopped parsley
4	lamb scallopini (from leg)
3 tbsp	(45 ml) melted butter
	salt and pepper

Preheat barbecue at MEDIUM.

Mix ground kidneys, breadcrumbs, parsley and pepper together. Spread over lamb, roll and secure with toothpicks.

Baste rolls with melted butter and season generously. Place on hot grill and cook 13 to 15 minutes depending on taste. Turn often and season once more.

Serve with julienne vegetables.

Rosemary Mint Lamb Chops

(serves 4)

1 SERVING	321 CALORIES	4g CARBOHYDRATE
37g PROTEIN	17g FAT	trace FIBER

½ cup	(125 ml) mint sauce
1 tsp	(5 ml) rosemary
2 tbsp	(30 ml) vegetable oil
8	lamb chops, fat trimmed
	salt and pepper

Preheat barbecue at HIGH.

Place mint sauce, rosemary and oil in deep dish; whisk together. Add lamb and mix; marinate 30 minutes.

Place chops on hot grill. Cook about 8 minutes depending on taste and size. Turn twice and season well.

Serve lamb with green beans.

STEEL

Lamb Chops Liza

(serves 4)

1 SERVING	303 CALORIES	2g CARBOHYDRATE
29g PROTEIN	19g FAT	trace FIBER

¼ cup	(50 ml) oil
1 tbsp	(15 ml) rosemary
2 tbsp	(30 ml) chopped parsley
1 tbsp	(15 ml) ground pepper
1	garlic clove, smashed and chopped
8	lamb chops, boned
	salt

Preheat barbecue at MEDIUM.

Mix oil with seasonings, parsley and garlic; brush generously over lamb chops.

Place lamb on hot grill. Cook 12 to 15 minutes, turning and basting frequently.

Serve with vegetables.

Lamb Kidneys

(serves 4)

1 SERVING	189 CALORIES	5g CARBOHYDRATE
21g PROTEIN	7g FAT	trace FIBER

8	lamb kidneys
1 tbsp	(15 ml) butter
3	shallots, chopped
1 tbsp	(15 ml) chopped parsley
½ cup	(125 ml) dry white wine
1 tbsp	(15 ml) tomato paste
	salt and pepper

Preheat barbecue at HIGH.

Remove fat from kidneys, rinse in water and slice in half; set aside.

Heat butter in saucepan over medium heat. Add shallots and cook 2 minutes.

Stir in parsley and wine; bring to boil. Continue cooking 3 minutes.

Remove saucepan from stove and stir in tomato paste. Let cool slightly.

Brush mixture over kidneys and place them on hot grill. Cook 4 to 5 minutes each side, basting often. Season to taste.

Skewered Lamb Cubes

(serves 4)

1 SERVING	684 CALORIES	2g CARBOHYDRATE
72g PROTEIN	42g FAT	trace FIBER

Marinade

½ cup	(125 ml) olive oil
2	garlic cloves, smashed and chopped
1 tbsp	(15 ml) rosemary
½ tsp	(2 ml) chili powder
1 tbsp	(15 ml) curry powder

Recipe

3 lb	(1.4 kg) lamb from leg, in 2 in (5 cm) cubes
	salt and pepper

Preheat barbecue at HIGH.

Mix marinade ingredients together; pour over lamb and refrigerate 2 hours.

Thread lamb cubes on skewers. Place on hot grill and cook 8 to 10 minutes depending on taste. Turn 4 to 5 times, baste and season.

Serve with rice.

London Broil — Lamb Style

(serves 4)

1 SERVING	824 CALORIES	3g CARBOHYDRATE
70g PROTEIN	57g FAT	trace FIBER

1 lb	(500 g) ground lamb
½ lb	(250 g) lean ground pork
½ lb	(250 g) lean ground veal
1	onion, chopped and cooked
2	garlic cloves, smashed and chopped
1 tbsp	(15 ml) chopped parsley
1	egg
4	10 in (25 cm) long strips beef sirloin (to wrap around lamb steaks)
	salt and pepper

Preheat barbecue at MEDIUM.

Blend ground meats, onion, garlic, parsley and egg in mixer until well incorporated.

Shape mixture into steaks, wrap sirloin around outside and secure with toothpicks.

Place on hot grill and cook 12 to 14 minutes depending on taste. Turn at least 4 times and season twice.

If desired serve with Soya Dipping Sauce.

Soya Dipping Sauce

1 SERVING	47 CALORIES	11g CARBOHYDRATE
.7g PROTEIN	--g FAT	--g FIBER

½ cup	(125 ml) water
4 tbsp	(60 ml) granulated sugar
1 tbsp	(15 ml) honey
2 tbsp	(30 ml) soya sauce
1 tsp	(5 ml) cornstarch
2 tbsp	(30 ml) cold water

Place ½ cup (125 ml) water, sugar, honey and soya sauce in saucepan; cook 3 minutes over medium heat.

Mix cornstarch with remaining water; stir into sauce and cook 1 more minute.

Remove and serve with barbecued lamb.

Rack of Lamb

(serves 4)

1 SERVING	712 CALORIES	4g CARBOHYDRATE
50g PROTEIN	48g FAT	trace FIBER

2 tbsp	(30 ml) butter
2 tbsp	(30 ml) finely chopped parsley
2	shallots, finely chopped
1	garlic clove, smashed and chopped
2 tbsp	(30 ml) breadcrumbs
2	1 lb (500 g) racks of lamb
	salt and pepper
	oil for basting

Preheat barbecue at MEDIUM.

Mix butter, parsley and shallots together. Add garlic, breadcrumbs and season well; set aside.

Prepare lamb by removing fat from between ribs. Wrap bones in foil to prevent charring.

Baste lamb with oil and set on hot grill with bone side down. Partially cover and cook 15 minutes; turn once. Season well.

Continue barbecuing 30 minutes partially covered. Turn often and baste with more oil.

About 2 minutes before lamb is cooked, spread reserved butter mixture over meat.

Serve with potatoes.

1 Prepare lamb by removing fat from between ribs.

3 Baste lamb with oil and place racks bone side down on hot grill.

2 Wrap bones in foil to prevent charring.

4 About 2 minutes before lamb is cooked to taste, spread butter mixture over meat. Replace on grill and finish cooking.

Barbecued Pork Medallions

(serves 4)

1 SERVING	642 CALORIES	17g CARBOHYDRATE
70g PROTEIN	27g FAT	trace FIBER

Marinade

¼ cup	(50 ml) soya sauce
½ cup	(125 ml) sherry wine
2 tbsp	(30 ml) honey
1 tbsp	(15 ml) brown sugar
1	garlic clove, smashed and chopped
2 tbsp	(30 ml) fresh chopped ginger
	juice ½ lemon
	salt and pepper

Recipe

2 lb	(900 g) pork tenderloin, fat removed and meat sliced in 1½ in (4 cm) medallions

Preheat barbecue at MEDIUM.

Mix marinade ingredients together, add pork and let stand 20 minutes.

Place pork medallions on hot grill. Cook 4 to 5 minutes, basting often, and turning once. Season well.

Grilled Pork Tenderloin

(serves 4)

1 SERVING	303 CALORIES	1g CARBOHYDRATE
26g PROTEIN	21g FAT	trace FIBER

2 tbsp	(30 ml) oil
2	garlic cloves, smashed and chopped
1 tbsp	(15 ml) soya sauce
1 tbsp	(15 ml) lemon juice
2	pork tenderloins, fat trimmed
	salt and pepper

Preheat barbecue at HIGH.

Mix oil with garlic, soya sauce and lemon juice; set aside.

Slice pork tenderloins open using long, thin knife. Be careful not to cut all the way through — they should remain in one piece.

Score meat on both sides, baste with lemon mixture and place on hot grill. Partially cover and cook 8 to 10 minutes each side. Turn 3 to 4 times, baste occasionally and season well.

When meat is cooked, slice and serve with wild rice and mushrooms.

Pork Meatballs

(serves 4)

1 SERVING	651 CALORIES	8g CARBOHYDRATE
36g PROTEIN	52g FAT	trace FIBER

½ cup	(125 ml) chopped white bread (no crust)
1½ lb	(750 g) lean ground pork
1	onion, chopped and cooked
1 tbsp	(15 ml) chopped parsley
1 tbsp	(15 ml) chopped fresh mint
¼ tsp	(1 ml) allspice
¼ tsp	(1 ml) chili powder
1	egg
3 tbsp	(45 ml) olive oil
2	garlic cloves, smashed and chopped
	lemon juice
	salt and pepper

Preheat barbecue at LOW.

Mix bread, pork, onion, parsley, mint, seasonings and egg together in mixer until well incorporated.

Shape into small meatballs, thread on skewers and set aside.

Mix remaining ingredients together. Brush over skewers and set on hot grill. Partially cover and cook 8 minutes. Turn skewers often and baste several times.

Serve with fries.

Sweet Orange Loin of Pork

(serves 4)

1 SERVING	693 CALORIES	33g CARBOHYDRATE
47g PROTEIN	38g FAT	trace FIBER

1 cup	(250 ml) dry white wine
1 tbsp	(15 ml) honey
2 lb	(900 g) boneless loin of pork, fat trimmed and meat scored
1 tbsp	(15 ml) butter
1	onion, diced
1 tbsp	(15 ml) vinegar
10 oz	(284 ml) can mandarin sections
1 cup	(250 ml) brown sauce, heated
	juice 2 oranges
	salt and pepper

Preheat barbecue at LOW.

Bring wine to boil in small saucepan; continue cooking 2 minutes.

Stir in honey and orange juice; cook 3 minutes.

Brush honey mixture over pork. Place meat on hot grill and cook, partially covered, 40 to 45 minutes depending on size. Turn frequently, baste occasionally and season once.

Before pork is done, prepare sauce. Heat butter in small saucepan. Add onion and cook 3 minutes over medium heat.

Stir in vinegar and half the juice from mandarins; cook 3 minutes.

Correct seasoning and stir in brown sauce and mandarin sections; simmer 3 to 4 minutes and serve with sliced pork.

Pork Chops Marinated in Beer

(serves 4)

1 SERVING	270 CALORIES	14g CARBOHYDRATE
24g PROTEIN	11g FAT	0.5g FIBER

Marinade

1 cup	(250 ml) beer
1 tbsp	(15 ml) teriyaki sauce
½ tsp	(2 ml) allspice
1 tbsp	(15 ml) tomato paste
	salt and pepper

Recipe

4	pork chops, ¾ in (2 cm) thick
2	apples, peeled, cored and sliced
¼ cup	(50 ml) crushed pineapple
1 tbsp	(15 ml) butter
½ tsp	(2 ml) cinnamon

Preheat barbecue at HIGH.

Mix marinade ingredients together and pour over pork; let stand 30 minutes.

Meanwhile, place apples, pineapple, butter and cinnamon on large double sheet of foil. Shape into basket and seal edges.

Drain pork and place chops along with foil basket on hot grill. Cook everything 8 to 10 minutes, depending on taste.

Turn chops over 3 to 4 times, baste occasionally and season well. Turn basket of apples over once.

Serve.

1 Trim excess fat from pork chops.

3 Add tomato paste and stir well.

2 Place beer, teriyaki sauce and allspice in bowl.

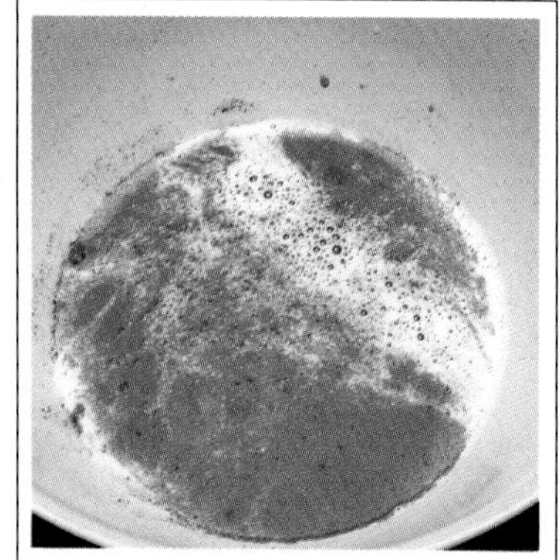

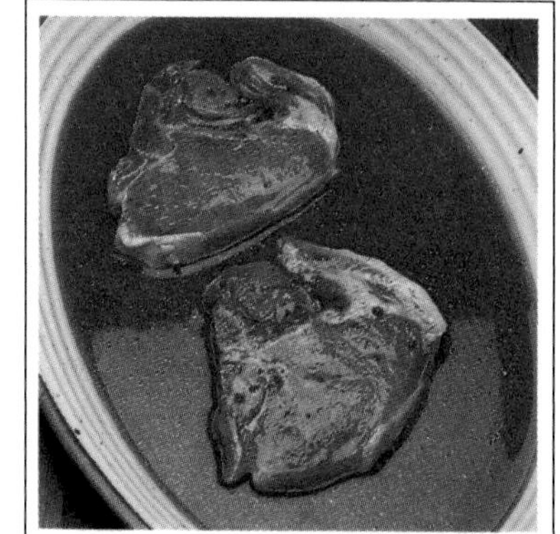

4 Marinate pork in mixture for 30 minutes.

Pork Cutlets with Mango Relish

(serves 4)

1 SERVING	673 CALORIES	79g CARBOHYDRATE
49g PROTEIN	20g FAT	1.0g FIBER

1	ripe mango
½ cup	(125 ml) cider vinegar
½ cup	(125 ml) brown sugar
¼ lb	(125 g) pitted dates
½ cup	(125 ml) Smyrna raisins
1 tbsp	(15 ml) chopped ginger
1 tsp	(5 ml) chopped garlic
¼ cup	(50 ml) grated coconut
8	pork cutlets, about ¾ in (2 cm) thick
	oil
	salt and pepper

Preheat barbecue at HIGH.

Slice mango in half and remove pit. Using small knife remove fibrous middle and discard. Dice remaining flesh and set aside.

Place vinegar and sugar in small saucepan; bring to quick boil. Reduce heat and cook 4 to 5 minutes.

Add dates and mix well. Stir in raisins, ginger, garlic and mango. Sprinkle in coconut and season lightly with salt. Cook 20 minutes over low heat.

Before relish is cooked, start preparing pork by basting with oil.

Place on hot grill and cook 6 to 8 minutes depending on thickness. Turn at least twice and season several times.

Serve pork with mango relish.

1 Slice mango in half and remove pit.

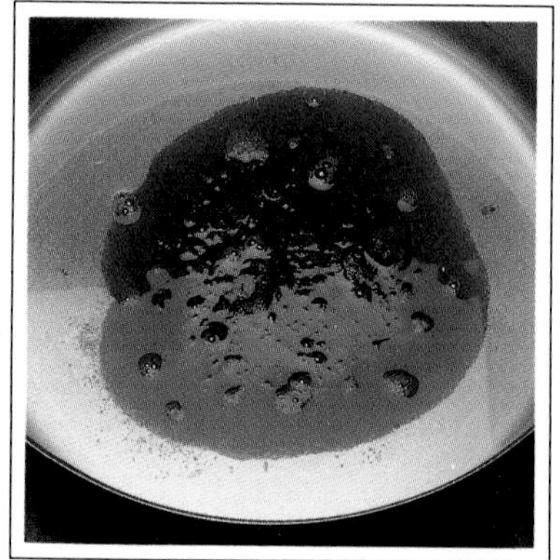

3 Place vinegar and sugar in small saucepan; bring to quick boil. Reduce heat and cook 4 to 5 minutes.

2 Using small knife, remove fibrous middle and discard. Dice remaining flesh and set aside.

4 Add dates and mix well. Stir in remaining relish ingredients and finish cooking 20 minutes over low heat.

Sausage Skewers

(serves 4)

1 SERVING	530 CALORIES	33g CARBOHYDRATE
19g PROTEIN	36g FAT	0.5g FIBER

Marinade

½ cup	(125 ml) cider vinegar
2 tbsp	(30 ml) corn syrup
2 tbsp	(30 ml) molasses
3	cloves
½ tsp	(2 ml) cinnamon

Recipe

2 lb	(500 g) Polish sausages, sliced ¾ in (2 cm) thick
2	apples, in wedges with skin
1	red pepper, in bite-size pieces
4	small onions, cut in half
	salt and pepper

Preheat barbecue at MEDIUM.

Place marinade ingredients in saucepan; boil 3 to 4 minutes.

Meanwhile, alternate kebab ingredients on skewers and set in deep platter. Pour marinade over kebabs and season well; let stand 10 to 12 minutes.

Place kebabs on hot grill. Cover and cook 10 to 12 minutes, turning 2 to 3 times. Baste frequently and season well.

Serve with fresh vegetable sticks.

Sweet and Spicy Spareribs

(serves 4)

1 SERVING	1189 CALORIES	24g CARBOHYDRATE
53g PROTEIN	146g FAT	0.6g FIBER

Marinade

2	garlic cloves, smashed and chopped
1 tsp	(5 ml) finely chopped jalapeno pepper
1 tsp	(5 ml) dry mustard
½ tsp	(2 ml) oregano
½ tsp	(2 ml) rosemary
3 tbsp	(45 ml) honey
1 cup	(250 ml) tomato sauce
	juice 2 oranges

Recipe

3½ lb	(1.6 kg) pork spareribs, about 4-6 in (10-15 cm) long
	salt and pepper

Preheat barbecue at LOW.

Place all marinade ingredients in small saucepan and cook 15 minutes over very low heat.

Meanwhile, blanch ribs in boiling water for 15 minutes.

Drain ribs and baste with marinade sauce. Place ribs on hot grill and partly cover. Cook 30 minutes depending on size. Turn frequently, baste occasionally and season well.

If desired serve any leftover marinade as sauce.

Pork Chops and Bell Peppers

(serves 4)

1 SERVING	517 CALORIES	6g CARBOHYDRATE
60g PROTEIN	27g FAT	1.0g FIBER

1 tsp	(5 ml) oregano
1 tsp	(5 ml) rosemary
2	garlic cloves, smashed and chopped
1 tsp	(5 ml) honey
½ tsp	(2 ml) olive oil
4	large pork chops, fat trimmed
2 tbsp	(30 ml) vegetable oil
4	bell peppers, halved and seeded
	salt and pepper

Preheat barbecue at MEDIUM.

Mix seasonings, garlic, honey and olive oil together. Spread over pork chops.

Place chops on hot grill and cook 15 to 18 minutes depending on size. Season and turn occasionally.

Brush bell peppers with vegetable oil. Barbecue 3 to 4 minutes.

Serve peppers with chops.

Half Chicken Dinner

(serves 2)

1 SERVING	1311 CALORIES	14g CARBOHYDRATE
124g PROTEIN	77g FAT	trace FIBER

Marinade

½ cup	(125 ml) dry white wine
¼ cup	(50 ml) lemon juice
1	garlic clove, smashed and chopped
1 tsp	(5 ml) tarragon
¼ tsp	(1 ml) paprika
1 tbsp	(15 ml) fresh chopped ginger
2 tbsp	(30 ml) oil
1 tbsp	(15 ml) honey
	salt and pepper

Recipe

3 lb	(1.4 kg) chicken, cleaned and split in half

Preheat barbecue at LOW.

Mix all marinade ingredients together and set aside.

Prepare chicken halves as described in Technique.

Place chicken in large roasting pan and pour in marinade; refrigerate 30 minutes.

Place chicken halves (bone side down) on hot grill. Cover and cook 30 minutes. Baste and season occasionally but do not turn halves over.

Now place halves with breast side down on grill. Continue barbecuing covered for another 30 minutes. Baste occasionally and turn halves over often.

1 Split chicken into two halves.

2 Use a small knife and make a hole in skin through flesh as shown. It should be big enough for your finger to fit through.

3 Push chicken leg through hole. This will help chicken maintain its shape during barbecuing.

4 Marinate chicken in refrigerator for 30 minutes before cooking.

Chicken Breasts, Devil Sauce

(serves 4)

1 SERVING	321 CALORIES	12g CARBOHYDRATE
29g PROTEIN	15g FAT	0.7g FIBER

½ cup	(125 ml) dry white wine
2 tbsp	(30 ml) red wine vinegar
2	shallots, chopped
3 tbsp	(45 ml) green peppercorns
1¼ cups	(300 ml) brown sauce, heated
2	chicken breasts, skinned, halved and boned
	salt and pepper

Preheat barbecue at MEDIUM.

Cook wine, vinegar and shallots in small saucepan over high heat; bring to boil. Reduce heat to medium and continue cooking 4 to 5 minutes.

Add peppercorns and brown sauce; correct seasoning. Bring to quick boil then remove from heat.

Season chicken and baste in sauce. Place breasts on hot grill and cook 10 minutes each side. Turn at least 4 to 5 times and baste occasionally.

Serve with salad.

Grilled Chicken Anchovy

(serves 4)

1 SERVING	416 CALORIES	trace CARBOHYDRATE
30g PROTEIN	32g FAT	trace FIBER

4	anchovy filets, drained
½ cup	(125 ml) soft butter
1 tsp	(5 ml) horseradish
½ tsp	(2 ml) lemon juice
2	chicken breasts, halved and skinned
	cayenne pepper to taste

Preheat barbecue at MEDIUM.

Pat anchovy filets dry to remove any oil, then mash in mortar. Mix butter, horseradish, lemon juice and cayenne pepper with anchovy until well blended.

Force mixture through sieve using wooden spoon, then spread on both sides of chicken breasts. Wrap chicken in double sheets of foil with 2 half breasts per bundle.

Place on hot grill and cook 35 minutes with cover. Turn twice.

Remove chicken from foil and set directly on grill. Finish barbecuing 5 minutes without cover; season to taste.

Some sauce will have collected in foil packages — serve with chicken.

Spicy Chicken Legs

(serves 4)

1 SERVING	282 CALORIES	11g CARBOHYDRATE
49g PROTEIN	15g FAT	trace FIBER

4	chicken legs
½ cup	(125 ml) catsup
¼ cup	(50 ml) wine vinegar
¼ tsp	(1 ml) Tabasco sauce
½ cup	(125 ml) clam/tomato juice
2	garlic cloves, smashed and chopped
¼ tsp	(1 ml) cumin
¼ tsp	(1 ml) curry powder
½ tsp	(2 ml) fines herbes
	salt and pepper
	paprika

Preheat barbecue at HIGH.

Slash chicken legs with knife, season with paprika and set aside.

Place catsup, vinegar, Tabasco and clam/tomato juice in bowl. Add garlic and seasonings; mix well with whisk.

Place chicken on hot grill and baste with tomato mixture. Cook 5 minutes.

Turn legs over; continue cooking 10 minutes. Turn once and baste several times; season.

Turn chicken over; finish barbecuing about 27 minutes (depending on size) at LOW. Be sure to cover this time; baste often and turn legs every 4 to 5 minutes.

1 Slash chicken legs with knife so that basting sauce will be able to soak into meat. Season chicken with paprika.

3 Mix well with whisk.

2 Place catsup, vinegar, Tabasco and clam/tomato juice in bowl. Add garlic and seasonings.

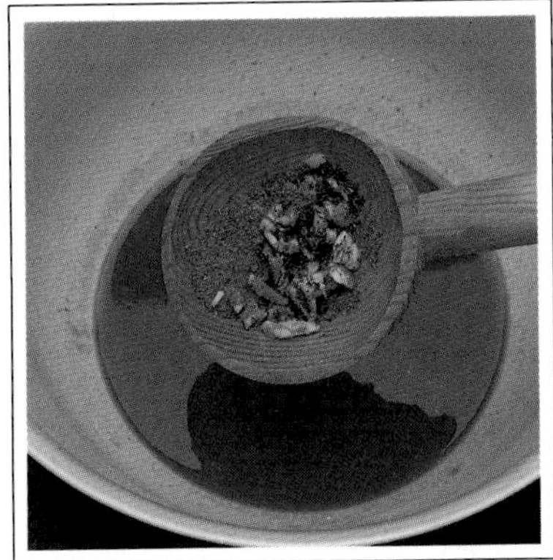

4 Begin cooking legs on hot grill for 5 minutes. Baste with tomato mixture.

Cornish Hens

(serves 4)

1 SERVING	636 CALORIES	2g CARBOHYDRATE
61g PROTEIN	41g FAT	trace FIBER

3	garlic cloves, smashed and chopped
3 tbsp	(45 ml) vegetable oil
2 tbsp	(30 ml) wine vinegar
1 tbsp	(15 ml) teriyaki sauce
4	Cornish hens, cleaned and split in half
	salt and pepper

Preheat barbecue at LOW.

Place all ingredients in roasting pan and let stand 15 minutes.

Set hens on grill (bone side down) and cook 35-40 minutes with cover. Baste occasionally, turn often and season well.

Chicken Pieces with Pineapple

(serves 4)

1 SERVING	714 CALORIES	15g CARBOHYDRATE
79g PROTEIN	20g FAT	trace FIBER

1 cup	(250 ml) crushed pineapple
2 tbsp	(30 ml) brown sugar
1 cup	(250 ml) rum
2	limes, cut in half
3½ lb	(1.6 kg) chicken, cut in pieces and skinned
	salt and pepper

Preheat barbecue at LOW.

Mix pineapple, sugar and rum together in small saucepan; bring to boil over medium-high heat.

Rub limes all over chicken pieces. Pour the pineapple mixture over and refrigerate 1 hour.

Place chicken pieces on hot grill. Cook, partially covered, for the following times: white meat — 8 to 10 minutes each side; dark meat — 15 minutes each side.

Season during cooking and baste occasionally.

Chicken with Orange Marinade

(serves 4)

1 SERVING	573 CALORIES	45g CARBOHYDRATE
62g PROTEIN	15g FAT	trace FIBER

Marinade

1	onion, finely chopped
1	garlic clove, smashed and chopped
½ cup	(125 ml) catsup
1 cup	(250 ml) orange juice
½ cup	(125 ml) orange marmalade
2 tbsp	(30 ml) soya sauce

Recipe

2½ lb	(1.2 kg) chicken parts, cleaned and skinned
	salt and pepper

Preheat barbecue at MEDIUM.

Mix marinade ingredients together in small saucepan; bring to boil.

Pour over chicken parts and marinate 4 hours in refrigerator.

Place chicken parts on hot grill. Cook, partially covered, for the following times: white meat — 8 to 10 minutes each side; dark meat — 15 minutes each side.

Season during cooking and baste with any leftover orange marinade.

Half Chicken for Two

(serves 2)

1 SERVING	1325 CALORIES	40g CARBOHYDRATE
127g PROTEIN	71g FAT	0.7g FIBER

Marinade

1 cup	(250 ml) catsup
⅓ cup	(75 ml) water
1 tbsp	(15 ml) oil
1½	onions, finely chopped
2	garlic cloves, smashed and chopped
2 tbsp	(30 ml) vinegar
½ tsp	(2 ml) chili powder
½ tsp	(2 ml) ground ginger
	pinch sugar
	few drops Tabasco sauce

Recipe

3 lb	(1.4 kg) chicken, cleaned and split in half
	salt and pepper

Preheat barbecue at LOW.

Mix catsup and water together; set aside.

Heat oil in small saucepan. Add onions and garlic; cook 2 minutes over medium heat.

Stir catsup into saucepan with remaining marinade ingredients. Bring to boil and cook 2 to 3 minutes.

Place chicken halves in large roasting pan. Pour sauce over and refrigerate 30 minutes.

Place chicken halves (bone side down) on hot grill. Cover and cook 30 minutes. Baste and season occasionally but do not turn halves over.

Now place halves with breast side down on grill. Continue barbecuing covered for another 30 minutes. Baste occasionally and turn halves over often.

Marinated Chicken Wings

(serves 4)

1 SERVING	559 CALORIES	18g CARBOHYDRATE
42g PROTEIN	33g FAT	0.5g FIBER

24	chicken wings
1 tbsp	(15 ml) sunflower oil
2	pickled hot cherry peppers, seeded and finely chopped
1	green pepper, finely chopped
2	garlic cloves, smashed and chopped
½ cup	(125 ml) crushed pineapple
¼ cup	(50 ml) brown sugar
1 tbsp	(15 ml) chopped parsley
2 tbsp	(30 ml) vinegar
¼ cup	(50 ml) dry white wine
2 tbsp	(30 ml) soya sauce
¼ tsp	(1 ml) paprika
	salt and pepper

Preheat barbecue at HIGH.

Cut off wing tips and reserve for stocks or other uses. Set wings aside in deep dish.

Heat oil in saucepan over medium heat. Cook cherry peppers, green pepper and garlic 3 minutes.

Stir in pineapple and brown sugar; cook 3 to 4 minutes.

Add parsley, vinegar, wine, soya sauce and seasonings; continue cooking 3 to 4 minutes.

Pour over wings and let stand 20 minutes.

Drain wings and place on hot grill. Cover and cook 14 to 16 minutes, turning 2 to 3 times. Season generously.

Serve with pasta salad.

1 Cut off wing tips and reserve for stocks or other uses. Set wings aside in deep dish.

3 Stir in pineapple and brown sugar; cook 3 to 4 minutes.

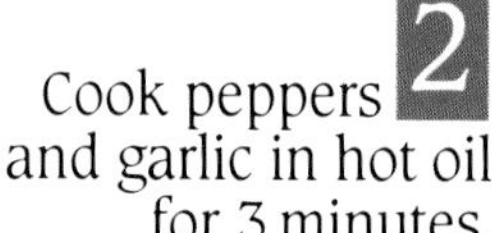

2 Cook peppers and garlic in hot oil for 3 minutes.

4 After other ingredients have been added to marinade, pour all over chicken and let stand 20 minutes before barbecuing.

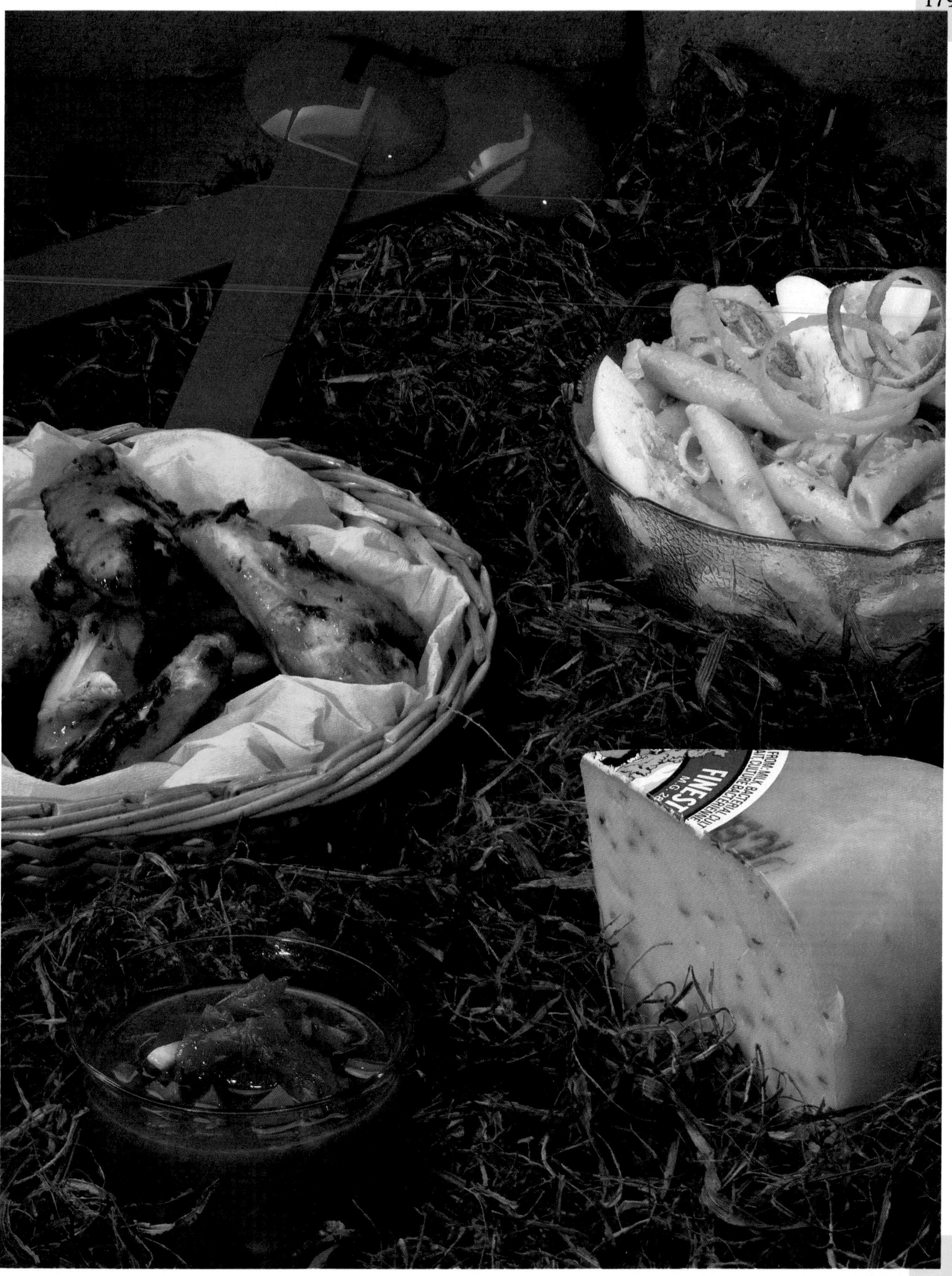
FINEST

Easy Wings

(serves 4)

1 SERVING	616 CALORIES	8g CARBOHYDRATE
42g PROTEIN	36g FAT	trace FIBER

Marinade

2 cups	(500 ml) dry red wine
2 tbsp	(30 ml) olive oil
1	garlic clove, smashed and chopped
1	small onion, thinly sliced
1	carrot, thinly sliced
1	bay leaf

Recipe

24	chicken wings, tips removed
	salt and pepper

Preheat barbecue at HIGH.

Mix marinade ingredients together; pour over wings and let stand 10 to 12 minutes.

Drain wings and place on hot grill. Cover and cook 14 to 16 minutes, turning 2 to 3 times. Season generously.

Serve with fries.

Chicken Strips

(serves 4)

1 SERVING	447 CALORIES	9g CARBOHYDRATE
62g PROTEIN	13g FAT	trace FIBER

Marinade

1½ cups	(375 ml) cider
2 tbsp	(30 ml) oil
2	garlic cloves, smashed and chopped
½ tsp	(2 ml) tarragon
2 tbsp	(30 ml) maple syrup

Recipe

2 lb	(900 g) chicken breast strips, about 3 in (7.5 cm) long
	salt and pepper

Preheat barbecue at MEDIUM.

Bring marinade ingredients to boil in small saucepan. Continue cooking 2 more minutes.

Pour over chicken and marinate 25 minutes.

Place chicken strips on hot grill. Cook 4 to 5 minutes each side depending on size. Baste and season twice.

Serve with potatoes.

Salmon Filets with Blender Hollandaise

(serves 4)

1 SERVING	778 CALORIES	1g CARBOHYDRATE
70g PROTEIN	53g FAT	trace FIBER

2 tbsp	(30 ml) melted butter
1 tsp	(5 ml) fennel seed
4	8 oz (250 g) salmon filets
1 tbsp	(15 ml) hot water
2 tbsp	(30 ml) horseradish
3	egg yolks
½ cup	(125 ml) melted butter
	few drops Tabasco sauce
	salt and pepper
	lemon juice

Preheat barbecue at HIGH.

Brush 2 tbsp (30 ml) butter over salmon; sprinkle with fennel seed. Place fish on hot grill and cook 5 to 6 minutes each side depending on taste.

Meanwhile, mix water, horseradish, egg yolks, Tabasco, salt, pepper and lemon juice in blender for 30 seconds at high speed.

Reduce blender speed to low; very slowly incorporate second measurement of butter. Keep mixing until butter is well blended, then correct seasoning.

Serve Hollandaise with salmon.

Lobster Tails

(serves 4)

1 SERVING	413 CALORIES	4g CARBOHYDRATE
36g PROTEIN	14g FAT	trace FIBER

4	lobster tails (small if available)
8	large shrimp, shelled
8	large scallops
4 tbsp	(60 ml) melted butter
1 tbsp	(15 ml) lemon juice
1 tbsp	(15 ml) soya sauce
1	garlic clove, smashed and chopped
	salt and pepper

Preheat barbecue at HIGH.

Remove shells from lobster tails, discard and place meat in bowl; add remaining ingredients and set aside 15 minutes.

Thread ingredients on skewers in the following order; shrimp, scallop, lobster, scallop and shrimp. Repeat until full.

Place skewers on hot grill. Cook 4 minutes each side depending on size of lobster tails. Baste and season.

Salmon Tail Supreme

(serves 4)

1 SERVING	563 CALORIES	3g CARBOHYDRATE
48g PROTEIN	39g FAT	trace FIBER

2	1 lb (500 g) salmon tails
2 tbsp	(30 ml) teriyaki sauce
2	garlic cloves, smashed and chopped
3 tbsp	(45 ml) olive oil
2 tbsp	(30 ml) lemon juice
	salt and pepper

Preheat barbecue at MEDIUM.

Slide knife along backbone of salmon tail. Set outer piece of fish aside. Slice along other side of bone and set second piece of fish aside — discard piece containing bone.

Mix remaining ingredients together and pour over fish; let stand 15 minutes.

Place fish on hot grill (skin side down) and cook 14 to 16 minutes with cover. Turn pieces twice, season lightly and baste occasionally.

1 Slide knife along backbone of salmon tail. Set the piece without the bone aside.

3 Marinate fish for 15 minutes.

2 Repeat the same procedure on the other side of backbone — this will give you a second piece of fish. Discard middle part containing bone.

4 Begin barbecuing by placing salmon pieces on hot grill with skin side down.

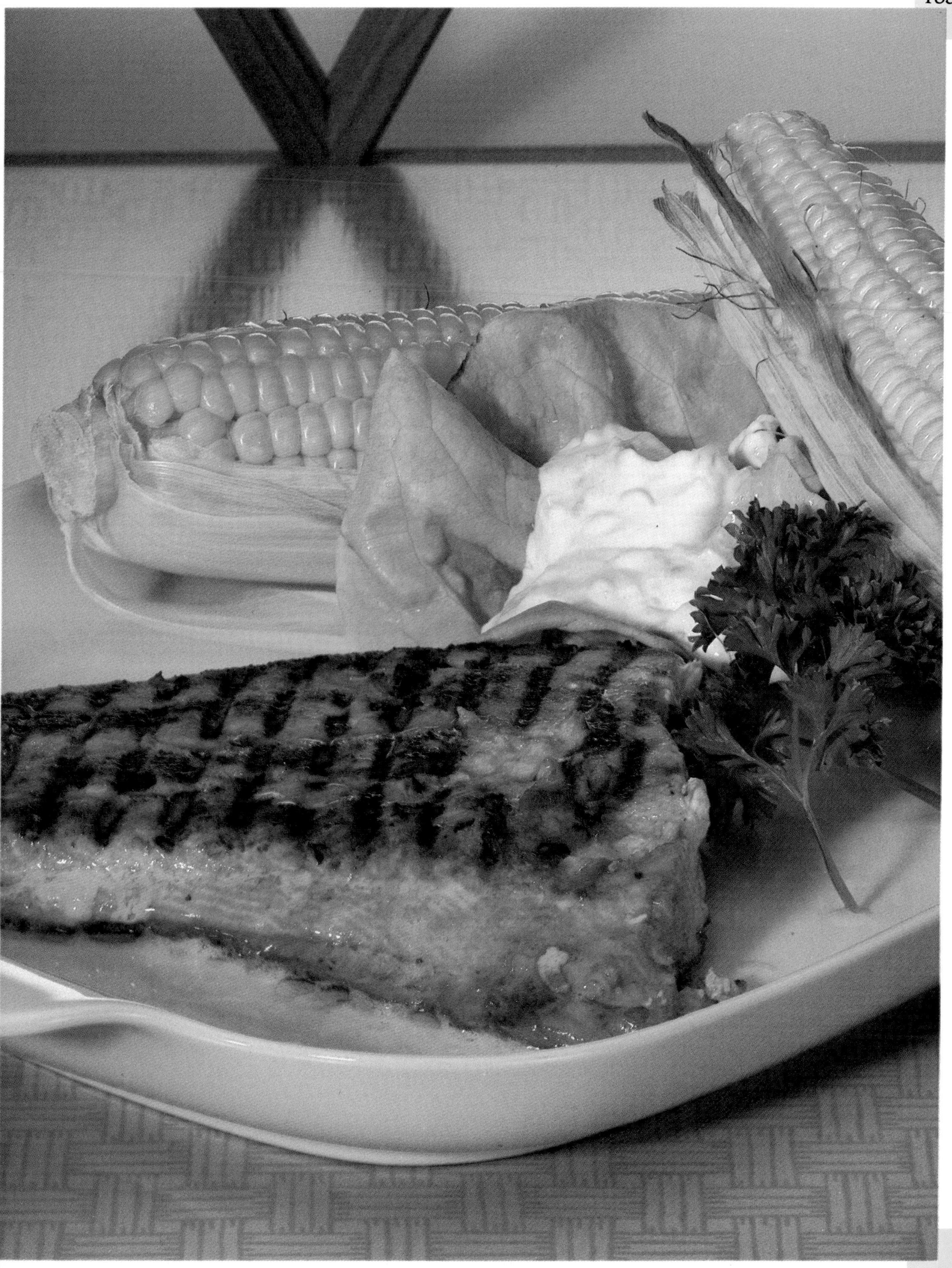

Flounder and Tomatoes

(serves 2)

1 SERVING	306 CALORIES	6g CARBOHYDRATE
28g PROTEIN	14g FAT	2.0g FIBER

2	large flounder filets
12	cherry tomatoes, cut in half
1	onion, chopped
2 tbsp	(30 ml) soya sauce
2 tbsp	(30 ml) melted butter
1 tsp	(5 ml) lemon juice
	salt and pepper

Preheat barbecue at HIGH.

Place all ingredients on triple sheet of foil. Cover with single sheet and seal edges well.

Place on hot grill and cover. Cook 15 minutes turning once.

Flounder and Vegetables

(serves 4)

1 SERVING	224 CALORIES	20g CARBOHYDRATE
26g PROTEIN	5g FAT	0.6g FIBER

1 tbsp	(15 ml) vegetable oil
2	green onions, chopped
2	small bamboo shoots, diced
1 tbsp	(15 ml) fresh chopped ginger
1	small carrot, pared and thinly sliced
1 tbsp	(15 ml) lemon rind
1¼ cups	(300 ml) hot chicken stock
2 tbsp	(30 ml) honey
2 tbsp	(30 ml) tomato paste
3 tbsp	(45 ml) wine vinegar
1 tbsp	(15 ml) cornstarch
3 tbsp	(45 ml) cold water
4	flounder filets
	salt and pepper

Preheat barbecue at HIGH.

Heat oil in saucepan. Cook onions, bamboo shoots, ginger, carrot and lemon rind 1 minute.

Season well and add chicken stock, honey, tomato paste and vinegar; bring to boil. Continue cooking 2 to 3 minutes.

Mix cornstarch with water; stir into sauce and cook 1 minute.

Spread mixture over fish and place on hot grill. Partially cover and cook 3 to 4 minutes each side according to taste.

Seasoned Whole Trout

(serves 4)

1 SERVING	380 CALORIES	trace CARBOHYDRATE
27g PROTEIN	29g FAT	--g FIBER

4	brook trout, cleaned
⅓ cup	(75 ml) melted butter
1 tbsp	(15 ml) lemon juice
	dash paprika
	few drops Tabasco sauce
	salt and pepper

Preheat barbecue at HIGH.

It is advisable to use a fish grill.

Using scissors, cut off all fins. Slash fish on one side with sharp knife and then baste with melted butter.

Sprinkle fish with remaining ingredients and place on hot grill. Cook 6 minutes each side; season when turning.

1 Be sure that trout are completely gutted and cleaned.

3 Slash fish on one side only with sharp knife.

2 Using scissors, cut off all fins.

4 Baste with melted butter.

Double Fish Kebabs

(serves 4)

1 SERVING	220 CALORIES	7g CARBOHYDRATE
27g PROTEIN	5g FAT	trace FIBER

Marinade

1 cup	(250 ml) dry white wine
1 tbsp	(15 ml) lime juice
2 tbsp	(30 ml) fresh chopped ginger
2	garlic cloves, smashed and chopped
¼ tsp	(1 ml) crushed chillies
2 tbsp	(30 ml) soya sauce
1 tbsp	(15 ml) vegetable oil
	salt and pepper

Recipe

¾ lb	(375 g) shrimp, peeled and deveined
1	large halibut steak, cubed

Preheat barbecue at HIGH.

Mix marinade ingredients together in bowl.

Place shrimp and halibut in marinade. Let stand 30 minutes.

Thread fish on skewers. Place on hot grill and cover; cook 8 minutes. Turn twice, baste occasionally and season well.

Serve with vegetables.

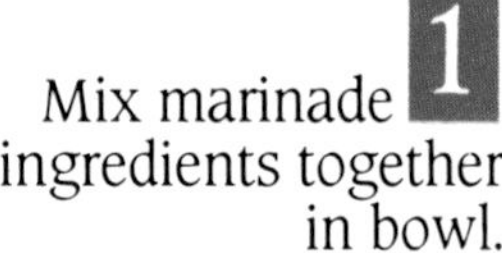

1 Mix marinade ingredients together in bowl.

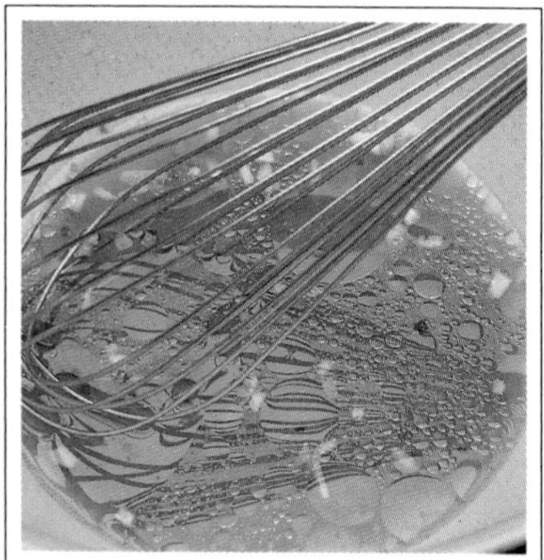

3 Place shrimp and halibut in marinade; let stand 30 minutes.

2 Peel and devein shrimp.

4 Thread seafood on skewers. Reserve marinade for basting.

Scallops Cartagena

(serves 4)

1 SERVING	166 CALORIES	12g CARBOHYDRATE
21g PROTEIN	4g FAT	0.8g FIBER

1 lb	(500 g) fresh sea scallops
¼ cup	(50 ml) lime juice
2 tbsp	(30 ml) olive oil
1 tbsp	(15 ml) chopped fresh parsley
1 tbsp	(15 ml) chopped shallot
1 tsp	(5 ml) basil
2	large tomatoes, peeled and diced
1	red pepper, diced
	salt and pepper

Preheat barbecue at MEDIUM.

Place all ingredients on double sheet of foil. Cover with single sheet and seal edges shut.

Place foil basket on hot grill. Cover and cook 8 minutes; mix occasionally.

Serve with rice.

Scallops in Foil Basket

(serves 4)

1 SERVING	211 CALORIES	17g CARBOHYDRATE
40g PROTEIN	7g FAT	1.0g FIBER

1 lb	(500 g) sea scallops
½ cup	(125 ml) lichee nuts (optional)
2	green onions, chopped
2 tbsp	(30 ml) garlic butter (hard)
⅓ lb	(150 g) mushrooms, diced
½ cup	(125 ml) pineapple chunks
	salt and pepper

Preheat barbecue at HIGH.

Place all ingredients on double sheet of foil. Cover with single sheet and shape into basket — seal edges well.

Place on hot grill and cover; cook 8 to 10 minutes. Open foil basket during cooking to stir twice.

Serve with rice.

Halibut Steaks

(serves 4)

1 SERVING	186 CALORIES	trace CARBOHYDRATE
26g PROTEIN	8g FAT	--g FIBER

2 tbsp	(30 ml) oil
1 tsp	(5 ml) lemon juice
½ tsp	(2 ml) teriyaki sauce
¼ tsp	(1 ml) paprika
4	halibut steaks
	salt and pepper

Preheat barbecue at HIGH.

Mix oil, lemon, teriyaki and paprika together; season to taste.

Brush mixture over fish and set steaks on hot grill. Cook 10 minutes turning once or twice. Baste occasionally.

GRILLED FISH AND SEAFOOD

GRILLED FISH AND COQUILLES

The seafood presented here is prepared according to two traditional cooking techniques: grilled or served in coquilles. Everybody has a favorite fish and a preferred method for cooking it, but it is hoped that you will find some exciting new concoctions among this selection that will earn their place on your top ten list. Fresh, frozen and canned fish are used in the recipes. Generally frozen and canned require little buying skill and depend more on quality control by the manufacturer. The best rule of thumb is to take note of brands and keep using those which you can depend upon. Fresh fish, however, takes a bit more scrutiny on your part. Always try to touch a whole fish before purchasing. It should feel firm and springy. Inspect the eyes, looking for clearness and fullness; avoid fish with sunken or drippy eyes. Contrary to some people's beliefs, fresh fish does not smell fishy — bad fish does. Granted, there are some species (shark for example) which do have a stronger odor. But on the whole, fish should smell clean. Cooking fish is so simple that few specialty items are needed. Aside from your regular frying pan, the only other requirement is a selection of scallop shells. These can be purchased quite inexpensively in the natural form, or you can find various replicas in porcelain. The advantage of these copy-cat versions is that they are often deeper, larger and more decorative. Now let's cast off...

Cod Steaks and Pickles

(serves 4)

1 SERVING	350 CALORIES	24g CARBOHYDRATE
45g PROTEIN	21g FAT	0.3g FIBER

4	cod steaks
1 cup	(250 ml) seasoned flour
2 tbsp	(30 ml) vegetable oil
2 tbsp	(30 ml) melted butter
1 tbsp	(15 ml) chopped parsley
2	large pickles, diced
1	lemon, peeled, seeded and diced
	salt and pepper

Preheat oven to 150°F (70°C).

Dredge cod in flour. Heat oil in large frying pan and add fish. Cook 4 to 5 minutes each side depending on thickness. Season well when turning fish over.

Remove fish from pan and keep hot in oven.

Add butter to pan and heat. Add all remaining ingredients and cook 2 minutes over medium heat.

Season and serve pickle sauce with fish.

Sautéed Sole Pieces

(serves 4)

1 SERVING	274 CALORIES	13g CARBOHYDRATE
22g PROTEIN	15g FAT	0.5g FIBER

4	sole filets, cut in 3 pieces
½ cup	(125 ml) seasoned flour
3 tbsp	(45 ml) melted butter
¼ lb	(125 g) mushrooms, sliced
½ cup	(125 ml) stuffed green olives
1 tbsp	(15 ml) chopped parsley
	salt and pepper
	juice 1 lemon

Dredge fish lightly in flour; set aside.

Heat half of butter in large frying pan. Add mushrooms, olives and parsley; season well. Cook 3 to 4 minutes over medium heat.

Transfer mushroom mixture to plate; set aside.

Replace frying pan on stove and add remaining butter. When hot, add fish and cook 3 to 4 minutes depending on size. Turn pieces over once and season well.

Replace mushroom mixture in pan with fish. Simmer everything 2 minutes, sprinkle with lemon juice and serve.

Grilled Sole Parmesam

(serves 4)

1 SERVING	453 CALORIES	3g CARBOHYDRATE
48g PROTEIN	27g FAT	-- FIBER

4	large sole filets
3	beaten eggs
1½ cups	(375 ml) grated Parmesan cheese
3 tbsp	(45 ml) vegetable oil
	salt and white pepper
	dash paprika
	lemon juice

Dip sole filets in beaten eggs.

Season grated cheese with pepper and paprika; thoroughly coat filets in mixture.

Heat oil in large frying pan. Add filets and cook about 2 minutes each side, depending on size, over medium-high heat. Season during cooking.

Serve with lemon juice.

Grilled Marinated Trout

(serves 4)

1 SERVING	346 CALORIES	5g CARBOHYDRATE
27g PROTEIN	18g FAT	trace FIBER

4	brook trout, cleaned, in filets and cut in 1 in (2.5 cm) slices
1½ cups	(375 ml) dry white wine
2 tbsp	(30 ml) lemon juice
1 tbsp	(15 ml) grated orange rind
1 tbsp	(15 ml) chopped fresh ginger
1 tbsp	(15 ml) chopped chives
2 tbsp	(30 ml) olive oil
2	fennel sprigs
	salt and pepper
	lemon wedges

Place fish, wine, lemon juice, orange rind, ginger and chives in bowl. Marinate 2 hours in refrigerator.

Drain fish well.

Heat oil in large frying pan. Add fish and fennel sprigs; season well. Cook 2 to 3 minutes over high heat, stirring once or twice.

Serve fish with lemon wedges.

Grilled Trout with Tomatoes

(serves 4)

1 SERVING	514 CALORIES	32g CARBOHYDRATE
32g PROTEIN	40g FAT	3.0g FIBER

2 tbsp	(30 ml) vegetable oil
4	small brook trout, gutted and cleaned
1 cup	(250 ml) flour
1	onion, chopped
1	red pepper, diced small
½	zucchini, diced small
1	garlic clove, smashed and chopped
½ cup	(125 ml) pitted black olives
¼ tsp	(1 ml) fennel seed
1 tbsp	(15 ml) green peppercorns
1 cup	(250 ml) chopped tomatoes
	salt and pepper
	few drops lemon juice

Preheat oven to 150°F (70°C).

Heat oil in large frying pan. Dredge trout lightly in flour and place in hot oil. Cook 5 to 6 minutes each side over medium heat, depending on size. Season well.

Transfer fish to serving platter and keep hot in oven.

Add onion, red pepper, zucchini and garlic to frying pan; cook 2 minutes over medium-high heat.

Stir in olives, fennel seed, peppercorns, tomatoes, salt and pepper; cook 2 to 3 minutes over high heat.

Spoon tomato mixture over bottom of individual plates. Rest trout on top and sprinkle with lemon juice. Serve immediately.

Red Snapper Filets with Fennel

(serves 4)

1 SERVING	331 CALORIES	36g CARBOHYDRATE
28g PROTEIN	11g FAT	0.8g FIBER

4	small red snapper filets
1 cup	(250 ml) flour
1 tbsp	(15 ml) vegetable oil
2 tbsp	(30 ml) butter
1	small red pepper, halved and thinly sliced
1	zucchini, cut in half lengthwise and thinly sliced
1	green apple, cored and sliced
1 tsp	(5 ml) green peppercorns
2	fresh fennel sprigs, chopped
	salt and pepper

Dredge filets lightly in flour.

Heat oil and butter in large frying pan. Add fish and cook 3 minutes over medium-high heat.

Turn filets over, season well and continue cooking 2 to 3 minutes.

Add red pepper, zucchini and apple to pan; cook 2 to 3 minutes over medium heat.

Stir in peppercorns and fennel; season well. Cook 2 minutes and serve.

1 Besides choosing the best fish available, search out fresh fennel as well.

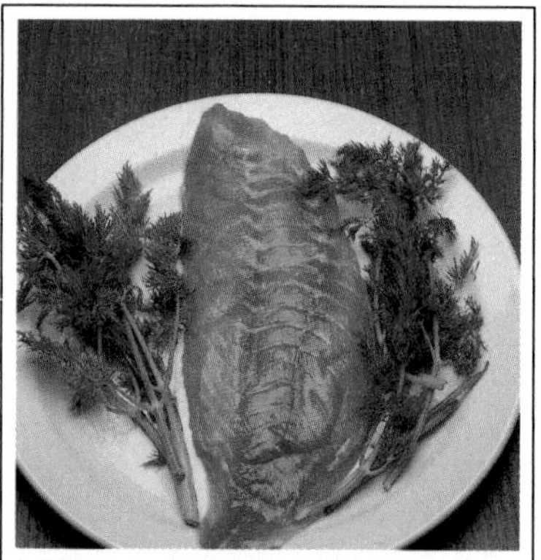

3 Turn fish over, season well and continue cooking 2 to 3 minutes.

2 Cook lightly floured fish in hot oil and butter for 3 minutes over medium-high heat.

4 Add vegetables and apple to pan with fish. Sauté 2 to 3 minutes over medium heat.

Snapper and Shrimp

(serves 4)

1 SERVING	446 CALORIES	27g CARBOHYDRATE
44g PROTEIN	18g FAT	0.6g FIBER

4	red snapper filets
1 cup	(250 ml) seasoned flour
2 tbsp	(30 ml) vegetable oil
2 tbsp	(30 ml) melted butter
12	medium shrimp, peeled, deveined and cut in ½ on angle
2 tbsp	(30 ml) capers
1	lemon, peeled, seeded and thinly sliced
2 tbsp	(30 ml) slivered almonds
	salt and pepper

Preheat oven to 150°F (70°C).

Dredge red snapper in flour. Heat oil in large frying pan and add filets. Cook 3 to 4 minutes each side, depending on size, over medium-high heat. Season when turning filets over.

Remove filets from pan and keep hot in oven.

Add butter and shrimp to pan. Season and add all remaining ingredients; cook 3 minutes over medium heat.

Remove red snapper from oven and serve with shrimp.

Red Snapper and Tomato

(serves 4)

1 SERVING	246 CALORIES	9g CARBOHYDRATE
27g PROTEIN	12g FAT	0.7g FIBER

4	red snapper filets
3 tbsp	(45 ml) olive oil
1	garlic clove, smashed and chopped
1	small onion, chopped
3	tomatoes, peeled, seeded and diced
¼ tsp	(1 ml) ground cloves
¼ tsp	(1 ml) sugar
	juice 1 lemon
	salt and pepper

Place filets in platter, sprinkle with few drops of oil and half of lemon juice; set aside.

Heat 1½ tbsp (25 ml) oil in large frying pan. Add garlic and onion; cook 2 to 3 minutes over medium heat.

Add tomatoes, cloves, sugar and remaining lemon juice. Season well and cook 7 to 8 minutes over medium heat.

Reduce heat to very low and let tomato mixture simmer.

Heat remaining oil in second frying pan. Cook fish 4 minutes on each side, depending on size, over medium heat. Season well when turning filets over and serve with tomatoes.

Fried Smelts

(serves 4)

1 SERVING	718 CALORIES	54g CARBOHYDRATE
38g PROTEIN	37g FAT	0.1g FIBER

24-28	smelts, cleaned and dried with paper towel
1½ cups	(375 ml) seasoned flour
1½ cups	(375 ml) milk
2	eggs
1 tsp	(5 ml) olive oil
1½ cups	(375 ml) crushed soda crackers
½ cup	(125 ml) peanut oil
	salt and pepper
	lemon juice

Dredge smelts in flour.

Place milk, eggs and olive oil in large bowl; beat together until well combined.

Dip smelts in milk mixture then roll in crushed cracker crumbs.

Heat half of oil in deep skillet until hot (about 375°F or 180°C). Carefully add half of smelts and cook 2 to 3 minutes, turning over once during cooking.

Using slotted spoon remove from oil and drain on paper towels.

Add second half of oil and repeat for remaining smelts.

Serve with lemon juice.

Herb Salmon Steaks

(serves 4)

1 SERVING	395 CALORIES	2g CARBOHYDRATE
41g PROTEIN	24g FAT	trace FIBER

2 tbsp	(30 ml) vegetable oil
4	salmon steaks, ¾ in (2 cm) thick
2 tbsp	(30 ml) butter
1 tbsp	(15 ml) chopped fresh mint
1 tbsp	(15 ml) chopped fresh chives
1 tbsp	(15 ml) chopped fresh parsley
	salt and pepper
	juice 1 lemon

Heat oil in large frying pan. Add fish and cook 3 to 4 minutes over medium heat.

Turn fish over, season and continue cooking 4 minutes.

Turn fish over again, season and cook another 7 minutes; turn fish once more during this time.

Transfer fish to heated serving platter.

Wipe frying pan clean with paper towel and add butter. Add herbs and pepper; cook 1 minute over high heat.

Add lemon juice, stir and pour over fish. Serve immediately.

Pernod Salmon

(serves 4)

1 SERVING	516 CALORIES	8g CARBOHYDRATE
43g PROTEIN	32g FAT	0.5g FIBER

1 tbsp	(15 ml) vegetable oil
2 tbsp	(30 ml) butter
4	salmon steaks, ¾ in (2 cm) thick
1	shallot, chopped
½ lb	(250 g) mushrooms, sliced
3 tbsp	(45 ml) Pernod
½ cup	(125 ml) heavy cream
1 tbsp	(15 ml) chopped parsley
	salt and pepper

Preheat oven to 150°F (70°C).

Heat oil and butter in large frying pan. When melted, add fish and season well; cover and cook 4 minutes over medium heat.

Turn fish over; continue cooking 4 to 5 minutes covered.

Remove fish from pan and keep hot in over.

Add shallot and mushrooms to frying pan; season well. Cover and cook 3 to 4 minutes.

Pour in Pernod and bring to boil; continue cooking 2 minutes over high heat.

Correct seasoning and mix in cream and parsley. Cook sauce 2 minutes over medium heat.

Pour over fish and serve.

1 Heat oil and butter in large frying pan. When melted, cook fish, covered, 4 minutes over medium heat.

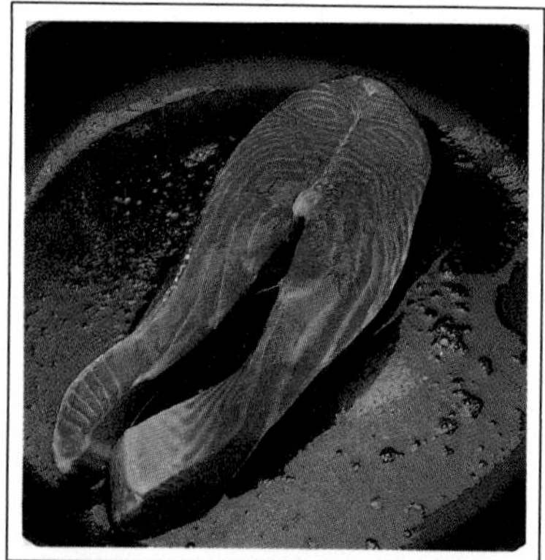

3 Add shallot and mushrooms to frying pan; season, cover and cook 3 to 4 minutes.

2 Turn fish over; continue cooking 4 to 5 minutes covered. Remove and keep hot in oven.

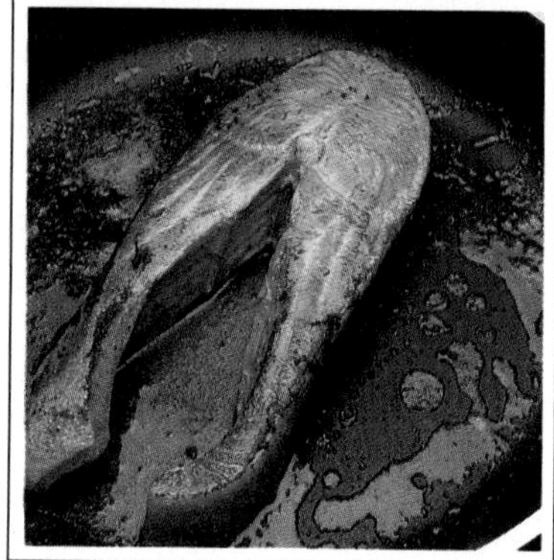

4 Pour in Pernod and bring to boil; continue cooking 2 minutes over high heat.

Salmon Steaks al Limone

(serves 4)

1 SERVING	566 CALORIES	30g CARBOHYDRATE
46g PROTEIN	29g FAT	0.3g FIBER

4	salmon steaks, ¾ in (2 cm) thick
1 cup	(250 ml) seasoned flour
¼ tsp	(1 ml) paprika
2 tbsp	(30 ml) butter
1	medium onion, chopped
1 tbsp	(15 ml) chopped chives
1 cup	(250 ml) light chicken stock, hot
¼ tsp	(1 ml) Tabasco sauce
1½ tbsp	(25 ml) cornstarch
4 tbsp	(60 ml) cold water
¼ cup	(50 ml) light cream, hot
2 tbsp	(30 ml) vegetable oil
1 tsp	(5 ml) butter
½	cucumber, seeded and sliced thick
	dash ground ginger
	salt and pepper
	juice 1 lemon

Dredge salmon in seasoned flour sprinkled with paprika; set aside.

Heat 2 tbsp (30 ml) butter in saucepan. Add onion and chives; cook 3 minutes over low heat.

Add lemon juice and continue cooking 1 minute over low heat.

Pour in chicken stock, add Tabasco, ginger and season well; bring to boil.

Mix cornstarch with water; stir into sauce and cook 1 minute over low heat.

Stir in cream and correct seasoning; bring to quick boil then remove from heat and set aside.

Heat oil in large frying pan. Add salmon and cook 4 minutes over medium-high heat.

Turn fish over and season well; continue cooking another 4 minutes.

Turn fish over again; cook another 7 minutes. Turn fish once more during this time.

Meanwhile, heat 1 tsp (5 ml) butter in second frying pan. Add cucumbers and cook 3 to 4 minutes over medium-high heat.

Simmer lemon sauce over low heat and when warmed, serve with fish and sauteed cucumbers.

1 Choose the freshest salmon available.

3 Cook onion and chives 3 minutes in hot butter.

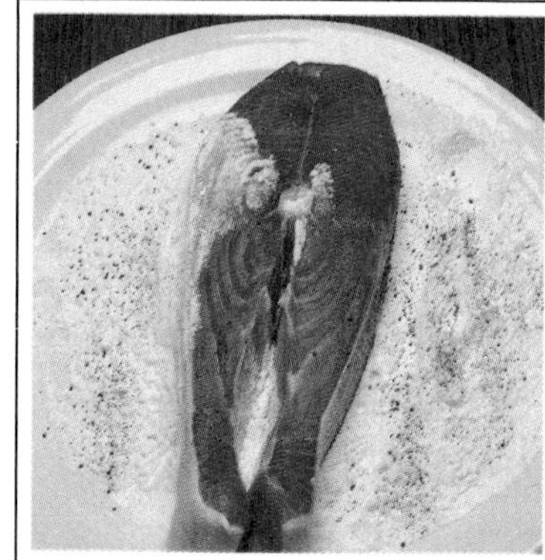

2 Dredge fish in seasoned flour sprinkled with paprika; set aside.

4 After lemon juice and chicken stock have been added, thicken sauce with diluted cornstarch.

Grilled Fish Cakes

(serves 4)

1 SERVING	475 CALORIES	38g CARBOHYDRATE
26g PROTEIN	24g FAT	0.6g FIBER

1¾ cups	(425 ml) cooked halibut, boned and flaked
2½ cups	(625 ml) mashed potatoes, hot
1 tbsp	(15 ml) chopped parsley
3 tbsp	(45 ml) chopped cooked onions
2 tbsp	(30 ml) soft butter
1	beaten egg
1 cup	(250 ml) flour
3 tbsp	(45 ml) peanut oil
	salt and pepper

Place fish, potatoes, parsley, onions, butter and beaten egg in food processor. Season well and blend until well incorporated.

Shape mixture into small balls and flatten. Dust lightly in flour.

Heat oil in large frying pan. Add fish cakes without crowding and cook 2 to 3 minutes over medium-high heat. Turn patties over once and adjust time depending on thickness.

Serve with tartare sauce.

Halibut with Fennel Sauce

(serves 4)

1 SERVING	228 CALORIES	4g CARBOHYDRATE
24g PROTEIN	13g FAT	0.5g FIBER

1 tbsp	(15 ml) vegetable oil
2	large halibut steaks, with skin, cut in 2
5	fresh fennel sprigs
1 tbsp	(15 ml) butter
½ lb	(250 g) mushrooms, sliced
1	shallot, chopped
	salt and pepper
	juice 1 lemon

Preheat oven to 150°F (70°C).

Heat oil in large frying pan. When hot, add fish and cover; cook 3 minutes over medium-high heat.

Turn pieces over, season and drop in 2 fennel sprigs. Continue cooking 3 to 4 minutes over medium heat.

Remove fish from pan and keep hot in oven.

Add butter to frying pan. Cook remaining fennel, mushrooms and shallot 3 to 4 minutes covered; season well.

Add lemon juice, mix well and pour over fish. Serve with vegetables.

Pan-Fried Breaded Perch

(serves 4)

1 SERVING	523 CALORIES	38g CARBOHYDRATE
45g PROTEIN	19g FAT	0.1g FIBER

2 tbsp	(30 ml) olive oil
2	beaten eggs
8	ocean perch filets
1 cup	(250 ml) seasoned flour
1 cup	(250 ml) breadcrumbs
2 tbsp	(30 ml) vegetable oil
	salt and pepper
	lemon slices

Beat olive oil into eggs.

Dredge fish in flour, dip in eggs and coat with breadcrumbs.

Heat vegetable oil in large frying pan. When hot, add fish and cook 4 to 6 minutes over medium-high heat. Turn filets over twice and season once.

Serve with tartare sauce and garnish with lemon slices.

Perch Filets with Red Pepper Sauce

(serves 4)

1 SERVING	547 CALORIES	36g CARBOHYDRATE
44g PROTEIN	25g FAT	0.8g FIBER

1 tbsp	(15 ml) melted butter
1	garlic clove, smashed and chopped
1	medium onion, thinly sliced
1½	red peppers, thinly sliced
1½ cups	(375 ml) hot white sauce
¼ tsp	(1 ml) Worcestershire sauce
¼ tsp	(1 ml) Tabasco sauce
8	small perch filets
1 cup	seasoned flour
2 tbsp	(30 ml) vegetable oil
	salt and pepper
	juice ½ lemon

Heat butter in saucepan. Add garlic and onion; cover and cook 3 to 4 minutes over medium heat.

Stir in red peppers and season; continue cooking 7 to 8 minutes over medium heat, uncovered.

Pour mixture into food processor and purée. Replace in saucepan and incorporate white sauce, Worcestershire, Tabasco and lemon juice.

Simmer sauce 8 minutes over low heat. Do not cover.

Meanwhile, dredge fish in flour. Heat oil in large frying pan and add filets. Cook 3 to 4 minutes each side depending on size. Season fish well when turning.

When fish is cooked, arrange on heated serving platter and top with red pepper sauce.

Curried Grouper

(serves 4)

1 SERVING	507 CALORIES	58g CARBOHYDRATE
46g PROTEIN	9g FAT	1.0g FIBER

4 tbsp	(60 ml) curry powder
2 cups	(500 ml) flour
4	7 oz (200 g) grouper steaks
2 tbsp	(30 ml) vegetable oil
½	large cantaloupe, flesh sliced thick
1	banana, sliced thick on angle
	juice 1 tangerine
	salt and pepper

Mix curry powder with flour and season well. Dredge grouper in flour and shake off excess.

Heat oil in large frying pan. Add fish and cook 3 to 4 minutes over medium-high heat.

Turn fish over; continue cooking 2 to 3 minutes.

Season and turn fish over again; finish cooking 3 to 4 minutes depending on size. When bone can be removed easily, the fish is cooked.

Transfer fish to heated dinner plates. Quickly add remaining ingredients to frying pan and cook 2 minutes. Serve fruit with fish.

1 Mix curry powder with flour and season well. Dredge grouper in flour and shake off excess.

3 When bone can be removed easily, the fish is cooked.

2 Cook fish 8 to 11 minutes depending on size. Turn steaks over twice.

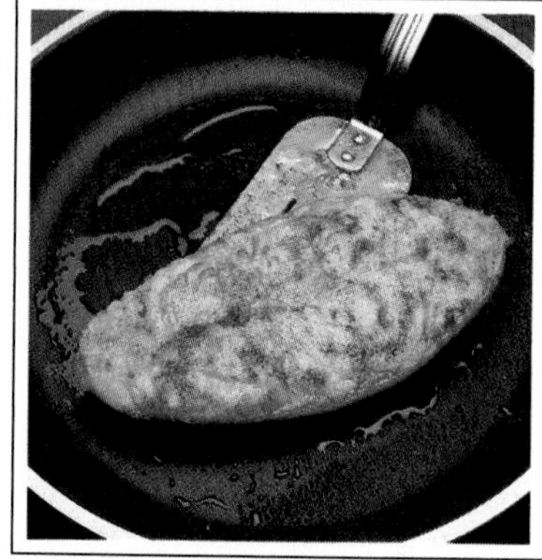

4 Quickly cook remaining ingredients in frying pan for 2 minutes.

Italian Style Grouper

(serves 4)

1 SERVING	352 CALORIES	15g CARBOHYDRATE
45g PROTEIN	12g FAT	1.0g FIBER

2 tbsp	(30 ml) olive oil
2	large shallots, chopped
1	garlic clove, smashed and chopped
1	small eggplant, diced with skin
28 oz	(796 ml) can tomatoes, drained and chopped
¼ tsp	(1 ml) basil
¼ tsp	(1 ml) marjoram
½	pickled hot cherry pepper, chopped
¼ tsp	(1 ml) sugar
1 tbsp	(15 ml) vegetable oil
4	7-8 oz (200-225 g) pieces grouper
	salt and pepper

Heat olive oil in large skillet. Cook shallots and garlic 2 minutes over medium heat.

Add eggplant and cover; cook 8 to 10 minutes over medium heat stirring occasionally.

Season eggplant very well; stir in tomatoes, seasonings, chopped cherry pepper and sugar. Bring to boil and cook 8 minutes over medium-high heat.

Meanwhile, heat vegetable oil in large frying pan. Add grouper and cook 4 minutes over medium heat.

Turn pieces over, season and continue cooking 4 to 5 minutes depending on size.

Serve fish with eggplant mixture.

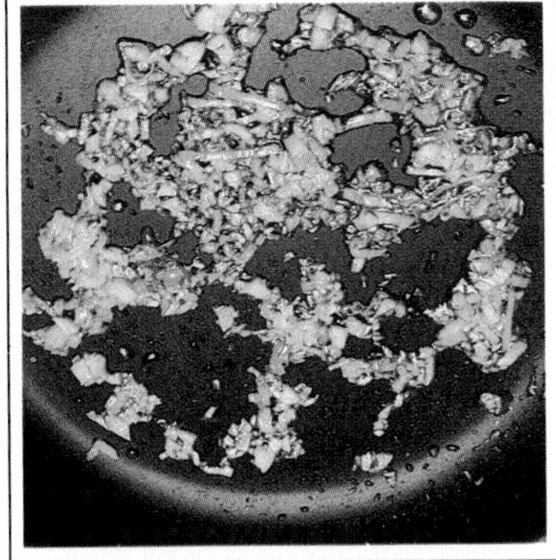

1 Heat olive oil in large skillet. Cook shallots and garlic 2 minutes over medium heat.

3 After 8 to 10 minutes of cooking, season eggplant very well.

2 Add eggplant and cover.

4 Stir in tomatoes, seasonings, cherry pepper and sugar. Bring to boil and cook 8 minutes over medium-high heat.

Grilled Shark Steaks

(serves 4)

1 SERVING	473 CALORIES	5g CARBOHYDRATE
41g PROTEIN	33g FAT	trace FIBER

2	1 lb (500 g) shark steaks
3 tbsp	(45 ml) olive oil
½ cup	(125 ml) lemon juice
2 tbsp	(30 ml) butter
1 tsp	(5 ml) chopped ginger
1	garlic clove, smashed and chopped
1 tbsp	(15 ml) chopped chives
1 tsp	(5 ml) brown sugar
1 tsp	(5 ml) lime juice
1 tsp	(5 ml) Worcestershire sauce
1 tbsp	(15 ml) vegetable oil
	salt and pepper

Place shark, olive oil and lemon juice in deep plate; marinate 20 minutes.

Drain fish well and pat dry; using heavy knife cut each shark steak into 2 pieces. A wooden mallet is useful to pound knife through bone.

Place butter, ginger, garlic, chives, sugar, lime juice and Worcestershire in small saucepan; heat until melted.

Brush butter mixture over fish.

Heat oil in large grill or frying pan. Add fish and cook 10 to 12 minutes over medium heat. Season during cooking and turn pieces over 2 to 3 times.

If desired, garnish servings with saudéed apples and steamed green beans.

1 A 1 lb (500 g) shark steak serves 2 people.

3 Place butter, ginger, garlic, chives, sugar, lime juice and Worcestershire in small saucepan; heat until melted.

2 After fish has been marinated, use heavy knife and mallet to cut it into 2 pieces.

4 Brush butter mixture over fish before cooking.

Boston Bluefish à la Nicoise

(serves 4)

1 SERVING	399 CALORIES	6g CARBOHYDRATE
42g PROTEIN	22g FAT	0.5g FIBER

1 tbsp	(15 ml) olive oil
2	shallots, chopped
1	garlic clove, smashed and chopped
1.75 oz	(50 g) tin anchovy filets, drained and chopped
2 cups	(500 ml) cherry tomatoes, halved
½ cup	(125 ml) pitted black olives
1 tbsp	(15 ml) vegetable oil
1½ lb	(750 g) Boston bluefish filets, in large pieces, lightly dredged in flour
	salt and pepper

Heat olive oil in large skillet. Cook shallots and garlic 2 to 3 minutes over medium heat.

Add anchovies and continue cooking 1 minute.

Season well, add tomatoes and olives; mix and continue cooking 1 minute over medium-high heat. Set aside.

Heat vegetable oil in large frying pan. Add fish and cook 4 to 5 minutes over medium heat.

Season and turn pieces over; continue cooking another 4 minutes.

Pour tomatoes over fish, simmer 1 minute and serve.

1 Add anchovies to pan and continue cooking 1 minute.

3 After cooking fish 4 to 5 minutes on one side, turn pieces over and continue cooking another 4 minutes. Be sure to season.

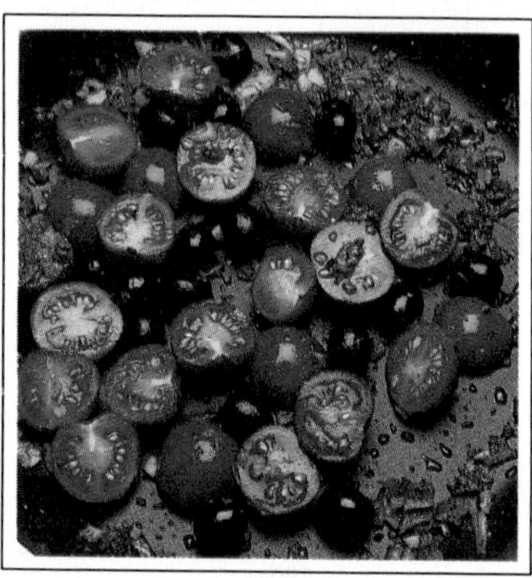

2 Season well, add tomatoes and olives; mix and continue cooking 1 minute over medium-high heat. Set aside.

4 Pour tomatoes over fish, simmer 1 minute and serve.

Sautéed Lobster Tails

(serves 4)

1 SERVING	330 CALORIES	14g CARBOHYDRATE
16g PROTEIN	2g FAT	trace FIBER

2 tbsp	(30 ml) melted butter
4	lobster tails, shelled and cut in 3
1	shallot, finely chopped
1 tbsp	(15 ml) chopped parsley
1 cup	(250 ml) tasty dill sauce
	salt and pepper
	few drops lemon juice

Heat butter in large frying pan. When hot, add lobster and cook 2 to 3 minutes over medium-high heat.

Season well and add shallot and parsley; continue cooking 1 minute.

Sprinkle with lemon juice and serve with tasty dill sauce (see following recipe).

Sweet and Sour Scampi

(serves 4)

1 SERVING	324 CALORIES	15g CARBOHYDRATE
33g PROTEIN	13g FAT	0.3g FIBER

1	green onion, chopped
3 tbsp	(45 ml) dry white wine
4 tbsp	(60 ml) white vinegar
1 tbsp	(15 ml) sugar
$\frac{1}{4}$ cup	(50 ml) orange juice
1 tbsp	(15 ml) chopped fresh ginger
1 cup	(250 ml) diced pineapple
1 cup	(250 ml) hot chicken stock
1 tbsp	(15 ml) cornstarch
3 tbsp	(45 ml) cold water
$1\frac{1}{2}$ lb	(750 g) scampi, peeled
3 tbsp	(45 ml) melted butter
$\frac{1}{2}$ tsp	(2 ml) fennel seed
	salt and pepper
	lemon juice

Prepare sauce by placing green onion in saucepan. Add wine and vinegar; season well with pepper. Bring to boil and cook 3 minutes over medium heat.

Add sugar, orange juice, ginger, pineapple and chicken stock; mix well. Bring to boil again.

Mix cornstarch with water; stir into sauce and cook 2 minutes.

Correct seasoning and simmer over very low heat.

Cook scampi in two batches to avoid overcrowding the pan. Heat butter in large frying pan. Add scampi, fennel seed and lemon juice; season well. Cook 3 to 4 minutes, stirring frequently.

Serve cooked scampi with sauce.

Marinated Lobster Tails

(serves 4)

1 SERVING	293 CALORIES	4g CARBOHYDRATE
16g PROTEIN	25g FAT	0.5g FIBER

4	large lobster tails, shelled and in 1 in (2.5 cm) pieces
4 tbsp	(60 ml) olive oil
2 tbsp	(30 ml) tarragon wine vinegar
1 tbsp	(15 ml) chopped parsley
1 tbsp	(15 ml) chopped tarragon
¼ tsp	(1 ml) paprika
3 tbsp	(45 ml) melted butter
2 tbsp	(30 ml) capers
	salt and pepper
	juice ½ lemon

Place lobster, oil, vinegar, parsley, tarragon and paprika in bowl. Season well with pepper and marinate 30 minutes.

Drain lobster.

Heat butter in large frying pan. When hot, add lobster pieces and sauté 3 to 5 minutes over high heat. Stir often and turn pieces over once.

Stir in capers and lemon juice and season well. Finish cooking 1 minute.

Serve on rice.

Halibut with Fresh Fruit

(serves 4)

1 SERVING	382 CALORIES	18g CARBOHYDRATE
21g PROTEIN	26g FAT	0.2g FIBER

3 tbsp	(45 ml) butter
2	halibut steaks, cut in 2
1	mandarin, peeled and sliced in rings
2	bananas, peeled and sliced thick
½ cup	(125 ml) heavy cream
1 tsp	(5 ml) chopped fresh parsley
¼ tsp	(1 ml) paprika
	salt and pepper
	juice 1 lemon

Preheat oven to 150°F (70°C).

Heat butter in large frying pan. When partly melted, add fish and season well. Cover and cook 4 minutes over medium heat.

Squeeze in lemon juice and turn fish over; continue cooking another 4 minutes covered. Season well.

Remove fish from pan and keep hot in oven.

Add mandarin and bananas to frying pan; cook 2 minutes over high heat.

Mix in cream, parsley and paprika; season well. Cook 2 minutes, then pour over fish and serve.

Fried Shrimp with Eggs

(serves 4)

1 SERVING	280 CALORIES	5g CARBOHYDRATE
39g PROTEIN	11g FAT	-- FIBER

1 ½ lb	(750 g) shrimp, peeled and deveined
2 tbsp	(30 ml) soya sauce
2 tbsp	(30 ml) lemon juice
¼ tsp	(1 ml) paprika
2 tbsp	(30 ml) vegetable oil
2	beaten eggs
	salt and pepper

Place shrimp in large bowl. Add soya sauce, lemon juice and paprika; marinate 15 minutes.

Heat oil in large frying pan. Meanwhile, dip shrimp in beaten eggs and add to pan. Cook shrimp 2 minutes each side over medium heat. Season well.

When shrimp are cooked, drain on paper towels. If desired, serve with dipping sauce such as plum sauce.

Butterflied Garlic Shrimp

(serves 4)

1 SERVING	304 CALORIES	8g CARBOHYDRATE
43g PROTEIN	11g FAT	0.6g FIBER

3 tbsp	(45 ml) butter
2 lb	(900 g) medium shrimp, peeled, deveined and butterflied
3	garlic cloves, smashed and chopped
1½	green peppers, in thin strips
1	large lemon, peeled and diced
1 tbsp	(15 ml) chopped parsley
¼ tsp	(1 ml) paprika
	salt and pepper

Heat butter in large frying pan. Add shrimp and cook 2 minutes each side over medium-high heat.

Add garlic and season well; continue cooking 1 minute.

Stir in green pepper and diced lemon; cook 1 more minute.

Correct seasoning, add parsley and paprika, mix and serve.

Shrimp with Pernod Sauce

(serves 4)

1 SERVING	648 CALORIES	12g CARBOHYDRATE
44g PROTEIN	44g FAT	trace FIBER

3 tbsp	(45 ml) butter
2 lb	(900 g) medium shrimp, peeled and deveined
1 tbsp	(15 ml) chopped parsley
1	shallot, finely chopped
1 tsp	(5 ml) chopped chives
¼ cup	(50 ml) Pernod
1½ cups	(375 ml) heavy cream
¼ tsp	(1 ml) Tabasco sauce
	salt and pepper

Heat butter in large frying pan. Cook shrimp, parsley, shallot and chives 2 minutes each side over medium-high heat.

Season well and pour in Pernod; cook 2 minutes over high heat.

Remove shrimp with slotted spoon and set aside.

Replace pan over heat and pour in cream and Tabasco; cook 1½ minutes over high heat or until thickened.

Correct seasoning, replace shrimp in sauce and simmer 2 minutes.

Serve with Parisienne potatoes.

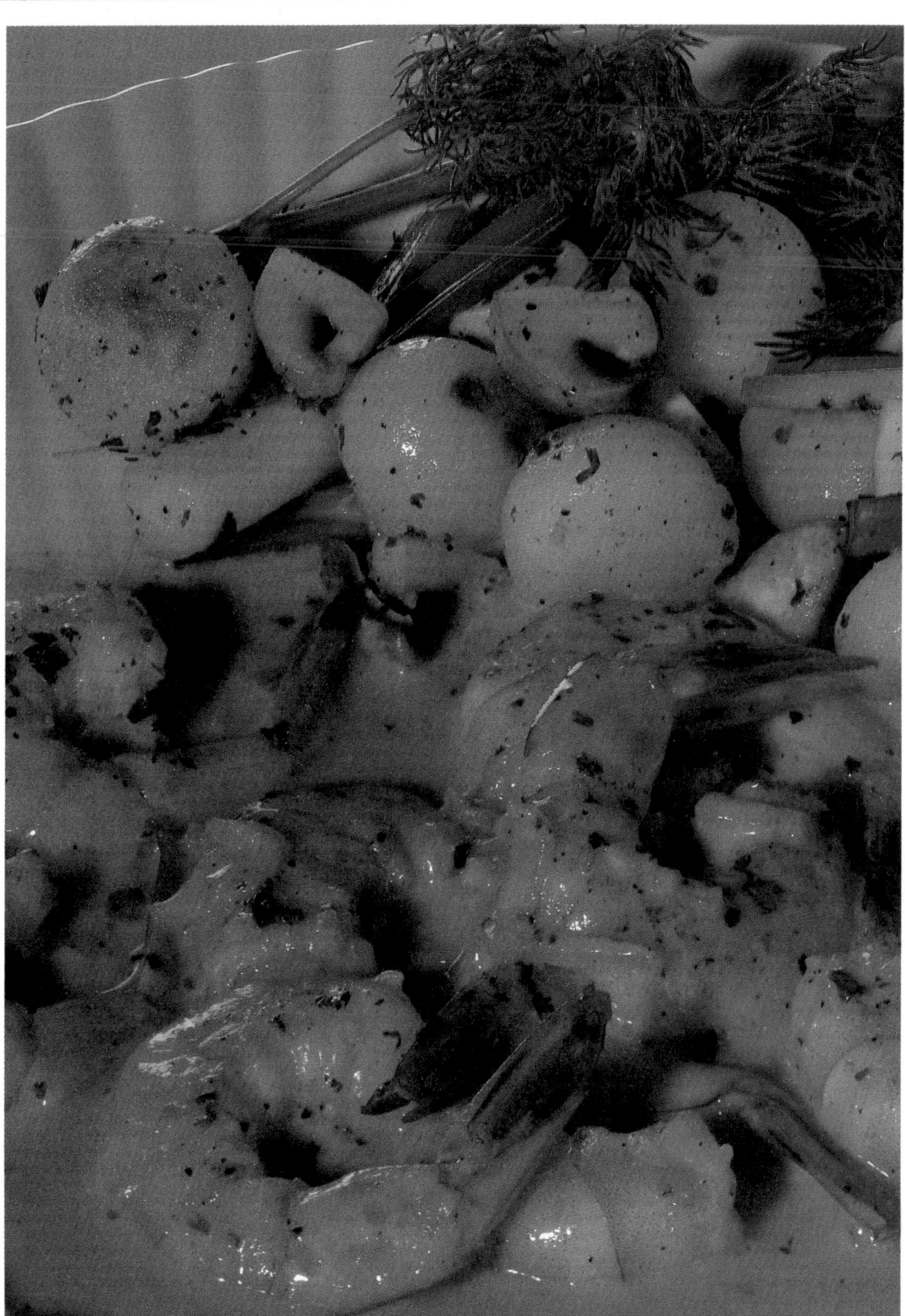

Grilled Sole and Shrimp

(serves 4)

1 SERVING	361 CALORIES	28g CARBOHYDRATE
43g PROTEIN	9g FAT	0.6g FIBER

¼ tsp	(1 ml) paprika
1 cup	(250 ml) flour
4	large sole filets
1 tbsp	(15 ml) vegetable oil
1 tbsp	(15 ml) butter
½ lb	(250 g) mushrooms, quartered
½ lb	(250 g) shrimp, peeled, deveined and cut in 3
1 tbsp	(15 ml) chopped chives
	salt and pepper
	juice 1 lemon

Preheat oven to 150°F (70°C).

Mix paprika with flour and season well. Dredge fish in flour and shake off excess.

Heat oil and butter in large frying pan. Add fish and cook 2 minutes over medium-high heat.

Turn filets over, season and continue cooking 2 minutes.

Remove fish from pan and keep hot in oven.

Place remaining ingredients in pan and cook 3 to 4 minutes over medium-high heat.

Serve with sole.

1 Mix paprika with flour and season well. Dredge fish in flour and shake off excess.

3 Turn filets over, season and continue cooking 2 minutes. Remove and keep hot in oven.

2 Add fish to hot oil and butter; cook 2 minutes over medium-high heat.

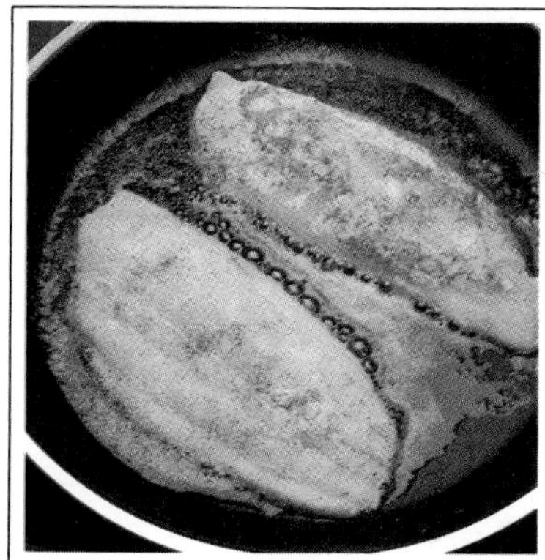

4 Place remaining ingredients in pan and cook 3 to 4 minutes over medium-high heat.

Fried Oysters

(serves 4)

1 SERVING	615 CALORIES	55g CARBOHYDRATE
20g PROTEIN	35g FAT	trace FIBER

2 cups	(500 ml) shucked oysters
1 cup	(250 ml) seasoned flour
2	beaten eggs
¼ cup	(50 ml) light cream
2 cups	(500 ml) crushed soda crackers
⅓ cup	(75 ml) peanut oil
	salt and pepper
	lemon juice

Dredge oysters in flour.

Mix eggs with cream; dip oysters in liquid. Coat with cracker crumbs.

Heat oil in deep skillet. When hot, add half of oysters and cook 4 minutes over high heat. Turn oysters over once.

Using slotted spoon remove cooked oysters and drain on paper towels.

Add remaining oysters to hot oil and repeat.

Serve with lemon juice and if desired with tartare sauce as well.

Quick Grilled Scallops

(serves 4)

1 SERVING	274 CALORIES	13g CARBOHYDRATE
32g PROTEIN	10g FAT	1.0g FIBER

3 tbsp	(45 ml) butter
1½ lb	(750 g) fresh scallops
1 lb	(500 g) mushrooms, quartered
1	shallot, chopped
1 tbsp	(15 ml) chopped parsley
1 tbsp	(15 ml) chopped chives
	salt and pepper
	juice 1 lemon

Heat butter in large frying pan. When hot, add scallops and season with pepper. Cover and cook 2 to 3 minutes over medium-high heat, turning scallops over once.

Add mushrooms and shallot to pan; continue cooking covered, for 1 minute.

Add remaining ingredients, mix well and correct seasoning.

Serve immediately.

Tasty Dill Sauce

1 RECIPE	1,172 CALORIES	77g CARBOHYDRATE
6g PROTEIN	93g FAT	0.4g FIBER

4	stems watercress
1	green onion, diced
3	sprigs fresh dill
2	garlic cloves, smashed and chopped
1 tbsp	(15 ml) chopped chives
1 cup	(250 ml) mayonnaise
3 tbsp	(45 ml) Port wine
⅓ cup	(75 ml) sour cream
	juice 1 lemon
	salt and pepper
	few drops Tabasco sauce
	dash paprika

Place watercress, onion, dill, garlic and chives in food processor; blend 1 minute.

Add remaining ingredients and continue blending 30 seconds or until smooth.

Correct seasoning and serve with a variety of grilled fish.

Mornay Sauce

1 RECIPE	936 CALORIES	46g CARBOHYDRATE
31g PROTEIN	71g FAT	trace FIBER

3 tbsp	(45 ml) butter
3 tbsp	(45 ml) flour
2 cups	(500 ml) hot milk
1	small onion
2	cloves
¼ tsp	(1 ml) nutmeg
1	egg yolk
1 tbsp	(15 ml) light cream
¼ cup	(50 ml) finely grated Gruyère Cheese
	salt and pepper

Heat butter in saucepan. When hot, add flour and cook 1 minute over low heat while mixing.

Pour in milk; mix well with whisk. Stud onion with cloves and add to saucepan along with nutmeg; season well.

Cook sauce 8 minutes over low heat. Stir occasionally.

Remove onion. Mix egg yolk with cream, then whisk into sauce. Add cheese and mix well. Serve sauce with fish.

Homemade Tartare Sauce

1 RECIPE	970 CALORIES	57g CARBOHYDRATE
2g PROTEIN	84g FAT	-- FIBER

1 cup	(250 ml) mayonnaise
2 tbsp	(30 ml) light cream
1	shallot, finely chopped
1 tsp	(5 ml) chopped parsley
1 tsp	(5 ml) chopped tarragon
1 tsp	(5 ml) dry mustard
	pinch sugar
	salt and pepper
	dash paprika
	lemon juice to taste

Place all ingredients in bowl and mix together until well incorporated.

Season to taste and serve sauce with fried fish.

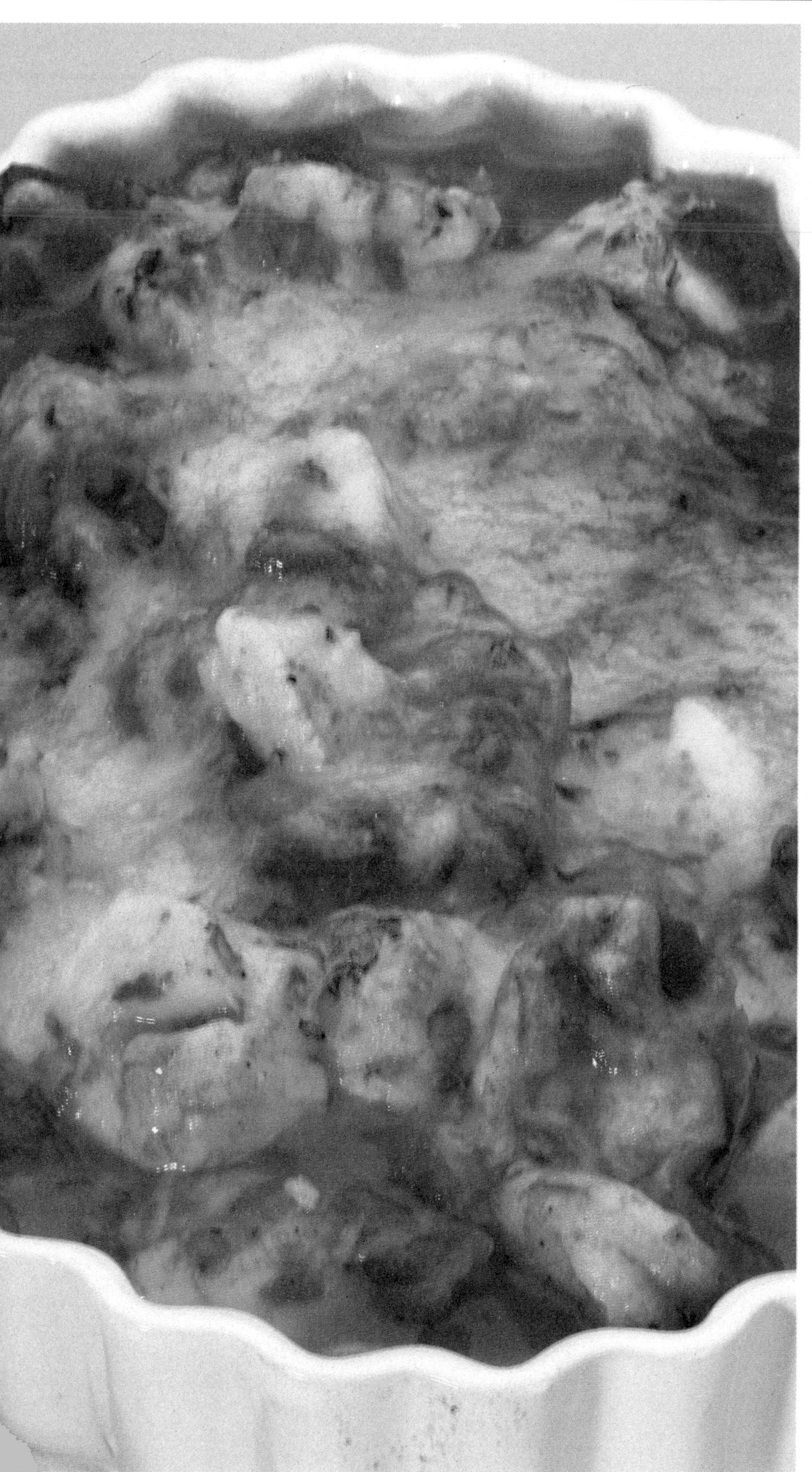

Seafood Mix

(serves 4)

1 SERVING	335 CALORIES	15g CARBOHYDRATE
40g PROTEIN	13g FAT	1.0g FIBER

2 tbsp	(30 ml) butter
1	garlic clove, smashed and chopped
1 cup	(250 ml) crabmeat, well drained
¾ lb	(375 g) scallops
½ lb	(250 g) shrimp, peeled and deveined
28 oz	(796 ml) can tomatoes, drained and chopped
2 tbsp	(30 ml) tomato paste
1 tbsp	(15 ml) chopped parsley
½ cup	(125 ml) grated Gruyère cheese
	salt and pepper

Heat butter in large frying pan. Add garlic, crabmeat, scallops and shrimp; season well. Cook 3 to 4 minutes over medium-low heat.

Mix in tomatoes, correct seasoning and simmer 2 to 3 minutes.

Stir in tomato paste and cook 1 minute over medium heat.

Pour mixture into large ovenproof dish. Top with parsley and cheese. Broil in oven until golden brown.

Serve in scallop shells.

Mixed Seafood Potato Coquilles

(serves 4)

1 SERVING	354 CALORIES	25g CARBOHYDRATE
31g PROTEIN	15g FAT	1.0g FIBER

2 cups	(500 ml) creamy mashed potatoes
2 tbsp	(30 ml) butter
1	garlic clove, smashed and chopped
1	green onion, chopped
1	shallot, finely chopped
⅔ lb	(300 g) mushrooms, thinly sliced
⅔ lb	(300 g) scallops, coarsely chopped
⅔ lb	(300 g) shrimp, peeled, deveined and coarsely chopped
2 tbsp	(30 ml) breadcrumbs
1 tbsp	(15 ml) chopped chives
1 tbsp	(15 ml) chopped parsley
	salt and pepper
	extra breadcrumbs
	extra butter

Force mashed potatoes through star nozzle of pastry bag and outline rims of scallop shells; set aside.

Heat 2 tbsp (30 ml) butter in large frying pan. Cook garlic, onion, shallot and mushrooms 3 to 4 minutes over medium heat. Season well.

Stir in scallops and shrimp; continue cooking 2 to 3 minutes.

Mix in breadcrumbs, chives and parsley. Fill scallop shells with mixture; top each with more breadcrumbs and dot with butter.

Broil in oven until golden brown.

1 Force mashed potatoes through star nozzle of pastry bag and outline rims of scallop shells; set aside.

3 Stir in seafood and continue cooking 2 to 3 minutes.

2 Cook garlic, onion, shallot and mushrooms 3 to 4 minutes over medium heat; season well.

4 Add breadcrumbs, chives and parsley, mix well and spoon into scallop shells. Top with more breadcrumbs and dot with butter. Broil.

Seafood on Rice

(serves 4)

1 SERVING	851 CALORIES	57g CARBOHYDRATE
39g PROTEIN	14g FAT	trace FIBER

1 lb	(500 g) scallops
½ cup	(125 ml) dry white wine
1 cup	(250 ml) water
1 tsp	(5 ml) melted butter
1 tbsp	(15 ml) chopped parsley
4	cooked lobster tails, shelled
2½ tbsp	(40 ml) butter
3 tbsp	(45 ml) flour
½ tsp	(2 ml) cumin
¼ cup	(50 ml) hot light cream
	salt and pepper
	juice 1 lemon
	cooked rice for 4

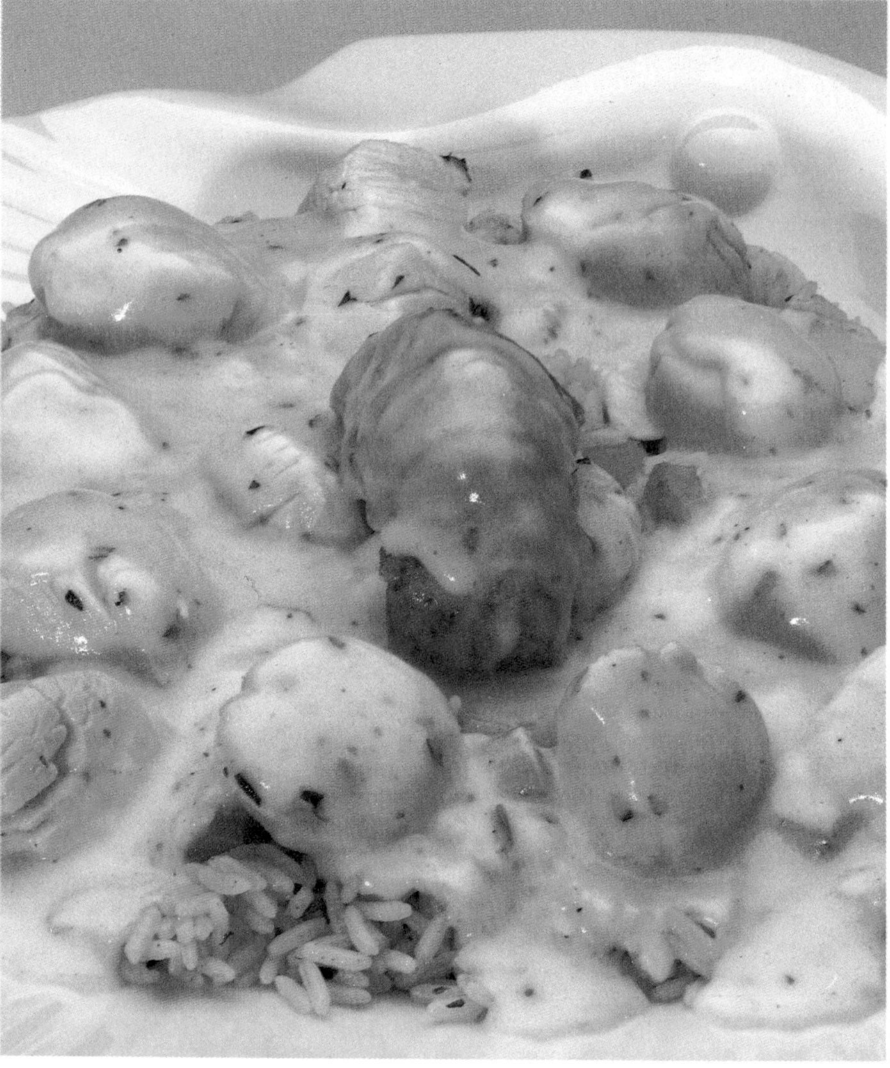

Place scallops, wine, water, melted butter, parsley, pepper and lemon juice in saucepan; bring to boil.

Add lobster. Cover saucepan and let stand 2 to 3 minutes on cold burner.

Remove scallops and lobster with slotted spoon and set aside.

Continue cooking liquid in saucepan 2 minutes over high heat. Set aside as well.

Heat 2½ tbsp (40 ml) butter in second saucepan. Add flour and cook 1 minute, stirring constantly.

Whisk in reserved cooking liquid from seafood. Add cumin and cook 1 to 2 minutes over medium heat.

Pour in cream, mix and cook 4 to 5 minutes over very low heat.

Place fish in sauce, mix and correct seasoning. Simmer 1 to 2 minutes to reheat.

Serve over rice.

Frog Legs Frita

(serves 4)

1 SERVING	347 CALORIES	11g CARBOHYDRATE
25g PROTEIN	22g FAT	0.5g FIBER

1 tbsp	(15 ml) butter
¼ cup	(50 ml) chopped celery
1	shallot, chopped
¼ tsp	(1 ml) fennel seed
½ lb	(250 g) mushrooms, halved
16	frog legs, cleaned
1 cup	(250 ml) dry white wine
½ cup	(125 ml) water
2	parsley sprigs
1½ cups	(375 ml) hot Bercy sauce
½ cup	(125 ml) grated Emmenthal cheese
	juice ½ lemon
	salt and pepper

Grease large frying pan with butter. Add remaining ingredients except sauce and cheese.

Cook frog legs, covered, 10 to 12 minutes over low heat depending on size. Check if cooked by removing meat from the bone.

When cooked, remove all meat from bones and place in scallop shells. Using slotted spoon, add mushrooms to shells.

Replace pan containing cooking liquid on stove over high heat; cook 3 to 4 minutes.

Mix in Bercy sauce and continue cooking 2 minutes; correct seasoning.

Pour sauce over meat and mushrooms in scallop shells. Top with cheese and broil in oven until bubbly.

Coquilles Saint-Jacques

(serves 4)

1 SERVING	427 CALORIES	16g CARBOHYDRATE
37g PROTEIN	20g FAT	0.5g FIBER

4 tbsp	(60 ml) butter
½ lb	(250 g) mushrooms, quartered
2	shallots, finely chopped
¼ tsp	(1 ml) paprika
1 tsp	(5 ml) finely chopped parsley
1½ lb	(750 g) scallops
½ cup	(125 ml) dry white wine
4 tbsp	(60 ml) flour
¼ tsp	(1 ml) fennel seed
1½ cups	(375 ml) hot light chicken stock or fish stock
2 tbsp	(30 ml) heavy cream
½ cup	(125 ml) grated Gruyère cheese
	salt and pepper

Wipe ½ tsp (2 ml) of butter over surface of frying pan with paper towel. Add mushrooms, shallots, paprika and parsley.

Add scallops and wine; season well with pepper. Cover and bring to boil over medium-high heat.

Turn scallops over and remove pan from heat. Let stand 30 seconds.

Remove scallops from frying pan using slotted spoon and set aside. Pour remaining contents in pan into bowl; set aside as well.

Heat remaining butter in saucepan until melted. Add flour and mix well; cook 1 minute over low heat while stirring constantly.

Pour mushrooms and liquid from bowl into saucepan. Add fennel seed and mix well to incorporate.

Pour in chicken stock, mix and season. Add cream and bring to boil. Cook 8 minutes over low heat.

Place scallops in sauce and simmer 1 minute to reheat. Spoon mixture into scallop shells set on ovenproof tray.

Top with cheese and broil in oven until melted.

If desired serve with a light fruit dessert.

1 Wipe ½ tsp (2 ml) of butter over surface of frying pan with paper towel. Add mushrooms, shallots, paprika and parsley.

3 After scallops have been cooked, remove from pan with slotted spoon and set aside. Pour remaining contents in pan into bowl for later use.

2 Add scallops and wine; season well with pepper. Cover and bring to boil over medium-high heat.

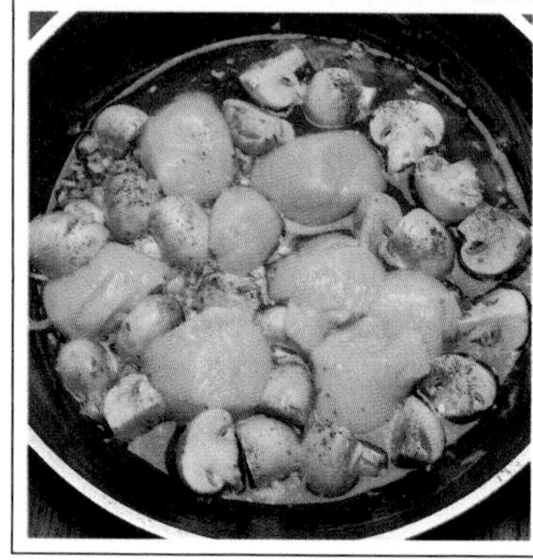

4 After flour mixture has cooked, add reserved mushrooms and liquid. Add fennel seed and mix well to incorporate.

Scallops Emmenthal

(serves 4)

1 SERVING	327 CALORIES	15g CARBOHYDRATE
30g PROTEIN	17g FAT	2.0g FIBER

2 tbsp	(30 ml) vegetable oil
1	medium onion, chopped
1	eggplant, diced small with skin
½ tsp	(2 ml) oregano
1 tbsp	(15 ml) chopped fresh ginger
1 lb	(500 g) scallops
1 cup	(250 ml) grated Emmenthal cheese
1 tsp	(5 ml) chopped parsley
	dash paprika
	salt and pepper
	lime slices

Heat oil in large frying pan. Cook onion, covered, 2 to 3 minutes over medium-low heat.

Add eggplant and seasonings; continue cooking 6 to 7 minutes, covered, over medium heat.

Stir in scallops and season well. Cook 3 to 4 minutes, covered, over low heat; stir occasionally.

Mix in half of cheese and cook 1 minute over low heat uncovered.

Spoon mixture into scallop shells, top with remaining cheese and broil in oven until lightly browned. Garnish with lime slices and sprinkle with chopped parsley.

Scallops in Garlic-Cream Sauce

(serves 4)

1 SERVING	371 CALORIES	16g CARBOHYDRATE
31g PROTEIN	19g FAT	0.6g FIBER

4 tbsp	(60 ml) butter
2	garlic cloves, smashed and chopped
1 tsp	(5 ml) chopped chives
¼ tsp	(1 ml) fennel seed
2	small zucchini, diced
3½ tbsp	(55 ml) flour
2½ cups	(625 ml) light chicken stock, hot
1¼ lb	(625 g) cooked scallops, cut in ½
3 tbsp	(45 ml) heavy cream
¼ cup	(50 ml) grated Parmesan cheese
	salt and pepper
	few drops lemon juice

Heat butter in saucepan. Add garlic, chives, fennel and zucchini; season well. Cook 4 to 5 minutes over medium heat, stirring several times.

Mix in flour and cook 1 minute over low heat.

Add chicken stock and mix well; bring to boiling point. Season and continue cooking 6 to 8 minutes over low heat.

Mix in scallops, cream and lemon juice; cook 1 minute.

Pour into scallop shells, top with cheese and serve.

Fish and Vegetable Coquilles

(serves 4)

1 SERVING	517 CALORIES	25g CARBOHYDRATE
30g PROTEIN	33g FAT	1.0g FIBER

4	large carrots, pared
1	potato, peeled
1 tbsp	(15 ml) butter
2-3 tbsp	(30-45 ml) hot light cream
2 cups	(500 ml) cooked boned salmon
1½ cups	(375 ml) hot white sauce
2 tbsp	(30 ml) coarse breadcrumbs
	salt and pepper
	few drops melted butter

Cook carrots and potato in saucepan of salted boiling water. When cooked, drain well and purée vegetables through food mill into bowl.

Add butter and cream; season well. Mix until well blended.

Border scallop shells with vegetable purée. Be sure to leave enough space in middle for the salmon. Set shells aside.

In another bowl, mix salmon with white sauce; season well. Spoon into scallop shells.

Sprinkle with breadcrumbs and few drops melted butter. Broil in oven until lightly browned.

Shrimp and Tomato in Shells

(serves 4)

1 SERVING	261 CALORIES	12g CARBOHYDRATE
35g PROTEIN	8g FAT	1.0g FIBER

2 tbsp	(30 ml) olive oil
1½ lb	(750 g) shrimp, peeled and deveined
2	garlic cloves, smashed and chopped
28 oz	(796 ml) can tomatoes, drained and chopped
1 tsp	(5 ml) chopped parsley
¼ tsp	(1 ml) fennel seed
½ tsp	(2 ml) lime juice
	salt and pepper
	pinch sugar

Heat oil in large frying pan. Add shrimp and garlic; season and cook 3 to 4 minutes over high heat. Stir occasionally.

Remove shrimp from pan and set aside.

Add tomatoes and parsley to pan. Season with salt, pepper and fennel seed; cook 4 to 5 minutes over high heat, stirring occasionally.

Stir in lime juice and sugar and replace shrimp in pan. Simmer 1 minute to reheat, then spoon into scallops shells and serve with vegetables.

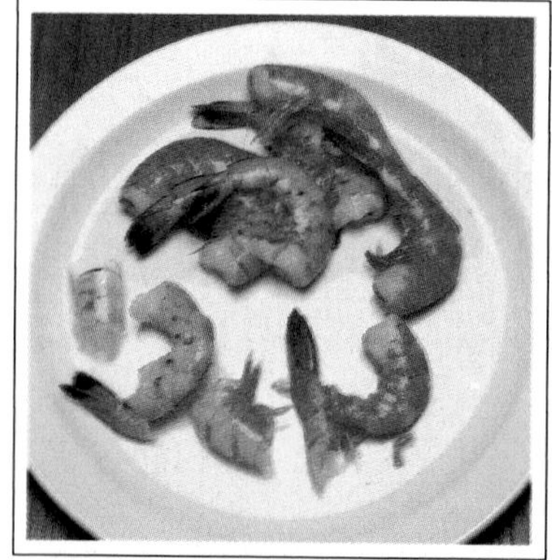

1 Peel and devein shrimp.

3 Remove shrimp from pan and set aside.

2 Cook shrimp and garlic in hot oil for 3 to 4 minutes over high heat.

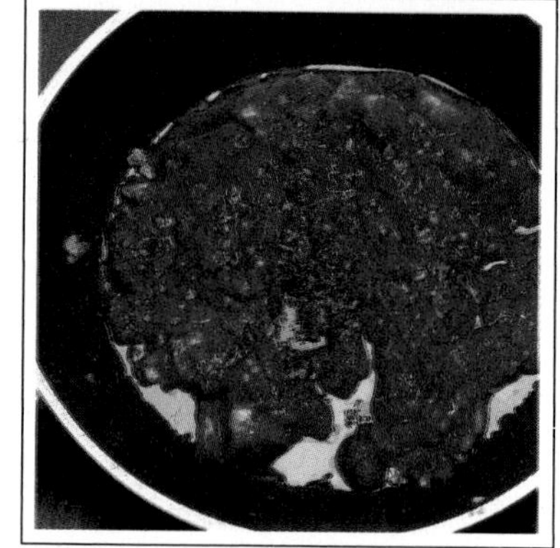

4 Add tomatoes and parsley to pan. Season with salt, pepper and fennel seed; cook 4 to 5 minutes over high heat.

Coastal Shrimp Coquilles

(serves 4)

1 SERVING	627 CALORIES	49g CARBOHYDRATE
48g PROTEIN	26g FAT	1.0g FIBER

3 tbsp	(45 ml) butter
1	small onion, chopped
1 cup	(250 ml) long grain rice, rinsed
1½ cups	(375 ml) light chicken stock, hot
¾ cup	(175 ml) grated Gruyère cheese
1½ lb	(750 g) small shrimp, peeled and deveined
1½ cups	(375 ml) hot paprika sauce
3 tbsp	(45 ml) coarse breadcrumbs
	salt and pepper

Preheat oven to 350°F (180°C).

Heat 1 tbsp (15 ml) butter in ovenproof casserole. Add onion and cook 2 minutes over medium heat.

Stir in rice and cook 2 minutes over high heat.

Pour in chicken stock, mix well and season. Cover and cook 18 minutes in oven.

Four minutes before end of cooking time, mix in cheese and continue cooking.

Remove cooked rice from oven, fluff with fork and set aside.

Heat remaining butter in frying pan. Cook shrimp 3 minutes over medium-high heat, stirring once and seasoning.

Spoon layer of rice in bottom of scallop shells. Add shrimp and cover with paprika sauce.

Top with breadcrumbs and broil in oven for several minutes.

Zucchini-Shrimp Coquilles

(serves 4)

1 SERVING	381 CALORIES	24g CARBOHYDRATE
30g PROTEIN	18g FAT	1.0g FIBER

1 tbsp	(5 ml) butter
1 lb	(500 g) shrimp, peeled and deveined
2	zucchini, sliced ½ in (1.2 cm) thick
¼ cup	(50 ml) dry white wine
1 cup	(250 ml) water
½ tsp	(2 ml) fennel seed
1½ cups	(375 ml) thick white sauce, hot
3 tbsp	(45 ml) breadcrumbs
	juice 1 lemon
	salt and pepper
	few drops Tabasco sauce

Grease bottom of deep skillet with butter. Add shrimp, zucchini, wine, water, fennel seed and lemon juice. Cover and bring to boiling point over medium heat.

Turn shrimp over and continue cooking 1 minute over medium heat, covered.

Using slotted spoon, remove shrimp and zucchini from skillet; set aside.

Bring liquid in skillet to boil; do not cover. Continue cooking 5 minutes over high heat to reduce by ¾.

Mix in white sauce, salt, pepper and Tabasco. Cook 1 to 2 minutes over medium heat.

Replace shrimp and zucchini in sauce and mix well.

Spoon mixture into scallop shells and top with breadcrumbs. Broil in oven several minutes or until hot.

Shrimp Provençale

(serves 4)

1 SERVING	292 CALORIES	7g CARBOHYDRATE
35g PROTEIN	13g FAT	0.5g FIBER

3 tbsp	(45 ml) olive oil
1½ lb	(750 g) shrimp, peeled and deveined
3	garlic cloves, smashed and chopped
1	red pepper, halved and thinly sliced
½	zucchini, halved lengthwise and thinly sliced
1 tbsp	(15 ml) coarsely chopped fresh oregano
1 tbsp	(15 ml) chopped parsley
3 tbsp	(45 ml) grated Parmesan cheese
	salt and pepper
	juice ½ lemon

Heat 2 tbsp (30 ml) oil in large frying pan. Add shrimp and garlic; season well. Cook 2 to 3 minutes each side over high heat; stir occasionally.

Remove shrimp from pan and set aside.

Add remaining oil to pan. Cook vegetables, oregano and parsley 2 to 3 minutes over medium-high heat. Season well and sprinkle with lemon juice.

Replace shrimp in pan, stir and cook 1 minute.

Spoon mixture into scallop shells, sprinkle with cheese and broil in oven until lightly browned.

Lobster and Leek Coquilles

(serves 4)

1 SERVING	334 CALORIES	10g CARBOHYDRATE
20g PROTEIN	24g FAT	trace FIBER

2 tbsp	(30 ml) melted butter
2 tbsp	(30 ml) chopped shallots
2	leeks, white part only, well washed and finely chopped
¼ tsp	(2 ml) fennel seed
1½ cups	(375 ml) cooked chopped lobster meat
1½ cups	(375 ml) hot white sauce
½ cup	(125 ml) grated Gruyère cheese
	salt and pepper

Heat butter in saucepan. Add shallots and cook 1 minute over medium heat.

Add leeks and fennel; season well. Cover and cook 8 to 10 minutes over medium-low heat.

Stir in lobster meat, then add white sauce; mix again. Season and simmer 3 minutes over low heat, uncovered.

Spoon into scallop shells and top with cheese. Broil in oven until bubbly.

Coquille Supreme

(serves 4)

1 SERVING	444 CALORIES	13g CARBOHYDRATE
57g PROTEIN	16g FAT	trace FIBER

1 tbsp	(15 ml) butter
4½ lb	(2 kg) mussels, cooked*, shelled and chopped
11.3 oz	(320 g) can lobster meat, chopped
1 tbsp	(15 ml) capers
2 tbsp	(30 ml) cornstarch
4 tbsp	(60 ml) cold water
¾ cup	(175 ml) grated Gruyère cheese
	salt and pepper
	chopped parsley

* Strain cooking liquid from mussels through cheesecloth and reserve for later use in recipe.

Heat butter in large frying pan. Add mussels, lobster and capers; cook 2 to 3 minutes over medium heat.

Season well with pepper and pour in reserved cooking liquid from mussels; bring to boil.

Mix cornstarch with water; stir into sauce and cook 1 minute over medium heat.

Add ⅓ cup (75 ml) cheese and continue cooking 1 minute.

Pour into large ovenproof dish, top with remaining cheese and parsley; broil in oven until golden brown. Serve in scallop shells.

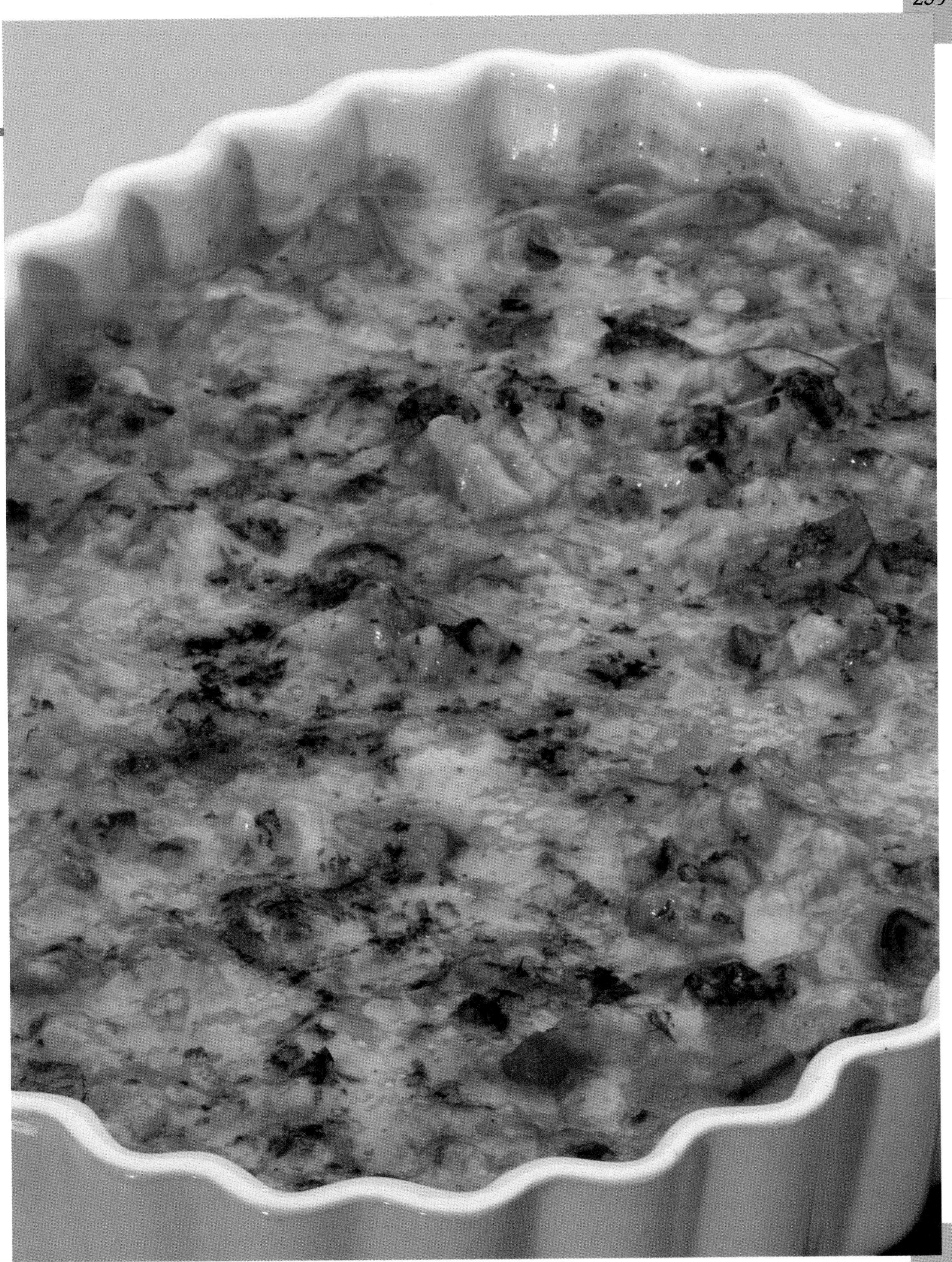

Lobster and Asparagus Coquilles

(serves 4)

1 SERVING	426 CALORIES	11g CARBOHYDRATE
35g PROTEIN	27g FAT	trace FIBER

3½ tbsp	(55 ml) butter
1	shallot, finely chopped
1 lb	(500 g) frozen lobster meat, thawed, drained and diced
1	bunch fresh asparagus, cooked and diced
¼ tsp	(1 ml) lemon juice
3 tbsp	(45 ml) flour
2 cups	(500 ml) hot milk
¼ tsp	(1 ml) nutmeg
1 cup	(250 ml) grated Emmenthal cheese
	salt and pepper
	pinch ground cloves

Heat 1 tsp (5 ml) butter in saucepan. Add shallot and cook 1 minute over medium heat.

Stir in lobster, asparagus and lemon juice; cover and simmer 6 to 7 minutes over very low heat.

Heat remaining butter in second saucepan. Mix in flour and cook 2 minutes over low heat, stirring constantly.

Pour in milk and season with nutmeg and cloves; blend well with whisk. Correct seasoning and cook sauce 6 to 7 minutes over low heat.

Transfer lobster and asparagus to saucepan containing sauce. Mix in half of cheese and simmer 1 to 2 minutes.

Spoon into scallop shells, top with remaining cheese and broil until golden brown.

Seaside Mussel Coquilles

(serves 4)

1 SERVING	252 CALORIES	12g CARBOHYDRATE
21g PROTEIN	11g FAT	0.7g FIBER

1 tbsp	(15 ml) melted butter
5	stems fresh basil, leaves chopped
3	large tomatoes, peeled, seeded and chopped
1	garlic clove, smashed and chopped
¼ cup	(50 ml) heavy cream
2 cups	(500 ml) cooked shucked mussels
½ cup	(125 ml) grated mozzarella cheese
	few drops lemon juice
	few drops Tabasco sauce
	salt and pepper

Heat butter in sauce pan. Add basil and cover; cook 3 to 4 minutes over medium-low heat. Stir twice during cooking.

Add tomatoes and garlic; season well and cook 5 to 6 minutes over high heat, uncovered.

Mix in cream and cook 2 minutes over high heat.

Add mussels, lemon juice and Tabasco; mix well.

Spoon into scallop shells, top with cheese and broil several minutes in oven.

Mussel Coquilles

(serves 4)

1 SERVING	575 CALORIES	17g CARBOHYDRATE
39g PROTEIN	36g FAT	-- FIBER

3 lb	(1.6 kg) fresh mussels, cleaned
4 tbsp	(60 ml) butter
½ cup	(125 ml) dry white wine
½ cup	(125 ml) cold water
1	shallot, chopped
1¼ cups	(300 ml) thick white sauce, hot
¼ tsp	(1 ml) paprika
¾ cup	(175 ml) grated Gruyère cheese
	salt and pepper

Place mussels, butter and wine in large saucepan.

Add water and shallot. Cover and bring to boil; cook until shells open.

Remove saucepan from heat. Separate mussels from shells, pouring juices back into saucepan. Set mussels aside and discard shells.

Strain cooking liquid from mussels through cheesecloth into clean saucepan. Bring to boil and continue cooking 4 to 5 minutes.

Mix in white sauce and paprika; season well. Cook 3 to 4 minutes over low heat.

Stir in ½ cup (125 ml) cheese; continue cooking sauce 1 minute over low heat.

Remove saucepan from heat and add mussels; mix well. Spoon into scallop shells and top with remaining cheese. Broil in oven until golden brown.

1 Before cooking mussels check for any opened shells and discard them.

3 As soon as the shells open, remove saucepan from heat.

2 Cook mussels in butter with wine, water and shallot. Cover pan.

4 Separate mussels from shells, pouring juices back into saucepan.

Crabmeat Coquilles

(serves 4)

1 SERVING	330 CALORIES	8g CARBOHYDRATE
34g PROTEIN	18g FAT	0.8g FIBER

2 tbsp	(30 ml) vegetable oil
1	yellow pepper, thinly sliced
1	shallot, finely chopped
½ lb	(250 g) mushrooms, finely chopped
2 tbsp	(30 ml) tomato paste
12	shrimp, peeled, deveined and cut in 3
7 oz	(200 g) can crabmeat, chopped
¼ tsp	(1 ml) fennel seed
1 tsp	(5 ml) chopped chives
1 cup	(250 ml) grated cheddar cheese
	salt and pepper

Heat oil in large frying pan. Add yellow pepper, shallot and mushrooms; season and cook 5 to 6 minutes over medium heat, covered. Stir mixture once.

Stir in tomato paste, shrimp, crabmeat, fennel seed and chives. Cover and cook 3 minutes over medium heat.

Mix in half of cheese and cook 1 minute uncovered.

Correct seasoning and spoon mixture into scallop shells. Top with remaining cheese and broil in oven until melted.

Crabmeat au Gratin

(serves 4)

1 SERVING	461 CALORIES	12g CARBOHYDRATE
33g PROTEIN	31g FAT	trace FIBER

1 tbsp	(15 ml) butter
½	small onion, chopped
¼	celery stalk, chopped
2	hard-boiled eggs, sliced
2 cups	(500 ml) cooked crabmeat, diced or chopped
2 cups	(500 ml) hot cheese sauce
½ cup	(125 ml) grated mozzarella cheese
	few drops lime juice
	salt and pepper

Heat butter in saucepan. Add onion and celery; cover and cook 3 minutes over medium heat.

Add eggs, crabmeat, lime juice and cheese sauce; mix carefully. Season well and simmer 2 to 3 minutes.

Spoon mixture into scallop shells and top with grated cheese. Broil in oven until melted.

Tasty Oyster Coquilles

(serves 4)

1 SERVING	264 CALORIES	12g CARBOHYDRATE
17g PROTEIN	16g FAT	trace FIBER

3 tbsp	(45 ml) butter
1	small onion, chopped
1	small carrot, pared and diced small
¼	celery stalk, diced
3½ tbsp	(55 ml) flour
2½ cups	(625 ml) hot chicken stock
½ tsp	(2 ml) basil
1¾ cups	(425 ml) cooked shucked oysters
½ cup	(125 ml) grated Gruyère cheese
	few drops Tabasco sauce
	salt and pepper

Heat butter in saucepan. Add onion, carrot and celery; cover and cook 5 minutes over medium heat.

Add flour and mix well; cook 1 minute over low heat.

Pour in chicken stock and mix well. Add basil, Tabasco sauce and season well. Cook 7 to 8 minutes over low heat uncovered.

Stir in oysters and simmer 2 to 3 minutes.

Spoon into scallop shells, top with cheese and broil several minutes in oven.

Hawaiian Coquilles

(serves 4)

1 SERVING	295 CALORIES	10g CARBOHYDRATE
32g PROTEIN	13g FAT	trace FIBER

4	small halibut steaks
4	thick rings fresh pineapple
1 tbsp	(15 ml) chopped parsley
1 tbsp	(15 ml) melted butter
2 cups	(500 ml) water
2 tbsp	(30 ml) cornstarch
4 tbsp	(60 ml) cold water
¼ cup	(50 ml) hot light cream
¼ tsp	(1 ml) paprika
¼ tsp	(1 ml) Tabasco sauce
4-6	small squares mozzarella cheese
	salt and pepper

Place fish, pineapple, parsley, butter and 2 cups (500 ml) water in frying pan. Cover and bring to boil.

Turn fish over; cover and continue cooking 3 minutes over low heat, depending on size.

When bone can be removed easily, the halibut is cooked. Remove from pan and set aside.

Replace pan on stove and bring to boil. Mix cornstarch with water; stir into liquid and cook 2 to 3 minutes over high heat.

Pour cream into frying pan, season and add paprika and Tabasco. Cook 2 minutes over medium-high heat.

Bone and flake fish; add to sauce with mozzarella. Cook 2 minutes over low heat.

Serve in scallop shells or on heated plates.

1 Fresh pineapple, if in season, is the best choice for this particular recipe, as it adds more flavor.

3 Turn fish over; cover and continue cooking 3 minutes over low heat, depending on size.

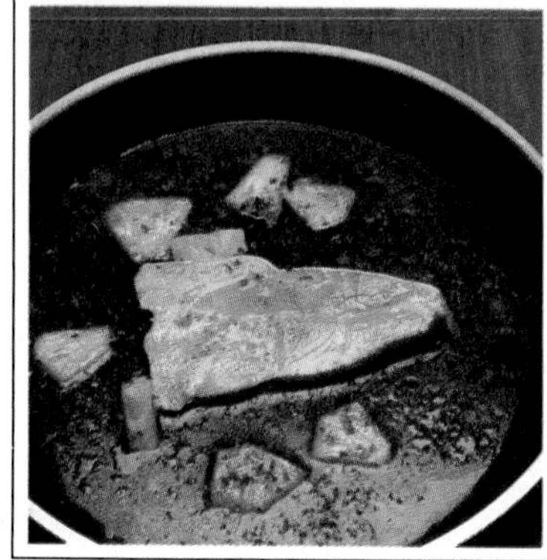

2 Place fish, pineapple, parsley, butter and water in large frying pan. Cover and bring to boil.

4 When bone can be removed easily, the fish is cooked.

Sole au Gratin

(serves 4)

1 SERVING	337 CALORIES	9g CARBOHYDRATE
29g PROTEIN	18g FAT	trace FIBER

4	sole filets
¼ tsp	(1 ml) fennel seed
3-4	fresh mint leaves
¼ lb	(125 g) mushrooms, sliced thick
½ cup	(125 ml) dry white wine
1 cup	(250 ml) water
3 tbsp	(45 ml) butter
3½ tbsp	(55 ml) flour
¾ cup	(175 ml) grated cheddar cheese
	extra butter
	juice 1 lemon
	salt and pepper

Lightly grease frying pan with a bit of butter. Add fish, fennel seed, mint, mushrooms and lemon juice; season well.

Pour in wine and water; cover and bring to boil.

Turn filets over, shut off heat and let stand 1 minute.

Remove fish and set aside.

Replace frying pan on stove and cook liquid 2 to 3 minutes over high heat; set aside.

Heat 3 tbsp (45 ml) butter in saucepan. Add flour and cook 1 minute, stirring constantly.

Add cooking liquid with mushrooms to saucepan; mix well and season. Cook 8 minutes over low heat.

Break fish into smaller pieces and place in scallop shells. Pour mushroom sauce over and top with cheese. Broil in oven until melted.

1 Place fish, fennel seed, mint, mushrooms and lemon juice in lightly buttered frying pan; season well.

3 After fish is cooked, remove from pan and set aside.

2 Pour in wine and water; cover and bring to boil.

4 Add cooking liquid with mushrooms to flour mixture in saucepan; mix well and season. Cook 8 minutes over low heat.

1 Place 3 tbsp (45 ml) butter and chopped mint in saucepan. Melt over medium heat.

2 Add shallot and curry powder; cook 1 minute over medium heat.

3 Mix in flour with wooden spoon and cook 2 minutes over low heat.

4 Pour in milk and whisk until well incorporated; season to taste. Cook sauce 7 to 8 minutes over low heat.

Almond Sole with Mint Sauce

(serves 4)

1 SERVING	377 CALORIES	16g CARBOHYDRATE
29g PROTEIN	22g FAT	trace FIBER

3 tbsp	(45 ml) butter
3	stems fresh mint, leaves coarsely chopped
1	shallot, chopped
1 tbsp	(15 ml) curry powder
3½ tbsp	(55 ml) flour
2 cups	(500 ml) hot milk
4	sole filets
1½ cups	(375 ml) water
1 tbsp	(15 ml) melted butter
1	onion, thinly sliced
1 tbsp	(15 ml) chopped parsley
4 tbsp	(60 ml) slivered almonds
	salt and pepper
	juice ½ lemon

Place 3 tbsp (45 ml) butter and mint in saucepan. Melt over medium heat.

Add shallot and curry powder; cook 1 minute over medium heat.

Mix in flour with wooden spoon and cook 2 minutes over low heat.

Pour in milk and whisk until well incorporated; season to taste. Cook sauce 7 to 8 minutes over low heat.

Meanwhile, roll filets (do not tie) and set in large frying pan. Add water, melted butter, onion, parsley, lemon juice, salt and pepper. Cover and bring to boil.

Turn fish rolls over; continue cooking 2 to 3 minutes over low heat, covered.

Transfer fish rolls to scallop shells. Top with mint sauce, sprinkle with slivered almonds and broil in oven until lightly browned.

Spinach Sole Coquilles

(serves 4)

1 SERVING	303 CALORIES	21g CARBOHYDRATE
24g PROTEIN	14g FAT	1.0g FIBER

1 tbsp	(15 ml) vegetable oil
4	thick slices tomato
½ cup	(125 ml) breadcrumbs
1½ cups	(375 ml) cooked spinach, well drained and chopped
3	cooked sole filets, in 1½ in (4 cm) pieces
1½ cups	(375 ml) hot curry sauce
4 tbsp	(60 ml) grated coconut
	salt and pepper

Heat oil in frying pan. Meanwhile, dredge tomato slices in breadcrumbs. Fry in hot oil until browned on both sides. Remove and drain on paper towels.

Arrange layer of spinach in bottom of large scallop shells. Add slice of tomato.

Spoon fish over tomato slices and spinach; cover with curry sauce. Season well.

Sprinkle with coconut and broil several minutes in oven.

Layered Coquilles

(serves 4)

1 SERVING	350 CALORIES	15g CARBOHYDRATE
30g PROTEIN	19g FAT	0.8g FIBER

2	10 oz (284 g) packages spinach, cooked
4	small turbot filets
½	zucchini, sliced
1	large parsley sprig
¼ tsp	(1 ml) celery seed
1-2	slices lemon
1½ cups	(375 ml) hot white sauce
½ cup	(125 ml) grated Gruyère cheese
¼ tsp	(1 ml) paprika
	salt and pepper
	melted butter

Shape cooked spinach into balls and squeeze out excess water. Chop and place in bottom of ovenproof dish; set aside.

Place fish, zucchini, parsley, celery seed, lemon, salt and pepper in large frying pan. Pour in just enough water to cover. Cover and bring to boil.

Remove cooked fish from pan and rest on spinach in baking dish. Discard remaining contents in pan.

Cover fish with white sauce and top with cheese and paprika. Moisten with a bit of melted butter and broil in oven until golden brown.

Serve in scallop shells.

1 Place chopped spinach in bottom of ovenproof dish; set aside.

3 Remove cooked fish from pan and rest on spinach.

2 Place fish, zucchini, parsley, lemon and seasonings in frying pan with just enough water to cover. Bring to boil, covered.

4 Cover fish with white sauce and top with cheese and paprika; broil in oven.

Turbot Coquilles Mornay

(serves 4)

1 SERVING	467 CALORIES	15g CARBOHYDRATE
44g PROTEIN	26g FAT	trace FIBER

$1\frac{1}{2}$ cups	(375 ml) water
1	small onion, quartered
1	clove
$\frac{1}{2}$	celery stalk, thinly sliced
2 lb	(900 g) fresh turbot filets, cut in 1 in (2.5 cm) pieces
2 tbsp	(30 ml) butter
$\frac{1}{4}$ lb	(125 g) mushrooms, diced
1 tsp	(5 ml) chopped chives
$1\frac{3}{4}$ cups	(425 ml) Mornay sauce, hot
$\frac{1}{2}$ cup	(125 ml) grated mozzarella cheese
	juice 1 lemon
	salt and pepper

Pour water into skillet. Stud one quarter of onion with clove and place all in pan. Add celery, lemon juice and salt; bring to boil.

Add fish and cook over low heat for 3 to 4 minutes.

Remove fish and drain well; set aside.

Heat butter in saucepan. Add mushrooms and chives; cook 3 minutes over low heat.

Stir in Mornay sauce and season well. Simmer 3 minutes.

Place fish in Mornay sauce mixture and stir well; simmer 1 minute.

Pour into scallop shells, top with cheese and broil in oven until golden.

Coquille of Turbot au Feta

(serves 4)

1 SERVING	167 CALORIES	12g CARBOHYDRATE
15g PROTEIN	5g FAT	1.0g FIBER

1 tbsp	(15 ml) butter
2	turbot filets, cut in 1 in (2.5 cm) pieces
2	shallots, chopped
$\frac{1}{2}$ lb	(250 g) mushrooms, sliced
1 tbsp	(15 ml) fresh tarragon, finely chopped
$\frac{1}{2}$ cup	(125 ml) dry white wine
$1\frac{3}{4}$ cups	(425 ml) spicy tomato sauce, hot
3 tbsp	(45 ml) feta cheese
	salt and pepper

Grease large frying pan with butter. Add fish, shallots, mushrooms, tarragon and wine. Cover with sheet of buttered waxed paper and bring to boiling point over medium heat.

As soon as liquid starts to boil, remove pan from heat and let stand 1 minute.

Remove fish from pan and set aside.

Replace pan on stove; cook 2 to 3 minutes at high heat. Add tomato sauce, mix well and season; bring to boil. Continue cooking 2 to 3 minutes over high heat.

Correct seasoning, replace fish in sauce and mix. Spoon into scallop shells and top with cheese; broil in oven several minutes.

Cold Coquilles

(serves 4)

1 SERVING	254 CALORIES	9g CARBOHYDRATE
21g PROTEIN	15g FAT	trace FIBER

3 oz	(90 g) blue cheese, mashed
1 tbsp	(15 ml) Dijon mustard
4-5 tbsp	(60-75 ml) lemon juice
¾ cup	(175 ml) light cream
1	garlic clove, smashed and chopped
¾ lb	(375 g) scallops, cooked and cooled
¼ lb	(125 g) mushrooms, well cleaned and sliced
1 tbsp	(15 ml) chopped parsley
	few drops Worcestershire sauce
	few drops Tabasco sauce
	salt and pepper
	green onions for decoration

In large bowl, mix together cheese and mustard.

Blend in lemon juice to taste. Add cream, garlic, Worcestershire, Tabasco, salt and pepper; mix until well incorporated.

Place scallops, mushrooms and parsley in second bowl. Pour in dressing and toss until evenly coated.

Serve in scallop shells with green onions as decoration. If desired, garnish with fruit and lettuce leaves.

Bercy Sauce

1 RECIPE	626 CALORIES	26g CARBOHYDRATE
14g PROTEIN	52g FAT	trace FIBER

4 tbsp	(60 ml) butter
1 tbsp	(15 ml) chopped parsley
1 tbsp	(15 ml) chopped chives
2	garlic cloves, smashed and chopped
1 tbsp	(15 ml) chopped fresh tarragon
3½ tbsp	(55 ml) flour
2 cups	(500 ml) light chicken stock, hot
	salt and pepper
	few drops Tabasco sauce

Heat butter in saucepan. Add parsley, chives, garlic and tarragon; cook 3 minutes over low heat.

Mix in flour and continue cooking 2 minutes.

Add chicken stock and season well with salt, pepper and Tabasco sauce. Mix and cook sauce 10 to 12 minutes over low heat, stirring twice.

Use in a variety of coquille recipes.

Paprika Sauce

1 RECIPE	942 CALORIES	75g CARBOHYDRATE
24g PROTEIN	65g FAT	5.0g FIBER

4 tbsp	(60 ml) butter
2	medium onions, thinly sliced
2 tbsp	(30 ml) paprika
4 tbsp	(60 ml) flour
1	large apple, peeled, cored and chopped
3 cups	(750 ml) light chicken stock, hot
3 tbsp	(45 ml) hot light cream
	salt and pepper

Heat butter in saucepan. Add onions and cook 4 minutes over low heat.

Stir in paprika and flour; mix well and cook 1 minute over low heat.

Add apple and chicken stock; mix well and season. Cook sauce 8 to 10 minutes over medium heat.

Remove sauce from heat and pour into food processor; blend until smooth.

Incorporate hot cream and serve.

Curry Sauce

1 RECIPE	672 CALORIES	39g CARBOHYDRATE
20g PROTEIN	52g FAT	3.0g FIBER

3 tbsp	(45 ml) butter
1	onion, finely chopped
1	small garlic clove, smashed and finely chopped
2 tbsp	(30 ml) curry powder
1 tsp	(5 ml) cumin
3 tbsp	(45 ml) flour
2½ cups	(625 ml) light chicken stock, hot
3 tbsp	(45 ml) hot light cream
	salt and pepper

Heat butter in saucepan. Add onion and garlic; cook 3 minutes over medium heat.

Mix in curry powder, cumin and flour; cook 4 to 5 minutes over low heat, stirring often.

Pour in chicken stock and season well. Mix and cook sauce 7 to 9 minutes over medium heat.

Incorporate cream, correct seasoning and serve.

SALADS

SALADS

Mmmmm... salads, is there any other combination of foods that is so fresh and crisp, so bursting with color and seemingly with the power to make you feel as though you are getting healthier with each and every bite? Salads are a wonderful way to balance out a heavy dinner, or start or finish a light meal, and just as wonderful served on their own as the star attraction. Their versatility is unlimited — only your preferences and produce availability will set any restrictions. Preparing the perfect salad is quite simple but begins long before you start the recipe — a fact that is often forgotten. First, you must search out the freshest vegetables you can find, inspecting items carefully for hidden blemishes or just plain poor quality. Secondly, it is essential that all vegetables be thoroughly washed in plenty of cold water — tomatoes, cucumbers, everything! Thirdly, they must also be thoroughly dried (especially greens), otherwise the dressing you so carefully blended will not adhere properly, causing the whole salad to taste watery. And lastly, they should be trimmed, pared, cut as suggested in the recipe and assembled in a large serving bowl for tossing. Even if the salad is small it should be tossed with the dressing in a large bowl to make sure everything is evenly coated. Enjoy.

Summer Salad

(serves 4)

1 SERVING	571 CALORIES	20g CARBOHYDRATE
5g PROTEIN	55g FAT	2.8g FIBER

1 tbsp	(15 ml) strong mustard
1 tsp	(5 ml) chopped chives
1 tsp	(5 ml) chopped parsley
1 tbsp	(15 ml) green peppercorns, mashed
¼ cup	(50 ml) wine vinegar
1 cup	(250 ml) olive oil
1	head Romaine lettuce, leaves in bite-size pieces
1 cup	(250 ml) cooked green beans
1 cup	(250 ml) cooked yellow beans
1 cup	(250 ml) cooked green peas
2	carrots, pared and in fine julienne
	salt and pepper
	few drops lemon juice

Place mustard, chives, parsley, peppercorns, salt and lemon juice in bowl. Whisk in vinegar.

Incorporate oil in thin stream, whisking constantly. Correct seasoning.

Place remaining ingredients in large salad bowl. Pour on vinaigrette to taste, toss and serve.

Vegetable Salad with Cheese Dressing

(serves 4)

1 SERVING	403 CALORIES	36g CARBOHYDRATE
25g PROTEIN	22g FAT	2.1g FIBER

1	Boston lettuce
1	small Romaine lettuce
1	celery stalk, thinly sliced
2 cups	(500 ml) cooked cauliflower
3	canned beets, in julienne
½ cup	(125 ml) well-cooked bacon, chopped
1 cup	(250 ml) garlic croutons
3 oz	(90 g) blue cheese
4 tbsp	(60 ml) sour cream
3 tbsp	(45 ml) lemon juice
1 tbsp	(15 ml) cider vinegar
3 tbsp	(45 ml) heavy cream
	salt and pepper

Wash and dry both lettuces. Tear leaves into smaller pieces and place in large bowl.

Add celery, cauliflower, beets, bacon and croutons.

Mix blue cheese, sour cream and remaining ingredients in food processor until smooth.

Correct seasoning, pour dressing over salad and toss well. Serve.

Mixed Vegetable Side Salad

(serves 4)

1 SERVING	165 CALORIES	7g CARBOHYDRATE
7g PROTEIN	12g FAT	2.9g FIBER

1	English cucumber
1	head broccoli, in flowerets, cooked
1	carrot, pared and grated
3 oz	(90 g) cheddar cheese, in julienne
	salt and pepper
	vinaigrette of your choice

Do not peel cucumber. Cut in half lengthwise, remove seeds and slice.

Place cucumber in bowl with cooked broccoli, carrot and cheese. Season and toss.

Pour in vinaigrette, toss again and serve.

Eggplant Salad

(serves 4)

1 SERVING	637 CALORIES	48g CARBOHYDRATE
12g PROTEIN	48g FAT	1.0g FIBER

2	garlic cloves, smashed and chopped
¼ cup	(50 ml) wine vinegar
¾ cup	(175 ml) olive oil
1 tbsp	(15 ml) lemon juice
1	small eggplant
4	potatoes, cooked in jackets and still hot
4	large tomatoes, skinned, cut in half and sliced
2	bunches asparagus, tips cooked and cut in half
1 cup	(250 ml) cubed pineapple, drained
4 tbsp	(60 ml) toasted slivered almonds
	salt and pepper
	vegetable oil

Preheat ovent to 400°F (200°C).

Place garlic, vinegar, olive oil, lemon juice, salt and pepper in small bowl; whisk together and set aside.

Cut eggplant lengthwise into slices ½ in (1.2 cm) thick. Cut into long strips and dice. Place eggplant on cookie sheet and brush generously with vegetable oil.

Cook 15 minutes in oven, turning pieces over often.

Transfer eggplant to large salad bowl.

Peel hot potatoes, cut in half and slice; add to salad bowl.

Add tomatoes, asparagus, pineapple and almonds to bowl. Pour in vinaigrette to taste, toss well, season and serve.

Lettuce and Fruit Salad

(serves 4)

1 SERVING	447 CALORIES	12g CARBOHYDRATE
3g PROTEIN	45g FAT	1.4g FIBER

4 tbsp	(60 ml) wine vinegar
⅔ cup	(150 ml) olive oil
1 tsp	(5 ml) sugar
1 tbsp	(15 ml) lemon juice
2	endives, separated, leaves cut in ½
1	small bunch watercress
1	Boston lettuce, in leaves
1	yellow pepper, cut in thin strips
2 cups	(500 ml) ripe strawberries, hulled
	salt and pepper

Using whisk, mix vinegar with oil, sugar and lemon juice; season well and set dressing aside.

Place endives and watercress in salad bowl. Tear lettuce leaves into smaller pieces and add to bowl with yellow pepper and strawberries.

Whisk dressing and pour over salad. Toss and serve.

The Best Bean Salad

(serves 4-6)

1 SERVING	420 CALORIES	35g CARBOHYDRATE
19g PROTEIN	26g FAT	2.0g FIBER

1½ cups	(375 ml) white beans, soaked in cold water overnight
1	carrot, sliced
1	onion, chopped
1 tsp	(5 ml) celery seed
2	bay leaves
1 tsp	(5 ml) basil
1 tsp	(5 ml) chopped parsley
1 cup	(250 ml) cooked red kidney beans
1 cup	(250 ml) black-eyed peas (ready to serve)
1 tsp	(5 ml) vegetable oil
4	slices back bacon, ¼ in (0.65 cm) thick, diced
1	medium onion, chopped
1	garlic clove, smashed and chopped
1 tbsp	(15 ml) strong mustard
¼ cup	(50 ml) raspberry wine vinegar
½ cup	(125 ml) olive oil
	salt and pepper

Drain beans and place in large saucepan. Add carrot, 1 chopped onion, celery seed, bay leaves, basil and parsley.

Pour in enough water to cover by 2 in (5 cm). Partially cover and cook 1½ hours, skimming as necessary during cooking.

Drain beans and vegetables; transfer to salad bowl.

Add kidney beans and peas; toss and set aside.

Heat vegetable oil in small frying pan. Cook bacon, remaining onion and garlic 3 to 4 minutes over medium-high heat or until browned.

Stir this into salad mixture.

Mix mustard, vinegar and oil together in small bowl; season well and whisk. Pour over beans, toss and serve warm or slightly chilled.

1 Drain beans and place in large saucepan with carrot, 1 chopped onion and seasonings. Cover with water and cook 1½ hours partially covered; skim as necessary.

3 Cook bacon with remaining onion and garlic in hot oil, then add to salad bowl.

2 Add kidney beans and peas to drained white beans and vegetables; toss and set aside.

4 Pour dressing over beans, toss and serve warm or cold.

Tomato Mustard Salad

(serves 4)

1 SERVING	553 CALORIES	8g CARBOHYDRATE
5g PROTEIN	67g FAT	0.8g FIBER

4	ripe tomatoes, cut in ½ and sliced
2	shallots, finely chopped
1 tsp	(5 ml) chopped parsley
1 tsp	(5 ml) chopped chives
2	hard-boiled eggs, sliced
1 tbsp	(15 ml) Dijon mustard
¼ cup	(50 ml) wine vinegar
1 cup	(250 ml) olive oil
	salt and pepper

Place tomatoes, shallots, parsley, chives and eggs in bowl; season well.

Place mustard, vinegar and oil in another bowl. Mix together with whisk and season well.

Pour vinaigrette over tomatoes to taste, toss and serve.

Light Side Salad

(serves 4)

1 SERVING	184 CALORIES	28g CARBOHYDRATE
4g PROTEIN	8g FAT	1.4g FIBER

3	bananas, peeled and sliced
2	celery stalks, thinly sliced
12	cherry tomatoes, halved
1 tbsp	(15 ml) lemon juice
4 tbsp	(60 ml) sour cream
¼ cup	(50 ml) chopped walnuts
	salt and pepper
	Boston lettuce leaves

Place bananas, celery and tomatoes in bowl. Mix in lemon juice and sour cream; season well.

Arrange lettuce leaves on side plates, add salad and sprinkle servings with chopped walnuts.

Cucumber Salad with Sour Cream Dressing

(serves 4)

1 SERVING	79 CALORIES	12g CARBOHYDRATE
3g PROTEIN	3g FAT	1.1g FIBER

1	cucumber, peeled, seeded and sliced
2	celery stalks, sliced
12	cherry tomatoes, halved
3	hearts of palm, sliced
1 tbsp	(15 ml) chopped parsley
4 tbsp	(60 ml) sour cream
¼ tsp	(1 ml) dry mustard
1 tsp	(5 ml) red wine vinegar
	juice 1 lemon
	pinch sugar
	salt and pepper
	alfalfa sprouts for decoration
	pinch paprika

Place cucumber, celery, tomatoes, hearts of palm and parsley in salad bowl. Toss gently.

Mix together remaining ingredients with the exception of alfalfa sprouts and paprika.

Pour dressing over salad and toss to coat evenly. Arrange servings on small bed of alfalfa sprouts and sprinkle with a dash of paprika.

Watercress Salad

(serves 4)

1 SERVING	614 CALORIES	12g CARBOHYDRATE
18g PROTEIN	57g FAT	1.7g FIBER

¼ cup	(50 ml) wine vinegar
½ cup	(125 ml) olive oil
½	zucchini, in julienne and blanched
¼ lb	(125 g) green beans, pared and cooked
2	endives, leaves separated
1	small bunch watercress
6 oz	(170 g) cheddar cheese, in julienne
2	hard-boiled eggs, sliced
½ cup	(125 ml) chopped walnuts
½	ripe avocado, sliced thick
	salt and pepper
	juice 1 lemon

Mix vinegar, salt, pepper and lemon juice together in small bowl. Very slowly incorporate oil while mixing constantly with whisk. Set dressing aside.

Arrange remaining ingredients in large salad bowl. Pour in dressing, toss and serve.

Endive Salad Robert

(serves 4)

1 SERVING	429 CALORIES	33g CARBOHYDRATE
22g PROTEIN	21g FAT	2.7g FIBER

6	artichoke bottoms, cut in 3
5	endives, leaves well washed
1	cooked chicken breast, skinned and in julienne
1	Boston lettuce
2	tomatoes, cored and in wedges
½	cucumber, peeled, seeded and sliced
1	onion, finely chopped
¼ cup	(50 ml) wine vinegar
1 cup	(250 ml) dry white wine
⅔ cup	(150 ml) brown sauce, heated
	salt and pepper
	your favorite vinaigrette

Place artichoke bottoms, endives and chicken in salad bowl.

Tear washed lettuce leaves into smaller pieces; add to bowl along with tomatoes and cucumber.

Place onion in small saucepan. Add vinegar and wine and season with pepper. Cook 4 minutes over medium-high heat.

Mix in brown sauce and season; continue cooking 2 minutes.

Mix this sauce to taste with your favorite vinaigrette, then pour over salad, toss and serve.

Refrigerate remaining brown sauce for other uses.

Endives with Cucumber Mayonnaise

(serves 4)

1 SERVING	576 CALORIES	24g CARBOHYDRATE
42g PROTEIN	35g FAT	0.7g FIBER

½	cucumber, peeled and seeded
1¼ cups	(300 ml) mayonnaise
¼ tsp	(1 ml) paprika
¼ tsp	(1 ml) Tabasco sauce
1 tsp	(5 ml) lemon juice
3	endives, separated, leaves cut in ½
1	apple, peeled, cored and sliced
4	slices Black Forest ham, in julienne
2 tbsp	(30 ml) pine nuts
	salt and pepper

Place cucumber in food processor and purée.

Add mayonnaise, paprika, Tabasco sauce, lemon juice, salt and pepper; blend 30 seconds. Set aside.

Arrange endives, apple and ham in large salad bowl. Add cucumber mayonnaise to taste, mix well and serve.

Garnish individual portions with pine nuts.

Potato Bacon Salad

(serves 4)

1 SERVING	263 CALORIES	31g CARBOHYDRATE
10g PROTEIN	22g FAT	0.8g FIBER

2	green onions, chopped
1	shallot, chopped
6	potatoes, cooked in jackets and still hot, peeled and cubed
1 tbsp	(15 ml) chopped parsley
4	slices crisp bacon, chopped
3 tbsp	(45 ml) wine vinegar
⅓ cup	(75 ml) olive oil
3 tbsp	(45 ml) dry white wine
	salt and pepper

Place onions, shallot, potatoes and parsley in large bowl; toss and season.

Add bacon and remaining ingredients; toss gently but well.

Cool before serving.

Warm Potato Salad

(serves 4)

1 SERVING	236 CALORIES	18g CARBOHYDRATE
5g PROTEIN	16g FAT	0.5g FIBER

4	medium potatoes
2	hard-boiled eggs, chopped
2 tbsp	(30 ml) wine vinegar
4 tbsp	(60 ml) olive oil
1 tbsp	(15 ml) chopped chives
	salt and pepper
	few sprigs fresh watercress

Cook potatoes in jackets in salted boiling water.

When cooked, drain well and let stand 5 minutes in saucepan.

Peel potatoes, cut in ½ and slice; place in bowl.

Add eggs and toss gently. Add remaining ingredients, except watercress, and toss well.

Serve salad decorated with watercress.

Potato Salad with Mussels

(serves 4)

1 SERVING	470 CALORIES	27g CARBOHYDRATE
20g PROTEIN	32g FAT	1.3g FIBER

1 tsp	(5 ml) curry powder
1 tsp	(5 ml) sugar
4 tbsp	(60 ml) wine vinegar
½ cup	(125 ml) olive oil
½ tsp	(2 ml) lemon juice
1 tbsp	(15 ml) chopped parsley
1	garlic clove, smashed and chopped
1	bunch asparagus tips, cooked
4	potatoes, cooked in jackets and still hot
2	hard-boiled eggs, quartered
1½ cups	(375 ml) marinated mussels, drained
2 tbsp	(30 ml) chopped sweet pimento
	few blanched snow pea pods
	salt and pepper

Mix curry, sugar, wine vinegar, oil, salt and pepper together in bowl. Whisk until completely incorporated.

Blend in lemon juice, parsley and garlic; set dressing aside.

Place cooked asparagus in large salad bowl.

Peel hot potatoes and cut into large cubes. Add to bowl along with remaining ingredients.

Whisk dressing again and pour over salad. Toss and serve.

Hot Veggie Side Salad

(serves 4)

1 SERVING	187 CALORIES	14g CARBOHYDRATE
3g PROTEIN	10g FAT	1.5g FIBER

½	red pepper, diced large
½	yellow pepper, diced large
1	onion, diced large
1 cup	(250 ml) dry white wine
1	celery stalk, sliced thick
3	green onion, in 1 in (2.5 cm) lengths
¼	head broccoli, in flowerets
⅓	cucumber, peeled, halved, seeded and sliced thick
⅓	zucchini, sliced thick
¼	Chinese cabbage, sliced thick
2	garlic cloves, smashed and chopped
1 tbsp	(15 ml) chopped parsley
2	bay leaves
1 tsp	(5 ml) basil
3 tbsp	(45 ml) olive oil
3 tbsp	(45 ml) wine vinegar
	salt and pepper
	fresh mint to taste
	fresh dill to taste
	juice ½ lime

Place peppers, diced onion, wine, celery and green onions in skillet. Season, cover and cook 3 minutes over high heat.

Add all remaining ingredients, except lime juice, and cook 6 minutes covered over medium-high heat.

Sprinkle in lime juice and serve immediately.

1 Cut and trim the vegetables as neatly as possible to further enhance the finished product.

2 Place peppers, diced onion, wine, celery and green onions in skillet. Season, cover and cook 3 minutes over high heat.

3 Add all remaining ingredients, except lime juice, and cook 6 minutes covered over medium-high heat.

4 Sprinkle in lime juice and serve immediately.

Marinated Mushrooms

(serves 4)

1 SERVING	335 CALORIES	14g CARBOHYDRATE
6g PROTEIN	31g FAT	1.8g FIBER

2 lb	(900 g) fresh mushrooms, well cleaned
1 tbsp	(15 ml) butter
1 tbsp	(15 ml) chopped parsley
1	lemon, cut in ½
1 cup	(250 ml) dry red wine
¼ cup	(50 ml) wine vinegar
½ cup	(125 ml) olive oil
1 tsp	(5 ml) tarragon
¼ tsp	(1 ml) ground cloves
1	shallot, chopped
	salt and pepper

Place mushrooms, butter and parsley in saucepan. Squeeze juice from lemon halves, add to saucepan and season well.

Pour in wine, vinegar and olive oil. Mix well.

Add remaining ingredients, season and cook 8 to 10 minutes over high heat with cover. Stir once or twice during cooking.

Cool mushrooms before serving.

Arrange on fresh lettuce leaves with slices of lemon if desired.

1 Place mushrooms, butter and parsley in saucepan. Squeeze juice from lemon halves, add to saucepan and season well.

3 Pour in vinegar.

2 Pour in wine.

4 Pour in olive oil.

Rice Salad with Lemon Dressing

(serves 4)

1 SERVING	622 CALORIES	33g CARBOHYDRATE
27g PROTEIN	43g FAT	1.3g FIBER

4 tbsp	(60 ml) lemon juice
1	egg yolk
¾ cup	(175 ml) sunflower oil
2 cups	(500 ml) cooked rice
1	red pepper, diced small
1	celery stalk, sliced
16	cooked shrimp, cut in 3
1	bunch asparagus, tips cooked and cut in 1 in (2.5 cm) lengths
¼ lb	(125 g) cooked green beans, cut in 2
1 tbsp	(15 ml) chopped parsley
	pinch sugar
	dash paprika
	salt and pepper

Place lemon juice, egg yolk, sugar, paprika, salt and pepper in small bowl. Whisk together until well incorporated.

Incorporate oil in thin stream while whisking constantly. Season very well.

Place remaining ingredients in large salad bowl. Pour in dressing, season and toss well. Serve.

Chick Pea Salad

(serves 4)

1 SERVING	521 CALORIES	50g CARBOHYDRATE
17g PROTEIN	6g FAT	3.3g FIBER

19 oz	(540 ml) can chick peas, drained
¼ lb	(250 g) cooked green beans
1½ cups	(375 ml) marinated cauliflower, drained
1 tbsp	(15 ml) chopped parsley
1	yellow pepper, diced
1 tbsp	(15 ml) tarragon
¼ cup	(50 ml) cider vinegar
½ tsp	(2 ml) sugar
½ cup	(125 ml) olive oil
1 tsp	(5 ml) fresh chopped mint
	salt and pepper
	few drops lemon juice
	Tabasco sauce to taste

Place chick peas, beans, cauliflower, parsley and yellow pepper in large salad bowl.

In separate bowl, mix together remaining ingredients, whisking until well incorporated.

Pour dressing over salad, toss and serve.

Hearty Pasta Salad

(serves 4)

1 SERVING	395 CALORIES	40g CARBOHYDRATE
13g PROTEIN	21g FAT	1.9g FIBER

1	garlic clove, smashed and chopped
1 tbsp	(15 ml) Dijon mustard
1	egg yolk
1	hard-boiled egg
¼ tsp	(1 ml) paprika
⅓ cup	(75 ml) olive oil
1½ cups	(375 ml) cooked medium pasta bows
1 cup	(250 ml) cooked red kidney beans
½ cup	(125 ml) cooked green peas
½ cup	(125 ml) blanched diced carrots
1	green onion, chopped
2	artichoke bottoms, sliced
1	celery stalk, sliced
1	leaf Chinese lettuce, sliced
	salt and pepper
	grated Parmesan cheese to taste
	juice 1 lemon

Place garlic, mustard and egg yolk in small bowl; whisk together.

Add hard-boiled egg by forcing through sieve. Whisk in paprika, salt, pepper, dash of Parmesan cheese and lemon juice.

Incorporate oil in thin stream while whisking constantly. Set dressing aside.

Place remaining ingredients in large salad bowl and pour in dressing. Toss, correct seasoning and serve.

1 Add hard-boiled egg to dressing ingredients by forcing through sieve.

3 Incorporate oil in thin stream while whisking constantly.

2 Whisk in paprika, salt, pepper, dash of Parmesan cheese and lemon juice.

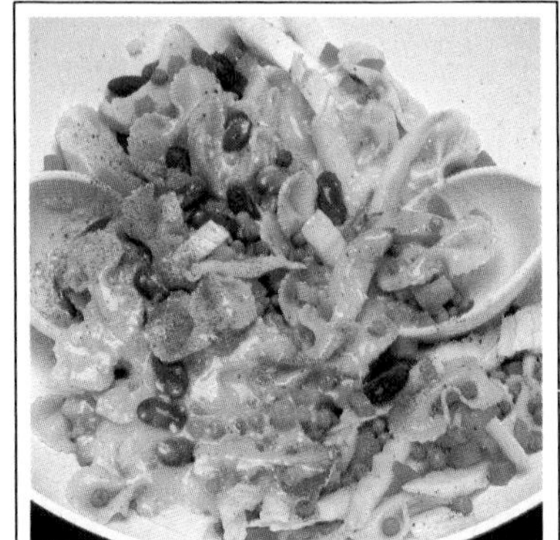

4 Pour dressing over salad ingredients, toss, correct seasoning and serve.

Chicken Salad

(serves 4)

1 SERVING	286 CALORIES	18g CARBOHYDRATE
32g PROTEIN	10g FAT	1.0g FIBER

2	chicken breasts, skinned and halved
1	celery stalk, sliced thick on angle
1	parsley sprig
4	lemon slices
1	onion, diced large
¼ tsp	(1 ml) celery seed
1	green onion, chopped
1	celery stalk, sliced
2	hard-boiled eggs, sliced
¼ tsp	(1 ml) paprika
6	water chestnuts, sliced
½ cup	(125 ml) seedless green grapes
2 tbsp	(30 ml) diced pimento
3 tbsp	(45 ml) mayonnaise
1 tsp	(5 ml) curry powder
	salt and pepper
	several cherry tomatoes, halved
	juice 1 lemon

Place chicken, first celery stalk, parsley sprig, lemon slices, diced onion, celery seed, salt and pepper in saucepan. Pour in enough water to cover. Cover and cook about 18 minutes over medium heat, depending on size of breasts.

When chicken is cooked, drain and discard other ingredients. Bone chicken and cut meat in large slices.

Place green onion, other celery stalk, eggs and paprika in bowl. Add chicken and season well.

Mix in water chestnuts, grapes, pimento and tomatoes; toss slightly.

Mix in remaining ingredients until well incorporated and serve salad on lettuce leaves.

1 Place chicken, first celery stalk, parsley sprig, lemon slices, diced onion, celery seed, salt and pepper in saucepan. Add water to cover and cook, covered, about 18 minutes over medium heat depending on size of breasts.

3 Add cooked chicken and season.

2 Place green onion, other celery stalk, eggs and paprika in bowl.

4 Add remaining ingredients, mix until well incorporated and correct seasoning.

Chicken and Beef Salad

(serves 4)

1 SERVING	621 CALORIES	7g CARBOHYDRATE
38g PROTEIN	49g FAT	0.9g FIBER

1 tbsp	(15 ml) Dijon mustard
1 tsp	(5 ml) chopped fresh tarragon
1	garlic clove, smashed and chopped
3 tbsp	(45 ml) wine vinegar
2 tbsp	(30 ml) lemon juice
¾ cup	(175 ml) olive oil
1	head Chinese lettuce
1	cooked chicken breast, skinned and boned
1 cup	(250 ml) leftover cooked steak, in strips
2	tomatoes, cut in half, then in wedges
1	celery stalk, sliced
2	hard-boiled eggs, sliced
	salt and pepper

Place mustard, tarragon, garlic, vinegar and lemon juice in small bowl; whisk together.

Incorporate oil in thin stream while whisking constantly. Correct seasoning and set aside.

Wash and dry lettuce; tear leaves into smaller pieces. Cut cooked chicken breast into strips; place in salad bowl with lettuce.

Add steak, tomatoes, celery and eggs to salad bowl. Toss everything well.

Whisk vinaigrette and pour over salad to taste. Toss well, season and serve.

Chinatown Salad

(serves 4)

1 SERVING	263 CALORIES	27g CARBOHYDRATE
19g PROTEIN	2g FAT	1.9g FIBER

1	cooked chicken breast, skinned, boned and sliced thick
1 tbsp	(15 ml) chopped fresh ginger
2	garlic cloves, smashed and chopped
1 tbsp	(15 ml) soya sauce
1½ cups	(375 ml) shredded radicchio
1 cup	(250 ml) cooked green peas
1 cup	(250 ml) bean sprouts
1	yellow pepper, thinly sliced
2	green onions, chopped
3 tbsp	(45 ml) red wine vinegar
¼ cup	(50 ml) sesame oil
	salt and pepper

Place chicken, ginger, garlic, soya sauce, radicchio and green peas in bowl. Season well.

Add bean sprouts, yellow pepper and green onions. Pour in wine vinegar and oil. Toss everything to incorporate well, correct seasoning and serve.

1 Place chicken, ginger, garlic and soya sauce in bowl.

2 Add radicchio and green peas; season well.

3 Add bean sprouts, yellow pepper and green onions. Pour in wine vinegar.

4 Pour in oil, toss and correct seasoning.

Elegant Strawberry and Shrimp Salad

(serves 4)

1 SERVING	459 CALORIES	70g CARBOHYDRATE
31g PROTEIN	6g FAT	1.8g FIBER

¾ lb	(375 g) cooked shrimp
12	canned baby corn on the cob
1	pear, peeled and sliced
½ lb	(250 g) ripe strawberries, hulled and halved
4 tbsp	(60 ml) sour cream
1 tsp	(5 ml) dry mustard
1 tbsp	(15 ml) apple cider
1 tsp	(5 ml) ground ginger
	juice 1 lemon
	pinch sugar
	few drops Tabasco sauce

Place shrimp, corn, pear and strawberries in salad bowl.

Mix sour cream with mustard; add lemon juice.

Whisk in cider, sugar, ginger and Tabasco sauce.

Pour over salad and mix well. Serve on lettuce leaves if desired.

Shrimp and Pepper Salad

(serves 4)

1 SERVING	412 CALORIES	9g CARBOHYDRATE
17g PROTEIN	35g FAT	1.5g FIBER

2 tbsp	(30 ml) vegetable oil
1	onion, thinly sliced
2	yellow peppers, thinly sliced
2	garlic cloves, smashed and chopped
1½ cups	(375 ml) thinly sliced eggplant
½ lb	(250 g) cooked shrimp
3 tbsp	(45 ml) wine vinegar
½ cup	(125 ml) olive oil
	salt and pepper

Heat vegetable oil in large frying pan. Cook onion, peppers, garlic and eggplant 7 minutes over medium heat with cover. Stir 2 to 3 times during cooking and season well.

Remove vegetables from pan and transfer to salad bowl; set aside.

Add shrimp, vinegar and olive oil to frying pan; season well. Cook 1 to 2 minutes over medium-high heat.

Drain most of the oil off, then add shrimp to salad bowl. Toss and cool slightly before serving.

Scallop Salad

(serves 4)

1 SERVING	309 CALORIES	28g CARBOHYDRATE
35g PROTEIN	6g FAT	1.6g FIBER

3	large potatoes, peeled and cut into balls
1 lb	(500 g) large mushrooms, quartered
1 tbsp	(15 ml) lemon juice
1 tbsp	(15 ml) oil
¼ tsp	(1 ml) fennel seed
1 lb	(500 g) scallops
1 tbsp	(15 ml) chopped parsley
3 tbsp	(45 ml) sour cream
1 tbsp	(15 ml) Dijon mustard
1 tbsp	(15 ml) chopped pimento
	juice 1 lemon
	salt and pepper

Place potato balls in saucepan, season with salt and pour in enough cold water to cover. Bring to boil. Continue cooking 5 minutes over medium heat.

Add mushrooms, 1 tbsp (15 ml) lemon juice, oil and fennel seed; continue cooking 2 minutes.

Drop in scallops and finish cooking 1 minute.

Drain well and transfer boiled ingredients to salad bowl; sprinkle with parsley.

Squeeze in juice of 1 lemon and season well. Mix in sour cream, mustard and pimento; toss until all is evenly coated.

Serve.

Fish and Vegetable Salad

(serves 4)

1 SERVING	431 CALORIES	18g CARBOHYDRATE
15g PROTEIN	35g FAT	2.1g FIBER

3 tbsp	(45 ml) wine vinegar
2	garlic cloves, smashed and chopped
1 tbsp	(15 ml) soya sauce
½ tsp	(2 ml) sugar
½ cup	(125 ml) olive oil
2 tbsp	(30 ml) vegetable oil
2	sole filets, cut in 1 in (2.5 cm) pieces
2 cups	(500 ml) broccoli flowerets, blanched
¼ lb	(125 g) snow peas, blanched
6	cooked asparagus, cut in 2.5 cm (1 in) lengths
6	cherry tomatoes, halved
2 tbsp	(30 ml) chopped fresh chives
6	water chestnuts, sliced
¼ tsp	(1 ml) ground ginger
½ tsp	(2 ml) ground cumin
	juice 1 lemon
	salt and pepper

Whisk vinegar, garlic, soya, sugar, olive oil and lemon juice together until well incorporated; set aside.

Heat remaining oil in large frying pan. Cook fish 2 minutes each side over high heat.

Add broccoli and pea pods; mix well.

Add remaining ingredients, season to taste and cook 3 to 4 minutes over high heat.

Transfer mixture to large salad bowl. Whisk dressing and pour over ingredients; toss well and serve immediately.

1 Cook fish in hot oil for 2 minutes on each side over high heat.

3 Add remaining ingredients, season to taste and cook 3 to 4 minutes over high heat.

2 Add broccoli and pea pods; mix well.

4 Pour prepared dressing over salad, toss and serve.

Penne with Crab

(serves 4)

1 SERVING	494 CALORIES	40g CARBOHYDRATE
14g PROTEIN	30g FAT	0.6g FIBER

¼ cup	(50 ml) wine vinegar
1 tbsp	(15 ml) chopped parsley
½ cup	(125 ml) olive oil
1 tbsp	(15 ml) Dijon mustard
1 tsp	(5 ml) sugar
1 tsp	(5 ml) tarragon
¼ cup	(50 ml) grated Parmesan cheese
1	shallot, finely chopped
2	garlic cloves, smashed and chopped
¼ tsp	(1 ml) Tabasco sauce
3 cups	(750 ml) cooked penne
5	cooked asparagus, diced
2	hearts of palm, sliced
4.25 oz	(120 g) can crabmeat, well drained
2 tbsp	(30 ml) chopped pickled sweet pimento
	salt and pepper
	lettuce leaves for serving

Whisk together vinegar, parsley and oil until well incorporated.

Add mustard, sugar, tarragon, cheese, shallot, garlic, Tabasco, salt and pepper; continue whisking until vinaigrette has thickened.

Place remaining ingredients in salad bowl. Pour in vinaigrette, season and toss. Serve on lettuce leaves.

1 Whisk together vinegar, parsley and oil until well incorporated.

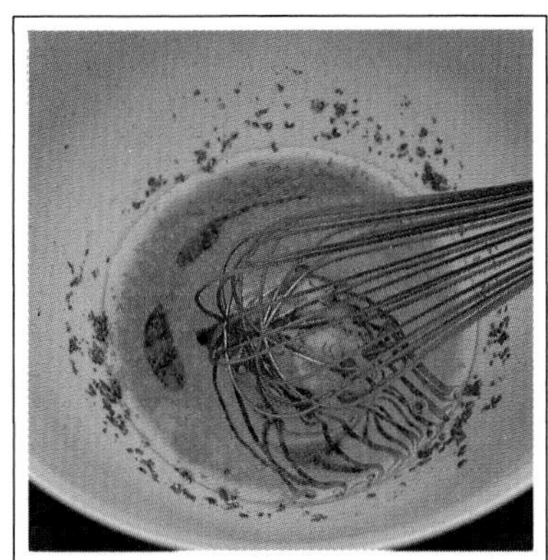

3 Place salad ingredients in bowl.

2 Add mustard, sugar, tarragon, cheese, shallot, garlic, Tabasco, salt and pepper; continue whisking until thickened.

4 Pour in vinaigrette, season and toss.

Fancy Meal Salad

(serves 4)

1 SERVING	306 CALORIES	41g CARBOHYDRATE
13g PROTEIN	13g FAT	4.2g FIBER

3	pears, peeled and cut in wedges
½ lb	(250 g) white mushrooms, in julienne
3 cups	(750 ml) cooked green beans
1	yellow pepper, thinly sliced
1 cup	(250 ml) seedless green grapes
5 oz	(142 g) can crabmeat, drained
1 tbsp	(15 ml) curry powder
3 tbsp	(45 ml) lemon juice
1 tbsp	(15 ml) horseradish
1 cup	(250 ml) sour cream
1 tbsp	(15 ml) chopped chives
	salt and pepper

Place pears, mushrooms, beans, yellow pepper, grapes and crabmeat in salad bowl.

Place curry powder, lemon juice and horseradish in small bowl; whisk together very well and season generously.

Add sour cream and chives; whisk again until incorporated. Season again to taste and pour over salad; toss and serve.

Herring Salad

(serves 4)

1 SERVING	595 CALORIES	29g CARBOHYDRATE
13g PROTEIN	49g FAT	1.0g FIBER

1	hard-boiled egg
1 tbsp	(15 ml) Dijon mustard
4 tbsp	(60 ml) wine vinegar
¾ cup	(175 ml) olive oil
1 tbsp	(15 ml) lemon juice
3	cooked marinated herring filets, cubed
3	apples, peeled, cored and sliced
3	cooked potatoes, peeled and sliced
2	pickles, in julienne
3	canned beets, sliced
	salt and pepper

Cut hard-boiled egg in half and force yolk and white through sieve into bowl.

Add mustard and vinegar; whisk well.

Incorporate oil in thin stream while whisking constantly. Mix in lemon juice and correct seasoning.

Place herring, apples, potatoes, pickles and beets in large salad bowl.

Pour in vinaigrette to taste, toss well and correct seasoning.

APPETIZERS

APPETIZERS

Appetizers, in their countless shapes and sizes, come to our tables in hopes of awakening sleepy palates by tantalizing our senses with a sampling of flavors and textures that are married to perfection. Whether served hot or cold, appetizers are meant to be eaten for the pure pleasure of eating, so they should never be to filling or so complicated that they prevent the diner from enjoying the fleeting moments with ease. From the simplest open-faced canapé to servings of fancy Lobster Liza, appetizers encourage spontaneity not just with ingredients but with the way in which they are presented. If you are serving an assortment of buffet-style appetizers, try arranging the platters on different levels surrounded by attractive plates, cutlery and napkins. Although hot appetizers require a little more care and planning (so they can be served promptly), take a few extra minutes to decorate portions with fresh herbs or condiments such as pickles and olives. The following recipes offer you an interesting selection of hot and cold dishes to choose from. Remember that an appetizer doesn't necessarily have to reflect what the main meal is about — so make your choice by what strikes your fancy and have fun with it!

Lobster Liza

(serves 4-6)

1 SERVING	326 CALORIES	27g CARBOHYDRATE
25g PROTEIN	11g FAT	0.9g FIBER

2 tbsp	(30 ml) butter
2	shallots, chopped
1	green pepper, chopped
1 lb	(500 g) chopped lobster meat, cooked
1¼ cups	(300 ml) thick tomato sauce, heated
1 tbsp	(15 ml) lemon juice
½ cup	(125 ml) grated Parmesan cheese
	salt and pepper
	toasted white bread

Heat butter in sauce pan. Cook shallots and green pepper 3 minutes over low heat.

Mix in lobster meat and tomato sauce; season well and add lemon juice. Cook over low heat 2 to 3 minutes.

Correct seasoning and spoon mixture over toast. Top with cheese and broil 2 to 3 minutes in oven.

Deep-Fried Fish

(serves 4-6)

1 SERVING	460 CALORIES	53g CARBOHYDRATE
29g PROTEIN	14g FAT	trace FIBER

2 cups	(500 ml) crushed soda crackers
1	garlic clove, smashed and chopped
1 tbsp	(15 ml) curry powder
1 tbsp	(15 ml) celery seed
4	large sole filets
1½ cups	(375 ml) seasoned flour
3	beaten eggs
	pepper
	peanut oil

Mix crackers with garlic, curry powder and celery seed; set aside in bowl.

Cut fish into strips ½ in (1.2 cm) wide. Throughly coat in flour.

Dip fish strips in beaten eggs, then in soda cracker crumbs. Season well with pepper.

Deep-fry in hot oil for 2 minutes.

Pat dry with paper towels and serve with lemon wedges.

Hot Shrimp Kebabs

(serves 4)

1 SERVING	422 CALORIES	20g CARBOHYDRATE
32g PROTEIN	24g FAT	0.7g FIBER

24	shrimp, peeled and deveined
3 tbsp	(45 ml) sesame oil
1 tbsp	(15 ml) lemon juice
¼ tsp	(1 ml) Tabasco sauce
24	large cubes fresh pineapple
24	wedges red apple
	salt and pepper
	melted butter seasoned with lemon juice

Place shrimp, oil, lemon juice and Tabasco sauce in bowl. Marinate 30 minutes.

Alternate shrimp, pineapple and apple on short wooden skewers. Baste with melted lemon butter and season very well.

Place skewers on ovenproof platter and broil 3 minutes each side in oven. Baste frequently.

Smoked Salmon Canapés

(serves 4-6)

1 SERVING	658 CALORIES	47g CARBOHYDRATE
34g PROTEIN	36g FAT	-- FIBER

1 lb	(500 g) sliced smoked salmon
½ cup	(125 ml) soft butter
1 tbsp	(15 ml) lemon juice
¼ tsp	(1 ml) Tabasco sauce
1	loaf French bread, sliced
3 tbsp	(45 ml) capers
	pepper
	sliced hard-boiled eggs

Place 4 slices of salmon in food processor. Add butter, lemon juice, Tabasco sauce and pepper; blend 30 seconds.

Butter bread with mixture and top with remaining smoked salmon. Sprinkle canapés with capers and decorate platter with sliced boiled eggs.

Rice Canapés

(serves 6-8)

1 SERVING	336 CALORIES	49g CARBOHYDRATE
12g PROTEIN	10g FAT	trace FIBER

5	hard-boiled eggs, chopped
1 cup	(250 ml) cooked saffron rice
½	celery stalk, diced small
2	green onions, finely chopped
1 tsp	(5 ml) chopped chives
3 tbsp	(45 ml) mayonnaise
2 tbsp	(30 ml) sour cream
1 tsp	(5 ml) Worcestershire sauce
	juice ½ lemon
	salt and pepper
	sliced Italian bread

Place eggs, rice, celery, onions and chives in bowl; mix well.

Add mayonnaise, sour cream, Worcestershire sauce, lemon juice, salt and pepper; mix again until incorporated.

Spread over sliced Italian bread and serve.

Party Canapés

(serves 6)

1 SERVING	289 CALORIES	39g CARBOHYDRATE
7g PROTEIN	10g FAT	1.0g FIBER

4	stems watercress, finely chopped
1	celery stalk, chopped
1	red apple, peeled, cored, quartered and chopped
1 tbsp	(15 ml) pine nuts
1 tbsp	(15 ml) chopped parsley
1 tsp	(5 ml) curry powder
2 tbsp	(30 ml) mayonnaise
1 tbsp	(15 ml) sour cream
1 tsp	(5 ml) lemon juice
10-12	slices "party" light rye bread with caraway seeds
	salt and pepper
	halved cherry tomatoes for garnish

Mix all ingredients together except bread and tomatoes.

Season to taste, spread mixture over bread slices and garnish with halved cherry tomatoes. If desired serve with blanched broccoli.

Cold Beef Appetizer

(serves 4)

1 SERVING	866 CALORIES	60g CARBOHYDRATE
31g PROTEIN	56g FAT	0.5g FIBER

½ lb	(250 g) soft butter
1	medium onion, finely chopped
1	garlic clove, smashed and chopped
1 tbsp	(15 ml) paprika
1	loaf French bread
½ lb	(250 g) thin slices cooked roast beef
	few drops lemon juice
	salt and pepper

Heat 1 tbsp (15 ml) butter in small saucepan. Cook onion and garlic 3 minutes over medium heat.

Mix in paprika and continue cooking 1 minute. Remove and purée in food processor; set aside to cool.

Mix onion mixture, remaining butter, lemon juice, salt and pepper together until well incorporated.

Slice bread and toast in oven. Spread butter over pieces of bread and top with roast beef.

Serve cold with pickles.

Fancy Pastrami Canapés

(serves 4)

1 SERVING	569 CALORIES	17g CARBOHYDRATE
31g PROTEIN	41g FAT	trace FIBER

10	thin slices deli bread
4 tbsp	(60 ml) butter
1 tbsp	(15 ml) mustard
1 tsp	(5 ml) horseradish
10	slices pastrami
1 cup	(250 ml) fine herb pâté
2 tbsp	(30 ml) sour cream
	shredded lettuce for garnish

Place slices of bread on cutting board.

Mix butter with mustard and horseradish; spread evenly over bread.

Place slice of pastrami on each slice of bread, trim crusts and cut into two triangles.

Arrange canapés on shredded lettuce.

Mix pâté with sour cream until well blended. Place in pastry bag and decorate canapés with mixture.

Cheesy Crab Bread

(serves 6)

1 SERVING	335 CALORIES	26g CARBOHYDRATE
13g PROTEIN	20g FAT	trace FIBER

3 tbsp	(45 ml) butter
1	onion, chopped
¼ lb	(125 g) mushrooms, chopped
5 oz	(142 g) can crabmeat, drained
1¼ cups	(300 ml) white sauce, heated
8-10	slices white bread, toasted
½ cup	(125 ml) grated Emmenthal cheese
	salt and pepper
	few drops Tabasco sauce

Heat butter in saucepan. Cook onion and mushrooms 2 to 3 minutes over medium-high heat; season well and add Tabasco sauce.

Mix in crabmeat, season and pour in white sauce. Cook 2 minutes over medium heat.

Spoon mixture over toast, top with cheese and broil 2 minutes in oven.

Camembert Treat

(serves 6-8)

1 SERVING	243 CALORIES	26g CARBOHYDRATE
11g PROTEIN	10g FAT	trace FIBER

1 cup	(250 ml) fine breadcrumbs
3	garlic cloves, smashed and finely chopped
1 tbsp	(15 ml) chopped parsley
1 tsp	(5 ml) celery seed
1 tsp	(5 ml) sesame seed
¼ tsp	(1 ml) paprika
1	small round of Camembert cheese, chilled
½	French baguette, sliced and toasted on both sides
	dash cayenne pepper

Mix breadcrumbs with garlic, parsley and seasonings; set aside.

Remove soft crust from sides of cheese. Lightly scrape top and bottom with knife.

Place cheese in bowl with breadcrumbs and coat. Remove cheese and set on cutting board; flatten with rolling pin.

Turn cheese over, sprinkle with more breadcrumbs and roll again.

Repeat procedure using all breadcrumbs and rolling until cheese is ¼ in (0.65 cm) thick.

Using cookie cutter about the same size as the bread slices, cut out pieces of cheese and set on bread.

Broil 2 minutes in oven.

Serve cold.

Beef Strips

(serves 8-10)

1 SERVING	314 CALORIES	26g CARBOHYDRATE
19g PROTEIN	15g FAT	trace FIBER

1 tbsp	(15 ml) vegetable oil
1½ lb	(750 g) strip loin steaks, 1 in (2.5 cm) thick, fat trimmed
1	shallot, chopped
1 tbsp	(15 ml) chopped parsley
1 tsp	(5 ml) lemon juice
1 tsp	(5 ml) Worcestershire sauce
1 tbsp	(15 ml) red wine vinegar
2 tbsp	(30 ml) olive oil
3 tbsp	(45 ml) butter
1 tsp	(5 ml) strong mustard
	salt and pepper
	sliced French baguette
	endive leaves for garnish

Heat oil in large frying pan or on nonstick grill. When very hot, add meat and sear 3 minutes over medium-high heat.

Turn meat over, season well and continue searing another 3 to 4 minutes.

Turn meat over again; finish cooking 3 minutes for rare meat.

Remove meat from pan and slice thinly on an angle; place pieces on plate.

Cover meat with shallot, parsley, lemon juice, Worcestershire sauce, vinegar, oil and pepper. Cover loosely with plastic wrap and refrigerate 2 hours.

Drain meat if necessary and set aside.

Mix butter with mustard, spread over bread and toast in oven.

Remove and top with marinated meat. Serve with endive leaves as garnish.

1 Trim excess fat from meat.

3 Remove meat from pan and thinly slice on an angle; place pieces on plate.

2 Sear meat a total of 9 to 10 minutes for rare.

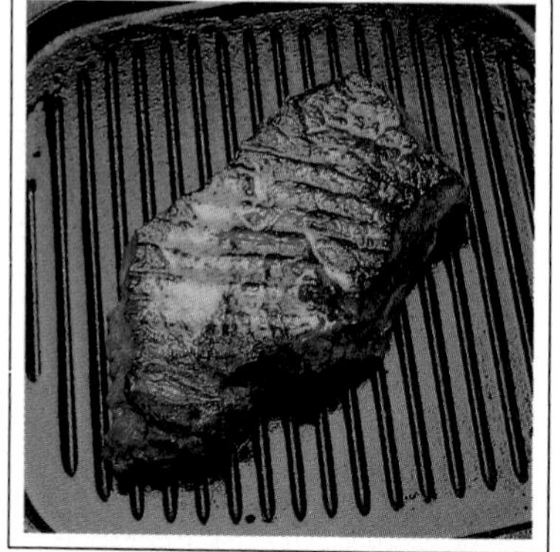

4 Cover meat with shallot, parsley, lemon juice, Worcestershire sauce, vinegar, oil and pepper. Cover loosely with plastic wrap and refrigerate 2 hours.

Cheesy Muffin Starter

(serves 4)

1 SERVING	413 CALORIES	25g CARBOHYDRATE
15g PROTEIN	29g FAT	2.0g FIBER

1 cup	(250 ml) stuffed green olives, sliced
4	green onions, chopped
1	celery stalk, chopped
2	slices processed Gruyère cheese, diced
¼ tsp	(1 ml) celery seed
¼ tsp	(1 ml) paprika
3 tbsp	(45 ml) mayonnaise
1 tbsp	(15 ml) Dijon mustard
1 tsp	(5 ml) lemon juice
¼ tsp	(1 ml) Worcestershire sauce
2	English muffins, halved
4	squares mozzarella cheese
	salt and pepper
	more paprika to taste

Place olives, onions, celery, Gruyère cheese, seasonings and mayonnaise in bowl; mix well.

Add mustard, lemon juice and Worcestershire sauce; mix again and correct seasoning.

Set muffin halves on ovenproof platter and top with olive mixture. Cover with mozzarella and dash of paprika.

Broil in oven until melted.

1 Place olives, onions and celery in bowl.

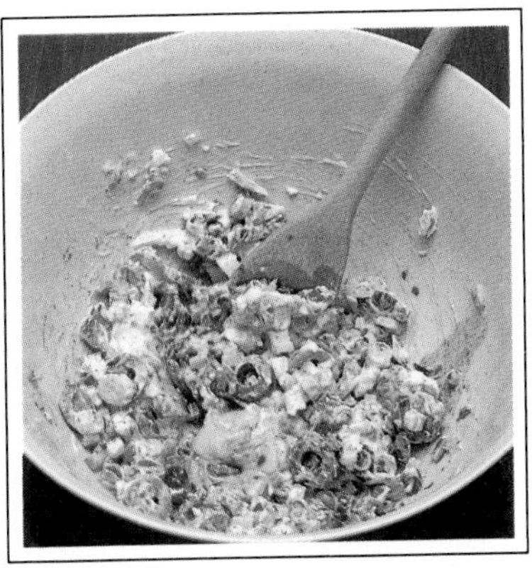

3 Add mustard, lemon juice and Worcestershire sauce; mix again and correct seasoning.

2 Add Gruyère cheese, seasonings and mayonnaise; mix well.

4 Set muffin halves on ovenproof platter and top with olive mixture. Cover with mozzarella and dash of paprika. Broil in oven until melted.

Ricotta Tomato Bread

(serves 4-6)

1 SERVING	429 CALORIES	58g CARBOHYDRATE
16g PROTEIN	14g FAT	1.0g FIBER

2 tbsp	(30 ml) vegetable oil
1	celery stalk, diced
½	green pepper, chopped
1	onion, chopped
2	garlic cloves, smashed and chopped
¼ tsp	(1 ml) paprika
¼ tsp	(1 ml) chili powder
28 oz	(796 ml) can tomatoes, drained and chopped
3 tbsp	(45 ml) tomato paste
⅓ cup	(75 ml) grated Parmesan cheese
1	French baguette, cut in half lengthwise
½ cup	(125 ml) ricotta cheese
	salt and pepper

Heat oil in large skillet. Cook celery, green pepper, onion, garlic, paprika and chili powder 4 to 5 minutes over low heat.

Mix in tomatoes and tomato paste; season well. Continue cooking 15 minutes.

Add Parmesan cheese and finish cooking 5 minutes.

Slice each bread half into 3 pieces and toast in oven.

Place bread on cookie sheet or ovenproof platter. Spoon tomato mixture over and top with ricotta cheese.

Broil 3 to 4 minutes or until melted.

Serve immediately.

1 Cook celery, green pepper, onion, garlic, paprika and chili powder in hot oil for 4 to 5 minutes over low heat.

3 Add Parmesan cheese and finish cooking 5 minutes.

2 Mix in tomatoes and tomato paste; season well. Continue cooking 15 minutes.

4 Place toasted bread on cookie sheet and add tomato mixture; top with ricotta cheese and broil in oven.

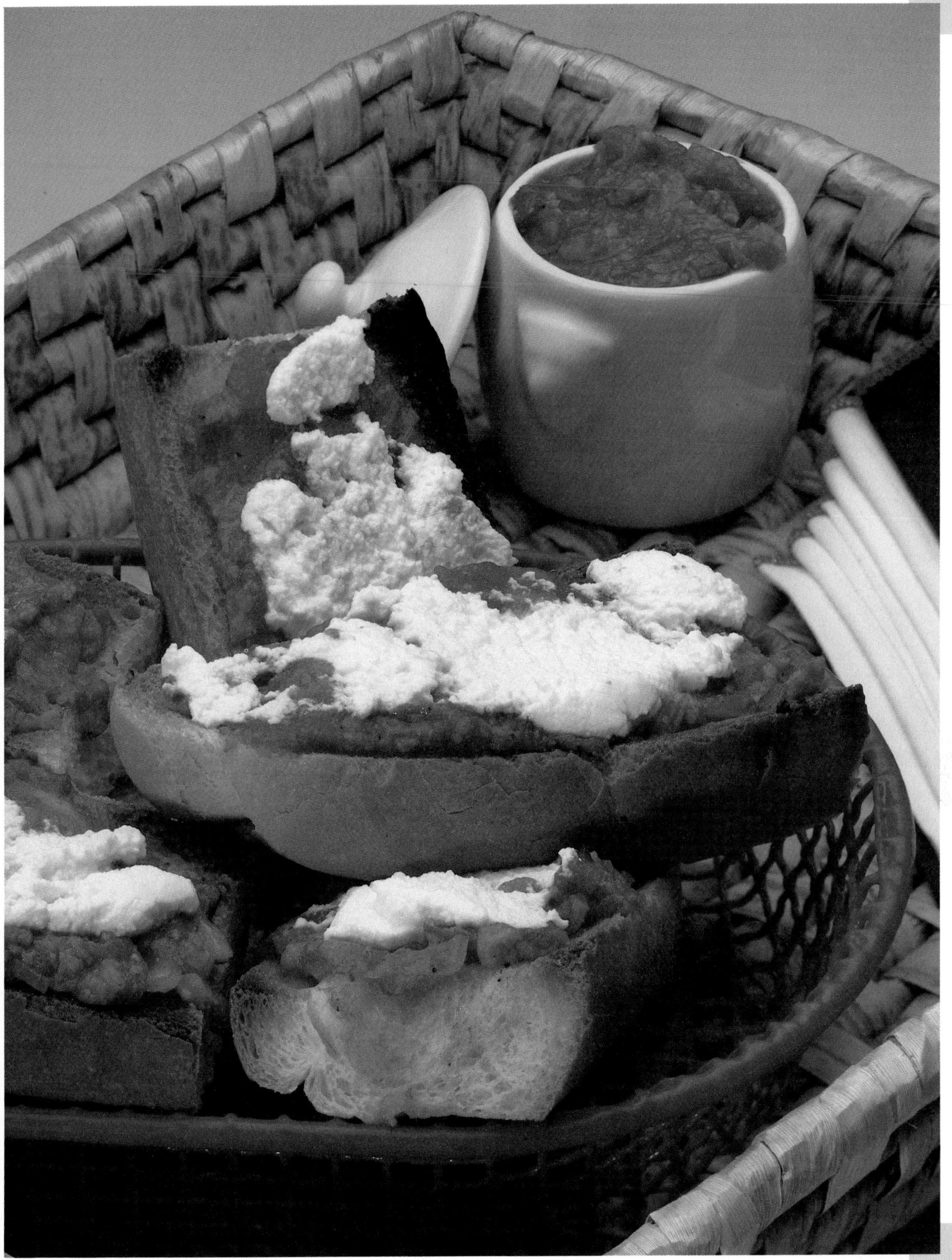

Vegetable Sandwich Loaf

(serves 6-8)

1 SERVING	323 CALORIES	42g CARBOHYDRATE
9g PROTEIN	13g FAT	trace FIBER

6 oz	(170 g) pepper cream cheese
3 tbsp	(45 ml) sour cream
1 tsp	(5 ml) chopped parsley
¼ tsp	(1 ml) paprika
1	loaf white bread, unsliced
½	English cucumber, thinly sliced
6	radishes, thinly sliced
1	small bunch asparagus, cooked
	salt and pepper

Mix cheese, sour cream, parsley, paprika, salt and pepper together in food processor until smooth.

Using long bread knife, slice off top and bottom crusts of loaf. Continue cutting loaf to obtain 4 slices. See Technique for visual help.

Spread first slice of bread with cheese mixture. Set on large sheet of aluminum foil and layer with cucumbers; season well.

Butter second slice of bread with cheese mixture on both sides and set over cucumbers. Layer radishes on bread and season well.

Butter third slice of bread with cheese mixture on both sides; place on sandwich. Arrange asparagus on bread, trimming to size; season well.

Butter last slice of bread with cheese mixture on one side only. Place, face down, over asparagus and cover sandwich loaf in foil. Use another sheet if needed.

Refrigerate overnight, then slice and serve. If desired trim off crusts before serving.

1 Mix cheese, sour cream, parsley, paprika, salt and pepper together in food processor until smooth.

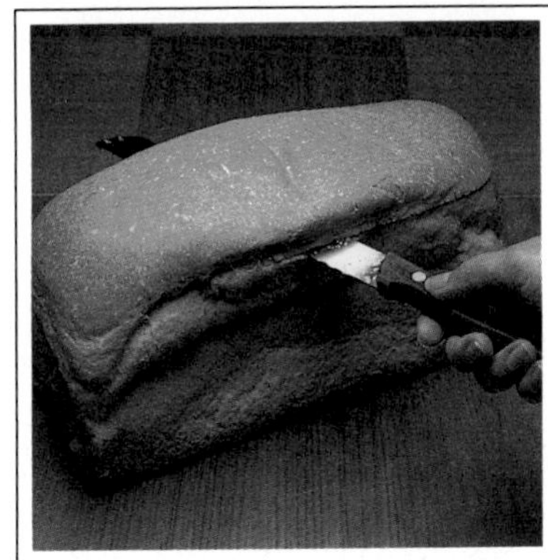

2 Using long bread knife, slice off top and bottom crusts.

3 Continue cutting loaf to obtain 4 slices.

4 Add the last vegetable layer of the sandwich.

Crêpes with Spinach

(serves 4)

1 SERVING	579 CALORIES	35g CARBOHYDRATE
22g PROTEIN	36g FAT	1.0g FIBER

1 cup	(250 ml) all-purpose flour
¼ tsp	(1 ml) salt
¼ tsp	(1 ml) paprika
¼ tsp	(1 ml) ground ginger
½ tsp	(2 ml) celery seed
3	whole eggs
1 cup	(250 ml) beer
3 tbsp	(45 ml) melted butter
½ cup	(125 ml) milk
2	10 oz (284 g) packages spinach, well washed and drained
½ cup	(125 ml) grated Parmesan cheese
¼ cup	(50 ml) olive oil
¼ tsp	(1 ml) nutmeg
½ cup	(125 ml) grated Romano cheese
1 tbsp	(15 ml) melted butter
	extra butter
	salt and pepper

Mix flour, salt, paprika, ginger and celery seed together in bowl.

Whisk in eggs until throughly blended. Add beer and whisk again. Stir in 3 tbsp (45 ml) melted butter.

Pass batter through medium-fine sieve (holes must be large enough for celery seed) into clean bowl.

Pour in milk and mix well. Refrigerate 2 hours uncovered.

Remove batter from refrigerator and mix well. If too thick, add a bit of milk.

Spread small amount of butter on crêpe pan with paper towel. Place pan over medium-high heat and when butter heats wipe off excess with paper towel.

Pour small ladle of batter on tilted crêpe pan and rotate to completely coat bottom. Allow excess batter to drip back into bowl.

Cook crêpe over medium-high heat until brown — about 1 minute. Then using long spatula knife turn crêpe over and cook other side about the same time.

After each crêpe, wipe pan with lightly buttered paper towel. Adjust heat as necessary to maintain an even temperature for all the crêpes.

Set cooked crêpes aside.

Steam spinach 3 minutes. Squeeze out excess liquid by pressing with spoon. Blend 2 minutes in food processor.

Add Parmesan cheese and blend 1 minute; season well.

Add olive oil through top in food processor while it is mixing. Correct seasoning and add nutmeg.

Lay desired amount of crêpes flat on cutting board. Spread puréed spinach over each crêpe but keep some filling for decoration.

Roll crêpes and place on cookie sheet. Sprinkle with Romano cheese and 1 tbsp (15 ml) melted butter. Broil several minutes in oven.

Decorate crêpes with reserved spinach filling.

1 Mix flour, salt, paprika, ginger and celery seed together in bowl.

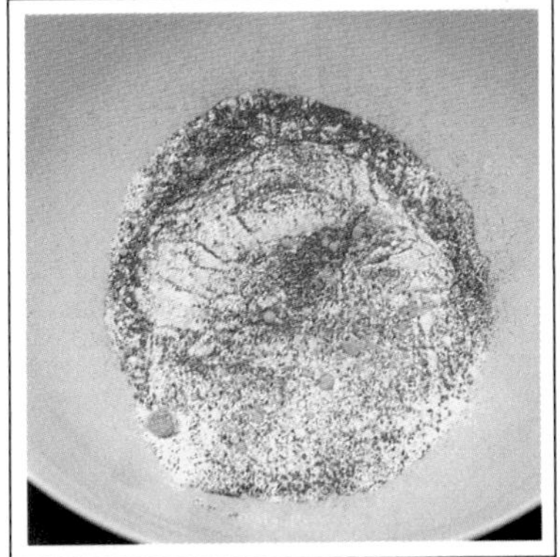

2 Whisk in eggs until thoroughly blended.

3 Cook crêpe over medium-high heat until brown — about 1 minute. Then using long spatula knife turn crêpe over.

4 Cook other side of crêpe about the same length of time.

Crab Vol-au-Vent

(serves 4-6)

1 SERVING	537 CALORIES	26g CARBOHYDRATE
16g PROTEIN	41g FAT	trace FIBER

3 tbsp	(45 ml) butter
1	shallot, chopped
½	celery stalk, chopped
8	large mushrooms, chopped
¼ tsp	(1 ml) anise
¼ tsp	(1 ml) paprika
2 tbsp	(30 ml) flour
1½ cups	(375 ml) hot milk
1 tsp	(5 ml) cumin
5 oz	(142 g) can snow crabmeat, drained
12	small vol-au-vent, cooked
1 cup	(250 ml) grated cheddar cheese
	salt and pepper

Heat butter in large skillet. Cook shallot 1 minute.

Add celery, mushrooms, anise, paprika and season well. Continue cooking 2 to 3 minutes over medium heat.

Mix in flour and cook 2 minutes over medium-low heat.

Add milk, mix well and bring to boil. Add cumin and continue cooking 4 to 5 minutes over low heat.

Stir in crab and finish cooking 2 minutes over low heat.

Spoon crab mixture into vol-au-vent set on ovenproof platter. Top with cheese and broil in oven until melted.

Decorate with olives if desired.

1 Add celery mushrooms, anise, paprika, salt and pepper to shallot in skillet. Continue cooking 2 to 3 minutes.

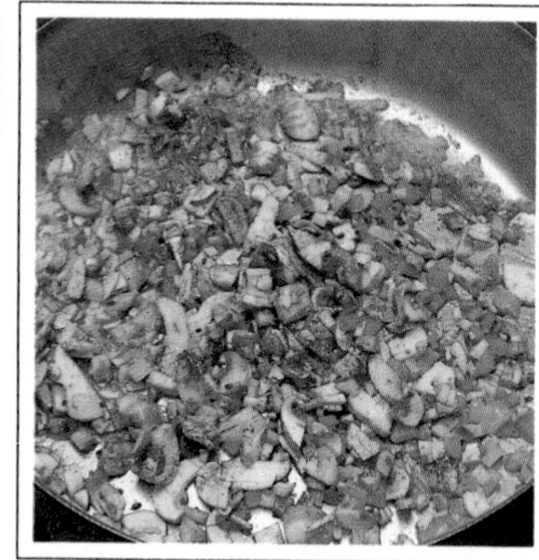

3 Add milk, mix well and bring to boil. Add cumin and continue cooking 4 to 5 minutes over low heat.

2 Mix in flour and cook 2 minutes over medium-low heat.

4 Stir in crab and finish cooking 2 minutes over low heat.

Scallops in Pastry Shells

(serves 4-6)

1 SERVING	514 CALORIES	27g CARBOHYDRATE
16g PROTEIN	34g FAT	trace FIBER

1 tbsp	(15 ml) butter
½ lb	(250 g) mushrooms, quartered
½ cup	(125 ml) dry white wine
1 tbsp	(15 ml) chopped shallot
1 tbsp	(15 ml) chopped parsley
½ lb	(250 g) scallops, halved
¾ cup	(175 ml) thick white sauce, hot
12	small vol-au-vent or tartlets, cooked and cooled
½ cup	(125 ml) grated Parmesan cheese
	salt and pepper

Heat butter in skillet. Add mushrooms, wine, shallot and parsley; cook 3 to 4 minutes over medium-high heat.

Stir in scallops and continue cooking 2 minutes over medium heat.

Pour in white sauce, season and cook 1 minute.

Place pastry shells on ovenproof platter and fill with scallop mixture. Top with cheese and broil 2 to 3 minutes in oven.

Serve on lettuce leaves if desired.

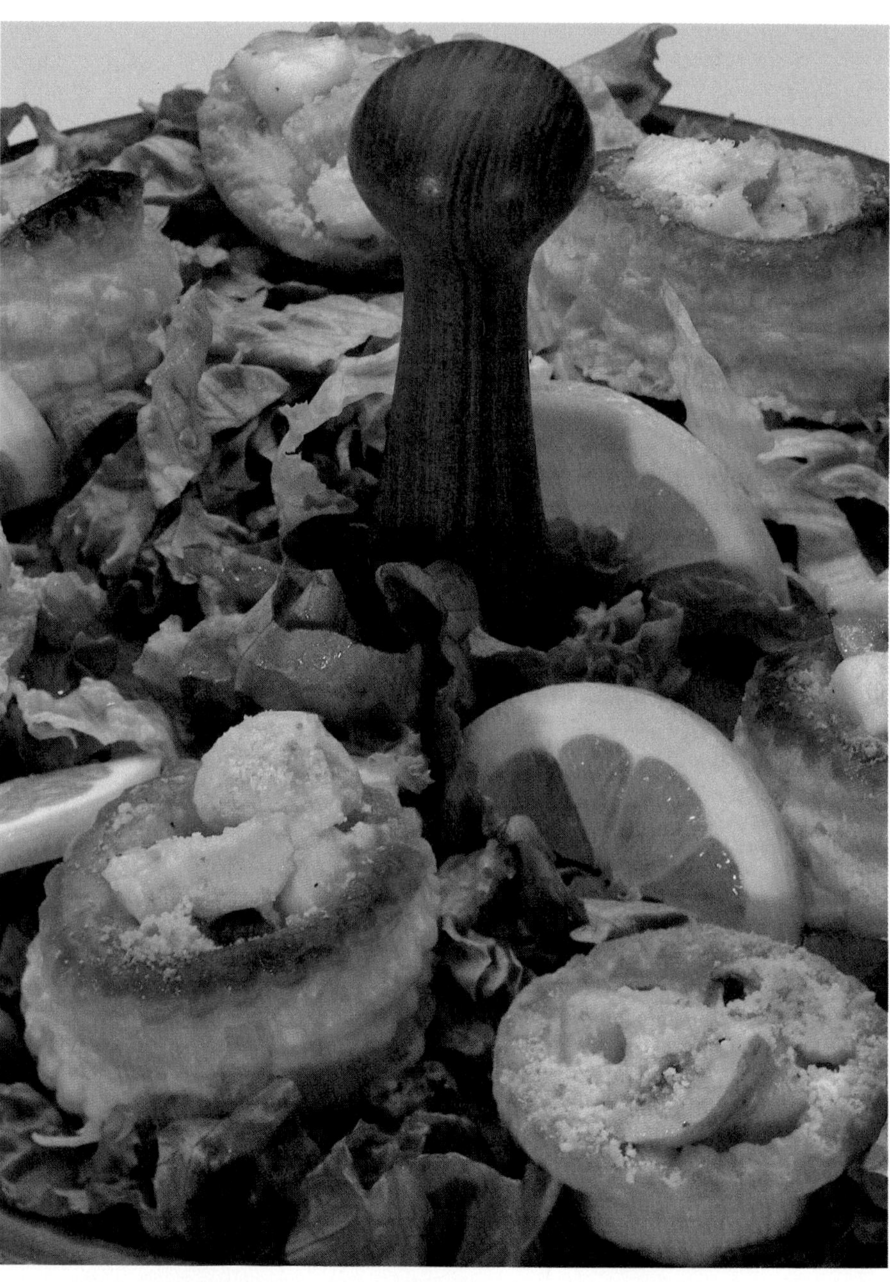

Mushroom Vol-au-Vent

(serves 4)

1 SERVING	692 CALORIES	27g CARBOHYDRATE
16g PROTEIN	57g FAT	0.5g FIBER

10 oz	(284 g) fine liver pâté
2 tbsp	(30 ml) sour cream
1 tbsp	(15 ml) Dijon mustard
2 tbsp	(30 ml) butter
1	shallot, chopped
1	garlic clove, smashed and chopped
½ lb	(250 g) mushrooms, finely chopped
3 tbsp	(45 ml) ricotta cheese
12	small vol-au-vent, cooked
	dash paprika
	salt and pepper

Blend pâté, sour cream and mustard together in food processor; set aside.

Heat butter in saucepan. Cook shallot and garlic 2 minutes over medium heat.

Add mushrooms and paprika; season well. Continue cooking 4 to 5 minutes.

Stir in cheese, correct seasoning and cook 2 minutes over low heat. Remove saucepan from heat and set aside to cool.

Fill vol-au-vent with cold mushroom mixture and arrange on serving platter.

Spoon pâté mixture into pastry bag fitted with plain nozzle. Decorate the tops of vol-au-vent. Keep leftover pâté for spreading on crackers.

Garnish with watercress and quartered black olives if desired.

Asparagus Pastry Bites

(serves 8-10)

1 SERVING	558 CALORIES	46g CARBOHYDRATE
9g PROTEIN	38g FAT	0.7g FIBER

3 tbsp	(45 ml) butter
1 tbsp	(15 ml) green peppercorns, mashed
1	red pepper, diced
1	green onion, sliced
1 tsp	(5 ml) chopped jalapeno pepper
3 tbsp	(45 ml) flour
1½ cups	(375 ml) hot milk
1 tsp	(5 ml) fennel seed
2	bunches asparagus, tips cooked and diced
24	tartlets, cooked and cooled
½ cup	(125 ml) grated cheddar cheese
	salt and pepper

Heat butter in skillet. Cook mashed peppercorns, red pepper, green onion and jalapeno pepper 3 minutes over medium heat.

Mix in flour and continue cooking 2 minutes over low heat.

Pour in milk, add fennel seed and season well. Mix and continue cooking 5 to 6 minutes over low heat.

Stir in asparagus, season and simmer 2 minutes.

Place tartlets on ovenproof platter and fill with asparagus mixture. Top with cheese and broil in oven until melted.

Serve on a bed of alfalfa sprouts if desired.

Vegetable Tartlets

(serves 4)

1 SERVING	569 CALORIES	40g CARBOHYDRATE
10g PROTEIN	40g FAT	0.6g FIBER

2 tbsp	(30 ml) butter
2	shallots, finely chopped
1	garlic clove, smashed and chopped
½ lb	(250 g) mushrooms, chopped
1 cup	(250 ml) white sauce, heated
8	tartlets, cooked
¼ cup	(50 ml) grated Parmesan cheese
	salt and pepper
	dash nutmeg

Heat butter in saucepan. Cook shallots and garlic 2 minutes over low heat.

Season and add mushrooms and nutmeg; cook 4 to 5 minutes over medium-high heat.

Pour in white sauce and continue cooking 2 to 3 minutes over medium heat.

Spoon mixture into tartlets set on cookie sheet. Add cheese and broil 3 minutes in oven.

Shrimp and Mushroom Tartlets

(serves 4)

1 SERVING	713 CALORIES	43g CARBOHYDRATE
31g PROTEIN	47g FAT	0.7g FIBER

2 tbsp	(30 ml) butter
18	mushrooms, diced
1	shallot, chopped
1 tbsp	(15 ml) curry powder
¾ lb	(375 g) cooked shrimp, diced
1½ cups	(375 ml) white sauce, heated
8	tartlets, cooked
½ cup	(125 ml) grated Gruyère cheese
	salt and pepper

Heat butter in frying pan over medium heat. Cook mushrooms and shallot 4 minutes.

Season and add curry powder and shrimp; continue cooking 1 minute.

Pour in sauce, mix well and cook 1 minute.

Fill tartlets with mixture and top with cheese. Broil 2 to 3 minutes in oven and serve.

Spinach-Stuffed Mushrooms

(serves 6-8)

1 SERVING	233 CALORIES	14g CARBOHYDRATE
12g PROTEIN	16g FAT	1.0g FIBER

3 tbsp	(45 ml) butter
1 lb	(500 g) spinach, cooked, chopped and well drained
2	garlic cloves, smashed and chopped
3 tbsp	(45 ml) flour
1½ cups	(375 ml) hot milk
¼ tsp	(1 ml) nutmeg
1¼ cups	(300 ml) grated mozzarella cheese
2 lb	(900 g) mushroom caps, cleaned
2 tbsp	(30 ml) melted butter
	salt and pepper
	juice ½ lemon
	dash paprika

Place 3 tbsp (45 ml) butter in large skillet and heat. When melted, add spinach and garlic; cook 3 to 4 minutes over medium-high heat.

Mix in flour and continue cooking 2 to 3 minutes over low heat while mixing constantly.

Pour in milk and season with nutmeg, salt and pepper; mix well. Add ½ cup (125 ml) cheese, mix and cook 2 to 3 minutes over medium heat.

Set mushroom caps on ovenproof serving platter; sprinkle with lemon juice, paprika and 2 tbsp (30 ml) melted butter. Broil 5 minutes in oven.

Fill mushroom caps with spinach stuffing and top with remaining cheese. Finish broiling about 5 minutes or until cheese starts to brown.

Vegetable Artichoke Bottoms

(serves 4)

1 SERVING	223 CALORIES	20g CARBOHYDRATE
5g PROTEIN	15g FAT	.4g FIBER

8	artichoke bottoms
1 tbsp	(15 ml) lemon juice
2 tbsp	(30 ml) olive oil
¼ tsp	(1 ml) Tabasco sauce
1	green pepper, diced small
1	carrot, pared and diced small
1	yellow pepper, diced small
⅓	celery stalk, diced small
3 tbsp	(45 ml) mayonnaise
¼ tsp	(1 ml) Worcestershire sauce
	salt and pepper

Place artichoke bottoms in bowl; sprinkle with lemon juice, oil, Tabasco sauce, salt and pepper. Marinate 30 minutes.

Place remaining vegetables in another bowl. Add mayonnaise, Worcestershire sauce, salt and pepper; mix well.

Fill artichoke bottoms with vegetable mixture and serve.

Fancy Artichoke Bottoms

(serves 4)

1 SERVING	378 CALORIES	25g CARBOHYDRATE
18g PROTEIN	26g FAT	5.0g FIBER

12	stuffed green olives, chopped
12	pitted black olives, chopped
4 oz	(113 g) can small shrimp, drained and rinsed
1 tsp	(5 ml) chopped parsley
1	celery stalk, chopped
½	pickled banana pepper, chopped
3 tbsp	(45 ml) mayonnaise
¼ cup	(50 ml) water
1 tbsp	(15 ml) butter
10	artichoke bottoms
10	small squares mozzarella cheese
	salt and pepper
	juice ½ lemon

Mix both olives, shrimp, parsley, celery, banana pepper and mayonnaise together. Correct seasoning and add extra mayonnaise if desired.

Place water, butter, artichoke bottoms and lemon juice in saucepan; bring to boil. Remove saucepan from heat and let stand 2 to 3 minutes on counter.

Remove artichoke bottoms from pan and transfer to ovenproof serving platter. Fill each with shrimp stuffing and top with squares of mozzarella cheese.

Broil about 2 to 3 minutes in oven or until cheese melts. If desired sprinkle with paprika for decoration.

Shrimp-Stuffed Eggs

(serves 6)

1 SERVING	280 CALORIES	1g CARBOHYDRATE
16g PROTEIN	23g FAT	-- FIBER

6	large eggs
4 oz	(113 g) can small shrimp, drained and rinsed
1 tsp	(5 ml) chopped parsley
2 tbsp	(30 ml) soft butter
3 tbsp	(45 ml) mayonnaise
¼ tsp	(1 ml) paprika
	few drops lemon juice
	few drops Worcestershire sauce
	salt and pepper
	extra chopped parsley
	extra mayonnaise

Cook eggs 10 minutes in gently boiling water. When cooked, drain and cool under running water for at least 3 to 4 minutes.

Peel eggs and cut in half, either lengthwise or widthwise.

Carefully remove yolks and place in sieve set over bowl. Force through with pestle and be sure to scrape the bottom of sieve to gather all the yolks. Set aside in bowl.

Pat shrimp dry with paper towel. Place in food processor along with parsley; purée.

Transfer shrimp to bowl containing sieved yolks. Add butter and mix well.

Stir in mayonnaise until well incorporated. Season with paprika, lemon juice, Worcestershire sauce, salt and pepper. Mix well with spatula.

Arrange the egg white halves on plate. Decorate several by coating tops in mayonnaise then dipping in chopped parsley.

Spoon shrimp filling into pastry bag fitted with large star nozzle. Force into egg white halves and, if desired, decorate with a bit of caviar.

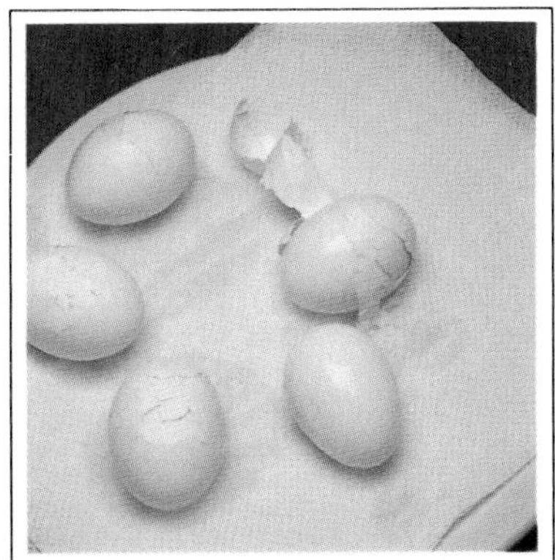

1 After eggs have cooled for at least 3 to 4 minutes in cold water, peel away shells.

3 With pestle, force egg yolks through sieve into bowl.

2 Cut eggs in half, either lengthwise or widthwise.

4 Purée shrimp with parsley in food processor.

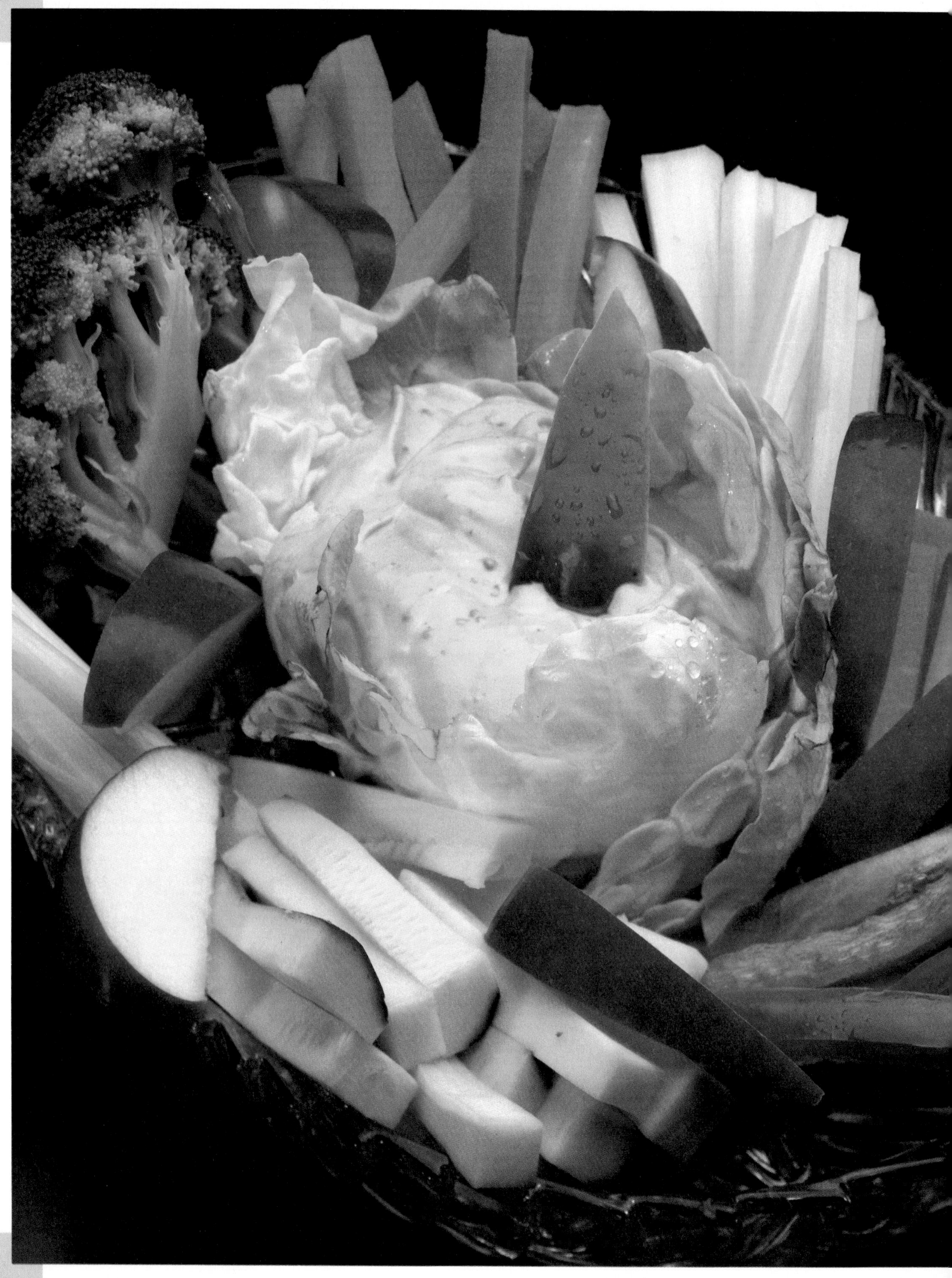

Vegetables with Cheese Dip

(serves 6-8)

1 SERVING	255 CALORIES	29g CARBOHYDRATE
16g PROTEIN	12g FAT	4.0g FIBER

6 oz	(170 g) blue cheese, in chuncks
1 tsp	(5 ml) Worcestershire sauce
½ cup	(125 ml) sour cream
¼ tsp	(1 ml) paprika
2 tbsp	(30 ml) caviar
1	head broccoli, flowerets blanched
2	carrots, pared, cut in sticks, and blanched if desired
6	green onion sticks
1	zucchini, peeled and in sticks
1	apple, cored and in wedges
1	celery stalk, in sticks
1	green pepper, sliced
	salt and pepper
	few leaves Boston lettuce

Place cheese and Worcestershire sauce in food processor; blend until puréed.

Add sour cream and paprika; continue blending until very smooth. Use spatula several times to clean sides of bowl.

Add caviar and blend another 30 seconds. Season with some salt and plenty of pepper.

Arrange lettuce leaves in middle of large serving platter. Spoon cheese dip over leaves and surround with vegetable and apple sticks.

1 Although the broccoli should be blanched it is a matter of taste as to whether or not you blanch the carrots.

3 Add sour cream and paprika; continue blending until very smooth. Use spatula several times to clean sides of bowl.

2 Place cheese and Worcestershire sauce in food processor; blend until puréed.

4 Add caviar and blend another 30 seconds. Season with some salt and plenty of pepper.

Spicy Dip for Vegetables

(serves 4)

1 RECIPE	948 CALORIES	13g CARBOHYDRATE
21g PROTEIN	92g FAT	1.0g FIBER

1 tsp	(5 ml) strong mustard
½ lb	(250 g) cream cheese
½ cup	(125 ml) finely chopped red pepper
½ tsp	(2 ml) cumin
1	garlic clove, smashed and chopped
1 tbsp	(15 ml) sour cream
1 tsp	(5 ml) finely chopped chives
¼ tsp	(1 ml) paprika
¼ tsp	(1 ml) celery seed
	few drops lemon juice
	salt and pepper
	assorted vegetable sticks

Blend mustard and cream cheese in food processor until smooth.

Add red pepper, cumin, garlic and sour cream; mix well.

Stir in chives, paprika, celery seed, lemon juice; season very well and blend together.

Serve with assorted vegetable sticks.

Versatile Cheese Dip

(serves 4)

1 RECIPE	1997 CALORIES	6g CARBOHYDRATE
65g PROTEIN	192g FAT	-- FIBER

½ lb	(250 g) strong cheddar cheese
¼ cup	(50 ml) sour cream
¼ lb	(125 g) soft butter
1 tbsp	(15 ml) finely chopped chives
1 tbsp	(15 ml) finely chopped parsley
	salt and pepper
	few drops Tabasco sauce
	few drops Worcestershire sauce
	assorted crackers

Blend cheese in food processor until quite smooth.

Add sour cream and butter; mix again until incorporated.

Add chives, parsley, salt, pepper, Tabasco and Worcestershire; blend again.

Serve dip on crackers.

Chicken Liver Appetizer

(serves 4)

1 SERVING	312 CALORIES	9g CARBOHYDRATE
34g PROTEIN	14g FAT	0.6g FIBER

1	head Boston lettuce
2 tbsp	(30 ml) olive oil
1 lb	(500 g) fresh chicken livers, cleaned, halved and fat trimmed
2	garlic cloves, smashed and chopped
1	onion, thinly sliced
3	anchovy filets, chopped
2 tbsp	(30 ml) capers
¼ tsp	(1 ml) sage
1½ cups	(375 ml) chicken stock, heated
1 tbsp	(15 ml) cornstarch
3 tbsp	(45 ml) cold water
	salt and pepper

Wash and dry lettuce; arrange leaves like baskets on four individual plates. Set aside.

Heat oil in frying pan. Cook livers, garlic and onion 3 to 4 minutes over medium heat; season well.

Stir in anchovies, capers and sage; continue cooking 1 minute.

Pour in chicken stock and bring to boil. Mix cornstarch with water; incorporate into sauce and cook 1 minute over low heat.

Spoon mixture into lettuce baskets and serve immediately.

DESSERTS

Desserts

«If I had to live the rest of my life as a food, I would choose to be a lone strawberry, covered ever so delicately in smooth chocolate sauce, set atop the highest mound of swirled vanilla ice cream surrounded by a tiny sea of colored sprinkles.»

Anonymous

It's a fact that no matter how hard we try to resist the temptation, desserts in their many forms and disguises win the tug-of-war almost every time!

For some it may be the cool elegance of a parfait, assembled so neatly in a tall, frosty glass that makes their eyes sparkle. For others, a generous portion of rich chocolate cake smothered in fluffy, cognac-laced whipped cream might be the ultimate reward. Whatever your enthusiasm, this collection of fruit and dessert recipes will surpass anything your palate has experienced before. You will discover the natural goodness of exotic fruit in recipes such as Mango Mousse and Passion Fruit Cream Dessert, and devour such favorites as Shortbread Cookies and Almond Brownies. And for those who relish a mysterious tinge to their cookery, you can try Apple Galette and Cherry Clafoutis.

Before reading on, remember one thing: desserts are not just another course — they are extra-special and need your complete concentration. So put your whole heart into the preparation of these recipes and no cutting corners — they will turn out every bit as sumptuous as you imagined!

Chocolate Frosting

¼ cup (50 ml) 248 CALORIES	35g CARBOHYDRATE	
2g PROTEIN	10g FAT	0.2g FIBER

4 oz	(125 g) unsweetened chocolate
2¼ cups	(550 ml) icing sugar
3 tbsp	(45 ml) hot rum
2	egg yolks
¼ cup	(50 ml) softened unsalted butter

Place chocolate in stainless steel bowl, set over saucepan half-filled with boiling water. Melt.

Remove bowl from heat and add icing sugar. Incorporate using electric beater.

Add hot rum and mix well with spatula.

Add egg yolks, one at a time, mixing well between each.

Add butter and mix very well with spatula or electric beater if necessary. Consistency should be smooth.

When cool, spread frosting over almost any type of cake.

Chocolate Sundae

(serves 4)

1 SERVING	598 CALORIES	55g CARBOHYDRATE
10g PROTEIN	37g FAT	0.9g FIBER

4 oz	(125 g) unsweetened chocolate
½ cup	(125 ml) granulated sugar
1 tbsp	(15 ml) maple syrup
¼ cup	(50 ml) water
2 tbsp	(30 ml) rum
½ cup	(125 ml) heavy cream
	vanilla ice cream
	chopped walnuts

Place chocolate in stainless steel bowl set over saucepan half-filled with boiling water and melt.

Remove bowl from heat and set aside.

Place sugar, maple syrup and water in saucepan. Bring to boil and continue cooking 2-3 minutes over medium heat.

Remove saucepan from heat and let cool slightly.

When sugar-syrup mixture is lukewarm, add rum and mix well.

Add melted chocolate and mix well. Slowly pour in cream while whisking constantly.

Pour chocolate sauce into bowl and refrigerate until cold.

Serve with vanilla ice cream and decorate with chopped walnuts.

Chocolate Layer Cake

(serves 8-10)

1 SERVING	479 CALORIES	57g CARBOHYDRATE
7g PROTEIN	25g FAT	0.4g FIBER

2 cups	(500 ml) pastry flour
1¾ cups	(425 ml) granulated sugar
⅔ cup	(150 ml) unsweetened cocoa
1 tsp	(5 ml) baking soda
1 tbsp	(15 ml) baking powder
¾ cup	(175 ml) all-vegetable shortening
1 cup	(250 ml) milk
3	eggs
	pinch salt
	whipped cream
	shaved chocolate

Preheat oven to 325°F (160°C). Butter 9 inch (23 cm) spring-form cake pan.

Sift flour, sugar, cocoa, baking soda, baking powder and salt into large bowl.

Add shortening and incorporate with pastry blender.

Pour in milk and beat well with electric beater until batter is smooth.

Add eggs, one at a time, beating 30 seconds after each addition.

Pour batter into prepared cake pan and bake 65 minutes or until toothpick inserted comes out clean.

When cake is cooked, remove from oven and let cool 10-15 minutes in pan.

Carefully unmold and let cool completely on wire rack at room temperature.

Slice cake into two or three layers and ice with whipped cream. Decorate with shaved chocolate.

Chocolate Mousse

(serves 4-6)

1 SERVING	376 CALORIES	9g CARBOHYDRATE
9g PROTEIN	34g FAT	0.5g FIBER

6 oz	(170 g) semi-sweet chocolate
3 tbsp	(45 ml) unsalted butter
¼ cup	(50 ml) water
4	egg yolks
2 tbsp	(30 ml) Tia Maria liqueur
4	egg whites, beaten stiff
½ cup	(125 ml) heavy cream, whipped
	shaved chocolate for decoration

Place chocolate, butter and water in saucepan and cook over low heat to melt. Mix constantly with wooden spoon.

Remove from heat and transfer chocolate to bowl.

Add egg yolks, one at a time, mixing between additions with whisk.

Add Tia Maria and continue whisking several seconds.

Incorporate egg whites using spatula, being careful not to overmix.

Add whipped cream and incorporate with spatula.

Mix well with whisk for several seconds.

Pour into glass bowls and refrigerate 4 hours before serving. Decorate with shaved chocolate.

Chocolate Berry Mousse

(serves 4-6)

1 SERVING	321 CALORIES	24g CARBOHYDRATE
3g PROTEIN	24g FAT	0.5g FIBER

3	squares semi-sweet chocolate
1	egg
½ cup	(125 ml) puréed strawberries
1 cup	(250 ml) hot heavy cream
3	egg whites
½ cup	(125 ml) sugar

Melt chocolate in stainless steel bowl set over saucepan half-filled with hot water, placed over medium heat.

Remove bowl from pan; mix in whole egg with whisk.

Add puréed strawberries and mix well. Pour into food processor and blend 1 minute.

Blend in hot cream and continue processing until well incorporated. Refrigerate to cool.

Beat egg whites until stiff. Slowly add sugar while beating until incorporated.

Fold egg whites into chilled mousse batter and spoon into glass dishes.

Refrigerate before serving.

Strawberry and Raspberry Mousse

(serves 6-8)

1 SERVING	226 CALORIES	28g CARBOHYDRATE
4g PROTEIN	11g FAT	1.6g FIBER

1½	small envelopes unflavored gelatine
¼ cup	(50 ml) hot water
⅔ cup	(150 ml) granulated sugar
3 tbsp	(45 ml) maple syrup
½ cup	(125 ml) boiling water
2 cups	(500 ml) fresh strawberries, hulled
1 cup	(250 ml) fresh raspberries
1 tbsp	(15 ml) grated lemon rind
5	egg whites
1 cup	(250 ml) heavy cream, whipped

Grease 8 cup (2 L) soufflé mold with oil.

Sprinkle gelatine over ¼ cup (50 ml) hot water placed in small bowl; set aside.

Place half of sugar, maple syrup and boiling water in saucepan. Bring to boil and continue cooking 2 minutes over medium heat.

Stir in both fruits and lemon rind; continue cooking 3 minutes.

Transfer contents to food processor and purée.

Replace mixture in saucepan and mix in gelatine; cook 1 minute.

Pour fruit mixture into bowl and refrigerate.

When fruit mixture starts to set, begin preparing egg whites by placing them in bowl.

Beat with electric beater until they peak. Add remaining sugar and continue beating 30 seconds.

Fold into fruit mixture using spatula.

Incorporate whipped cream and pour mixture into prepared mold. Refrigerate 8 hours.

Unmold and serve with a fruit sauce.

Strawberry Omelet

(serves 4)

1 SERVING	369 CALORIES	28g CARBOHYDRATE
13g PROTEIN	23g FAT	1.8g FIBER

2 cups	(500 ml) strawberries, hulled and sliced in 3
4 tbsp	(60 ml) butter
3 tbsp	(45 ml) sugar
1 cup	(250 ml) orange juice
2 tsp	(10 ml) cornstarch
3 tbsp	(45 ml) cold water
8	eggs, well beaten

Set strawberries aside in bowl.

Heat half of butter in frying pan. Add 2 tbsp (30 ml) sugar and cook 2 minutes over high heat while stirring constantly.

Continue stirring, pour in orange juice and bring to boil. Cook 2 more minutes over high heat.

Mix cornstarch with water; stir into sauce. Cook 1 minute over high heat, stirring occasionally.

Pour over strawberries and let stand 15 minutes.

Heat remaining butter in large nonstick frying pan or omelet pan. When hot, pour in eggs and cook 30 seconds over high heat while mixing with fork.

Continue cooking another 30 seconds or until top is set.

Add half of strawberries and cook another 20 seconds.

Carefully roll omelet while tilting pan, then turn onto ovenproof serving platter.

Sprinkle with remaining sugar and broil several minutes in oven.

Meanwhile, heat remaining strawberries in small saucepan.

When ready to serve, pour strawberries over omelet and garnish with shredded coconut if desired.

1 Using spatula, cream together the butter and brown sugar.

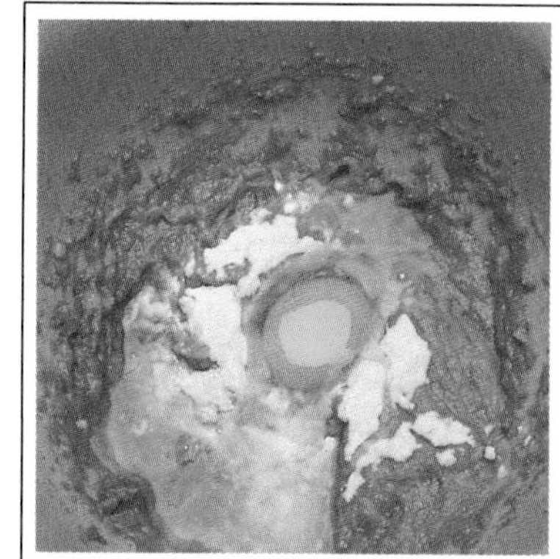

3 Add second egg and 2 tbsp (30 ml) of flour to bowl; beat well with electric beater.

2 Add first egg and beat well with electric beater.

4 Add last egg, flour and beat again. Pour in coffee and rum; beat well. Pour in cream, beat and add cherries.

Cherry Clafoutis

(serves 4-6)

1 SERVING	362 CALORIES	42g CARBOHYDRATE
6g PROTEIN	19g FAT	0.1g FIBER

¼ cup	(50 ml) softened butter
½ cup	(125 ml) brown sugar
3	eggs
½ cup	(125 ml) all-purpose flour
1 tsp	(5 ml) baking powder
¼ cup	(50 ml) strong black coffee
2 tbsp	(30 ml) rum
1 cup	(250 ml) light cream
14 oz	(398 ml) can pitted Bing cherries, well drained
1 tbsp	(15 ml) granulated sugar
	whipped cream

Preheat oven to 350°F (180°C). Butter 10 inch (25 cm) glass pie plate.

Place butter and brown sugar in bowl; using spatula cream together.

Add first egg and beat well with electric beater.

Sift flour and baking powder together.

Add second egg and 2 tbsp (30 ml) of flour to bowl; beat well with electric beater.

Add last egg and rest of flour; beat again.

Pour in coffee and rum; beat well. Pour in cream, beat and add cherries.

Pour batter into prepared pie plate; bake 45-50 minutes or until toothpick inserted comes out clean.

About 5 minutes before clafoutis is cooked, sprinkle with a bit of granulated sugar and resume cooking.

Serve warm with whipped cream.

Bavarian Cream with Cherries

(serves 6-8)

1 SERVING	260 CALORIES	22g CARBOHYDRATE
5g PROTEIN	17g FAT	0.3g FIBER

6	egg yolks
½ cup	(125 ml) sugar
2 cups	(500 ml) hot milk
1 tbsp	(15 ml) vanilla
2 tbsp	(30 ml) gelatine
¼ cup	(50 ml) cold water
1 cup	(250 ml) heavy cream
2 cups	(500 ml) pitted cherries

Place egg yolks and sugar in stainless steel bowl. Mix together with electric beater for 2 minutes.

Add hot milk and vanilla; mix well to incorporate.

Have ready a saucepan filled with hot water placed over medium heat. Set bowl over saucepan and cook cream until it coats the back of a spoon. Stir constantly.

Remove bowl from saucepan and set aside. Dilute gelatine in cold water; let stand 2 minutes.

Incorporate diluted gelatine into cooked cream. Set bowl over larger bowl filled with ice water.

As soon as the cream mixture starts to set, whip the heavy cream.

Incorporate cherries, then whipping cream into gelling mixture. Pour into oiled mold and refrigerate overnight.

Cottage Sundaes

(serves 4)

1 SERVING	305 CALORIES	38g CARBOHYDRATE
20g PROTEIN	8g FAT	0.9g FIBER

¾ lb	(375 g) pitted cherries
¼ cup	(50 ml) sugar
¼ cup	(50 ml) water
1 tbsp	(15 ml) grated lemon rind
1 tsp	(5 ml) cornstarch
2 tbsp	(30 ml) cold water
2½ cups	(625 ml) cottage cheese
	whipped cream for topping
	maraschino cherries for decoration

Place cherries, sugar, ¼ cup (50 ml) water and lemon rind in saucepan. Cover and cook 2 to 3 minutes over medium heat, stirring occasionally.

Mix cornstarch with 2 tbsp (30 ml) water; stir into cherry sauce and continue cooking 1 minute. Remove pan from heat and let cool.

To build sundaes, alternate cherry sauce and cottage cheese in tall dessert glasses.

Top with whipped cream and decorate with maraschino cherries if desired.

Pastry Cream

1/4 cup (50 ml)	81 CALORIES	8g CARBOHYDRATE
3g PROTEIN	4g FAT	0g FIBER

4	egg yolks
1/4 cup	(50 ml) granulated sugar
4 tbsp	(60 ml) flour
2 cups	(500 ml) hot milk
2 tbsp	(30 ml) slivered almonds

Place egg yolks in bowl. Add sugar and beat well with whisk.

Add flour, mix with whisk, and pour in milk. Continue mixing until well incorporated.

Stir in almonds and pour mixture into saucepan. Cook over medium heat, stirring constantly, until mixture reaches boiling point.

Continue cooking 2 minutes or until cream starts to thicken.

Pour cream into bowl and let cool slightly. Cover with plastic wrap (it must touch surface of cream) and refrigerate until cold.

Use this pastry cream recipe in a variety of dessert dishes.

Pears with Pastry Cream

(serves 6)

1 SERVING	179 CALORIES	36g CARBOHYDRATE
6g PROTEIN	1g FAT	4.8g FIBER

4 cups	(1 L) water
1 1/2 cups	(375 ml) granulated sugar
1 tbsp	(15 ml) lemon juice
2 tbsp	(30 ml) light rum
6	pears, cored and peeled
1 1/2 cups	(375 ml) pastry cream
4	egg whites, beaten stiff
1/4 cup	(50 ml) hot rum

Place water, sugar, lemon juice and light rum in saucepan; bring to boil and continue cooking 4 minutes over medium heat.

Add whole pears and reduce heat. Cook 6 to 7 minutes over low heat.

Remove saucepan from heat and let pears cool in syrup.

Pour pastry cream into ovenproof baking dish. Arrange pears in cream and decorate sides of dish with beaten egg whites. It is best to use pastry bag and nozzle for this.

Broil 2 minutes or until lightly browned.

Remove from oven, pour in hot rum and flambé. Serve immediately.

Sugared Pears

(serves 4)

1 SERVING	514 CALORIES	87g CARBOHYDRATE
3g PROTEIN	17g FAT	7.2g FIBER

1/2 cup	(125 ml) sugar
2 cups	(500 ml) water
1/2 cup	(125 ml) orange juice
4	large pears, cored, peeled and halved
1 tbsp	(15 ml) cornstarch
3 tbsp	(45 ml) cold water
3 tbsp	(45 ml) shredded coconut
1 cup	(250 ml) crushed macaroons
1 tbsp	(15 ml) butter

Place sugar, 2 cups (500 ml) water and orange juice in saucepan. Bring to boil over medium heat and continue cooking 3 to 4 minutes.

Add pears and cook 3 minutes over low heat.

Remove saucepan from heat and let pears stand in syrup 5 to 6 minutes.

Remove pears from saucepan and place in baking dish; set aside.

Replace saucepan of syrup on stove; cook 4 to 5 minutes over high heat.

Mix cornstarch with 3 tbsp (45 ml) cold water; stir into syrup and continue cooking 1 minute over low heat.

Pour half of syrup over pears. Top with coconut and macaroons; dot with butter. Broil 3 minutes in oven.

Orange Pears

(serves 4)

1 SERVING	181 CALORIES	42g CARBOHYDRATE
0g PROTEIN	0g FAT	4.7g FIBER

½ cup	(125 ml) sugar
2½ cups	(625 ml) water
1 tsp	(5 ml) vanilla
4	Bartlett pears
½ cup	(125 ml) orange juice
2 tbsp	(30 ml) grated orange rind
1 tsp	(5 ml) cornstarch
2 tbsp	(30 ml) cold water
2 tbsp	(30 ml) orange liqueur

Place sugar, 2½ cups (625 ml) water and vanilla in saucepan. Bring to boil.

Meanwhile, carefully core pears without removing stem. Peel and place pears in syrup mixture in saucepan.

Cook 4 to 5 minutes over low heat. Remove saucepan from heat and let pears cool in syrup.

Remove pears and set on serving platter; set aside.

Remove 1 cup (250 ml) of syrup and transfer to clean saucepan. Bring to boil.

Add orange juice and rind; bring to boil again and continue cooking 3 minutes over high heat.

Mix cornstarch with 2 tbsp (30 ml) water; stir into orange syrup and cook 1 minute.

Mix in liqueur and pour sauce over pears. Cool before serving.

Buckwheat Crêpes with Peaches

(serves 6-8)

1 SERVING	264 CALORIES	32g CARBOHYDRATE
5g PROTEIN	13g FAT	1.1g FIBER

1 cup	(250 ml) buckwheat flour
¼ cup	(50 ml) all-purpose flour
½ tsp	(2 ml) salt
1½ cups	(375 ml) milk
3	beaten eggs
2 tbsp	(30 ml) melted butter
4 tbsp	(60 ml) butter
4 tbsp	(60 ml) brown sugar
5	large peaches, blanched, peeled and sliced
3 tbsp	(45 ml) rum
	icing sugar

Stir both flours and salt together in large bowl. Mix in milk until well incorporated, then add eggs; mix vigorously with whisk. Pass through sieve.

Stir in melted butter and refrigerate batter 1 hour.

Lightly butter crêpe pan and place over medium-high heat. Whisk batter well.

As butter melts, wipe off excess with paper towel. When pan is hot, pour in small ladle of batter and rotate pan to completely coat bottom.

Replace pan over heat and cook crêpe 1 minute until lightly browned.

Turn crêpe over (use long spatula rather than flipping) and continue cooking 1 minute.

Repeat for rest of batter, stacking cooked crêpes on large plate. During cooking wipe pan with butter as needed and monitor heat to keep it at medium-high.

For crêpe filling, heat 4 tbsp (60 ml) butter in saucepan. Add brown sugar and peaches; cook 2 minutes over medium-high heat.

Mix in rum and spoon peaches on middle of flat crêpes (keep some peaches for garnish). Fold crêpes into 4 and place on ovenproof platter.

Sprinkle with icing sugar and broil several minutes.

Serve with remaining peach slices.

Delicious Fruit Trifle

(serves 10-12)

1 SERVING	305 CALORIES	43g CARBOHYDRATE
5g PROTEIN	11g FAT	2.1g FIBER

4	egg yolks
½ cup	(125 ml) sugar
1 cup	(250 ml) boiled milk, tepid
1 tbsp	(15 ml) dark rum
1 cup	(250 ml) mixed berries
2 cups	(500 ml) blueberries
2 cups	(500 ml) diced watermelon
1	small angel or sponge cake, sliced into 3 layers
⅓ cup	(75 ml) light rum
3 cups	(750 ml) strawberries, hulled and halved
2½ cups	(625 ml) whipped cream

Place egg yolks and sugar in stainless steel bowl; beat together with electric beater until mixture forms ribbons.

Mix in milk until well incorporated. Stir in dark rum and set bowl over saucepan half-filled with hot water. Cook over medium heat while stirring constantly with wooden spoon. Do not boil.

When cream coats the back of the spoon, remove bowl from saucepan and set aside to cool.

Toss mixed berries, blueberries and watermelon together in small bowl.

When custard cream has cooled, begin building trifle in large glass bowl or substitute. Set one layer of cake in bottom followed by sprinkling of rum.

Continue with layer of strawberries, whipped cream, custard cream and mixed fruit.

Repeat layers until ingredients are used, ending with a generous topping of whipped cream.

If desired decorate trifle with glaze.

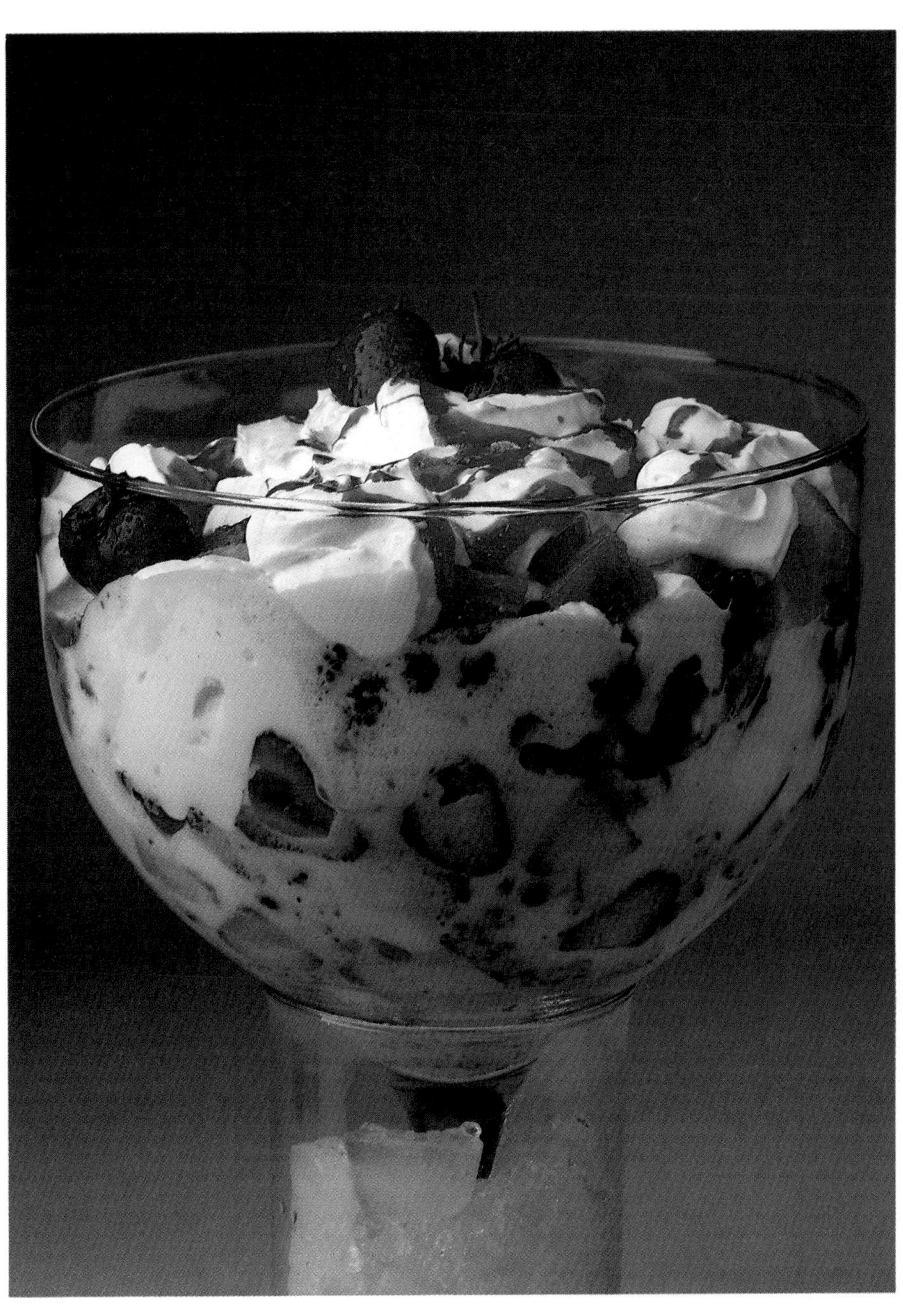

Fruit in the Shell

(serves 2)

1 SERVING	390 CALORIES	79g CARBOHYDRATE
2g PROTEIN	7g FAT	8.5g FIBER

1	small pear, peeled and diced
1	nectarine, diced
1	slice watermelon, seeded and diced
12	strawberries, hulled and halved
1	kiwi fruit, peeled and sliced
6-8	blackberries
¼ cup	(50 ml) blueberries
1 tbsp	(15 ml) soft butter
2 tbsp	(30 ml) sugar
3 tbsp	(45 ml) rum
1	pineapple
	juice 1 orange
	juice 1 lemon
	several pitted cherries
	few whole strawberries for decoration

Place pear, nectarine, watermelon, halved strawberries, kiwi fruit, blackberries and blueberries in mixing bowl; set aside.

Heat butter in frying pan over medium heat. Add sugar and cook 3 minutes over high heat while stirring constantly — mixture should become golden in color.

Add orange and lemon juices; mix well. Stir in rum and cook 3 minutes.

Pour syrup over fruit in bowl, toss and marinate 30 minutes.

Slice pineapple in half, lengthwise. Using sharp knife and spoon, cut and scoop out insides from shells. Reserve pineapple flesh for other recipes.

When fruit is ready, spoon into hollowed shells and decorate with cherries and whole strawberries.

Berries and Broiled Cream

(serves 4)

1 SERVING	355 CALORIES	39g CARBOHYDRATE
1g PROTEIN	22g FAT	2.4g FIBER

1 cup	(250 ml) strawberries, hulled and halved
1 cup	(250 ml) raspberries
2	kiwi fruit, peeled and sliced
1 cup	(250 ml) heavy cream, whipped
½ cup	(125 ml) brown sugar
½ cup	(125 ml) hot rum

Divide fruit among 4 individual baking dishes.

Top fruit with whipped cream and sprinkle with brown sugar. Broil for 1 minute in oven.

Remove from oven, sprinkle with rum and flambé.

Fruit à la Mode

(serves 4)

1 SERVING	398 CALORIES	63g CARBOHYDRATE
4g PROTEIN	13g FAT	4.2g FIBER

¼ cup	(50 ml) sugar
1 tsp	(5 ml) vanilla
1 cup	(250 ml) water
4	large peaches, blanched, peeled and halved
1 cup	(250 ml) strawberries, hulled and halved
1 cup	(250 ml) raspberries
2 tbsp	(30 ml) fine sugar
2 tbsp	(30 ml) Cointreau
4	large scoops vanilla ice cream
	whipped cream

Place sugar, vanilla and water in saucepan; bring to boil. Continue cooking 2 to 3 minutes over medium heat.

Add peaches and cook 2 minutes over medium heat. Remove pan from heat and let fruit cool in syrup.

Purée strawberries and raspberries in food processor. Transfer to nonstick frying pan and stir in fine sugar. Cook 3 minutes over medium heat.

Add liqueur and cook 1 more minute over high heat. Force mixture through sieve into bowl.

Spoon a bit of berry sauce into bottom of glass dessert dishes. Add a half peach and follow with scoop of ice cream.

Cover with another peach half, top with berry sauce and decorate with whipped cream.

Cheese Fruitcup

(serves 4)

1 SERVING	348 CALORIES	31g CARBOHYDRATE
5g PROTEIN	23g FAT	2.1g FIBER

2	kiwis, peeled and diced
2	bananas, peeled and sliced
1	apple, cored, peeled and sliced
4 tbsp	(60 ml) yogurt, flavor of your choice
2 tbsp	(30 ml) your preferred liqueur
8 oz	(250 g) package cream cheese, softened
	juice 1 orange

Place kiwis and bananas in food processor and purée.

Add apple and orange juice; continue blending several seconds.

Add yogurt, liqueur and cream cheese; blend well until quite smooth.

Spoon into small cup-like glasses and refrigerate before serving.

Blueberries in Syrup

(serves 4)

1 SERVING	295 CALORIES	46g CARBOHYDRATE
5g PROTEIN	10g FAT	2.1g FIBER

4 tbsp	(60 ml) brown sugar
1 tsp	(5 ml) vanilla
1 tbsp	(15 ml) grated lemon rind
1 tbsp	(15 ml) grated orange rind
1 cup	(250 ml) water
2 cups	(500 ml) blueberries
4	large scoops ice cream

Place sugar, vanilla, fruit rinds and water in saucepan; mix well and bring to boil. Cook 2 to 3 minutes over low heat until syrup thickens.

Stir in blueberries, remove saucepan from heat and let fruit cool in syrup.

Spoon blueberries over ice cream and serve.

Wally's Watermelon Punch

(serves 10-12)

1 SERVING	129 CALORIES	21g CARBOHYDRATE
0g PROTEIN	0g FAT	0.5g FIBER

½	watermelon, seeded and cubed
½ cup	(125 ml) lime juice
1 cup	(250 ml) light rum
4 cups	(1 L) orange juice
1 cup	(250 ml) pineapple juice
½ cup	(125 ml) fine sugar
	plenty of ice

Purée watermelon in food processor. Pass through sieve into large punch bowl.

Add remaining ingredients, mix very well and refrigerate 3 to 4 hours.

If desired, decorate with slices of fruit and serve in a bowl with plenty of ice.

Watermelon Compote

(serves 4)

1 SERVING	129 CALORIES	31g CARBOHYDRATE
1g PROTEIN	0g FAT	1.5g FIBER

¼ cup	(50 ml) brown sugar
½ cup	(125 ml) water
1 tbsp	(15 ml) grated lemon rind
2 cups	(500 ml) diced watermelon
2	large peaches, blanched, peeled and thinly sliced
½ cup	(125 ml) seedless green grapes
	juice 2 limes

Place sugar, water, lemon rind and lime juice in small saucepan. Bring to boil.

Add fruit and mix well; cover and cook 3 to 4 minutes over low heat.

Remove pan from heat and let fruit cool in syrup. Serve over ice cream.

Cantaloupe Tarts

(serves 4)

1 SERVING	605 CALORIES	71g CARBOHYDRATE
9g PROTEIN	32g FAT	1.4g FIBER

1 cup	(250 ml) milk
1 tbsp	(15 ml) water
1 tsp	(5 ml) Pernod
½ cup	(125 ml) sugar
3	egg yolks
¼ cup	(50 ml) all-purpose flour, sifted
1	small ripe cantaloupe
8	cooked pastry tarts
	green maraschino cherries

Pour milk and water into medium-size saucepan. Bring to boil over medium heat. Stir in Pernod, remove from heat and set aside.

Place sugar and egg yolks in stainless steel bowl. Beat together with electric beater for 3 to 4 minutes or until eggs become foamy and almost white in color.

Mix in flour with whisk until well incorporated.

Gradually pour half of hot milk into bowl containing egg mixture, stirring constantly with whisk. Incorporate well.

Incorporate remaining milk and immediately place bowl over saucepan half-filled with hot water.

Cook over medium heat while whisking constantly until very thick and cream coats the back of a spoon.

Pour cream into clean bowl and let cool. Cover with buttered waxed paper and chill before using.

To prepare tarts, remove all seeds from cantaloupe. Slice into quarters and thinly slice flesh on slight angle.

Spread pastry cream in bottom of cooked tarts and arrange cantaloupe slices decoratively on top.

Serve tarts immediately or glaze if desired. Decorate with green maraschino cherries.

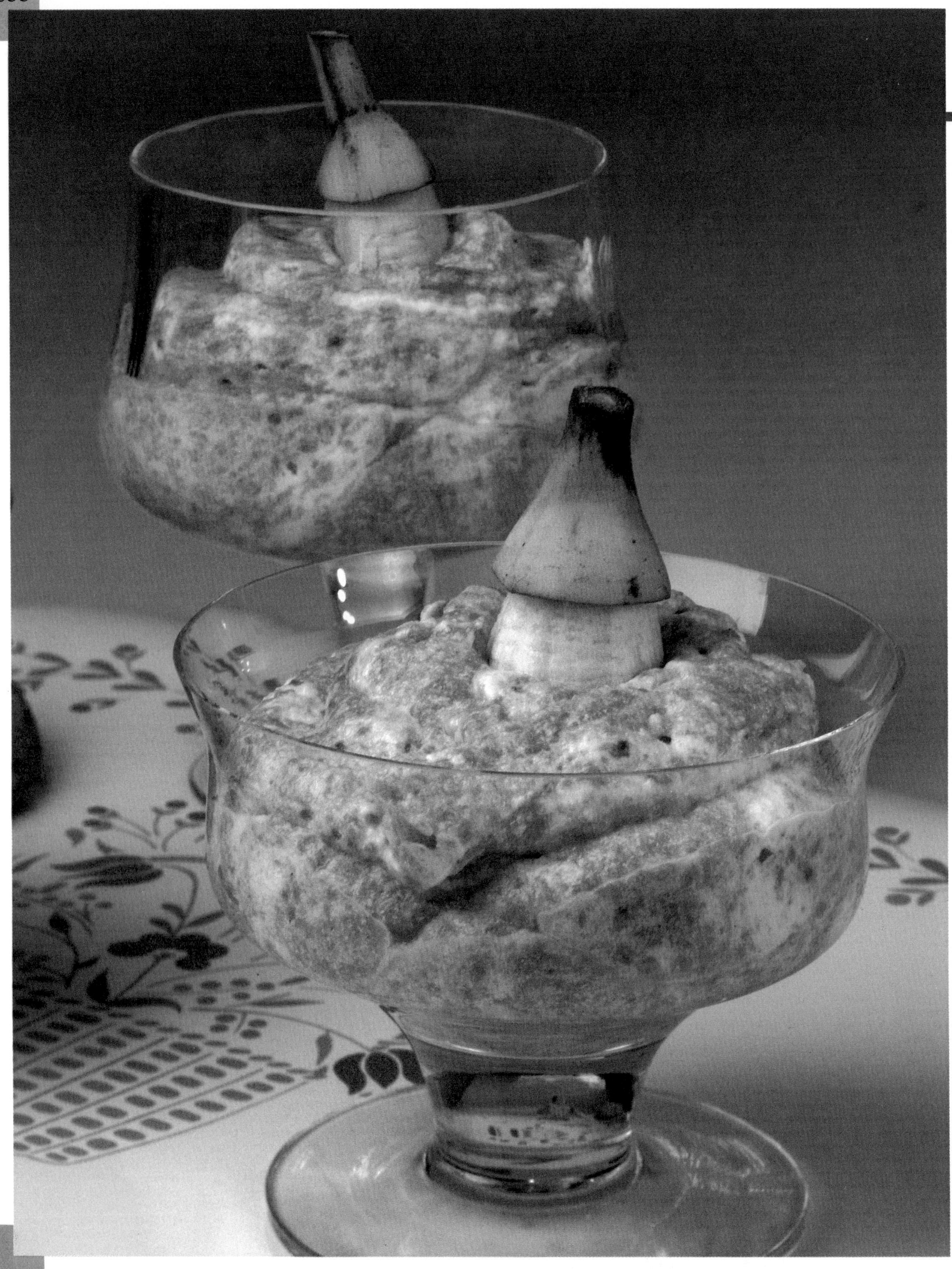

Banana Mousse

(serves 4)

1 SERVING	369 CALORIES	39g CARBOHYDRATE
4g PROTEIN	22g FAT	2.4g FIBER

1/4 cup	(50 ml) sugar
1/3 cup	(75 ml) water
4	ripe bananas, peeled and sliced
1/4 tsp	(1 ml) cinnamon
3	egg whites, beaten stiff
1 cup	(250 ml) heavy cream, whipped

Cook sugar and water together in saucepan 1 minute over medium heat.

Add bananas and cinnamon; cook 3 minutes over medium-high heat.

Transfer bananas to food processor and blend until puréed. Chill.

Transfer puréed bananas to mixing bowl. Fold in stiff egg whites until well incorporated.

Have whipped cream ready in large bowl. Fold banana mixture into cream using spatula until well incorporated.

Spoon into dessert dishes and chill before serving.

Macaroon Bananas

(serves 4)

1 SERVING	574 CALORIES	73g CARBOHYDRATE
8g PROTEIN	28g FAT	4.9g FIBER

4	large bananas
1/4 cup	(50 ml) bourbon
1 tsp	(5 ml) lime juice
2	beaten eggs
1 1/2 cups	(375 ml) crushed macaroons
3 tbsp	(45 ml) butter

Peel bananas and place them on large platter. Add bourbon and lime juice; marinate 1 hour.

Dip bananas in beaten eggs and roll in crushed macaroons.

Heat butter in large frying pan. Add bananas and cook 2 to 3 minutes over medium heat, turning to brown all sides.

If desired, flambé with heated marinade before serving.

Banana Flip

(serves 4)

1 SERVING	224 CALORIES	25g CARBOHYDRATE
4g PROTEIN	12g FAT	1.2g FIBER

2	bananas, peeled
1 1/2 cups	(375 ml) cold milk
1 cup	(250 ml) cold light cream
2 tbsp	(30 ml) maple syrup
1/4 cup	(50 ml) dark rum
	few drops lime juice
	orange slices for decoration

Place bananas in blender and purée.

Add milk, cream, maple syrup, rum and lime juice; continue blending until well mixed and frothy.

Pour into tall-stemmed glasses and decorate with orange slices.

Passion Fruit Cream Dessert

(serves 4)

1 SERVING	333 CALORIES	49g CARBOHYDRATE
7g PROTEIN	12g FAT	–g FIBER

4	egg yolks
½ cup	(125 ml) sugar
1 cup	(250 ml) boiled milk, tepid
1 tbsp	(15 ml) rum
4	passion fruits
3 tbsp	(45 ml) heavy cream

Place egg yolks and sugar in stainless steel bowl; beat together with electric beater until mixture forms ribbons.

Mix in milk until well incorporated. Stir in rum and set bowl over saucepan half-filled with hot water. Cook over medium heat while stirring constantly with wooden spoon. Do not boil.

When cream coats the back of the spoon, remove bowl from saucepan and set aside to cool.

Slice passion fruits in half, widthwise. Using spoon, scoop out pulp and seeds and place in blender. Add heavy cream and blend at medium speed for 1 minute.

Pour blended fruit into custard cream and mix. Serve cold in dessert bowls.

Mango Sherbet

1 SERVING	174 CALORIES	40g CARBOHYDRATE
0g PROTEIN	0g FAT	0.9g FIBER

3½ lb	(1.6 kg) ripe mangoes
1 cup	(250 ml) granulated sugar
⅔ cup	(150 ml) water
3 tbsp	(45 ml) white rum
	juice 3 limes

Peel mangoes and slice off flesh from pits. Purée fruit in food processor and transfer to bowl.

Place sugar and water in small saucepan; cook 5 minutes over high heat.

Remove saucepan from heat and let syrup cool.

Add syrup, rum and lime juice to mangoes in bowl; mix well.

Freeze following the directions for your particular brand of ice cream maker.

Mango Salad

(serves 4)

1 SERVING	176 CALORIES	31g CARBOHYDRATE
8g PROTEIN	2g FAT	0.9g FIBER

2	large mangoes
3 tbsp	(45 ml) fine sugar
1-1½ cups	(250-375 ml) cottage cheese
1½ cups	(375 ml) raspberries
	juice 2 limes

Using sharp knife, run blade around mangoes against the large flat pit. Peel one half and slice flesh in wedges. Repeat for other side.

Place all wedges in bowl; add lime juice and sugar. Marinate 30 minutes.

Scoop cottage cheese onto dessert plates or in bowls. Surround with mangoes and top with raspberries. Serve.

Mango Mousse

(serves 4)

1 SERVING	260 CALORIES	35g CARBOHYDRATE
3g PROTEIN	12g FAT	1.4g FIBER

3	mangoes, peeled and sliced
3 cups	(750 ml) water
¼ cup	(50 ml) sugar
½ cup	(125 ml) heavy cream, whipped
3	egg whites, beaten stiff
	juice ½ lemon
	chocolate shavings

Place sliced mangoes in saucepan. Add water, sugar and lemon juice; cook 5 to 6 minutes over medium heat.

Force mixture through sieve into bowl; set aside to cool.

Incorporate whipped cream, then fold in beaten egg whites until well incorporated.

Chill before serving and decorate with chocolate shavings.

Mango and Prosciutto

(serves 4)

1 SERVING	138 CALORIES	23g CARBOHYDRATE
7g PROTEIN	2g FAT	1.4g FIBER

3	mangoes, peeled
¼ lb	(125 g) prosciutto slices
	lime slices
	ground pepper

Slice mangoes into 1 inch (2.5 cm) pieces.

Cut prosciutto slices into 3 and wrap around mango pieces; secure with toothpicks.

Serve with lime slices and season well with pepper.

Raspberry Rice Pudding

(serves 4-6)

1 SERVING	355 CALORIES	72g CARBOHYDRATE
7g PROTEIN	4g FAT	1.7g FIBER

2½ cups	(625 ml) salted water
1 cup	(250 ml) long grain rice, rinsed
3 cups	(750 ml) milk
1 cup	(250 ml) sugar
1 tsp	(5 ml) vanilla
½ tsp	(2 ml) nutmeg
1½ cups	(375 ml) raspberries

Pour salted water into saucepan and bring to boil. Mix in rice, cover and cook 19 to 21 minutes over low heat.

Add milk, half of sugar, vanilla and nutmeg; bring to boil. Mix rice well and cover saucepan; cook 30 to 35 minutes over low heat. Stir 2 to 3 times.

Transfer cooked rice to 8 cup (2 L) soufflé mold; refrigerate to cool.

Meanwhile, place raspberries and remaining sugar in small saucepan. Partially cover and cook 4 to 5 minutes.

Purée in food processor and spread over rice pudding. Serve.

Chestnut Parfait

(serves 4)

1 SERVING	395 CALORIES	47g CARBOHYDRATE
7g PROTEIN	20g FAT	0.8g FIBER

⅓ cup	(75 ml) granulated sugar
4	egg yolks
2 tbsp	(30 ml) rum
1 cup	(250 ml) hot milk
¼ cup	(50 ml) candied fruit
1 cup	(250 ml) canned puréed chestnuts
2 cups	(500 ml) whipped cream

Place sugar, egg yolks and rum in bowl. Mix together with electric beater until fluffy — about 2 minutes.

Pour in hot milk and whisk well. Cook cream in double-boiler until it coats the back of a spoon. Whisk constantly!

Stir in candied fruit.

Choose tall dessert glasses and spoon layer of puréed chestnuts in bottom. Follow with layer of custard cream and repeat until ingredients are used.

Top parfaits with whipped cream and if desired decorate with icing.

1 Place sugar, egg yolks and rum in bowl.

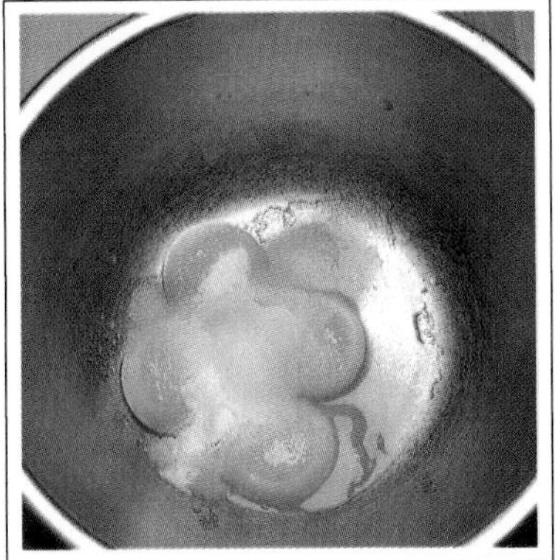

2 Mix together with electric beater until fluffy — about 2 minutes.

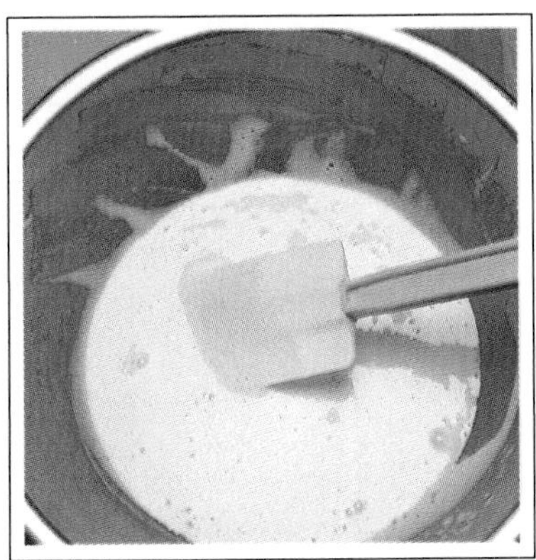

3 Pour in hot milk and whisk well.

4 After cream has cooked, begin layering the puréed chestnuts and custard cream in tall dessert glasses.

1 Place flour, $\frac{3}{4}$ cup (175 ml) butter and cinnamon in bowl.

2 Add granulated sugar.

3 Add 2 eggs and vanilla.

4 Incorporate with pastry blender.

Apple Galette

(serves 6-8)

1 SERVING	536 CALORIES	77g CARBOHYDRATE
5g PROTEIN	23g FAT	1.8g FIBER

2 cups	(500 ml) all-purpose flour
¾ cup	(175 ml) softened butter
1 tsp	(5 ml) cinnamon
¾ cup	(175 ml) granulated sugar
2	eggs
1 tsp	(5 ml) vanilla
2 tbsp	(30 ml) cold water
2 tbsp	(30 ml) butter
4	apples, cored, peeled and sliced
⅓ cup	(75 ml) brown sugar
1 tbsp	(15 ml) grated lemon rind
1 cup	(250 ml) icing sugar
2 tbsp	(30 ml) lemon juice
1 tbsp	(15 ml) hot water
	beaten egg

Place flour, ¾ cup (175 ml) butter and cinnamon in bowl. Add granulated sugar, 2 eggs and vanilla; incorporate with pastry blender.

Add cold water and pinch dough to incorporate. Shape into ball and cover with waxed paper; refrigerate 2 hours.

Preheat oven to 350°F (180°C).

When ready to prepare galette, cut dough in half. Roll both on floured surface until about ¼ inch (0.65 cm) thick. Dust with more flour if needed. Place 9 inch (23 cm) plate on dough and trace galettes. Cut away excess dough to form circles.

Place galettes on separate buttered and floured cookie sheets; brush lightly with beaten egg. Bake 10 minutes.

Set aside to cool while you prepare the filling.

Melt 2 tbsp (30 ml) butter in frying pan. Add apples and cook 15 minutes over high heat, stirring frequently.

Sprinkle in brown sugar and lemon rind; continue cooking 3 minutes.

Remove frying pan from heat and set aside to cool.

Meanwhile, prepare icing by placing icing sugar, lemon juice and hot water in small bowl. Mix together.

To assemble dessert, place one galette on bottom of serving platter. Cover with cooled apples and top with second galette. Generously spread lemon icing over top, letting it drip down sides. Decorate with additional colored icings if desired.

Slice (carefully) and serve.

Rhubarb and Raspberry Compote

(serves 4)

1 SERVING	319 CALORIES	64g CARBOHYDRATE
2g PROTEIN	6g FAT	5.3g FIBER

1 cup	(250 ml) sugar
1¼ cups	(300 ml) water
1½ lb	(750 g) diced rhubarb
1¼ cups	(300 ml) raspberries
3 tbsp	(45 ml) grated orange rind
	juice 1 lime
	heavy cream

Place sugar and water in large saucepan. Cook 4 to 5 minutes over medium-low heat or until sugar is melted.

Stir in rhubarb and lime juice; cook 10 minutes over low heat.

Add raspberries and orange rind; mix well. Continue cooking 3 minutes.

Spoon compote into dessert bowls and serve with heavy cream.

Super-Moist Cheesecake

(serves 10-12)

1 SERVING	410 CALORIES	32g CARBOHYDRATE
6g PROTEIN	29g FAT	0.1g FIBER

2	8 oz (250 g) packages cream cheese, softened
½ cup	(125 ml) granulated sugar
3 tbsp	(45 ml) Tia Maria liqueur
2 tbsp	(30 ml) cornstarch
4	egg yolks
1 cup	(250 ml) heavy cream, whipped
4	egg whites, beaten stiff
14 oz	(398 ml) can pitted Bing cherries
¼ cup	(50 ml) granulated sugar
1 tbsp	(15 ml) cornstarch
3 tbsp	(45 ml) cold water
	graham crumb bottom crust, cooked in 10 inch (25 cm) spring-form cake pan

Preheat oven to 300°F (150°C).

Place cheese and ½ cup (125 ml) sugar in bowl of electric mixer. Mix at medium speed until creamed.

Add liqueur and 2 tbsp (30 ml) cornstarch; continue mixing until completely incorporated and smooth.

Add egg yolks and mix very well — about 2 minutes.

Add whipped cream and continue mixing until incorporated.

Remove bowl from mixer and fold in beaten egg whites with spatula. Continue folding until well incorporated.

Pour batter into cake pan prepared with crumb crust and bake 1¼-1½ hours or until toothpick inserted comes out clean.

Remove cake from oven and let cool in pan.

Unmold and refrigerate 1 hour.

Meanwhile, begin preparing topping. Pour cherry juice (set cherries aside) and ¼ cup (50 ml) sugar in small saucepan. Bring to boil and continue cooking 2-3 minutes.

Mix 1 tbsp (15 ml) cornstarch with 3 tbsp (45 ml) cold water; stir into sauce and continue cooking 1 minute over medium heat.

When sauce has thickened enough, stir in cherries and set aside on counter to cool.

Spread cherries over cheesecake, slice and serve.

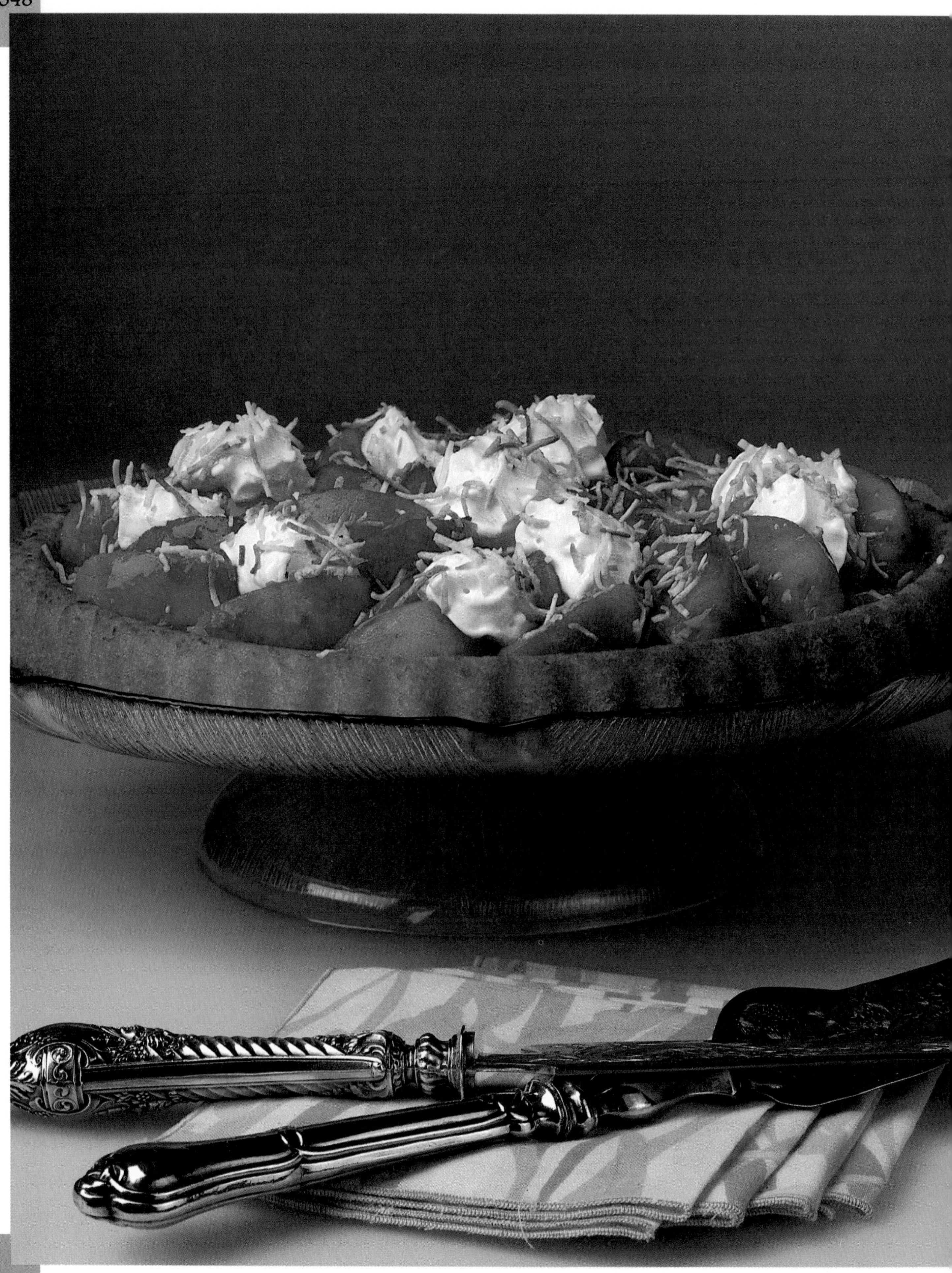

One Layer Fruit Cake

(serves 4-8)

1 SERVING	262 CALORIES	51g CARBOHYDRATE
3g PROTEIN	5g FAT	0.9g FIBER

4	ripe nectarines
2	ripe peaches
½ cup	(125 ml) sugar
1 cup	(250 ml) water
1	1.2 oz (34 g) package glaze mix, prepared
1	6 oz (169 g) shortcake layer
	juice 1 orange
	whipped cream for decoration

Cut fruit in half to remove pits — if they are not ripe this might be difficult.

Cut halves into quarters and set aside.

Place sugar, water and orange juice in saucepan; bring to boil. Continue cooking 3 to 4 minutes over high heat.

Add fruit to hot liquid in saucepan and bring to boiling point. Reduce heat to medium-low and continue cooking 2 minutes.

Remove fruit from liquid, peel and cut quarters in half; set aside on plate.

Replace saucepan containing syrup over heat and bring to boil.

Remove from heat and mix ⅓ cup (75 ml) of syrup into prepared glaze mix. Generously spread glaze over bottom of cake.

Arrange fruit on cake over glaze and brush with any remaining glaze.

Refrigerate before serving. Decorate with whipped cream and if desired, sprinkle with coconut.

1 Cut fruit in half to remove pits — if they are not ripe this might be difficult.

3 Mix ⅓ cup (75 ml) of syrup into prepared glaze mix.

2 Add fruit to syrup mixture in saucepan and bring to boiling point. Reduce heat to medium-low and continue cooking 2 minutes.

4 Generously spread glaze over bottom of cake and arrange fruit on top. Brush with leftover glaze.

Afternoon Rum Cake

(serves 8-10)

1 SERVING	524 CALORIES	51g CARBOHYDRATE
9g PROTEIN	32g FAT	0.3g FIBER

1¼ cups	(300 ml) softened butter
1 cup	(250 ml) granulated sugar
5	eggs
3 cups	(750 ml) all-purpose flour
1 tsp	(5 ml) cinnamon
2 tsp	(10 ml) baking powder
2 tbsp	(30 ml) dark rum
1 cup	(250 ml) milk
½ cup	(125 ml) slivered almonds
	grated rind 1 lemon
	pinch salt
	icing sugar

Preheat oven to 325°F (160°C). Generously butter 9 inch (23 cm) spring-form cake pan.

Place butter and lemon rind in large bowl; work butter until pliable.

Add sugar and cream together using spatula.

Add 1 egg and 3 tbsp (45 ml) flour and cinnamon; beat together with electric beater.

Add remaining eggs and beat until completely incorporated.

Place remaining flour with baking powder and salt in small bowl; mix together.

Sift half into egg batter and mix very well with spatula.

Pour in rum and incorporate with spatula.

Add remaining flour and continue incorporating.

Pour in milk and with spatula, mix until incorporated. Fold in almonds.

Pour batter into prepared cake pan and rap bottom against counter to settle mixture. Bake 40 minutes or until toothpick inserted comes out clean.

Remove pan from oven and cool 5-6 minutes.

Unmold onto wire rack and set aside until cold.

Place icing sugar in wire sieve and dust cake just before serving.

1 Place butter and lemon rind in bowl; work butter until pliable.

3 Add 1 egg, 3 tbsp (45 ml) flour and cinnamon; beat together with electric beater.

2 Add sugar and cream together using spatula.

4 After remaining eggs have been added, start adding the rest of the flour.

Midnight Snacking Cake

(serves 6-8)

1 SERVING	240 CALORIES	25g CARBOHYDRATE
4g PROTEIN	14g FAT	0g FIBER

½ cup	(125 ml) softened butter
½ cup	(125 ml) granulated sugar
1 tsp	(5 ml) cinnamon
3	eggs
4 tbsp	(60 ml) rum
1¼ cups	(300 ml) all-purpose flour
1 tsp	(5 ml) baking powder
	pinch salt

Preheat oven to 350°F (180°C). Butter 8½ inch (21 cm) spring-form cake pan.

Place butter, sugar and cinnamon in bowl; cream together.

Add first egg and beat well with electric beater.

Add remaining eggs, one at a time, beating well after each addition. Add rum during this time.

Mix flour with baking powder and salt; sift into batter and mix with spatula until smooth.

Pour batter into prepared cake pan and bake 30-35 minutes or until toothpick inserted comes out clean.

Cool in pan about 10-15 minutes before unmolding cake onto wire rack for continued cooling.

Ice with vanilla icing or another one of your favorites.

* Make recipe twice for two-layer cake.

1 Place butter, sugar and cinnamon in bowl; cream together.

3 Mix flour with baking powder and salt; sift into batter and mix with spatula until smooth.

2 Add eggs, one at a time, beating well after each addition. At some point during this time, add the rum too.

4 Pour batter into prepared cake pan.

Raisin Almond Fruit Cake

(serves 8-10)

1 SERVING	619 CALORIES	59g CARBOHYDRATE
9g PROTEIN	39g FAT	2.1g FIBER

1¾ cups	(425 ml) all-purpose flour
1 tbsp	(15 ml) baking powder
¾ cup	(175 ml) sultana raisins
1 cup	(250 ml) chopped walnuts
1 cup	(250 ml) slivered almonds
1 cup	(250 ml) all-vegetable shortening
½ cup	(125 ml) brown sugar
½ cup	(125 ml) granulated sugar
4	eggs
½ cup	(125 ml) chopped candied mixed fruit
¼ cup	(50 ml) Tia Maria
	pinch salt
	pinch powdered ginger

Preheat oven to 325°F (160°C). Butter 8 inch (20 cm) square cake pan.

Sift flour, baking powder, salt and ginger into bowl.

Place raisins, walnuts and almonds in another bowl; add ⅓ of flour mixture. Toss and set aside.

Place shortening, brown and granulated sugar in bowl containing just flour. Incorporate well with pastry blender.

Add eggs and blend well with wooden spoon.

Incorporate raisin/flour mixture along with candied fruit; mix very well with wooden spoon.

Pour in Tia Maria and blend well. Pour batter into prepared cake pan and bake 1 hour or until toothpick inserted comes out clean.

Cool cake in pan before unmolding onto wire rack.

Serve with tea, coffee, as a snack or in your children's lunches as a nutritious dessert.

1 Sift flour, baking powder, salt and ginger into bowl.

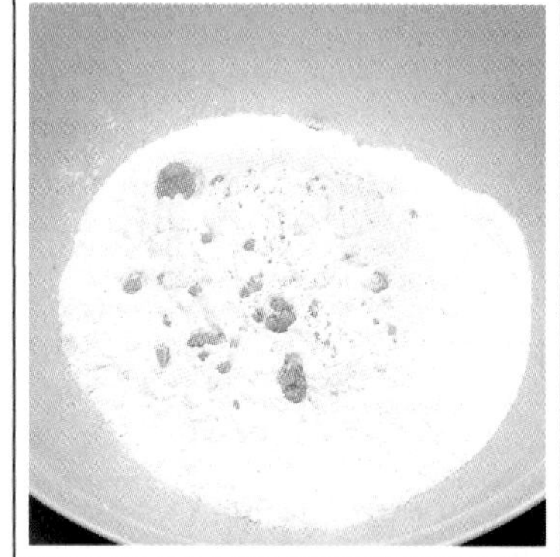

3 Place shortening, brown and granulated sugar in bowl containing just flour. Incorporate well with pastry blender.

2 Place raisins, walnuts and almonds in another bowl; add ⅓ of flour mixture. Toss and set aside.

4 Add eggs and blend well with wooden spoon.

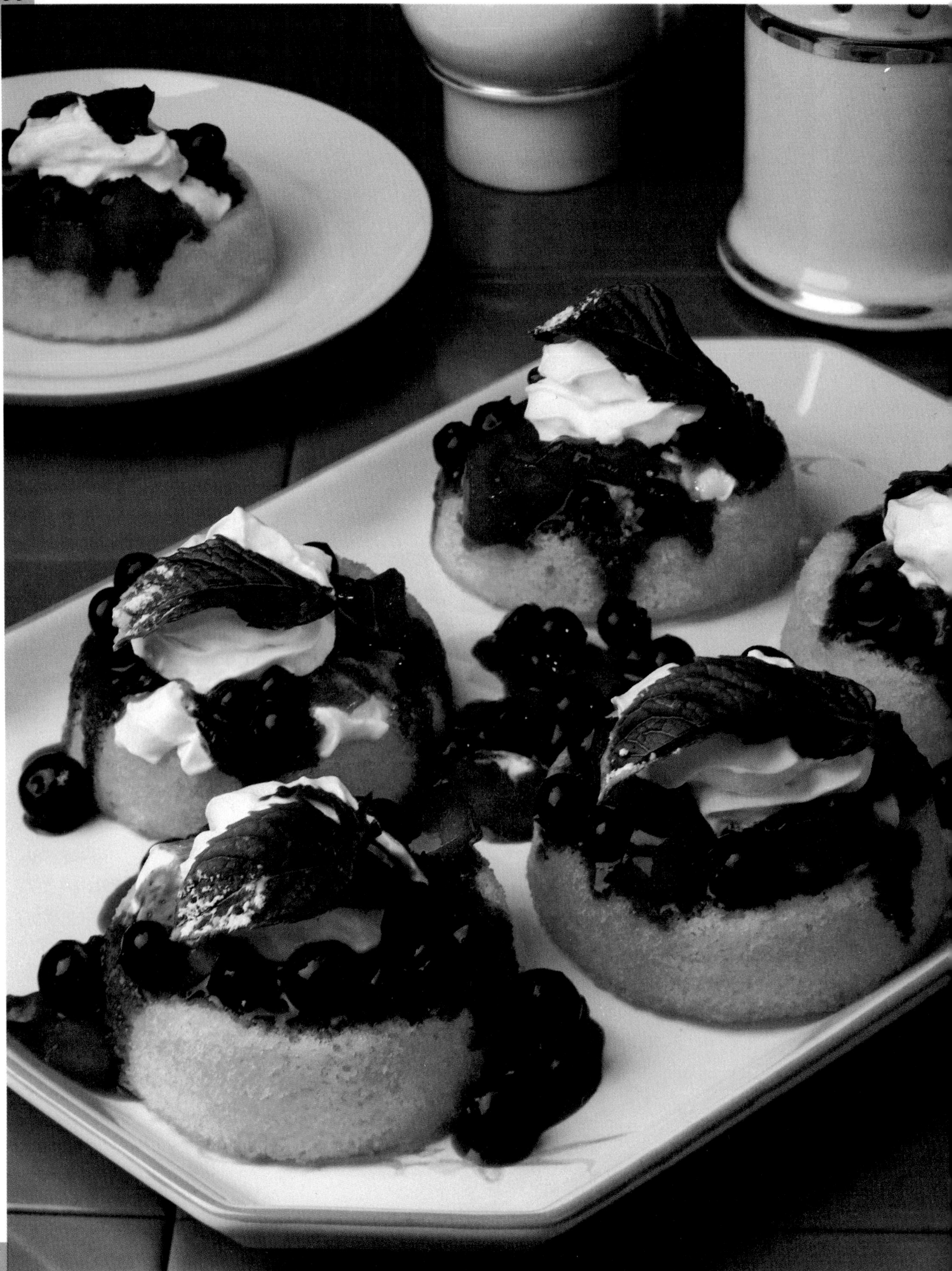

Blueberry and Papaya Cakes

(serves 6)

1 SERVING	233 CALORIES	43g CARBOHYDRATE
4g PROTEIN	5g FAT	1.3g FIBER

½	papaya
⅓ cup	(75 ml) sugar
¼ cup	(50 ml) water
1½ cups	(375 ml) blueberries
¼ cup	(50 ml) orange juice
2 tsp	(10 ml) cornstarch
3 tbsp	(45 ml) cold water
6	cake dessert shells
	dash grated lemon rind
	whipped cream to taste

Slice half papaya in half again, lengthwise. Seed, peel and dice flesh.

Place papaya in saucepan with sugar and ¼ cup (50 ml) water. Bring to boil over medium heat and continue cooking 3 minutes.

Stir in blueberries, orange juice and lemon rind; bring to boil again.

Mix cornstarch with 3 tbsp (45 ml) water; stir into cooking fruit and cook 1 more minute.

Pour into bowl and refrigerate until cold.

Fill cakes with whipped cream to taste; arrange on attractive serving platter.

Spoon fruit topping over cream, letting it drip down sides of cakes. Decorate with more whipped cream and serve.

Orange Cake Sauce

¼ cup (50 ml)	93 CALORIES	23g CARBOHYDRATE
0g PROTEIN	0g FAT	0.5g FIBER

1	small orange
1	lime
½	lemon
½ cup	(125 ml) strawberries, hulled
½ cup	(125 ml) brown sugar
½ cup	(125 ml) granulated sugar
⅔ cup	(150 ml) water
1 oz	(30 ml) rum

Slice orange and lime in half; remove seeds and dice with rind. Dice ½ seeded lemon with rind as well.

Place diced fruit in food processor and mix well. Add strawberries and blend 30 seconds; set aside.

Place both sugars and water in saucepan; bring to boil. Continue cooking until temperature reaches 260°F (125°C). If you do not have a candy thermometer, drop a bit of syrup in cold water — if it forms a soft ball, it has reached the correct temperature.

Remove saucepan from stove, cool 5 minutes, then add fruit and rum.

Cool sauce before serving over cake.

Almond Brownies

(serves 6-8)

1 SERVING	410 CALORIES	33g CARBOHYDRATE
7g PROTEIN	28g FAT	0.7g FIBER

2 oz	(60 g) unsweetened chocolate
½ cup	(125 ml) softened butter
¾ cup	(175 ml) granulated sugar
3 tbsp	(45 ml) honey
1 tsp	(5 ml) vanilla
2	eggs
½ cup	(125 ml) sifted all-purpose flour
1 cup	(250 ml) slivered almonds
1	egg white, beaten stiff
	pinch salt

Preheat oven to 350°F (180°C). Butter 8 inch (20 cm) square cake pan.

Place chocolate in stainless steel bowl. Melt over saucepan half-filled with boiling water.

Place butter, sugar and honey in large bowl. Add melted chocolate and mix well.

Add vanilla and eggs, one at a time, beating well after each addition. It is best to use electric beater.

Fold in flour and salt and mix until completely incorporated. Stir in almonds and incorporate stiff egg white.

Pour batter into prepared cake pan and bake 25-30 minutes or until toothpick inserted comes out clean.

Cool brownies in pan 10-15 minutes, then finish cooling on wire rack. Serve with cold milk if desired.

1 Add melted chocolate to butter, sugar and honey placed in large bowl. Mix well.

3 Fold in flour and salt and mix until completely incorporated.

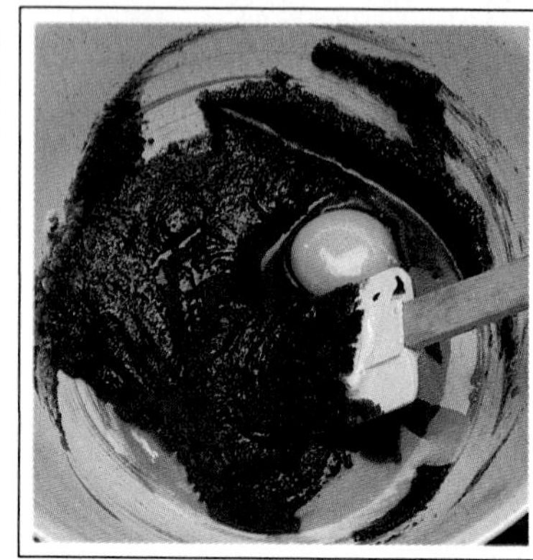

2 Add vanilla and first egg; beat well before adding second egg.

4 Stir in almonds and incorporate stiff egg white.

Papaya Pie

(serves 6-8)

1 SERVING	336 CALORIES	47g CARBOHYDRATE
3g PROTEIN	15g FAT	1.0g FIBER

4	large ripe papayas, peeled
¾ cup	(175 ml) granulated sugar
1 tsp	(5 ml) nutmeg
1 tsp	(5 ml) cinnamon
2 tbsp	(30 ml) butter
2 tbsp	(30 ml) cornstarch
1	beaten egg
	enough dough for bottom and top crusts*

Preheat oven to 425°F (220°C).

Cut papayas in half, seed and slice ½ inch (1.2 cm) thick. Place in bowl with sugar, nutmeg, cinnamon, butter and cornstarch; mix well.

Line 10 inch (25 cm) pie plate with half of rolled dough.

Add papaya filling and brush edges of dough with a bit of water.

Cover with top crust and pinch edges shut. Score top several times and brush with beaten egg.

Bake 7 minutes.

Reduce heat to 350°F (180°C) and continue baking 35-40 minutes. Note: If upper crust browns too quickly, cover with small sheet of aluminum foil.

Let cool slightly before serving.

* If desired you can use the dough recipe from the Blueberry Pie.

Cold Lime Soufflé

(serves 4-6)

1 SERVING	326 CALORIES	32g CARBOHYDRATE
7g PROTEIN	19g FAT	0g FIBER

2	small envelopes unflavored gelatine
¼ cup	(50 ml) cold water
4	egg yolks
¾ cup	(175 ml) super-fine sugar
4	egg whites, beaten stiff
1 cup	(250 ml) heavy cream, whipped
	juice of 6 large limes

Sprinkle gelatine over water poured into small bowl; set aside.

Place egg yolks and sugar in large bowl; mix together with whisk.

If bowl is stainless steel, set over saucepan half-filled with boiling water. Otherwise, use double-boiler.

Reduce heat to low and cook while whisking constantly until mixture becomes thick enough to coat the back of a spoon.

Whisk in gelatine and cook 1 more minute.

Squeeze in lime juice, whisk quickly and remove from heat. Set aside to cool.

When egg yolks are cool, incorporate beaten egg whites by folding in with spatula.

Fold in whipped cream, incorporating with spatula.

Attach a foil collar around the outside edge of 4 cup (1 L) soufflé mold. Tape to secure.

Pour in soufflé mixture and refrigerate 4 hours.

Remove collar and serve with a fruit sauce if desired.

Lime Pie

(serves 6)

1 SERVING	443 CALORIES	48g CARBOHYDRATE
9g PROTEIN	24g FAT	0g FIBER

9 inch	(23 cm) pie shell
1¼ cups	(300 ml) can sweetened condensed milk
3	egg yolks
2 tbsp	(30 ml) grated lime rind
½ cup	(125 ml) lime juice
2	egg whites, beaten stiff
½ cup	(125 ml) heavy cream, whipped stiff

Bake pie shell in oven preheated at 425°F (220°C) for 12 to 15 minutes. Remove and set aside to cool.

Place milk, egg yolks, lime rind and juice in stainless steel bowl. Set over saucepan half-filled with hot water on medium-low heat. Cook mixture until thickened, stirring constantly.

Transfer bowl to counter and let cool.

Fold in egg whites, then whipped cream, with spatula.

Pour filling into pie shell and refrigerate overnight. Garnish pie with roasted almonds or with slices of lime if desired.

Blueberry Pie

(serves 6-8)

1 SERVING	433 CALORIES	65g CARBOHYDRATE
3g PROTEIN	18g FAT	2.1g FIBER

2 cups	(500 ml) all-purpose flour
⅔ cup	(150 ml) all-vegetable shortening
5-6 tbsp	(75-90 ml) cold water
1¼ cups	(300 ml) granulated sugar
3 tbsp	(45 ml) cornstarch
4 cups	(1 L) thawed blueberries
1 tbsp	(15 ml) melted butter
1 tbsp	(15 ml) grated lemon rind
	several pinches salt
	light cream

Sift flour with one pinch salt into large bowl. Add shortening and incorporate with pastry blender.

Knead in enough cold water to form a ball. Wrap in waxed paper and refrigerate 2-3 hours.

Preheat oven to 425°F (220°C).

Cut dough in half. Roll out on floured surface and line 10 inch (25 cm) pie plate. Set aside.

Place sugar, cornstarch and remaining ingredients in saucepan; mix well. Cook 15 minutes over low heat.

Pour cooled berry mixture into pie shell. Cover with top crust and pinch edges shut. Score top several times and brush with light cream.

Bake 10 minutes.

Reduce heat to 375°F (190°C) and continue baking 45 minutes.

Let cool slightly before serving.

1 Sift flour and salt into large bowl.

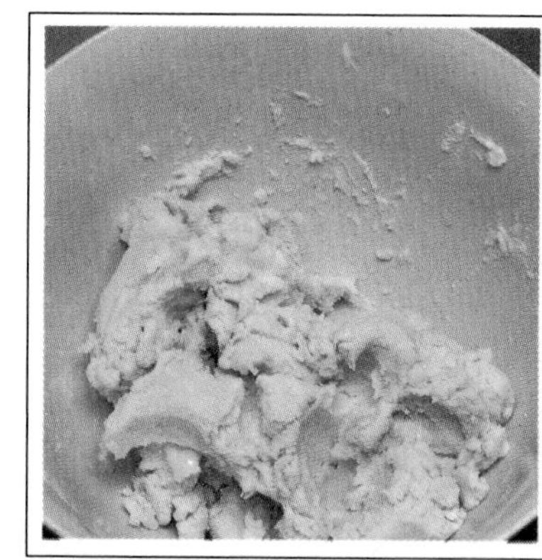

3 Add water as required and knead dough to form ball. The dough should be pliable and all ingredients completely combined.

2 Add shortening and incorporate with pastry blender — the dough will begin to take shape.

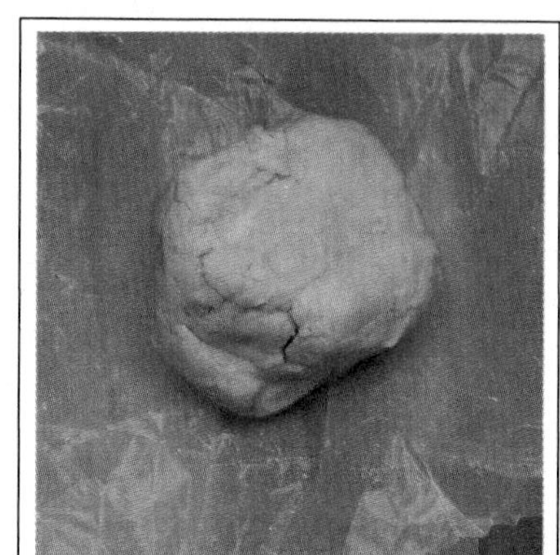

4 Wrap dough in waxed paper and refrigerate 2-3 hours.

Rum Graham Pie

(serves 6-8)

1 SERVING	419 CALORIES	43g CARBOHYDRATE
7g PROTEIN	23g FAT	0.5g FIBER

1½ cups	(375 ml) graham crumbs
½ cup	(125 ml) brown sugar
¼ cup	(50 ml) softened butter
¼ cup	(50 ml) cold water
1	small envelope unflavored gelatine
3	egg yolks
¼ cup	(50 ml) granulated sugar
¼ cup	(50 ml) rum
¼ cup	(50 ml) light cream
3	egg whites, beaten stiff
1 cup	(250 ml) heavy cream, whipped
	grated rind 1 orange

Preheat oven to 375°F (190°C).

Place graham crumbs and half of brown sugar in bowl; mix together.

Add butter and incorporate well. Press mixture into 10 inch (25 cm) spring-form cake pan. Bake 8 minutes. Remove from oven and set aside.

Pour cold water into small bowl. Sprinkle in gelatine and let stand without stirring.

Place egg yolks in large bowl. Add remaining brown sugar and all of granulated sugar; beat well with electric beater.

Mix in orange rind. Pour in rum and light cream; mix well.

Cook pastry cream in double-boiler until it coats the back of a spoon. Whisk constantly!

Incorporate gelatine and whisk 30 seconds. Remove from heat and refrigerate.

When custard cream is cold and almost settled, incorporate egg whites and whipped cream with whisk.

Make a collar from double sheets of foil that can be placed around the cake pan to help keep the cream mixture in position during chilling. Tape securely to pan.

Once the collar is positioned correctly, pour in the rum cream mixture and refrigerate overnight.

Unmold. Serve plain or with a variety of fruit toppings.

1 Place egg yolks in large bowl with remaining brown sugar and all of granulated sugar; beat well.

3 Be sure to beat the egg whites until stiff. Notice how they form peaks.

2 Mix in orange rind. Pour in rum and light cream; mix well.

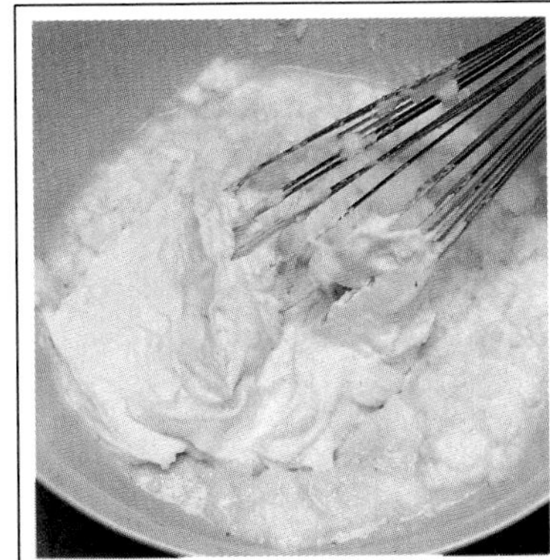

4 When custard cream is cold and almost settled, incorporate egg whites and whipped cream.

Rhubarb Pie

(serves 6)

1 SERVING	476 CALORIES	71g CARBOHYDRATE
5g PROTEIN	19g FAT	2.4g FIBER

1½ lb	(750 g) cubed rhubarb
¾ cup	(175 ml) granulated sugar
¾ cup	(175 ml) brown sugar
2 tbsp	(30 ml) grated lemon rind
2½ tbsp	(40 ml) cornstarch
2	large eggs
2 tbsp	(30 ml) heavy cream
	pastry dough for pie shell and top crust

Preheat oven to 425°F (220°C).

Mix rhubarb with sugars, lemon rind and cornstarch; toss to evenly coat.

Beat eggs with cream; pour half over rhubarb and mix.

Spoon rhubarb into uncooked pie shell. Cover with top crust, crimp edges and prick with fork or knife. Brush with remaining beaten eggs.

Bake 25 minutes in oven.

Reduce heat to 350°F (180°C) and continue baking 15 minutes.

Cool before serving.

Rum Cream Pie

(serves 6-8)

1 SERVING	260 CALORIES	23g CARBOHYDRATE
2g PROTEIN	16g FAT	0g FIBER

3	egg yolks
½ cup	(125 ml) granulated sugar
1 tbsp	(15 ml) grated lemon rind
1 cup	(250 ml) hot milk
4 tbsp	(60 ml) rum
1	small envelope unflavored gelatine
½ cup	(125 ml) heavy cream, whipped
3	egg whites, beaten stiff
9 inch	(23 cm) pie shell, precooked
	grated sweet chocolate

Place egg yolks and sugar in large bowl and mix with electric beater until color changes to nearly white.

Stir in lemon rind. Pour in hot milk and whisk very well.

Pour rum into small bowl and sprinkle in gelatine; set aside.

Cook milk mixture in double-boiler until cream coats the back of a spoon. It is essential to whisk constantly.

Add gelatine and continue cooking 1 more minute, whisking constantly.

Refrigerate cream until it settles and starts to cling to the sides of the bowl.

Remove cream from refrigerator and fold in whipped cream. Incorporate with whisk.

Fold in beaten egg whites and gently whisk to finish incorporating. Refrigerate 5-6 minutes.

Whisk mixture again and pour into prepared pie shell. Refrigerate 6 hours.

Dust with grated chocolate just before serving.

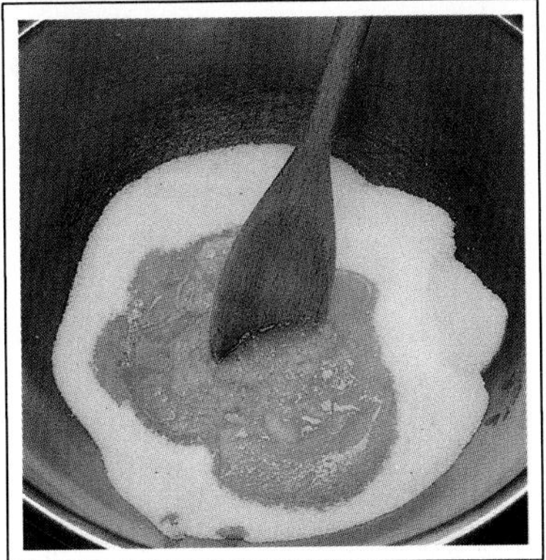

1 Place egg yolks and sugar in large bowl, preferably stainless steel for use later as double-boiler.

3 Pour in hot milk and whisk very well.

2 Mix with electric beater until color changes to nearly white. Stir in lemon rind.

4 After cream has been cooked and chilled, fold in whipped cream and incorporate with whisk.

Honey Walnut Clusters

(yield: 24-36)

2 CLUSTERS	140 CALORIES	13g CARBOHYDRATE
2g PROTEIN	9g FAT	0.2g FIBER

1/3 cup	(75 ml) granulated sugar
1/2 cup	(125 ml) softened butter
1 tsp	(5 ml) vanilla
1 1/4 cups	(300 ml) all-purpose flour
3/4 cup	(175 ml) chopped walnuts
1/4 cup	(50 ml) light cream
1/4 cup	(50 ml) liquid honey

Prepare cookie sheet by lining it with sheet of lightly buttered aluminum foil; set aside.

Place sugar and butter in large bowl; cream together.

Add vanilla and flour; combine with pastry blender.

Mix in walnuts. Add cream and blend everything together (best to use your hands) until well incorporated.

Knead with heel of your hand and shape into ball. Cover with waxed paper and refrigerate 30 minutes.

Preheat oven to 350°F (180°C).

Drop about 1 tbsp (15 ml) of cookie dough onto prepared sheet. Flatten slightly with fork, brush tops with honey and bake 18-20 minutes.

Cool cookies on wire racks.

1 Place sugar and butter in large bowl; cream together.

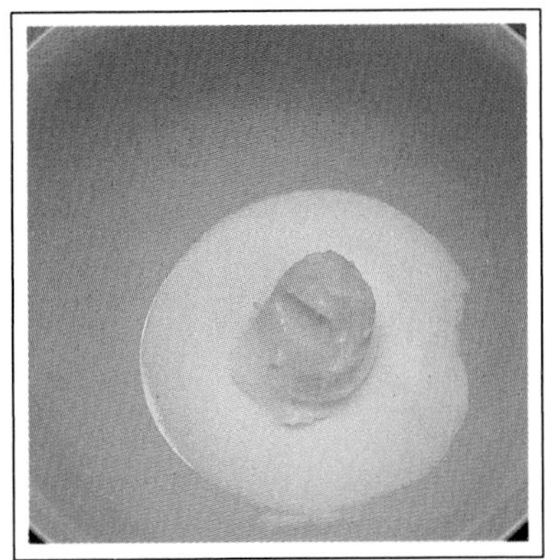

3 Mix in walnuts. Add cream and blend everything together.

2 Add vanilla and flour; combine with pastry blender.

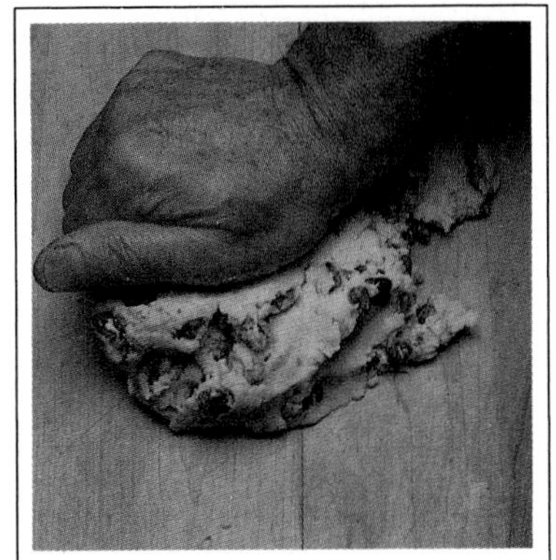

4 Knead dough with the heel of your hand and shape into ball for chilling.

Lemon Glazed Cookies

(yield: 24-36)

2 COOKIES	145 CALORIES	16g CARBOHYDRATE
0g PROTEIN	9g FAT	0g FIBER

2 cups	(500 ml) all-purpose flour
½ cup	(125 ml) all-vegetable shortening
1 tsp	(5 ml) nutmeg
½ cup	(125 ml) granulated sugar
2	egg yolks
¼ cup	(50 ml) softened butter
⅓ cup	(75 ml) light cream
1 cup	(250 ml) icing sugar
2 tbsp	(30 ml) lemon juice
1 tbsp	(15 ml) hot water
	pinch salt
	grated rind 1 orange

Preheat oven to 350°F (180°C).

Place flour, salt, shortening, nutmeg, granulated sugar and orange rind in bowl.

Add egg yolks and butter; incorporate well with pastry blender.

Add cream and pinch dough to incorporate. Roll on floured surface until about ¼ inch (0.65 cm) thick. Dust with more flour if needed.

Using assorted cookie cutters, cut shapes and place on buttered cookie sheet. Bake 12 minutes.

Meanwhile, mix remaining ingredients together for glaze.

As soon as cookies are done, brush tops with lemon glaze.

Cool cookies on wire racks.

1 Place flour, salt, shortening and nutmeg in bowl.

3 Add egg yolks.

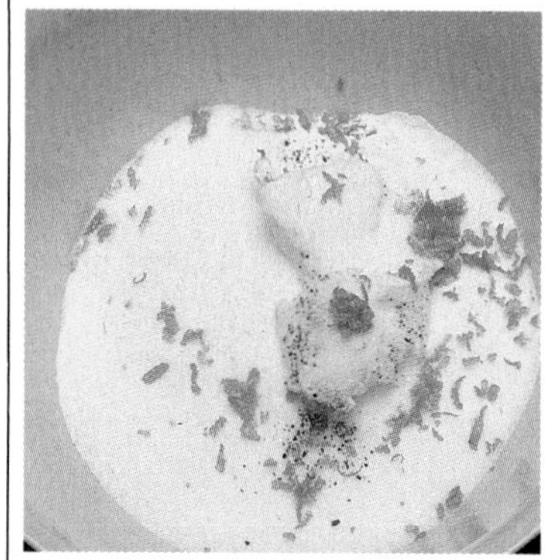

2 Add granulated sugar and orange rind.

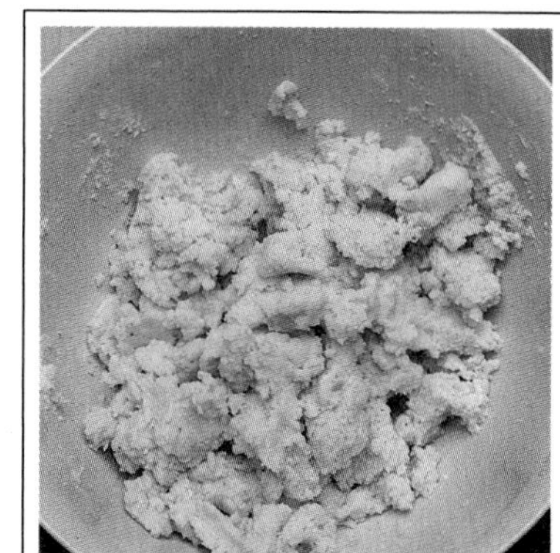

4 Add butter and incorporate well with pastry blender.

Almond Cookies

(yield: 24-36)

2 COOKIES	152 CALORIES	15g CARBOHYDRATE
3g PROTEIN	9g FAT	0.1g FIBER

$\frac{3}{4}$ cup	(175 ml) softened butter
$\frac{1}{2}$ cup	(125 ml) granulated sugar
$\frac{3}{4}$ cup	(175 ml) ground almonds
$1\frac{3}{4}$ cups	(425 ml) all-purpose flour
$\frac{1}{4}$ cup	(50 ml) light cream
2 tbsp	(30 ml) cold water

Place butter, sugar and almonds in bowl; cream together.

Add flour and incorporate with pastry blender.

Pour in cream and pinch dough with fingers.

Add water, incorporate and shape dough into ball. Cover with waxed paper and refrigerate 1 hour.

Preheat oven to 350°F (180°C).

Place dough on floured surface and roll until about $\frac{1}{4}$ inch (0.65 cm) thick. Dust with more flour if needed.

Using assorted cookie cutters, form shapes and place on buttered cookie sheet. Bake 10-12 minutes.

Cool cookies on wire racks.

Anise Cookies

(yield: 24-36)

2 COOKIES	102 CALORIES	21g CARBOHYDRATE
2g PROTEIN	1g FAT	0.1g FIBER

3	eggs
1 cup	(250 ml) granulated sugar
2 cups	(500 ml) all-purpose flour
1 tsp	(5 ml) baking powder
1 tbsp	(15 ml) anise seeds

Place eggs in large bowl and add sugar; mix together.

In separate bowl, sift flour with baking powder. Drop in anise seeds and mix.

Incorporate flour into wet batter. Cover with waxed paper and refrigerate dough overnight.

Preheat oven to 350°F (180°C).

Place cookie dough on floured surface and roll dough until about ¼ inch (0.65 cm) thick. Sprinkle with additional flour to avoid sticking.

Using cookie cutters (of different shapes if desired), form shapes and place cookies on buttered cookie sheet. Bake 10 minutes.

Cool cookies on wire racks.

Party Cookies

(yield: 24-36)

2 COOKIES	119 CALORIES	13g CARBOHYDRATE
1g PROTEIN	7g FAT	0g FIBER

½ cup	(125 ml) softened butter
¾ cup	(175 ml) granulated sugar
1 oz	(30 g) grated semi-sweet chocolate
1	egg
¼ cup	(50 ml) shredded coconut
1¼ cups	(300 ml) all-purpose flour
1 tsp	(5 ml) baking powder
	pinch salt
	green sprinkles

Place butter, sugar and chocolate in bowl; cream together with electric beater.

Add egg and continue beating.

Mix in coconut. Sift flour with baking powder and salt; incorporate into wet batter. Cover with waxed paper and refrigerate 3 hours. Preheat oven to 350°F (180 °C).

Place cookie dough on floured surface and roll dough until about ¼ inch (0.65 cm) thick. Sprinkle with additional flour to avoid sticking.

Shower dough with green sprinkles and cut into shapes with cookie cutters.

Place cookies on buttered cookie sheet and bake 10 minutes. Cool on wire racks.

1 Place butter, sugar and chocolate in bowl; cream together with electric beater.

3 Mix in coconut. Sift flour with baking powder and salt; incorporate into wet batter. Cover with waxed paper and refrigerate 3 hours.

2 Add egg and continue beating.

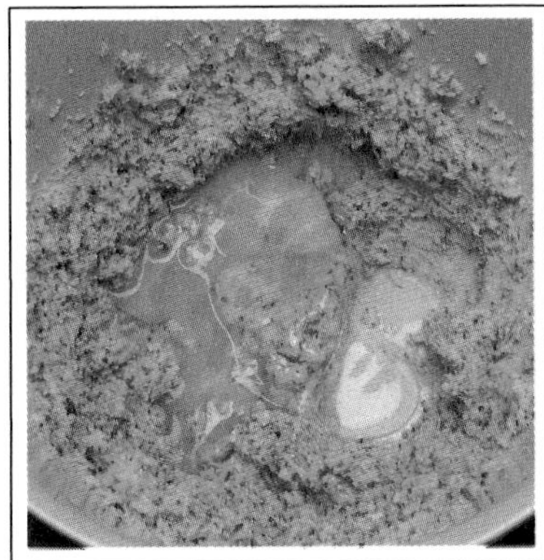

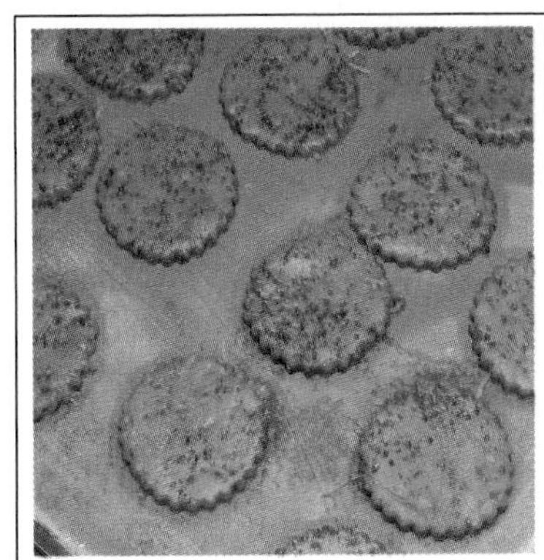

4 Place prepared cookies on buttered sheet and bake 10 minutes.

Chocolate Tube Cake

(serves 8-10)

1 SERVING	424 CALORIES	27g CARBOHYDRATE
10g PROTEIN	31g FAT	0.2g FIBER

8 oz	(250 g) sweet chocolate
½ cup	(125 ml) strong black coffee
2 tbsp	(30 ml) Tia Maria liqueur
10	egg yolks
½ cup	(125 ml) granulated sugar
10	egg whites
1½ cups	(375 ml) heavy cream, whipped with dash vanilla
½ cup	(125 ml) slivered almonds

Preheat oven to 350°F (180°C). Butter 2 cookie sheets and cover each with sheet of buttered waxed paper.

Place chocolate, coffee and liqueur in stainless steel bowl (or double-boiler) and place over saucepan half-filled with boiling water. Allow chocolate to melt, then remove and set aside to cool.

Place egg yolks in bowl and add granulated sugar; beat with electric beater about 3-4 minutes.

Stir in melted chocolate and continue beating 2-3 minutes. Place bowl in refrigerator 5-6 minutes.

Beat egg whites until stiff. Incorporate ⅓ into cooled chocolate mixture, mixing with spatula.

Add remaining egg whites and fold in with spatula, scraping bottom of bowl to incorporate. Turn bowl during this procedure and be careful not to overmix!

Pour batter onto prepared cookie sheets and spread evenly with spatula. Bake 15 minutes.

Turn off oven. With door ajar, let cakes stand 10 minutes.

Remove from oven and let cool 5-6 minutes.

Spread whipped cream over cakes and sprinkle with almonds. Delicately detach cake from waxed paper while rolling it onto itself.

Completely rid of old waxed paper, wrap chocolate tubes in new waxed paper and refrigerate 12 hours before serving.

1 Place egg yolks in bowl and add granulated sugar; beat with electric beater about 3-4 minutes.

3 Incorporate ⅓ of beaten egg whites into cooled chocolate mixture. Mix with spatula.

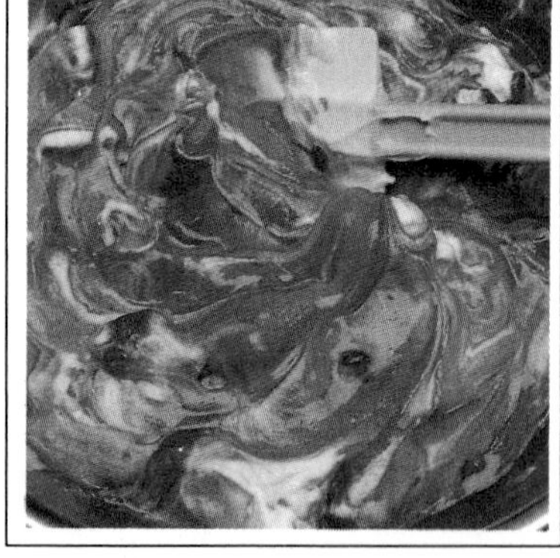

2 Stir in melted chocolate and continue beating 2-3 minutes.

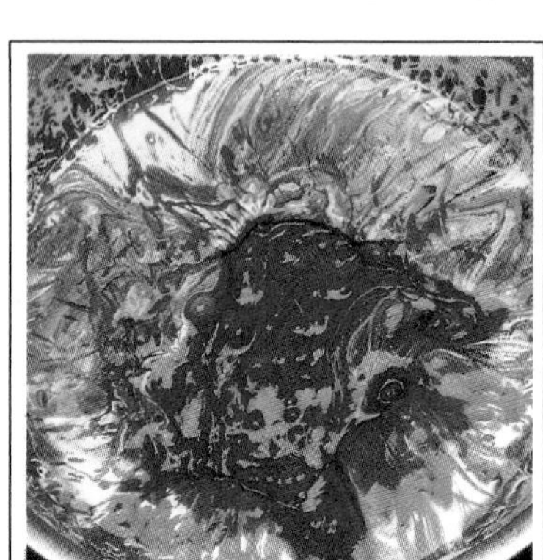

4 Add remaining egg whites and fold with spatula, scraping bottom of bowl, to incorporate.

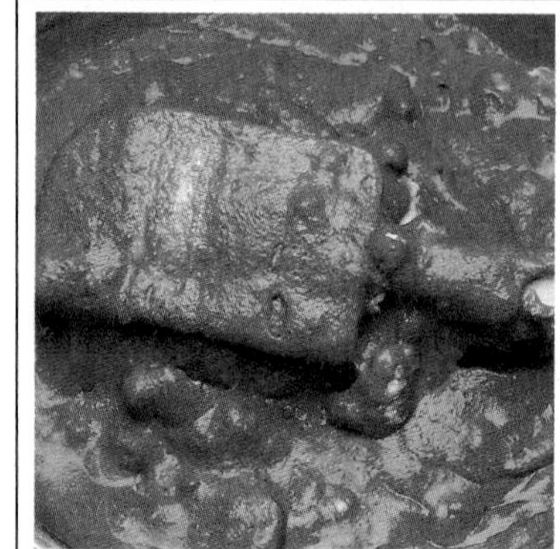

Demi
Demi

Shortbread Cookies

(yield: 24-36)

2 COOKIES	179 CALORIES	19g CARBOHYDRATE
1g PROTEIN	11g FAT	0.1g FIBER

½ lb	(250 g) softened, unsalted butter
½ cup	(125 ml) icing sugar
½ cup	(125 ml) cornstarch
1½ cups	(375 ml) all-purpose flour
1 tsp	(5 ml) cinnamon
	pinch salt
	candied cherries, halved

Preheat oven to 325°F (160°C).

Place butter in food processor. Add sugar and mix 2-3 minutes.

Add cornstarch, flour, cinnamon and salt; continue mixing until well blended.

Roll dough between the palms of your hands into small balls. Place on buttered and floured cookie sheet and flatten with tines of fork. Top with candied cherries.

Bake 14 minutes. Cool cookies on wire racks.

1 Place softened, unsalted butter in bowl of food processor.

3 Mix 2-3 minutes.

2 Add icing sugar.

4 Add remaining ingredients, except cherries, and continue mixing until well blended.

Royal Biscuits

(yield: 24-36)

2 COOKIES	155 CALORIES	21g CARBOHYDRATE
2g PROTEIN	7g FAT	0.3g FIBER

1 cup	(250 ml) all-purpose flour
¾ tsp	(3 ml) baking soda
1 tsp	(5 ml) baking powder
½ tsp	(2 ml) ground cloves
1 cup	(250 ml) brown sugar
½ cup	(125 ml) softened butter
1	beaten egg
1 tsp	(5 ml) vanilla
1 cup	(250 ml) quick-cooking rolled oats
½ cup	(125 ml) shredded coconut
	pinch salt

Place flour, baking soda, baking powder, cloves and salt in bowl; stir and set aside.

Cream brown sugar and butter in another bowl using spatula.

Stir in egg and vanilla; mix with electric beater.

Add rolled oats and coconut; incorporate well with spatula.

Fold in flour mixture and mix until completely incorporated. Cover with sheet of waxed paper and refrigerate 2-3 hours.

Preheat oven to 350°F (180°C).

When ready to bake cookies, roll dough on floured surface until about ¼ inch (0.65 cm) thick.

Using assorted cookie cutters, form shapes and place on buttered cookie sheet. Bake 10 minutes.

Cool cookies on wire racks.

These wholesome biscuits are a perfect companion for afternoon breaks.

1 Cream brown sugar and butter together using spatula.

3 Add rolled oats and coconut; incorporate well with spatula.

2 Stir in egg and vanilla; then mix with electric beater.

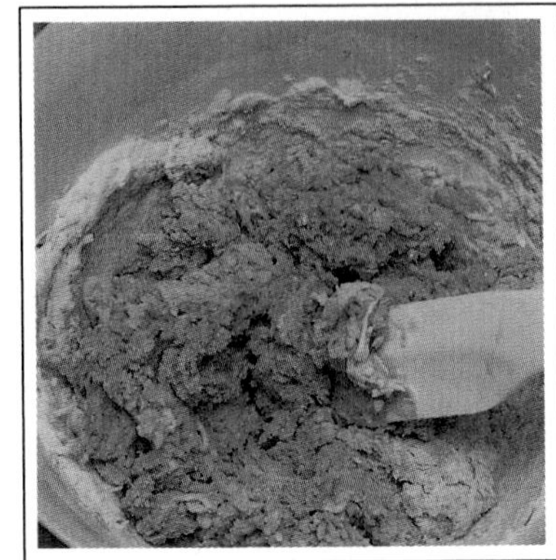

4 Fold in flour mixture and mix until completely incorporated.

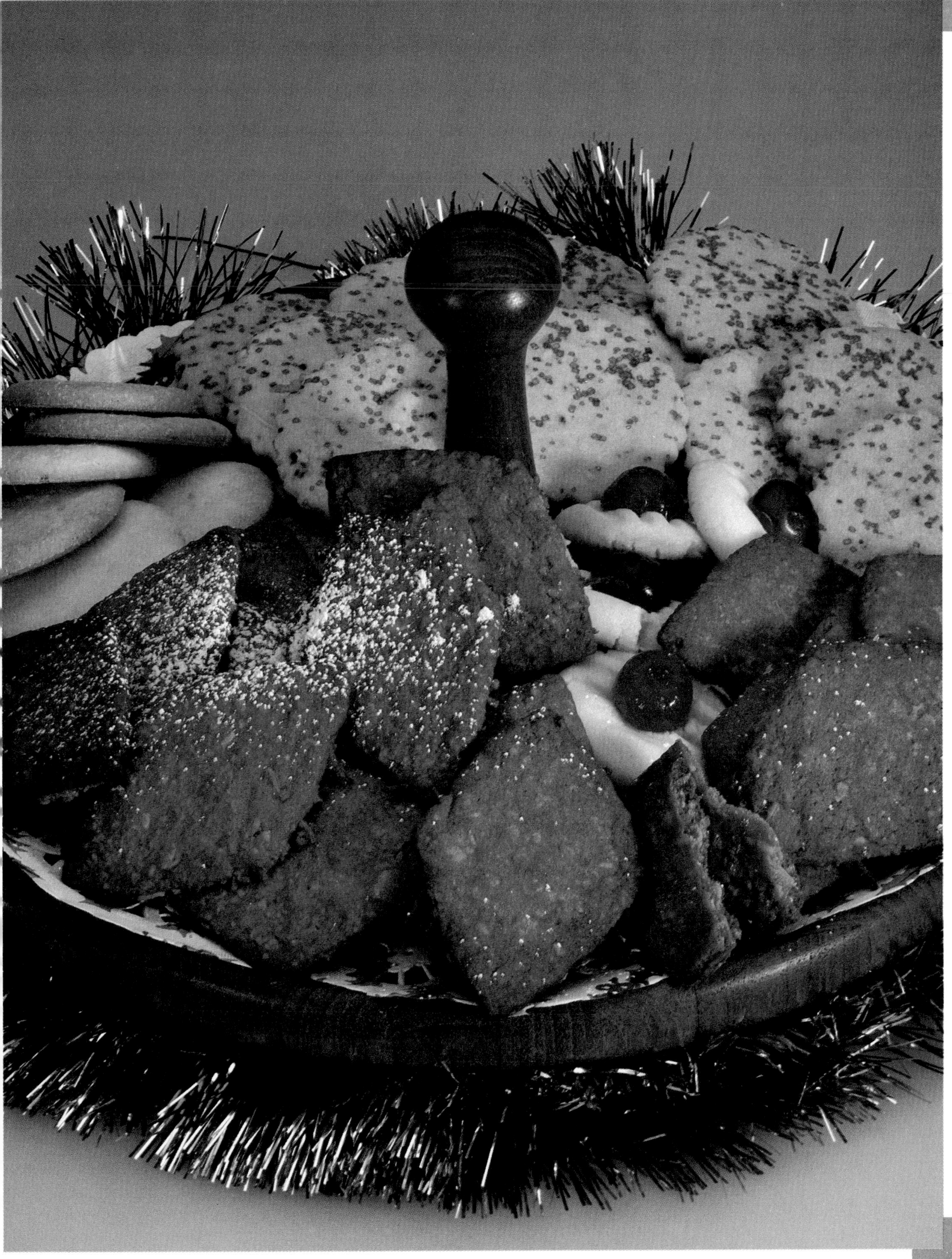

Cheese Parfait

(serves 2-4)

1 SERVING	505 CALORIES	19g CARBOHYDRATE
6g PROTEIN	45g FAT	3.1g FIBER

8 oz	(250 g) package cream cheese, softened
3 tbsp	(45 ml) brown sugar
2 tbsp	(30 ml) Tia Maria liqueur
½ cup	(125 ml) heavy cream, whipped
1 cup	(250 ml) chopped fresh strawberries
	whole fresh strawberries for decoration

Place cheese in bowl of electric mixer. Add sugar and mix well for 2 minutes.

Add Tia Maria and continue mixing 30 seconds.

Add whipped cream and chopped strawberries; incorporate using spatula until well blended.

Spoon mixture into parfait glasses and refrigerate 3-4 hours before serving.

Decorate with fresh strawberries.

Walnut Chocolate Chewies

(serves 6-8)

1 SERVING	298 CALORIES	24g CARBOHYDRATE
6g PROTEIN	20g FAT	1.0g FIBER

1 cup	(250 ml) chopped walnuts
1 cup	(250 ml) slivered almonds
½ cup	(125 ml) liquid honey
2 tbsp	(30 ml) strong black coffee
	sweet cocoa to taste

Place walnuts and almonds in small bowl and toss together. Transfer to food processor and blend several minutes.

Replace nuts in small bowl and add honey; mix together.

Transfer nuts back to food processor and add coffee; blend about 1 minute.

Spread mixture on large plate and cover with sheet waxed paper, pressed against surface. Refrigerate 2-3 hours.

Remove and shape into small balls with hands. Roll in cocoa and continue to chill another hour before serving.

1 Place walnuts and almonds in small bowl and toss together.

3 Transfer nuts back to food processor and add coffee.

2 Replace blended nuts in bowl and add honey; mix together.

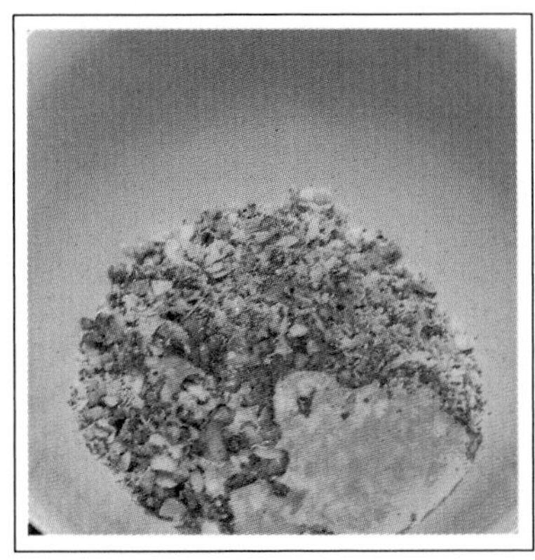

4 Blend about 1 minute.

Coffee Custard Pudding

(serves 6)

1 SERVING	174 CALORIES	12g CARBOHYDRATE
5g PROTEIN	12g FAT	0g FIBER

1 cup	(250 ml) hot milk
1 cup	(250 ml) hot, light cream
2 tbsp	(30 ml) hot expresso coffee or very strong coffee
1 tbsp	(15 ml) rum
⅓ cup	(75 ml) granulated sugar
4	eggs
	whipped cream

Preheat oven to 350°F (180°C).

Pour milk, cream and coffee into bowl; whisk together.

Add rum and beat with electric beater.

Add sugar and continue beating to incorporate.

Lightly beat eggs with fork. Pour into bowl containing custard mixture and whisk well until incorporated.

Place 6 individual custard dishes in roasting pan and pour in 1 inch (2.5 cm) hot water.

Fill custard dishes with mixture and bake 40 minutes.

Cool before unmolding and refrigerate. Before serving decorate with whipped cream.

Molasses Custard

(serves 6)

1 SERVING	183 CALORIES	14g CARBOHYDRATE
5g PROTEIN	12g FAT	0g FIBER

1 cup	(250 ml) hot milk
1 cup	(250 ml) hot, light cream
4	eggs
⅓ cup	(75 ml) molasses
½ tsp	(2 ml) vanilla
	pinch salt
	whipped cream

Preheat oven to 350°F (180°C).

Pour milk and cream into bowl; whisk well.

Lightly beat eggs with fork. Add to bowl along with molasses, salt and vanilla; whisk very well.

Place 6 individual custard dishes in roasting pan and pour in 1 inch (2.5 cm) hot water.

Fill custard dishes with mixture and bake 40 minutes.

Cool before unmolding and refrigerate. Before serving decorate with whipped cream.

Eggnog

(serves 4-6)

1 SERVING	257 CALORIES	21g CARBOHYDRATE
8g PROTEIN	12g FAT	0g FIBER

4	eggs, separated
½ cup	(125 ml) fine sugar
¼ cup	(50 ml) rum
2 tbsp	(30 ml) cognac
2 cups	(500 ml) cold milk
1 cup	(250 ml) cold, light cream
2	egg whites
	pinch nutmeg

Beat egg yolks with electric beater. Add half of sugar and continue beating until thick.

Pour in rum and cognac; beat 1 minute.

Add milk and cream; continue beating 30 seconds.

Place all egg whites in bowl. Beat with electric beater until they peak. Add remaining sugar and continue beating 1 minute.

Using spatula, fold in egg whites until well incorporated.

Serve in glasses with dash of nutmeg.

MICROWAVE

Microwave Notes:

Understanding how your microwave works is easy — just think of it as a chain reaction. As microwaves penetrate the food, they cause the food molecules to vibrate. This in turn causes heat which cooks the food; the cooking process spreads from the outside towards the center.

Because food cooks from the outside in, there are some techniques you should use to avoid uneven cooking:

— position the thickest portion of irregularly shaped food toward the walls of the microwave where it will receive more microwave energy.

— when stirring foods, move the food from the outside of the dish towards the center and vice-versa.

— rotating is a technique used with such foods as cakes or puddings which cannot be stirred. If a recipe calls for this procedure, simply rotate the dish a quarter or half turn (depending on the size of the mold).

You can cover food with the matching casserole top or in some cases with sheets of paper towel, plastic wrap or waxed paper. When you use plastic wrap be sure to pierce the wrap or tuck up one corner to allow excess steam an escape.

Although it is not essential to have a cupboard stacked with special microwave utensils, it is advisable to invest in at least several casserole dishes, plus perhaps a serving platter and a rectangular glass dish. Some dessert recipes call for particular cake molds; refer to the recipe for a description.

Because microwave ovens vary in terms of maximum power and power settings, you should study the following chart before you begin any recipes. Our test microwave was 650 watts.

Setting	Approximate wattage	Percent of power
HIGH	650	100
MEDIUM-HIGH	485	75
MEDIUM	325	50
LOW	160	25

Please consult your manufacturer's guide booklet if you are not already familiar with your microwave's controls and settings.

Mozza Sticks

(serves 2)

1 SERVING	352 CALORIES	17g CARBOHYDRATE
30g PROTEIN	22g FAT	0.5g FIBER

Setting: HIGH

Cooking Time: 14 minutes

Utensil: Roasting Rack
8 cups (2 L) casserole with cover

8	slices bacon
8	2 in (5 cm) carrot sticks
8	2 in (5 cm) mozzarella sticks
	salt and pepper

Arrange bacon on roasting rack; microwave 7 minutes. Cover with paper towel to prevent spattering.

Remove bacon from rack and set aside. Clean rack for later use.

Place carrot sticks in casserole; pour in about 1 cup (250 ml) water. Cover and microwave 6 minutes.

Drain carrots and rinse under cold water for several seconds.

Team carrot sticks with cheese sticks; carefully wrap with bacon. Secure with toothpicks.

Place bundles on roasting rack and season generously. Microwave 1 minute uncovered.

Snacking Eggs

(serves 4)

1 SERVING	594 CALORIES	20g CARBOHYDRATE
34g PROTEIN	42g FAT	trace FIBER

Setting: HIGH

Cooking Time: 6½ minutes

Utensil: 8 cups (2 L) casserole with cover

1 tbsp	(15 ml) butter
1	onion, diced
1	garlic clove, smashed and chopped
1	green pepper, diced
¾ lb	(375 g) piece Italian sausage, sliced
4	large eggs, beaten
1 cup	(250 ml) cubed mozzarella
4	large hot buns
	salt and pepper

Place butter, onion, garlic and green pepper in casserole. Cover and microwave 2 minutes.

Add sausage slices and microwave 1 minute covered.

Pour in beaten eggs and season well; mix with wooden spoon. Microwave 1½ minutes uncovered.

Stir eggs well and add cheese. Microwave 1 minute uncovered. Stir again; microwave 1 minute uncovered.

Serve on hot buns.

Stuffed Mushrooms

(serves 4)

1 SERVING	211 CALORIES	5g CARBOHYDRATE
5g PROTEIN	15g FAT	1.0g FIBER

Setting: MEDIUM

Cooking Time: 3 minutes

Utensil: Stoneware serving platter

1	bunch fresh watercress
3 tbsp	(45 ml) walnuts
1	tomato, cut in chunks
1	garlic clove, smashed and chopped
¼ cup	(50 ml) olive oil
4 tbsp	(60 ml) grated Parmesan cheese
16	large mushroom caps
	few drops Tabasco sauce
	few drops Worcestershire sauce
	salt and pepper

Wash watercress well and dry. Place in food processor and blend until almost puréed.

Add walnuts and tomato; blend until puréed.

Add garlic and oil; blend several seconds. Add cheese, Tabasco, Worcestershire, salt and pepper; blend again for several seconds.

Stuff mushroom caps with mixture and arrange on stoneware plate. Microwave 3 minutes.

Serve as an appetizer.

1 Place washed dried watercress in bowl of food processor. Blend until almost puréed.

3 After oil and garlic have been incorporated, add cheese and remaining ingredients; blend for several seconds.

2 Add walnuts and tomato; blend until puréed.

4 Stuff mushroom caps with mixture. Microwave 3 minutes.

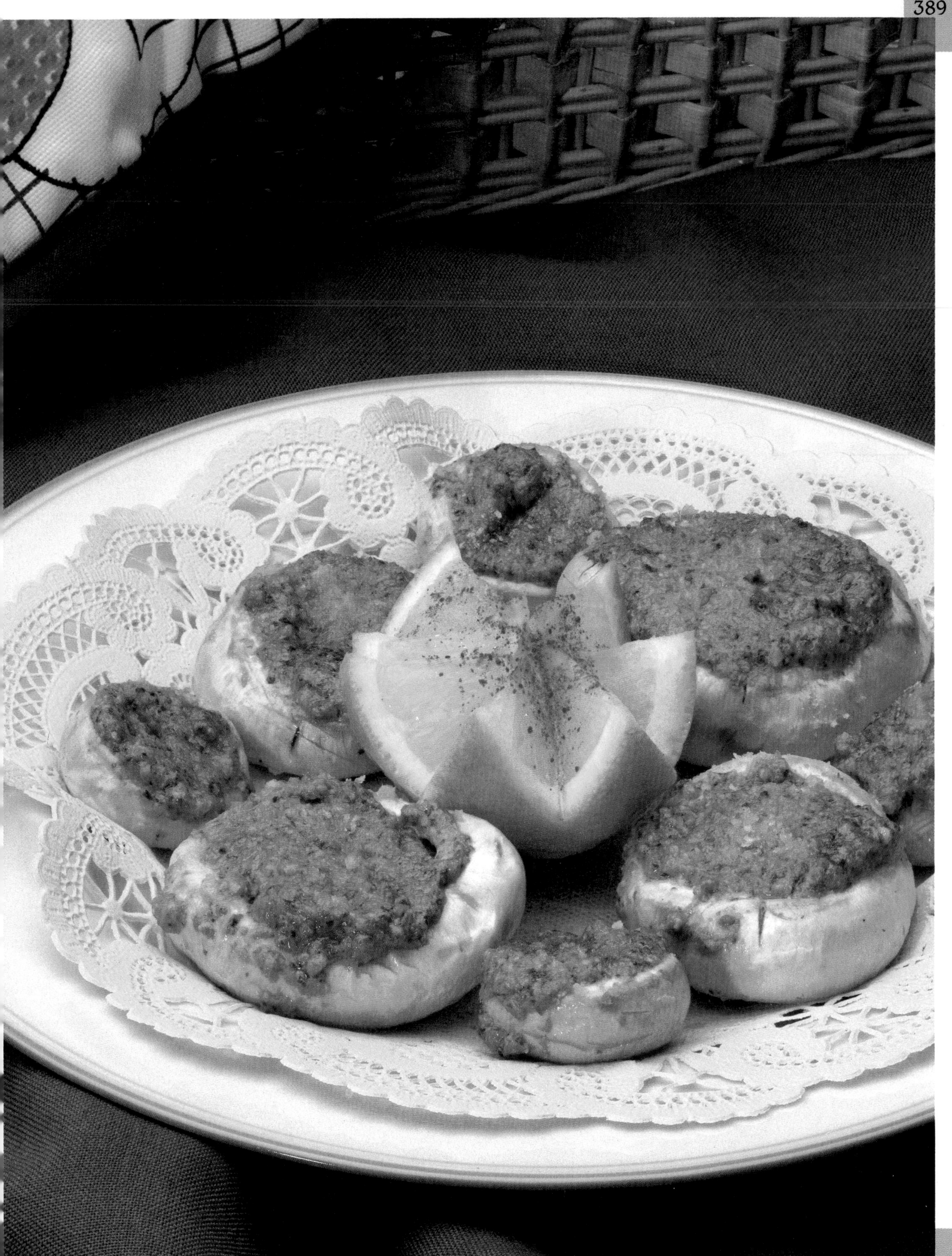

Artichoke Appetizer

(serves 4)

1 SERVING	166 CALORIES	13g CARBOHYDRATE
9g PROTEIN	10g FAT	1.0g FIBER

Setting: HIGH and MEDIUM-HIGH

Cooking Time: 5 minutes

Utensil: 8 cups (2 L) casserole with cover
Stoneware serving platter

14 oz	(398 ml) can artichoke bottoms, drained and rinsed
2 tbsp	(30 ml) butter
½ lb	(250 g) mushrooms, sliced
½	celery stalk, very finely chopped
1	small onion, finely chopped
2	slices crisp bacon, chopped
1	garlic clove, smashed and chopped
3 tbsp	(45 ml) ricotta cheese
	salt and pepper

Arrange artichoke bottoms on stoneware platter; set aside.

Place butter, mushrooms, celery and onion in casserole. Cover and microwave 3 minutes at HIGH.

Mix in bacon, garlic and cheese; season well.

Fill artichoke bottoms with mixture. Microwave 2 minutes at MEDIUM-HIGH uncovered.

Sausage Sloppy Joes

(serves 4)

1 SERVING	376 CALORIES	35g CARBOHYDRATE
16g PROTEIN	21g FAT	2.0g FIBER

Setting: HIGH

Cooking Time: 10 minutes

Utensil: 12 cups (2.8 L) casserole with cover

1 tbsp	(15 ml) butter
1	onion, sliced
1	green pepper, thinly sliced
28 oz	(796 ml) can tomatoes, drained and chopped
½ cup	(125 ml) stuffed green olives, chopped
2	small pepperoni sausages, sliced
1 tbsp	(15 ml) cornstarch
2 tbsp	(30 ml) cold water
4	hamburger buns, toasted open
1¼ cups	(300 ml) grated mozzarella cheese
	salt and pepper

Place butter, onion and green pepper in casserole. Cover and microwave 5 minutes.

Stir in tomatoes and season to taste. Add olives and pepperoni; microwave 4 minutes covered.

Mix cornstarch with water; stir into casserole and microwave 1 minute uncovered.

Separate hamburger buns and place tops over bottoms. Set on cookie sheet and spoon sausage mixture over bread. Top with cheese and broil in conventional oven until melted.

Serve immediately.

Meatloaf Muffins

(serves 4)

1 SERVING	293 CALORIES	55g CARBOHYDRATE
41g PROTEIN	6g FAT	1.0g FIBER

Setting: HIGH

Cooking Time: 5 minutes

Utensil: Muffin Ring

2	small potatoes, peeled and grated fine
2	carrots, pared and grated
1 lb	(500 g) lean ground beef
1	egg
2	medium onions, chopped and cooked
¼ tsp	(1 ml) allspice
½ tsp	(2 ml) chili powder
	salt and pepper

Combine potatoes and carrots in large bowl. Add beef and mix together well.

Add remaining ingredients and mix until thoroughly incorporated.

Press mixture into cups of muffin ring. Microwave 5 minutes uncovered.

Remove and let cool slightly before serving. These are ideal for after-school snacks and are handy to have on weekends.

1 Combine potatoes and carrots in large bowl.

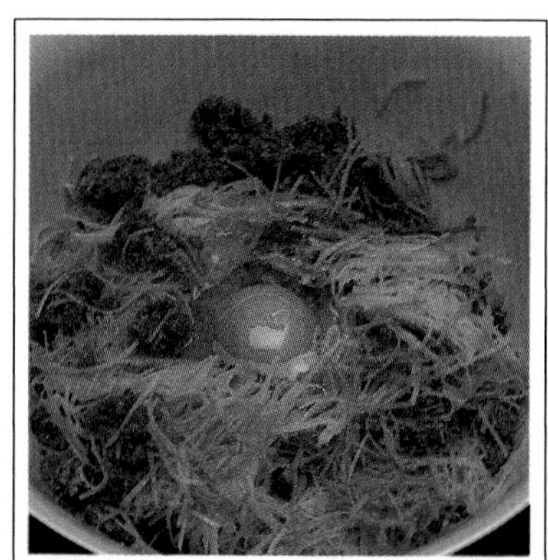

3 Add egg and remaining ingredients and mix until thoroughly incorporated.

2 Add beef and mix together well.

4 Press mixture into cups of muffin ring.

Shrimp on Muffins

(serves 4)

1 SERVING	472 CALORIES	40g CARBOHYDRATE
23g PROTEIN	23g FAT	1.0g FIBER

Setting: HIGH

Cooking Time: 8 minutes

Utensil: 12 cups (2.8 L) casserole with cover

3 tbsp	(45 ml) butter
1 lb	(500 g) mushrooms, diced
1	shallot, chopped
4 tbsp	(60 ml) flour
1½ cups	(375 ml) hot milk
4 oz	(113 g) can shrimp, drained and rinsed
¼ tsp	(1 ml) nutmeg
4	English muffins, lightly toasted whole
1 cup	(250 ml) grated cheddar cheese
	salt and pepper

Place butter, mushrooms and shallot in casserole. Cover and microwave 4 minutes.

Mix in flour. Pour in milk and season; mix again. Microwave 4 minutes uncovered.

Add shrimp and nutmeg; mix well.

Using small knife pare away some of bread in the middle of each muffin. Place on cookie sheet and fill holes with shrimp mixture. Top with grated cheese and broil in conventional oven until melted.

Serve as a light lunch.

Bacon Bite

(serves 4)

1 SERVING	131 CALORIES	7g CARBOHYDRATE
37g PROTEIN	8g FAT	1.0g FIBER

Setting: HIGH

Cooking Time: 5 minutes

Utensil: 8 cups (2 L) rectangular dish

4	slices fast-fry back bacon
4	rings yellow pepper
4	thick slices tomato
4	slices Camembert or Brie cheese

Arrange bacon in rectangular dish; top each with ring of yellow pepper.

Cover loosely with plastic wrap and microwave 3 minutes.

Add tomato slices and cheese; finish microwaving 2 minutes covered.

Serve as snack or for breakfast.

Bacon Potato Treats

(serves 4)

1 SERVING	379 CALORIES	28g CARBOHYDRATE
26g PROTEIN	25g FAT	1.0g FIBER

Setting: HIGH

Cooking Time: 10 minutes

Utensil: 8 cups (2 L) rectangular dish

5	potatoes, unpeeled, sliced ½ in (1.2 cm) thick
1	onion, grated and cooked
24	stuffed green olives, chopped
½ tsp	(2 ml) chopped jalapeno
6	slices crisp bacon, chopped
1½ cups	(375 ml) grated Gruyère cheese
	salt and pepper

Arrange slices of potato in rectangular dish — this may require a couple of layers depending on the size of potatoes. Cover dish with plastic wrap and microwave 4 minutes. Rotate and microwave another 4 minutes.

When potatoes are cooked, top with grated onion. Mix olives with jalapeno and sprinkle over; add bacon and cheese.

Season very well and microwave 2 minutes uncovered. Serve as an afternoon snack or at lunchtime.

Watercress and Leek Soup

(serves 4)

1 SERVING	202 CALORIES	22g CARBOHYDRATE
8g PROTEIN	8g FAT	trace FIBER

Setting: HIGH

Cooking Time: 23 minutes

Utensil: 12 cups (2.8 L) casserole with cover

2 tbsp	(30 ml) butter
2	green onions, chopped
1	large leek, white part only, chopped
3 tbsp	(45 ml) flour
4	medium potatoes, peeled and sliced
4 cups	(1 L) hot chicken stock
¼ tsp	(1 ml) thyme
¼ tsp	(1 ml) anise
1	bunch fresh watercress, chopped
	salt and pepper

Place butter, onions and leek in casserole. Cover and microwave 4 minutes.

Mix in flour, salt and pepper. Microwave 4 minutes uncovered.

Add potatoes, chicken stock and seasonings; cover and microwave 7 minutes.

Stir well. Add watercress, season, and microwave 5 minutes covered.

Remove cover; finish microwaving 3 minutes.

1 Open leek by cutting it in 4 lengthwise. Do not, however, cut through the base. Wash well in cold water.

3 After the onions and leek have been microwaved 4 minutes, sprinkle in flour, salt and pepper. Mix well and continue microwaving 4 minutes uncovered.

2 Depending on the recipe you can use the entire leek or as in this recipe, discard the green portion and use only the white part. In either case check that sand has all been washed away.

4 Add potatoes, chicken stock and seasonings; cover and microwave 7 minutes.

Green Soup

(serves 4)

1 SERVING	260 CALORIES	24g CARBOHYDRATE
12g PROTEIN	14g FAT	2.0g FIBER

Setting: HIGH

Cooking Time: 19 minutes

Utensil: 12 cups (2.8 L) casserole with cover

3 tbsp	(45 ml) butter
1	small onion, chopped
2	small stalks broccoli, pared and diced
5 tbsp	(75 ml) flour
2 cups	(500 ml) hot chicken stock
1 tsp	(5 ml) basil
2 tbsp	(30 ml) tomato paste
2 cups	(500 ml) hot milk
1	large head broccoli, in flowerets
	salt and pepper
	dash paprika

Place butter, onion and diced broccoli stalks in casserole. Cover and microwave 3 minutes.

Mix in flour and season with salt, pepper and paprika; mix very well with wooden spoon. Cover and microwave 3 minutes.

Stir in chicken stock and basil; correct seasoning. Add tomato paste and mix well. Cover and continue microwaving 4 minutes.

Pour in milk and mix well; cover and microwave another 4 minutes.

Add broccoli flowerets, cover and finish microwaving 5 minutes.

1 After 3 minutes of microwaving, add flour to vegetables. Sprinkle in paprika and season to taste.

3 Stir in chicken stock and basil; correct seasoning. Add tomato paste and mix well. Continue microwaving 4 minutes.

2 Mix well with wooden spoon. Cover and microwave 3 minutes.

4 Pour in milk. Add broccoli flowerets. Cover and finish microwaving 5 minutes.

Squash and Macaroni Soup

(serves 4)

1 SERVING	136 CALORIES	15g CARBOHYDRATE
8g PROTEIN	5g FAT	2.0g FIBER

Setting: HIGH

Cooking Time: 18 minutes

Utensil: 12 cups (2.8 L) casserole with cover

1 tbsp	(15 ml) butter
1	leek, washed and thinly sliced
½	squash, seeded and diced small
1	carrot, pared and thinly sliced
1	zucchini, peeled and sliced
5 cups	(1.2 L) hot chicken stock
1	bay leaf
¼ tsp	(1 ml) thyme
½ tsp	(2 ml) basil
½ cup	(125 ml) elbow macaroni
	salt and pepper

Place butter, leek and squash in casserole. Cover and microwave 6 minutes.

Add remaining ingredients; cover and microwave 12 minutes.

Serve hot.

Red Pepper Soup

(serves 4)

1 SERVING	141 CALORIES	16g CARBOHYDRATE
5g PROTEIN	7g FAT	1.0g FIBER

Setting: HIGH

Cooking Time: 20 minutes

Utensil: 12 cups (2.8 L) casserole with cover

2 tbsp	(30 ml) butter
1	celery stalk, diced
2	green onions, diced
4 tbsp	(60 ml) flour
2	large red peppers, seeded and sliced
2 cups	(500 ml) tomato clam juice, heated
2 cups	(500 ml) chicken stock, heated
¼ tsp	(1 ml) celery seed
1 tsp	(5 ml) sugar
	salt and pepper

Place butter, celery and onions in casserole; microwave 4 minutes covered.

Mix in flour; microwave 4 minutes covered.

Add red peppers and remaining ingredients; mix well. Cover and finish microwaving 12 minutes.

Transfer soup to food processor and purée.

Country Soup

(serves 4)

1 SERVING	289 CALORIES	11g CARBOHYDRATE
32g PROTEIN	12g FAT	1.0g FIBER

Setting: HIGH
Cooking Time: 48 minutes
Utensil: 12 cups (2.8 L) casserole with cover

2 tbsp	(30 ml) butter
1	celery stalk, diced
1	carrot, pared and diced
1	medium onion, diced
1	garlic clove, smashed and chopped
½ tsp	(2 ml) chervil
1	bay leaf
½ cup	(125 ml) yellow split peas
½ lb	(250 g) flank steak, thinly sliced and seared in oil
5 cups	(1.2 L) light beef stock, heated
6	large mushrooms, diced
	salt and pepper

Place butter, celery, carrot, onion, garlic, seasonings and bay leaf in casserole; cover and microwave 5 minutes.

Mix in peas, meat and beef stock; correct seasoning. Cover and continue microwaving 40 minutes.

Stir in mushrooms and finish microwaving 3 minutes uncovered.

Fennel Soup

(serves 4)

1 SERVING	246 CALORIES	11g CARBOHYDRATE
7g PROTEIN	20g FAT	trace FIBER

Setting: HIGH
Cooking Time: 22 minutes
Utensil: 12 cups (2.8 L) casserole with cover

4 tbsp	(60 ml) butter
1	leek, slit lengthwise in 4, washed and thinly sliced
1	medium fennel bulb, leaves and bulb thinly sliced
5 tbsp	(75 ml) flour
4 cups	(1 L) hot light chicken stock
½ cup	(125 ml) hot light cream
	pinch chervil
	salt and pepper
	lemon juice

Place butter, leek and fennel in casserole. Cover and microwave 10 minutes.

Mix well and add remaining ingredients, except cream. Continue microwaving 10 minutes covered.

Force mixture through fine sieve or food mill; stir in cream and replace in casserole. Microwave 2 minutes uncovered.

Serve hot.

Potato Onion Cream

(serves 4)

1 SERVING	313 CALORIES	42g CARBOHYDRATE
15g PROTEIN	11g FAT	1.0g FIBER

Setting: MEDIUM-HIGH and MEDIUM

Cooking Time: 31 minutes

Utensil: 12 cups (2.8 L) casserole with cover

2	slices bacon, diced
3	medium onions, diced
4 tbsp	(60 ml) flour
4 cups	(1 L) hot milk
3	large potatoes, peeled and thinly sliced
1 tsp	(5 ml) tarragon
	salt and white pepper
	dash paprika

Place bacon and onions in casserole; cover and microwave 6 minutes at MEDIUM-HIGH.

Mix in flour. Pour in milk, stir, and add tarragon, salt, pepper and paprika.

Add potatoes and cover. Microwave 14 minutes at MEDIUM-HIGH.

Stir mixture well and microwave 11 minutes at MEDIUM, covered.

Serve hot.

Thick Leftover Vegetable Soup

(serves 4)

1 SERVING	289 CALORIES	27g CARBOHYDRATE
20g PROTEIN	11g FAT	1.0g FIBER

Setting: HIGH

Cooking Time: 23 minutes

Utensil: 12 cups (2.8 L) casserole with cover

2 tbsp	(30 ml) butter
2	leeks, white part only, thinly sliced
1	garlic clove, smashed and chopped
1	green pepper, diced
2	potatoes, peeled, quartered and thinly sliced
1	large sweet potato, peeled, quartered and thinly sliced
½ tsp	(2 ml) basil
¼ tsp	(1 ml) celery seed
¼ tsp	(1 ml) anise
5 cups	(1.2 L) hot chicken stock
1 cup	(250 ml) diced cooked chicken
	salt and pepper

Place butter in casserole; cover and microwave 1 minute. Add leeks and continue microwaving 5 minutes covered.

Stir in garlic and green pepper; season well. Cover and microwave 3 minutes.

Stir and add potatoes, sweet potato and seasonings; cover and microwave 3 minutes.

Pour in chicken stock; mix well and microwave 10 minutes uncovered.

Add diced chicken and correct seasoning. Finish microwaving 1 minute with cover.

Perch Soup

(serves 4)

1 SERVING	209 CALORIES	23g CARBOHYDRATE
21g PROTEIN	4g FAT	2.0g FIBER

Setting: MEDIUM-HIGH and MEDIUM

Cooking Time: 31 minutes

Utensil: 12 cups (2.8 L) casserole with cover

2	slices bacon, diced
1	celery stalk, diced
1	garlic clove, smashed and chopped
4 tbsp	(60 ml) flour
4 cups	(1 L) light chicken stock, heated
2	large potatoes, peeled and diced
1/4 tsp	(1 ml) fennel
1 tsp	(5 ml) chopped parsley
1	bay leaf
1/2 tsp	(2 ml) thyme
2	perch filets, cubed
1	red pepper, diced
	salt and pepper

Place bacon, celery and garlic in casserole. Cover and microwave 5 minutes at MEDIUM-HIGH.

Mix in flour, pour in chicken stock and mix again. Add potatoes, fennel, parsley, bay leaf and thyme. Cover and microwave 20 minutes at MEDIUM-HIGH; stir once during this time.

Mix in fish and red pepper; correct seasoning. Microwave 6 minutes at MEDIUM uncovered.

Serve hot.

Chicken Casserole

(serves 4)

1 SERVING	361 CALORIES	22g CARBOHYDRATE
31g PROTEIN	16g FAT	1.0g FIBER

Setting: HIGH

Cooking Time: 16 minutes

Utensil: 12 cups (2.8 L) casserole with cover

4 tbsp	(60 ml) butter
2	potatoes, peeled and cubed
2	carrots, pared and cubed
2	celery stalks, pared and cubed
1 tbsp	(15 ml) chopped fresh parsley
2	chicken breasts, skinned, halved and boned
¼ tsp	(1 ml) anise
3 tbsp	(45 ml) flour
1½ cups	(375 ml) hot chicken stock
1 cup	(250 ml) cooked pearl onions
	salt and pepper

Place butter, potatoes, carrots, celery and parsley in casserole. Cover and microwave 8 minutes.

Add chicken breasts and anise; season generously.

Mix in flour until well incorporated. Pour in chicken stock, cover and microwave 6 minutes.

Stir in onions and microwave 2 minutes uncovered.

1 Place butter, potatoes, carrots, celery and parsley in casserole. Cover and microwave 8 minutes.

3 Add chicken breasts and anise; season generously.

2 Check if vegetables are cooked by piercing with knife.

4 Mix in flour until well incorporated.

Chicken and Shrimp Casserole

(serves 4)

1 SERVING	644 CALORIES	35g CARBOHYDRATE
84g PROTEIN	13g FAT	1.0g FIBER

Setting: MEDIUM-HIGH
Cooking Time: 10 minutes
Utensil: 12 cups (2.8 L) casserole with cover

2 tbsp	(30 ml) butter
1 tbsp	(15 ml) chopped shallot
1 lb	(500 g) mushrooms, diced
24	large shrimp, shelled and deveined
2	chicken breasts, skinned, halved, boned, meat cut in 1 in (2.5 cm) chunks
2 cups	(500 ml) cooked elbow macaroni
1 cup	(250 ml) grated mozzarella cheese
½ cup	(125 ml) tomato sauce, heated
1 cup	(250 ml) brown sauce, heated
	salt and pepper

Place butter, shallot, mushrooms, shrimp and chicken in casserole. Cover and microwave 5 minutes.

Season well and mix. Add remaining ingredients and finish microwaving 5 minutes covered.

Serve with green salad.

Chicken and Melon Casserole

(serves 4)

1 SERVING	334 CALORIES	14g CARBOHYDRATE
30g PROTEIN	13g FAT	1.0g FIBER

Setting: HIGH
Cooking Time: 13 minutes
Utensil: 12 cups (2.8 L) casserole with cover

3 tbsp	(45 ml) butter
2	chicken breasts, skinned, halved, boned, and cut in large pieces
1 tbsp	(15 ml) chopped parsley
1 tsp	(5 ml) tarragon
1	celery stalk, sliced
20	mushrooms, halved
3 tbsp	(45 ml) flour
1¼ cups	(300 ml) beer
1	cantaloupe melon, cut in half
	salt and pepper

Place butter and chicken in casserole. Add parsley, tarragon, celery, salt and pepper. Cover and microwave 6 minutes.

Add mushrooms and mix in flour; pour in beer. Microwave 6 minutes uncovered.

Using melon-ball cutter, scoop out melon flesh and add to casserole. Mix very well and finish microwaving 1 minute uncovered.

Chicken Chili

(serves 4)

1 SERVING	387 CALORIES	37g CARBOHYDRATE
31g PROTEIN	13g FAT	2.0g FIBER

Setting: HIGH

Cooking Time: 95 minutes

Utensil: 12 cups (2.8 L) casserole with cover

1 tbsp	(15 ml) butter
1	onion, chopped
2	celery stalks, chopped
1	small leek, washed and chopped
1½ cups	(375 ml) diced raw chicken, dark meat preferably
3 cups	(750 ml) white beans, soaked in water overnight
¼ tsp	(1 ml) crushed chillies
½ tsp	(2 ml) oregano
½ tsp	(2 ml) cumin
½ tsp	(2 ml) allspice
2	hot banana peppers
	hot chicken stock
	salt and pepper
	grated mozzarella cheese

Place butter, onion, celery, leek, salt and pepper in casserole. Cover and microwave 5 minutes.

Mix well and add raw chicken, beans (with liquid), seasonings and banana peppers. Pour in enough hot chicken stock to cover by 2 in (5 cm). Cover casserole and microwave 75 minutes. Stir at least 2 or 3 times.

Note: At some point during this cooking time the banana peppers must be removed. The exact time will depend on how spicy you desire the chili — leaving them in 15 minutes will produce a medium-hot flavor.

Also, if at any time the chicken stock reduces considerably, add more.

Stir in mozzarella cheese to taste and correct seasoning. Cover and finish microwaving beans 15 minutes.

Meat and Potato Casserole

(serves 4)

1 SERVING	473 CALORIES	33g CARBOHYDRATE
61g PROTEIN	11g FAT	2.0g FIBER

Setting: HIGH

Cooking Time: 25 minutes

Utensil: 12 cups (2.8 L) casserole with cover

1 tbsp	(15 ml) butter
½	red onion, finely chopped
1½ lb	(750 g) lean ground beef
¼ tsp	(1 ml) chili powder
¼ tsp	(1 ml) allspice
½ tsp	(2 ml) thyme
3	potatoes, peeled and thinly sliced
¼ tsp	(1 ml) paprika
28 oz	(796 ml) can tomatoes, drained and chopped
1 cup	(250 ml) tomato sauce, heated
	salt and pepper
	chopped parsley to taste

Place butter, onion and meat in casserole. Season well with chili powder, allspice and thyme. Cover and microwave 6 minutes.

Mix well and cover with ½ of sliced potatoes; sprinkle with paprika.

Add tomatoes, tomato sauce and chopped parsley. Cover with remaining potatoes and season well.

Cover and microwave 12 minutes.

Mix well and continue microwaving 7 minutes covered.

1 Place butter, onion and meat in casserole. Season well with chili powder, allspice and thyme. Cover and microwave 6 minutes.

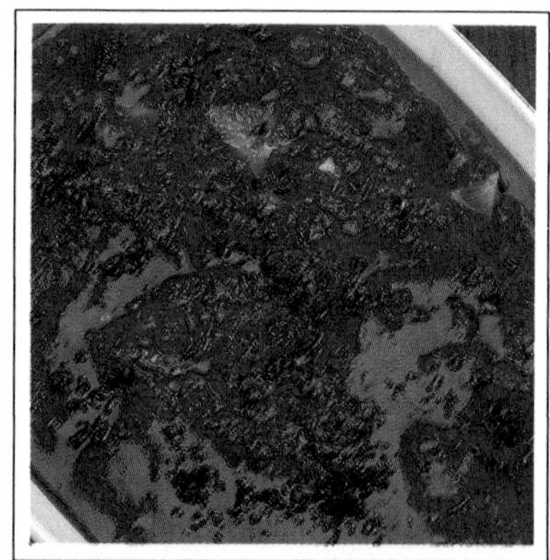

3 Add tomatoes, tomato sauce and parsley.

2 Mix well and cover with ½ of sliced potatoes; sprinkle with paprika.

4 Cover with remaining potatoes and season well. Cover and microwave 12 minutes. Stir and finish microwaving 7 minutes.

Ground Veal Casserole

(serves 4)

1 SERVING	498 CALORIES	15g CARBOHYDRATE
55g PROTEIN	24g FAT	2.0g FIBER

Setting: HIGH

Cooking Time: 10 minutes

Utensil: 12 cups (2.8 L) casserole with cover

2 tbsp	(30 ml) butter
1	medium onion, chopped
1	green pepper, diced
1	yellow pepper, diced
1 tsp	(5 ml) oregano
1½ lb	(750 g) lean ground veal
28 oz	(796 ml) can tomatoes, chopped with juice
2 tbsp	(30 ml) tomato paste
1 cup	(250 ml) diced cheddar cheese
	salt and pepper

Place butter, onion, peppers and oregano in casserole. Cover and microwave 3 minutes.

Add veal, mix and season. Continue microwaving 3 minutes covered.

Add remaining ingredients and mix well. Correct seasoning and microwave 4 minutes covered.

Serve with fresh bread.

Meaty Tomato Casserole

(serves 4)

1 SERVING	446 CALORIES	13g CARBOHYDRATE
60g PROTEIN	17g FAT	1.0g FIBER

Setting: HIGH

Cooking Time: 10 minutes

Utensil: 12 cups (2.8 L) casserole with cover

2 tbsp	(30 ml) butter
1	small onion, finely chopped
2	garlic cloves, smashed and chopped
½ lb	(250 g) mushrooms, diced
1 tbsp	(15 ml) chopped chives
½ tsp	(2 ml) chili powder
1½ lb	(750 g) lean ground beef
1½ cups	(375 ml) tomato sauce, heated
¼ cup	(50 ml) sour cream
	salt and pepper

Place butter, onion, garlic, mushrooms, chives and chili powder in casserole. Cover and microwave 4 minutes.

Season well and mix in ground beef; cover and continue microwaving 3 minutes.

Stir and pour in tomato sauce; microwave 3 minutes covered.

Remove from microwave, mix in sour cream and serve over noodles.

Leftover Casserole

(serves 4)

1 SERVING	681 CALORIES	50g CARBOHYDRATE
63g PROTEIN	24g FAT	1.0g FIBER

Setting: HIGH

Cooking Time: 7 minutes

Utensil: 12 cups (2.8 L) casserole with cover

1 lb	(500 g) leftover cooked ham, in strips
½	onion, thinly sliced
2 tbsp	(30 ml) garlic butter
2	garlic cloves, smashed and chopped
1 tbsp	(15 ml) chopped parsley
28 oz	(796 ml) can tomatoes, chopped, with ½ of juice
3 cups	(750 ml) leftover cooked macaroni
½	green pepper, thinly sliced
1 tbsp	(15 ml) tomato paste
1 cup	(250 ml) grated cheddar or other leftover cheese
	salt and pepper

Place ham, onion, garlic butter, garlic, parsley, salt and pepper in casserole. Cover and microwave 3 minutes.

Mix in tomatoes, macaroni and green pepper; season generously.

Add tomato paste and cheese; stir well. Cover and microwave 4 minutes.

Lima Bean Dinner

(serves 4)

1 SERVING	261 CALORIES	42g CARBOHYDRATE
15g PROTEIN	8g FAT	2.0g FIBER

Setting: HIGH
Cooking Time: 56½ minutes
Utensil: 12 cups (2.8 L) casserole with cover

1 tbsp	(15 ml) butter
1	medium onion, chopped
½ tsp	(2 ml) marjoram
½ tsp	(2 ml) chervil
4	slices bacon, diced
3	celery stalks, diced
14 oz	(400 g) dried lima beans, soaked in water overnight
2 tbsp	(30 ml) brown sugar
2 tbsp	(30 ml) molasses
1 tsp	(5 ml) dry mustard
1 tbsp	(15 ml) cornstarch
2 tbsp	(30 ml) cold water
	salt and pepper
	dash paprika
	hot chicken stock

Microwave butter ½ minute in casserole uncovered.

Add onion, marjoram and chervil. Cover and microwave 2 minutes.

Stir in bacon and microwave 4 minutes uncovered. Mix well; microwave another 3 minutes.

Spread celery over bacon. Cover with beans (including liquid). Sprinkle in brown sugar and molasses.

Mix in mustard and season with salt, pepper and paprika; mix again.

Pour in enough hot chicken stock to cover. Cover casserole and microwave 30 minutes.

Mix well; continue microwaving 17 minutes covered.

Mix cornstarch with water; stir into bean mixture, let stand ½ minute and serve.

1 Microwave onion, marjoram and chervil for 2 minutes covered.

3 Add celery, beans, brown sugar and molasses.

2 Microwave bacon a total of 7 minutes but be sure to stir about halfway through.

4 Mix in mustard, salt, pepper and paprika. Pour in enough chicken stock to cover. Microwave a total of 47 minutes covered, stirring once.

Watercress Rice

(serves 4)

1 SERVING	124 CALORIES	18g CARBOHYDRATE
4g PROTEIN	5g FAT	trace FIBER

Setting: HIGH

Cooking Time: 20½ minutes

Utensil: 12 cups (2.8 L) casserole with cover

1 tbsp	(15 ml) butter
2	green onions, chopped
½	medium white onion, chopped
1 cup	(250 ml) long grain rice, rinsed
2 cups	(500 ml) hot chicken stock
3 tbsp	(45 ml) finely chopped watercress
1 tbsp	(15 ml) chopped parsley
1 tbsp	(15 ml) chopped chives
	salt, pepper, paprika
	pinch tarragon
	butter to taste

Microwave butter ½ minute in casserole uncovered.

Add both onions; cover and microwave 2 minutes.

Stir in rice, salt, pepper and paprika. Pour in chicken stock and mix again. Cover and microwave 18 minutes, mixing halfway through.

Stir in remaining ingredients and serve.

1 After onions have microwaved 2 minutes, stir in rice, salt, pepper and paprika.

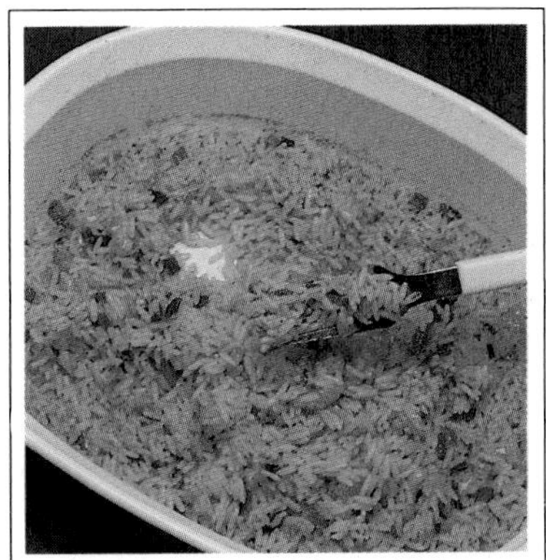

3 Cooked rice should be moist and fluffy.

2 Pour in chicken stock and mix again. Cover and microwave 18 minutes.

4 Stir in remaining ingredients and serve.

Vegetable Pasta Casserole

(serves 4)

1 SERVING	407 CALORIES	56g CARBOHYDRATE
17g PROTEIN	14g FAT	2.0g FIBER

Setting: HIGH

Cooking Time: 14 minutes

Utensil: 12 cups (2.8 L) casserole with cover

1 tbsp	(15 ml) butter
½	yellow pepper, diced large
½	red pepper, diced large
½	green pepper, diced large
1	very small eggplant, diced
3 tbsp	(45 ml) flour
1½ cups	(375 ml) hot milk
2	celery stalks, sliced
½	cucumber, peeled, seeded and sliced
8	lichees
3 cups	(750 ml) cooked medium conch shells
1 cup	(250 ml) grated mozzarella cheese
¼ tsp	(1 ml) nutmeg
¼ tsp	(1 ml) celery salt
1 cup	(250 ml) tomato sauce, heated
	salt and pepper

Place butter, peppers, eggplant, salt and pepper in casserole. Cover and microwave 4 minutes.

Mix in flour, pour in hot milk and stir well.

Mix in remaining ingredients and correct seasoning. Cover and microwave 10 minutes.

If desired decorate servings with sliced tomatoes.

Macaroni and Eggs

(serves 4)

1 SERVING	818 CALORIES	59g CARBOHYDRATE
54g PROTEIN	41g FAT	1.0g FIBER

Setting: HIGH and MEDIUM-HIGH

Cooking Time: 10 minutes

Utensil: 12 cups (2.8 L) casserole with cover

2 tbsp	(30 ml) butter
⅓ lb	(150 g) mushrooms, diced
1 tsp	(5 ml) chopped parsley
1	shallot, chopped
4 cups	(1 L) leftover cooked macaroni
5	hard-boiled eggs, sliced
1½ cups	(375 ml) diced cooked ham
1 cup	(250 ml) grated Gruyère cheese
2½ cups	(625 ml) hot light white sauce
	salt and pepper
	few drops lemon juice

Place butter, mushrooms, parsley, shallot, salt, pepper and lemon juice in casserole. Cover and microwave 4 minutes at HIGH.

Drain mushrooms, reserving liquid, and set aside.

Spread ½ of macaroni in bottom of casserole. Top with all sliced eggs.

Cover with ham and drained mushrooms; top with ½ of cheese. Add remaining macaroni.

Mix reserved cooking liquid from mushrooms with white sauce. Pour this over macaroni and finish with grated cheese.

Cover casserole and microwave 6 minutes at MEDIUM-HIGH.

Scallop Salad

(serves 4)

1 SERVING	395 CALORIES	8g CARBOHYDRATE
20g PROTEIN	31g FAT	1.0g FIBER

Setting: MEDIUM-HIGH

Cooking Time: 3 minutes

Utensil: 12 cups (2.8 L) casserole with cover

1 lb	(500 g) sea scallops
2 tbsp	(30 ml) lime juice
1 tbsp	(15 ml) butter
1/4 tsp	(1 ml) anise seed
1/4 cup	(50 ml) dry white wine
1	celery stalk, sliced
1/2 cup	(125 ml) radishes, thinly sliced
2	green onions, chopped
1 tbsp	(15 ml) Dijon mustard
3 tbsp	(45 ml) raspberry wine vinegar
1/2 cup	(125 ml) olive oil
	salt and fresh ground pepper
	lemon juice
	few drops Tabasco sauce

Place scallops, lime juice, butter, anise seed, wine and pepper in casserole. Cover and microwave 3 minutes.

Drain scallops and transfer to bowl. Mix in celery, radishes and onions; set aside.

In second bowl, whisk mustard, vinegar, salt and pepper together.

Incorporate oil in thin stream while whisking constantly. Correct seasoning, add lemon juice and Tabasco sauce and pour vinaigrette over salad to taste.

Toss and serve.

Haddock Casserole

(serves 4)

1 SERVING	414 CALORIES	45g CARBOHYDRATE
25g PROTEIN	15g FAT	2.0g FIBER

Setting: HIGH

Cooking Time: 21 minutes

Utensil: 12 cups (2.8 L) casserole with cover

4 tbsp	(60 ml) butter
2	celery stalks, sliced thick
1	onion, in chunks
1	fennel bulb, cut in ½ and cubed
5 tbsp	(75 ml) flour
3 cups	(750 ml) hot chicken stock
10 oz	(300 g) haddock filets, cut in 1 in (2.5 cm) wide strips
8	small round potatoes, peeled and cooked*
1	sweet potato, peeled, cooked and cubed*
	salt and pepper

Place butter, celery, onion and fennel in casserole; season well. Cover and microwave 5 minutes.

Mix in flour. Cover and microwave 2 minutes.

Pour in chicken stock, mix and microwave 5 minutes uncovered. Stir well; continue microwaving 5 minutes uncovered.

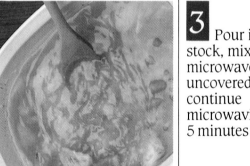

Correct seasoning and add fish, potatoes and sweet potato. Microwave 4 minutes uncovered.

* The canned variety serves as an excellent substitute for fresh produce.

1 Place butter, celery, onion and fennel in casserole; season well. Cover and microwave 5 minutes.

3 Pour in chicken stock, mix and microwave 5 minutes uncovered. Stir well; continue microwaving 5 minutes uncovered.

2 Mix in flour. Cover and microwave 2 minutes.

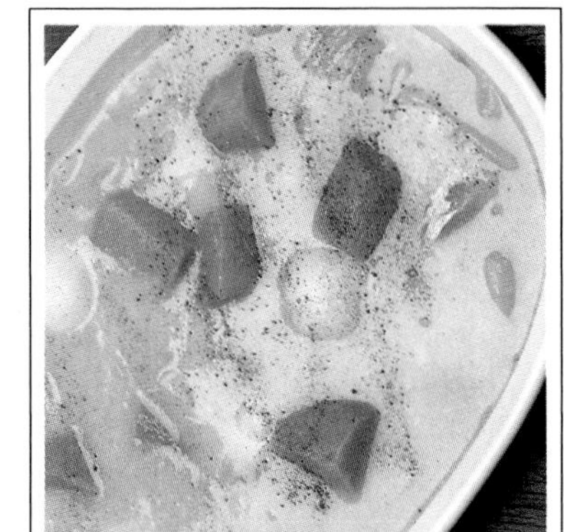

4 Correct seasoning and add fish, potatoes and sweet potatoes. Microwave 4 minutes uncovered.

Shrimp Bisque

(serves 4)

1 SERVING	315 CALORIES	13g CARBOHYDRATE
24g PROTEIN	20g FAT	trace FIBER

Setting: HIGH

Cooking Time: 25 minutes

Utensil: 12 cups (2.8 L) casserole with cover

4 tbsp	(60 ml) butter
1	carrot, pared and diced small
1	celery stalk, diced small
1	shallot, chopped
12	large shrimp, unpeeled
¼ tsp	(1 ml) fennel
1 tsp	(5 ml) chopped chives
5 tbsp	(75 ml) flour
4 cups	(1 L) hot fish stock
½ cup	(125 ml) hot light cream
	salt and pepper

Place butter, vegetables, shallot, shrimp, salt and pepper in casserole. Cover and microwave 8 minutes.

Remove shrimp from casserole and shell. Set shrimp and shells aside.

Add seasonings and flour to vegetables in casserole; mix well. Place shrimp shells and fish stock in casserole. Cover and microwave 15 minutes.

Pass mixture through sieve using pestle and pour back into casserole.

Chop shrimp and stir into soup. Add cream and season to taste. Microwave 2 minutes uncovered.

Boston Bluefish with Vegetables

(serves 4)

1 SERVING	169 CALORIES	8g CARBOHYDRATE
19g PROTEIN	6g FAT	1.0g FIBER

Setting: HIGH and MEDIUM-HIGH

Cooking Time: 12 minutes

Utensil: 12 cups (2.8 L) casserole with cover

1	leek, cut in 4 lengthwise, washed and chopped
1 tbsp	(15 ml) chopped parsley
1 tbsp	(15 ml) butter
¼ tsp	(1 ml) fennel
12 oz	(350 g) Boston Bluefish filets
8	lichees nuts
2	tomatoes, sliced
	salt and pepper

Place leek, parsley, butter and fennel in casserole. Cover and microwave 4 minutes at HIGH.

Lay filets in casserole; add lichees and tomato slices. Cover and microwave 5 minutes at MEDIUM-HIGH.

Turn filets over and correct seasoning. Cover and microwave 3 minutes at MEDIUM-HIGH.

Grilled Rainbow Trout

(serves 2)

1 SERVING	370 CALORIES	1g CARBOHYDRATE
28g PROTEIN	27g FAT	--g FIBER

Setting: HIGH

Cooking Time: 5½ minutes

Utensil: 12 cups (2.8 L) casserole with cover

1 tbsp	(15 ml) butter
2	rainbow trout, gutted and cleaned
	lime juice
	salt and pepper
	melted butter
	toasted slivered almonds

Place butter in casserole and microwave ½ minute uncovered.

Season insides of trout with lime juice, salt and pepper. Place in casserole, cover and microwave 3 minutes.

Turn trout over; continue microwaving 2 minutes covered.

Serve with melted butter and garnish with slivered almonds.

Vermouth Scallops

(serves 4)

1 SERVING	336 CALORIES	14g CARBOHYDRATE
28g PROTEIN	17g FAT	1.0g FIBER

Setting: MEDIUM-HIGH and HIGH

Cooking Time: 11 minutes

Utensil: 12 cups (2.8 L) casserole with cover
4 individual microwave coquille dishes

1 lb	(500 g) fresh scallops
3 tbsp	(45 ml) butter
1 tbsp	(15 ml) chopped parsley
½ lb	(250 g) mushrooms, quartered
1 tbsp	(15 ml) lime juice
3 tbsp	(45 ml) dry vermouth
3 tbsp	(45 ml) flour
½ cup	(125 ml) hot milk
¼ tsp	(1 ml) fennel seed
1 cup	(250 ml) grated mozzarella cheese
	salt and pepper
	dash paprika
	few drops lemon juice

Place scallops, butter, parsley, mushrooms and lime juice in casserole.

Pour in vermouth, cover and microwave 3 minutes at MEDIUM-HIGH.

Mix in flour. Continue microwaving 3 minutes, covered, at MEDIUM-HIGH.

Remove scallops and set aside.

Add hot milk, fennel, salt, pepper and paprika to casserole; mix well and sprinkle in lemon juice to taste. Microwave 4 minutes at HIGH uncovered.

Replace scallops in casserole and mix well. Spoon mixture into coquille dishes and top with cheese; microwave 1 minute at HIGH uncovered.

1 Place scallops, butter, parsley, mushrooms and lime juice in casserole.

3 Mix in flour. Continue microwaving 3 minutes covered at MEDIUM-HIGH.

2 Pour in vermouth, cover and microwave 3 minutes at MEDIUM-HIGH.

4 Remove scallops and set aside.

Haddock Topped with Cheese

(serves 4)

1 SERVING	166 CALORIES	2g CARBOHYDRATE
21g PROTEIN	7g FAT	trace FIBER

Setting: MEDIUM-HIGH

Cooking Time: 8 minutes

Utensil: 12 cups (2.8 L) casserole with cover Microwave serving platter

12.3 oz	(350 g) package frozen haddock filets
1 tbsp	(15 ml) lime or lemon juice
3	green onions, chopped
1 tbsp	(15 ml) butter
¼ tsp	(1 ml) fennel seed
¼ tsp	(1 ml) tarragon
½ cup	(125 ml) grated mozzarella cheese
	salt and pepper
	paprika to taste

Grease casserole and add frozen fish, lime juice and onions.

Sprinkle in butter, fennel seed and tarragon; season well. Cover and microwave 5 minutes.

Turn filets over; cover and continue microwaving 2 minutes.

Transfer fish to serving platter, season with paprika and top with cheese. Finish microwaving 1 minute uncovered.

Serve with small salad and vegetables.

1 Use fish straight from the freezer.

3 Turn filets over; cover and continue microwaving 2 minutes.

2 Place frozen fish, lime juice and onions in greased casserole. Add butter, fennel seed and tarragon; season well. Cover and microwave 5 minutes.

4 Transfer fish to serving platter, season with paprika and top with cheese. Finish microwaving 1 minute uncovered.

Oyster Bake

(serves 4)

1 SERVING	390 CALORIES	10g CARBOHYDRATE
48g PROTEIN	16g FAT	trace FIBER

Setting: HIGH

Cooking Time: 13 minutes

Utensil: 8 cups (2 L) rectangular dish

2 tbsp	(30 ml) butter
4	large sole filets
1 tbsp	(15 ml) chopped shallot
1 tbsp	(15 ml) chopped parsley
24	shrimp, shelled and deveined
1 cup	(250 ml) halved mushrooms
1 cup	(250 ml) shucked oysters
½ cup	(125 ml) dry white wine
½ cup	(125 ml) hot light cream
	pinch fennel
	salt and pepper
	lemon juice

Place half of butter and all filets in rectangular dish. Season well and cover with pierced plastic wrap; microwave 3 minutes.

Turn filets over and continue microwaving 4 minutes covered.

Remove fish and transfer to serving platter; set aside.

Add remaining butter, shallot, parsley, shrimp and mushrooms to rectangular dish; cover with plastic wrap and microwave 4 minutes.

Season well with fennel, salt, pepper and lemon juice. Add oysters and wine; mix well. Cover and continue microwaving 2 minutes.

Stir in cream and correct seasoning.

Pour over fish and serve.

Scampi Parisienne

(serves 4)

1 SERVING	494 CALORIES	23g CARBOHYDRATE
66g PROTEIN	15g FAT	1.0g FIBER

Setting: HIGH

Cooking Time: 5½ minutes

Utensil: 12 cups (2.8 L) casserole with cover

4 tbsp	(60 ml) butter
32	scampi, shelled
2	garlic cloves, smashed and chopped
1 cup	(250 ml) water chestnuts
1 cup	(250 ml) cooked Parisienne potatoes
2	tomatoes, peeled and diced
1 tbsp	(15 ml) chopped parsley or chives
1 tsp	(5 ml) soya sauce
1 tsp	(5 ml) chopped pickled banana pepper
	salt and pepper

Place butter in casserole and microwave ½ minute uncovered.

Add scampi and garlic; season well. Cover and microwave 2 minutes.

Mix in remaining ingredients and correct seasoning. Finish microwaving 3 minutes covered.

Ocean Perch and Cabbage

(serves 4)

1 SERVING	228 CALORIES	11g CARBOHYDRATE
31g PROTEIN	6g FAT	1.0g FIBER

Setting: MEDIUM-HIGH
Cooking Time: 12 minutes
Utensil: 12 cups (2.8 L) casserole with cover

½	cabbage, thinly sliced, cooked
4 tbsp	(60 ml) grated Parmesan cheese
4	ocean perch filets
2 tsp	(10 ml) butter
½ tsp	(2 ml) fennel seeds
¼ tsp	(1 ml) anise
¼ tsp	(1 ml) paprika
14 oz	(398 ml) tomato sauce, heated
	salt and pepper

Lightly grease casserole. Add half of cabbage and top with half of cheese.

Add filets flat and dot with butter. Sprinkle in seasonings followed by remaining cheese and cabbage.

Season again with salt and pepper and pour in tomato sauce. Cover and microwave 12 minutes.

Serve with spaghetti squash.

Baked Apples

(serves 4)

1 SERVING	87 CALORIES	11g CARBOHYDRATE
trace PROTEIN	2g FAT	1.0g FIBER

Setting: HIGH

Cooking Time: 9 minutes

Utensil: 8 cups (2 L) casserole with cover

2	apples, hollowed
2 tsp	(10 ml) butter
½ tsp	(2 ml) cinnamon
	lemon juice

Using small knife score apples around middle to prevent skin from splitting during cooking.

Place apples in casserole and sprinkle remaining ingredients over. Cover and microwave 9 minutes.

When apples are cooked, cut each into half and serve as garnish with flounder filets.

Pineapple Flounder Filets

(serves 4)

1 SERVING	163 CALORIES	8g CARBOHYDRATE
15g PROTEIN	4g FAT	1.0g FIBER

Setting: HIGH and MEDIUM-HIGH

Cooking Time: 6 minutes

Utensil: 8 cups (2 L) rectangular dish

1 tbsp	(15 ml) butter
4	flounder filets
1 tbsp	(15 ml) chopped parsley
1	yellow pepper, thinly sliced
4	fresh pineapple rings
	salt and pepper
	dash paprika
	lemon juice

Arrange all ingredients in rectangular dish and cover with pierced plastic wrap; microwave 4 minutes at HIGH.

Turn filets over and continue microwaving 2 minutes at MEDIUM-HIGH, covered with plastic wrap.

Serve with baked apples.

Sweet, Sweet Potatoes

(serves 4)

1 SERVING	173 CALORIES	41g CARBOHYDRATE
2g PROTEIN	trace FAT	1.0g FIBER

Setting: HIGH

Cooking Time: 23 minutes

Utensil: Stoneware serving platter

2	large sweet potatoes
1 tbsp	(15 ml) brown sugar
1 tsp	(5 ml) cinnamon
¼ cup	(50 ml) orange juice
2 tbsp	(30 ml) molasses

Wrap each potato in plastic wrap, prick several times and place in microwave. Microwave 20 minutes depending on size, turning 3 to 4 times.

Remove and slice with skin about ½ in (1.2 cm) thick. Arrange pieces on stoneware plate and top with remaining ingredients. Microwave 1½ minutes uncovered.

Turn pieces over; continue microwaving another 1½ minutes uncovered.

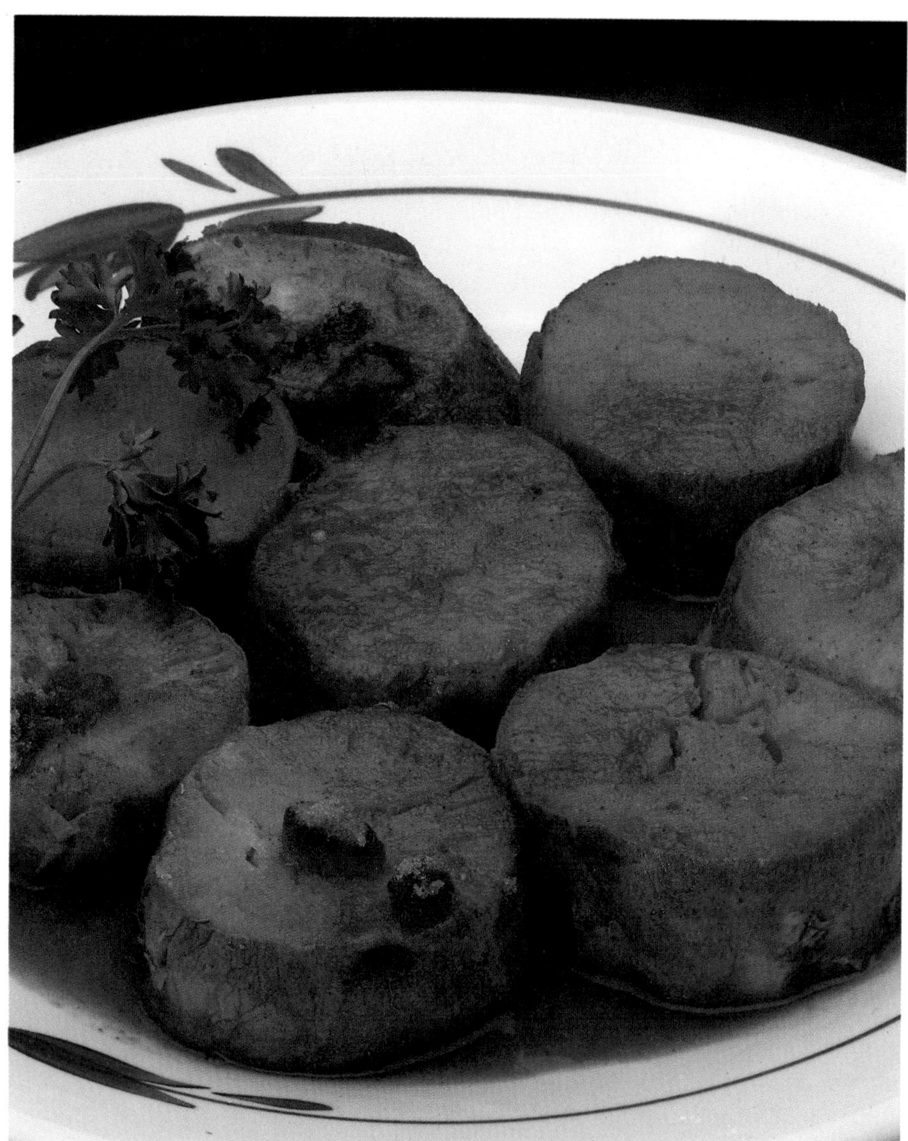

Garlicky Sweet Potatoes

(serves 4)

1 SERVING	349 CALORIES	62g CARBOHYDRATE
12g PROTEIN	6g FAT	2.0g FIBER

Setting: HIGH

Cooking Time: 23 minutes

Utensil: None

4	large sweet potatoes
3	slices crisp bacon, chopped
2	garlic cloves, smashed and chopped
1 tbsp	(15 ml) chopped parsley
½ cup	(125 ml) cooked shrimp, chopped
4 tbsp	(60 ml) sour cream
	salt and pepper

Wrap each potato in plastic wrap; prick each several times with knife. Place in microwave for 8 minutes.

Turn potatoes over; continue microwaving 15 minutes. Remove and unwrap.

Mix remaining ingredients together; season to taste.

Slit potatoes open and top with mixture. Serve.

Endive Ham Bake

(serves 4)

1 SERVING	350 CALORIES	11g CARBOHYDRATE
26g PROTEIN	11g FAT	1.0g FIBER

Setting: HIGH

Cooking Time: 23 minutes

Utensil: 12 cups (2.8 L) casserole with cover

4	endives
2 tbsp	(30 ml) butter
1 tbsp	(15 ml) lemon juice
1 tbsp	(15 ml) chopped parsley
½ tsp	(2 ml) tarragon
½ cup	(125 ml) light chicken stock
4	large slices Black Forest ham, fat removed
1½ cups	(375 ml) light white sauce, heated
1 cup	(250 ml) grated mozzarella cheese
	salt and pepper

Slit endives in four lengthwise without cutting through the base. Wash well in cold water and shake off excess.

Place endives, butter, lemon juice, parsley, tarragon and chicken stock in casserole; season well. Cover and microwave 20 minutes; turn endives over halfway through.

Remove endives from casserole and discard ½ of cooking liquid.

Wrap endives in slices of ham and secure with toothpicks; replace in casserole. Pour in white sauce, season and top with cheese. Microwave 3 minutes uncovered.

Quick Vegetable Mix

(serves 4)

1 SERVING	182 CALORIES	22g CARBOHYDRATE
10g PROTEIN	8g FAT	3.0g FIBER

Setting: HIGH

Cooking Time: 24 minutes

Utensil: 12 cups (2.8 L) casserole with cover

1 tbsp	(15 ml) butter
1	medium onion, chopped
1	garlic clove, smashed and chopped
3	slices bacon, diced
1 lb	(500 g) fresh okra, ends snipped
4	tomatoes, peeled, seeded and chopped
1	green pepper, diced
1 tsp	(5 ml) chopped jalapeno pepper
1 tbsp	(15 ml) curry powder
1 tbsp	(15 ml) cumin powder
1 tsp	(5 ml) olive oil
	salt and pepper

Microwave butter 1 minute in casserole uncovered.

Add onion, garlic and bacon; cover and microwave 6 minutes.

Add okra and mix; microwave 2 minutes covered.

Stir in tomatoes, green pepper, jalapeno, seasonings and oil; cover and microwave 7 minutes.

Mix well; finish microwaving 8 minutes covered.

Sprinkle with cheese if desired.

1 Trim ends from fresh okra.

3 Microwave onion, garlic and bacon 6 minutes covered. Then, add okra and microwave 2 minutes.

2 An easy way to peel fresh tomatoes is to blanch them in boiling water for 2 to 3 minutes. The skin should separate quite easily from the flesh.

4 Stir in tomatoes, green pepper, jalapeno, seasonings and oil; cover and microwave 7 minutes.

Spaghetti Squash

(serves 4)

1 SERVING	57 CALORIES	2g CARBOHYDRATE
1g PROTEIN	6g FAT	trace FIBER

Setting: HIGH
Cooking Time: 25 minutes
Utensil: none

1	spaghetti squash
2 tbsp	(30 ml) butter
	salt and pepper
	butter to taste

Cut squash in half lengthwise; remove all seeds and hair-like fibers.

Divide butter between halves and season very generously. Wrap loosely in pierced plastic wrap and place in microwave.

Microwave 25 minutes.

Remove from oven, scoop out squash and place in bowl. Add more butter to taste and serve as garnish with ocean perch.

Creamy Cauliflower

(serves 4)

1 SERVING	213 CALORIES	17g CARBOHYDRATE
5g PROTEIN	11g FAT	2.0g FIBER

Setting: HIGH
Cooking Time: 9 minutes
Utensil: 12 cups (2.8 L) casserole with cover

1 tbsp	(15 ml) butter
1	small cauliflower, in flowerets
2	large potatoes, peeled, cooked and diced
1	cucumber, peeled, seeded and diced
2	garlic cloves, smashed and chopped
1 tbsp	(15 ml) chopped parsley
2 tbsp	(30 ml) chopped pimento
1 cup	(250 ml) hot light cream
	salt and pepper
	few drops lemon juice

Place butter and cauliflower in casserole; season with salt, pepper and lemon juice. Cover and microwave 5 minutes.

Add potatoes, cucumber, garlic, parsley and pimento; mix well. Continue microwaving 2 minutes covered.

Mix again and stir in cream; finish microwaving 2 minutes uncovered.

Layered Asparagus Dish

(serves 4)

1 SERVING	174 CALORIES	14g CARBOHYDRATE
16g PROTEIN	15g FAT	1.0g FIBER

Setting: HIGH
Cooking Time: 15 minutes
Utensil: 12 cups (2.8 L) casserole with cover

1 lb	(500 g) fresh asparagus, pared
½ cup	(125 ml) water
1 cup	(250 ml) tomato sauce, heated
1 cup	(250 ml) white sauce, heated
¼ tsp	(1 ml) nutmeg
1 cup	(250 ml) grated Gruyère cheese
	salt and pepper

Place asparagus and water in casserole. Season with salt, cover and microwave 6 minutes.

Using tongs bring asparagus at bottom of casserole towards top; replace cover and microwave 6 more minutes. (If asparagus are very large continue microwaving an extra minute.)

Discard liquid from casserole and remove half of asparagus.

Add half of each: tomato sauce, white sauce, nutmeg and cheese.

Cover with remaining asparagus and repeat above layers. Cover and microwave 3 minutes.

Broccoli and Asparagus

(serves 4)

1 SERVING	79 CALORIES	6g CARBOHYDRATE
3g PROTEIN	5g FAT	1.0g FIBER

Setting: HIGH

Cooking Time: 9 minutes

Utensil: 12 cups (2.8 L) casserole with cover

1	bunch fresh asparagus, tips only
1 tbsp	(15 ml) butter
1	head broccoli, in flowerets
1 tbsp	(15 ml) chopped fresh ginger
3 tbsp	(45 ml) toasted slivered almonds
	salt and pepper

Slice asparagus tips in half lengthwise. Cut each half into 2 pieces. Place in casserole with butter, salt and pepper. Cover and microwave 4 minutes.

Add broccoli, ginger and almonds; mix well. Cover and microwave 5 minutes.

Serve.

Almond Cake

(serves 10-12)

1 SERVING	298 CALORIES	35g CARBOHYDRATE
5g PROTEIN	16g FAT	trace FIBER

Setting: MEDIUM
Cooking Time: 19 minutes
Utensil: 12 cups (3 L) bundt mold

1⅔ cups	(400 ml) all-purpose flour
1 cup	(250 ml) granulated sugar
¼ cup	(50 ml) powdered almonds
1 tsp	(5 ml) baking soda
¼ tsp	(1 ml) salt
¼ tsp	(1 ml) nutmeg
1 cup	(250 ml) milk
½ cup	(125 ml) vegetable oil
1	egg
1 tsp	(5 ml) vanilla
¼ cup	(50 ml) slivered almonds
½ cup	(125 ml) crushed pineapple
2	egg whites, beaten stiff

Lightly oil bundt mold and set aside.

Sift flour, sugar, powdered almonds, baking soda, salt and nutmeg into bowl of mixer. Using whisk attachment, mix at low speed for 2 minutes.

Add milk, oil, whole egg and vanilla; beat 2 minutes or until well incorporated.

Add almonds and pineapple; blend 2 minutes at low speed.

Using spatula fold in stiff egg whites until thoroughly incorporated.

Pour batter into mold and rap bottom on counter to settle mixture. Microwave 19 minutes, rotating 4 times.

Let cake stand in mold to cool. When ready to serve, ice with your favorite frosting.

1 Sift flour, sugar, powdered almonds, baking soda, sait and nutmeg into bowl of mixer.

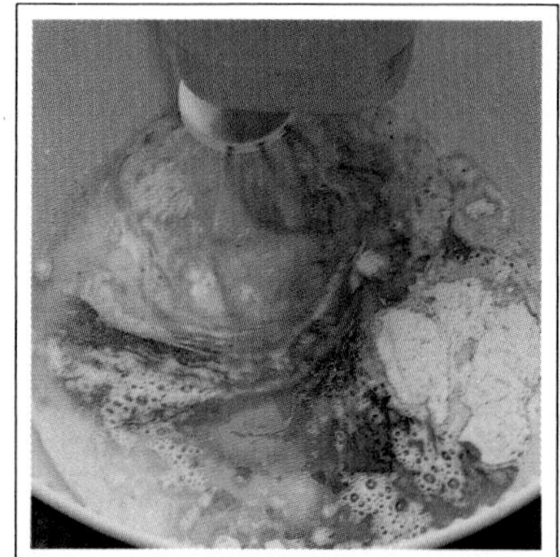

3 Beat milk, oil, egg and vanilla for 2 minutes or until well incorporated.

2 Using whisk attachment, mix at low speed for 2 minutes.

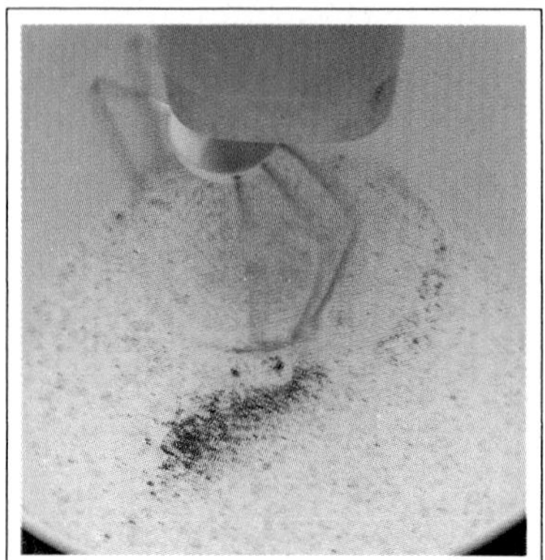

4 Add almonds and pineapple; blend 2 minutes at low speed.

Almond Brownies

(serves 8)

1 SERVING	445 CALORIES	42g CARBOHYDRATE
8g PROTEIN	28g FAT	trace FIBER

Setting: HIGH

Cooking Time: 5½ minutes

Utensil: 8 cups (2 L) square plastic mold

½ cup	(125 ml) butter
¾ cup	(175 ml) granulated sugar
¼ cup	(50 ml) brown sugar
3	beaten eggs
1 tbsp	(15 ml) rum
4 tbsp	(60 ml) heavy cream
1 cup	(250 ml) sifted all-purpose flour
½ cup	(125 ml) cocoa
1 tsp	(5 ml) baking powder
1	egg white, beaten stiff
½ cup	(125 ml) slivered almonds

Grease plastic mold and set aside.

Place butter in glass bowl and microwave 1 minute uncovered or until melted.

Pour butter in large mixing bowl. Incorporate both sugars using electric hand beater.

Add beaten whole eggs, rum and cream; continue beating until well combined.

Sift dry ingredients into bowl; incorporate very well.

Using spatula fold in egg white and almonds. Pour batter into plastic mold and rap bottom on counter to settle mixture.

Microwave 4½ minutes uncovered. Rotate twice.

Remove from microwave and set aside to cool before serving.

Crêpes Stuffed with Bananas

(serves 4)

1 SERVING	313 CALORIES	53g CARBOHYDRATE
6g PROTEIN	13g FAT	1.0g FIBER

Setting: MEDIUM-HIGH

Cooking Time: 4 minutes

Utensil: 8 cups (2 L) casserole

1 tbsp	(15 ml) butter
1 tbsp	(15 ml) maple syrup
4	bananas, sliced 1 in (2.5 cm) thick
2 tbsp	(30 ml) Caribbean Cream liqueur
3	egg whites
2 tbsp	(30 ml) granulated sugar
4	crêpes
	juice 1½ oranges

Place butter and maple syrup in casserole; microwave 1 minute uncovered.

Add bananas, liqueur and orange juice; mix and microwave 3 minutes uncovered.

Meanwhile, beat egg whites until stiff. Add sugar slowly and continue beating 1 minute.

Spread banana mixture on crêpes, roll and place on platter. Top with dollops of meringue and brown in conventional oven set at broil.

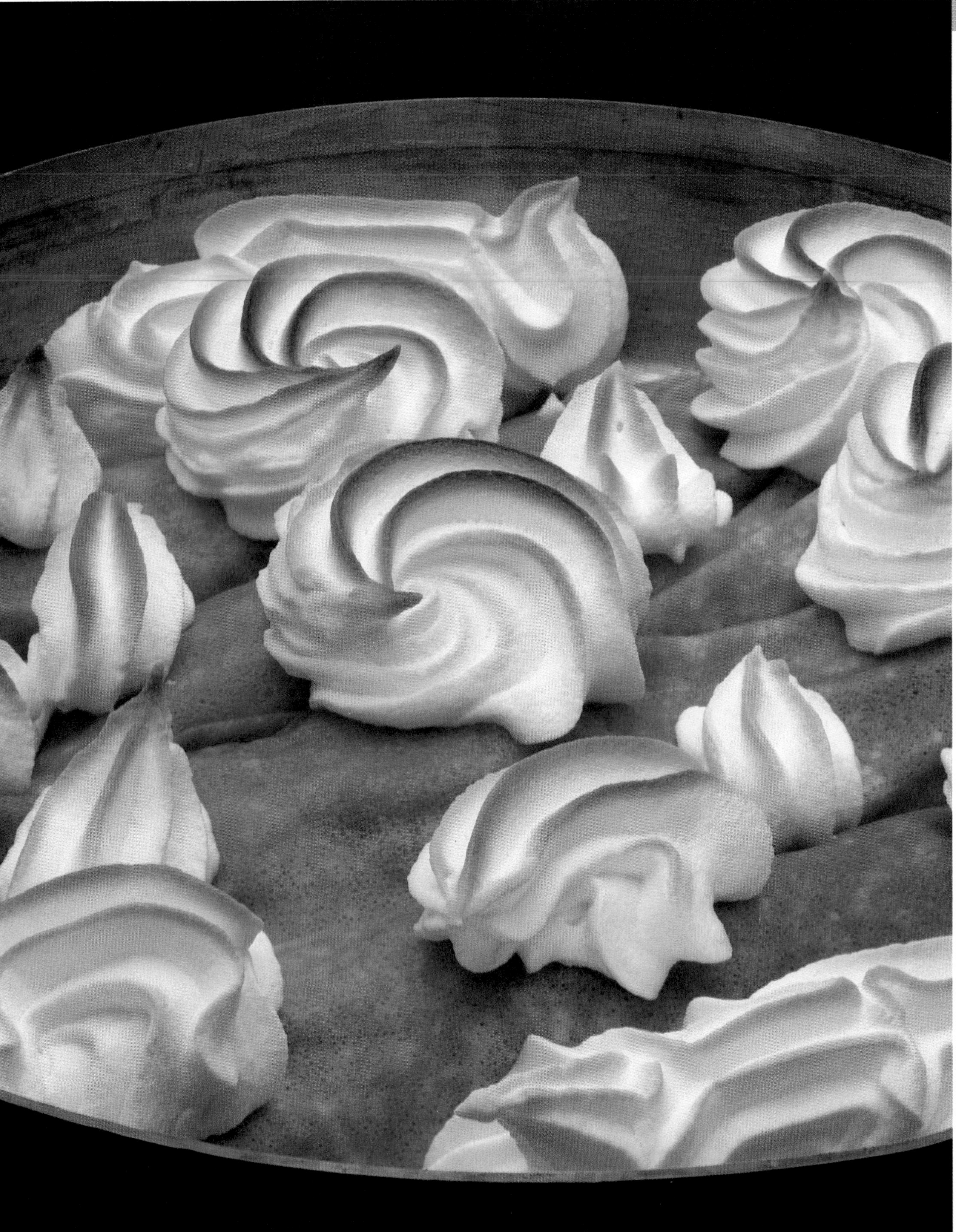

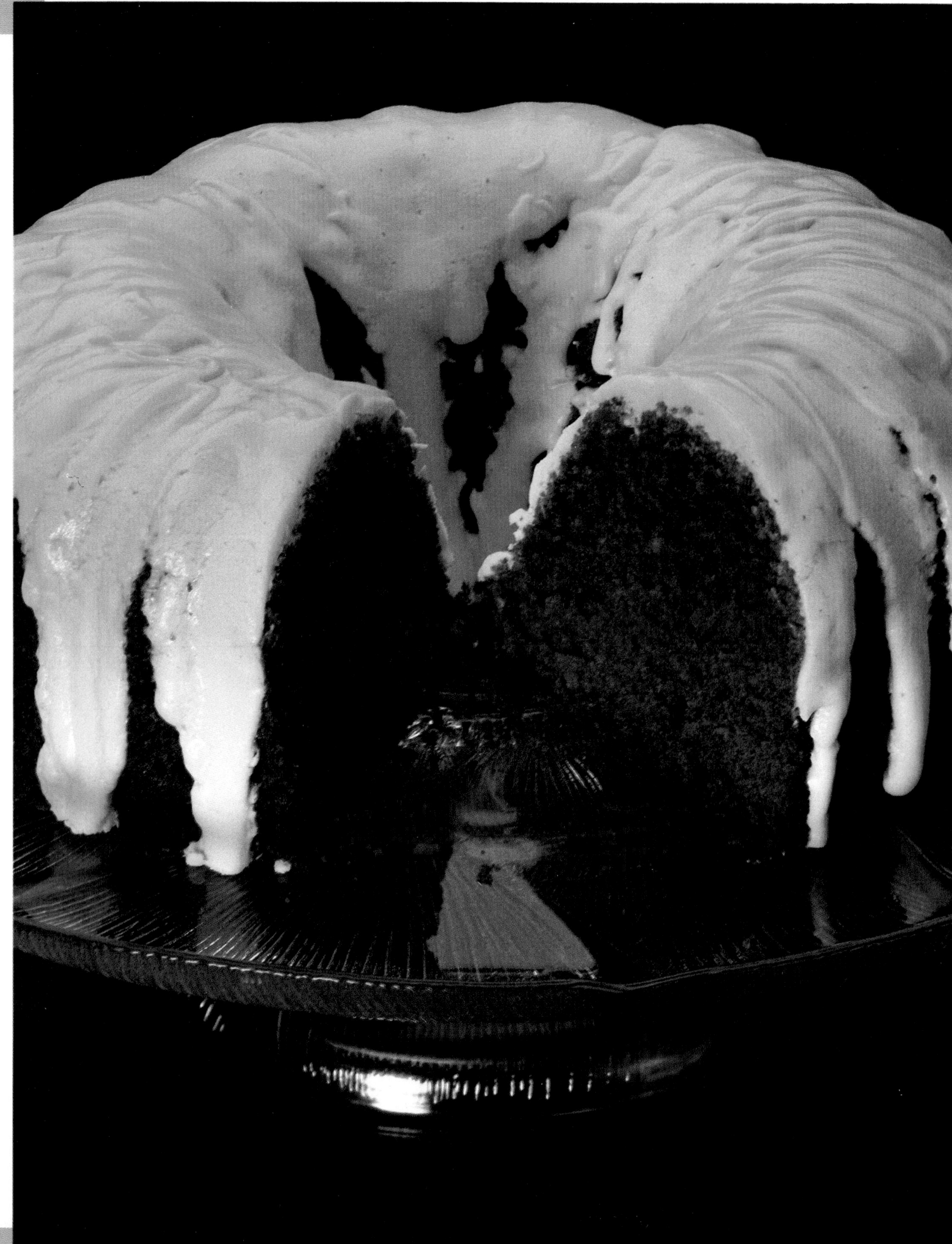

Chocolate Cake

(serves 10-12)

1 SERVING	396 CALORIES	38g CARBOHYDRATE
6g PROTEIN	24g FAT	trace FIBER

Setting: MEDIUM

Cooking Time: 29 minutes

Utensil: 12 cups (3 L) bundt mold

1 cup	(250 ml) granulated sugar
1½ cups	(375 ml) all-purpose flour
½ cup	(125 ml) cocoa
1½ tbsp	(25 ml) baking powder
¼ tsp	(1 ml) salt
¼ cup	(50 ml) powdered almonds
1 cup	(250 ml) soft unsalted butter
1 cup	(250 ml) milk
2 tbsp	(30 ml) Tia Maria
2	egg yolks
2	whole eggs
3	egg whites, beaten stiff
	oil

Lightly oil bundt mold and set aside.

Sift granulated sugar, flour, cocoa, baking powder, salt and powdered almonds into bowl of mixer. Using dough hook, mix at low speed for 2 minutes.

Add butter to bowl; continue mixing at medium speed until well incorporated. If necessary use spatula occasionally to prevent mixture from riding up sides.

Reduce mixer speed to low. Add milk and Tia Maria; blend for 1 minute.

Replace dough hook with whisk attachment. Increase speed to medium and add yolks and whole eggs; beat about 4 to 5 minutes.

Using spatula, fold in stiff egg whites until thoroughly incorporated.

Pour batter into mold and rap bottom on counter to settle mixture. Microwave 29 minutes, rotating 4 times.

Let cake stand in mold to cool. When ready to serve, ice with your favorite frosting.

Tasty Strawberry Sauce

1 RECIPE	800 CALORIES	187g CARBOHYDRATE
7g PROTEIN	.5g FAT	2.5g FIBER

Setting: HIGH

Cooking Time: 7 minutes

Utensil: 8 cups (2 L) casserole

15 oz	(425 g) package frozen strawberries
4 tbsp	(60 ml) black currant jelly
2 tbsp	(30 ml) orange liqueur
2 tbsp	(30 ml) cornstarch
4 tbsp	(60 ml) cold water

Thaw strawberries according to directions on package.

Place strawberries, jelly and liqueur in casserole. Microwave 4 minutes uncovered.

Mix cornstarch with water; stir into sauce and continue microwaving 3 minutes.

Cool and pour over ice cream or drizzle over sponge cake.

Rhubarb Sauce

1 RECIPE	1661 CALORIES	344g CARBOHYDRATE
4g PROTEIN	27g FAT	trace FIBER

Setting: HIGH

Cooking Time: 31 minutes

Utensil: 12 cups (2.8 L) casserole with cover

4 cups	(1 L) frozen rhubarb
3 tbsp	(45 ml) light rum
1 cup	(250 ml) granulated sugar
½ cup	(125 ml) brown sugar
¼ cup	(50 ml) freshly squeezed orange juice
2 tbsp	(30 ml) butter
2 tbsp	(30 ml) cornstarch
5 tbsp	(75 ml) cold water
	chopped rind 1 lemon
	chopped rind 1 orange

Place rhubarb in casserole and pour in rum.

Add both sugars, orange juice, butter and chopped rinds.

Mix slightly and cover; microwave 30 minutes.

Mix rhubarb sauce well. Mix cornstarch with water; stir into sauce. Microwave 1 minute uncovered.

Serve with cake or over ice cream.

1 It is not necessary to defrost the rhubarb before microwaving.

3 Add both sugars.

2 Place rhubarb in casserole and pour in rum.

4 Add orange juice, butter and chopped rinds.

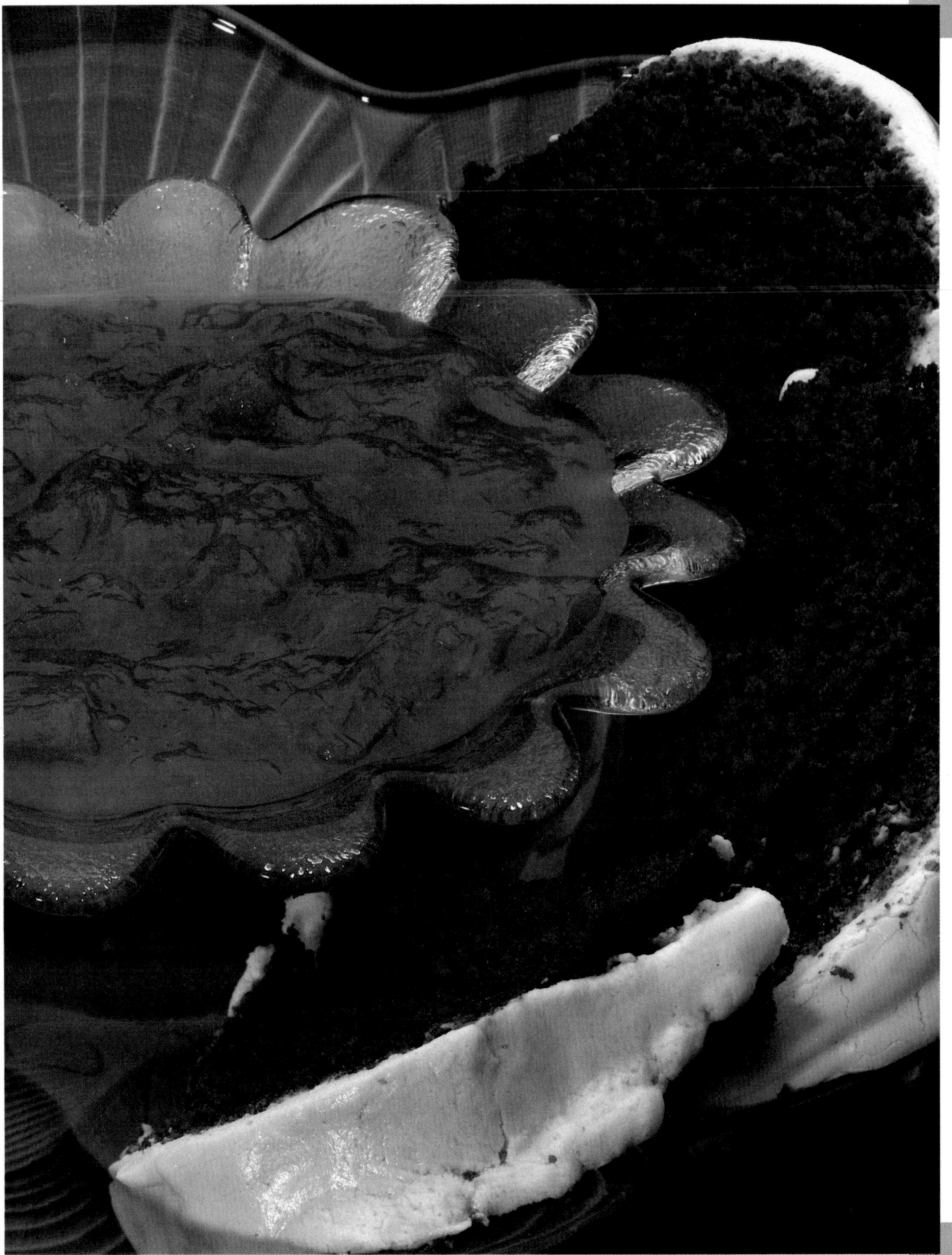

Baked Apples

(serves 4)

1 SERVING	298 CALORIES	39g CARBOHYDRATE
1g PROTEIN	10g FAT	1.0g FIBER

Setting: HIGH

Cooking Time: 12 minutes

Utensil: 8 cups (2 L) casserole with cover

4	large baking apples
3 tbsp	(45 ml) brown sugar
2 tbsp	(30 ml) butter
2 tbsp	(30 ml) heavy cream
¼ tsp	(1 ml) nutmeg
½ cup	(125 ml) light rum
1 tbsp	(15 ml) cornstarch
2 tbsp	(30 ml) cold water
	rind 1 orange in julienne

Core apples and using small knife score around middle. This will prevent skin from cracking during cooking.

Cut away a bit of apple flesh at one end to make hole wider for filling. Place apples in casserole.

Mix brown sugar with butter in small bowl. Stir in cream and nutmeg.

Pour rum into bottom of casserole and fill apple cavities with cream mixture.

Cover and microwave 11 minutes.

Remove apples from casserole and set aside.

Add orange rind to juices in casserole. Mix cornstarch with water; stir into sauce to thicken. Microwave 1 minute uncovered.

Pour sauce over apples and serve.

1 Core apples.

3 Cut away a bit of apple flesh at one end to make hole wider for filling. Place apples in casserole and pour in rum.

2 Using small knife score apples around middle to prevent skin from cracking during cooking.

4 Fill apple cavities with cream mixture.

Dessert Drink

(serves 4)

1 SERVING	248 CALORIES	19g CARBOHYDRATE
1g PROTEIN	17g FAT	trace FIBER

Setting: HIGH

Cooking Time: 2 minutes

Utensil: 12 cups (2.8 L) casserole

4	lemon slices
3	cinnamon sticks
1 tbsp	(15 ml) grated orange rind
2	cloves
3 tbsp	(45 ml) dark rum
3 tbsp	(45 ml) brown sugar
1 tbsp	(15 ml) honey
4 cups	(1 L) strong black coffee, hot
¾ cup	(175 ml) heavy cream, whipped
	granulated sugar
	dash cinnamon

Coat rims of 4 tall-stemmed glasses with lemon. Dip in granulated sugar and set aside.

Place remaining ingredients, except cream and cinnamon, in casserole. Microwave 2 minutes uncovered.

Pour into glasses and top with dollops of whipped cream. Sprinkle with dash of cinnamon and serve immediately.

Creamy Rice Pudding

(serves 4-6)

1 SERVING	345 CALORIES	53g CARBOHYDRATE
9g PROTEIN	7g FAT	1.0g FIBER

Setting: MEDIUM-HIGH and LOW

Cooking Time: 39 minutes

Utensil: 12 cups (2.8 L) casserole with cover

1 cup	(250 ml) long grain rice, rinsed
½ cup	(125 ml) brown sugar
3½ cups	(875 ml) hot milk
1 tbsp	(15 ml) grated lemon rind
¼ cup	(50 ml) sultana raisins
½ cup	(125 ml) light cream
2 tbsp	(30 ml) mixed candied fruit
1 tbsp	(15 ml) cinnamon
1	beaten egg

Place rice in casserole and sprinkle in sugar. Mix in milk and lemon rind. Cover and microwave 18 minutes at MEDIUM-HIGH, stirring twice.

Add raisins, cream, fruit and cinnamon; incorporate well. Continue microwaving 19 minutes covered, stirring occasionally.

Add egg, mix well and finish microwaving 2 minutes at LOW uncovered.

Serve plain or drizzled with maple syrup.

Creamy Cheesecake

(serves 8-10)

1 SERVING	403 CALORIES	28g CARBOHYDRATE
7g PROTEIN	30g FAT	--g FIBER

Setting: HIGH

Cooking Time: 8¾ minutes

Utensil: 6 cups (1.5 L) glass pie plate

¾ cup	(175 ml) crushed chocolate wafers
¼ cup	(50 ml) fine granulated sugar
¼ cup	(50 ml) soft butter
2	8 oz (227 g) packages cream cheese, soft
½ cup	(125 ml) fine granulated sugar
3 tbsp	(45 ml) orange liqueur
1 tbsp	(15 ml) grated lemon rind
1 tbsp	(15 ml) grated orange rind
1 tbsp	(15 ml) cornstarch
3	large eggs
½ cup	(125 ml) heavy cream, whipped
1	egg white, beaten stiff

First, prepare crust by combining wafers, ¼ cup (50 ml) sugar and butter until thoroughly blended. Press into pie plate and microwave ¾ minute uncovered. Set aside to cool while filling is being prepared.

Place cheese and second measure of sugar in bowl of mixer; blend until smooth.

Add liqueur, rinds and cornstarch; mix to incorporate.

Add eggs one at a time, mixing well between additions.

Fold in whipped cream and egg white with spatula.

Pour filling into cooled crust and smooth with spatula. Microwave 8 minutes uncovered. Rotate every 2 minutes.

Remove from microwave and set aside to cool. Refrigerate 2 hours before serving.

04902663

THE TSAR'S DRAGONS

Tsar Alexander II decided to drag Russia into the industrial age. He began by inviting Welsh businessman John Hughes to build an ironworks. A charismatic visionary, John persuades influential people to invest in his venture, while concealing his greatest secret – he couldn't even write his own name. John recruited adventurers prepared to sacrifice everything to ensure the success of Hughesovka (Donetsk, Ukraine). In a place where murderers, whores, and illicit love affairs flourish, *The Tsar's Dragons* is their story of a new beginning in Hughesovka, a town of opportunity.

THE TSAR'S DRAGONS

THE TSAR'S DRAGONS

by

Catrin Collier

Magna Large Print Books
Long Preston, North Yorkshire,
BD23 4ND, England.

British Library Cataloguing in Publication Data.

Collier, Catrin
The tsar's dragons.

A catalogue record of this book is
available from the British Library

ISBN 978-0-7505-4107-7

First published in Great Britain in 2014 by Accent Press Ltd.

Cover illustration by arrangement with Accent Press

Published in Large Print 2015 by arrangement with Accent Press Ltd.

Magna Large Print is an imprint of Library Magna Books Ltd.

Printed and bound in Great Britain by
T.J. (International) Ltd., Cornwall, PL28 8RW

For
ROSS MICHAEL WATKINS
12.02.1980 – 04.02.2013

To me there needs no stone to tell
'Tis Nothing that I loved so well.

Lord Byron, 'Elegy on Thyrza'

When one has nothing left ... but memories, one guards and dusts them with especial care.

Saki (H. H. Munro)
The Wolves of Cernogratz

Press article

Nikita and Mrs Khrushchev's ten-day state visit to Britain, April 1956

Premier and Mrs Khrushchev were guests of honour at a state banquet in Buckingham Palace yesterday. During the course of the evening Mr Khrushchev questioned the Duke of Edinburgh and the Prime Minister, Sir Anthony Eden, as to the history of Welshman John Hughes, who founded the town where Mr Khrushchev was born, Donetsk (formerly Hughesovka) in the Ukraine.

Neither the Duke nor the Prime Minister had heard of John Hughes. Therefore they could give Mr Khrushchev no information regarding the man, or even confirm his existence.

Prologue

Soon I will draw my last breath where I drew my first. But for now this room is my kingdom, this oak-framed bed my county. A compact yet comfortable domain, and I have learned that nothing outweighs comfort in old age. I am clean, well-fed, warm, cared for ... lovingly, beautifully cared for. And I have my memories, no small consolation for loss of strength and independence.

The past is my last and most precious possession. My recall absolute, but I'm no longer certain what I've seen with my own eyes and what I've been told.

I'll concede that some events, some experiences, may have come to me second-hand, but I'll not admit the great events I've witnessed have been tainted by forgotten conversations. What's the harm if I was told about these things so many times by those who were there, that they've been absorbed into my own history? It doesn't make the past less valid or true.

I've often wondered if memories and emotions, like disease, can be transmitted from one person to another. If so, that would explain why I've always felt so acutely the pleasures and pain of those I've loved.

I've had a good life, a long one, richer in every way than the one of poverty and bondage to iron and coal I was born into. I've seen and done things and travelled to places beyond most people's imaginations.

I've lived like royalty in a St Petersburg palace and cowered, a hunted animal, in a burrow in the ground without a kopek or crust to my name. But the steepest climb I made was out of the Merthyr hovel where I lost my innocence and abandoned my childhood. I've broken more commandments than I care to dwell on, including *Thou shalt not kill*. But I feel no remorse for that sin – if sin it was. Some men are evil and deserve death. If saying that makes me a poor Christian then so be it.

Perhaps that's why I've lived so long. Ninety-nine years on this earth and still God doesn't want me in his heaven. Possibly He's asked Satan to prepare a place for me but the Devil is also reluctant to extend an invitation.

I sense my thoughts meandering into philosophy; the hobby of the ancients, the bane of the young. I'm not so decrepit that I can't recall my irritation when I was on the receiving end of lectures from my elders. I believed I knew everything then, just as my grandchildren and great-grandchildren do now. They sit next to my bed with grave, unlined faces, solemn-eyed in the face of my old age and impending death, so sure of their knowledge and themselves.

They try to fool me and themselves that I have a future. That my life isn't coming to an end.

It is, but it's not over ... not while I can still dream...

A shaft of light pierces the darkness. The door opens. I keep my eyes closed but I sense him creeping in, wary of disturbing me. It's too dark for me to see his face but I don't need the light. His features are imprinted on my memory. They are those of his great-grandfather, alive again.

He steals to the bed, removes the photograph album from my hands, and lays his fingers gently on my forehead.

His touch is soft, cool, like the whisper of the spring wind brushing over the Russian Steppe...

Chapter One

Owen Parry's ironworker's cottage
Broadway, Treforest, Pontypridd, 1956

So many papers to put into order. So much history to be preserved.

As I sift through the dry, brittle, letters, diaries, plans, age-tarnished albums, and photographs – Glyn's photographs – scents rise from the papers and the long-dead flowers pressed between their pages. The perfume of old summers fills the air, drifting through the mist that shrouds the years, evoking memories of *my* Russia more vivid and redolent than those conjured by mere words alone.

Where to begin?

I recall Glyn Edwards' letters, written on the same day from the same house and yet so very different. I search for them and look once more on his strong firm hand. The first is a detailed letter to his brother Peter and sister-in-law Sarah, the second, shorter, little more than a note, to his wife Betty.

Strange to think Glyn penned these before a single brick of the ironworks had been laid. Before John Hughes imported the Welsh metal-workers and colliers and long before the gamblers and adventurers flocked to colonise the Iron Master's new town. Men and women who saw the possibility of making their own fortunes in the enterprise of Mr Hughes's New Russia Company. They came, first in their hundreds, then their thousands.

Salesmen, shopkeepers hoteliers, priests, whores and whoremongers, murderers, thieves, the steadfastly moral and downright criminal of every nationality, all crowded into a few square miles. Forced to live next to, if not respect, their neighbours. Every one of them drawn by one man's vision of a brave new industrial town that promised freedom, equality, wealth, and a better life for all who had the strength to work and the courage to join him, no matter what their class, creed, or lineage.

John Hughes had the vision but he couldn't have realised it alone. It was Glyn Edwards who recruited the men who built the town. I look at the words etched on the thick cream paper, engraved with the address of the Beletsky Dower House and beyond the page I see them as they were.

Glyn, over six and a half feet tall in his stockinged feet, heavily built, as handsome, swarthy, black-haired and eyed as a gypsy. My brother, Richard Parry, just out of boyhood, with the dark curly hair and blue eyes of the Irish; Russian aristocrat Alexei, with blond hair and mischievous blue eyes that belied his angelic features; Nathan Kharber and his sister Ruth, slight, dark, with Jewish features and piercing eyes that penetrated the soul; Huw Thomas, born to subservience, mousy in looks and nature; Dr Peter Edwards; Count and Countess Beletsky; and myself, Anna Parry, the youngest, smallest, and least significant emigrant, taken to Russia as a charity case because I was the subject of salacious interest and gossip in Merthyr. The women who became closer to me than sisters. Sarah Edwards, healer, mentor, friend; Cossack Praskovia, who could have modelled for Titian with her voluptuous figure, red hair, and emerald eyes. And Sonya, who saved us all in the end with her self-sacrificing, unconditional love.

Every one of us over-shadowed by John Hughes, who strode over the steppe and through life with the air of a medieval king born to govern, to command, and above all to build and create...

Letter from Glyn Edwards to his brother, Dr Peter Edwards, and sister-in-law Sarah
Oakleigh, High Street, Merthyr Tydfil

The Beletsky Dower House
The Donbas region of the Ukraine
Saturday April 10th 1869

Dear Peter and Sarah,

We've been here four days and for the first time since our arrival I've found time to write to you. This trip with Mr Hughes is the journey of a lifetime. Believe me when I say you can't begin to imagine the size of Russia. There are no mountains where we'll be living. Not a one. So there's nothing to stop the wind blowing across a plain (the Russians call it steppe, although the ground is as level as a Welsh cake) that stretches as far as the eye can see. Little wonder the peasants, or Mujiks, *as they're called here, believe the world to be flat.*

Mr Hughes has commissioned a German architect and master builder to design the buildings, including your twelve-bed hospital and accommodation for his key workers (you as the company doctor as well as the managers), and after looking at the preliminary plans, I can confidently say that when they are built our houses will be fine ones, with ten family rooms, plus bathroom, kitchens, pantries, and separate living space for up to six indoor servants. There'll also be outbuildings and rooms above them for a coachman and outside staff. As agreed, Betty and I will share a house with you, but only until sufficient are built to accommodate all the senior management.

Mr Hughes has arranged mortgages for the senior employees of the New Russia Company, repayments to be taken directly from our wages. He doesn't want company houses as he believes people look after their own possessions better than those of others. He asked me to warn you that the furnaces, plant, collieries, and hospital will take precedence over domestic accommodation. I told him you and our wives are prepared for initial hardships, which will be more than compensated for by the excitement of seeing life in a foreign land, but most of all being part of his enterprise.

Tomorrow morning we'll be viewing the site Mr Hughes has marked for his works. Our party will be thirty in number, and as the Tabernacle minister's wife would say, 'very select'. There's a prince, two counts, three dukes (including one grand duke; Mr Hughes explained the difference. I'll pass the information on when I see you), several landowners, and two Russian ironmasters, Mr Pastukov and Mr Levsky. Every man other than me and Mr Hughes's deputy, Huw Thomas, is immensely wealthy and every man aside from Mr Hughes, Huw, and me again, high born.

Mr Hughes, Huw, and I are guests of a local landowner, a charming widow, Mrs Catherine Ignatova. Her Dower House is a twenty-minute ride from the Beletsky Mansion where her daughter Olga and son-in-law Count Nicholas Beletsky reside. Mrs Ignatova has a companion, an orphaned distant relative, Sonya, a young girl who bears a striking resemblance to Botticelli's Venus. *Well educated by Mrs Ignatova and multilingual in Russian, French, English, and Polish, she's sixteen and promises to become a real beauty.*

The Beletsky and Ignatova families will be our nearest neighbours. Count Beletsky is a cultivated man, well-educated, well-manicured, well-dressed, and he speaks several languages, including English, French, German, and Russian, but he couldn't be more different from Mr Hughes. He insists on everyone deferring to him because of his exalted birth. That doesn't make him a bad man, only narrow-minded, arrogant, and overbearing

His wife has invited Mr Hughes, Huw, and I to dine with her family tomorrow. Apparently she's a perfect hostess and mother, but she has the advantage of a staff of forty indoor servants as well as coachmen, stable boys, gardeners, and estate workers whose sole purpose in life is to ensure the Beletsky Mansion is perfectly run. The count and countess have six sons but only their eldest, Alexei, lives with them. He's a bright, inquisitive boy who puts me in mind of poor Mary's son Richard. Their five younger sons are in a military academy in Allenstein in East Prussia. They also have four daughters who are being educated at home by an English governess, a Miss Smith, who will dine at the count's table with their eldest daughter, Katya, in honour of our visit. When the count and countess called on us, Katya interpreted for her mother as the countess (unlike her mother) doesn't speak English, only French, German, and Russian.

Nicholas Beletsky has sold Mr Hughes several parcels of land but he has made it clear he believes industry is for the lower classes, not aristocrats. He owns houses in St Petersburg and Moscow as well as the mansion, which his wife inherited from her father. It's enormous, half as large again as Cyfarthfa Castle.

Unlike me, Mr Hughes has adopted Russian outer dress. His hat and coat are sable, costly even here, his suits are hand-tailored in London, but expensive as his clothes are, he wears them as a workman would his overalls. I don't know if you realised when you met him in Greenwich, but there's no false 'show' with Mr Hughes, which is just one of many reasons I admire and respect him. He's never forgotten his origins which are as humble as ours.

Did he tell you he started his apprenticeship before his thirteenth birthday in Cyfarthfa ironworks just like me and our brother Edward?

I digress. The purpose of this letter was to tell you about Russia. In many ways the country resembles the Britain of a century ago. Outside of Moscow and St Petersburg, which are beautiful cities, it has few of the modern luxuries we take for granted, like train travel, good roads, well-stocked shops, or towns that offer hotels, inns, restaurants, libraries, museums, and hospitals. After living in London I hope you won't miss city life when you reach here. On reflection, you probably won't, considering you've lived in Merthyr for the last few months but I warn you, the journey here and the first few years won't be easy.

Shipping the vast amount of supplies and materials we need to build the works is daunting. Everything is being manufactured in Britain and transported to Southampton. From there, Mr Hughes has charted a fleet of ships to take the goods and all his workers, including us, round the Bay of Biscay through the Mediterranean, on to the Sea of Azov and the port of Taganrog. There, the supplies will be loaded on bullock carts for the last eighty-mile leg of the journey.

Mr Hughes has bought thousands of the animals and we'll be reliant on them for transport until the works has produced enough rails to lay a line to the Donbas.

Mr Hughes hopes to have all the arrangements finalised, the licences signed, and the materials shipped before next summer, so you and Sarah can make preparations to leave Merthyr early next spring.

The dinner gong has sounded so I must end this. The lawyers are preparing more government forms and leases that will have to be signed on behalf of the New Russia Company so Mr Hughes and I will be back in our Moscow office before the end of the month. Please write to me there. I want you to know there is nothing Mr Hughes has not thought of. You and Sarah will sleep as safe in Russia as you do in Merthyr, if not safer and in time just as comfortably.

Good night, God bless and keep you until we are together again. Look in on Betty now and again for me if you can spare the time.

Your loving brother,

Glyn

P.S. I spoke to Mr Hughes after dinner this evening about our plans to open an independent coal mine. He's agreed to lend us company money at a preferential rate and offered to take our entire output provided it's of suitable grade. After studying the geologist's reports I've chosen a site and tomorrow will open discussions with the Cossack owners on the possibility of taking a fifty-year option on the mineral rights. So the 'Edwards Brothers Colliery' may rise alongside The New Russia Company's ironworks. God willing, we'll fulfil Mr Hughes's prophecy and become the Russian Crawshays. Who'd have thought when we were growing up in Georgetown that we'd have the opportunity to become as wealthy as the coal and iron barons of Wales?

I imagined Glyn writing the letter, full of enthusiasm and plans for the future. Pictured the people who'd taken it out of the envelope over the years to read and re-read his words; all wanting to find out about the initial steps John Hughes had taken to transform his dream of a Russian industrial city into reality.

Beneath the envelope I found the second letter I'd sought; a single page written the same day, but shorter, more formal, hardly the letter of a lover to his sweetheart – or a man of thirty to his wife of ten years.

Letter from Glyn Edwards to his wife Betty
Boot Inn, High Street, Merthyr Tydfil

The Beletsky Dower House
The Donbas region of the Ukraine
Saturday April 10th 1869

My dear wife,

I've seen the plans for our house and assure you it will be comfortable and spacious. You asked in your last letter if Russia is cold. It is, but only in winter, and I promise to buy you a fur coat before the first snow falls. You may think our new country barren and inhospitable at first, but I'm confident that given time we'll make a fine life for ourselves here and, God willing if he sends them, our children.

I have to rise early to make a site visit with Mr Hughes so I will say goodnight, Betty. I only wanted to reassure you that there is nothing Mr Hughes has not thought of when it comes to your comfort and safety.

Good night, God bless, and keep you until we are together again, which given my work in Russia, Greenwich, and my added duty of recruiting workers for Mr Hughes's new enterprise, is not likely to be before Christmas. Prepare to leave Merthyr for Russia early next spring. I have written to Peter and Sarah and asked them to do the same. If possible, I will travel to Merthyr to fetch you so we can travel to our new lives together.

Your husband,
Glyn

Letters – words on paper.

They can communicate thoughts, feelings, even emotions, but to return there, to relive the birth of Hughesovka, all I have to do is close my eyes…

Chapter Two

The Donbas region of the Ukraine
April 1869

A chill dry breeze gusted across the plain that stretched flat, vast, and endless beyond the tight-knit group of people. It whipped at the hems of their coats and teased the ends of the mufflers wound around their mouths.

One man, of a square, heavy build with white hair and beard, dressed in a sable hat and coat, dominated the group. He wasn't the tallest or even the most prepossessing but all eyes looked to him as he thrust his walking stick into the ground.

'Here,' John Hughes shouted against the wind. 'The largest ironworks in Russia will stand on this spot and not just an ironworks.' He glanced at Glyn who, as usual, was busy with his camera and tripod. 'There's coal here?'

'More than the Cossacks are digging out.' Glyn looked north. In a scene reminiscent of a woodcut of England's Middle Ages, miniature men and beasts swarmed around skeletal wooden frames clustered on a scar hewn in the steppe.

'That's because their methods haven't changed since that old one-eyed warrior Cossack, Krivoi Rog, settled here in the 1600s and gave his name to the area,' Nicholas Beletsky commented.

'The geologist guaranteed there are thicker, richer seams of quality anthracite beneath this steppe than there are in the Welsh Valleys, sir,' Glyn interposed. 'They haven't been exploited because no Russian has the vision of a Crawshay – or John Hughes. There's more here than even you or I can remove.'

'More than the Cossacks can dig out, certainly. Possibly even more than you can hew, Glyn,' John agreed, 'but I wouldn't go taking any bets on my prowess if I were you.'

The men around them laughed – Count Nicholas Beletsky longest and loudest.

John didn't join in. He turned his back to the Cossacks and looked intently at the barren steppe as if he could already see his ironworks.

'As well as the works there'll be pitheads and brickworks and not just to service the furnaces,' John mused. 'We'll need houses for the workers, a hospital, schools – Russian and English – shops, churches, theatres, inns, hotels, bath houses, roads and once we've produced the tracks a railway station, goods yards, warehouses, workshops, sidings...' He faltered when he realized he'd become carried away, talking too fast for his interpreter to translate, as if words alone could fashion his dream. A sheepish smile creased his broad, round face. 'We won't just be creating an ironworks, gentlemen, but a town, the first and most prosperous industrial town in Russia. Three years from now, the Tsar will have his railway tracks, rolling stock, turntables, armour plating, and munitions and you, I and our fellow investors, will be making money. More than the Crawshays made in Wales. More, even than we dreamed of.'

'My dreams are enormous, Mr Hughes,' Glyn pressed the button on his equipment and took another photograph.

John's Russian interpreter, Turchin, translated Glyn's comment into French for the benefit of the non-English-speaking Russians.

That time John joined in the laughter. He walked over to Glyn and slapped him on the back. 'Ten years from now we'll be aristocrats, boy. Princes of the Russian Industrial Age.' He turned to the Russian delegation and beckoned to Turchin. 'Please inform Prince Serge Kochubei: it's a deal. I'll buy the concession to build the works and rail-producing factory on this land. But tell him I'll also need more than twice as much adjoining land on both sides of the river, including all the mineral rights.'

'Yes, sir.'

John and Glyn waited while the interpreter translated John's request into French.

The Prince smiled at John and nodded. John extended his hand and the two men shook on the deal.

John's gaze was drawn to the distant workers filling bullock carts with coal. 'Ask the Prince if our agreement will create problems with the Cossacks?'

Turchin spoke. The Prince shook his head before replying.

'The Prince assures you there won't be any trouble, sir,' Turchin explained, 'because you will be bringing paid work to the steppe. As you see, the Cossacks labour as their forefathers have done for centuries. They've no idea of efficiency or mechanization.'

'Would you agree with the Prince's opinion, Count Beletsky?' John questioned Nicholas.

'If you pay the Cossacks more in wages than they make from selling the coal they dig out, they'll welcome you,' Nicholas asserted.

Turchin translated the count's comment.

The Prince replied in Russian. 'The Cossacks will welcome John Hughes, as will everyone else who comes here.'

'"Everyone else who comes here,"' John repeated in Russian.

'You are learning our language and learning it well,' the Prince complimented.

'Once word of your town gets out, John Hughes, people will flock here,' Turchin continued to interpret for the Prince who'd switched back to French. 'People are ambitious. They want to better their lives for their children, if not themselves.'

'Seems to me working people want the same the world over, Mr Hughes,' Glyn gathered his photographic equipment as the group broke up and headed for the count's carriages.

'Enough money to secure a future for their children,' John climbed the steps of the carriage that Count Beletsky's driver had rolled down. 'Turchin, we passed a village and a hamlet on the way here.'

'The Cossack village of Alexandrovka and a

Jewish shtetl,' Turchin concurred.

'Tell the driver I'd like to stop at both and introduce myself.'

'I wouldn't advise stopping at either,' Nicholas took the seat alongside John, leaving the backward facing seats for his son Alexei and Glyn. 'If you want to see the Cossack Hetman, that's what the Cossacks call their head man, I'll send for him. As for the shtetl, no Christian would set foot among the dwellings of Christ killers. Not in Russia.'

'You're thinking of the etiquette of precedence.' John raised his eyebrows. 'Higher caste never visits lower and lower caste always comes running when higher demands.'

'Exactly,' Nicholas concurred.

'Seems to me this country is as hidebound as Britain.' John settled back in his seat.

'More so.'

'You think so, Nicholas?' John took a cigar case from his pocket and offered it to the count.

The count helped himself to one of John's Havanas. 'When I travelled in your country, I noticed a class who were not as wealthy or cultured as your aristocrats but more intelligent than your peasants. Some of the men had even received a smattering of education. We have no such social strata in Russia to raise the ambitions or challenge the primitive beliefs of our peasants, which is why Russia's Mujiks live, work, and breed as ignorant as they did before Christ walked this earth.'

'Not for much longer, Nicholas,' John challenged. 'Change is coming even to Russia. My town will need engineers, chemists, metallurgists, architects, doctors, lawyers, managers, the collieries...'

'You'll attract them, John. They'll come from England, Germany, France...'

'Moscow, and St Petersburg once investment has been made in your education system and universities,' John interrupted.

'Only if both cities attract foreign students. The Mujik is too stupid, superstitious, and dull-witted to study or see beyond his own bestial needs and the aristocrats have neither the need nor inclination to dirty their hands. They'll leave industry to the foreigners.'

'Industry is the future, Father,' Alexei interrupted. 'Without it, Russia will remain locked in a medieval enclave while the rest of the world forges ahead.'

'Let the rest of the world forge its way to the devil,' Nicholas snapped, 'while the sons of Mother Russia remember and worship the God that made her.'

Alexei struck a noiseless match, leaned forward, and lit John's and his father's cigars. 'God wouldn't allow men like Mr Hughes to be successful if industry was the work of the devil, father.'

'Russia will remain Russia and Godly while the rest of the world hurtles to its own damnation.' Nicholas frowned. 'I've told you, industry is an occupation for lower orders, not gentlemen.'

'Father...'

'I've spoken, Alexei.' The rebuke had the desired effect. Alexei retreated into silence. It wasn't the first time John and Glyn had heard Alexei attempt to discuss the modernisation of Russia with his father.

Nicholas broke the silence that had fallen over the carriage. 'When will you begin constructing your ironworks, John?'

'As soon as the brick factory has produced enough bricks and I have shipped all the materials needed out of Britain through the port of Taganrog.'

'Winter sets in early here, even in the ports around the Sea of Azov,' Nicholas warned.

Undeterred, John persisted. 'I'm confident the works will be completed two years from now and producing the finest quality iron in three.'

'Your families? They'll accompany you?' Nicholas asked.

'Mrs Hughes will remain in Greenwich with my younger children for the present, my older sons are in university.'

'You intend to build a house for them here?'

'The furnaces, plant, factory, and collieries will take precedence,' John replied.

'My wife will return with me.' Glyn tried to picture his petite, dark-haired and -eyed Welsh wife, Betty, on the steppe.

'Has Betty any idea what it's like here?' John questioned.

'I've told her what to expect in my letters. She's looking forward to making the move.'

'Have you emphasised the primitive conditions? Stressed it will take time to build the works and they'll take priority over workers' housing.'

'I have, but you know women.' Glyn shrugged.

'I do. Which is why I insist Elizabeth's place is

with our younger children in Greenwich.' John looked ahead and saw a group of pretty adolescent girls dressed in red, blue, and white embroidered dresses and headdresses standing outside the Cossack village of Alexandrovka. They were holding platters covered by linen cloths, and clay jugs and bowls. 'Looks like the Cossacks don't pay much heed to precedence, Nicholas. It appears they've sent a delegation to meet us. Ask the driver to stop, Turchin.'

The girls walked forward when they saw the driver reining in the horses. Two of them uncovered the wooden plates of bread and salt and all twelve burst into song.

'They are welcoming you, Mr Hughes.' Alexei leapt from the carriage before it stopped. Glyn reached for his camera, tripod, and fresh photographic plates.

John ignored the count's disapproval. 'Bring the girls over here please, Alexei?'

'Stand them close to the carriage but looking at me please, Alexei.' Glyn climbed down and set up his equipment.

The boy ushered the group forward. The girls curtsied and the two with plates offered them to John and Glyn.

John addressed them in the first phrases of Russian he'd learned. 'Thank you for bread and salt, and thank you for the traditional Russian greeting.' He tore a piece from the bread, dipped it into the salt, and proceeded to eat it while the girls offered the plate to the count, Turchin, Glyn, and the driver.

John finished one piece of bread, started another, and drank beer directly from the jug the girls handed him. 'Tell them their bread is excellent, Alexei, say I appreciate their welcome and I'm looking forward to being their neighbour.'

When Alexei finished translating he wrapped his arm around a stunning redhead and kissed her cheek, an embrace Glyn captured.

'Too familiar, boy,' Nicholas growled in English, which his son spoke fluently. 'Get back in the carriage.'

'I can't ignore my foster sister, Father.'

'Carriage! Now!'

Alexei's meekness bordered on sarcasm. 'Yes, Father.' He stole another kiss, released the girl, waved to the others, and helped Glyn load his camera and plates back into the carriage.

'Charming custom,' John finished his bread and dusted the salt from his hands.

'You think so?' Nicholas questioned when they left the cluster of rough-built wood and stone houses behind them.

Sensing the tension between John and Nicholas, Glyn intervened. 'There's one thing you haven't thought of, sir.'

'What's that?'

'A name for this Russian industrial town of yours.'

John placed the tips of his leather-gloved fingers together. 'Crawshay named Williamstown, Thomastown, and Georgetown for his sons. But they were only suburbs of Merthyr. This will be no suburb but a town that will grow into a city. What do you think of Hughestown? Every member of my family, old, young, and those not yet born will relate to that.'

'As it's in Russia shouldn't it be Hughesovka, sir?' Glyn suggested.

'What do you think?' John asked Nicholas.

The count addressed the driver and interpreter in Russian. 'Vlad, Turchin, what do you think of Hughesovka?'

'Yuzovka?' A smile creased Vlad's broad Asiatic face. 'A good name, sir. A very good name for a town. Yuzovka.' He indicated a procession walking down the dirt road towards them. 'Yuzovka will look better on a tombstone than Alexandrovka.'

'That's not a cheerful thought.' John tossed his cigar stub out of the carriage.

'You understood, Vlad?' Nicholas asked.

'Yes, and I accept that the Russianization of my name, if there is such a word, is inevitable.' John studied the column of heavily muscled, coal-blackened Cossack miners and shorter slighter women as they drew alongside. To his dismay he realised they were carrying an injured man on a stretcher lashed from pit props and coats.

'Another mining accident! Little wonder given their primitive mining methods,' Nicholas scorned.

'Accidents happen, no matter how much care and investment is expended on safety,' John said soberly.

'Babushka Razin, who's hurt?' Alexei shouted to one of the women. They were dressed in blackened smocks and headscarves. Given the state of their hands and faces it was obvious they'd been labouring alongside the men.

'My Pavlo, Alexei,' she whispered without

breaking step as the procession drew alongside.

'Excuse me, Mr Hughes, Mr Edwards, Father.' Without a care to his safety, Alexei jumped from the carriage a second time.

'Alexei. Damn you!' Nicholas shouted. 'The boy's incorrigible. He's developed a taste for low life. The more degraded the better.' He glared at his son, but oblivious to his father's annoyance and the Cossacks' filthy clothes Alexei embraced the middle-aged woman he'd spoken to.

Vlad slowed the horses.

'Drive on, we don't want to be out on the steppe all night,' Nicholas ordered.

'Sir,' Vlad cracked his whip alongside the leading horse but didn't touch its back.

'Be careful, John,' Nicholas pointed his kid-gloved finger back at the procession. 'Cossacks are lazy brutes and drunks. Incidents like this, they look for someone to blame for their own shortcomings. If they take it into their heads that your British workers are stealing their work and wages they'll have no compunction about murdering them.'

'I admit I've anticipated trouble, which is why I discussed policing with the Tsar's representatives. They've agreed to station two regiments to act as peacekeepers and law enforcers alongside my works.'

'Lifeguards?' Nicholas asked.

'No.'

'Dragoons? Hussars?'

'No,' John permitted himself a small smile. 'Cossacks.'

The Donbas region of the Ukraine
April 1869

Nathan Kharber paused at the gate of the shtetl cemetery and watched the progress of the long line of carriages, every one drawn by thoroughbreds. Behind them, silhouetted against the sun, was the settlement he called home, although since his return he felt more outsider than native.

When he'd returned from Paris three months before, the wooden houses were smaller than he remembered; older, more weathered, their walls greyer. The largest building in the shtetl, the synagogue, had shrunk from the imposing edifice he recalled from his days in the Cheder, the religious school the rabbi tutored. But that had been before he'd seen the cathedral of Notre Dame and towering medieval stained glass windows of San Chappelle.

He opened the gate to the graveyard. The elders had built a stone wall around it while he'd been away, a wise precaution given that wolves congregated around the memorials during the worst of the winter weather. He walked along the aisles of headstones towards the marker he'd paid for and he and his uncle had erected two months after his father's death.

He read the chiselled names, recognised most and conjured images of people he'd known, dressed in shrouds standing behind the monuments; in some cases two and three to correspond with an extended family sharing a single stone.

So many deaths in ten years. Ruth and his

uncle had written about the epidemics that had ravaged the community during his absence but their letters had seemed abstract, relating details of remote tragedies he hadn't equated with the lives of his friends and former neighbours.

He arrived at the section that had been erected the year his mother had died. He'd replaced the simple marker his father had bought from the stone mason with a grander stone that had taken most of his inheritance. He'd given his Uncle Asher most of what remained, including the family home which his uncle had sold. In return his uncle and Aunt Leah had agreed to care for his younger sister Ruth. Grossly underestimating his expenses he'd kept back only eighty roubles to pay for his journey to Paris, never suspecting that it would take him fourteen months to work his way to the city.

The headstone he'd paid for had worn well. He ran his fingers over the Hebrew lettering, first his father's name, Nathan Kharber, and below it his mother's, Ruth Kharber. The day of her death was the same as his sister's birth. After his mother had drawn her last breath, his father lost all interest in life. When his shell had died from pneumonia six years later, the carpenter's only thought, even in delirium, was of being reunited with his wife.

The white marble pebble he'd placed on the memorial the day he'd left for Paris was still balanced on the grave. He picked it up and gazed at the array that had been placed alongside it since. Tributes from visitors, who'd left stones in the time-honoured tradition to show people had passed, stopped, and prayed for the souls of Nathan and Ruth, taking a moment from their lives to remember his parents.

He removed his hat and bowed his head. 'I'm home, Papa. Nothing is as I expected although I am finally a doctor. I returned intending to set up practice so I could earn enough to take care of Uncle Asher and Aunt Leah in their old age to repay them for caring for Ruth. But I work as you did, as a carpenter. All that studying was for nothing. Even worse, Ruth refuses to marry Abraham Goldberg. The son of the wealthiest man in the shtetl ... I don't know what to do...'

'You'll do what our people have always done, my boy. Wait and hope that something good will come along to end your troubles.'

His uncle and aunt stood behind him.

Asher beamed. 'Yelena Razin has sent for you. Her husband Pavlo has been injured in an accident in the mine.'

'Make him well again and you will have your practice as a doctor,' Leah added.

Nathan's spirits rose along with excitement at the prospect of his first non-Jewish patient. 'I'll get my bag.'

'Hurry,' Asher advised. 'The messenger has brought a horse for you.'

'Nathan ... thank God, you're still here.' Breathless Ruth ran through the gate, her friends Miriam and Rivka close on her heels.

'Noise in the cemetery...'

Ruth cut her uncle short. 'Miriam said Yelena Razin sent for you. Don't go.'

'I have to. I've sworn an oath to heal the sick

wherever and however I can.'

'Praskovia gave the boy who brought the message a note for me. Her father is dying. If he breathes his last after being treated by you the Cossacks will blame you.'

'Ruth is right,' Leah began to tremble. 'The Cossacks hate us. If Pavlo dies after you've seen him, the Cossacks will bring torches to burn down the shtetl...'

'I'm a doctor. I've been sent for. I have to go.' Nathan strode down the path.

'Please, Nathan, if you won't think of yourself think of the children in the shtetl. If Pavlo Razin should die...'

'And if he should live?' He faced Ruth. 'Pavlo's recovery will give me everything I've worked for. I'll finally have a practice that will enable me to earn money from treating the Cossacks, and once word spreads the Mujiks and God willing the aristocrats, I'll be able to care for you, Uncle Asher and Aunt Leah the way you should be cared for.'

Ruth realised words wouldn't sway Nathan but she wasn't going to walk away without trying to protect him. She turned towards the Dower House and started running.

The Razins' house, Alexandrovka
The Donbas region of the Ukraine, April 1869

A novice rider who'd only ever ridden the old cart horses from the shtetl, Nathan was relieved when they reached the village. He slid from the saddle of the borrowed horse, grateful to be on firm ground. Shaking from more than the effect of the ride, he walked down the steps to the Razins' front door. Ducking his head he entered.

The room was crowded with miners and women blackened by coal dust. Pavlo Razin was lying on a cushioned bench, his head in his wife's lap. Praskovia was kneeling on the floor beside them, bathing her father's face. Pavlo's eyes flickered but his breath was laboured, ragged, and the hand Yelena grasped was limp.

A murmur of voices greeted him. 'The doctor, the Jewish doctor ... the doctor ... Kharber's son ... Paris...'

Nathan crouched beside Praskovia. She folded back the blanket that covered her father and exposed his chest.

One glance was enough. Nathan knew why Praskovia had sent Ruth the note. Pavlo's chest had caved in, his shattered ribs protruded through his blackened skin and blood oozed from the wounds. Dark blood mixed with bright. The major blood vessels had ruptured.

Although there was nothing he, or any doctor could do for Pavlo Razin, Nathan kneeled beside Praskovia.

Praskovia leaned close and whispered. 'At the last breath, people will wail. I'll lead you to the window. Climb out. There's a cellar in the ruined monastery below the Christmas candle fir tree. Hide until help comes. Don't worry about your bag.'

Chapter Three

The Beletsky Mansion
The Donbas region of the Ukraine, April 1869

'Thank you for the excellent dinner, Olga, Nicholas.'

The gentlemen rose when Catherine Ignatova left the table. She extended her hand to John.

'Please don't go on my account, Mr Hughes. The second carriage will convey you, Mr Edwards, and Mr Thomas, when you are ready to leave my daughter and son-in-law's house. I look forward to seeing you at supper in the Dower House.'

'Until then, Mrs Ignatova.' John had acquired continental manners on his travels and kissed Catherine's hand.

'Ladies, gentlemen, forgive me for breaking up the party and taking Sonya with me. I trust you will all sleep well and with God this night.' Catherine went into the hall. Alexei, Sonya, Nicholas, and Olga followed.

Alexei took his grandmother's fur from the footman and draped it over her shoulders.

'I wish you would stay, Mother-in-law,' Nicholas complained. 'At least until coffee and brandy has been served to our important guests.'

Catherine knew 'important' to her son-in-law meant titled. 'Thank you for your hospitality,

Nicholas, but if Sonya and I remain it will be too late for us to pay our respects to the Razin family.'

'Cossacks, really, Mother-in-law,' he bristled. 'It isn't expected of you. You'll embarrass the Razin family, who have no idea how to receive a lady of your station.'

Catherine's spine stiffened along with her resolve. 'Have you forgotten Yelena Razin was wet nurse to three of your sons?'

'She was paid,' Nicholas countered.

'The payment was necessary for Yelena to provide for her own babies. No amount of money could have compensated her for the love she gave your children, which was equal to the love she bore for her own. The least we can do is show Christian sympathy in her time of sorrow. Come, Sonya, Alexei.'

'Alexei!' His father exclaimed as the footman handed Alexei his and Sonya's capes.

'Grandmother and Sonya can hardly travel to Alexandrovka without an escort at this time of night, Father. Mother.' He kissed his mother's cheek before returning to the open door of the dining room. 'Your honours, Mr Hughes, Mr Edwards, Mr Thomas, gentlemen, please excuse me.'

'Alexei, you're being infernally rude to our guests,' Nicholas snapped. 'As the son of the host...'

'Precisely, Father. You are the host. I won't be missed.'

Catherine interrupted. 'I hear carriage wheels. Alexei, we mustn't keep the driver waiting on an evening as cold as this. Goodnight, Nicholas,

Olga. I'll see you tomorrow at luncheon in the Dower House?'

'Until tomorrow, Mother.' Impassive, tired, and heavy from her advanced pregnancy, Olga kissed her mother and Sonya and returned to the dining room.

'Alexei, if you promise those Cossacks charity or give them one kopek of my money, I will throw you out of my house. Do you understand?'

'Yes, Father.'

'We need to discuss your behaviour.'

'There will be time to continue this conversation when I return, Father.'

'Depend on it,' Nicholas threatened.

Alexei offered his grandmother his arm. She tucked her hand into the crook of his elbow. The footman opened the double doors.

The oil lamps had been lit sending shadows dancing and flickering beneath the marbled portico and its supporting Corinthian columns. A full moon shone down attended by a litter of surrounding stars, silvering the formal gardens and chestnut-tree-lined drive that led to the main gates.

The coachman had lowered the steps of the carriage. A groom held the reins of Alexei's horse, Agripin.

Nicholas watched his mother-in-law and Sonya climb into the carriage then turned on his heel. His footsteps echoed over the marble floor until the footman closed the doors.

'Your father will die of apoplexy if you continue to goad him, Alexei.' Catherine made room for Sonya on the seat.

'I don't deliberately goad him. But neither will I live my life the way he wants me to.' Alexei closed the cab, took the reins of his horse, and swung himself up on the saddle. He held Agripin in check, content to trot quietly behind the carriage. He glanced back as the driver negotiated the gates.

The classical sculptures his maternal grandfather had acquired in Italy half a century ago during a youthful 'Grand Tour' gleamed, pale transplanted ghosts from another civilization among the manicured glades.

He could hear his father's voice.

'One day, Alexei, this estate will be yours to care for and enhance; a place of beauty created by generations of men who lived their lives according to the edicts of the ancient intellectuals of Greece and Rome. Art is everything. Outside of art, life is low, bestial, and never more so than when tainted by the grime of modern industry with its constant spewing of filth.'

Alexei continued to gaze at the house and gardens. His father was right, the family house and estate was a place of beauty, but it was also an anachronism peopled by phantoms that had no place in the new world of engineering and progress. The industrial society he burned to enter – John Hughes's world.

He looked down the road. The carriage was a speck on the horizon.

'Alexandrovka, Agripin.' He dug in his heels. His mount lowered his head and quickened from a canter into a gallop.

The Razins' house,
The Cossack village of Alexandrovka, April 1869

Alexei tried not to think how his father would vent his annoyance. The last time Nicholas had discovered he'd visited the Razin household, the servants had been ordered to fumigate every room he'd entered on his return with foul-smelling disinfectant and his allowance had been cut off. If it hadn't been for his grandmother he would have had a bleak six weeks until his father capitulated to his mother's pleadings and forgave him.

It took them twenty minutes to reach the village. The coachman left the rough track on the open steppe and negotiated the narrow lanes between the houses, halting outside the Razin house, blocking the narrow walkway that separated it from its neighbour. At home in the village and with the Razins, Alexei led Agripin around the side of the wooden house to the backyard and the watering trough beside the barn.

The windows were open despite the cold, and the sonorous sound of religious hymns wafted out as Alexei tethered his horse. He recognised the practised tones of Father Grigor's baritone leading the Cossacks in a musical version of the Lord's Prayer.

Like all Cossack houses, the Razins had been dug in partially underground to lessen the amount of planking needed for the walls. Alexei walked round to the front and was dazzled by a bright light. The coachman had lifted down one of the carriage lamps and was using it to illuminate a path for his grandmother and Sonya.

'Alexei, you know the Razins better than us, so please, go ahead.' Catherine moved to allow him to pass.

He ran down the short flight of rickety stones. Someone opened the door before he reached it. He knew why the windows had been thrown wide as soon as he entered. The atmosphere was thick, as warm and humid as a bath house, and so packed with bodies he wondered they were able to make room for him.

As befitting a house in mourning, the mirror and all the glass objects in the house had been covered by black cloth. Candles had been lit and placed around the open pine coffin on the table that held the corpse of Pavlo Razin. Praskovia sat next to her mother at the head, her slow-witted brother Pyotr curled like a cat at their feet.

Washed clean of the coal dust that had covered him in later life, dressed in his Sunday best tunic, trousers, and boots, his hair neatly brushed, trimmed, and combed, Pavlo was barely recognisable as the grubby, hard-drinking, foul-tempered man who'd made his wife and children's lives a misery for the last five years.

Death had transformed his features, softening them until he was once again the loving and much loved 'Papa Pavlo' Alexei remembered from his childhood. The mentor who'd taught him, Sonya, and his brothers and sisters, along with the local children, to ride, fish, aim a pistol and rifle, and hunt without scaring away the game. But most important of all, Pavlo had imparted the single piece of knowledge his father neither knew nor understood. How to enjoy life.

Yelena, Praskovia, and Pyotr rose to their feet when they saw him, Catherine, and Sonya. Every man in the room bowed, every woman curtsied, which wasn't easy for those perched precariously on the stairs or hemmed in so tightly they could only move after their neighbours had shifted.

'Please, sit down, good people.' Catherine removed her gloves. 'We've come to pay our respects to Pavlo Razin.' She looked around and knew why her grandson spent so much time in the house.

The downstairs living room was warm, welcoming, typically Cossack, more of a home than any of the rooms in the Beletsky Mansion Nicholas had so lavishly and expensively furnished. The fitted shelves, chests of drawers, cupboards, and chairs, resplendent with carvings, bore testimony to Pavlo Razin's carpentry skills before drink had destroyed his sure touch. Everything was spotlessly clean, and ornamented by hand-made lace and blue and red embroidered cushions and cloths.

'We are so sorry, Babushka Razin, Praskovia, Pyotr.' Alexei looked down on the dead, grey-lined face and made the sign of the cross with three fingers in deference to the Cossacks adherence to the old church beliefs as opposed to the new believers who signed using two fingers.

He stood back while his grandmother and Sonya crossed themselves over the corpse before kissing Yelena, Praskovia, and Pyotr. Alexei drew close to Praskovia.

She slipped her hand into his. 'Thank you for coming; I know how difficult it must have been for you to get away.'

'I have my grandmother to protect me.' He watched Catherine take the chair the priest vacated and offered to her. Father Grigor leaned over Catherine and Yelena and all three began to speak too low for him to hear.

'When is the funeral, Praskovia?' Sonya asked.

'Dawn, the day after tomorrow. The miners voted to delay their shift. After the ceremony the crosses from the church will be carried down to the river and dipped into the water. Then we'll return to eat the funeral porridge and meats.'

'We had such fun when we were children. He was a friend to us all...'

'Please,' Praskovia couldn't bear to hear more. 'Those days have long gone, Alexei.'

'What happened?' Sonya asked.

'The roof of the seam my father was working caved in. His chest was crushed but he was awake and talking when they brought him out. As soon as I saw his injuries I knew he couldn't survive but my mother insisted on sending for Nathan Kharber.' Praskovia softened her voice. 'He came quickly but my father died a few minutes after he arrived. You know how the men are about Jews...'

'Is Nathan all right?' Alexei clenched his fists. The Cossacks hatred of the Jews frequently led to murder even without provocation. A Jewish doctor's failed attempt to save a Cossack life could start a pogrom.

'I helped Nathan get away. I told him to hide in your place.'

Alexei nodded to show he'd understood.

'You'll...'

Sonya noticed people staring at Alexei and Praskovia and began talking loudly. 'I'll attend the funeral with Aunt Catherine, Praskovia. Is there anything we can do? Perhaps send food for your guests?'

'Food is always a welcome gift at a funeral.' Praskovia answered Sonya, but continued to look at Alexei. 'Please, don't get into trouble with Count Beletsky on our account.'

'We won't,' Sonya assured her. 'Aunt Catherine will want to help your mother.'

'I'll escort my grandmother and Sonya to the funeral.'

'You'll be very welcome, Alexei.' Mindful of the people watching, Praskovia released his hand.

Father Grigor left the women and stood over the corpse. Swinging an incense burner he began to pray, a moving invocation that culminated in one of the Cossacks' best-loved hymns, 'Deliver O God Thy People.'

Catherine waited until the last note had echoed around the room before rising. 'Next Sunday is Easter by the Julian Calendar. I will provide a feast for everyone in Alexandrovka at the Dower House to celebrate Christ arisen. There we will eat, drink, and raise a glass to the memory of Pavlo Razin. I will also send food to the shtetl. The Jews may not celebrate Easter but I understand Nathan Kharber came to help Pavlo Razin. I will thank him for you the only way I know.'

An angry murmur rose from the people crammed into the room.

'That Nathan Kharber could not help Pavlo Razin was God's will, not Nathan's. The Jews are our brethren and my friends. We all make use of their skills, none more than me. I ask all of you to join me in looking out for them as the Good Samaritan did the stranger in the Bible. Please, live beside them in peace and remember, he who hurts my friend, hurts me. God bless all in the house of mourning. God bless the soul of Pavlo Razin. Father Grigor, escort me to my carriage please.'

Yelena and Praskovia pushed ahead, forging a path for her through the crowd. Alexei snatched Praskovia's hand and pulled her into the shadows when they reached outside. 'If you need anything before the funeral, send a message through one of our maids or footmen.'

Praskovia returned his hug.

'Will you, your mother, and Pyotr stay in Alexandrovka?'

'My mother has been nagging me to accept Efim Litvin again.'

'For pity's sake, Praskovia. He's sixty if he's a day.'

'Sixty-eight, but he has money. He suggested she keep house for us. It would mean she'd be able give up carting coal from the mine. It's not that she minds the work but she hates me working in Efim's potato fields. She keeps saying it's filthy heavy work but it's no worse than what she's doing.'

Father Grigor overheard Praskovia. 'You must send for Misha, Praskovia. He can apply for exemption from military service as he is now the family's sole breadwinner. When he returns from St Petersburg he can take your father's place in the mine...'

'Over my dead body, Father,' Yelena retorted. 'Misha is already a lieutenant in the regiment. The last thing I want for my eldest son is the slow death that took his father. My Pavlo died years ago. The mine sucked the life out of him. All that was killed was a walking corpse.'

'But how will you, Praskovia, and Pyotr manage, Yelena?' the priest enquired.

'We may not have the strength to dig out the coal but I have the ox and cart and can load as well as any man. Pyotr can drive the cart and Praskovia will continue to work in Efim's fields until she finds a husband. God will provide.'

'The ox is old, Yelena.'

Catherine interrupted. 'Yelena, Praskovia, Pyotr. You will visit me at the Dower House the day after Pavlo's funeral?'

'If you wish us to call on you, Madam, we will be happy to.' Yelena lifted her head. 'But we want no charity and my Misha stays in St Petersburg.'

'That decision is yours and Misha's to make, Yelena. No one else's.' Catherine inclined her head. 'We have disturbed you long enough. God bless you, Yelena, Praskovia, Pyotr, and all in this house of mourning.'

Sonya climbed in beside Catherine. Alexei closed the door and signalled to the coachman. As the vehicle moved away, he walked into the back yard to fetch Agripin. Praskovia was stroking his horse's nose.

'You're as fond of Agripin as I am.'

'I was the one who chose him for your mount out of all the foals born on your father's estate that year. Do you remember?'

'I remember.'

She glanced over her shoulder to make certain no one was close. 'Hide it.'

Alexei took the doctor's bag she lifted out from behind the wood pile, fastened it to his saddle-bag, and covered it with a blanket.

'Thank you again for coming, Alexei.' She stood on tiptoe and kissed his cheek.

'Remember if you need anything...'

'You'll be the first to know. Take care, especially with your father. And...'

'I'll see the bag and him safe.' He gripped his horse's mane and hauled himself into the saddle. 'Changes are coming, Praskovia. Changes that will improve all our lives.'

'Since Ivan died, I've had no life.'

Alexei didn't contradict her, but grasped her hand again. 'Be strong for your mother and Pyotr. Mr Hughes has great plans for this place. You'll visit my grandmother?'

'My mother has promised. But what can your grandmother do for us in the face of your father's disapproval?'

'You'll be surprised.' He bent his head to hers and kissed the top of her head before spurring Agripin and racing after the carriage.

Dower House, Beletsky Estate
April 1869

'How did you know Nathan Kharber tried to treat Pavlo Razin?' Alexei asked his grandmother when he helped her from her carriage.

'His sister called on me this afternoon. She told me he'd been sent for. She was afraid the Cossacks would hurt him if Pavlo died.'

'They would have if Praskovia hadn't helped Nathan get away.'

'He's back in the shtetl?'

'He will be by morning,' Alexei promised.

'Be careful...'

'I always am, Grandmother.'

'You coming inside?'

'Not tonight, I have things to do before I face my father. Goodnight, and bless you for saving not just Nathan but the shtetl.'

'I will pray the Cossacks stay in Alexandrovka tonight.' Catherine watched Alexei mount his horse.

'After what you said, they will.'

Alexei swung low in the saddle, kissed his grandmother and Sonya, and galloped off.

Dower House, Beletsky Estate
April 1869

After a late supper Glyn went straight to his room. He was pushing his collar studs from his shirt when he was disturbed by a knock at his bedroom door. John Hughes was outside, two brandy balloons in one hand and a bottle of French cognac in the other. Many of the New Russia Company's most important decisions had been mulled over and refined during nightcap sessions with his boss.

John pulled a chair up to the desk and poured

the cognac. He raised his glass. 'To Hughesovka.'

'Hughesovka.' Glyn drank before taking a chair and waited. He knew there was no point in trying to prompt John Hughes into speaking before he was ready to talk, no matter how long a day they'd shared.

'What do you think of Alexei Beletsky?' John topped up their balloons.

'Keen, intelligent, a linguist. He could be an asset to the company if his father allowed him to join us.'

'Given the boy's enthusiasm and thirst for knowledge, as more than an interpreter?' John questioned.

'He has no experience of engineering or industry.'

'But he wants to learn and there's nothing like learning while you work. We've plenty of people who'd be glad to teach the boy.' John took two cigars from his pocket and handed one to Glyn. 'We have to return in Moscow to check the contracts before they're signed, but I'm thinking of leaving Huw here to oversee the building and offering Alexei a post as his assistant. The architect and builders will be arriving from Germany next month; they and Huw, if he agrees to stay, will need help from the locals. Not just in recruiting and communicating with workers but in coping with the climate, the natives, and their customs. Given the different communities I've a feeling it's going to be easy to annoy some of them, and that's before we import the Welsh.'

'I'm sure the boy will prove invaluable to Huw, but what about Count Beletsky? He's not going to be pleased at the idea of his aristocratic son working for industrialists.'

'The count has invested in the company. Not as much as Catherine Ignatova. You wouldn't call it substantial but I thought I'd suggest his son work with Huw to safeguard the Beletsky family interests.'

'Nicholas might swallow that, sir, and Huw will be grateful for a willing helper who can speak the language.'

'Willing and brave to the point of recklessness.'

'Brave?' Glyn eyed John quizzically.

'If the count was your father, would you cross him by nagging to be allowed to forge a career in industry?'

'Possibly, if I had a grandmother like Mrs Ignatova prepared to fight my corner.'

'She has more imagination, foresight, and common sense than her son-in-law.' John sipped his brandy. 'You're sure about the boy?'

'Absolutely.'

'Good. And Mr Levsky?'

'Too thick with Count Beletsky. I don't trust him.'

'Pastukov?'

'Knows what he's talking about and seems sound.'

John stroked his beard. 'Strange how your opinions invariably coincide with mine.'

'Not really, sir, you've taught me to be as wise and astute a judge of character as yourself.' Glyn wasn't entirely joking.

'As soon as the contracts are signed, I'll return to Greenwich with the information you've compiled on weather conditions so we can begin manufacturing furnace components able to withstand the Russian extremes of temperature. If we haven't found a Moscow-based accountant conversant with the Russian tax system by then you'll have to carry on interviewing after I've left. Downe in the Moscow office can help you. We want an honest firm with a spotless reputation that will ensure all the New Russian Company affairs will be open, and above suspicion.'

'Between us, Downe and I will find a competent firm, sir.'

'Can you stop off in Paris, Warsaw, and Berlin on your return journey to interview the metallurgists we've been corresponding with? The laboratory needs to be up and running before the furnaces so it can test the quality of our first output.'

'Of course, sir.'

'Hire the most likely experts and tell them to get here by next spring. I'm sorry, Glyn, between the contracts and the interviews I doubt you'll be able to return to Merthyr and your wife much before Christmas. I'll need you back in Greenwich and Southampton early in January to oversee the assembling of equipment.'

'I don't mind, sir. I like being busy and we'll have plenty of time to put down roots when we return here for good.'

'For good?' John repeated the colloquialism. 'We have to ensure it will be "for good", Glyn. Not just for us but all the company workers.'

'It will be, sir.'

'With you and Huw to help me, I think it will.'

John opened his pocket watch. 'It's late. See you at breakfast.'

Glyn smiled but only after he closed his door. He suspected his boss's opinion on Levsky and the decision to offer Alexei a position had been formed before they'd shared a nightcap. But he found it flattering to be used as a sounding board.

Abandoned monastery on the banks of the Kalmius River
April 1869

Alexei rode slowly, stopping every few yards to check he wasn't being followed. When he heard the river, he reined in Agripin and listened intently. An owl hooted before swooping low in search of prey. Something splashed close to the bank – a freshwater turtle, river rat, or insomniac duck? A lone wolf howled, but aware how sound echoed over the steppe, he knew from hunting trips the animal was probably half a day's journey away.

When he was certain the only noises were of the land and the night, he cupped his hands around his mouth and mimicked birdsong. Before he'd finished, an answering call came from within the broken walls of the old chapel. He made the sign of the cross and blessed Pavlo for teaching him and the local children, animal and bird cries. He dug in his heels and Agripin picked a way over the stone walls into what remained of the monastery. He slid from the saddle. The moon was bright, but he knew every inch of the ruins and could have found his way around them blindfolded.

'Nathan?'

'Alexei?' The voice came from a carved stone sacristy screen to the side of the altar. Behind it, a broken slab and a conifer partially covered the entrance to a cave that had been enlarged to make a cellar. Nathan's head and shoulders were in silhouette as he peered above ground. 'My doctor's bag...'

'Is safe. Praskovia gave it to me.' Alexei made his way to the spot, crouched down, and handed Nathan a metal flask.

Nathan unscrewed the top, drank, and coughed. 'It's brandy.'

'What did you expect?'

'Water. I'm not used to spirits.'

'Thought you'd need courage as well as warmth. What insanity possessed you to go to the Razin house?'

'Yelena Razin sent for me. Pavlo was hurt. I'm a doctor.'

'You're a Jew. Have you forgotten the Cossacks still blame your people for bringing the Black Death to the steppe five hundred years ago and that's without the more recent outbreaks of cholera and scarlet fever?'

'No, but...' Nathan faltered.

'Ten years in Paris made you forget how the Cossacks feel about your race?'

'I heard Pavlo was alive. I thought I could keep him that way.'

'You realise you've given the Cossacks an excuse to kill everyone in the shtetl, including your sister?'

'Is Ruth the only Jew you care about, Alexei?' Nathan didn't wait for Alexei to answer. 'They said Pavlo was conscious and talking when they brought him out of the mine. I took an oath, Alexei, a Hippocratic oath to save life whenever I could.'

'Save lives by all means, but not at the risk of your own, your sister's, and everyone in your shtetl.'

Despite his insistence that he wasn't used to spirits, Nathan took another draught before returning the flask. 'It's not just saving lives. It took me over a year to walk to Paris, eight years of working nights in a mortuary and studying by day to qualify as a doctor, and a full year to walk back. I'm a good doctor, Alexei. All my patients and everyone I've worked with have said so.'

'I believe you.'

'I returned to set up a practice so I could pay my uncle and aunt for caring for my sister while I studied. But no one will consult me.'

'Surely the people in the shtetl do?' Alexei said in surprise.

'They have no money to pay for medicine, let alone a fee. The largest payment I received this week was a pail of milk and five eggs.'

'How are you surviving?'

'As my father did, by working as a carpenter.'

'Pavlo used to say you weren't just a carpenter but the best.'

'That's no consolation. If I could get some Cossack, Mujik, or aristocrat patients...'

'You can forget about the Cossacks after today. And you know how superstitious Mujiks are. They regard Jews as demons. As for my father, if he was dying he'd crawl to Taganrog or St Petersburg on his hands and knees rather than consult you. Unfortunately for you, my grandmother, Sonya, and I are bursting with health. If I thought my grandmother could persuade her servants to consult you I'd ask the cook to poison their soup, but after Pavlo's death I doubt they would allow her to send for you.'

Nathan sank his head in his hands. 'Perhaps I should return to Paris or Vienna. I worked in hospitals in both cities. I was offered a good position in Vienna...'

'Vienna's a beautiful city.'

'You want me to leave?'

'No.' Alexei protested.

'No?' Nathan mocked. 'Alexei ... you and my sister ... for the first time since I returned home her behaviour makes sense. Abraham Goldberg wants to marry her. She's refused him. She sneaks out in the early morning, says she's going to the cemetery to put flowers on our parents' grave. Praskovia sent me to your place – this place. Ten minutes' walk from the cemetery. I should have put a stop to the friendship between you and Ruth when you were inseparable as children.'

Seeing denial was futile Alexei said, 'You couldn't have parted us then or now, Nathan. We're meant to be together.'

'You might think so. I don't.' There was anger in Nathan's voice.

'Ruth wanted to tell you about us when you returned.'

'Us! There can be no us when it comes to you

and Ruth, Alexei. Miriam told me what you and Praskovia are doing. Trying to make everyone believe you are in love to give Praskovia an excuse to refuse Efim Litvin's offer of marriage. Now I see the pretence not only serves Praskovia's purpose but also distracts attention from you and Ruth.'

Alexei decided Praskovia's dislike of Efim was a safer topic of conversation than Ruth. 'Praskovia doesn't love Efim.'

'I doubt any girl of eighteen would consider an old man a good catch, even a wealthy one. But what happens when Praskovia gets over losing Ivan Kalmykov, falls in love, and wants to marry?'

'I'll ask another Cossack girl to pretend to be in love with me.'

'So you can continue to keep your love for Ruth a secret from your family?'

'Until I'm old enough to marry without my father's consent. My father hates me enough without me giving him more reason to lock me up or send me away.'

'What about Ruth's family, Alexei? Have you thought of consulting them?'

'I wanted to call on your aunt and uncle and formally ask their permission to court your sister, but Ruth warned me they are as prejudiced, bigoted, and bunkered as my father. Please don't tell me you are too.'

'I won't allow you to marry my sister, Alexei. That's my final word on the subject. You're not of our faith.'

'We worship the same God, don't we?' Alexei demanded.

'I've no intention of debating scripture with you.'

'There's more to life than faith.'

'A Jew without religion is a candle without a flame.' Nathan had no idea why he'd repeated the hackneyed phrase other than it had come easily.

'What about love?'

'You and Ruth are children.'

'We're not.' Alexei struggled to keep his temper in check. 'I love her and I know she loves me. I'll take care of her.'

'How?'

'I'm ambitious.'

'You can't eat ambition, Alexei, as you'll di-cover when your father disinherits you when he finds out about Ruth.'

Alexei sat back on his heels. He and Ruth needed all the friends, Russian, Jew, Mujik, and Cossack they could make. He couldn't afford to make an enemy of Ruth's brother. 'I admired you when you left here after your father died. You seemed so grown-up, so determined to make something of yourself. Yet you couldn't have been much older than I am now.'

'I was sixteen. Two years younger.' Nathan hoisted himself out of the cave.

'You were like a knight going on a quest. You insisted nothing and no one was going to stop you from studying medicine in Paris. Everyone said you were mad except Papa Pavlo. Ruth told me the rabbi warned you that you'd end up starving and sleeping on the streets.'

'I did both. Before I reached Paris and after I was there.'

'But you did what you set out to do. You ignored

everyone's warnings and listened only to Papa Pavlo who encouraged you.'

'Papa Pavlo was a dreamer who wanted to believe fairy tales come true. They don't, Alexei.'

'Yours did. You're a doctor.' Alexei pocketed his flask.

'One the Cossacks would like to kill, who has no paying patients.'

'You'll have them when Mr Hughes builds his town.'

'You think Mr Hughes will consult a Jew?' Nathan was sceptical.

'Anything is possible in a modern city.'

'Anything in science and industry perhaps, but not marriage between a Jew and a gentile. That will never be possible, Alexei. Give up Ruth for her sake and safety and your own.'

'You may as well ask me to stop breathing.'

'It will end in tragedy.'

'Not if I can help it.' Sensing further argument was futile; Alexei looked up at the sky. 'Clouds are about to cover the moon. When they do, we should get you back to the shtetl. We can't risk being seen by any hunters or fishermen who've decided to make an early start. My grandmother has spoken to the Cossacks and warned them on pain of her displeasure to treat all Jews well.'

'Your grandmother! How did she know I went to Alexandrovka?'

'Ask Ruth. Once you're home, be sensible, stay within the walls of your house and workshop for the next few months.'

'While allowing Ruth to walk out anytime she chooses to?'

'I respect her, Nathan, and I will marry her.'

'In a church or a synagogue?'

'The place doesn't matter, only the ceremony. I hope you'll be there to wish us well.'

'I couldn't do that.'

'Because of your religion?'

'Because I care deeply about Ruth.'

'I refuse to argue with you, Nathan. In time I hope you'll think well of me.'

'Even as a child you were better than most of your kind, Alexei. But the more I've considered it, the more I realise your father was right. No good came of Pavlo's efforts to foster friendship between Cossack, Jew, Mujik, and aristocrat. We should only mix with our own kind.'

'There's no difference between races other than the way people see us.'

'And the way we see ourselves.'

'We could discuss that all night but if I'm to keep my promise to Praskovia and get you back to the shtetl in one piece before dawn we have to move. No talking on the way. You know how sound carries at night.'

'You've met Ruth here?'

'A few times,' Alexei admitted.

'At night?'

'I wish we could meet openly but seeing your reaction makes me glad we never tried.' Alexei rose from his haunches and straightened his back.

'And now?'

'You'll stop us from meeting?' Alexei challenged.

'I'll talk to Ruth.'

'And forbid her to see me?'

'I'll advise her not to.'

'If she refuses?'

'I won't lock her up, Alexei. But as I've already said, the only result of this mutual infatuation can be tragedy.'

Alexei whistled for Agripin. He led the horse out of the chapel onto the scrubland that had once been a tended monastery garden, climbed into the saddle, extended his hand, and hauled Nathan up behind him. They rode in silence until they reached the wall of the Jewish cemetery east of the shtetl.

Nathan tapped Alexei's shoulder and whispered in his ear. 'Leave me here. There's no one around. I want to visit my parents' grave.'

Alexei pulled on the rein, Agripin halted. Nathan slid to the ground.

'Give her my love, Nathan.'

'I won't, Alexei. But thank you for this.'

The shtetl near Alexandrovka
April 1869

Nathan saw them as he left the cemetery and closed the gates behind him.

Ruth must have been watching and waiting for him and seen Alexei. The two of them stood, caught in a stray beam of moonlight in the shadow of the Goldbergs' barn. Two lovers locked in one another's arms as though the power of their embrace was sufficient to keep all the hatred and injustice of the world at bay.

He wished it could be true.

Chapter Four

Georgetown, Merthyr Tydfil
June 1870

Light-headed from exhaustion, Glyn Edwards walked out of the railway station and headed for High Street and the Boot Inn. He'd left John Hughes superintending the despatching of the last of the equipment they'd ordered, out of the Greenwich yards into the Southampton warehouses prior to loading on the company's charted ships. He'd wanted to stay with his boss, but John had insisted he return to Merthyr so he could accompany his wife, brother, and the colliers and ironworkers he'd recruited on the first leg of their journey from Wales to the Steppe.

He suspected the main reason John had sent him to Merthyr was guilt. Aside from a week's break at Christmas, during which he'd spent five days interviewing those who'd answered advertisements for workers for the New Russian Company, he'd worked solidly on company business since the day he and John had left Hughesovka, over twenty months before.

He returned the smile of a pretty girl before remembering he was on home territory where people talked, and more often than not, to his wife.

'Good to see you looking so well, Gwilym.' He

kept his smile and passed it on to a one-legged vinegar and salt seller who'd pushed his hand cart into an alleyway between two shops.

'Mr Glyn, good to see you back.'

'Good to be back, Gwilym.'

'Here for long?'

'Until I leave next week for Russia.'

'Come back to make sure everyone who's signed up to Mr Hughes's new company gets on the train, Mr Glyn?'

'Can't you see my whip?'

'Always the joker, Mr Glyn.'

'Mr Glyn.' A title that reminded him he was in the same town as his brothers. He shook his head at the army of small boys who offered to carry his bag for a farthing and avoided colliding with gangs of men, filthy from the colliery and iron-works' morning shifts, who were streaming into the pubs to slake their thirst before going home to sleep.

Butchers' and grocers' boys raced past on delivery bicycles without giving leeway to pedestrians. Carts blocked the narrow streets; women hauled shopping baskets, tiptoeing past piles of filth swept up by shopkeepers who were fighting a losing battle to keep the frontage of their premises clear.

He was home, in the heart of dirty, noisy Merthyr. His thoughts turned to the peaceful Russian steppe. How much progress had Huw made with building the works and the town? How long would it be before John Hughes's town turned into bedlam like this, or even worse? Chaos resembling London?

He raised his hat to an elderly woman he recognised and stepped into the gutter to avoid a group of women walking four abreast with shawls wrapped around them and their babies, Welsh fashion.

He was tired, stiff, and hungry after travelling on the overnight train from Greenwich via London to Cardiff. In contrast to the fast service from the city, the train from Cardiff to Merthyr had been slow, stopping at every village to drop off and take on passengers who took for ever to climb in and out of the carriages with their arrays of bags, bundles, and packages.

He finally reached the Boot Inn and walked around the draymen rolling barrels into the cellar and the manure dropped by their shire horses. Entering the passageway, he pushed his way through a crowd of colliers in the main bar and headed for the flap that separated barmaids from the customers. He lifted it and dropped his case alongside an empty crate.

'Hey! What do you think you're doing? Customers are not allowed behind the bar.' Betty whirled round, her sleeves rolled to her elbows, the black curls that had escaped the bun at the back of her neck tumbling around her red cheeks.

'I think I've come home, but if you'd like me to leave, say the word and I'll go to Edward's or Peter's. They might have a warm welcome for a weary traveller.'

'Glyn!' Betty's hands fluttered from her hair to her elbows. Flustered, she unrolled her sleeves. 'I wasn't expecting you until tomorrow.'

Glyn had whiled away time on the journey by

planning his homecoming down to the smallest gesture. He'd intended to lift Betty into his arms, whirl her around, and plant a kiss full on her lips. After only the one week working Christmas visit in over a year he'd lived this moment many times in his imagination even down to the length of the kiss. But it was too late for kisses. The surprise and the emotion – if there'd been any – had come and gone.

Settling for restraint he leaned over the bar and pecked Betty's cheek.

Betty stepped back. 'Look at me, I'm a sight.'

'For sore eyes, love.'

'Do you want a drink?' She slipped into barmaid mode.

'I wouldn't say no. I left Greenwich before midnight. It's been a long dry journey.'

'You've grown a moustache.'

'I have.' He moved his fingers to his upper lip. He wanted to ask if she liked it, but fear of censure held him back.

'You must be starving.' She talked at high speed as she pulled him a pint, as much to hide her embarrassment as to update him. 'The Sunday dinners will be served as soon as I whip the girls in the kitchen into shape. The minute I turn my back they stop working and start gossiping but you know what they're like. Hark at me, dropping my problems on you back the minute you walk through the door.' She glanced at the clock. 'The dinners shouldn't be more than ten minutes. Why don't you go upstairs and put your feet up. I'll bring your meal up as soon as it's ready. Would you prefer beef or lamb?'

Glyn felt his eyelids droop as he leaned against the bar. 'Beef, please, Betty.'

She looked down at his tapestry carpetbag. It was lightly packed. 'How long are you stopping this time?' She picked up on a sharp edge to her voice she hadn't intended.

'Until we leave next week. I've moved out of my lodgings in Greenwich. Tom Station will be up with my trunk and photographic equipment this afternoon. I'll sort through my clothes before we go, throw away the worn ones and replace them. We won't be able to buy anything in the Donbas. Shopping will mean a trip to Moscow or St Petersburg and both are several days' journey from where we'll be living, so we'll need to stock up. On winter as well as summer clothes. Enough to see us through the next few years.'

'You haven't left me much time for shopping.'

'I thought a day in Cardiff would be enough for us to pick up the things we can't buy in Merthyr.'

'It'll have to be, won't it?' That edge again. She saw he'd noticed it too. 'I'll get Tom Station to carry your trunk upstairs when he arrives. You go on up. I'll be with you as soon as the dinners are dished out and I can get away from the bar.'

Glyn picked up his beer and his bag. His father-in-law, Bert, was coughing behind the bar in the saloon. He lifted his mug to him and mouthed 'see you later' over the heads of the customers before climbing the stairs.

He pushed open the door to the private sitting room. It was as well the weather was warm. The fire had burned out in the grate, the mantel was dusty, and the room had a musty, disused air.

The pub was always busy, allowing Betty and Bert little free time to spend outside of the public rooms.

Leaving the living room and a pile of mail addressed to him on the table, he went to the bedroom, dropped his bag on the floor, and set his pint pot on the marble washstand so it wouldn't leave a mark.

The bed was made, the dressing table and washstand newly dusted, the floorboards swept. Betty obviously spent more time here than she did the living room.

He sat on the bed and unlaced his boots. After kicking them off, he lifted his legs on the bed and lay back on the pillows. He felt oddly flat as well as tired, yet he couldn't have expected more of a welcome from Betty. Married for over ten years, he doubted they'd lived together more than six months in all that time.

With no children to occupy her and him away working, Betty had been glad to help her father out in the pub after her mother died. It was hardly fair of him to expect his wife to wait for him to make one of his once, or at the most twice, yearly visits while leaving her father to run the Boot Inn without a landlady.

Things would be different in Russia. They'd be living together, seeing one another every day, eating breakfast and dinner if not lunch at their own table. Sharing their evenings, visiting Mr Hughes's other workers and their families, and together with his brother Peter and wife Sarah, hosting dinner parties.

Mr Hughes had talked about setting up clubs.

Music and drama societies for the workers and their wives, arranging lectures, dances, bridge parties ... workmen were damming a river to create a reservoir to supply water for the works that could also be used for boating, sailing, and swimming...

'Mr Edwards. Mr Edwards, sir?'

Glyn opened his eyes and realised he'd fallen asleep. A young girl was standing in front of the bed. Little more than a child, she had long dark hair and blue eyes, which in Merthyr meant fish heritage. She reminded him of someone. He sat up, rubbed his eyes and tried to think who she resembled.

'I'm sorry I woke you, sir, but Mrs Edwards asked me to bring up your dinner.'

'Thank you.' He swung his legs over the side of the bed.

'I'll put the tray here, shall I, sir? On the dresser?'

'Please.' He ran his hands through his hair. 'Are you Mary Parry's daughter?'

'Yes, sir.'

'You don't have to "sir" me. I'm almost your uncle. It's Anna, isn't it?'

'Yes, sir ... Mr Edwards, I mean.'

'How long have you been working here?'

'Two years. Mrs Edwards offered me a job when she heard I wanted to leave the tunnel mines.'

'Isn't the work hard here?' He poured water from the jug on the washstand into the china basin and splashed his face.

'I'm not afraid of hard work, Mr Edwards, and I see daylight all day every day, which I didn't when I worked the traps.'

'How are your brothers and sisters?'

'All three of my brothers are fine, sir.'

Three! There had been six boys and three girls. Had so many of the Parrys died in the last cholera outbreak? Had Betty told him? He had no memory of it and he was sure he would have if Betty had written to him. He sensed the girl watching him. 'And your mother?'

'Mam's managing, Mr Edwards, thank you for asking.' She looked at the tray. 'Do you have everything you need, because if you do, I should go back downstairs? Dishing out time is busy. Mrs Edwards told me to tell you she'll be up as soon as she can get away.'

'I have everything I need, Anna. Thank you for bringing this up. Here.' Accustomed to living in hotels, he tossed her a sixpence.

'Oh, Mr Edwards, you shouldn't.'

''Course I should, you did something nice for me and that warrants a tip. Now go downstairs. The sooner you help my wife, the sooner she'll be finished and can come up and join me.'

The girl smiled, turned, and ran down the stairs.

He'd grown up next door to her mother, Mary. Watched his brother Tom court and marry her and witnessed Mary's grief when Tom had been killed 'by the iron' a week after their wedding.

Mary had married again two years later. As far as he knew, she'd been happy, until her second husband had also been killed when the boiler he'd been working next to in Treforest ironworks had exploded.

If Tom had lived, Anna and her brothers would

have been his niece and nephews. Pushing the thought from his mind, he picked up the tray, went into the living room, and set it on the dusty table. He looked at the pile of letters and reached for the first one, which John had told him to expect. He slit the envelope with his pocket knife, sat down and began to eat and read.

New Russia Company Ltd,

Dear Glyn,

Enclosed are the formal papers for your records setting out the terms and conditions of the loan you requested, including the repayment schedule postponed for two years as agreed.

I am delighted to ratify your request. Your purchase of the rights to sink a colliery in the Donbas is indicative of your support for the New Russia Company and the work the company has undertaken.

No doubt we'll face difficulties but I also know no man is better placed to assist me in overcoming them.

See you next week in Southampton.

John Hughes.

My compliments to your wife.

The letter was neatly written, Glyn assumed by one of John's confidential secretaries, since Huw Thomas, who'd dealt with John's correspondence when they'd travelled in Russia, had remained in the Donbas.

John Hughes's signature was little more than an indecipherable squiggle. Glyn knew better than to expect different. He was party to John's great secret. The man who'd persuaded dozens of the richest railway contractors, armaments manufacturers, and engineers in Britain to invest a total of £300,000 in his New Russia Company could neither read nor write. Not even to sign his own name.

Betty opened the purse she kept in her pocket, took out three coins, and dropped them into Anna's hand.

'Nine pence, Mrs Edwards. Are you sure?' Anna looked down at the three silver joeys in her palm.

'We couldn't have managed without you doing double work today.' Betty glanced around the kitchen. The dishes had been washed and stacked ready for the next meal, the tables cleaned, and the floor swept. Dinner rush over, the kitchen staff were taking their break. There were two barmaids on duty to help her father. She was free to go upstairs to see Glyn. She should be excited and happy after seeing so little of her husband for the past few years but all she felt was a sick sense of nervous apprehension.

'Mr Edwards gave me sixpence for taking up his dinner,' Anna blurted, uncertain despite Mr Edwards' assurance that she should have taken the money.

'I'm not surprised. He's used to living in hotels where people splash their money around like water and no one does a good turn for nothing. Spend it on yourself, Anna; you deserve it, the hours you put in here.'

'Thank you, Auntie Betty, but if it's all the same to you I'll give it to Mam. We need every penny the way the boys are growing out of their clothes. Can I take your washing down for Mam now? It will save her walking up to get it in the morning.'

''Course you can, Anna. Sure it won't be too much for you with the basket?'

'I'll manage.'

Betty went into the outhouse and helped Anna pile the pub's dirty laundry into the centre of a large sheet. When all the linen bins had been emptied she knotted the ends together to make a bundle. 'I could ask one of the boys to carry this home for you.'

Knowing none of them would do it without being paid a halfpenny Anna shook her head. 'I can do it, thank you, Mrs Edwards.'

The cook left the table where the kitchen staff ate and handed Anna her basket. Betty opened the door. She watched Anna struggle around the corner, lifting the bundle high, taking care to hold the washing above the dirty pavement.

'I feel sorry for Anna.' Betty closed the door. 'A full shift here, and then home to all that washing. I've heard she does most of it these days because Mary's not up to the job.'

'Anna's a godsend to her mother. I wish my Kate was half as helpful.' The cook settled in front of the range and poured herself a fresh cup of tea.

'Anna has an old head on her shoulders. She's as much of a mother to those boys as Mary. Comes of losing her father at a young age, I suppose.' Betty untied her apron and hung it on the back on the door. 'If anyone wants me I'll be upstairs.'

'Given how long Mr Edwards has been gone,

we won't be disturbing you unless the place catches fire.' The cook winked.

Betty glared but refrained from speaking her mind lest the woman take offence. Good cooks were hard to come by and harder to hold on to. Those who wanted an easy life worked for the managers in private houses catering for just one family. The better ones who weren't afraid of hard work were fought over by every cook shop owner, publican, and innkeeper in the town.

The cook knew she'd annoyed Betty but persisted. 'Must be like a second honeymoon every time he comes home.'

'I remember our first honeymoon well enough, thank you.' Betty slammed the door as she left the kitchen.

Betty entered the private sitting room on the second floor. For the first time in years she looked at it critically. A dirty, dusty, neglected room, papered in a small blue flowered print that was peeling at the corners and ceiling where it was stained by damp. The navy satin drapes had faded to grey where sunlight had bleached the cloth. The furniture was deal, hand-me-downs that should have been consigned to the firewood bin years ago. Strange she hadn't noticed until now, when she was on the point of leaving the Inn.

The tray Anna had brought up lay on the table. Glyn had eaten barely half his dinner and the remains were covered by a congealing skim of fat. A pile of empty envelopes lay next to his plate. She noticed he'd taken his letters.

She wondered who'd written to him at the pub. Had he intended to return home early and made arrangements for the New Russia Company to redirect his mail to Merthyr? Even when he was home he didn't discuss his business, or his life away from her.

She found Glyn stretched out on the bed in his trousers, shirt, and braces. His shoes had been neatly placed side by side next to the washstand, his jacket, waistcoat, collar, and tie hung on the back of a chair. The first thing she'd learned about Glyn after marrying him was he was tidy. Since then his orderly ways had almost reached the point of obsession. She assumed he'd become even more organized during his travels with Mr Hughes because he had to fend for himself.

'There's room on the bed if you'd like to join me.' His eyes were closed.

She'd thought he was asleep. 'I have to go back downstairs. The evening rush will be starting in an hour.'

'Can't your father manage by himself for once?' He patted the bed beside him but didn't open his eyes.

'It wouldn't be fair on him.'

'I haven't seen you in over five months, Betty.'

She felt suddenly – and considering the length of time they'd been married – ridiculously shy. 'I'll make us up a tea tray.'

'I've just eaten.'

'You didn't manage much of your dinner. Tea is always good after a meal and there's a tray of fresh bread pudding...'

He opened his eyes. 'I'd rather you came to bed.'

'It's three o'clock in the afternoon!'

'Thank you for reminding me.'

'Glyn... I couldn't... It's Sunday...'

'I'm aware of that too.'

'Now you're being sarcastic.'

'No, I'm not, Betty,' he protested.

'I'll get that tea.' She left the room.

He closed his eyes.

Ten years was a long time. Too long for any man and woman to keep alive the flicker of the romance that had brought them together. He'd been a fool to hope it could be otherwise.

Basement house in a court off John Street
Georgetown, Merthyr, June 1870

'You're dressing early for chapel, Richard.' Mary Parry didn't look up from the dishes she was washing in a tin bucket.

'Mr Edwards always arrives half an hour before the service. I help him get the place ready and set out the hymnals. It's the least I can do after everything he's done for us.' Richard finished cleaning his shoes and replaced the rags he'd used in the wooden box next to the hearth.

Mary eyed her eldest son suspiciously. He'd galloped into manhood and she resented the loss of the boy she'd loved. Only just seventeen, he was already over six feet tall. He'd inherited his father's good looks, deep blue eyes, black curly hair, and easy charm and she was terrified he'd meet a conniving girl who'd entice him away from her and his younger brothers and sister. Life was difficult enough with Richard's wages; without them it would be impossible.

She pursed her lips, which all her children knew was a sign of disapproval. 'As long as it is Mr Edwards you're going to see.'

'Who else would I be seeing in High Street chapel other than Mr Edwards and the minister?' Richard queried.

'If I knew, I wouldn't be asking. I wish you'd come to Evensong in our chapel with Anna, me, and the boys. It was good enough for you when you were growing up.'

'It's good enough for me now, Mam.' He kissed her cheek in an attempt to mollify her. 'But we owe Mr Edwards. If he wasn't my overman I'd be on boy's wages, not working as a collier, and if he hadn't put a word in with Management our Morgan wouldn't be an apprentice coal cutter or Owen a trapper. Have you any idea how many try to get their young ones the ventilator jobs in the tunnel mines?'

'None of your wheedling, now. You'll get soapy water over your Sunday best.' She elbowed him away. 'I don't need reminding how good Mr Edwards has been to us. I'll grant you the mines are better than the ironworks. No one with a brain in their head wants their children working close to the furnaces. It's just that...' She didn't finish the sentence.

Anxious to avoid further argument, Richard didn't press her. He stooped so he could see his reflection in the broken mirror he'd balanced between two nails he'd driven into the wall.

'I know who you're going to see,' ten-year-old

Morgan chanted from the outside steps, where he and eight-year-old Owen were playing 'toss and pick up' with sticks and stones they'd scavenged.

'You know nothing, squirt.' Richard left the mirror and cuffed his brother none too gently on the head before wiping his face in the flannel he'd wrung out in a cold tap in the shared yard.

'I do so. Judy Callaghan said she saw you with a girl on the mountain last Sunday.'

'Judy Callaghan's stupid and can't see for looking.' Richard pretended he hadn't noticed Morgan follow him inside, or his hand rise for a farthing bribe.

'She's clever enough to know you when she sees you.' After checking their mother's back was still turned, Morgan lifted his hand even higher.

'You can tell Judy Callaghan from me, she's an interfering gossiping bitch.'

'Language! That's no way to talk about a girl, Richard, and no way to talk on a Sunday.' Anna struggled down the steps with the enormous bundle and her basket.

'Judy Callaghan's not a girl. She's a poisonous cleckerbox. Here, let me, sis.' Richard took the bundle from her and swung it into a corner. 'If you'd sent word I would have come up to the Boot to carry this down for you.'

'I managed. It's tomorrow's washing from Auntie Betty, Mam. She said I could bring it to save you making the trip to the Boot tomorrow.' Anna set the three silver joeys Betty had given her and the sixpence next to the bowl.

'What's this?' Mary wiped her hands in her

apron and pushed her straggling grey hair from her eyes. She'd once been regarded as handsome, but double widowhood, nine pregnancies, and the deaths of five of her children in the cholera epidemic that had decimated the population of Merthyr had exacted a heavy toll. Now she only glanced in the mirror to check her hair was tied back and her face clean, because she couldn't bear the sight of the old woman who looked back at her.

'Threepence extra from Auntie Betty because I cleaned the vegetables as well as washed the pots. We were rushed off our feet. Auntie Betty had orders for seventy-two bachelors' dinners and Jinny Gibbs didn't come in. The cook and Auntie Betty said they couldn't have coped without me.'

'Jinny ill again?' Mary asked in concern.

'So her brother said. Auntie Betty asked if I could do Jinny's job as well as my own until Jinny recovers. It'll mean me working an extra four hours a day.'

'I hope you said yes.'

'Of course I did, Mam.'

'That girl's fading fast. Once lung disease gets hold of someone Jinny's build there's no stopping it. I'm sorry for her but the extra money will come in useful. And the sixpence?' Mary picked up all four coins.

'Mr Glyn Edwards is back from London. I took him his dinner and he gave me sixpence.'

'Just for bringing him his dinner?' Richard was amazed.

'Auntie Betty said he was used to living in hotels. I suppose you have to pay people to wait on you in those places.'

'Something the likes of you and me will never find out, sis.'

Richard made a face at his reflection.

Mary dropped the coins in the cracked jug where she kept the money she and Anna earned day to day. Richard, Morgan, and Owen were paid by the company every three months. She counted herself lucky if their wages covered the 'draw' the family made against them for food, boots, and clothes in the company shop. The washing she took in and Anna helped with when she wasn't working in the pub, coupled with what Anna earned, covered the rent most weeks. When it didn't, they took money from the draw instead of food and lived on bread, tea, and margarine.

Richard turned from his reflection. 'Did Auntie Betty give you anything besides her dirty washing?'

'Nothing I'm in the mood to share with a foul-mouthed brother.' Anna lifted a cloth from the top of her basket and removed a plate wrapped in a second clean tea towel. She unfolded it. Morgan and Owen ran over.

'Bread pudding,' Owen gasped.

'With currants, sultanas, and sugar on top.' Morgan raised his hand intending to break off a piece. Anna knocked him away. 'Good boys with clean hands and faces can have a slice after they've eaten the mutton sandwiches Auntie Betty gave me. But no one gets anything until I've made Mam and me a cup of tea.'

'Is there enough for us all to have big slices, Anna?' Owen begged.

'Very big ones. Now go and play, so Mam and I can sit down in peace. I've been on my feet since five o'clock.'

'The agreement was that sandwiches are part of your wages. Nothing was said about extras. Did Betty give you the bread pudding out of charity?' Mary enquired.

'There was a load of bread going to waste. Auntie Betty told the cook to make a couple of trays. She gave me a plateful because she said it would be hard by tomorrow and she can't sell it when it's stale. I'll put the kettle on. Anyone else want a cuppa?'

'Not me, I'm out of the door.' Richard had returned to the mirror and was trying to flatten his hair with a finger of grease he'd scooped from his mother's lard pot.

'Me, please, Anna,' Morgan and Owen shouted in unison.

'Move, boys, so Mam can sit out on the step and get some fresh air. I'll bring the tea to you when it's ready, Mam.' Anna picked up the kettle and carried it to the cold tap in the yard.

When Richard Parry senior had been killed in the Taff Vale Ironworks in Treforest, Pontypridd nine years ago, the Parrys had lost their tied cottage as well as their breadwinner. Destitute and pregnant, Mary had gratefully accepted her one-time brother-in-law, Edward Edwards' offer to find jobs for three of her eight children in the drift mine he managed in her home town of Merthyr. She sold most of her furniture to the new occupants of her company cottage to finance the nine-mile journey from Pontypridd to Merthyr and rented a one-up-one-down basement house because it was the cheapest on offer.

Built below street level it was cold and damp in summer, freezing and soaking wet in winter. The front door was reached by a short flight of steps that opened directly into the kitchen. As the only window downstairs was small and high level the door was never closed in fine weather so the place could benefit from natural light and what Mary termed 'a good drying out and airing'. But the open door made little difference. Summer and winter, water seeped up from the floor and ran down the walls, even high on the bedroom "shelf" that had a slightly larger window than the downstairs area.

'See you later, Mam.' Richard kissed her cheek. 'Keep me a sandwich and a slice of pudding please, sis.'

'I'll think about it, but it won't be the biggest slice of pudding.'

'Medium will do.'

Anna smiled. She could never be angry with Richard for long and he knew it.

'And you two,' Richard ruffled Owen and Morgan's hair. 'No more listening to Judy Callaghan or spreading stories about me.'

Before Morgan could think of a retort, Richard was away, striding across the yard.

Chapter Five

Oakleigh, Dr Peter Edwards' rented house
High Street, Merthyr, June 1870

'Here, wife, I want you.' Peter locked his hands around Sarah's waist.

She dropped the pile of woollen long johns she'd been stowing in a trunk. 'Don't, Peter, it's too hot.'

'And about to get warmer.'

'There's too much to do.' She giggled when he tickled her.

'We're not going anywhere for a week.'

'Our trunks are. They're being picked up first thing tomorrow. Remember?'

'I'll help you pack later.'

'You pack? Later when? Your brother and his wife are coming for supper. Edward will give us an hour-long lecture if he catches either of us doing anything he regards as "work" on a Sunday.'

'Edward won't be poking his nose upstairs.'

'I hope not.' She looked at the piles of clothes that littered every surface. 'If he does, he'll think I'm the most appalling housekeeper.'

'So you are.'

'Peter!'

'I didn't marry you for your housekeeping abilities. I married you because I want to spend the rest of my life looking into your beautiful brown eyes and running my hands though your beautiful long brown hair and stroking your beautiful, smooth, preferably naked skin.' He lowered her on to the bed, pulled the pins from her chignon and climbed up beside her. Catching the heel of his slippers with his toes, he kicked them off and kissed her.

'Your brother,' she murmured when he allowed her to draw breath.

'Won't be here for hours. I want to celebrate our eight-month anniversary by making love to you, Mrs Dr Peter Edwards.' He loosened the knot on his tie.

She pushed his hands aside and untied it for him 'What's "I love you" in Russian?'

'I've no idea.' He tossed his jacket and tie on top of a pile of shirts.

'We'll have to learn the language if we have Russian as well as Welsh patients.'

'More like we'll teach the Russians English.'

'Or Welsh.'

'Given your limited knowledge of my native tongue that isn't a good idea, sweetheart.' He slipped the loops from the pearls that fastened her muslin blouse and pulled at the lace on her bust shaper. 'Why do women wear so many clothes? It's summer.'

'Dare I suggest protection from their husbands' sweaty hands?'

'My hands aren't sweaty.'

'Yet.' She left the bed, slipped off her blouse, and hung it on a hook on the back of the door. She undressed slowly, deliberately tantalizing him. Her cotton bust shaper and muslin skirt followed. She swished them through the air before dropping them on top of the blouse. Peter undressed swiftly and lay naked on top of the bed.

'Three petticoats?' He watched her step out of two, only to start on the waist ribbons of a third.

'This muslin is thin. I don't want to scandalize Edward. His wife wears flannel even in summer.'

'She would.'

'That's enough! Judith is kind.'

'A man needs more than kindness in a woman to inspire him.'

She raised an eyebrow at his erection. 'Some would say you're inspired enough.'

'Only by you, my sweet.'

She unlaced her corset but it remained stuck to her skin. She eased it from her body.

'I wish you wouldn't wear stays. Whalebone leaves such ugly marks.' He left the bed and massaged the angry red weal that encircled her waist.

'In that case to please you I'll let myself go in Russia. I'll forgo my corset and wear my stockings rolled down to my ankles. Dress in loose smocks and lie on a chaise longue all day long reading novels while our servants bring me sweet tea and cream cakes.'

'I can't wait to see you get fat. But not from cream cakes.' He pulled down her bloomers. She stepped out of them.

'No, leave your stockings,' he ordered when she reached for her garters.

'Whatever makes you happy.' She wrapped her arms around his neck.

'You make me happy.' He lifted her off her feet and entered her standing up.

'You, dear husband, are insatiable.'

'If I am, sweetheart, you have only yourself to blame.' He fell back onto the bed, carrying her with him.

Mountain above Cyfarthfa Castle
Merthyr, June 1870

Richard left Georgetown and looked past the ironworks up the hill to the massive ornamental gates that marked the entrance to Cyfarthfa Castle. The first season he'd worked in Merthyr he'd accompanied Alf Mahoney, the senior miner he'd 'buttied' or trained under, to the Castle to help clean the guns for the annual rabbit shoot.

The drive was out of bounds to all except the Crawshays and their guests, so they'd followed the other workers who'd been pressganged to assist, and entered the grounds by a side road. He'd caught a glimpse of the gardens that swept down the hill from the front of house. An opulent, exotic wonderland of blooms set against the grim background of the smoking furnaces and chimneys that floored the valley.

The 'help' had been shown to wooden benches and tables in the yard outside the stables. After they'd finished working on the guns they'd been given beer and food. The back doors to the house had been open and he recalled palatial painted passages and corridors floored with marble.

Richly dressed men and women had ferried trays of food and drink and cleared the dirty plates and beakers. The women wore lace caps and collars and a few had made a fuss of him because he'd been the youngest there, ruffling his hair and feeding him sugar pastries. He'd assumed they were Crawshays but afterwards Alf told him they'd only seen the outdoor staff, not even the indoor servants, let alone the Crawshays themselves.

Since then, he'd thought of the mansion as a palace. He imagined Robert Crawshay and his family living within its walls like royalty looking down the hill at the workers who'd made them rich – a million and a half pounds rich, or so rumour had it. Not for the first time he wished he'd been born in Cyfarthfa Castle. If he had he'd…

He kicked a stone out of his path. Some dreams were so fanciful they weren't worth dreaming.

He left the road that led to the high street chapel and continued to climb. The trees were blackened and stunted, the grass dry. Smoke from the works hung heavy, tainting the atmosphere with a metallic tang but he knew when he reached the summit, the air would be cleaner.

He passed a farmhouse that had been old before the Crawshays had arrived in the valley. A mile to the left was a field with a dry-stone-wall sheep pen. A century ago trees had been planted inside it to shelter the animals during winter storms but the trees had outgrown the pen and their roots had damaged the walls, causing falls in a few places.

He headed for a May tree that leaned precariously close to the ground, took a red handkerchief from his pocket, and spread it on the grass before sitting down. His mother had an eagle eye when it came to dirt on his clothes and he didn't want to have to explain how his hand-me-down father's Sunday best had acquired grass stains when he was supposed to be in chapel.

He leaned against the tree, turned his face to the sun, and breathed in deeply. He relished his one day off a week. The Tunnel Pits never seemed to have enough air, no matter how fast the trappers worked the ventilators.

Seductive as the summer's day and smell of grass was; he grew restless. He envied the older workers their watches. He'd intended to start saving for a pocket watch on his first day at work, but he was no nearer buying one than he'd been then. One day, he'd buy himself a watch and an eight-day clock for his mother, but not until they moved out of the basement. He couldn't bear to watch the polished wood of a clock case turn white and warp the way his mother's dresser and table had after they'd been forced to move out of their cottage in Treforest.

Church bells tolled in the distance and he wondered if Alice Perkins would be able to get away. He imagined her pleading a headache to be excused from Sunday worship; pictured her father, mother, and sister leaving their double bay-windowed manager's house for church – not chapel. Like most of the managers Alice's father had abandoned chapel to join the same congregation as the Crawshays.

Richard had seen the Perkinses' cook, maid-servants, and man of all work walking behind the family as they made their way to their chapel two streets below the church. Alice had told him her father had given their housekeeper permission to attend morning services on condition she remain behind on Sunday afternoons and evenings to look after the house. He also knew Alice wouldn't be able to get away unless the housekeeper stayed in the servants' quarters.

He visualised Alice's family joining the congregation of elite (or, in Welsh terms, *crache*) in the church. Alice left behind in her pink and white wallpapered bedroom she'd described at such length he felt he'd visited it.

When the house was quiet and Alice was certain the housekeeper would remain in the servants' quarters, she'd leave her bed, lace on her boots, and pick up her cape – she'd need the hood to conceal her face. She'd run down the main staircase, out through the French doors of the dining room, and into the garden. Avoiding the basement windows, she'd walk through the shrubbery to the back gate that opened on to the mountain.

In his mind's eye he followed Alice every step of the way. It was easier to picture her walking up to meet him than it was to imagine the town hall clock. No matter how hard he concentrated, he couldn't hazard a guess at the time. If Alice didn't come soon, church and chapel services would be over and they'd have no time together – that's if she turned up. She had to come ... she had to... He picked up a blade of heather and pulled off the tiny flowers one by one.

'She'll come ... she won't ... she'll come ... she won't...'

His chant ended on 'she won't'. He cheated, broke a piece from the stem and whispered 'she'll come'.

Irritated, he discarded what was left of the heather and tried counting the time away. Mr Edwards had told him it took a full second to say twenty-one – slowly. He tried to repeat 'twenty-one' sixty times but forgot how many he'd said after thirty.

He peered over the wall of the pen. The hillside sprawled below him, devoid of life apart from sheep cropping grass. Just as he was about to give up and make his way back, he heard humming. A lively music hall tune, unsuitable for the Lord's Day, laced with a catchy chorus of, 'tap tap tap and click click click.'

He recognised 'The Telegraph', Alice's current favourite. Ducking low, he caught a glimpse of the hem of Alice's frock. He'd seen it before, a blue cotton with an over pinafore, the only concession Alice's mother would allow to placate Alice's craving for a bustle; a fashion Alice's father had decreed unsuitable for any girl below the age of eighteen.

He'd learned a lot about women's clothes since he'd been stepping out with Alice Perkins. Not that they actually 'stepped out'. Not anywhere where there was any danger of them being seen. Alice had warned him her father would be furious if he discovered his youngest daughter was secretly seeing any boy, let alone a common collier.

Richard heard the clatter of stones as Alice climbed over the dry-stone wall. Raising his head he watched her from behind the tree, admiring the sweep of her fair hair as it rippled down her back. Alice couldn't wait to pin it up, but like the bustle, 'grown-up' hairstyles had to wait until her eighteenth birthday. Alice found her father's edict hard to bear. He was glad she was too young to wear it up. It was soft and silky as he'd discovered when she'd allowed him to run his fingers through it.

'Richard!' Alice caught sight of his cap as he bobbed behind the tree and ran towards him. He leapt to his feet, caught her when she tripped, and led her to his handkerchief.

'I've missed you terribly this week.' She flung her arms around him and pressed her lips inexpertly against his.

He pulled her close and dared to do something he'd been thinking about all week. He slid his tongue past her teeth into her mouth.

She jumped back. 'You've never done that before.'

'It's been a long week without you.'

'I told you. No liberties. Not until we're married.'

His face burned. Blood rushed to his cheeks. He pointed to his handkerchief. 'Let's sit down.'

'Only if you promise to be good.'

'I promise, but damn it, Alice...'

'And no swearing,' she added.

'You're worse than the minister.'

'Because I expect you to respect me?' she challenged.

'Because you criticise everything I do.'

He pulled a second, green handkerchief from his pocket, set it next to the one she was sitting on and knelt beside her. He knew he was still blushing. It didn't help he couldn't stop staring at the curve of her breast beneath her bodice. He would have liked to have stroked it but he knew she wouldn't hesitate to slap him.

'I don't mean to criticize. I'm sorry.' She moved towards him.

He cupped her face in his hands, kissed her, and dared to allow his right hand to slip lower ... and lower.

She wriggled closer. He left his hand, resting between them. Her hair smelled of lavender, her skin lemon, her breath of mint.

'I love you, Alice Perkins. One day we'll be married.'

'I know.' She kissed him with unpractised enthusiasm.

He pushed her on to the grass and slid his hand beneath her skirt until his little finger rested on the garter above her knee.

'No! Richard!'

There was fear in her voice that came from more than her reaction to the 'liberty'.

He opened his eyes and saw terror in her eyes. Whirling around, he was aware of dark shapes crowding in on them.

Something large and heavy crashed on the back of his head. Stunned, lost in a violent, red-tinged explosion he tumbled headlong into agonising darkness.

The last thing he heard before pain overrode his senses was Alice screaming his name.

Chapter Six

Basement house in a court off John Street
Georgetown, Merthyr, June 1870

Mary stared at the archway that linked the court with John Street so intently, Anna felt as though her mother was willing Richard to return.

'Your brother's found himself a girlfriend, hasn't he?'

'If he has, he's not told me, Mam. But, he wouldn't, would he?' Anna handed Mary her tea and sat beside her on the narrow step.

'If he gets married we won't be able to manage. It'll be the workhouse for the rest of us.'

'Richard knows his responsibilities, Mam. He won't let us go into the workhouse.'

'You're young; you don't know what men are like once their heads have been turned. They stop thinking with their brains and...' Mary faltered. It wasn't easy to keep a young girl innocent, living in close proximity to their neighbours in the yard. Anna had seen and heard things Mary had rather she hadn't but still she struggled to keep Anna in ignorance of the more brutal and physical side of men's natures.

'Like you turned Dad's head?' Anna had become skilled at dispelling her mother's black moods.

The ghost of a girlish smile played at the corners

of Mary's mouth. 'That was a long time ago.'

'Richard will look after you, me, and the boys for as long as we need looking after.'

'I don't know what I would have done without Richard after your father was killed.' Mary looked inwards, as she always did whenever she spoke about either of her husbands. 'I can't believe he's been gone nine years. Richard never shed a tear at the time. Never murmured, even when I took him out of Treforest School. The schoolmaster said Richard was bright. With the right education he could have gone a long way. Become an engineer even. But I had you and the others. I couldn't afford to feed all of you without Richard's help. I had no choice but to put him, David, and you to work. Mr Edwards' offer to find the three of you places in the tunnel mines was a Godsend. If the cholera hadn't taken George and Victor along with David and your sisters, the younger ones would have had to join you as soon as they were old enough. It's the only way I could have kept them.'

'I know, Mam, and Richard knows you had no choice, but we're better off now than we've been for a long time, and it'll be better still once I start doing extra hours in the Boot.'

Mary ignored Anna's attempt to reassure her with the promise of increased wages. 'Richard's right. We've a lot to be grateful to Mr Edwards for. Without his help Richard and the boys wouldn't have found work away from the iron that killed your father.'

Anna knew it was useless to point out there were as many, if not more dangers in the tunnel mines where her brothers worked as in the ironworks where her father had been killed.

'When the new colliery in Merthyr Vale goes into production, the boys can get jobs there. We'll move out of this damp house into one of the new ones they're building in Aberfan. Mrs Parfitt said they're going to have their own backyards with ty bach and tap, not one shared between six families like here. Just think, Anna, there'll be no more breaking our backs, hauling water in buckets. It'll be better for all of us, healthier...'

Anna stopped listening. She'd heard it all before, many times.

'Mr Edwards says it could be five years before the Merthyr Vale pit goes into production, Mam,' Morgan broke in.

'Not that long, surely?' Mary looked to Anna to contradict him.

'It could, Mam,' Anna was reluctant to tell a lie, even a comforting one. 'And, it'll cost money we haven't got to move.'

'No point in hiring a cart to take furniture from here. It's all been ruined by the damp. We'll leave with what we carry and make do with a roof over our heads. Five years...'

'A lot can happen in that time. Richard's doing well and knowing him, he'll soon be doing even better. There are plenty of new pits being dug beside Merthyr Vale. Richard's ambitious.'

'A fat lot of good Richard doing well will be to us if he spends the money he earns on a girl.'

'Don't start that again, Mam. You're looking for trouble where there's none.' Even before her father had been killed, her mother had been prone to grim predictions that the family would end up in the workhouse. But the last few weeks she'd been worse than usual.

'Mark my words. Trouble's coming, girl,' Mary said darkly. 'When it does it'll be in the shape of a no good, red-lipped, bright-eyed, flibbertigibbet who's set her cap at your brother. And he'll be too blind and taken with her to see it – or think of us.'

Before Anna could answer, a gang of urchins burst through the archway into the court shouting, 'Auntie Mary, quick! It's your Richard!'

Mary turned, stumbled, and fell up the steps in her haste to reach the yard.

'Your Richard's been beaten to death...' the young boy paused for effect and to catch his breath.

'Richard ... dead.' Mary swayed and fainted.

Anna caught her but not before Mary's head hit the cobbles. 'You stupid boys!' Anna shouted, shock manifesting in anger. 'Where is he?'

'Tom Farmer's bringing him now,' the boy mumbled shamefaced. 'He and Bert Farmer have him in their cart.'

'See to Richard. I'll take care of your mother.' Maggie Two Suits, so named because her husband, Tim Two Suits, had inherited a second from his brother that he'd refused to pawn, was a large woman accustomed to taking control. She swept Mary into her arms and carried her into her own house.

Anna charged through the archway. Tom and Bert were lifting Richard from their cart.

'Bert and me were working with the sheep and dogs in the top field, training a couple of pups, when we saw a crowd of men coming up from the works. We knew a gang that size would be up to no good.' Tom took Richard's legs and signalled to Bert to take Richard's shoulders. 'They went into the west field, the one with the sheep pen. Next thing, we heard a girl scream as if she was being murdered. I ran down with the dogs while Bert went back to the farm to get the shotgun.'

Bert took up the story. 'Dad had harnessed the cart ready for him and Mam to go Sunday visiting. I told him what me and Tom had seen. We stopped to get the gun and took the cart so we reached the field before Tom. We saw the men – ten or eleven of them beating your Richard. He was on the ground out cold. Couldn't have lifted a finger to save himself if he'd wanted to.

'Ianto Paskey was kicking him and Ianto's brother Mervyn was holding the girl. She was trying to fight but she didn't stand a chance against those louts. Dad tried to bring her off the mountain along with Richard but the girl's father was with the men and wouldn't have it. In the end we thought it best to leave her, so we could get your Richard seen to.'

Anna was too concerned about Richard to take in what Tom and Bert were saying. 'I'll send for the doctor.'

'Already done, Anna. Mr Edward Edwards saw us coming down off the mountain. He told us where you lived and said he'd bring his doctor brother here, quick as he could.' Spreading Richard's weight between them, Tom and Bert hoisted him from the cart and carried him through the archway into the court. 'Which is your house?'

Anna pointed to the open door.

'Best get him to bed.' Tom advised.

Anna shouted to her brothers. 'Morgan, run upstairs and turn down your bed.' He raced into the house. 'Owen, stir the fire under the kettle, doctors always need boiling water, and fill the water buckets, both of them.'

Tom eyed the narrow entrance and took Richard from Bert who immediately pulled off his cap to show respect. Lifting Richard over his shoulder Tom descended into the kitchen.

'I've turned down our bed, Anna.' Morgan peered at her from the top rung of the ladder that led up to the sleeping shelf.

'Richard's in no state to go up there, Anna,' Tom warned. 'You'd best make him a bed down here for the time being.'

'How is he?' Maggie walked in, followed by half a dozen women from the court.

'As you see. How's Mam?' Anna asked urgently.

'Out of it and best that way from the state of your Richard. I've settled her in my Tim's easy chair. May Twp's looking after her.'

May Twp's husband Dai had gained his nickname after a pit prop had fallen on his head. He hadn't been right since.

'Bed, Anna,' Tom prompted.

Flustered, Anna realized Tom was wilting under Richard's weight. 'Morgan, throw down the clothes from Mam's and my bed.' Anna pulled the rag rug her mother had made from the boys' outgrown trousers to the side of the hearth. She grabbed the bedding Morgan tossed down, covered the rug with a blanket, and spread a sheet on top.

Tom set Richard on the makeshift bed, removed his cap, and rubbed his aching shoulder muscles.

'Your shirt's covered in blood!' Anna exclaimed.

'It'll wash.' Tom spoke with the assurance of a man who'd never washed a shirt in his life.

'Blood's terrible to get out of coarse linen,' Anna warned.

'Mam's got out worse.'

'I've filled the water buckets and the kettle's steaming, Anna.' Owen pushed his way through the throng of neighbours.

'Good boy.' She covered Richard with a sheet and blanket. 'Morgan come down; fetch me a bowl of hot water and a clean flannel, soap, and towel.'

'Give the boy some room, ladies,' Tom pleaded as the neighbours settled on every available surface.

'We're here to help,' Maggie retorted.

'You'd help us more by looking after Mam,' Anna countered.

'You'd help Bert, me, and the Parrys by clearing out so we have enough air to breathe.' Tom wasn't renowned for his tact.

Morgan scurried between the legs of the adults and brought Anna everything she'd asked for.

Wiping the tears from her eyes with the back of her hand Anna examined her brother. Every inch of skin that wasn't broken was bloody, black, and swollen. His lips were torn, split, and bleeding. His eyelids glued shut by blackened clots, his black curls wet with blood. The brown twill jacket, trousers, and linen shirt that had been their father's was torn and stained beyond repair. He wasn't recognisable as her adored and handsome brother who'd walked out of the door, happy and whistling less than two hours before.

She wrung the flannel out in warm water and rubbed soap on it.

'Don't!'

Alarmed, Anna dropped the soap into the bowl.

Bare-headed Peter Edwards pushed aside the neighbours, who'd retreated no further than the door, and strode into the room with his doctor's bag, his brother Edward close on his heels. Edward removed his hat and nodded to the women.

Peter laid a hand on Anna's shoulder. 'Don't disturb those blood clots. If you touch them you could cause haemorrhaging.'

'Sorry...' Anna swallowed hard.

'You've done well to make your brother comfortable. Richard is your brother?' Peter checked.

Anna's voice was unsteady but she managed, 'Yes, sir.'

'You're?'

'Anna, sir.'

Peter glanced over his shoulder. The room wasn't much larger than the pantry of his rented house, yet twenty or more people were crammed into it and more still were caught up in a crush in the doorway. 'This patient needs quiet. Everyone except his family and the men who brought him here, out!'

No one dared argue with a doctor.

'One at a time and, quietly,' Edward warned when two women jostled and squabbled in the doorway.

Peter turned to Tom and Bert. 'You brought this man here?'

'Yes, Dr Edwards. I'm Tom, this is my brother Bert. We help our father at the top farm.'

'You saw this man being beaten?'

Tom repeated the story he'd told Anna.

'Was Richard conscious when you found him?' Peter asked.

'He was out cold. I know him well, sir. He's not a fighter, not like some round here. That's not to say he won't punch back if someone comes after him,' Tom elaborated.

'No man would have lain there and taken the kicking the Paskey boys and their cronies were giving him if he'd been in a fit state to do anything about it,' Bert added.

'Did you recognise any of the men who attacked Richard beside the Paskeys?' Edward watched Peter kneel beside Richard and begin his examination.

'They were all from the Rolling Mill, sir. Deputy Perkins was with them. Not that he did anything besides order the men to keep hammering Richard after they wanted to leave off.'

'I know the Paskeys and what they're capable of Like their father and uncles they're...' Edward moderated his language in front of Anna, '...nasty pieces of work. But why would Deputy Perkins order men to beat Richard Parry? I doubt he knows the boy. I understand why men would obey Mr Perkins given his power to hire and fire but it doesn't make sense.'

'Richard was with Alice, Deputy Perkins's daughter, Mr Edwards,' Bert divulged.

Anna began to shake uncontrollably.

'Take a deep breath and sit back against the wall.' Peter was too concerned about Richard to help her.

Edward shook his head. 'Stupid boy, chasing skirt at his age. You'd think the girl would have warned him about her father. Deputy Perkins puts on more airs than the Crawshays.'

'He keeps a close eye on his daughters.' Tom sounded bitter.

Edward recalled there'd been gossip about Tom and one of the Perkins girls. Gossip that had ended when she'd married a solicitor thirty years her senior.

'With his three older daughters married to businessmen I doubt Mr Perkins would be happy to see either of the younger ones walk down the aisle with a collier.' Peter returned his stethoscope to his bag.

'You know a lot about the Perkins family for someone who's spent the last eight years in London,' Edward commented.

'Sarah helped the second daughter, Margaret, organise the young wives' bazaar. I met the father there.' Peter took a brown glass bottle, upended it on a wad of cotton wool, and cleaned the worst of the cuts on Richard's face. 'Richard's a brave but foolish boy to set his sight on a Perkins.'

'Mr Perkins won't hurt Richard any more, will he, Mr Edwards?' Anna looked to Edward for reassurance. Since they'd lived in Merthyr, her mother's brother-in-law had always been there to help them.

'I'll talk to Deputy Perkins, Anna, but I can't

promise anything. He must be very angry with Richard to get his men to do this. My brother's right. Richard set his sights too high when it came to courting a Perkins and he's suffering for it.'

'Richard will be all right though, won't he, Dr Edwards?'

Peter wanted to comfort the girl but his experience in East End hospitals had taught him the worst mistake a doctor could make was to give false hope. It put his reputation and personal safety at risk. Recovery from a bleak diagnosis was invariably greeted by tears of relief and jubilation. An unexpected death the relatives hadn't been prepared for could result in loss of face and a bloody nose for whoever delivered the bad news.

'The next few hours will be critical. Your brother has four broken ribs, severe bruising around his eyes, face, and torso and open wounds on his head. Painful as those injuries are they'll mend, given time, care and rest. As for the injuries that can't be seen, they're impossible to diagnose. There's no obvious skull fracture, but that's not to say there isn't one. He's deeply unconscious, bordering on coma. A great deal depends on the state he'll be in when he wakes. He's going to need careful nursing for the next few hours. I'll stay as long as I can but I'll have to leave if someone else needs me.'

'Thank you, Dr Edwards. You're most welcome to stay but I have to tell you...' Anna hated bringing up the subject of payment with her brother in dire need of doctoring but felt she had no choice. 'About your fee...'

'Your family pay the penny a week?' Peter asked.

'Yes, sir.' For the first time Anna noticed the doctor's shirt buttons were undone, he wasn't wearing a tie, and his waistcoat and jacket had been flung on.

He saw her looking at him. 'I was changing for church when my brother told me someone had been hurt. I didn't wait to dress properly.'

Embarrassed, Anna blurted, 'Our penny a week goes to Dr Jones, Dr Edwards.'

'No matter.' Peter glanced around. There was only one wooden chair, rickety and swollen with damp. He sat on a bench, the only other seat in the room, and leaned against the wall until he realised the stonework was wet.

Anna remembered her manners. 'Would you like a cup of tea, Dr Edwards, Mr Edwards? Tom, Bert?'

Recognising Anna's need to do something, Edward answered. 'Thank you, Anna; we could all do with one.'

'Not for me and Bert if you don't mind, Anna.' Tom went to the door. 'We left the dogs when we went to see to your brother. The old ones will be fine but the pups can be skittish. They may have run off. If they have, they'll take some tracking down.'

'I can't thank you enough for rescuing Richard and bringing him home.'

'I wish we could have got to him before he was hurt, Anna.' Tom twisted his cap in his hands. 'If you walk up our way, our Mam will have a cup of tea and a slice of bara brith ready for you, the boys, and your Mam anytime.'

Too overcome to speak, Anna nodded her thanks.

'We came the minute I found a barmaid to cover for me,' Betty gushed when Edward opened the Panys' door. 'Oh, my poor love.' She rushed to Anna who was sitting on the floor next to Richard. She knelt beside her and hugged her. 'How are you holding up, pet?'

Anna turned her tear stained face to Betty. 'I'm all right, Auntie Betty. But Richard ... and Mam...'

'Where's Mary?' Glyn asked Peter.

'Maggie Two Suits is looking after her. You heard what happened?' Edward checked.

'The version that's being bandied around the Boot. Deputy Perkins set his men on Richard and ordered the boy beaten to death. Is Mary hurt as well?'

Edward took Glyn outside so he could relate what had happened out of Anna's earshot.

Betty removed her bonnet and shawl before joining Glyn and Edward in the court. 'There's a spare bed in the maids' attic at the Inn. I could take Anna back there. The other girls would look after her and keep her busy to take her mind off what's happened.'

'You won't get her away from Richard, her mother, or her younger brothers. With Richard and Mary ill she believes she's the only one who can care for them,' Edward pointed out.

Peter appeared in the doorway. 'Do me a favour, Betty. Go next door and check on Mary. I don't want to leave Richard longer than I have to.'

'You're worried about Mary as well as Richard?'

Betty saw Anna standing behind him. Alarm registered on the young girl's face. Betty wished she could retract her words.

'I'm not as worried about Mary as I am about Richard. But I'm concerned about the neighbours' ability to care for her. They mean well but Mary needs proper nursing and you've had experience after looking after your mother.'

Betty was flattered by the confidence Peter placed in her. 'Don't worry, I'll take good care of her.'

'I can spare five minutes to check on her again now. Any change in Richard's condition, knock the wall, Anna, and I'll be right back.' Peter steered Betty to the head of the steps that led down to the Jefferies' house.

Mary was propped up in the only easy chair in Maggie's house, her feet on a stool, an old grey army blanket wrapped around her.

'Dr Edwards, Betty, can I get you a cup of tea?' Maggie pushed aside the pile of boys' socks she'd been darning.

'No, thank you, Maggie, I've just eaten,' Betty refused.

'I couldn't drink another teaspoonful of tea after all the pots Anna has brewed in the last couple of hours. There's no change?' Peter checked the pulse at Mary's wrist.

'None, Dr Edwards. I haven't left her side except when I had to visit the ty bach, and then May stayed with her.' Maggie indicated a bench next to the hearth.

'She hasn't stirred, Dr Edwards,' May confirmed.

'Both of you must be exhausted,' Betty sympathised.

'It's not been easy keeping the boys out so Mary can get some peace,' Maggie conceded. 'I haven't had time to make tea for them.'

'If you send two of your boys up to the Boot, I'll give them a note for the cook. She can pack enough cheese sandwiches and bread pudding for your and May's families,' Betty offered.

'Your boys can eat in my place, Maggie,' May suggested. 'Then they'll have no excuse to bother you until bedtime.'

'Good idea, May,' Betty agreed. 'I'll stay here, so you can both take a break. When the boys bring the food, eat with them, Maggie. Take as long as you like, I've arranged cover for me in the Boot. While Mary's quiet I'll work out the ordering and menus for the Boot for next week.' Betty opened her bag and took out a pencil and notebook.

'I'll return to the Parrys.' Peter went to the door. 'Knock the wall if you need me.'

'I will.' Betty pulled a kitchen chair to the table and started to write.

Night fell over the court, darkening the Parrys' kitchen to coalface gloom. Apart from a candle that danced in a draught on a stool next to Richard, the only light emanated from the hearth. It was barely enough to make out the shape of the door, windows, and shelf where the two boys were sleeping.

'Will Richard recover?' Edward whispered to Peter as they sat side by side, stiffly upright on the bench. Whether it was the result of inertia or damp, Edward was shivering.

'I'll be able to make a clearer diagnosis when he regains consciousness. One thing's certain; he won't survive another beating as severe.' Peter reached for his pocket watch. He held it close to the candle. The hands pointed to midnight.

Anna was lying on the rug next to her brother, her hand closed around his blackened, bloodied, and bruised fingers. She'd fallen asleep hours ago. As had the boys she'd sent up the ladder to their shared bed. Even Glyn had succumbed and was slumped over the kitchen table.

'Given the involvement of the Paskeys I'm surprised Richard's alive. The police sergeant was telling me the other day that he suspects them of having a hand in the murder of the collier who was killed walking over the mountain to Aberfan a couple of months ago.' Edward reached for his pipe.

'We should send for the sergeant now,' Peter advised.

'You've been in London too long. If we involved the police, Deputy Perkins would produce a dozen witnesses to contradict anything Tom, Bert, or their father said. The deputy wouldn't allow Alice to testify and Richard wouldn't live long enough to reach a courtroom.'

'So much for law and order in Merthyr.' Peter conceded. 'I can't wait to leave.'

'You don't know what you're going to.'

'According to Glyn, an empty plain waiting for John Hughes's works and town to be built.'

'That doesn't mean Mr Hughes will be able to create Utopia. There are good and bad everywhere, including Russia.'

'There are, but if my experiences in East London are any indication, foul living conditions, filthy air, and abject poverty breeds more bad than good. After meeting John Hughes I believe he's a fair man who intends to build a town that's worth living in and pay every one of his workers a decent wage.' Peter fell silent when he heard the ring of metal boot studs cross the yard.

Edward lifted his finger to his lips, went to the door and opened it a crack. 'We're jumping at our own shadows. It's Iestyn Swine going to the ty bach.'

'Iestyn Swine who married Jenny who used to be Jones?'

'I'd forgotten you courted her before you went to London.'

'I heard she married Iestyn but I haven't seen her since I returned. How is she?'

'Just about surviving like everyone else in this court. She has eleven children.'

'Eleven!'

'Three sets of twins. They run in Iestyn's family. He lost his leg last year when he fell under a tram in the rail yard but scrapes a living collecting pigswill for farmers. He's also developed a side line in gelding livestock and selling the potions Jenny brews to doctor animals.'

'Glyn's awake.' Peter smiled at the confused expression on Glyn's face.

'I haven't recovered from the journey yet,' Glyn sat up. 'I can't wait to get to Russia so I can sleep in the same bed for more than one night. I need fresh air.'

'You won't find that this low in the valley the way the furnaces belch out.' Edward warned.

'Look in on Betty and Mary if you're heading for the ty bach,' Peter asked when Glyn left his chair.

'Will do.' Glyn slipped out.

'Do you think Perkins will send his thugs after Richard again?'

Edward made certain Anna was really asleep before answering Peter. 'I'd say certainly and soon. But you're the one who's met the man.'

'Met isn't the same as know. My patients tell me Perkins rules his section of the ironworks like a medieval baron. Everyone who works under him lives in fear. Sarah says he controls every minute of his wife and daughters' lives. He married the three eldest off to businessmen decades older than them.'

'This isn't the Middle Ages. The girls could have said no if they didn't want to marry.'

'According to Sarah none dared. Deputy Perkins threatened to throw them naked into the street if they didn't do as he ordered. Sarah believes him capable of it.'

'Then God help Alice Perkins.'

'I hope God's listening. Sarah said he didn't do much to aid her sisters.' Peter left the bench and monitored Richard's pulse and breathing.

'Any improvement?'

'He doesn't appear to be quite as deeply and unnaturally unconscious as earlier.'

They were interrupted by a soft tap at the door.

'Come in, Mrs Jeffries.' Edward assumed it was Maggie who'd been in and out of the house all evening to see if there was any change in Richard's condition.

'It's not Mrs Jeffries, Mr Edwards.'

'Alf?' Edward rose when the collier who worked under him in the mine entered, cap in hand. Alf Mahoney was Irish, and what he lacked in brain power he made up for in brawn. He was large, even by mining standards, although not as tall as Glyn, but at six feet two inches he was considerably wider, with muscles honed and hardened by ten years of hewing coal.

'I heard you were here, sir, sir.' He nodded to both brothers. 'I came because I thought you ought to know what the Paskeys were saying about Richard in The Chandlers Arms.' He hovered in the doorway. 'How is the lad, sir?'

'The boy's holding his own at the moment.' Peter wished he could offer more reassurance.

'No thanks to Ianto and Mervyn Paskey. Richard's a good lad. The best of the young ones I've trained up.'

'The Paskeys were in The Chandlers?' Edward reminded.

'Mervyn was boasting they'd as good as killed Richard and it was going to stand them in good stead with Deputy Perkins. Ianto was trying to hush him but Mervyn was having none of it. He was telling anyone who'd listen that Deputy Perkins would promote them and pay them a guinea bonus apiece when Richard drew his last breath.'

'Did anyone say anything about the girl?' Peter asked.

'Alice Perkins?' Alf stared, mesmerized by the damage to Richard's face. 'The barmaid said she'd heard from one of the Perkins's housemaids that Deputy Perkins has locked her in her bedroom. Mousy Tinker said he saw Josiah Wilkins going into the Perkinses' house. Everyone knows Josiah is looking for a wife.'

'Josiah Wilkins is over sixty. He's a deacon. The deputy could have sent for him to talk to the girl.'

'No, he wouldn't, Peter,' Edward interrupted. 'Josiah's chapel, Perkins works for the Crawshays and will do anything to ingratiate himself with them, which is why he left the chapel to join the church when he was promoted head of the Rolling Mill. The deputy would send for a vicar to talk to Alice, not a deacon if he wanted someone to discuss religious matters or filial obedience with the girl.'

'Josiah Wilkins has buried three wives, the last six months ago. He has eight children living. But the man's so mean no woman will keep house for him. It's common knowledge he starved all his wives to death.' Alf repeated gossip that ignored the fact that two of Josiah's three wives had died of consumption and the last in childbirth.

'He owns a boot and shoe shop, which would impress Deputy Perkins. And a gossip-soiled sixteen-year-old would appeal to a man of his age,' Edward said thoughtfully.

'Gossip-soiled!' Peter was shocked by the expression.

'That's how Deputy Perkins and Josiah Wilkins would see it,' Edward explained. 'It wouldn't matter to them whether the girl had done anything to warrant the talk. As far as those two are concerned, she'd be no better than a common streetwalker. Knowing Richard, I doubt he's laid a hand on Alice – not in the way her father thinks.'

'I thought you ought to know what the Paskeys were saying, Mr Edwards, and they're still after Richard.' Alf went to the door.

'Thank you for coming.'

'Least I could do. Like I said, sir, Richard's a good lad.'

Edward looked at him thoughtfully. 'Are you afraid of the Paskeys?'

'Not the brothers on their own, sir, but whenever they set about hammering someone, they do it after they've had a few jars of ale with their hangers-on. From what I heard in the Chandlers, someone – and I'm betting, though I wouldn't say so outside of this room, that someone was Deputy Perkins – gave the Paskeys money to buy a few rounds of ale before Richard was beaten to a pulp. There's plenty in Merthyr willing to throw punches in exchange for free beer and there's only so much one man can do against a mob turned ugly by drink.'

'There are enough men in this court who'd help you if it came to a fight with the Paskeys and their mob, but hopefully it won't come to more blows. If I send for a carpenter to strengthen the door could you hold off the Paskeys and their riff-raff for as long as it would take one of the court boys to fetch the police?'

'You want me to look after Richard and his family, sir?'

'It's an idea. What do you think?' Edward turned to Peter and Glyn who'd arrived in time to hear Edward's suggestion.

'We can't leave the boy and his family without protection,' Peter agreed. 'As you said, the police won't make a move against the deputy without cast-iron proof, which we're not likely to get.'

'Betty wants to move the younger children into the Boot,' Glyn stepped down into the room. 'But your idea is better, Edward. It would be impossible to keep track of every customer drifting around the bars or intent on creeping upstairs when Betty and her father's backs are turned.'

'How would you like to move in here for a week or two, Alf, and look after Mrs Parry and the children?' Edward asked. 'We'll make up a bed on the floor.'

'But the pit…'

'Can manage without you for a short while. I'll keep your job open and pay you a pound a week bonus while you're here. How much did you take home last week?'

'One pound six shillings and three pence, sir.'

'I'll guarantee you two pounds six shillings and three pence a week while you're here. What do you say?'

'Yes please, sir. Provided you keep my job open.'

'You have my word on it, Alf.' Edward extended his hand to shake on the deal.

'I'll fetch my things, sir.'

'The Paskeys still in The Chandlers?'

'They were when I left, sir,' Alf confirmed.

'Drunk?'

'Too drunk to think straight or do anything in a hurry, sir,' Alf concurred.

Edward turned to Peter. 'Given the threats the Paskeys have made in public against Richard,

Mrs Parry and the children will be safer if we get the boy out of here. Can we move him into your house, Peter? You've enough spare rooms.'

'Sarah and I will look after the boy to the best of our ability but you can't move Richard yet, Edward.'

'You'd rather see the boy dead?'

'No but...'

'There are no "buts". If we get Richard out of this house now, right away, chances are the Paskeys won't find out where we've taken him. Alf, go up to Tom at the farm and tell him to bring his cart down. Pick up your things from your lodgings on the way. If we shift Richard at this time of night while the Paskeys are drunk and most of the town asleep or on shift no one will be any the wiser. Tom won't open his mouth.'

'Richard's at a critical stage.' Peter opened his bag.

'You'd rather the Paskeys finished what they started and killed the boy?'

Peter looked down at Anna lying on the rug before glancing up at the boys on the shelf. 'You really think Alf will be able to protect Richard's family by himself?'

'Not alone, but with the neighbours, long enough to get word to me or the constables, yes. Any sign of trouble or the Paskeys, don't be a hero, Alf, send for me and the police. But I doubt the Paskeys will bother the family once they realize Richard isn't here. It's Richard Deputy Perkins is paying them to kill.'

'When Richard recovers? What then?' Peter crouched over the boy.

'You still looking for colliers to take to Russia, Glyn?' Edward asked.

'We haven't recruited enough to sink and work the pits to supply coal to all the furnaces John Hughes intends to build.' Glyn followed his brother's train of thought. 'Is Richard a good collier?'

'He has the makings of the best. Not only good at digging out coal, but shoring too. I was thinking of promoting him to trainee repairman. I've lost two this year to lung disease.'

'If he's going to Russia, he'll have to be fit to travel next week. He won't be up to it,' Peter declared.

'Train from here to Cardiff, then on to the docks, ship out of Southampton through the Mediterranean. Summer voyage with sea air and wholesome food is just what the boy needs, and he'll have you and Sarah to nurse him back to health. His own private physician and nurse.'

'Given his present state I won't predict a recovery. Aren't you forgetting his mother, sister, and brothers,' Peter reminded. 'He won't want to leave them.'

'He will when he finds out the alternative is another pasting from the Paskeys. Hasn't John Hughes offered to pay half his workers' wages to their families back here?' Edward asked.

'He has,' Glyn confirmed.

'Richard's mother will miss him but she won't be worse off financially, not when you take the cost of his clothes and food into account,' Edward said.

'I'll draw up a contract for him tomorrow.'

'I hope he lives long enough to sign it, Glyn.' Peter checked Richard's pulse, yet again.

Alf opened the door. 'I'll get Tom Farmer and his cart.'

'For all the good I'm doing here, I'll go with you. Mountain air has to be fresher than the fug in that court. I'll tell Betty to wait until I come back. I don't want her making her way to the Boot alone in the dark at this time in the morning.'

'I'll walk you to the arch.' Edward followed Alf.

They could hear cats yowling but the yard was quiet and in darkness apart from the shadowy blue light of the gas lamp that shone through from John Street.

'Be as quick as you can.' Edward didn't know why he'd asked. Alf wasn't likely to dawdle, not after he'd taken the trouble to inform them of the Paskeys' threats.

'Be back before you know it, sir.'

'You and Peter will be all right?' Glyn checked with Edward.

'As all right as we've been for the last four hours with you sleeping. How's Mary?'

'No change.'

'I'll tell Peter.' Edward watched his brother and Alf walk away before descending into the damp basement. Peter was still crouched beside Richard.

'He's...'

'The same.' Peter stretched. 'I need to feel the wind on my face if I'm going to keep my eyes open.'

Edward returned to the court with Peter. He pulled the door behind them but didn't latch it. The atmosphere was thick with smoke.

Peter leaned against the wall. 'It will be as good to get away from here as it was to leave London. I can't wait to look up at a night sky and see stars.'

'You won't see them for long after John Hughes has built his works. The furnaces will smoke the same in Russia as they do here.'

'Only after they've been commissioned. We've at least a year, maybe two, of clear skies to look forward to.' He patted his pockets. 'I wish I'd brought my cigarettes.'

'I have a couple of cigars.' Edward took two from his top pocket. He handed Peter one and struck a Lucifer. 'No second thoughts about dragging Sarah off to follow Glyn and John Hughes in this crazy Russian enterprise?'

'John Hughes knows what he's doing. He's going to build more than an ironworks in Russia. Mark my words, he'll...'

'Start a revolution?'

'A non-violent one.'

'With liberty, fraternity, and equality for all. The cry of the French Revolution and look what happened there. Despite the high ideals and fine speeches it culminated in a bloodbath, and not just for the aristocrats. It's a dream, Peter, and dreams have a habit of ending in tragedy. You've not long qualified. You and Sarah have the world at your feet. You could make a fine life for yourselves here.'

'In Merthyr?' Peter looked around the grim dank court. 'It's even more crowded and unsanitary than the East End slums.'

'Not in Merthyr. I'm tied here by my position,

but you could go anywhere. Back to London – Cardiff – anywhere. This country is full of beautiful towns and villages.'

'Not brand new ones, with a history waiting to be written. This is a strange time to start arguing with me about Russia again when Glyn's returned to fetch Betty so we can all travel together.'

'I suppose it is.' Edward was finding it difficult to resign himself to losing both his brothers and sister-in-laws to John Hughes's Russian enterprise. 'If it doesn't work out, if you find yourselves unhappy...'

'Ships sail both ways, and trains make return journeys. John Hughes would offer you a contract tomorrow if you asked him, and for better pay than you're getting here. Have you thought of joining us?'

'I have.'

'Really?'

'Judith wouldn't countenance the idea of leaving her mother, brothers, sisters, and their families. She idolises her nieces.'

'If Judith changed her mind?'

'She won't. You and Glyn have adventurous wives. I don't.' It was the closest Peter had heard Edward come to criticizing his wife.

'Time I returned to my patients.' Peter walked down to Maggie's house. He lifted the latch.

Tim was sleeping on the shelf, his nine boys in a separate bed alongside his. Maggie was on a wooden stool, slumped against the wall snoring.

Betty was holding Mary's hand. She gazed up at Peter. 'I knocked the wall.'

'I didn't hear. I was outside.' He looked down

at Mary. Her face was grey, bloodless. Her eyes slightly open. He took Mary's hand from Betty. Felt for her pulse. Kneeled and moved his fingers from Mary's wrist to her neck. He turned to the open door. Edward was watching him.

'You did all you could for her.' Edward's voice was hoarse with supressed grief.

'It wasn't enough. If you can still pray, Edward, pray I don't lose the boy too.'

Chapter Seven

Oakleigh, Dr Edwards' rented house
High Street, Merthyr, June 1870

Richard lay, bruised and battered, in the bed in Peter and Sarah Edwards' spare room. Four days after his beating, he was still too weak to stand unaided. He was also devastated by Dr Edwards' refusal to allow him to attend his mother's funeral. Peter had warned that although he was recovering, his injuries were so severe that even a slight infection could result in a major setback and possibly permanent, crippling damage.

It was the threat of damage that would prevent him from working that silenced him. With his mother dead, he knew if he were to keep his family together he had to remain healthy and earn enough to support his younger brothers and sister.

The curtains had been drawn against the afternoon light. Dr Edwards didn't open them when he ushered Glyn and Edward in before they had to leave for St Tydfil's cemetery. After discussions with Richard and Anna, Edward had arranged for Mary to be buried beside her first husband, Tom, and her children by Richard Parry in the grave she'd bought with the proceeds of Tom's life insurance. Money had been so short when Richard had been killed, he'd been interred in a pauper's grave in Pontypridd. A common grave was a dismal prospect, and one Edward wouldn't countenance for Mary's final resting place.

Weak, resenting his dependence on the doctor and his wife for his every need, weary of the monotony of convalescence, Richard welcomed the three brothers.

He listened absently to Glyn's account of the New Russia Company and the venture in the Ukraine, and looked at the photographs Glyn passed around without evincing the slightest interest, because he couldn't see how the enterprise was relevant to him. When Sarah brought in a bottle of laudanum, he used the interruption to ask if anyone had seen or heard anything of Alice Perkins. Sarah glanced at Peter before answering.

'No one's seen Alice, her mother, or sister since last Sunday. Her father works, but from I've heard he hasn't said a word about his family.' Sarah set the bottle on the bedside cabinet. 'I'll plump the pillows if you help Richard up, Peter.'

Peter eased Richard forward while Sarah rearranged the bed.

Richard grimaced when Peter lowered him back. 'Could you get a letter to Alice please, Mrs Edwards?'

'No, she couldn't.' Edward was unequivocal. 'If we'd left you at home, boy, you'd be in a coffin alongside your mother, and if the Paskeys discover your whereabouts it won't be just you who'll get hurt. Should they find out you're in this house, none of our lives will be worth living. That goes for Sarah as well as my brothers.'

'I'm sorry. I hadn't thought about it. I've caused all of you a great deal of trouble as well as killing my mother.'

'You can't blame yourself for your mother's death, Richard,' Peter insisted. 'She fainted and hit her head. It was an accident. It could have happened at any time.'

'But it happened after she saw me unconscious.'

'Before she saw you,' Peter contradicted. 'Everyone who was in the court when the Farmers brought you home was clear on that point.'

For the first time Richard realized what a risk Dr Edwards and his brothers had taken in caring for him. 'My sister and brothers...'

'Are fine,' Edward reassured. 'Alf Mahoney hasn't left them since we moved you here and the neighbours are looking out for them as well. They've promised to send word if the Paskeys go anywhere near the court.'

'You're lucky to be alive, Richard.' Sarah counted off half a dozen drops of laudanum and stirred them into a glass of water.

Richard's hand shook but he took the glass and drained the contents.

'Put all thoughts of Alice Perkins from your mind, Richard,' Edward advised. 'Not just now – for ever. For her sake as well as yours.'

Richard had to ask. 'Do you think her father has hurt her?'

'No, because he *is* her father. But I wouldn't like to speculate as to what he'd do to you if he caught the two of you together again.' Sarah took the glass.

'Because he hates the thought of her marrying a common collier?' There was self-pity in Richard's voice.

'No, because both of you are too young to think about marriage.' Sarah left the room.

Edward, Glyn, and Peter had discussed the Parry family and made decisions about the children's future that seemed eminently sensible – to them. But they still had to put them to Richard.

Glyn opened the discussion. 'My wife's arranged for your brothers and sister to move into the Boot Inn after your mother's funeral. You won't have to worry about paying rent, Anna will be living where she's working and other colliers are lodging there so the boys will have company when they walk back and fore to work. They'll live "all found", so Anna won't have to buy food, make meals, or do the laundry as it's all sent out. Even the lodgers.'

'But they'll return to our house when I'm fit? I know it won't be easy without my mother and the money she made from taking in washing but we'll manage with what the boys and I make in the mine and Anna brings in. Anna and I can take care of the boys. We've been doing it for years. Mam hasn't been well since Dad died. It was Anna and me who kept the house going. Not that Mam didn't do her best for us,' Richard added loyally. 'We couldn't have asked for a better mother.'

'We know that, boy, but given this trouble with the Paskeys it's best you don't return to the court.'

'What do you mean, Mr Edwards?' Richard challenged.

Glyn decided the best way to suggest Richard join Mr Hughes's Russian expedition was straight out. 'My brother tells me you have the makings of a fine collier and repairman, Richard. How would you like to come with me, my wife, Dr and Mrs Edwards and travel to Russia with Mr Hughes to help set up his new enterprise?'

'Me? Go to Russia? Go here!' Richard picked up Glyn's photographs and stared at the one of Alexei Beletsky kissing a Cossack girl. The laudanum was beginning to take effect and he wasn't sure he'd heard Glyn correctly.

'You, boy. You have to admit the girls there are as pretty as the ones here.' Reluctant as he was to see his brothers leave, Edward realised Glyn had offered Richard a lifeline. 'You've made a powerful enemy in Deputy Perkins.'

'But my sister and brothers ... they'll never keep the house on without me and I won't let them go into the workhouse.'

'No one is going into the workhouse,' Edward promised.

'Mr Hughes has an agreement with his Welsh workers,' Glyn interposed. 'Up to half their wages can be paid direct to their families in Wales. Provided you agree, he will arrange for a share of your wages to go to your sister.'

'Half my wages won't be enough to pay for Anna and the boys to live in the Boot or pay the rent on the house without Mam's washing money.'

'We've worked out the expenses. Your brothers and sister will be able to live permanently in the Boot. Mrs Edwards won't be there, as she's going to Russia with me, but her father's taking on a housekeeper. Anna's job at the Inn is safe. In fact, from what my wife tells me, they couldn't manage in the kitchen without her. As she'll be working full time in future her wages will double. The boys' and Anna's wages taken together will cover their board, lodge, and washing but there won't be anything left. Their clothes and other expenses will have to be funded by you.'

'But I won't be there to look after them.'

'I'll be around and Mrs Edwards' father will keep an eye on them.' Edward added his persuasive voice to Glyn's. 'Russia's the only option open to you, boy. If you stay here the Paskeys will kill you – and if you're living with your brothers and sister, probably harm them as well.'

'I'd be happy to give Anna and the boys half my wages, but will I be left with enough to live on?'

'More than enough,' Glyn said. 'Because you'll be lodging with me and Dr and Mrs Edwards. All Mr Hughes's Welsh workers are guaranteed a minimum of eighty roubles a month, which is about £10.'

'Ten pounds...'

'Five after your sister's been paid,' Glyn qualified. 'Which will go a long way as Anna won't have the expense of feeding you, or buying your clothes. Your board and lodge will amount to no more than two pounds, or at the most two pounds ten shillings a month, so you could send your sister even more money if you wanted to.'

'I'd work as a fully-fledged collier?' Richard's eyes shone as he saw the possibilities.

'To begin with. But a new pit brings greater opportunity.' Glyn recognised Richard's enthusiasm and pressed his advantage. 'As soon as the pits are operational, Mr Hughes will need repairmen, foremen, managers, and engineers. You'll be on site and have received on-the-job training so you'll be first in line for promotion.'

'A repairman or foreman...'

'Aim as high as you like, Richard, there'll be nothing to hold you back in Russia except the limit of your ambition. You'll be part of a new venture in a country untouched by modern progress.' Happy to be talking about his favourite subject there was no stopping Glyn. He handed Richard copies of the landscape photographs he'd taken. 'These don't do the country justice. Russia's vast. When you stand on the plain where the furnaces will be built, all you can see in every direction is sky, and beneath it a thin purple line of horizon. The spot Mr Hughes has chosen has few trees and scrub grass. Perhaps the best way of putting it is that it's an almost empty country; empty of people, and empty of buildings, apart from a few isolated villages of wooden houses and the odd grand mansion. A land that's like a book of blank pages waiting to be written on. Since I've returned here I can't help thinking that Wales seems to be over-full of people, especially Merthyr.'

'I'll agree with you there,' Peter chimed in. 'Most of the slum houses are so crowded I wonder where everyone sleeps at night.'

Glyn took his pipe from his pocket but made no move to fill it. 'Mr Hughes commissioned geological surveys for the area. There's coal there, good anthracite and coking coal which is what's needed for smelting iron, and I won't just be managing the New Russia Company's coal mines. I've raised enough money to sink a pit of my own and Mr Hughes has agreed to take every ton I produce. You're just the sort of boy I want working for me. A few years from now you could be managing a coal face and shortly after that, who knows? A pit perhaps.'

'A manager!'

'If you're prepared to work, I don't see why not. Indications suggest there are huge seams underground. Wider, longer, and more accessible than any in Merthyr. They'll make for an easier day's work for all the colliers in the Edwards Brothers' pit.'

'"Edwards Brothers"?' Edward raised his eyebrows.

'Sarah and I have agreed to fund Glyn and Betty's living expenses in exchange for shares in the colliery,' Peter explained.

'Two women in the same house, in the same kitchen! They'll be at each other's throats and have you and Peter wanting to kill one another inside a week.'

'As matron of the hospital Sarah will be too busy helping to set up the medical facilities to interfere in Betty's domestic arrangements,' Glyn pointed out.

'Don't know what the world's coming to.

Married women shouldn't be working but staying at home caring for their husbands.'

'In Hughesovka it's going to be all hands to the coal face, both literally and metaphorically for the first few years,' Glyn predicted. 'It'll be different when everything's established but until it is, everyone, women as well as men will have to do their bit.'

Edward couldn't resist a final doom-laden pronouncement. 'There'll be a lot of empty pockets if Mr Hughes fails.'

'John Hughes won't fail himself or those who've put their trust in him,' Glyn countered. 'This will be the making of you, Richard, and the making of all our fortunes. Ten years from now you'll be thanking the Paskey boys for the pasting.'

'I doubt, I'll ever do that, Mr Edwards, sir,' Richard grimaced in pain.

'Then you'll go to Russia with my brothers, boy?' Edward asked.

'Seems I haven't much choice, Mr Edwards, but from what Mr Edwards,' he nodded to Glyn, 'says, this could be the chance of a lifetime.'

'It could at that, boy.'

'If I go...'

'When you go,' Glyn corrected.

'Will you really look after Anna, Morgan, and Owen for me, Mr Edwards?'

'I promise, boy.' Edward opened his watch. 'We'll talk again later. It's time we were going, Glyn?'

'I'm coming with you.' Peter picked up his jacket.

Glyn lowered his voice after they'd left the room.

'Aren't you taking a risk in leaving Sarah and the boy alone in the house?'

'No one knows the boy is here other than Alf, Tom Farmer, and our family.' Peter straightened his black tie. 'The servants are downstairs, it's broad daylight, and the police station is a few minutes away.'

'It would be suspicious if Peter wasn't at the funeral after attending Mary and issuing her death certificate.' Edward glanced back through the door at Richard. 'Concentrate on getting better, boy. In a few days you'll be on a train going to Russia.'

'Can I see my sister and brothers before I go, Mr Edwards?'

'I'll bring them back with me this evening if you feel up to talking to them.'

'I'd like that, sir.' Richard's voice dropped to a whisper. He closed his eyes but it was Alice he was thinking about, not Anna.

If he gave his sister a note she should be able to find some way of smuggling it to Alice. Once he was in Russia, working and earning, he'd start saving. If the prospects were as good as Glyn Edwards promised he'd soon be in a position to send Alice tickets to join him.

Basement house in a court off John Street
Georgetown, Merthyr, June 1870

'It's time, Anna.' Edward Edwards leaned over her as she kneeled on the floor, hands clasped on the edge of her mother's coffin. He slipped his arm around her shoulders.

Anna kissed Mary's cold grey forehead for the last time and stroked her hair. 'I don't understand why I can't go to the cemetery, Mr Edwards. She was my mother. Morgan and Owen are only children.'

'They're boys, Anna. Women don't go to funerals.' Edward drew Anna away to give Tim room to screw down the coffin lid. Betty moved behind him, holding a wreath of white marguerites she and the other women had helped Anna make.

'Here, Anna, you're the one who has to arrange this.' Edward took the wreath and handed it to the girl.

Anna waited until Tim finished fastening the lid before setting the wreath on the pinewood box. She watched Mr Edwards, his brothers, Tim Two Suits; Iestyn Swine, and Dai Twp manhandle her mother's coffin out of the narrow door and up the steps. Morgan and Owen walked behind it with Alf who hadn't left them – or her – since the morning after her mother's death.

When the last of the men climbed the steps Anna followed. The mourners who'd crowded into the court and spilled out on to John Street stood silently, caps and hats in hand, waiting for the cortège to pass so they could walk behind.

Anna watched the six bearers lift her mother's coffin on to their shoulders. At Edward Edwards' command they marched in step through the arch and out of view.

Anna ran behind so she could watch the cortege's progress. She pictured her mother inside the dark interior of the coffin; tried to absorb that she would never, ever, see her in life again.

An old woman laid a hand on her shoulder. 'They've gone, love,' she said when the procession turned a corner. 'Time you went home.'

Anna didn't recognise the woman. She retraced her steps. The thought came to mind that she had so much to tell her mother about the events of the last few days before the realisation hit anew. Fighting tears she leaned against the wall.

Betty Edwards found her. 'We need you to see to the food for the wake, Anna.'

Anna straightened her back. 'Sorry...'

'Nothing to say sorry for, love. Come inside and help us uncover the plates. People have brought enough food to feed an army. You can take comfort that your mother was well thought of. Some old neighbours even travelled up from Treforest on the train, finding their fare and losing a day's wages just so they could pay their respects.'

'We need more plates and cups, Maggie. Can you bring what you've got from your house?' Jenny shouted as Betty ushered Anna down the steps.

'I've never seen such a crowd for a funeral,' Maggie said. 'I'm betting most will come back for a cuppa and a bite to eat. Particularly the ones from Treforest. We need to be prepared.'

The room was crowded. Every female who lived in the court was there and a few more besides. Anna felt hemmed in and realised she hadn't been alone for more than a few minutes since Mr Edwards had woken her to tell her that her mother had died and he was moving Richard out of the house – and out of harm and the Paskeys' way.

'You can arrange the sandwiches, Anna.'

'No, Auntie Betty. Please, it's boiling hot in here. I'll fill the water buckets.' She tried to push past.

'No, you don't, young lady, you're shocked and upset. You need to sit quietly with us, and drink a nice cup of hot sweet tea.' Jenny picked up a stool and dropped it in front of Anna.

'Please, I need air.' Anna struggled to the door and reached for the buckets.

'Anna...'

'What?' Anna glared at Maggie.

An embarrassed silence fell over the room.

'We – Jenny, all of us, we only want to help,' Maggie explained. 'When something like this happens we know nothing and no one can take away the pain but we feel we have to try. We do what we think is best. Sometimes, like now, we get it wrong and only make it worse.'

Ashamed of her outburst, Anna apologised. 'I'm sorry. None of you have made me feel worse, Auntie Maggie. It's just that...' choked she couldn't say another word.

'Get some fresh air, Anna. Take as long as you like,' Betty advised. 'We'll manage until you come back.'

Anna walked up the steps and stood in the deserted court.

All the children except the smallest had trailed behind the cortège in the hope of seeing something of the mysterious rituals of death adults tried to hide from those 'too young to understand'.

Anna knew little about funerals but even she'd realised the minister's suggestion that the ceremony begin so late in the day was unusual. He'd argued the timing was necessary because it meant friends could travel up from Pontypridd to join those who'd finished their day shifts. Mr Edwards reminded him that the Paskeys would have also finished their shifts and might be tempted to join the cortège to cause trouble. The minister won his point after reminding Mr Edwards the Parrys were popular and half the men in Merthyr would want to pay their respects to Tom Edwards' and Richard Parry's widow. He'd insisted that not even the Paskeys would be foolish enough to start anything in front of so many witnesses. Especially, as every decent person in the town had been horrified by their treatment of Richard.

Anna hoped the minister was right. Because after seeing what the Paskeys had done to Richard she never wanted them near any of her brothers again. She shivered and not from cold. Black smuts fell thickly, carried by the smog belching out of the ironworks. Her mother had christened the flakes 'the devil's snow' when she was in one of her dark moods.

Ignoring a peculiar, skin-crawling feeling of apprehension, she carried the buckets to the pump. She placed a bucket beneath it but instead of pumping, leaned against the iron stand and looked up at the overcast sky. Rain began to fall; a light, misty drizzle that coated the court with a film of damp, sealing in the pollution, and sliming the yard and the walls and roofs of the houses.

She closed her eyes and pictured her mother as she'd been in life, her thin face pinched by sadness and hunger as she sat, shoulders hunched on the step outside their home, nursing a cup of tea. She wished she could remember her mother smiling but she hadn't seen her happy since the day her father's workmates had carried his body through the door of their cottage in Treforest. Sometimes it seemed as though the sun had stopped shining that day. Had any of her family been truly happy since?

When her mother had moved them to Merthyr, Richard confided he'd felt they were leaving the green hills of Treforest for a black hole. That had been bad enough. But when cholera had raged through the town, taking her two sisters and three of her brothers...

She wrapped her arms tightly around herself, digging her nails into her shoulders, longing for Richard's presence with a pain that was almost physical. She wanted to see her brother, for him to put his arms around her and tell her they'd stay together out of the workhouse and be able to look after Owen and Morgan. But she couldn't blot an image of Richard as he'd been when she'd last seen him. Battered unconscious, his face torn and bruised, his hair plastered with clotted blood. Would he ever be strong enough to work or care for them again?

She opened her eyes. The rain was falling thicker and faster. Her face and hair were wet. She had a sudden very real image of her mother waiting at the door with a towel to dry her. So real she turned to her house. Tears started in her eyes, yet again. A heavy lump rose in her chest and suffocated her. Mary Parry was no more. She would never again sit out on the step, never walk to the pump, never reprimand the boys, or look for her as she came home from the pub...

She took a handkerchief from her pocket.

It had been her mother's. A treasured gift trimmed with real lace her father had bought her mother before they'd married. She opened it and touched the lock of faded, grey-brown hair she'd secreted in its folds before returning it to her pocket.

She could almost hear her mother's voice sharp with exhaustion. 'Pull yourself together, Anna, for your brothers' sake.'

She wiped her tears in the sleeve of the scratchy crepe mourning frock that had been her mother's. It was too long for her and the hem trailed, dragging across the dirt in the yard. She caught at the skirt, pinched the cloth between her fingers, lifted it out of the muddy water around the pipe, and began pumping.

When she changed the full bucket for the empty one, she saw the head of a single white daisy beneath the archway. She had the strangest feeling it was a last and final gift from her mother. She abandoned the buckets and ran towards it. As her fingers closed over it, a shadow moved in from John Street. A hand clamped across her mouth.

Her head was wrenched back. She stared up into the pockmarked, salivating face of Ianto Paskey.

'Your brother owes us and he hasn't paid his debt, Missy. As we can't get to him, we'll collect it from you.'

Chapter Eight

Oakleigh, Dr Edwards' rented house
High Street, Merthyr, June 1870

Richard woke when someone tapped his bedroom door. 'Come in,' he croaked

'I thought you might like company. But I see I've disturbed you. I'll go.'

'Please don't, Mrs Edwards.' Richard moved restlessly in the bed. 'I'm spending so much time sleeping in the day I'm not sleeping at night.'

'If you're lying awake, Peter can give you a draught. Every doctor and nurse knows the best medicine is unbroken sleep.'

'Thank you. You and the doctor are very kind. All the Mr Edwardses have done so much for my family. Taking care of Anna and my brothers as well as me and arranging my mother's funeral. I don't know how I can ever repay you.'

'Edward, Glyn, and Peter saw to everything for your mother's sake. If their brother Tom hadn't been killed a few weeks after he'd married her, you, your brothers, and Anna would be their nephews and niece. As for Peter and me, we've enjoyed having our personal patient to practise on. You helped us keep our hand in while our travel arrangements are being finalised.' She straightened the bed cover. 'I'm sorry,' she apologised when Richard gritted his teeth. 'It's the nurse in me. I can't get used to caring for a patient without Matron checking my bed making.'

'What's the time, Mrs Edwards?'

'The clock's just struck six. The funeral service will begin any minute.' She opened the curtains wide enough for him to see the sun hanging low over the rooftops across the road.

'I can't believe Mam's dead.'

'It won't be easy for you to come to terms with her loss, as you're in no condition to attend her funeral. But your mother would have been more concerned that you conserve your strength than go to the ceremony. Do you want to pass urine or open your bowels?'

Richard blushed.

'Both are perfectly natural functions, Richard.'

'I didn't mind you doing everything for me when I was helpless, but I'm getting stronger.'

'Not strong enough to look after yourself quite yet. But as you're coming to Russia with us we should get you out of bed tomorrow, if only for an hour.' She folded back the bedclothes, handed him a glass urine bottle, and left him in privacy.

She returned five minutes later, disposed of the bottle, and brought him a bowl of warm water, soap, and a towel so he could wash his hands. She frowned when she saw him bring his knees up in pain.

'The bruise in your groin?'

He nodded.

'I hoped it would heal without rupturing. The last thing we want is an open wound that will attract infection. Do you mind if I take a look?'

He was grateful for her tact in asking, but he

was in too much pain to refuse.

She untied the string on his pyjama trousers, took a pad of clean gauze, and pressed the ugly black and purple wound in the crease between his thigh and abdomen.

Richard was grateful for Sarah's gentle touch but to his mortification, on this occasion, he found it too gentle. The more he tried to divert his thoughts from Sarah the larger and harder his erection.

'This will hurt.' Sarah made a fist and punched his penis at the base.

It had the desired effect.

'I'm sorry you had to do that, Mrs Edwards.'

'No need to apologise.' She dressed the wound and retied his pyjamas. 'I'll clear this bowl and dressings and bring you a snack.'

Sarah returned five minutes later with a tray that held a plate of biscuits and two glasses of lemonade. 'You've recovered from my poking and prodding?' She pulled a chair up to the bed.

'Yes.'

'Liar, I see pain lines at the corners of your mouth.' She handed him a glass.

He looked past her to the window.

'Dr Edwards was right when he said your mother's death wasn't your fault, Richard. You do believe him, don't you?'

'If I hadn't gone up the mountain to meet Alice Perkins, her father wouldn't have been angry with me, and none of this would have happened.'

'Your mother fainted and hit her head. It could have happened any time.'

'It happened because she was told I was hurt.'

'Or for one of any number of reasons, Richard. Had she fainted before?'

He didn't give her a direct answer. 'She would never eat enough. Always tried to keep most of our food for my brothers, me, and Anna because she thought we needed it more than her.'

'She was right, Richard, growing children do need more food than adults. She'd be horrified at the thought of you feeling guilty about the way she died. If you want to honour your mother and her life, the best thing you can do is to live as she would have wanted you to, in an honourable way. What would she have thought of you going to Russia with Mr Hughes's expedition?' Sarah deliberately moved the conversation on.

'I think she would have been pleased. None of us thought of leaving Merthyr after we came here but only because we didn't have enough money to buy a train ticket to go as far as Pontypridd, let alone leave the country.'

'Mr Hughes will be paying the travelling expenses of everyone who's going with him.'

'I hoped he would from what Mr Edwards said. It's not just travelling to a whole other country, it's the idea of helping build a new works and town. I never thought I'd be part of anything like that. The way Mr Edwards talked, it seems so exciting. Starting a new life and a new job where I'll be able to work my way up. Perhaps become a foreman and in time even a manager.'

'It is exciting, Richard. That's why the doctor and I decided to join Mr Hughes. We want to be part of his dream.'

'Do you know him?'

'Peter and I met Mr Hughes in London when he interviewed Peter for the post of medical advisor to his company. He's a remarkable man who cares for his employees and not only by paying decent wages. He organises lectures and concerts for the workers in his shipyard in London. Not many men intent on constructing a new ironworks in a foreign country would think about medical facilities. Mr Hughes is building a twelve-bed hospital there that Peter will oversee and I will manage as matron. For us it's the chance of a lifetime. Neither the doctor nor I expected we'd ever be in charge of our own medical facility.'

'Will you stay there – in Russia?'

'We've no intention of travelling all that way to return within a year or two. The journey will take weeks, possibly months.'

'Months?' Richard echoed.

'How were you at geography at school?'

'Not as good as I was at mathematics and science.'

'I'll get the atlas. Then you can see for yourself how far we have to go. Right across the Mediterranean, Black Sea, and the Sea of Azov. We'll dock in Taganrog. Glyn said the new works are being built about sixty-five miles as the crow flies inland from the port.'

'Taganrog,' Richard repeated.

'You've heard of it?'

He shook his head. 'It sounds as though it should be in a country full of jungles, lions, and elephants.'

'There won't be any jungles or lions. Although Glyn said there are wolves, bears, boar, deer, and elk as well as the foxes and badgers we have here. There'll also be freezing cold snowy winters, wet springs, and hot dry summers. As soon as you get out of bed we'll have you measured by the tailor and order you a new winter wardrobe.'

'I've no money for clothes, Mrs Edwards.'

'Mr Hughes will be taking a stock for all his workers to purchase when needed. I'll make sure some are in your size.' She left her chair. 'I'll get that atlas.'

After Sarah walked out Richard realised she'd stayed with him to stop him from dwelling on the service in St Tydfil's cemetery. He loved Alice desperately but he wasn't blind to her faults. He doubted she'd have taken the time to distract or comfort someone in mourning. From her reaction to the few 'liberties' he'd dared take, he suspected she'd have disposed of his untimely erection in a far more brutal manner.

He suppressed the disloyal thought. Mrs Edwards was a nurse and the profession demanded kindness. Alice was years younger and, through no fault of her own, naïve and barely educated. She had no interest in reading, and couldn't understand why he borrowed so many books from Mr Edwards. But he was confident that, given time, he'd change Alice. She'd be different when he took her away from her father's house and introduced her to a life outside of gowns, fashion, and trivia. She'd become more considerate and caring, just like Mrs Edwards. He was certain of it.

Court off John Street Georgetown, Merthyr, June 1870

Anna kicked and lashed out. She tried to scream but Ianto split the side of her lips by forcing his fist further into her mouth, effectively gagging her. The more she struggled, the tighter Ianto's right arm banded around her, pressing her arms painfully against her ribcage. Ensnared, immobilised, it took all her strength to draw breath.

Ianto must have sensed the fight ebbing from her. He relaxed his hold slightly. She made a supreme effort, clamped her jaw down, and sank her teeth into the hand Ianto had rammed into her mouth.

He reacted by jamming his fist even further down her throat. Her teeth cracked. She retched. The world around her darkened, blotting out the sky.

Ianto lifted her off her feet. She heard subdued laughter and sensed another presence. Someone grabbed her ankles, lifting her horizontally. She looked up, saw the bricks of the archway, and knew she was being carried back into the court.

She tried to cry out, but the only sound she managed was muffled. She was aware of being carried downwards. The mixed aromas of kippers, smoke, tobacco, and rotting food filled the air. Pigswill?

Was she in Iestyn and Jenny Swine's house?

She picked up whispered snatches of conversation.

'The women are all in the Parrys'...'

'...no one will come...'

'...keep her quiet...'

'...not a sound...'

Ianto moved his fist from her mouth. She gasped. Before she had time to scream he clamped his fingers over her lips and nose, preventing her from drawing a second breath. Her legs swung free. He clasped her tightly, the back of her head to his chest. He was holding her so close, his belt buckle dug painfully into the base of her spine.

Her eyes widened in terror when Mervyn Paskey moved in front of both of them. His tongue darted from his mouth like a lizard's, moistening his lips. He leered. Saliva dribbled down his chin as he grabbed her breast, and squeezed it through the bodice of black crepe.

She kicked, hammering her heels into the front of Ianto's shins.

'Bitch!' Ianto growled.

Mervyn pulled a steel blade from his boot. He inserted the point in the high necked collar of her dress and sliced downwards.

Anna's mouth filled with the iron taste of blood as she bit down again with every ounce of strength.

'Cow!'

A deafening ringing resounded in her ears. Her head snapped back. She heard her bones crack.

The world went black.

Parrys' House, court off John Street
Georgetown, Merthyr, June 1870

'Anna's been gone a while, Betty, shouldn't someone check she's all right?' Jenny asked.

Betty carried on spreading margarine on the scones Jenny had baked for the wake. 'The poor girl hasn't had a minute to herself since Mary died.'

'I'll go along with that,' Maggie said. 'What, between finishing off the washing Mary had taken in and looking after the boys. Alf Mahoney wasn't much help. I understand why Mr Edwards moved him in with the Parrys,' she added, remembering Edward Edwards was Betty's brother-in-law. 'The children needed someone around in case the Paskeys came looking for Richard but, when all's said and done, Alf's a man. We all know how useless they are inside the house. Only good for filling their faces and putting their feet up on chairs. When I spoke to Anna this morning she was that worried about Richard and not being able to see him...'

'I think it's worth checking on her,' Jenny interrupted. 'She looked peaky when she went out. I'll go if you don't want to, Betty.'

'Give her a few more minutes,' Betty pleaded.

'I'll see to her. If she doesn't want company I'll leave her be.'

Maggie knew if Jenny went, she'd hover around Anna whether the girl wanted her to or not. She set down the knife she'd been using to cut slices of bara brith, wiped her hands on her overall, squeezed past the women gossiping in the doorway, and walked up the steps.

She stood at the top. The court was empty. The only noise the conversation coming from the house behind her. She saw the buckets under the pump, looked to the archway and called, 'Anna?' When there was no reply she shouted again. 'Anna?'

Despite the rain, the front doors of the houses were open, but she knew no one was home because all the men who weren't working were at the funeral and all the women in the Parrys.

She repeated, 'Anna?' and walked to the archway. The street outside was deserted. She walked few steps to the right and looked up and down. After shouting 'Anna' one final time as loudly as she could she headed back to the court.

She felt something beneath her boot. It was the head of one of the marguerites she'd helped weave into the wreath for Mary Parry's coffin. She picked it up. Beneath it was a fine muslin handkerchief. It had real lace trimming. She recognised it. Mary Parry had kept it in her pocket and referred to it as her most precious possession. The last time she'd seen it, Anna had folded a lock of her mother's hair into it. She opened it. The grey lock, tied with a tiny scrap of red ribbon, was inside.

Heart pounding, Maggie cried, 'Anna!' before picking up her skirts putting her head down and running. She stopped, suddenly realising that any one of the younger women would reach the cemetery and Edward Edwards before her, even allowing for the time it would take her to return to the Parrys.

She turned and charged back as quickly as she could, sensing that Anna's life depended on it.

St Tydfil's Cemetery
Merthyr, June 1870

Morgan and Owen had been accorded the position of chief mourners. Conscious of the gravity of the occasion they stood, side by side at the head of the grave, manfully holding back their tears. Edward, Peter, Glyn, and Alf had ranged themselves behind the boys, facing the sea of men who'd crowded into the cemetery. Hundreds stood, heads bowed, hats and caps removed. The only sound was the sonorous voice of the minister. He crouched down, picked up a clump of sodden clay, broke it one handed, and dropped the clods on the coffin. They fell with loud, dull thuds.

'Ashes to ashes ... dust to dust...'

Glyn recalled his childhood. Mary Parry – Williams, as she'd been then – was the stunning girl next door who'd been courted by every bachelor in their neighbourhood. He, along with his entire family, had been delighted when his eldest brother Tom, had won her. But Tom and Mary's joy had been short lived. Days after their marriage Tom was killed 'by the iron'. Nineteen years later he could still taste the raw grief and feel the effect of Tom's death on his parents and Mary. Within a year both his parents had joined Tom in the family grave. Mary married Richard Parry two years after she'd been widowed, but something had gone from her for ever. The brightness of her smile. A lilt in her voice. Her zest for life. Richard Parry had married a shadow of the girl she'd been.

He'd assumed Richard engineered the move to

Treforest in an attempt to help Mary forget Tom. He doubted Richard's ploy had been successful. Despite the death of both her parents within a year of her and Richard moving away, Mary had seized Edward's offer to help her and her children return to Merthyr after Richard had been killed.

He looked into Mary's grave. Mary had married Tom on her sixteenth birthday, which made her thirty-five. He was thirty-one and the last time he'd seen Mary, at Christmas, he'd commented to Betty that Mary looked fifty.

He wondered if there was a grave waiting for him in his near future. Would it be in Merthyr, or in Russia? The thought was sobering. There was so much more living he wanted to do. And there was Betty. It wasn't as though he had anything to complain about. His wife never openly nagged or grumbled at his absences. She was an excellent housekeeper, kept the Inn's public rooms as clean as possible given the human traffic that wandered in and out of the building. She supervised the cooking of fine meals, welcomed him every time he returned from his travels and said she was looking forward to spending more time with him in Russia. But he couldn't help feeling it wasn't what was said, more what was left unsaid between them.

Betty never mentioned the subject, but he sensed she regretted they hadn't had children. Would children have brought them closer together? Cemented whatever he'd felt when he'd proposed to her He must have felt something, but if he had, he had no recollection of strong emotion. Would they have children in the future...?

The minister finished his address with an 'Amen'.

The mourners shuffled into a queue and began to file past the grave, murmuring low words of comfort to the two boys as they shook their hands. Recognising most of them, Glyn nodded to the men but his thoughts remained fixed on John Hughes and the new life that awaited him. It was peculiar how he was having difficulty picturing Betty a part of it.

Court off John Street
Georgetown, Merthyr, June 1870

Maggie rushed into the court the same moment Ianto Paskey left Iestyn Swine's house. He was hitching up his trousers as he climbed the steps, fastening the belt, but his flies were open, exposing hairy dirty flesh and a blood-stained penis.

Maggie screamed. Within seconds a crowd of women charged out of the Parrys'.

Ianto held up his hands. 'Don't want no trouble...'

'What you doing in my house, Ianto Paskey!' Jenny ran straight for him. She stopped in her tracks when Mervyn appeared in her doorway.

'Where's Anna, Ianto?' Maggie drew strength from the women behind her.

Ianto edged back down the steps.

'What have you done to her?' Maggie joined Jenny.

'You filthy men get out of my house and stay out. Both of you,' Jenny added when Mervyn ducked back inside the doorway.

'Where's Anna?' Betty repeated. Concern for the girl, and guilt at stopping Jenny and Maggie from looking for her earlier, overrode caution. Betty pushed past Maggie and caught up with Ianto at the door. Ianto tried to close it, but too late. Maggie joined Betty and she'd had the foresight to jam her foot between the door and the stoop. Ianto was no match for Maggie, who had the weight of the women behind her.

Maggie, Betty, and May burst into the house. Ianto and Mervyn backed towards the wall and the ladder that led to the sleeping platform.

The men had nowhere to go and they were terrified. Because on the rag rug in front of the hearth lay the stripped, broken, bleeding body of Anna Parry.

'Bastards!' Maggie rushed at Ianto and pounded him with her fists.

'We didn't do nothing to her she didn't want done,' Ianto blustered.

Betty took off her shawl and covered Anna with it.

'She was asking for it...'

Those were the last words Ianto spoke before Maggie and the other women surrounded him and Mervyn.

'Get them out of my house,' Jenny demanded.

The women dragged the two men out of the door and up the steps.

Betty lifted Anna's head on to her lap. The girl opened her eyes and stared blindly at the ceiling. Betty wrapped her arms around her, crooning to her as if she were a baby. 'You'll be all right. I'll look after you, darling. You'll be all right...'

Jenny waited until the women had heaved the men up the steps into the court before looking along the shelves where Iestyn kept his tools.

She picked up his gelding irons.

St Tydfil's cemetery
Merthyr, June 1870

'Do you intend to stay there all night, Glyn?' Edward called from the gates where he was waiting with Peter, Alf, and the Parry boys.

Glyn looked up from the grave. The mourners had left. The cemetery had emptied and he'd been too deep in thought to notice.

'Head in Russia?' Edward suggested.

'Back in the Quarr.' Glyn referred to the area where he and his brothers had grown up alongside Mary and her family. He looked down at the coffin and remembered the pretty, smiling girl she'd been.

Edward joined him. 'Mary had a hard life.'

'Only after she'd been widowed. She had a happy childhood. I don't think she recovered from losing Tom. Then to lose another husband and five children,' Glyn paused. 'The ultimate tragedy has to be burying your children. I don't know how Mary found the strength to carry on.'

'She was happy the day she married Tom,' Edward murmured. 'I'm glad they had a little time together.'

'It wasn't long enough.'

'Did you ever look at Mary and Tom when they

were together? Really look at them? I'd exchange ten years of my married life for one hour of theirs.' Edward saw Glyn staring at him. 'I don't mean that I loved her...' Realising his brother had seen through his protest Edward stopped talking.

'But you did.' Glyn had made a statement.

Realising denial was futile, Edward confessed. 'Even before Tom realised he was in love with her.'

'You wanted to marry her?'

'We were the same age, sixteen. Too young for a boy to consider marriage. Not too young for a girl. By the time I realised the strength of my feelings, Tom had proposed and Mary accepted.'

'So that's why you helped her and the children after Richard Parry was killed.'

'I would have done more if she'd let me but I think she guessed how I felt about her. So did Judith. It didn't help that Judith and I haven't had children. Every time I look at Richard I think he could have been my nephew – or...'

'Your son,' Glyn suggested.

'I shouldn't have started this conversation. Forget I said anything.'

Glyn was shocked by the thought that Edward had anything more than fraternal feelings for Mary. But even as he assured Edward he would disregard what had been said, he knew neither of them would. The words had been spoken. They couldn't be forgotten.

They went to the gate. Owen and Morgan were looking back at their parents' grave, their eyes damp from more than rain.

Glyn jammed his hat on his head. A police

whistle shrilled. A constable raced up.

'Dr Edwards?'

'Yes?' Peter answered.

The constable placed his hands on his knees and kept his head low, gasping in air. 'People have been hurt in a fracas in a court off John Street. It's bad. The women told the sergeant you'd be here. He sent me to fetch you and check on the Parry boys.'

'Why check on the Parry boys?' Peter asked. When the constable wouldn't meet his eye he started running.

Chapter Nine

Court off John Street
Georgetown, Merthyr, June 1870

The constable hadn't exaggerated. The situation was bad. The yard in front of Iestyn Swine's house was awash with blood. A constable was attempting to clean it but as there was no drainage all he could do was sweep the congealing mess from one spot to another, staining even more of the cracked flagstones.

Two officers were attempting to interview the neighbours who'd gathered in front of the Parrys' house. The women were shrieking and gesticulating, the constables shouting their questions above the din. One was scribbling with a pencil in his notebook although Peter doubted he'd heard anything intelligible.

The sergeant saw Peter and Edward and went to meet them. The police doctor, Dr Evans, finished superintending the loading of a patient on a stretcher and joined them.

'What happened?' Edward asked. 'Is Anna Parry...?'

The sergeant drew Edward and Peter away from the crowd. Dr Evans caught sight of Morgan and Owen entering the court with Alf and Glyn.

'The young Parrys would be better off elsewhere.'

'Glyn, Alf, take Morgan and Owen to the Boot, we'll meet you there,' Edward called.

The sergeant waited until Glyn shepherded the boys away before continuing. 'Mervyn and Ianto Paskey raped the Parry girl.'

'Anna! In heaven's name, she's a child!' Edward blanched.

Dr Evans addressed Peter. 'She's conscious, in deep shock, bruised, and covered in cuts and abrasions. Her injuries need stitching but I thought that would best be done away from here. I've administered laudanum. Physically she should recover. Mentally... Have you experience of dealing with children who've been raped?'

'Unfortunately,' Peter replied.

'After I dressed her wounds I left her with your sister-in-law. She wants to take the girl to the Boot Inn. Frankly I don't think a public house the best place for her.'

'The blood,' Edward asked. 'Is it Anna's?'

'No,' the sergeant revealed. 'Ianto's. The women got to him before the constables arrived.'

'That was Ianto being carried out,' Dr Evans said.

'The women beat him?' Peter asked the sergeant.

'Castrated him. They were about to do the same to Mervyn when my officers stopped them.'

'Pity.' Edward meant it.

'We have both Paskeys in custody; Mervyn in the cells, Ianto in the infirmary.'

'Ianto shouldn't be in the infirmary for more than a week or two,' Dr Evans predicted. 'He lost a lot of blood but Iestyn Swine's wife knew what she was doing. She made a neat job of the gelding.'

'Too neat for my liking,' the sergeant added. 'Bastard deserves to swing for what he did to Anna Parry. As you said, Edward, she's a child.'

'The Paskeys deserve to dance at the end of a rope but they won't.'

'Rapists can't be sentenced to death these days, Edward. But if I have my way, the Paskeys will be going down for a long time over this.'

'You'll want Anna to give evidence?' Edward checked. 'Knowing what that will do to her reputation?'

'If she refuses to give evidence they won't be convicted.'

'You have other witnesses,' Peter reminded.

'None of them saw the actual rape.' Anxious to avoid argument; the sergeant opened his notebook. 'Your sister-in-law Betty and Maggie Two Suits said you paid Alf Mahoney to stay with the Parry children after their mother died because you were expecting trouble from the Paskeys?'

'That's right,' Edward concurred.

'I heard they'd attacked Richard and he was lucky to be alive. I was expecting you to visit the station to make an official complaint.'

'Against Deputy Perkins and the Paskeys? How far would we have got?'

'Nowhere against Deputy Perkins, because no one would be prepared to go up against him in court. The Paskeys are a different matter, which is why it's important Anna testifies against them,' the sergeant stressed. 'If you'd come to the station with the Farmer boys who carted Richard off the mountain we might have made something stick against them days ago.'

'Like what?' Edward demanded. 'Assault? Affray?'

'Either would have been better than nothing. As it is the Paskeys have got away with beating Richard and raping Anna.'

'Not quite, thanks to the gelding irons,' Peter interposed.

'If you'd charged the Paskeys with assault or affray all you'd have succeeded in doing is annoying them and making them more determined to injure Richard, and possibly the Farmers for helping the boy. I thought it best to leave things until we could get Richard away from Merthyr. I was wrong. I should have gone after the Paskeys.'

'And done what, Edward?' the sergeant questioned. 'Killed or injured them? If you had, you'd be in the dock. That wouldn't help Richard Parry or his sister. You told Alf to care for the Parry children. Were you expecting the Paskeys to attack the girl?'

'Not on the day of her mother's funeral.' Edward was bitter.

'I should have taken Anna to the cemetery. She wanted to go.'

'The Paskeys are nasty pieces of work. You couldn't have protected the children for ever,' the sergeant consoled.

'I could have damned well tried.'

Peter had never heard Edward swear before. 'You did what you could, Edward.'

'I failed and that's an end to it.'

'I asked the sergeant to send for you, Dr Edwards, because I didn't know what to do with the girl,' Dr Evans appealed to Peter. 'She needs stitching and nursing care, but neither the Boot Inn nor the infirmary is suitable for someone her age, in her condition. Her neighbours are well meaning but they have no medical knowledge. There are no parents...'

'My wife and I will take care of her,' Peter interrupted.

'I hoped you'd offer. I'll take you to her.' Dr Evans led the way. The sergeant followed.

Peter looked for Edward. He was striding through the arch. 'Where are you going?'

'To put a stop to this hounding of the Parrys.'

'The Paskeys are in custody, sir.'

'They're not the only thugs in Merthyr willing to kill for a pint of ale, sergeant. The only way to finish this is by talking to the man who put a price on Richard's head.'

Peter turned. 'I'll come with you.'

'No.' Edward put his hand on Peter's shoulder. 'Take care of Anna and tell Betty to pack the

Parrys' possessions, especially their clothes, then send word with one of the lads to Tom Farmer. Tell him to notify the landlord that the Parrys are moving out and ask him to contact me if there's any outstanding rent. I'll pay Tom to clear the house and cart the contents to the Boot. Ask Betty to find room for their bits and pieces. If Glyn and Betty take the boys for the time being and you take Anna, Alf can return to his lodgings. We'll make a decision about the Parrys' future tomorrow.'

'You're going to see Deputy Perkins.' Peter guessed.

'He should be home at this time in the evening.'

'You're going alone?'

'I've known Perkins since he was a boy.'

'Edward...' Peter was talking to Edward's back. 'At least take Alf with you.' His plea fell on deaf ears. His brother was half way up the street.

The sergeant appeared at his elbow. 'Don't worry, Dr Edwards, I'll send a couple of constables after him.'

'To arrest Deputy Perkins?'

'Only if you can suggest a charge that will stick, sir?'

'We know he paid the Paskeys to beat up Richard. And probably paid them to rape Anna – a child...'

'The Paskeys will be punished for the rape, because Anna's testimony can be corroborated by witnesses who saw her injuries before the Paskeys left the crime scene. But knowing Deputy Perkins paid the Paskeys to beat Richard and suspecting that he paid them to rape Anna isn't the same as being able to prove it. Courts demand proof. All I can do is set men to watch the deputy. I don't think he'll harm your brother for calling at his house but I'd rather be safe than sorry.' The sergeant eyed the constables in the yard. 'Jenkins, Kelly.'

The two largest officers stepped forward and snapped to attention. 'Sir.'

'You know where Deputy Perkins lives?'

'Yes, sir,' Kelly confirmed.

'Mr Edward Edwards is on his way there. Follow at distance and keep a friendly eye. Only interfere if you have to.'

'Got it, sir,' Jenkins answered.

Deputy Perkins' house
High Street, Merthyr, June 1870

Edward strode through the gate of Perkins's substantial villa. He stepped into the porch and rang the bell. It was answered by a middle-aged woman in a black dress and mob cap. Emotionally shattered by Anna's rape, he wasn't too distressed to notice Deputy Perkins dressed his parlour maids in a replica of the uniform worn by the Crawshays' indoor staff.

'Edward Edwards to see Mr Perkins.'

'I'll see if the master's in, sir.' The maid bobbed a curtsey and closed the door in Edward's face.

He looked through the etched glass panel and watched her blurred outline as she walked down the passage, knocked a door, presumably waited for an 'enter', and disappeared. She reappeared a few moments later, closed the door behind her, and opened the front door. Unable to meet his eyes she focused on the floor tiles.

'The master's not in, sir.'

'Please return to your master and tell him I will now call on Mr Robert Crawshay to voice my concern at the conduct of one of his deputies and the methods used by that deputy to promote workers to positions of junior authority within the rolling mill of Crawshays' Ironworks.'

Deputy Perkins emerged into the hall. 'Go to the kitchen.' He waited until the maid disappeared before addressing Edward. 'I have nothing to say to you, Edward Edwards.'

'I have something to say to you. Would you like me to move to the gate so I can shout it in the street?'

Perkins went as far as the porch. 'You have two minutes.'

'Perhaps a visit to Cyfarthfa Castle would be more productive. Mr Crawshay doesn't put a time limit on his callers if they have matters of business to discuss.'

'You can have no business to discuss with Mr Crawshay that concerns me.'

'You paid the Paskeys to beat Richard Parry and promised them a bonus when they killed him.'

'Prove it.' Perkins challenged.

'The police are doing that now. They have both Paskeys in custody and they're questioning them. Vigorously.'

Perkins latched the front door and pulled it behind him. He looked up the street and saw the constables across the road watching him and Edward. 'I know nothing about any doings of the Paskeys.'

'They work under you in the rolling mill.'

'What they do in their own time is no concern of mine. You can't prove anything...'

'The Paskeys boasted in the Chandlers Arms that you promised them promotion and a guinea bonus if they killed Richard Parry.'

'They were lying.'

'You deny ordering the Paskeys to beat Richard?'

'Whatever argument the Paskeys have with Richard Parry is none of my concern or yours.' Momentarily forgetting the constables' presence, Perkins pushed his face close to Edward's.

'What is my business, and Mr Crawshay's, is you promised promotions in Crawshay's ironworks in exchange for ... what would you call it, Perkins? "Personal favours"?'

'It's a criminal offence to slander a man.'

'You'll be amazed how quickly the sergeant will prove these accusations when he's finished questioning the Paskeys.'

'They're ruffians.'

'Everyone in Merthyr knows that,' Edward agreed.

'Unscrupulous, unreliable thugs.'

'Undeniable. The only question is why you employ them.'

'I was about to fire them.'

'Don't you need a reason?'

'They talk a lot of nonsense.'

'Such as?'

'They're lying if they said I paid them more than any other worker.'

'Tell me,' Edward continued conversationally. 'How much did you pay them to rape Anna Parry?'

'Rape...?'

'A doctor is caring for the child now. She's twelve years old, Perkins. You have daughters. Can you remember them at that age? Can you imagine grown men the size of the Paskeys raping your girls?'

'Even if it was the Paskeys...'

'Oh, it was the Paskeys all right. The women who live in the court caught them, unfortunately after, not before the act. They meted out their own justice on Ianto. They castrated him. He's in the infirmary. Pain is wonderful for concentrating the mind, which is why I'm confident Ianto will give the sergeant a full account of who paid him to attack Richard and rape Anna Parry.'

'Ianto Paskey wouldn't dare incriminate me...' Perkins only realized what he'd said when the constables moved closer.

'Why wouldn't he?' When the deputy failed to answer Edward dropped the mask of politeness. 'If so much as one more hair on Anna, Richard, Morgan, or Owen Parry's head is damaged, watch your back.'

'Are you threatening me?'

'I'm suggesting you should employ men with integrity in the rolling mill who don't attack young men and rape children.'

'I refuse to be held responsible for what my workers do when they leave the mill.'

'You don't try to exert a good influence on them?' Edward asked.

'How do you propose I do that?'

'By telling the men under your supervision to look out for orphans like the Parry family.'

'If the Parrys get hurt it will be nothing to do with me.'

'No?' Edward queried.

'No,' Deputy Perkins reiterated. 'And it's nothing to do with me that they've been hurt.'

'There are a lot of narrow alleyways and dark streets in Merthyr.'

'So you are threatening me?'

'Just conversing, one manager to another.'

'You can tell Richard Parry one thing. I'll kill him if he comes sniffing after my daughter again.'

'You feel that strongly about her?'

'She's my daughter.'

'Anna Parry is my goddaughter, Perkins.'

'You'd arrange to have my daughter...'

'I'm not stupid nor a coward. I don't employ others to do my dirty work, nor do I attack defenceless women, children, and young boys. I leave those things to the likes of the Paskeys – and you. As I said, Perkins, watch your back.'

Dr Edwards' house
High Street, Merthyr, June 1870

Sarah stood next to the kitchen table Anna was lying on; drip feeding chloroform onto the Clover apparatus she'd secured over Anna's nose and mouth. The sedative Dr Evans had given the girl had worked. Anna hadn't opened her eyes since Peter had carried her into the hired carriage that had conveyed them to their house.

Sarah continued to drop liquid slowly on to the mask until Anna's muscles contracted in a spasm. A few seconds later Anna fell, limp and relaxed on to the table.

'Watch her pupils...'

'And pulse and breathing. I've done this before, Peter.'

'I know, sorry. It's...'

'We're both upset.'

Peter lifted his hands from a bowl of antiseptic and dried them in a linen towel. 'I've seen dozens if not hundreds of rape victims, but never one as bad as this. You?'

'No,' she whispered.

'Damn Dr Evans. I wish I had a junior doctor I could pass Anna onto.'

'No, you don't, because you know no one else will care for her as well as you.' She folded back the sheet that covered Anna's body.

'It's as though she's been torn to pieces by a wild animal. Her rectum, anus, and blood vessels are shredded, her vagina ripped, her labia bruised and cut. She's going to be in agony for weeks. How could the beasts have done this...'

'Beasts don't inflict pain for no reason.' Sarah checked Anna's pupils were still dilated. Chloroform was a tricky substance. She'd witnessed sudden deaths due to overdose during lengthy operations. Determined this wouldn't happen to Anna, she checked her breathing, pulse, and pupils every few seconds.

The clock ticked on and she sensed the servants moving behind the door. The cook and kitchen maid had resented being turfed out of the kitchen so close to dinner time. She'd ordered them to clean the pantries but she could hear the housemaids' and manservant's voices in the servants' dining room and suspected precious little work was being done.

Oblivious to everything except Anna's injuries, Peter worked steadily. As always when operating, he closed out everything except the task in hand; repairing and stitching torn and damaged tissue to the best of his ability.

'Pulse?' he asked after half an hour.

'Pulse and respiration steady. Pupils dilated.'

'Almost finished. With this number of stitches pray she doesn't get an infection.'

'You're repairing the hymen?'

'You think I shouldn't?'

'You know my views on virginity.'

'A commodity over-prized by promiscuous men.' He recited one of her mantras.

'The damage the Paskeys inflicted won't be healed by a counterfeit virginity.'

'We're only a doctor and nurse, sweetheart, not God. All we can do is tend to Anna's physical injuries to the best of our ability and although I don't think she's begun menstruating, give her abortifacients to ensure she doesn't have a child.'

'I want to kill the Paskeys. Or at least castrate the one the women didn't.'

'Gelding him won't help Anna.'

'It might save the next victim.'

'I can't think further than Anna. Like her brother she's young. She'll heal in time, all except for the worst wounds. The ones that can't be seen.'

Boot Inn
High Street, Merthyr, June 1870

Glyn sat up in bed, a sheaf of plans and a notepad balanced on his knees. He was checking the quantities of pipework needed to convey waste gas from the furnaces against what had been delivered to the warehouses in Southampton.

Betty entered, closed the door, set her candle on the washstand, and blew out the flame. 'The poor Parry boys are asleep, bless them. They're worn out.'

'Hardly surprising after everything's that happened on top of the strain of their mother's funeral. What did you tell them about Anna?' Glyn gave up trying to make sense of his figures, gathered his papers, and shuffled them into a pile.

'The Paskeys beat her like they beat Richard.'

'They accepted that?'

'Morgan asked a few awkward questions. That boy knows too much for his age.'

'That boy was working the trap in Edward's drift mine when he was four years old and he's been cutting coal since his eighth birthday,' Glyn reminded. 'Miners don't watch their mouths, even among children.'

'He stopped being difficult when I pointed out he was upsetting Owen. They wanted to know where Richard and Anna were. I told them they'd been taken to the infirmary and wouldn't be allowed visitors until the doctor gave his permission.'

'Why the infirmary?'

'I didn't want to tell the boys Richard and Anna were staying with Peter and Sarah.'

'With both Paskeys in custody my brother should be safe enough.'

'Unless another of Deputy Perkins's ruffians decides to finish what the Paskeys started.'

'The police promised to keep a close eye on the deputy and his thugs.'

'I've never known the coppers in Merthyr to keep a close eye on anything other than the free hand-outs they extort from publicans and shop-keepers.'

'Trouble in the bar tonight?' Glyn asked.

'No worse than usual.'

'Your life will be more peaceful in Russia with only a house to run.'

'The way you men talk, you'd think there's nothing to keeping house.'

'We'll be able to afford servants. A cook, house-keeper, maids, an indoor man of work, as well as a groom and stable boy.'

'Seeing is believing.'

'You can afford to employ more help here on the allowance I give you,' Glyn protested.

'Affording to pay workers and getting those worth paying are two different things. Few people are prepared to put in a full day's work for a full day's pay. I don't expect servants to be different in Russia. Most expect wages for sitting round on their backsides. Anna Parry, God bless, heal, and keep her, working part time did twice as much as the full-time, full-grown slatterns in the kitchen.'

Glyn held his tongue. Betty had managed to

engineer an argument every night since his return. He'd actually caught himself regretting the loss of the peace and quiet, if not the loneliness, of the impersonal hotel rooms he'd slept in for the last few years.

'Have you finished working?' Betty eyed the pile of papers.

'For tonight.'

'The Parry boys didn't want to eat, but I gave them sandwiches and a drop of brandy in milk to help them sleep. There's no way I'll allow them to work tomorrow.'

'Edward wouldn't want them to.' Glyn tried to pre-empt argument. He set the papers beside the oil lamp on his bedside table.

'They've had it hard, and now on top of losing their Dad and Mam, this business with Richard and Anna. They're good boys. They carried their plates into the kitchen and would have washed them if I'd let them.'

'You moving them into the lodgers' dormitory tomorrow?' Glyn asked.

'Not until their future's been decided. They're so young.'

'There are younger than Owen in the dormitory, Betty.'

'None who've just lost their mother.'

'Most are orphans like Morgan and Owen. A couple of days, we'll be gone, on our way to Russia.'

'I don't need reminding. Your brothers said we'd discuss the Parry children tomorrow. I thought it best to wait to see what's decided then.' She tipped water from the jug into the china bowl on the washstand, dropped in a cake of soap and lathered it, spreading the suds over her hands and face.

'We all packed?'

'Apart from the clothes we'll need for the next few days. Turn off the lamp.'

Glyn almost refused but decided against it. Betty had never undressed in front of him. In over ten years of marriage he'd never seen her naked. He turned down the wick, punched his pillow into a more conducive shape, and lay back.

The rustle of clothing filled the air when Betty removed her dress and hung it on the back of the door. She took her nightdress from beneath her pillow, pulled it over her head without slipping her arms through the sleeves, allowed the hem to fall and continued undressing beneath the tent like garment. She unfastened and stepped out of her petticoats, stockings, corset, bust shaper, and bloomers. After she removed each item, she folded it and placed it on the chair.

When she finished, she slipped her arms through the sleeves of the nightgown and knelt beside the bed. Resting her forehead on the back of her hands, she recited the Lord's Prayer and continued with a list of names Glyn thought would never end and a final plea that 'God bless and keep them all.'

Glyn wasn't unsympathetic towards the rituals of Betty's Baptist religion. He prayed. On occasion several times a day, when invoking the Lord's blessing on Mr Hughes's business endeavours. In imminent danger, like the time the horses drawing Mr Hughes's hired carriage had bolted through crowded Berlin streets, his prayers had been desperate. But no matter how urgent, his supplications were always silent.

Eventually Betty rose from her knees folded back the bedclothes on her side of the bed, climbed in, and lay on her back beside him.

He glanced across at her, a shadowy grey hump in the shadowy grey gloom. Her voice, strained disembodied floated in the darkness.

'You want your rights?'

He sensed her waiting for him to break the silence that had fallen since she'd asked the question. 'Not if you're tired.'

'Give me a minute.' She sat up in the bed and pulled her nightgown to her waist.

He knew it would be too much to ask her to remove it.

'I'm ready.'

Glyn remembered his last visit to a 'lady'. He'd paid for the privilege but there'd been fun, laughter, and more emotion in the brief encounter than all the nights he'd spent with Betty.

'I said I'm ready.'

He knew what would follow if he moved on top of his wife. Her martyred rigidity while he 'took his rights'. Lovemaking wasn't a word that could be used to describe what he and Betty did.

'I'm tired, Betty. Perhaps tomorrow?'

'I wish you'd said something before I made preparations. Don't you want children?'

'Give me a minute.' He tried to recall some of the women he'd spent time with in the bordellos in Europe ... then remembered the pretty dark-haired Russian in Moscow who knew exactly how to revive a jaded sexual appetite.

The memory resulted in a performance even he rated perfunctory.

When he finished, Betty rolled on her side and rearranged her nightdress.

He was almost asleep when she spoke again. 'I want children. But with you away so much...'

'We'll talk in the morning, Betty.'

'We need to do more than talk. You might not be so tired first thing.'

He didn't answer. His thoughts were with a girl in Greenwich. Light brown hair, blue eyes, and a bewitching smile that had made him feel as though he were the most important being in the world – until her next customer had arrived.

Dr Edwards' house
High Street, Merthyr, June 1870

Sarah waited until nine o'clock before knocking on Anna's bedroom door. Peter had dosed the girl with laudanum twice during the night to help her sleep as much as deaden her pain but when Sarah walked in Anna's eyes were open. Dark, desolate as she lay curled in the foetal position in the bed.

'I brought you breakfast, Anna. Tea and toast. I put two sugars in the tea and brought the bowl in case you want more.' Sarah set the tray on the dressing table and opened the drapes.

Anna's face was swollen, her throat and cheeks marred by scratches and bruises that had darkened to deep purple. If she'd cried in the night, there was no trace left of her tears.

Sarah had become expert at concealing her feelings while working in London. But she found it impossible not to show anger towards the men who'd so cruelly abused Anna. After Peter carried Anna upstairs he'd had to physically restrain her from going to thank the women who'd emasculated Ianto Paskey. He only succeeded in stopping her by reminding her they had to keep Richard and Anna's whereabouts secret from other thugs who might be tempted by the rumours of bounty payable by Deputy Perkins.

Sarah sat on the bed and offered Anna the cup but Anna continued to stare blankly through large, frightened, and Sarah suspected, unseeing eyes.

'I don't know if you remember what we talked about last night, Anna. Richard's here. The doctor and I have been looking after him. You can see him.'

'No!' Anna focused on Sarah. 'Does Richard know what the Paskeys did to me?'

Sarah returned the untouched teacup to the tray. 'No, but you'll have to tell him. He'll want to know how you came by those bruises.'

'I couldn't bear Richard to know what they did to me. I don't want anyone to know.'

'I understand how you feel...'

'Did anyone ever do the vile things to you that the Paskeys did to me? Do you know what's it's like to be stripped naked ... to be ... to be...'

'Anna, don't think about it,' Sarah pleaded. 'You have your life ahead of you.'

'I have nothing...' Anna dropped her voice to a

whisper. 'I ... don't ... have ... anything... Please! Don't tell Richard.' She grabbed Sarah's arm. 'Please, promise me you won't tell him.' Anna turned her head to the wall. 'I wish the Paskeys had killed me.'

There was nothing theatrical in the pronouncement. Sarah's heart went out to the girl. 'I know you're hurting and you think your life is over, but it's not. You'll recover and when you do, you'll realise life is precious and worth living.'

'Everyone knows what the Paskeys did to me. No decent person will want to come near me.'

Peter knocked the door and opened it. Unable to face him, Anna buried her head in the pillow. He handed Sarah a bottle of laudanum and slipped outside.

Sarah gathered her thoughts. 'The Paskeys beat Richard; we could tell him they beat you.'

'Just a beating?'

Sarah poured water into a glass and added drops of laudanum. 'If that's what you want.' She couldn't bring herself to remind Anna that as the women in the court knew what the Paskeys had done to her, the story would have been related in every pub, street, and court in the town by now. 'Drink this.' She gave Anna the glass.

'Richard will find out, won't he? He and everyone will know just by looking at me. Auntie Maggie and Auntie May saw me; saw what those men had done...'

'What happened wasn't your fault. No man should do what the Paskeys did to you to any woman, especially a girl your age. The Paskeys are pure evil and they'll be punished.' Sarah set down the glass and the bottle, sat next to Anna, and wrapped her arms around her.

'They said I wanted them to do it. I heard them. They told Auntie Betty and Auntie Maggie that I was asking for it ... that...'

'No one believed them, Anna.'

'Auntie Maggie, Auntie Betty, and Auntie Jenny did something to the Paskeys. I heard screaming.'

'They hurt one of them and both the Paskeys are in custody. Try to forget them.' Sarah stroked Anna's hair away from her face.

'The sergeant said I'd have to tell people what the Paskeys did...' Anna sobbed. 'I should have fought harder. I should have run away. I should have...'

'Perhaps the police can find a way to punish the Paskeys without you having to go to court. I'll ask the doctor to talk to the sergeant.'

'Will you? Please! I never want to see them again. Ever! Please, Mrs Edwards, don't make me...'

'No one's going to make you do anything you don't want to, Anna. Not if I can help it.' Sarah settled her back on the pillows. 'Try to rest. There's a bell on the bedside cabinet. If you need anything ring and I'll come. I'll leave the tea and toast. Don't let the tea go cold.'

Chapter Ten

Dr Edwards' house
High Street, Merthyr, June 1870

Peter was leaving Richard's room when Sarah walked on to the landing.

'Have you told him about Anna?'

Peter held his finger to his lips. He didn't answer her until they were downstairs. 'I told him the Paskeys attacked her. I didn't tell him they raped her.'

'I don't think he should be told.'

'Better we tell the boy than he hears it from someone else. He will find out sooner rather than later, Sarah.'

'It will devastate Anna if he does. Consider Anna's feelings, Peter.' She led the way into the drawing room. 'She's been shamed.'

'For pity's sake, it's not her fault the Paskeys raped her.'

'I know that but she doesn't. She even said she should have fought harder.'

'Against those louts? No grown woman, let alone a young girl would have stood a chance.'

'She can't bear the thought of people knowing what the Paskeys did to her. People talk, Peter.'

'Of course they do. I've no doubt they already are.'

'Her reputation will be ruined.'

'It already is. Do you think the women in the court will keep quiet? Even if by some miracle they did, Ianto's in the infirmary. Nurses, porters, and doctors talk. It'll be all over the valley by now that he's been emasculated.'

'I've been thinking.' She sat in the chair next to the hearth.

'And?' he asked warily sitting opposite her.

'Richard's travelling to Russia with us, why don't we take Anna as well?'

'A young girl! For heaven's sake, Sarah. What's she going to do there? Given her precarious mental condition...'

'Which is hardly her fault. With care, rest, and help, she will recover.'

'Are you sure about that?'

'Not entirely,' she replied truthfully.

'Whether she will or won't, she'll need more care than we can give. We won't have time to look after her.'

'We'll have nothing else to do on the journey, especially on the boat, but care for Richard and Anna.'

'And if they haven't recovered by journey's end?'

'As you said, they're young, strong. With you to doctor them, they'll recover.'

'Flattery won't win you this argument, Sarah. How is Anna going to earn a living in Russia? Mine coal alongside her brother?'

'She can work with me in the hospital. I'll start her as a ward maid. If she shows promise I'll train her as a nurse.'

'Nurse? She's twelve years old.'

'I left the Whitechapel workhouse and began as

a ward maid in the infirmary on my tenth birthday. Richard will be living with us. He and his sister will be company for one another when they're not working.'

'And the two younger brothers? Are you suggesting we take them as well?'

'They could lodge with us. They're working in the drift mine now. Russia? Here? What's the difference, the work's the same.'

'We haven't been married a year. We're barely used to living with one another. The last thing I want is to adopt four orphans before we have our own children.'

'I'm not suggesting we adopt them and it's not as though they would be a financial drain. Glyn said there's enough work for everyone who wants it. He'll find positions for the boys in his colliery once it's sunk, and until it is they can labour for the construction workers.'

'I'll grant you that's the boys taken care of, apart from their accommodation, but that could be a problem.' Peter wrapped his arms around her after she moved from her chair onto his lap. 'Glyn warned conditions are going to be rough for everyone at first, and rough means shortages, including housing. I categorically refuse to share a bedroom with the Parry boys. So you can stop trying to wheedle me into this.'

'There'll be dormitories for the male workers. Won't there?'

'Probably, but there might not be enough beds in them for the boys and what about Anna? I understand you feeling sorry for the girl but are you sure you're prepared to take responsibility for her, especially after what she's been through? You'll have a hospital to run. That has to come first.'

'It will after you and our marriage.' Sarah left his lap and went to the window. 'I've told you everything there is to know about me, Peter. But I'm not sure you understand what it's like to be orphaned and grow up in a workhouse.'

'No one's going to send Anna to the workhouse. She has a live-in position in the Boot. She's been working for Betty for some time.'

'Betty's going to Russia with Glyn. Who's going to run the Boot Inn when she leaves?'

'Her father. He owns the place.'

'Busy as he'll be, he's going to care for Anna?' Sarah was sceptical.

'He's hired a housekeeper to take Betty's place.'

'Do you think a housekeeper will be able to give Anna the care she needs? Think what it will be like for her if she stays in Merthyr where everyone knows she's been raped. Girls who've been used that way once are considered "fair game" by men.'

'That's outrageous!'

'Is it, Peter?'

'Not all men think that way. I wouldn't.'

'You're a saint. I had a friend in the workhouse who'd been raped by her uncle when she was nine years old. Her father took her to the parish guardians because he didn't want her around her younger sisters lest she lead them astray. The guardians decided she was in need of moral guidance and sent her to the workhouse. Every time she went in the yard the boys called her a slut and tried to pull up her dress. She couldn't stand it. The day after her tenth birthday she walked to the top floor of the workhouse and threw herself down the stairwell. She killed herself but it wasn't quick. She took three days to die.'

'You had a foul childhood.'

'No inmate of the orphanage wing of Whitechapel Workhouse had a childhood.'

'Do you think Anna will try to kill herself?' Peter asked seriously.

'If she's left in Merthyr with people who know what happened to her, yes.'

'You really want to take her to Russia with us?'

She looked down the street. A crowd of women were gossiping outside the grocer's. She imagined their conversation. 'Have you heard about Anna Parry and what the Paskeys did to her ... stripped stark naked ... raped ... beaten...'

'Sarah?' Peter prompted.

She faced him. 'A fresh start away from this town and people who know what the Paskeys did to her might help Anna. But you're right, there's no way of knowing for certain whether she'll recover or not.'

'She'll be travelling and living with us and we know what happened to her. As do Glyn and Betty.'

'She knows we can be trusted not to tell anyone about it.'

'You want us to try to keep the knowledge of what the Paskeys did from her brother?'

'The Paskeys beat Richard. We'll tell him they did the same to her.'

'You've already made the decision to take her

with us, haven't you?'

'If I'd done that I wouldn't be discussing it with you.'

He smiled. 'Sweetheart, you'd better ask Edward, Judith, Glyn, Betty, and the boys over for tea tonight and see what they make of your scheming.'

'I've had a word with Glyn and Edward. They called when you were at the infirmary.'

'Did they now?' He left his chair and locked his arms around her waist.

'Glyn said Betty's grown fond of the two younger boys in the short time she's been looking after them and Richard and Anna are more or less old enough to look after themselves.'

'I'd say given the present state of them, rather less than more.'

'They'll recover thanks to your doctoring. You won't mind adding an extended family to our household in Russia, will you?'

'You accept the Parrys are too young to be independent?'

'At the moment but they'll soon grow up.'

'I give in. We'll take the Parrys with us but I reserve the right to have a quiet word in Mr Hughes's ear about that hospital he's building. It might be advantageous if a set of rooms for the use of the resident doctor and matron is incorporated in the plans so we can live on site until our house is ready, and if we do, the Parrys will have to live elsewhere.'

'We'll need dormitories in the hospital for the ward maids and porters. The Parrys can sleep there and share meals with us. I knew you'd understand.'

He kissed her. 'You're a soft touch, my love. But then if you weren't, you wouldn't have married me.'

Merthyr Railway Station
July 1870

Peter reflected it was as well they were leaving for Russia on a weekday morning, not Sunday when only the furnace crews were 'on shift'. As it was, everyone who could get time off – plus those who'd decided to play sick – had walked down to the station to see off the emigrants.

The travellers' luggage was piled at the end of the platform where the guard's van would draw up. Betty alone had refused to relinquish her trunk and was sitting perched on top of it, Owen and Morgan standing like sentinel dogs either side of her. Alf, Glyn's latest collier recruit, much to Edward's annoyance, was watching over all three of them.

'Anna, Richard...' the boys ran to greet their brother and sister the moment Edward, Peter, and Sarah helped them from the carriage.

Richard stared at his brothers. 'You're clean and well-dressed. New suits, caps, boots, shirts, where did you get them?'

'Mr Edwards took us to the draper's to be fitted out,' Owen divulged.

'He said we'd make enough money in Russia to pay him back.' Morgan turned around so Anna and Richard could admire his clothes.

'Given the way Mr Hughes and I intend to

work you in Russia, you will, young man.' Glyn walked over to them.

'You and Anna look awful bad, Richard,' Morgan commented.

'Be glad you weren't caught by the Paskeys or you'd look the same,' Edward admonished.

'Sorry, Richard, Anna.'

Anna strained to give her brothers a smile. 'I've never seen you two so well turned out. I hope you thanked Mr and Mrs Edwards.'

'They did,' Glyn answered for them. 'You'd better go into the Ladies' waiting room before my brother's arm drops off and you fall down, my girl. That goes for you too, Richard, only it'll have to be the general waiting room for you.'

'Do you want a hand?' Alf asked gruffly, choked by the sight of the bruises on Anna's face.

'We'll manage, but thank you for asking, Mr Mahoney.' Sarah took Anna's weight from Peter at the door of the 'Ladies Only', while Edward and Peter helped Richard into the general waiting room.

'Can we come with you, Anna?' Morgan and Owen cried.

'Not into the Ladies' Waiting Room,' Sarah said. 'You'll see your sister on the train.'

'Stay with Mrs Edwards and help her with the luggage, boys.' Weakened by the effort it had taken to get this far, Richard could barely stand.

'We'll see you and Anna on the train, Richard?' Owen needed to hear confirmation.

'Don't forget to introduce yourselves again. I'm used to ragamuffins, not princes.' Richard reached out to ruffle Owen's hair and almost fell.

Impatient, on edge, Glyn checked his pocket watch for the tenth time in as many minutes before pacing the length of the platform past the workers he'd recruited. Few were taking their families and several women were crying at the prospect of being parted from their husbands and sons.

'The train will come when it's ready, not before, Glyn.' Amused by his younger brother's uncharacteristic nervousness, Edward followed him.

'It's late.' Glyn slipped his watch back into his waistcoat pocket.

'Only by your watch, not the station clock.' Edward gripped his younger brother's shoulder. 'I can't believe we're actually saying goodbye. I never thought John Hughes would make this insane scheme of his a reality. But here you are, off halfway across the world and not just on one of your trips.'

'The trips will be the other way from now on.'

'I'll see you again?' Edward's question was a plea.

Glyn's voice was hoarse. 'Of course. I'll be back and forth, sorting out things. Not too often though given the length of the journey.' Suddenly aware of the enormity of the step he was taking, Glyn was barely aware of what he was saying.

'That sounds like a train.' Sarah appeared in the doorway of the waiting room.

'You're right,' Glyn confirmed as the engine steamed noisily into sight and drew up alongside the platform.

Whistles blew. The guards flung open the doors of the carriages and luggage van. Porters swarmed forward, grabbing the trunks and packages heaped on the platform and hauling them on to the train.

'Well, this is it, Edward.' Glyn wanted to hug his eldest brother but aware of the people around them and not wanting to appear "soft" he held out his hand.

Edward shook it vigorously before turning to Peter who'd emerged from the waiting room with Richard. 'Both of you take care of one another and Sarah and Betty. And you, young man and young lady,' he addressed Richard and Anna as Alf helped Richard to the train, 'take care of yourselves and your brothers.' He shook Richard's hand and kissed Anna's cheek, moving back when she shrank from his touch.

'Edward, thank you for welcoming me into the family and all you've done for Peter and me. I'll get Richard and Anna settled on the train.' Sarah picked up her travelling bag.

'I'll never understand how my brother managed to persuade you to marry him, Sarah, I'm just glad for the sake of our family he did.' Edward kissed her.

Sarah returned his embrace, wrapped her arm around Anna, and ushered her forward, leaving Peter to say goodbye to Edward in privacy.

'Thank you for everything, Mr Edwards. I'll write.' Richard called back to Edward.

'Mind you do but I won't be worrying about you, Anna, or your brothers. You'll be in safe hands with my brothers and Alf. Make the most of the voyage. Get all the rest you can, while you can.'

'Thank you for everything, Mr Edwards.' Anna

climbed the steps and disappeared into the train.

Glyn looked for Betty. She was still sitting on her trunk. 'Betty? It's time to move. Our luggage will be perfectly safe in the guard's van.'

Betty continued to sit, impervious to the combined efforts of three porters and Alf to dislodge her.

'Time to go, Betty.'

'I'm sorry, Glyn.'

'For what?'

'I can't go and I won't. I've been thinking about it all morning and the more I've thought, the more I realise I don't want to live in Russia among a lot of heathens and foreigners.'

'We'll be the foreigners in Russia, Betty.'

'There's no point in arguing, Glyn. I'll go back to the Boot and tell the woman my father hired she's not needed. The boys can come with me and give Dad a hand to run the place. They're too young to travel all that way. They can go in a year or two when you've had time to sort out a proper house for them.'

'Betty...' Glyn realised she was right. There was no point in arguing. She'd made up her mind to stay and wouldn't be dissuaded. He only wished he felt regret instead of relief.

'Guard's about to blow the whistle, Glyn,' Edward warned.

Owen and Morgan ran up to the train, Alf followed.

'Looks like you'll have to do without your helpers, Betty, they appear to be joining us,' Glyn said when the boys banged on the window of the carriage Richard, Anna, Peter, and Sarah were sitting in.

Sarah pulled down the window.

Morgan looked at Owen, who nodded. He'd sensed what Morgan intended to do.

Morgan shouted above the noise of the steam, 'We're staying with Auntie Betty. Bye, Anna, Richard. See you when you get back from Russia.'

'Yes, see you.' Owen waved.

Alf looked at the boys, then Anna, through the carriage window. He hesitated for a few seconds before stepping up into the carriage. The guard blew his whistle. Alf glanced at Glyn, who was still with Betty. He kept the door open.

Glyn ran across the platform when the train started moving. He took Alf's hand, jumped in, and slammed the door behind him.

Train somewhere between Merthyr and Southampton
July 1870

'I don't blame Betty for wanting to stay in Merthyr.' Glyn drew a last puff from his cigarette, stared at the glowing tip, then squashed it in the ashtray. He and Peter had lunched in the dining car with Sarah and Alf, but they'd lingered after the others had taken meals back to their carriage for Richard and Anna. Glyn had ordered coffee and brandy, and wanting to support his brother through his domestic crisis, Peter stayed.

'It's a lot to ask a woman to leave her home, her country, and her friends. Since Betty's mother died, her father's relied on Betty to help him run the Boot. It was her idea to turn the attics and rooms over the stables into dormitories for bachelors. That income would go if she wasn't there to supervise the cook and maids and keep an eye on the accounts. Her father was never any good at book-keeping. If she left the Boot she'd be leaving it for what? Life in a foreign country where no one speaks English and she wouldn't know a soul.'

'She'd know you.' Peter was irritated by Glyn's determination to excuse Betty's behaviour, 'as well as me and Sarah, there are over a hundred others in this convoy who speak English and Welsh. I'd be furious if Sarah left me to travel a thousand miles by myself so she could work in a family business.'

'Sarah hasn't a family, let alone a family business.'

Concerned for Glyn, Peter refused to allow his brother to side-track the conversation. 'You know what I mean.'

'I know Betty's an expert when it comes to running a pub.' Glyn swirled his brandy around in the balloon before sipping it.

'Are you saying you're happy for your wife to put her father's pub before your marriage?'

'I'd be the first to admit I've spent more time travelling with Mr Hughes and working with him in Greenwich since I married than I have with Betty. These last three years there's been so much to do to finalise the setting up of the New Russia Company. We had to order equipment for the new works, and given the extremes of Russian weather none of it could be standard because standard wouldn't tolerate the severe frosts of

Russia. It took time to work out the specification and even more time to arrange the manufacture of the components.' He gave Peter a rueful smile. 'I can recite the dimensions of the boilers we're taking to Russia but I haven't a clue what dress size Betty wears.'

'Small. I know because Sarah had one made for her as a birthday present. It's not me you should be telling this to, but Betty. You were home for over a week. Didn't you talk to her?'

'Of course I did.'

'About how you felt you'd neglected her for work?' Peter probed.

'There wasn't time.'

'In a week?'

'The first couple of days I was exhausted from travelling. After that, what little time Betty spent away from the Boot was taken up with shopping and packing. Once the Parry boys moved in, the remaining time simply vanished.'

'There's always bedtime. Sometimes Sarah and I spend half the night talking.'

'You and Sarah talk?' Glyn finished his brandy and lifted his finger to summon the waiter.

'About everything. You and Betty don't?'

'Other than, "What do you want for dinner?" or "Do you want me to put your shirts in the laundry?" not much. Another two brandies and coffees, please,' Glyn asked the waiter. 'I should never have married Betty.' When Glyn saw Peter watching him he said, 'It was a selfish relationship on my part from the outset.'

'Edward mentioned at the time he was concerned for you – both of you. He thought you and

Betty were a couple of kids playing at rushing up the aisle. He didn't believe either of you had considered what would happen the day after the wedding ceremony, let alone a year later.'

'That might be true of Betty, but I assure you at the time I thought no further than the wedding night. If there'd been one girl in our circle who hadn't adhered strictly to the moral teachings of the chapel on chastity before marriage I wouldn't have considered putting a ring on Betty's finger before our twentieth birthdays.'

'Looking back, my discussion with Edward was more of a lecture from him on the perils of marrying young,' Peter mused. 'Even then, I was aiming to leave Merthyr to study medicine.'

'Given your age at the time it's strange Edward discussed my marriage with you and not me.'

'Edward probably thought you'd bite his head off.'

'I probably would have – then.'

'You did love Betty when you married her?'

'I thought I did. Doesn't that amount to the same thing? As I've just admitted, lust played a large part and you know Merthyr. It was what was expected. You court a girl – you marry her. Betty was my childhood sweetheart.'

'We all have childhood sweethearts,' Peter observed. 'Not many end up marrying them.'

'You certainly didn't marry Jenny.'

'I knew I was heading for serious poverty. It was bad enough you and Edward had to support me through six years of medical studies. It would have been too much to expect you to keep my wife and possibly children as well. I thought Jenny would be best left in Merthyr where she could find someone else. I didn't wish her ill and I certainly didn't wish a man who'd lose his leg like Iestyn Swine on her.'

'She's surviving given the sideline she's developed in doctoring animals. Not to mention gelding them.'

'When I told Jenny to forget me I believed I was being noble and self-sacrificing. After meeting Sarah I realised I'd made the right and selfish decision. There's a world of difference between love and infatuation. But we're talking about you and Betty.'

'There's not much more to say other than I should have told Betty it was over between us nine years ago when I accepted the position of Mr Hughes's assistant. It's not Mr Hughes's fault. He warned me the job would mean travelling with him. It was an incredible opportunity for me but I hadn't expected him to spend quite so much time on the Continent.'

'You would have left Betty after only a year of married life?' Peter handed the waiter his empty glass in exchange for a full one. 'Thank you.'

'Yes, thank you. We'll have the bill please.' Glyn turned from the waiter. 'Not a year, six months to be exact.'

'You knew something was wrong between you and Betty that early on?'

'Truth is, probably before we walked down the aisle. At the time I was excited about only one thing – my work with Mr Hughes.'

'But your wedding ... the moment you put the ring on Betty's finger.'

'I can't remember it.'

'I remember every second of every moment I've spent with Sarah. I can tell you exactly how I felt when I saw her for the first time just over seven years ago.'

'Which was?'

'The world was brighter, more colourful. Truly, wondrously beautiful. It was as though I'd opened my eyes for the first time.'

'Betty never made me feel like that.'

'Never?' Happier than he'd believed possible in his own marriage, Peter wanted his brother to feel the same.

'I couldn't say with certainty how much of what I felt about Betty was down to habit. Whenever I called in the Boot when I was still working for the Crawshays in Merthyr she was always waiting with a smile, a friendly word, and a pint of ale. Edward warned me that if I continued to spend time talking to her, people in general, and her parents in particular, would expect me to marry her. He was right but I ignored his advice just as I discounted most of what he told me before I was old enough to think for myself.'

'I remember Edward's cautionary lectures. Much as I love him, they're boring and he always chose to deliver them when I was burning to do something other than listen.'

'I agree with you about Edward's "talks" but it's all water long flowed under the bridge. When Betty or her father – or perhaps both – first broached the subject of marriage, I did what was expected of me. I saw the minister and booked the chapel. Wasn't it like that for you and Sarah?'

'No, because I didn't want to imagine living a

day without her. When I started work in the hospital, I used every excuse to visit the women's surgical ward where she worked, just so I could see her and experience the feeling of excitement that still overwhelms me whenever I look at her. That goes for our wedding day. Every year of waiting until I qualified seemed like a century.'

'You sound like a bad romance novel.'

'My lack of eloquence doesn't make the way I feel about Sarah less real.'

'She must love you to traipse all the way to Russia,' Glyn allowed.

'That sounds like jealousy, despite what you said about Betty making the right decision to stay in Merthyr.' Peter's smile was so disarming, Glyn had to smile back.

'I am jealous,' Glyn admitted. 'Not of you and Sarah. Only the feelings you have for one another. The way you talk about Sarah...'

'Yes,' Peter prompted.

'I've only ever felt that about this expedition. The thought of building something new, something huge for the future that will last long after Mr Hughes, me, and everyone travelling with us will be long gone from this earth. It's as though we're writing history. I know an ironworks will never be regarded as a great work of art like the pyramids, the Coliseum in Rome, or a Greek temple, but we'll build furnaces that will dominate the Russian steppe for centuries. They'll be the hub and originator of other projects that will change the face of Russia. Trains and tracks will cross the country, from Poland to China, Siberia to the Balkans, because of our work. People will be able to travel a thousand miles in a few days. Massive railway stations will be built to rival those in London, with iron pillars and roof supports. Have you looked – really looked – at Brunel's Paddington? For sheer scale of engineering and beauty of design it rivals the greatest medieval cathedrals. We'll create edifices as magnificent, impressive, and splendid in Russia. Mr Hughes and his New Russia Company are about to hurl a medieval country into the modern age, bringing prosperity, wealth, and education to its people, and we are a part – granted, a very small part – of his enterprise and his dream.'

'That sounds as though you've invented industrial poetry.'

'Mock all you like.'

'I wasn't, Glyn. Only admiring the intensity of your dream. But there's one thing wrong with it.'

'What?'

'All the work is ahead of us and from what you've said it's not going to be a picnic.'

John Hughes's convoy, Mediterranean waters
July 1870

It was John who suggested that Sarah assume responsibility for the women and children in his party after they'd boarded the vessels he'd chartered. She formed a women's committee to help the stewards allocate the cabins, and organised meetings where the women could drink tea, gossip, and interrogate John and Glyn about Russia. She ran classes for school-age children so they wouldn't slip behind with their education, and song and play sessions for babies and their mothers.

It was Sarah who made the decision that men be kept out of the salon while the women held their meetings and women should leave the salon every night at ten o'clock so the men could enjoy sole occupancy, and as she said to John, Glyn, and Peter, 'Do whatever it is men do when women are out of the way.'

As Sarah expected, the men used their late night 'bachelor hour' to drink ale and brandy, and play cards. Richard was flattered when Glyn invited him to join them as soon as he was well enough, but disappointed when he discovered that most men didn't discuss engineering when women were out of the way.

Salon, John Hughes's ship, Mediterranean waters
July 1870

'How did your talk go down with the women this morning, Glyn?' John picked up the hand Richard had dealt. Under the tutelage of Glyn and Peter the boy was becoming a proficient poker player.

Glyn stroked his moustache and studied his cards. 'I resisted the temptation to tell them they'd be living in igloos and eating wolves.'

'If Huw's done his job it shouldn't come to that. You did warn them it would be cold?'

'I gave them the full weather breakdown.'

'You told them about the locals?'

'I mentioned there was little difference between Cossacks and the working class in Merthyr.'

'Is that an insult to the Welsh or the Cossacks?' Peter shuffled his cards in random order. He'd discovered to his cost that both John and Glyn were adept at reading their opponents' hands unseen.

'Both. I also told Mrs Cohen that she and her husband will be able to practise their Yiddish in the shtetl.'

Richard laid down his cards. 'I'm out.'

Peter looked at him with a professional eye. 'You're paler than usual. Bed for you, young man.'

'I'll not argue, sir.'

'I keep telling you, I'm not sir. It's Doctor or Peter. Do me a favour,' he said when Richard left his chair, 'look in on your sister.'

'Anna still seasick?' John asked.

'Today was the first day she's kept water down.'

'I'll make sure she's all right.' Richard went to the door. 'Good night, sir. Mr Edwards, doctor.'

'Good night to you, Richard, sleep well. We need strong colliers at journey's end. And tell your sister I've a job for her as soon as she's fit enough to leave her cabin,' John called after him.

Sarah had placed Anna in a cubicle between her and Peter's cabin and the one Glyn occupied with Richard. Anna was sharing with a female steward, a motherly soul who would have cared for Anna if she'd had a moment to spare after seeing to the wants of the more demanding passengers.

Richard stepped out on deck and shivered. A

cold breeze was blowing. Since they'd entered Mediterranean waters the daytime temperature had been higher than anything he'd experienced. He looked forward to the cool of early morning and evening but found the nights cold. He walked along the deck until he came to the entrance to the corridor that led to the cabins. He knocked Anna's door.

'Come in.'

Anna was sitting up in her bunk reading by the light of a hurricane lamp.

'You look almost human.'

'I am now I've stopped retching.'

'What are you reading?'

'*Jane Eyre*, Mrs Edwards lent it to me. She said I should be well enough to get up for breakfast tomorrow. Look?' she held out an empty plate.

'You've eaten?'

'Two ham sandwiches and they stayed down. I'm glad you called in. I've been thinking about the boys.'

'They'll be fine in the Boot with Mrs Edwards.'

'I know. She's kind, she'll look after them as well, if not better than us, because she makes sure that all the lodgers in the inn get enough to eat.'

'But you're still worried about them?'

'Have you thought they might not want to join us later but stay with her?'

'It's occurred to me.'

'They're our brothers, Richard. We should be looking after them.'

'Neither of us is in a position to look after anyone other than ourselves at the moment.' He leaned against the door.

'I suppose you're right.'

'You did want to come with me, didn't you?' He dreaded her answer but had to ask.

'I wanted to get away from Merthyr and like Mrs Edwards said, it's a good opportunity for you, and if I become a nurse, me.'

'You could have been a nurse in Merthyr.'

'Not at my age.'

'You could have started as a ward maid.' He frowned.

'About the Paskeys...'

'I don't want to talk about them, Richard. Not now, not ever. Please...'

'It's the same for both of us, Anna, we were both beaten. You do know they might not go to prison.'

'Of course they'll go to prison.'

'I overheard Mr Edwards talking to Dr Edwards. Without us to testify against them in court they might be acquitted.' He expected her to say something. When she didn't, he changed the subject. 'Mr Hughes told me to tell you he has a job for you as soon as you're well enough to leave your cabin.'

'What kind of a job?'

'He didn't say, but he seems kind for such an important man. It might be something to do with helping to look after the younger children.'

'Would I get paid?'

'I wouldn't have thought so. Not when Mr Hughes is covering our fares.' He stepped out of the cabin. 'Sleep tight, see you at breakfast.'

'Richard.'

He turned back.

'About what happened in Merthyr, it's not the same for both of us. You said you can't remember what the Paskeys did to you.'

'They knocked me out cold, you know that.'

'They didn't knock me out. I remember everything they did to me. That's why I don't want to talk about it.'

'Forget them. We'll never see them again. Get some sleep and don't worry about the boys. Knowing those two they're sitting up in bed right now, gorging themselves on a whole tray of Auntie Betty's bread pudding.'

'With a sugar crust, sultanas, and raisins.' She almost smiled.

'Night, Anna. Glad you're with me.' He meant it.

Chapter Eleven

Old house on fringe of Beletsky Estate
Ukraine, July 1870

Catherine Ignatova walked into the hall of her childhood home, stood at the foot of the staircase, and studied the decay. The walls had discoloured, the plasterwork was crumbling, and the few flakes of paint that still adhered to the woodwork were peeling.

'I wish I'd thought of this house when Mr Hughes was here. He could have looked it over and made a judgement as to whether it was worth renovating for one of his managers.'

Huw Thomas stood behind her. 'I'm glad you thought of it now, Madam. Given the builders' lack of progress, Mr Hughes will be grateful for any accommodation for the company workers. It would be dreadful if they arrived to find they didn't have a roof over their heads.'

'Especially with winter coming,' Catherine observed. 'Mr Thomas, please look around, give me your opinion, and be frank. I'm undecided whether to pay for renovations or tear the place down.'

'Shall we start upstairs, Mr Thomas? Sonya?' Alexei bounded up the sweeping staircase.

'Excuse me, Madam.' Huw followed at a sedate pace.

'If you've any sense you'll flatten the place.' Nicholas Beletsky sniffed. 'It's damp and rotting. I can smell it. Your father should have demolished this place when he built the new house fifty years ago.' He eyed the dirt on the marble floor, touched the wall, and rubbed the fingers of his gloved hand together. 'It's filthy.'

'So would you be if you'd been left to moulder for twenty years. My father didn't demolish this house because he thought my stepbrother could make use of it.'

'You mean he didn't want the drunk living with him.'

Catherine ignored the comment. There was no denying her stepbrother Sergei, the product of her stepmother's disastrous first marriage, had been a drunk, but she wished Nicholas would refrain from mentioning the fact. For all Sergei's faults she'd liked him when he'd been sober. Even as a child she'd sensed her father and stepmother's relief whenever Sergei left the Donbas for Moscow or St Petersburg. Trips that invariably resulted in his return sooner than hoped for, always the worse for wear financially, and frequently physically.

Alexei descended the stairs with Sonya and Huw. 'The bedrooms aren't too bad, Grandmother.'

'Mr Thomas?' Catherine asked Huw.

'All the rooms need cleaning and decorating, and the roof needs repairing. A few small leaks have resulted in damp patches in the corners of some of the rooms. But nothing appears too serious. I agree with Alexei, Madam. This house could be made serviceable and given the generous size of the rooms and their light and airy aspect, very comfortable.'

Alexei opened the double doors that led into the drawing room. He left footprints in the dust on the wooden floor. The furniture was shrouded in calico, the marble hearth, ash strewn. He pulled back one of the sheets to reveal a brass-inlaid mahogany table. 'This looks solid.'

'Apart from being old-fashioned it probably is.' Catherine walked in behind him. 'Few pieces were taken to the new mansion. My father wanted everything new; house, furniture, hangings, linen, dinner service, even silverware, so he left this place furnished for Sergei. Seeing everything shrouded like this is odd. I feel as though I'm lost in a nightmare. An abandoned child waiting for my parents to return to bring the house back to life.'

'I remember coming here with you when the steward lived here.' Alexei lifted another sheet to reveal a carved gilded chair upholstered in green velvet. The cloth was blotched by dark patches of mould.

'The poor man didn't stay long. He said the rooms were too big to heat in winter and to clean in summer when the dust storms blow. Alexei, go to the kitchens and bring Yelena and Praskovia here, please.'

'Not the Razins,' Nicholas snapped.

'Nicholas, forget this ridiculous prejudice you have against Yelena and Praskovia.' Catherine spoke in French, a language she knew Huw wasn't conversant with. 'If I'm going to rent or sell this house to one of Mr Hughes's managers, Yelena will make the perfect cook and Praskovia an excellent housekeeper. They have a right to comment on any restoration. Fetch them, Alexei.'

Alexei returned a few minutes later with the two women, Pyotr, and Yelena's brother, Feodor, who maintained most of the houses in Alexandrovka and built the few new ones that were needed.

'What do you think of the house, Yelena?' Catherine asked.

'The kitchens and servants' quarters need cleaning and painting, Madam. The stove is sound, although it needs a good scrub with a wire brush.'

'Everything could do with a good scrub, but not necessarily with a wire brush,' Catherine concurred.

'The staff quarters and store rooms are dry, the ice house cool and watertight, but the stables and banya need work, Madam.'

'You know your grandmother was cook here in my father's day, Yelena?'

'I remember visiting her here, Madam.'

'Would you like to take her place as cook and work here for the new occupants?'

'And live here, Madam?'

'In the servants' quarters with Praskovia and Pyotr. The three of you won't be able to manage on your own but you could hire people to help you, provided the new tenants or owners agree. Praskovia is old enough to take the position of housekeeper and Pyotr can do the heavy work and care for the horses. I'm sure you and Praskovia will be able to bring the place back to its former glory.'

'After the necessary repairs have been made to the roof and windows, certainly, Madam,' Yelena agreed. 'But our own house...'

'If you're prepared to consider renting it, Mrs Razin, the New Russia Company would be delighted to use it to accommodate company employees,' Huw interrupted.

Yelena looked at Praskovia.

Thinking of the income, Praskovia said, 'You can have it as soon as we've taken out our personal possessions, Mr Thomas.'

'Thank you, Praskovia.'

Catherine turned to Yelena's brother. 'What will it take to restore this house, Feodor?'

'Paint, paper, lead, new roof tiles to replace the broken ones; wood and glass to repair the windows, and a great many hours of labour, Madam.

You'll need an expert carpenter but Nathan Kharber is back.'

'He went to Paris to study medicine, not carpentry.'

'He did.'

'But now he's working as a carpenter?'

Feodor was too embarrassed to continue. Alexei wasn't.

'Nathan lacks paying patients, Grandmother.'

Nicholas burst out laughing. 'A Jewish doctor. Whoever heard of such a thing? Does he really expect people to consult him?'

'I don't see why not.' Alexei wanted to say more in Nathan's defence, but was afraid of arousing his father's curiosity as to where he'd acquired the information. If his father suspected his friendship extended to the Jewish as well as Cossack community he'd definitely lock him up.

'I suppose the Jews might trust him,' Nicholas conceded. 'But as they have no money it's no surprise he's returned to his father's trade. Surely he didn't expect things to have changed so much under this "progressive Tsar" Russia's been cursed with, that Jews would be entrusted with the health of Russians?'

Supressing her anger with Nicholas, Catherine changed the subject. 'How much will it cost to renovate the house, Feodor?'

'At least a thousand roubles for materials and labour, Madam. I won't be able to give you a definite figure until I've completed my survey.'

'A thousand roubles!' Nicholas exclaimed. 'My butler doesn't earn that much in five years.'

'Your butler has his living expenses and livery

paid for,' Catherine said. 'It's what I expected. A year's pay for a miner, and given the number of people that can be accommodated in this house, a tenth of its value if I sell and two years' rent if I lease. Come to the Dower House as soon as you have a detailed estimate, Feodor. I won't hold you to it until you've had time to study the damage but roughly how long will it take you to complete the renovation?'

'If the right craftsmen are available and there are no surprises hidden in the roof, under the floors, or behind the plasterwork, about three weeks, Madam.'

'Is that acceptable, Mr Thomas?'

'I'm not expecting Mr Hughes and his party to arrive before the end of the month, Madam.'

'If they do, we'll have to find them temporary lodgings in your house or mine, Nicholas.' Catherine saw Nicholas's mouth open and continued before he could begin another tirade. 'Hire as many men as can work together without getting in one another's way, Feodor. Begin in the servants' quarters so Yelena, Praskovia, and Pyotr can move in as soon as possible.'

'I will. Thank you, Madam.'

'Then it's settled. Hopefully the renovations will be completed by the time Mr Hughes and his party arrive, Mr Thomas.'

'Thank you for your concern, Madam. Finding sufficient accommodation is not going to be easy given the delays in the manufacture of bricks. If you've no objection, I'll move in here myself as soon as a suitable room can be made ready. I or rather the company will pay you rent until a sale is agreed. This is so much more comfortable than my room behind the site office.'

'I'd be delighted to have you as a tenant, Mr Thomas. I'm sure Praskovia and Yelena will look after you.'

'Thank you. Please, let me know when it's convenient for me to move in. Excuse me, Madam, Count, Miss Sonya. I have a meeting with the German contractor. Alexei, I'll see you in the office?'

'Thank you for sparing the time to look at this house, Mr Thomas.' Catherine shook Huw's hand.

'Considering the shortage of decent houses in the area, it's conceivable John Hughes might want this house for himself until he can build a better one,' Nicholas said as Huw rode away.

'Mr Hughes has accepted my offer to reside at the Dower House. Nicholas.'

Nicholas was astounded. 'When was this arranged?'

'Before Mr Hughes and Mr Edwards left for St Petersburg.'

'Where will you go?'

'I'm not moving out.'

'You don't have the staff to cater for long-term guests at the Dower House.'

'Which is why Mr Hughes will be bringing his own with him. The South Wing has a separate kitchen and entrance; it's taken very little organizing to make that section of the house self-contained.' Catherine turned to Yelena. 'Would you and Praskovia please begin by removing the dust covers and listing the contents of every room so I can check there's nothing here I want and it really is fully furnished.'

'I'll look in the study as I'm here. There may be something that Olga or I might find useful.' Nicholas went to the door. 'List all the books, paintings, and sculptures as well as the furniture, Praskovia. Don't forget to note their condition.'

'Yes, sir.' Praskovia acknowledged.

'Looking at this place, Catherine, you should sell it. If you rent it you may well find yourself facing a bill of another thousand roubles next year,' Nicholas advised.

'I'll only sell if I receive a reasonable offer. Don't forget, Nicholas, I'm a poor widow. Additional income would be useful,' Catherine watched him uncover a painting and check the artist's signature.

'Your husband left you well provided for, Catherine.'

'He also left me many expenses. Mr Hughes's contribution to my finances will be very welcome. The upkeep of the Dower House is not inconsiderable. There's also the maintenance of the roads to the village and shtetl...'

'Which is not down to you.'

'We all use the roads, Nicholas, even you, although you contribute nothing. Sometimes I think you forget our prosperity is linked to that of our neighbours. I look forward to receiving the lists of the house contents, Praskovia. Let me know what you've taken, Nicholas. Take me to my carriage please, Alexei, Sonya.'

'Grandmother.' Alexei offered her his arm.

'Yelena, Praskovia, Pyotr, would you like me to convey you back to the village?'

'There are hours of daylight left,' Praskovia took

an apron from her pocket. 'We'll begin making the lists. Uncle Feodor will drive us home in his cart, but thank you for the offer, Madam.'

'You have paper and pencil?' Alexei asked Praskovia.

'Uncle Feodor does. I'll borrow what I need from him.'

'I'll see you back at the house this evening, Alexei.' Nicholas returned from the study. 'Don't be late. Father Theodore will be waiting to give you your lesson in theology. Catherine, a word before you go. There are books I'd like to remove to my own library.' Nicholas glanced at his son. 'Isn't Mr Thomas waiting for you?'

'I'll see you tomorrow at lunch, Alexei?' Catherine offered her grandson her cheek.

Alexei took the hint, kissed his grandmother, said goodbye to Praskovia and Sonya, and whistled to the groom to bring his horse.

Nicholas waited for Catherine to enter the study; he followed and closed the door, shutting out Sonya, Praskovia, and Yelena.

'I'd forgotten my father ordered a door put into the back wall of his study that gave direct access to the kitchen and servants' quarters.'

'Wine cellar, you mean,' Nicholas corrected.

'My father was fond of his burgundy, but I think he had the door put in for the sake of convenience to his steward's office, which was off the corridor behind this room.' Catherine walked to the door and opened it. 'Strange how returning here has brought so many memories flooding back. Happy memories. I had a wonderful childhood.'

'Your father was a singularly indulgent man.'

'If by that you mean he knew how to enjoy life and make the lives of other people pleasant, I agree. Which books do you want?'

'I'll let you know when I see the list. Don't think I don't know what you're doing, Catherine.' He went to the window and watched Alexei mount his house.

'What do you think I'm doing, Nicholas?'

'Don't play the innocent with me.'

'I wouldn't dream of it, Nicholas, but I would like to know what you're accusing me of.'

'Alexei is infatuated with that ... that ... Cossack and you approve.'

'Cossack? You mean Praskovia?'

'Precisely. You throw them together every chance you get. You offer her and her family employment. You were instrumental in procuring the girl's mother the job of Alexei's wet nurse. Olga would never have thought of taking Yelena into my household if you hadn't suggested it.'

'If I was responsible for securing Yelena as Alexei's wet nurse, it was before Praskovia was born. You can hardly blame me for throwing her and Alexei together before she was even in her mother's womb. Alexei needed playmates...'

'He has his brothers,' Nicholas interrupted.

'He's your eldest son and had no brothers when he arrived. Yelena' s son Misha was the same age.'

'It's not Misha I'm talking about, it's Praskovia.'

'Alexei regards her as a younger sister.'

'Really, Catherine, do you think I'm stupid?'

'You can't expect me to answer that question

with any degree of honesty, Nicholas.'

Nicholas's face darkened. 'I've seen the way Alexei looks at the girl and the way she looks at him.'

'So have I, and all I've seen is affection. Alexei thinks no more of Praskovia than he does of Misha.'

'Rubbish! And, he can't think anything of Misha when the boy's in St Petersburg.'

'Out of sight doesn't mean out of mind. Five of your sons are in Allenstein. Do you never think of them because they don't live with you?'

'They're family.'

'Misha is Alexei's friend.'

'And Sonya?'

'What about Sonya?'

'You're not doing her any favours keeping her with you. She's developing a taste for a life and society she wasn't born into and isn't entitled to experience.'

'She's my stepbrother's child.'

'Possibly, possibly not, given Sergei's indiscriminate habits and the low women he consorted with. I've always had doubts as to the girl's paternity but one fact is inescapable: you're getting on, Catherine.'

'Now you're reminding me of my age. A most ungallant thing for a gentleman to do to a lady.'

'Instead of taking offence at what I say, don't you think it's time you thought of the girl? It's commendable you took her in considering her antecedents, but whether she's Sergei's child or not, she's undeniably illegitimate and for all you know the spawn of some other profligate. Her mother was a dancer.'

'A dancer with the Imperial Russian Ballet.'

'Imperial whores, more like. Hired for their looks and expected to sleep with aristocrats. Every one I've met had the morals of a farmyard cat.'

'The voice of experience, Nicholas?'

Nicholas refused to take Catherine's bait. 'You gave the girl a home when her mother died. You educated her with a view to her having to earn her own living, now it's time for her to do just that. If you don't know of any families who require a governess, I can put you in touch with several.'

'Sonya has a job. She's my companion.'

'If you moved out of the Dower House and into the Beletsky Mansion you wouldn't need a companion.'

'Nicholas, we both know we could never survive beneath the same roof for a day, so let's not pretend otherwise. I need Sonya's companionship and she will continue to live with me.'

'As long as you understand you're harming the girl by allowing her to mix with people above her station. When she becomes a governess...'

'Sonya's future is my concern, Nicholas.'

'My God, you don't intend to leave the girl any money ... surely you've made a will in my or at least Olga's favour...'

'You and Olga inherited fifty per cent of my late husband's estate, Nicholas. Aren't you content with that much?'

'You received as much...'

'It's mine, to dispose of as I wish, Nicholas. Good day.'

Catherine opened the door.

Nicholas hadn't finished. 'You've persuaded Alexei to stay here instead of accompanying me to St Petersburg.'

'It appears the boy is more interested in John Hughes's and Huw Thomas's plans than your lessons in aristocratic superiority.'

'I can't force Alexei to come with me.' Nicholas's grey eyes turned to steel. 'But I've employed Father Theodore to give the boy a thorough grounding in theology. I've also instructed him to keep the boy in his sight at all times after I leave and ordered him to sleep in Alexei's room. Across the doorway.'

'Do you really think that necessary?'

'Yes.'

'Aren't you being paranoid, Nicholas?'

'It's my way of ensuring the boy doesn't go tomcatting at night. I'll have no Cossack brats in my family, legitimate or otherwise.'

'Shouldn't that be "no more Cossack brats", Nicholas?' She looked him coolly in the eye. 'When do you intend to take Alexei to the whorehouse in Taganrog? Or have you already done so?'

'Who says...'

'It's obvious, Nicholas, as the boy's refused to visit St Petersburg with you. Did you think I was unaware of the delights you sample on your "business trips"?'

'My personal life is none of your concern.'

'Nor do I want it to be, but my daughter's and grandson's lives are. The boy has more sense than you, Nicholas. It's a pity you can't see it.' She swept out of the front door. Sonya was already in the carriage, talking to Praskovia through the open door.

Catherine had the grace to smile and wave to Nicholas as Praskovia helped her inside.

Beletsky Dower House Evening,
July 1870

'You're family, Alexei, and family don't use the kitchen door,' Catherine's cook, Lyudmila, admonished when Alexei walked into the servants' quarters of the Dower House.

'If I didn't, yours wouldn't be the first smiling face I see, Lyudmila.' He grabbed her ample waist, kissed her cheek, and waltzed her around the table.

'Get off with you.' She pushed him away. 'I suppose you want Kvass and pork blinis?'

'It's a long, thirsty, and hungry ride from my house, dinner was hours ago, and nectar in heaven won't match your home-brewed bread beer and savoury pancakes.'

'From the way you talk I swear you live on honey.' She poured him a glass of her fermented dark beer and set two of her savoury pancakes on a plate.

He took the plate and tankard, carried them to the window and hauled himself up on the sill before taking a bite from one of the pancakes. 'Is Sonya holding her English class in the servants' dining room?'

'She is, but before you ask, Praskovia isn't with them. Your grandmother has set your love and

Yelena to work in the old house.'
'I know.'
'You're well informed.'
'I was there earlier today with my father.'
Lyudmila 'humphed.' It was a sound Alexei had often heard his grandmother's servants' make whenever the count was mentioned.
'As your love isn't here you should go and see your grandmother.'
'Is she with anyone?'
'Father Grigor. He came to dinner and brought the charity list for the parish. It's longer than ever. The way some people expect your grandmother to pay their debts is not only scandalous but sinful.'
'As most of the money owed is to my father I suppose it stays in the family.'
'Not for long the way your father splashes his money around St Petersburg. He thinks we don't know what he gets up to, but people talk. The seed merchant told me your father dines every evening in the new Nevsky Hotel where one plate costs as much as a month's food for a family here.' Lyudmila would have never dared speak to any other Beletsky the way she did Alexei, but the servants knew he could be trusted not to repeat a conversation. Especially one that would land them in trouble with the count.
Alexei finished his beer and jumped down. 'I'll help Sonya with her lesson until Father Grigor leaves.'
'You should sit with Father Grigor and your grandmother. One day you'll have to take over her charity work. There isn't anyone else here who will

care for the poor.' Lyudmila managed to discount his father without actually saying his name.

'There's no need for me to take over because Grandmother will live to be a hundred.'

'Not if you keep worrying Her Excellency with your endless quarrels with your father.'

'The excitement I generate keeps Grandmother young. Thank you, Lyudmila, for a supper that has fed my soul as well as body.' He handed her his tankard and plate and opened the door to the servants' dining room.

Sonya had ranged a row of fruit down the centre of the table. Her students, all female, were repeating the English names as she held up each item in turn.

'Apple.'

'*Apple.*'

'Pear.'

'*Pear.*'

Sonya eyed Alexei. 'You've come to disturb us?'

'To help.'

'By flirting noisily with Lyudmila in the kitchen? Family should use the front door.'

'So Lyudmila told me, but I have my suspicions about Boris. He might be in my father's pay and my father doesn't like me visiting Grandmother, especially this late in the evening.'

'Boris has been in your grandmother's employ for over fifty years.'

'He's just the sort to turn traitor. He knows old age is coming and needs every kopek to keep himself in bread and vodka.' He pulled a chair out and sat beside Yulia and four Cossack girls, facing Ruth and two Jewish girls.

'Alma, Vera,' he gave the two Russian Mujiks who were sitting at the head of the table the benefit of his most charming smile. 'Glad to see you in Sonya's English class.'

'We'd better get jobs working for the new people after this.' Alma picked up a melon from the table and said, 'M-e-l-o-n,' slowly in a deep, guttural voice.

'Sonya's a good teacher. I'm sure you'll all get jobs the moment your new employers hear you speak.'

'Won't you be missed at home?' Sonya was irritated because her pupils had begun to primp and send flirtatious glances Alexei's way.

'No, because my father thinks I'm learning Greek in my study with Father Theodore. The priest fell asleep after dinner.'

'You mean you fed him enough wine to fall asleep,' Sonya suggested.

'Doesn't take much. Anyway, I decided I'd make the most of a fine evening, go for a ride, and visit here.'

'Your grandmother is talking to Father Grigor in the salon.'

'Lyudmila told me. I won't disturb them. That way Father Grigor won't have to lie if my father asks if he's seen me.' He opened the cutlery drawer and lifted out a selection of spoons, forks and knives. 'Who knows the English names for these?' He was careful to distribute his smiles and winks evenly among the girls but he was conscious of the presence of only one.

Ruth sat opposite him, her hands in her lap, her eyes downcast as she repeated the English words after Alexei and the others but he knew she was as aware of him as he was of her.

Soon, very soon, the sun would sink low and the girls would leave. He'd stay in the Dower House until darkness fell then ride out to the ruined monastery. If he were lucky he'd find Ruth waiting for him in the chapel.

Two years of secret meetings and still the only time he felt alive was during the minutes he stole from his everyday life to spend with her.

Chapter Twelve

Ships' convoy en route to the Donbas
September 1870

Anna Parry sat opposite John Hughes at a table in the salon, a writing tablet, bottle of ink, and cardboard file in front of her. A dozen other people were in the public area, reading, talking, and drinking tea. The tension was palpable. Every time someone left their seat to look out of a porthole people strained to hear their comments. Land was within sight but it was too distant to make out much beyond a grey strip of horizon.

Ignoring the excitement, John pressed his fingertips together, a sign he was deep in thought. He hesitated then continued dictating, '*...and so, Owen, I will finish this letter because we'll be docking shortly. I will write to you as often as I can, but once we disembark at Taganrog...*'

'Please slow down, sir.' Anna opened her file and copied Taganrog from her spell sheet into the letter she was writing to John Hughes's son Owen Tudor. The 'job' Mr Hughes had given her was to write letters he dictated to his youngest son. After she completed every letter, Mr Hughes encouraged her to add notes of her own composition.

'Owen Tudor will be more interested in what a young girl close to his own age has to say about the sights we've seen than his ancient father.'

She'd enjoyed writing the letters and looked forward to receiving Owen's replies to the missives Mr Hughes had posted in the ports they'd docked.

'Ready?' Mr Hughes checked when she dipped her pen nib in the ink.

'Yes, sir.'

'To continue ... *I will have little free time. I'm not looking forward to the journey from the port...*' he smiled at Anna, 'no Taganrog that time.'

'Thank you, sir. I always mix the letters up.'

'*...which will be overland to Hughesovka. We'll be using bullock carts and it promises to be hard, slow work, as we have a great deal of equipment and machinery to haul. After our arrival, there will be even more to do, not just for me, but also Anna Parry who has been kind enough to pen these letters from me to you. I look forward to hearing from you, Owen, when we are finally settled in Hughesovka.*

Never forget the town is named for every member of our family. Work hard in school, obey your masters and learn from them. Treat everyone you meet, no matter where they were born, what they do, or where they come from, as your equal. Live your daily life truthfully and honestly and no man will ask any more of you. I pray God will look after you and keep you, your brothers, sister, and mother safe. Your loving and proud father, John Hughes.'

'You can add your bit now, Anna.' John handed her a sovereign. 'As this is the last letter you will pen for me on board this ship, it's time you received your payment.'

'No, sir. I couldn't.'

'You've worked for me and work demands payment.'

'This isn't work, sir, I've enjoyed writing to your son.'

'The best work is the work we enjoy that doesn't seem like labour, but it still requires payment. Everyone should have a little money in case of emergency, Anna. You may be glad of that sovereign one day. Take it. I hope to see more of you and get to know you even better when we're in Hughesovka, where I hope you won't be too busy in the hospital to write my letters to Owen.' John dropped the coin into her file.

Sensitive to the needs of others, he'd realised that Anna couldn't bear to be touched by men, even before Glyn had confided the horrors inflicted on Anna by the Paskey brothers. 'Have you finished packing?'

'I've finished mine, sir, but I should check on Richard.'

'Last I saw, his clothes and the books he's borrowed were strewn from one end of his bunk to the other.' Glyn Edwards joined them.

'If you'll excuse me, Mr Hughes, sir, I'd better help him. I'll give you the letter, as soon as I've added my bit.' She gathered her writing materials.

'I'll send it from Taganrog.' He smiled as she ran off. 'You were right, Glyn, she's a good girl, and I've a feeling she'll prove to be a hard worker.'

'It's good of you to spend time with her, sir.'

'She's been the one helping me, not the other way round. Dictating letters made a pleasant change from poring over diagrams and plans for the furnaces. But,' he lowered his voice, 'she's still nervous around strangers. She's going to need careful handling, Glyn.'

'I know, and Peter and Sarah know. They've done a fine job of nursing her and her brother back to health.'

'Given the state of them when they came aboard, your brother's performed miracles. It's obvious those two had it rough without what happened to them just before they left Merthyr. When I listen to Richard talk about coal faces and engineering it puts me in mind of what I was like at his age. Precious little schooling except in the academy of hard knocks and a burning ambition to get on and learn all there is to know about modern industry.'

'Given what lies ahead, we need the ones who've learned to survive.'

'Let's hope they'll receive their just rewards in Hughesovka. Want to walk out on deck to see our new country?' John handed Glyn a cigar.

'Wouldn't miss it, sir.'

'Darling,' Sarah retreated as far from Peter as she could in their cramped cabin. 'Would you please find Glyn and Richard and walk on deck with them.'

'I'm not helping?'

'Not one little bit, and I'd like to leave the boat when we drop anchor.' She took a bundle of shirts from him and dropped them on to their bunk.

'I really can't help you?'

The expression on his face reminded her of the naughty child look the trainee nurses had given her whenever she caught them eating the last of the biscuits in the staff cupboard. 'No, you can't. Off with you, so I can finish what needs to be done.'

'Love you.' Peter kissed her cheek and grabbed his coat.

'I'll love you more when you're not under my feet.'

'I'm gone.' Peter walked on to the main deck. John was holding court in the centre of a crowd of men. They were looking at the seven ships sailing alongside their own, all loaded to the gunwales. Four with enormous metal boilers strapped to their decks.

Peter saw Glyn and Richard leaning on the rail. Like every man present, they were listening to every word John was saying. Steadying himself against the roll of the vessel, Peter joined them. The sun was shining but a stinging breeze dispelled its warmth. He felt the tang of an early autumn in its draught.

'...Problem is we're landing later in the year than I intended,' John declared. 'It's going to cause difficulties but there's nothing we can do, except meet them head on. I wanted to leave Britain months ago but so much of the equipment had to be manufactured bespoke it wasn't possible. A solemn warning, gentlemen: as Mr Edwards and I've discovered, winters can be cruel on the steppe.'

'I suspect we're about to find out just how cruel.' Peter looked to the horizon and the buildings slowly emerging into view. 'Is my nose playing tricks or is that the smell of Russia?'

A few men clamped handkerchiefs over their faces.

'Neither,' Glyn informed him. 'As there are no railways going our way, I wired ahead to have bullock carts ready. I know they've been kept waiting, but I assumed Huw Thomas would make arrangements to clear the manure.'

'As long as it is just bullock manure,' Peter qualified.

The men's laughter was subdued. No one other than John and Glyn knew what to expect. Peter sensed he wasn't the only emigrant harbouring doubts at the monumental step they'd taken.

'I've travelled widely in Russia and I promise you the country doesn't smell differently, or worse than Britain,' Glyn assured Peter.

'You're so easy to tease,' Peter leaned on the rail next to Glyn.

'The ferry boats and tugs are leaving port.' John spotted a flotilla of small craft heading out from land. 'If you haven't finished your packing, gentlemen, now is the time. The minute those boats reach us we'll begin disembarking.'

The men around them began to drift away.

'Shouldn't you be helping Sarah?' Glyn asked Peter.

'She threw me out of the cabin. Said she'd be better off doing everything herself.'

'Given the way she's taken care of everyone during this voyage, I've no doubt she will.' John studied the approaching boats through binoculars. 'It's going to take hours to offload our equipment. The captain warned me the sea's too shallow to allow ships close to the landing stages at this time of year. We'll have to transfer everything in the ferries.'

Peter eyed the massive boilers lashed to the decks. 'Which is fine for people, not so fine for equipment, especially my instruments. Some are very delicate.'

'Glyn, order the crew to handle all packages marked with a red cross carefully,' John warned.

'I'll tell them to watch them with the same care as my photographic equipment. I hate this waiting.'

'Another hour, we'll be on Russian soil. The waiting will be over and we can travel to the steppe,' John consoled.

'Are there really no roads?' Peter looked to John to contradict Glyn.

'If there had been I wouldn't have bought bullock carts. But,' John wrapped his arm around Richard's shoulders, 'we've plenty of young muscle with us. A few days of heavy hauling and we'll be at our new home.'

'If the rain holds off.' Glyn scanned the clouds.

'The rest of the journey is going to be rough, isn't it?' Peter questioned.

'It won't be pleasant, but don't worry about your wife. She'll hold up fine. As this lad and his sister will.' John smiled at Richard. 'Now, I have to visit the captain and finalise the arrangements.'

'I'll come with you,' Glyn volunteered.

'So you can stand next to us on the bridge and look important?'

'You know me so well, sir.'

'No hurry.' John looked back at the shoreline. 'Give it half an hour.'

'There are some things I'll never understand about John Hughes,' Peter said after John left.

'Like what?' Glyn asked.

'He's wealthy?' Peter offered Glyn and Richard his cigarettes.

'Beyond our dreams.' Glyn helped himself. 'He has a mansion in Greenwich that's larger and more luxurious than Cyfarthfa Castle. He has shares in the shipyard in Millwall that produced the *Great Eastern* in 1854. His wife is rumoured to have jewels the Queen covets, his sons are all studying or will study at university. His daughters are, or will be, debutantes, and he's invested a fortune in the New Russia Company.'

'So, he can afford to buy whatever he wants,' Peter continued.

'That must be wonderful.' Richard was envious.

'As you'll discover if you live long enough, Richard, money isn't everything. When you get older your wants diminish,' Glyn struck a match.

'Why on earth has Mr Hughes embarked on this expedition?' Peter persisted. 'If I was his age with his money I wouldn't put up with all this discomfort and uncertainty, not to mention separation from my wife and family. Especially when you consider this venture could fail.'

'Don't let John Hughes hear you say "fail",' Glyn warned. 'You haven't worked it out, Peter?'

'Worked out what?'

'Even in a mansion there's nothing worse than boredom and domestic day-to-day tedium that's crushed all excitement and challenge. Merthyr's bad enough, think what it must be like for Mr Hughes in Greenwich. I've stayed with him and seen the endless round of social functions and refined dinner and tea parties his neighbours expect him and his wife to attend. You're lucky to have Sarah. It wouldn't hurt to let her know how much you appreciate her sense of adventure and lack of interest in female frippery and the social niceties. Compared to most of her sex, she's a diamond.'

Port of Taganrog, Sea of Azov
September 1870

The first familiar face Glyn saw on the quayside was Alexei Beletsky. The boy was standing in the middle of a throng of black-coated, top-hatted dignitaries. All were monitoring the small boats that were carrying personnel and luggage from John's convoy that had been forced to anchor some distance out from the dock.

The moment John climbed out of a small boat he was mobbed by personnel from the consulate, distinguishable from the locals by the cut of their clothes. Alexei was in the centre of the group, but when he saw Glyn step out of one of the ferries he muttered his apologies to John and fought his way through the mob to join them. He drew Glyn past the porters hauling luggage; the food venders crying their wares, and the carriage drivers touting for trade.

'Mr Thomas isn't here. The construction workers went on strike in Hughesovka two weeks ago. Mr Thomas managed to get them back to work the day I left, but they were still grumbling. He didn't want risk leaving them, so he sent me to meet you.' Alexei looked at the ships. 'It's not going to be easy to unload those boilers.'

'So Mr Hughes understands.' Glyn looked around. Luggage was strewn from one end of the quay to the other. John was hemmed in on all sides. Hordes of people were milling around aimlessly and Glyn had no idea what he should do first, other than that he should do 'something'.

Alexei moved closer to Glyn so he could make himself heard above the cries of an old woman selling pickled cucumbers. 'I've hired porters and brought the bullock carts down to the dock. They're lined up behind the warehouses so the supplies can be loaded directly onto them.'

Glyn recalled the arguments between Nicholas Beletsky and his son about 'industry' and hoped the count wasn't lurking somewhere nearby waiting to make a scene. 'Does your father know you're here?'

'He's been in St Petersburg for the last three months attending to business. I'm here with my tutor, Father Theodore.'

'He's teaching you engineering and metallurgy?'

'Theology and ancient Greek. Useless subjects but Father Theodore says the mind is like a muscle that needs constant exercise. The only problem is the amount of valuable time he insists my muscle spend on the tedious lessons he gives me.'

'Where's Father Theodore?' Glyn saw no priest in high hat and black robe.

'Sick. He ate bad oysters last night.'

'You didn't?' Glyn was suspicious.

'I don't like oysters. My tutor will recover.' Alexei shrugged.

'From discussions with your father, I don't believe he'd be happy with your presence here.'

'My mother and grandmother know where I am,' Alexei countered.

'We didn't expect so many people to meet us. I hope someone's given a thought as to where we're going to sleep. I don't relish the thought of returning to my cabin.'

'Mr Hughes, you and your family party are staying at the British consulate. The address is Petrovskaya Street. Number 67.'

'You're well informed.'

'As Mr Thomas trusted me to meet you I've tried to think of everything. As soon as I arrived in Taganrog I went to your consulate. They told me your ships were expected today and they'd made arrangements to accommodate you in the consulate. If they hadn't, I'd have organised rooms and meals in one of the better hotels.'

Peter was overseeing the removal of the second tranche of their luggage from one of the boats. Glyn walked over to where Sarah, Richard, Anna, and Alf were standing guard over the more valuable items of their luggage. 'Everyone, this is Alexei Beletsky. He and his family will be our nearest neighbours.'

Alexei bowed and kissed Sarah and Anna's hands although Anna pulled hers away before his lips could touch her glove. 'I am pleased to meet you, ladies.'

'My brother, Dr Edwards.'

'Have rooms been booked for us at a hotel, Mr Beletsky?' Peter winced as a stevedore lifted a packing case marked with a large red cross from a boat only to drop it on the stone quayside.

'It's Alexei, Dr Edwards.' He shouted at the man who'd dropped the packing case in Russian and the porter took better care of the next box he unloaded.

'We're staying at the consulate,' Glyn answered Peter.

'I've been assured that the rooms there are comfortable, I haven't seen them...'

'I'm sure they'll be adequate, Alexei.' Glyn snatched a box of photographic plates from a dock worker. 'Peter, Alf, we need to safeguard our personal baggage and the hospital's equipment.'

'Leave it to me.' Alexei whistled and a man Glyn recognised as Nicholas Beletsky's coachman appeared. Alexei spoke rapidly to him in Russian and showed him the labels Sarah had affixed to her, Peter, Richard, Anna, and Glyn's luggage. 'Vlad will take care of your trunks, sirs.'

'And all the boxes marked with a red cross?' Peter added.

'And all those marked with this sign.' Glyn

pointed to the 'DELICATE' signs he'd pasted on to the crates that held his photographic equipment.

Alexei finished giving Vlad linstructions. 'All your luggage and the crates marked with a cross and that sign will be kept together in separate carts that Vlad will take care of.'

Glyn glimpsed John beckoning. 'I have to go.'

'We all do, Mr Edwards.' Alexei indicated a raised dais that had been erected at the far end of the quay. 'You will be expected to listen to the "Welcome to Russia" speeches the town council has rehearsed. There are chairs for the ladies...'

The remainder of Alexei's sentence was drowned out by a brass band striking a barely recognisable rendition of 'God Save the Queen'.

The ceremony Taganrog had organised to welcome John Hughes and his party was over an hour long, and because the speeches were in Russian, incomprehensible to most of the colliers and ironworkers. Given the wind that blew in from the sea, it was also cold. As soon as the brass band finished playing their final piece – the Russian National Anthem, 'God Save the Tsar' Glyn looked found Alexei.

'Will you take Mrs Edwards, Richard, and Anna to the consulate, while my brother, Alf, and I, make sure that all our luggage has been loaded?'

'I would be delighted and I will look after them well. Have no concern.' Alexei offered Sarah his right arm and Anna his left. 'Please, ladies, come with me.'

'You'll be safe with Alexei,' Glyn assured Sarah

and Anna. 'Peter and I will join you as soon as we're certain the more delicate boxes have been loaded.'

Sarah gave Anna, who was clinging to Richard, a reassuring smile. 'You men do what you have to, we'll be fine.'

'Can't I help you and Dr Edwards?' Richard asked.

Conscious the boy was still weak, Glyn drew him aside. 'Peter and I would appreciate it if you'd stay with Sarah and Anna. I know Alexei, but not well. I'd be happier if you were with them.'

Richard suspected Glyn's motives in asking him to stay with the women but didn't argue.

'I have a carriage here.' Alexei shouted to a stevedore in Russian.

'What a language! I'll never learn it. What on earth did he say?' Sarah asked.

'He asked the porter to carry your overnight bags to the carriage he's hired.' Glyn picked up Sarah's hat box.

'I didn't know you spoke Russian?' Sarah was dumbfounded.

'I understand more than I can speak, unlike Mr Hughes, who's proficient.'

Alexei led Sarah to the carriage. The coachman climbed down from the box and opened the door.

Alexei continued to bark orders in Russian before switching to English. 'I told the driver to load your luggage,' he explained. Anna and Sarah climbed inside, Alexei and Richard sat opposite them.

Peter handed Sarah the small case she'd packed

with her most personal possessions. 'Don't get used to travelling in style.' He indicated the quilted leather interior of the carriage, 'Glyn's hoping we'll leave tomorrow morning and we'll be travelling by cart.'

'Do we have far to go?' Anna hadn't shown much interest in either the journey or their destination. Sarah took her question as a positive sign of recovery.

'One hundred versts which is approximately,' Alexei stared at the roof of the carriage as if the answer was written there, 'sixty-two and a half of your English miles as a stork flies but eighty miles or more if we're to avoid rough ground.'

'One day or two's travelling?' Peter asked.

'By ox cart, a week, possibly longer.'

'You're joking?'

'Not at all, the ... how do you say it ... I know ... the terrain is difficult, Dr Edwards. Even for ox carts.'

Glyn joined them. 'The packages marked with a red cross are easily sorted but I need you to identify the rest, Peter.'

'I'm with you.' Peter blew Sarah a kiss and followed Glyn.

'Russian sounds impossible,' Sarah commented.

'I will teach you to speak it,' Alexei spoke with supreme confidence. 'Two months from now you'll be conversing like a native.'

'I doubt it. Not your ability to teach, but mine to learn.' Sarah returned the blue-eyed, blond, fresh-faced young man's smile. 'I think Mr Hughes, Mr Edwards, and my husband are lucky to have you to help us.'

'They are,' Alexei assured her. 'So are you. I will show you Taganrog. The town has many beautiful buildings. It was founded by our forward-looking Tsar Peter the Great in 1698.'

'We get a history lesson too,' Sarah teased gently.

'I try to be knowledgeable about my country. First I will take you to the consulate so you can drink tea. You English always drink tea in the afternoon, don't you?'

'Yes, please, but we're not English, we're Welsh,' Richard corrected.

'Wales is the Western part of England?'

'We're a separate country,' Richard growled.

'You can educate me about the geography of your country of Wales. So few people in Russia know anything about foreign lands, it's difficult to decide which travellers' tales to believe.' Alexei smiled at Anna.

She didn't return his smile or look him in the eye. After what the Paskey brothers had done to her she found it difficult to look at any man other than Richard. But she'd noticed that Alexei was good-looking. Very possibly the best-looking boy she'd ever seen.

British Consulate, Taganrog
Evening, September 1870

The grand hall was hot, noisy, and odorous. The sweet, occasionally sickly perfumes of the ladies vied with the pungent, acrid scents of human perspiration and bullock dung carried in on shoes from the street. The place would have been considered heaving with half as many people crammed within its walls.

The conversation was raucous, and in so many languages, all but one indecipherable, that Richard felt as though he'd been incarcerated in a madhouse.

The reception the consulate staff had organised for John Hughes, his senior managers, and their relatives had been scheduled to last an hour, but three hours after the first guests arrived, waiters were still pouring champagne and handing out caviar, and porters were ushering latecomers towards the master of ceremonies so they could be announced.

Richard gave up trying to decipher what was being said and retreated to a sofa set below the staircase. His hopes of indulging in quiet reflection ended when Alexei joined him.

'You are an ironworker?' Alexei handed him one of the glasses of champagne he'd taken from a waiter.

'I was a collier, but when I left I was training to be a repairman,' Richard said grandly.

'What does a repairman do?' Alexei shattered Richard's hope that the title 'repairman' would impress.

'Checks the props that keep the ceiling up in the tunnels are solid, makes sure the walls and ceiling of the shaft are sound and there's no danger of falls or collapse.'

'That's an important job. So, you won't be working in Mr Hughes's ironworks but one of the mines Mr Hughes will sink to dig out coal to fuel his furnaces?'

'It's not been decided, but I may be working in the mine Mr Edwards hopes to open. It was Mr Edwards' brother who recommended I join this expedition. He was my boss in Merthyr.'

'Merthyr. That's where Mr Crawshay has an ironworks?'

'You know about Crawshay's ironworks?' Richard was surprised.

'I have read everything I could find on modern industry. You're young. How long have you been a collier?'

'I started working as a trapper when I was eight years old. I worked the ventilator to get air into the shaft,' Richard added when he saw Alexei's puzzled look.

'In Russia only the children of the very poor work in the mines.'

'My father died when I was eight.'

'So you were poor?'

'My mother was left with nine children and no breadwinner.'

Realising he'd been tactless, Alexei said, 'You must have gained a great deal of experience as you started work so young.'

'Some, not as much as many of the colliers Mr Hughes has recruited. Why are you so interested in mining, Mr Hughes, and his affairs?' Richard was suspicious.

'I'm interested in progress. I've travelled a little, not as much as I would have liked, but I've seen Paris, Berlin, Rome, Venice, and London. Of all the cities, I thought London the most interesting. Your country has built so much since it entered the industrial age, yet it's so small. When Russia embraces modernisation, I believe it will become a rival for Britain's crown as the pioneering engineering nation of the world. My family owns land where Mr Hughes will sink his mines and build his ironworks, so we will be neighbours. I hope we're going to become great friends.'

Richard avoided commenting. 'Will your family develop your land?'

'My father has sold some to Mr Hughes. I would like to develop the rest, which is why I want to learn all I can about the production of metals, mining, and engineering.'

'Mr Edwards told me there'll be nothing to hold me back in Russia except the limit of my ambition.

'You are ambitious?'

'Very. I have two younger brothers and…' Richard fell silent when he realised he was about to mention Alice to someone he'd only just met. But Alexei wasn't like anyone he'd known.

'You'd like to own your own mine one day?' Alexei suggested.

'That really is a dream.'

'Why? I have land, you have the skills, and you seem to be a thoroughly nice fellow. I think we could work well together.'

'I'm only seventeen.'

'I'm eighteen. The right age to make dreams happen. It's boring here. Would you like to creep out and look round the town? There are a few places that sell good vodka and can offer young people fun.'

'Mr Edwards said we'll be leaving very early tomorrow,' Richard cautioned.

Alexei laughed. 'By bullock cart? All the animals have to be harnessed. Even if the drivers begin work before sunrise they won't finish until late afternoon. We won't be leaving early tomorrow. So what do you say to tasting the nightlife of Taganrog?'

Richard looked at Glyn. 'I'll have to ask Mr Edwards, but he won't mind as long as we're not out too late.'

'Tell him you're going to share my hotel room. There are two beds and that way he won't know how late we stay out.' Alexei winked. 'We'll be back before breakfast. I'll get my coat and ask the porter to hire us a carriage.'

Chapter Thirteen

Taganrog
Evening, September 1870

Richard gazed out of the carriage window at the broad streets and palatial white stone and red brick buildings illuminated by brilliant street lights. 'I didn't expect this.'

'This what?' Alexei asked.

'This incredible city. It's beautiful. The street lighting is so bright, so clear. So different from the gas lamps back home.'

'The lighting's oil and Taganrog's a town, not a city.'

'So's Merthyr.'

'You surprise me. With the ironworks there I thought it would be a city. I wanted to visit the place when my father took me on a tour of Europe but when we reached Great Britain he wouldn't leave London.'

'Dr and Mr Edwards talk about London sometimes. I've never been there.' Richard wondered if he'd ever have the opportunity to visit the city now he'd left Britain.

'What's Merthyr like?'

'Small compared to this, with narrow streets. The ironworks are in the centre, and pump out smoke day and night, dirtying the air and the streets. This is so clean and there are so many enormous buildings. It's how I imagined ancient cities like Rome. Is that a church?'

'Greek Orthodox, St Helen and St Konstantine.' Alexei ecited like a tour guide. 'Taganrog has to cater for many religions because it's a port and sailors are of many faiths. There's a German Lutheran church, a Greek monastery, a synagogue, the Russian Orthodox St Mikhall, you can see two of its five domes over there, shining in the moonlight.'

'Do you have a Catholic church?'

'You are Catholic?' Alexei found a pack of cigars, opened it, and extracted two.

'Welsh chapel.'

Alexei laughed. 'Whatever that is, I don't think Taganrog has a church to cater for it. That's the library, the assembly hall, the court...'

'That is beautiful, like a palace.' Richard pulled down the window of the carriage and leaned forward to get a better view.

‘It’s the theatre.’ Alexei gave him a cigar.

Richard took it, not wanting to tell Alexei he’d never smoked a cigar in his life. ‘That one?’

‘A school, but there are several mansions here because many wealthy men live in Taganrog, government officials as well as businessmen who own shipping companies.’ Alexei struck a Lucifer.

Richard drew in cigar smoke and coughed. ‘That mansion to the left is huge even though it’s only one storey. It looks bigger than Cyfarthfa Castle – that’s where Mr Crawshay who owns the ironworks in Merthyr lives,’ he spluttered.

‘That is a palace. Tsar Alexander died there in 1825, that’s why we have so many monuments to him in the town. He’s Taganrog’s most famous resident. Didn’t Mr Hughes and Mr Edwards tell you Taganrog was a town?’

Richard rested the hand that was holding the cigar outside the carriage window so he wouldn’t have to breathe in smoke. He was tempted to drop it but he didn’t want to hurt Alexei’s feeling by appearing ungrateful. ‘Mr Edwards told me we were going to an empty plain. He called it a step...’

‘You spell it with two p’s and an e,’ Alexei broke in. ‘S-t-ep-p-e.’

Richard suddenly realised that Alexei had learned English as a second language – and not only learned it, but mastered its spelling. Awed and envious, he said, ‘You’ve been well educated.’

‘You wouldn’t say that if you saw the military academy I attended. Two hours every morning and two every evening were wasted in useless drills and weapon training.’

'You obviously learned a great deal there.'

'I'd have expanded my knowledge to include more of the things I'm interested in, like engineering, if I'd been allowed to read what I wanted to instead of wasting time on drills. As for where Mr Hughes intends to build his town, Mr Edwards is right, it's a plain. There's very little there. A Cossack village of wooden houses, my father's house and estate, my grandmother's house, and a Jewish shtetl – what you call a hamlet because it's smaller than a village. I've been working for Mr Thomas since Mr Hughes and Mr Edwards visited my grandmother last year. Mr Hughes left him to oversee the construction. Considering the trouble he's had with the builders, he's made good progress. The foundations for the furnaces are laid and there's a wooden office he uses as headquarters for Mr Hughes's company. When I left three weeks ago the hotel was finished and they were beginning to put a roof on the hospital.' Alexei glanced out of the window. 'Here we are. Petrovskaya Street. The Cossacks always stay at the Hotel Bristol.'

'Cossacks, real Cossacks?'

'Unlike fairies, they exist.' Alexei reached for the door handle. 'The regiment will escort Mr Hughes's convoy to the new town, garrison, and police it.'

'That's a hotel?' Richard admired a white-colonnaded building that resembled sketches of the Parthenon.

'That's Gairabetov's mansion. Beautiful, isn't it. One day I will make enough money to build one like it, but not here, in St Petersburg. Now that's a wonderful city. People call it the Venice of the North. The hotel is higher up the street. The redbrick building.' Alexei knocked the roof of the carriage but the driver was already slowing the horses.

Dozens of men dressed in dark blue jackets and trousers with red stripes down the sides filled the street. They were cheering two men who were standing to attention on the saddles of cantering horses. One was smoking, the other drinking from a tankard. Both waved, as calm and confident as if their booted feet were on firm ground.

'They say Cossacks are born in the saddle. Those two haven't begun to show off. A few more pails of vodka they'll be riding two horses apiece with a foot on the back of each. Come, I'll introduce you.' Alexei opened the door. Before he could step out, a tall, dark haired officer with a moustache, dressed in a startling white uniform and cap, picked Alexei off the step as if he were a child.

The two men started talking. Richard couldn't understand a word either was saying. He doubted they could, as they were speaking at speed and over one another. After a few minutes Alexei stepped back.

'Richard Parry, meet my very good friend, almost brother, and Cossack lieutenant, Mikhall Razin. Misha, Richard is English.'

'It's not lieutenant, it's captain,' Misha corrected Alexei in strongly accented English, 'but as you are a friend of Alexei, it's Misha, Richard.'

Richard braced himself as Misha favoured him with the same strength bear hug he'd given Alexei.

'I'm Welsh, not English,' Richard protested when Misha released his iron grip.

'You'll have to get used to people saying you're English, no one understands Welsh in Russia.' Alexei turned to Misha. 'When did you learn to speak English, *Captain* Razin?'

'The officers were sent to classes when orders came through posting the regiment to the new town Mr John Hughes is building.'

'You were posted? You didn't volunteer?'

Misha fingered the insignia on his officer's jacket. 'They offered me promotion. I wasn't going to turn it down, nor the chance of eating my mother's cooking again. Come.' He hooked his arms around Alexei and Richard's shoulders. 'I have a fresh pail of vodka, and the scrambled eggs and ham in this hotel have to be tasted to be believed. We'll eat a few slices of heaven while catching up on one another's news.'

Hotel Bristol, Taganrog
Late evening, September 1870

The vodka pail was a metal cylinder with a cap that could be used as a measure. It reminded Richard of his mother's milk can but the contents couldn't have been more different. Drinking the strong spirit was worse than smoking a cigar. Gasping, he struggled for breath as soon as he took a sip.

'There are a few things you need to learn about Russia, Richard.' Alexei's eyes were already glazed by alcohol. 'First, never try to ride like a Cossack.'

'I've never ridden a horse,' Richard whispered. When he found his voice it was faint and squeaky.
'You have no horses in England?' Misha was horrified.
'Rich people have horses in Britain,' Richard croaked. 'Poor people use their legs.'
'I couldn't live without my horses.' Misha refilled his own and Alexei's glasses. 'Drink up.'
Richard manfully lifted his glass to his lips and pretended to sip the fiery liquor.
'The Cossack nations have to breed horses. Without them we couldn't fulfil our obligation to the Tsar.' Misha raised his glass at the mention of Tsar and drained the contents.
'Every male Cossack has to serve in the military for twenty years,' Alexei explained.
'We have to supply our own horse and uniform. But the Tsar gives us our weapons,' Misha added.
'Twenty years! That's a lifetime.' Richard was shocked.
'It's not so bad. The last five are served in the reserves. Then we leave our station, return to our villages, marry, and breed children.' Misha winked at a pretty blonde waitress.
'To continue your Russian education, Richard,' Alexei's speech as well as his eyes was now affected by vodka. 'Never try to outdrink a Cossack if you have plans for the following day. The Cossack will rise with the sun. You'll be lucky to see the sunset.'
Misha shouted at the waitress he'd winked at. 'Elise?'
She left the lap of an officer and joined them. Misha lifted her on to his knee. 'Elise, say hello to Alexei and Richard.'

'Pleased to meet you.' Her English was heavily accented. The sultry look she sent Richard's way set his pulse racing.

'We would like ham and eggs.'

'You mean you would like me to get them.' She nibbled Misha's ear.

'Thank you for offering. Are Marie and Colette free tonight?'

She wriggled from his lap. 'What do you think? A whole regiment and only three girls. No chance.'

'Pity,' Misha slipped his arm around her waist, 'my friends are fine strapping men who know how to give a girl a good time.'

'The regiment's full of fine strapping men; as for giving a girl a good time, none of you have a clue.' She removed Misha's cap and ran her fingers through his hair.

Misha slapped her thigh. 'Ham and eggs for three, woman.'

'On your bill, Misha?'

'On me,' Alexei slipped his hand into his pocket and pulled out a banknote.

'Thank you, sir.' Elise snatched it from Alexei's fingers.

'He'll want change,' Misha warned.

'Or personal service?' Elise leaned over Alexei.

He grabbed her hand before her lips could touch his. 'Thank you for the offer, but the love of my life would object.' He kissed her fingertips.

'But it's worth paying a few kopeks for good waitress service. No?' Elise cooed.

'No more than five.' Misha watched her hips sway as she walked away. 'She's an expert between the sheets, Alexei; you should have taken her up on her offer, if not tonight then tomorrow. It will take us days to get to Alexandrovka.'

'I'm spoken for.'

'My sister's a woman of the world. She'll forgive a passing encounter after all the rutting she did with Ivan Kalmykov before he was killed.'

'Who told you?'

'Igor.'

'Yulia's brother? He's wrong.'

'You're not courting Praskovia?' Misha reached for the pail again, and slopped more vodka into his glass. 'If it's not Praskovia then...' his features hardened along with his suspicions. 'Surely you've grown out of your boyish infatuation.'

'It's not an infatuation. I will marry her when I come of age.'

'You'll be an idiot if you do.'

'Misha, you know her...'

'I know what she is.' Misha slammed his glass on the table so hard the vodka shot out. 'Decent people will be sickened by the pair of you. Damn Praskovia for allowing you to use her.'

'She offered after Kalmykov was killed.'

'Stupid girl. If your father discovers the race of your intended,' Misha drew a line across his throat with his forefinger, 'neither you nor your bride will live long enough to enter the church. That's if Father Grigor is crazy enough to allow a Christ killer inside the holy walls.'

Alexei glared at Misha. 'When did you begin to call the Jews "Christ killers?"'

'When the regiment taught me to see sense.'

'You grew up alongside Jews...'

'I grew up alongside you, Alexei. Marry the bitch and you'll be likened to the horned goat in the fairy tale that wanted to fuck a duck to sire an egg.'

Lightheaded, dizzy, unable to focus for more than a few seconds, Richard didn't see Alexei throw the punch that floored Misha.

He was aware of people around them. Of a cacophony of noise. Men cheering. Skin splitting. Blood spattering and spraying the walls. A thud when Alexei crumpled to the ground. Misha and Alexei hammering at one another as they rolled on the floor. The slap of fists connecting with flesh. The crunch of bone connecting with bone.

A middle-aged man, in a uniform adorned with more gold braid and medals than any other officer, pushed his way through. He shouted in Russian, succeeded in taking control, and separated the protagonists.

The men began to disperse. The middle-aged officer continued to bark orders. He gripped Misha's shoulder with one hand, Alexei's with the other and shouted until they reluctantly extended their hands. After they shook hands he returned to his table and Misha and Alexei sat, still glowering at one another.

'Colonel Zonov reminded Misha that a gentleman doesn't insult his guest, and me, that a guest has no business attacking his host. But this isn't finished.' Alexei clenched his teeth to contain his anger.

Hoping he looked more alert than he felt, Richard nodded. When he felt it was safe to move without colliding with anyone, he abandoned his glass and rose to his feet. The room swung alarmingly around him. He gripped the table to steady himself.

Misha snapped. 'Where are you going?'

Richard felt as though his lips were made of India rubber and his mouth stuffed with cotton wool. 'I shhhould returnsh to the Conshulate.'

'There's no need to hurry. I told you it will take the drivers all morning to harness the bullock carts.' Alexei emptied his glass.

Misha refilled it with bad grace but only because his colonel was watching him. 'We're moving out early. Mr Hughes ordered the drivers to begin getting the carts ready hours ago.'

'Your ham and eggs.' Elise set three plates on their table. Misha held out his hand. She dropped a few coins into his palm. He glanced at them but didn't attempt to hand them to Alexei. Elise added two more. Misha still didn't move.

'That's enough, Misha,' Alexei ordered.

'Five kopeks is generous. She's kept fifteen. Ten buys an hour of her company, be sure to claim it.'

'I give you ten kopeks' worth of Elise's time and five kopeks to her. My gift.' Alexei pocketed the coins Misha dropped on the table.

'I don't want your cursed gift,' Misha retorted.

'You want your colonel to come back over here?' Alexei goaded. 'Raise your voice again and he will. He's looking our way.'

Taking advantage of Misha and Alexei's taunting, Elise dropped the coins she'd kept down the front of her gown. 'Don't expect me to serve you ham and eggs during that hour, Misha.' She walked away.

'Colonel Zonov's watching every move we make,' Misha hissed.
'I know,' Alexei snapped.
'Truce?'
'You expect me to forget what you said?'
'For tonight. But you should know, Alexei, everyone in the regiment holds the same opinion about Jews.'
'Then you're all fools.'
'John Hughes and your father will be the fools if they leave the shtetl standing once the regiment occupies the barracks. But,' Misha picked up his fork. 'A truce is a truce.'
'Only until morning,' Alexei pushed his plate away.

When Alexei's untouched plate and Richard's and Misha's half-full ones had been cleared, Richard rose again.
'I wantsh to pay for the vodkash, but I have no Russhiansh money. I will get some from Mr Edwardsh...'
Misha fastened his hand on Richard's shoulders and pressed him back on to his chair. 'I invited you and Alexei to join me. I pay for the vodka.'
'Rule number three; never refuse a Cossack's hospitality. He'll kill you if you do.' Alexei pushed his chair away from the table.
Turning his back to his colonel, Misha clamped his right hand on the hilt of his sword. 'Drink up, Richard, you're falling behind.' He refilled his own and Alexei's glasses with his left hand, without relinquishing his grip.
The atmosphere darkened, spawning fear. It

even percolated through Richard's addled brain. He picked up his vodka and lifted it, intending to toast Mr Hughes in an attempt to reconcile Alexei and Misha, but before he could speak he fell forward out of his chair.

He landed face down in a welter of splintering glass; his last thoughts were confused. He simply couldn't understand why the floor felt so soft.

Chapter Fourteen

Road from Taganrog to Alexandrovka
The Donbas, September 1870

Richard woke in broad daylight. He sensed he was moving and squinted up at the sky. By the height of the sun it was mid-afternoon. He turned his head and a stabbing pain shot through his eyes. His mouth was dry, his head hurt, and his stomach churned; nauseated by a barnyard smell, which wasn't surprising as he was lying on damp, dirty sacks. He heard a bullock low and realised he was in the back of a cart.

'How are you feeling?'

He tried to focus. The sun had never shone brighter. Something moved to block his vision. He looked up at Alexei.

'Where am I?'

'About two versts outside Taganrog. I carried you back to your room to prove to Mr Edwards and your sister that you were still alive. I packed your belongings but your sister checked I hadn't left anything behind. I don't think she approves of me.'

'Right now, I don't approve of you or me.' Richard struggled upright.

'Your head hurts?'

'A dozen little men are clog dancing in my brain.'

'Explain clog dancing?'

'Another time.'

'This should make you feel better.' Alexei dropped the reins of his horse, reached down into his boot, and pulled out a silver flask. He passed it to Richard.

Richard unscrewed the top and sniffed the contents. 'It's water, you funny fellow.'

'Just checking it's not what we were drinking last night.'

'I bought a few pails of vodka for the journey. If you join me tonight we can continue our discussion without Misha and the Cossacks.'

'I'm busy.'

'Doing what, in a bullock train?'

'I'll think of something.'

'Richard, about last night...'

'I don't remember much.'

Alexei leaned closer to Richard and lowered his voice. 'You remember I had a fight with Misha?'

'You shook hands afterwards.'

'Don't say anything about it to anyone. Or repeat what Misha said about the Jews.'

'I didn't understand half of what Misha said.'

'Promise you won't say anything, especially to Mr Edwards or Mr Hughes.'

Richard almost nodded then decided he'd only make his head ache even more. 'Where's my sister?'

'With the driver and Mrs Edwards at the front of this cart.'

Head pounding, Richard clambered to his knees and climbed over the sacks to the bench seat where Anna was sitting withMrs Edwards. He moved behind them.

Sarah greeted him. 'Good morning – or rather afternoon, Richard.'

'Mrs Edwards. I'm sorry.'

'It's your sister you should apologise to. She thought you'd been kidnapped when you didn't return to the consulate last night.'

'I was worried about you,' Anna reproached.

'We tried to convince her Alexei would look after you. It appears he did.'

'I remember him advising me not to drink vodka with a Cossack. As we were both doing just that it seemed a peculiar thing for him to say. I promise you, Mrs Edwards,' he sat alongside Anna and wrapped his arm around her. 'I'll never drink vodka again.'

'Spoken like a man with a hangover who's feeling sorry for himself. Your good intentions will be forgotten the moment your head clears.'

'I won't argue with you, Mrs Edwards, but I mean what I say.'

'I'm certain at this moment you do.'

The convoy crawled slowly forward as far as Richard's eye could see. At its head he made out the heavily built figures of John Hughes and Glyn Edwards. They'd reined in their horses and were watching the column. He turned. The line of carts behind them was endless as the one in front.

'Two versts behind us, only another ninety-eight to go.' Alexei was still riding alongside them. He tipped his cap to Sarah and Anna. 'I have friends who live close by. I'll ride ahead and see if they can provide accommodation for you ladies tonight.'

'Please don't trouble yourself, Alexei. I believe Mr Hughes has made provision for people to sleep in the carts.'

'You'd be more comfortable in a house.'

'I'd also miss my husband and Anna her brother.'

'So we all camp, like gypsies?'

'I believe that's the intention – but thank you for the offer, Alexei.'

'I hope the place we're going to isn't like this,' Anna said.

'In what way?' Richard asked.

'Flat and empty.'

'Even if it is, it won't be for long,' Sarah predicted. 'A few years of hard work and we'll build a town as elegant and imposing as Taganrog.'

'First we have to get there.' Richard's head was aching unbearably. He longed to stand somewhere still and quiet.

'A few more days. We're almost at journey's end.' Sarah waved to Peter who was walking ahead of the cart.

'Journey's end,' Anna repeated. 'That sounds good.'

Richard squeezed her hand. He hoped when

they were settled in their new home they would regain the close familiarity that had bound them together in the basement house in the court. But for the moment he couldn't help feeling Anna was slipping away from him.

As John had warned, and every emigrant in the convoy soon discovered, there were few roads over the steppe and none of any substance between Taganrog and Hughesovka. What John and Glyn hadn't expected were the substantial tolls every landowner exacted before allowing their carts to cross their estates. Even with Alexei to negotiate, their progress was expensive – and slow.

Rain began to fall two days after they left the port. The Russians assured them rain at that time of year was rare and the weather would soon turn dry. But the downpour proved relentless. By the fifth day everyone and everything in the column was drenched.

The blankets they wrapped themselves in and their clothes, even the ones stored in trunks, were sodden. Most people saw no point in changing out of the dripping outfits they were wearing. The cooks did their best to make tea and warm soup under canvas in the back of the carts but as soon as the liquid was served it became so diluted by rainwater it lost all vestige of warmth.

John instructed the senior members of the party to remain resolutely cheerful, but by the fifth day even Glyn was beginning to show signs of strain. That night the camp was quieter than any evening since they'd left Taganrog. The drivers, too tired to talk let alone sing, huddled on top of the feed carts, sheltering as best they could beneath canvas, sharing their vodka pails. Glyn and John had taken their brandy flasks and retired early, crawling into a boiler they'd lined with straw and transformed into a temporary bedroom.

Peter alone braved the glutinous mud, tramping from cart to cart dispensing shots of brandy and cough syrup. By the time he finally struggled back to the cart he and Sarah were sharing with Richard, Anna, and Alexei he felt as though he'd been swimming fully clothed in a river. But there was nothing he could do other than wrap himself in a blanket slightly less sodden than his clothes and lie down next to his wife in the hope that sleep would come.

Three versts from Hughesovka, the Donbas
Late afternoon, day six, September 1870

'Looks like this cart, along with a dozen others, will be staying here tonight – and probably, given the quagmire it's sunk into, even longer, sweetheart.' Peter squelched from the back of the cart loaded with his and Glyn's luggage to the front where Sarah sat between Anna and the driver. 'The axle is glued firm. As fast the men are shovelling out the mud it's oozing back in.'

'The two largest boilers are stuck.' Glyn splashed towards them. 'The drivers say we've no chance of shifting them until the ground freezes. Then we might be able pickaxe them out but there'll only be a small window between the frost and the first snow. Apparently snow causes as much of a problem as mud.'

'In which case I take it we'll be camping here overnight?' Sarah tried to sound matter-of-fact. They'd been forced to leave so many carts full of supplies behind that Glyn had lost count, and there was still no sign of civilization on the horizon. 'Is there a relatively dry spot within wading distance?' She looked at the black slime that caked Peter's boots, trousers, and coat.

Glyn leaned against the cart. 'Alexei left an hour ago to fetch fresh horses and carriages from his father's house. Our destination is only three versts ahead. That's not even two miles.'

'Where?' Sarah rose from the bench seat and peered all around. 'I can't see anything other than rain and a few trees.'

'If our new home isn't behind a tree I suppose it could be down a rabbit hole.' Glyn tugged at his knee to heave his right foot out of the mud. He succeeded in freeing his leg, but at the cost of soaking his trousers.

'We're really almost there?' Anna asked.

'Home,' Peter smiled. 'Not before time, looking at you ladies. Wash and brush ups all round, a hot meal, followed by sleep in a warm, dry, clean bed under a roof...'

'Wash and brush up! Have you looked at yourself in a mirror lately?' Sarah interrupted.

'I did say "all round". But unlike you ladies, we men are used to roughing it. You delicate hothouse creatures can't wait to enjoy the luxury of indoors.'

'After what Mrs Edwards and Anna have been

through since Taganrog, I will never call them delicate again,' John went to inspect the back of the cart.

'I listened to the grumbles around the camp fires last night, and as every one of them came from men. I'd argue we're no more fragile than you, Peter,' Sarah rebuked. 'As for "indoors", would you prefer to sleep in a wagon than beneath a roof?'

'I wouldn't turn down a warm bed and hot bath,' Glyn rubbed his hands together in an effort to warm them.

'I'd prefer not to think of either until I have them in sight.' Peter stared at the horizon. 'My eyes are playing tricks. I can't see any difference between land, air, and water. Thank heavens you arranged for Alexei to meet us, Glyn. This journey would have been unbearable without him to advise us.'

'Neither Mr Hughes nor I arranged anything. The boy met us because he likes working for the New Russia Company and hopes to continue doing so. But I've heard his father's views on industrialisation. Alexei may not be allowed to work for us much longer if the count discovers he's acted as our guide on this distinctly un-aristocratic trek.'

'Alexei's father is the count who's to become our neighbour? The count you wrote to me about?' Peter asked.

'That's the one. If he finds out Alexei's been getting his hands dirty he'll probably throw him out of the Beletsky ancestral home. He considers aristocrats above manual labour.' Glyn surveyed the wagons ahead of them. Alf and Richard were helping the stockmen and Cossacks unharness bullocks from the marooned carts. Despite the drivers' best efforts, several of the animals were too tired to extricate themselves. They'd lost over a hundred beasts. Given the conditions, he suspected they'd lose more despite their proximity to Hughesovka.

Glyn was pleased with Richard. The boy had made friends of the drivers and stockmen by working harder than any of the hired hands after he recovered from his hangover. With Alexei's help, he'd also begun to learn the rudiments of Russian as well as ride a horse and drive a bullock cart.

'I wish doctors were above manual labour.' Peter rubbed his shoulder. 'I've strained a muscle trying to shift this cart.'

'You're about to strain another one, Dr Edwards,' John warned. 'It's going to take a lot of persuasion to get these animals out on to what passes for dry ground. Here, let's see what our combined weight can do.'

Glyn and Peter slid through the puddles of mud to the back board and put their shoulders alongside John's.

Ten back-breaking minutes later the cart was sunk even deeper in the mud.

'When Alexei returns with the horses and carriages, you should go on ahead with Mrs Edwards, Anna, and Richard, Dr Edwards, so you can start organising the hospital. A doctor with strained muscles is no use to man or beast.' John smiled when Sarah leaned over the back of the cart and handed him, Glyn, and Peter tin mugs. 'You're an angel.'

'Tea?' Peter asked.

'And rainwater.'

'Tastes divine.' John lifted his mug to Sarah.

'You and Glyn going to sleep in the boilers again tonight, Mr Hughes?'

'They're drier than the carts, and cosy once we've wrapped straw around ourselves.'

'I'll take your word for it, sir.' Sarah slipped her arm around Anna when the girl joined her.

Glyn drank his tea and returned the mug to Sarah. 'Troikas coming. Alexei's in the leading one. I've no idea what breed of horses he's driving but we should get a herd of them. They don't seem bothered by the mud.'

John stood on the nearest firm patch of ground and wiped the rain from his face with the back of his hand. 'Glyn, go ahead with Peter, Richard, and the ladies. Tell Huw we'll arrive early tomorrow. Given the conditions we may need the hospital soon. It'll be a wonder if we don't have at least one case of pneumonia after this rain.'

'Are you sure, sir?' Even this close to their destination Glyn was reluctant to leave his boss.

'No one's indispensable, Glyn. I'll manage without you for one night. Take Alf with you too, you'll need his muscle if the troikas get stuck. Alexei can guide you. We're so close to Hughesovka the drivers will be able to get the rest of us there blindfolded. Warn Huw we'll need hot food and dry blankets as well as accommodation.'

'I'll tell Sarah and arrange for our luggage to be transferred into the troikas.' Peter left.

Glyn lingered.

A driver handed John a spade. He waved it in front of Glyn. 'Even the boss of this bullock train has to work. See you tomorrow, Glyn.'

Realising he'd been dismissed, Glyn shook John's hand. 'See you, sir.'

'In Hughesovka.'

Glyn walked towards the carriages. Alexei was loading blankets into one of the troikas. Richard and Alf were packing the second troika with their own, Anna's, and the Edwards' personal luggage.

'If we leave now, Mr Edwards, we might get to your house before dark.' Alexei watched Sarah help Anna into the carriage. He'd stopped offering Anna assistance after he'd noticed her trembling every time he went near her.

Peter joined Sarah and Anna in the back of the troika. Alexei took the driver's seat.

'I'll drive this carriage.' Alexei said to Glyn. 'You, Richard, and Mr Mahoney need have no worries about the other. The driver's been working in my father's stables for years.'

'I remember him from our last visit.' Glyn waved to the man who waved back.

Richard and Alf climbed into the carriage, Glyn sat alongside them. Alexei shouted to Vlad and the horses moved, hock deep through the mire.

Glyn Edwards' house, Hughesovka
September 1870

Alexei's prediction that they'd arrive at their new home before dark proved optimistic. Darkness fell hours before they drove into the courtyard of the substantial villa that had been Catherine Ignatova's childhood home.

The moment the horses' hooves hit the gravel drive, the front doors opened. Praskovia, Yelena, and Pyotr lined up to greet them. Alexei helped Sarah from the carriage and made the introductions.

'Welcome to your new home, Mrs Edwards,' Praskovia said in heavily accented English.

'Thank you.' Sarah stepped inside and looked around in astonishment. 'You've bought this house, Glyn?'

'The company's renting it, but from what I've seen so far it may do nicely. Huw did well to arrange it.'

'It may do! It's ... a palace.' Sarah checked the condition of her muddy boots and began to unlace them.

Glyn shook the rain from his cape and Pyotr took it from him.

'Marble floors and walls,' Peter noted. 'Just as well they can be easily washed given the state of us.'

Primed by Alexei, Praskovia said, 'Everything's prepared for your arrival, Mr Edwards, Mrs Edwards, Dr Edwards, Mr and Miss Parry, Mr Mahoney, Alexei.'

'You speak English very well, Praskovia,' Sarah complimented.

'I attended Miss Sonya's English classes, Madam. Alexei said if I wanted to be your housekeeper I would have to speak your language. My mother and brother do not yet, but I will interpret until they learn. My mother will cook for you, my brother Pyotr will do the heavy work. I hope you will be satisfied with our efforts.'

'I'm sure we will, Praskovia.' Sarah noticed Pyotr holding out his hand to take her boots. She handed them to him.

'There's hot water in your bedrooms and a fire lit under the boiler in the bathhouse. The meal will be ready when you are. My mother has made Ukrainian borsch to warm you, and shashlik.'

'Shashlik?' Sarah repeated.

'You'll love it,' Glyn stripped off his wet coat.

'It's very good,' Alexei explained. 'Lamb and onion on skewers with rice marinated in pomegranate juice. What's the dessert, Praskovia?'

'Kisel with cranberries and blackcurrants.'

'You won't be eating any, Alexei!'

A grey-haired man stood in the doorway, his face contorted in anger. 'I warned you never to enter this house again. Where's your tutor?'

'Father Theodore's ill. He had to stay in Taganrog.'

'I will terminate his employment.'

'It's not his fault he's ill.'

'Home now, Alexei.'

The silence intensified. The sense of suspense escalated. But instead of answering his father, Alexei left the house without another word.

Moments later the sound of horses' hooves echoed through the open door.

Chapter Fifteen

Glyn Edwards' house, Hughesovka
September 1870

'Sheer bliss.' Glyn reached up from the high-level wooden bench he was lying on, scooped a ladle of water from the tank above the stove, and poured it over the stones on the hotplate. Steam hissed and rose, intensifying the broiling atmosphere.

'I could get used to this,' Peter murmured from a bench two levels below Glyn.

Glyn rolled on his back. 'You will; there's nothing like relaxing in a banya – bathhouse to you until you learn Russian – after days of hard graft or travelling over a rain-sodden steppe.'

'Do all Russian houses have a bath house?'

'The manor and estate houses I've visited with Mr Hughes all had their own. Even the smallest village has a communal one.'

Peter was curious. 'With separate bathing times for men and women?'

'The rules are laid down by the head man and council. They vary between villages. Some allow mixed bathing, some discourage it. Apparently Peter the Great tried to outlaw it because he thought it might lead to orgies.'

'Might? If there was a mixed bath house in Merthyr and girls were reckless enough to patronise it, every male within walking distance would be fighting to get in.'

'I've never visited a banya that caters for both sexes but I've been told they're surprisingly chaste, with men occupying one side of the steam room, women the other. Given that anyone, including the priest, can walk in any time, they're probably models of propriety.'

'Apart from the nudity.'

'Nothing disgraceful in nudity. God gave us all a body. I've been told a communal bath house is a good way to check out the credentials of a woman you fancy as long as you realise they're giving you the once-over too.'

'I don't like the thought of a woman eyeing me when I'm naked.'

'You prefer them to do it when you're clothed?' Glyn asked.

'I'd prefer they didn't do it at all.'

'It's what we do to them. Or was it different for you and Sarah? Did her intellect mesmerize you, not her looks?'

There were some things Peter considered too private for discussion, even with his brother. 'Why are there half a dozen brushes over there?'

'The bundles of birch twigs?'

'They look like miniature witches' brooms.'

'Veniks, used for massage or masochism, depending on your preference and whether you like being lightly or severely thrashed. The Russians believe a gentle beating stimulates the circulation and opens the pores.'

'I'll take the Russians' word for it.'

'The peasants call the banya the first Russian doctor. No matter what the ailment, their first call is to the steam room.'

'The second their physician?' Peter was mindful of his potential earnings.

'Vodka.'

'From the drivers' brews I sampled on the journey, that's more likely to finish off someone who's under the weather. Especially if they drink it in bath house temperatures.'

'The third Russian doctor is raw garlic.'

'Which explains the stench of the drivers. Would it be too much to hope the fourth Russian doctor is a qualified man?'

'I've never heard mention of a fourth.'

'Which says something for the contempt my profession is held in this country.'

'The locals have no opinion on doctors because few medical men have ventured onto the steppe.' Glyn turned over again. 'I pity Sarah and Anna in the house bathroom. There's no plumbing; the only boiler is in the kitchen, so all the water will have to be hauled by hand. We'll have to set up a timetable so you and Sarah can enjoy the banya together – and experiment with the venik.'

'It wouldn't be fair for us to hog it when we're the only married couple in the house.' Peter ran his fingers through his damp hair. 'I would have said this is more like a Turkish bath than a Russian.'

'There are similarities. Cleanliness through perspiration.'

'From Alexei's description, I expected a rough wooden hut with a smoky stove next to a stream so you could jump in after you'd been baked.'

'He was talking about black banyas,' Glyn explained. 'They haven't a chimney. This is a white banya, because the smoke from the oven is ducted out. But every banya experience should culminate in a quick dip in icy water or a roll in snow. Cooling and invigorating.'

'Sounds more painful than energising.'

'It's a shock to the system.'

'I didn't know you were an expert on Russian baths.'

'Mr Hughes asked me to look into them. He wants to build a few for his workers.' Glyn poured another ladle of water on the stones.

Suddenly faint and dizzy, Peter sat up slowly.

Glyn looked down in time to see the door close. He followed Peter into the washing room.

Peter had climbed into a tub of cold water and was pouring it over himself. 'I felt light-headed.'

'It's easy to overdo the steam. Leave by the entrance room and give the steam a miss until tomorrow.'

The door opened, and Huw Thomas stepped in, stark naked.

'You're letting in one hell of a draught,' Glyn complained.

Huw shut the door. 'Praskovia said you'd arrived. How are you? Did you have a good journey? Is Mr Hughes with you? Have you brought everything we need to finish the furnaces and sink the pits?' Huw offered Glyn his hand. 'You've no idea how glad I am to see you.'

'Spoken like a man who's missed his fellow countrymen,' Glyn shook Huw's hand. 'My brother Dr Peter Edwards.'

'You're very pink. First time in a banya?'

'It shows?' Peter fought nausea.

'I turned bright red on my first visit – before I passed out. Pleased to meet you.' Huw pumped Peter's hand. 'Glyn told me about you. Your services are sorely needed. We've had a number of accidents, not just among the builders but in the brickworks. A kiln exploded yesterday. Two men were burned and the best we could come up with was goose-grease salve.'

Peter didn't venture an opinion on the efficiency of animal fat as a remedy. 'I'm pleased to meet you too. May I call you Huw?'

'Certainly, as we're going to be living in the same house until more are built. Given the builders' lack of progress that's likely to take some time. Have you heard about the problems I've had with the construction workers, Glyn?'

'Alexei told me.'

'They've quietened down but they won't stay calm.' Huw filled a tub with warm water and rinsed himself off.

Glyn sat on a bench. 'To answer your questions, Huw, no, we didn't have a good journey, not after Taganrog and not after the rain started. Mr Hughes should reach here tomorrow morning. Yes, we did bring everything we need to finish the furnaces although I don't want to think about how many carts of supplies we've abandoned in the mud.'

'Praskovia said you've brought young people with you.'

'Richard and Anna Parry, distant members of our family,' Glyn didn't offer a more detailed explanation. 'Richard's a collier and Peter's wife,

Sarah, intends to train Anna as a nurse. We've also brought a collier, Alf Mahoney. He's occupying one of the servants' rooms in the house.'

'I'll ask Praskovia if there are any spare rooms that can be furnished. I've booked the available accommodation in the hotel but I doubt we'll get all the workers Mr Hughes has brought in there,' Huw said. 'I've also had wooden dormitories erected for the colliers until something better can be built.'

'Everyone will have to make do,' Glyn declared. 'Mr Hughes asked me to check you've made provision for the workers' arrival. Accommodation, warm food...'

'It's done. I have spies on the steppe. There are four bedrooms in the main part of the house. If your guests take two and your brother and his wife the third...'

'I told Praskovia to make me up a bed in the alcove off the downstairs study,' Glyn interrupted. 'You have an office in town, Peter in the hospital...'

'If the hospital's ever finished.'

'It's Peter's hospital, Huw. He can galvanise the builders.'

'Thank you, brother.' Peter was still feeling ill but felt he had to say something.

'Meanwhile, I'll move into the ground floor study and use it as an office and bedroom.'

'You're renting this place; you should have the largest bedroom, Glyn.'

'After seeing it, I'll be buying not renting it – if Catherine Ignatova agrees.'

'She spent a fortune on renovations. It had

been empty for years. I could move into the hotel.'

'I wouldn't hear of it, Huw.' Glyn insisted. 'By the way, a Cossack Regiment is travelling with Mr Hughes. They have three girls with them.'

'To join Madam Koshka?'

'Koshka from Moscow is here?'

'She turned up a couple of weeks ago. She and a dozen of her girls moved into the hotel but the house she's building should be ready this week. She paid her Austrian builder treble the going rate to finish it. She could afford to, the money she's made from the men here. It was those wages that triggered the trouble with our builders. They wanted the same and refused to listen when I told them the company couldn't afford to pay that much, but we could offer them longer-term contracts. They only backed down when her builder started laying off tradesmen. I'm hoping now her brothel's nearly finished there'll be no more grumbles about our rates of pay.'

'Is Koshka staying in Hughesovka?' Glyn splashed water on his face.

'So she says. She'll want to see you, Peter. She's been asking when a doctor's going to be appointed. She likes her girls medically checked on a weekly basis.' Huw opened the door to the steam room. 'You've got this temperature about perfect, Glyn.'

'You thought I'd forget? Join you in a couple of minutes.'

Peter reached for a towel. 'You know this Madam Koshka?'

'Intimately. Koshka's "cat" in Russian. The

name suits her. She's sleek, smooth, and sensual. You wouldn't believe the tricks she knows and has taught her girls, but you can find out for yourself after I introduce you.'

'I'm happily married.' Peter left the tub, opened the door to the entrance room, and filched a robe from one of the hooks.

'The difference between a Koshka girl and a wife can be likened to the difference between tripe and wine-marinated beefsteak.' Glyn opened the door of the steam room.

'Not my wife.' Peter called after him.

Glyn Edwards' house, Hughesovka
September 1870

'Will Alexei's father hurt him?' Sarah asked.

She and Anna were bathing in slipper baths. The indoor bathroom was small, its floor, walls, and stove tiled with blue and white Dutch tiles that gave the place a jaunty air.

'I don't know, madam.' Praskovia folded towels on the stove.

'I'm Sarah. I'll never get used to "madam".' Sarah finished soaping herself and rinsed out her sponge.

'I'm your servant. You're the mistress. It wouldn't do for me to call you by your given name.'

'I'm not your mistress. My brother-in-law is master of the house, not my husband. How about we keep "madam" for when there are guests, and "Sarah" when there's only family.'

'It would never do, madam.'

'What difference does it make how we address one another in private?'

'We might forget when people visit. If anyone overhears us it wouldn't look good for either of us.' Praskovia offered Sarah a towel. 'They would say I didn't know my place and you didn't know how to put me in it. Will Mr Edwards' wife be arriving?'

'I'm not sure.' Sarah stepped out of the bath.

'I hope you won't call me madam, Praskovia,' Anna said shyly.

'You are a young lady, so you are "Miss Anna".' Praskovia tried to ignore the faded bruises and marks on Anna's body. The young girl had done her best to conceal them and Praskovia realised she was sensitive about them.

Encouraged by Praskovia's friendliness, Anna asked, 'Why doesn't Alexei's father want him to visit us?'

'In Russia nobility do not mix with Mujiks – in English you call them peasants – or Cossacks. Count Beletsky would prefer not to be reminded of the existence of those he regards as "low", or is it "lowly"? Alexei, unlike the rest of the nobility, makes friends with everyone, whether they live in a palace or a pit.'

'I don't know him well, but Alexei seems kind.'

'He is, Miss Anna.' Praskovia took Anna's robe from the back of the door.

'Cleaning this room will be a lot of bother, between emptying the baths, and mopping the floor,' Sarah observed. 'If there's an outside bath house – what did you call it, Praskovia?'

'Banya, madam.'

'We should draw up a timetable so we can use it when the men don't need it.'

'Pyotr – that's my brother – does the heavy work, madam. He'll empty the baths.'

'Six extra people will create a lot of work. You must talk to Mr Edwards about increasing the staff.'

'I intend to, madam.'

'Thank you for getting the house ready. You've made it warm and welcoming.' Sarah slipped on her robe and waited for Anna to finish drying.

'I enjoy working here, madam. Dinner will be served as soon as you are dressed.'

'Thank you.' Sarah handed Praskovia the towel. She left and Anna followed.

'What's your room like?' Sarah asked as they walked along the landing.

'Beautiful. Come and see.'

The wooden floorboards had been stained dark but the effect was lightened by blue and red rugs. The drapes and bedcover were red wool, embroidered with white and blue crewelwork.

A mahogany table stood next to the window with two matching upright chairs. A vast wardrobe and chest of drawers of the same rich dark wood filled the wall opposite the bed. A cheval mirror and red plush upholstered chaise longue completed the furniture.

'My two dresses are going to look lost in the wardrobe and I only have two sets of underclothes to place in the drawers. But it's a wonderful room.'

'The first of your own?' Sarah guessed.

'How did you know?'

'From your expression. I was brought up in a workhouse and went from there to a post as a ward maid in a hospital. I didn't have a room of my own until I qualified as a nurse and was able to move out of the trainees' dormitory into a cubicle. I thought it was a palace. Compared to this it was a cupboard. As for clothes, you'll soon have your hospital uniform and you'll be able to buy more after you're paid.' Sarah walked to the stove. Someone had unpacked Anna's bag and laid her damp clothes on the tiles. 'Did you do this?'

'No. I just dropped my bag before I went to the bathroom. I didn't want to drip everywhere.'

'Praskovia's a treasure.' Sarah opened the drapes. Stars shone brightly in a moonless sky. 'If you want me, Peter's and my room is next door. Richard is on the other side of you. Dress warmly. Stoves have been lit in every room but this country is piercingly cold and it's not even winter yet.'

Banya, Glyn Edwards' house, Hughesovka
September 1870

Huw returned to the washing room to find Richard crouched in one of the tubs, washing the mud from his legs. He held out his hand.

'You must be Richard. I'm Huw Thomas, the overseer Mr Hughes left to supervise the building. I'll be living with you.'

'That will be nice, Mr Thomas.' Richard had been shocked by the casual attitude of the Edwards brothers to nudity on board ship. Both men had stripped off in the communal bathroom without showing the slightest sign of embarrass-ment. He'd deliberately hung back in his room that evening in the hope he'd be able to wash in privacy, only to be greeted by a man who held a senior position in the company who thought no more of his state of undress than Dr and Mr Edwards.

He was accustomed to men unbuttoning and relieving themselves underground, but no collier would dream of undressing to bare skin and parading in front of their fellows the way Huw Thomas and the Edwards' brothers did.

Huw took an empty tub, dragged it below a brass tap, and turned it on. Cold water bubbled out. 'I always need to cool down after ten minutes in the steam room.' He tested the water before climbing into the tub. He lifted a jug from the shelf above the taps, crouched down, sank the jug between his legs, filled it with water, and poured it over his head. 'Glyn said you're a collier.'

'I worked for Mr Edward Edwards – Mr Glyn Edwards' brother – in a drift mine in Merthyr.'

'You must have started work young to be a collier now.'

'I started when I was eight.' Richard climbed out of his tub and self-consciously turned his back.

'There's a difference between drift and deep mines.'

'I talked to Mr Edwards about that on the journey here. Excuse me.' Richard wrapped a towel around his waist. He opened the door to the steam room. The atmosphere was close, heavy. He could hardly breathe.

'Lie on one of the lower benches, it's hottest

close to the ceiling, and don't push it the first time,' Glyn advised. 'I'll ask Praskovia to put some of the felt hats the Russians wear to stop their heads from overheating in here. Leave the moment you feel light-headed, go back into the wash room, and tip a cold jug of water over yourself.'

'That's what Mr Thomas is doing now.'

'He's used to the banya.'

Richard lay face down on the wooden slats. He heard the door open and close. The wood he was lying on creaked when Huw Thomas placed his foot on it to climb on to a higher bench.

'Are we on schedule with the building work, Huw?' Glyn asked.

Richard tried to listen to Huw's reply but his eyelids grew heavy. Within minutes he was asleep, lost in a dream of collieries that bore the name *Parry Brothers*.

Glyn Edwards' house, Hughesovka
September 1870

'That was excellent, Praskovia. Please thank your mother for us.' Sarah shook her head when Praskovia approached with the wine decanter. 'I couldn't eat or drink another thing.'

'The soup and meat tasted like soup and meat, which is more than can be said for what we were served on the journey,' Peter complimented.

'Goulash and kebabs are a speciality of Yelena's. Bring the brandy please, Praskovia, then clear the table. I'm sorry, Glyn,' Huw apologised. 'Living on my own, I've grown accustomed to giving orders. Praskovia, I hereby order you to ignore me in future.'

'Yes, sir.' She looked expectantly at Glyn.

'We need to talk about domestic arrangements, Praskovia. Now there are so many of us you'll need extra help.' Glyn took the brandy from her. 'We'll retire to the drawing room. You can talk to me there when you've finished clearing up.'

'Thank you, sir.' Praskovia bobbed a curtsey as first Sarah and Anna left, then Richard and the men.'

'Brandy, Richard, Alf?' Glyn asked.

'I've never drunk it, sir. If you don't mind I'll have an early night. I've been tired since I left the bath house,' Richard apologised.

'Comes of falling asleep in there. You have to be careful. A steam room can drain your strength if you're not used to high temperatures,' Peter warned.

'Yes, sir. Goodnight.'

'I'll say goodnight too, sir.' Alf regarded the Edwards' brothers as his betters and wasn't comfortable in their company. He was looking forward to the arrival of the rest of the party and hoped to move in with the colliers.

Glyn, Peter, and Huw retreated to the drawing room. Glyn poured the brandies and handed them out.

Huw closed the door. 'Why don't we visit Koshka? You can renew your acquaintance, Glyn, and introduce Peter to his Russian patients.'

'Tonight!' Peter protested. 'We've only just arrived.'

Huw saw Glyn eyeing him. 'It's not what you think.'

'How do you know what I'm thinking, Huw?'

'Koshka's organised a salon like Moscow. It's a good place to meet people, converse in English, have a drink or two.'

'Pick up a girl?'

'A couple of them are very pretty,' Huw said defensively.

'On that note, gentlemen, please excuse me.' Peter finished his brandy. 'I have a wife waiting. If we're going to begin organising the hospital tomorrow we need a good night's rest.'

'Sleep well.' Glyn sat in a leather chair next to the hearth.

'Enjoy the rest of your evening, gentlemen.' Peter left.

Huw looked at Glyn. 'And then there were two.'

'Do you think Koshka will remember me?'

'Remember you! She hasn't stopped asking about you since she arrived. All I get every visit is "where's my Mr Glyn?".'

'How far is the hotel?'

'Ten-minute walk.'

'Really?'

'Five if we walk quickly.'

Glyn hesitated, but only for a few seconds. 'Lead the way.'

Beletsky House
September 1870

Catherine Ignatova swept into the drawing room

of the Beletsky mansion without waiting for the footman to announce her.

'Mother-in-law.' Nicholas rose. 'We weren't expecting you.'

'Where's Olga?'

'She went to bed early. Hardly surprising...'

'When she's pregnant again less than a year after giving birth to her twelfth child.'

Stung by the condemnation in Catherine's voice, Nicholas retorted, 'Childbirth is a natural function.'

'So is vomiting. People who care about their well-being try not to do it to excess. Is Olga very upset?'

'Why should she be upset?'

'If she witnessed your ridiculous behaviour towards Alexei...'

'I never behave in a ridiculous fashion.'

'This stupid attitude you've adopted towards your eldest son...'

'Don't tell me. That uncouth Cossack girl sent a message to the Dower House from your father's old house.'

'It's no longer my father's old house, Nicholas. It's Mr Edwards' house.'

'You've sold, not rented it to him?'

'That's my affair. If "uncouth Cossack" is a reference to Praskovia, she didn't send a message. I heard what happened from Alexei.'

'How could you? Alexei's upstairs. I locked him in his bedroom myself.'

Catherine stared at him.

Nicholas ran from the room across the hall. He charged up the staircase. Catherine heard a rattle of keys a door being unlocked a door and waited until Nicholas returned, red-faced and breathless.

'Where is he? Tell me, or so help me...'

'You'll what, Nicholas?' Gathering her long skirts she sat calmly on the sofa.

'I'll horsewhip the boy.'

'You'll do no such thing.'

'Where have you hidden him?'

'I'd hardly tell you, given your present mood.'

'Alexei's no son of mine. Mixing with the dregs of humanity. Chasing after that ... that...'

'If he's chasing Praskovia, he's no different from his father. The entire countryside knows Yelena's idiot son is yours.'

'You admit Alexei is sleeping with...'

'I admit nothing for Alexei. He has a tongue in his head. You want to talk to the boy, do so, in my house in front of my lawyer with my manservants at hand. This ridiculous feud you have with him has to stop, Nicholas. He's a good boy and intelligent.'

'You always take his side.'

'He came to me tonight to ask me to lend him money so he could go to St Petersburg.'

'To do what?' Nicholas sneered.

'You know what the boy wants to do. He's told you often enough. In my opinion my money will be safer with Alexei than it is in the bank. Unlike you, he has an over-developed sense of honour.'

'You want him to study engineering so he can sink to the level of a filthy miner?'

'I want him to follow his dream.'

'I'm protecting the boy from himself. He could

apply for a position at court.'

'As what?'

'If you used your influence he could be posted a gentleman of the bedchamber.'

'Wasting his days in useless chit-chat about clothes and etiquette? How little you know him, Nicholas.'

'He would be mixing with his own kind.'

'My offer stands. You may visit my house tomorrow morning and talk to the boy. However, the first threat against him, or sign that you're about to lose your temper, I'll order my servants to show you the door and send the boy to a foreign university.'

'What will he live on?'

'The annuity I'll pay him. He's proved himself capable by working for Huw Thomas this past year. If you can bring yourself to leave him alone I'll employ Alexei to develop my estate and land in partnership with Mr Hughes's New Russia Company.'

'You'd sell out your house and grounds to industry?'

'It's the future, Nicholas. Even an old woman like me can see that. Alexei is eighteen. Not quite a man, yet he has a man's sense. I recall what you were like at that age. Alexei is more mature.'

'But your house is close to mine.'

'Close to the one Olga inherited from her father on his death, yes.' Catherine rose. 'Will I see you tomorrow morning in the Dower House?'

'You'll allow me to talk to the boy?'

'In the presence of my lawyer, manservants, and me,' she reiterated.

'You're determined to negate my influence?'

'I'd have thought the events of this evening proved Alexei is determined to run as far and fast as he can from your influence.'

'The boy...'

'The boy knows his own mind. I'll do all I can to allow him to develop his interests.'

'In other words you want to drag him down to the level of this Welshman, John Hughes.'

'You were happy to take the money John offered to lease some of your land.'

'Not the land in my back yard. I'm an aristocrat...'

'You, Nicholas, are the past. Alexei is the future. If you're too stupid to see that, stay away from him and my house. You have other sons you can mould to your image. They may prove more tractable than Alexei. But, if they've any brains that haven't been knocked out of them by that nonsensical military education you insisted on subjecting them to, they may prove just as obdurate as their brother.'

'Fine! Employ Alexei to manage your estate and affairs. I hope you lose every kopek.' Nicholas followed his mother-in-law into the hall, where the footman was waiting with her cloak.

'Thank you for your kind wishes, Nicholas.'

'Sarcastic woman! You've never listened to reason...'

'Alexei has a dream which is more than you've allowed my daughter. If you don't call tomorrow I'll assume you have no interest in the boy.'

'Alexei is *my* son.'

'Then for your sake as well as my daughter's behave like his father.' Catherine walked to the door. The footman ran to open it before she reached it. She sailed through without breaking step.

Chapter Sixteen

Glyn Edwards' house, Hughesovka
September 1870

The temperature in the kitchen was on a par with that of the steam room. Yelena was at the stone sink, washing dishes; Pyotr was hunched on a stool, cleaning Mr Edwards' boots.

Praskovia walked in and sat at the table. 'I can't find Mr Edwards or Mr Thomas.'

'I haven't seen them since they went in to the drawing room with the doctor when I was clearing the table.' Her mother rubbed at a stubborn spot on a bowl with the dishcloth.

'The doctor's in the garden,' Pyotr added helpfully in his slow drawl.

'They're not with him, I looked.' Praskovia turned the tap on the samovar and filled a glass with tea. 'Mr Edwards said he would discuss hiring extra people with me.'

'He probably forgot,' her mother said.

'In a few minutes?'

'It's not urgent. Your talk can wait until morning.' Yelena lifted the bowl from the water and set it on the wooden draining board. 'When you speak to the master, don't forget we need kitchen and laundry maids as well as indoor maids. And, if he intends to buy horses, a carriage, and sleigh, another man to help Pyotr look after them. He'll need a gardener too if he wants it planted.'

'I have the list we worked on. Those boots are shining like glass, Pyotr. Leave them outside the master's door then go to bed. You have to get up early to see to the stoves. Sleep with one ear open. Mr Thomas has a key but the master doesn't. If they're out and return separately you may have to let the master in.'

'Yes, Miss Housekeeper Praskovia.' Pyotr clambered awkwardly to his feet.

'God bless and keep you, son.' Yelena kissed his cheek.

'Do you want me to pour you a glass of tea?' Praskovia asked Yelena.

'Yes, please.' Yelena sat at the table and took four lumps of sugar from the bowl. 'The master's very good-looking.'

'He is.'

'He's married?' Yelena phrased the comment as a question.

'You know he is,' Praskovia confirmed irritably.

'Strange he hasn't brought the mistress with him.'

'Mr Hughes hasn't brought his wife here either. From what Mr Mahoney said when I showed him to his room, most of the men with the company have left their wives at home.'

'Be careful, my girl. I saw the way he looked at you when he arrived.'

'If he looked at me at all, it was a friendly look.'

'You think so?'

'Yes, I think so,' Praskovia countered.

'I know what masters are like, and for all the Tsar – God bless and keep him–'Yelena crossed herself, 'abolishing serfdom, the ones who pay our wages still think they can treat us like slaves. This master's rich, good-looking. His bed is empty. He'll be looking to fill it. After the shameless way you behaved with Ivan Kalmykov before he was killed, who better than to fill it than a housekeeper who's missing a man between her thighs. Be warned, my girl, a married man isn't the answer to your loneliness.'

'You've no idea how much I miss Ivan.'

'I lost your father...'

'When he was an old man. Ivan was nineteen. We hadn't begun our lives together.'

'You're mourning Ivan. That's your right. But when I saw the way the master looked at you and the way you looked him full in the eye back...' Yelena saw the tears on Praskovia's cheeks but was driven by the need to prevent her daughter from making the same mistake she had. 'Any girl, let alone one mourning the loss of a lover, would be attracted to him. But if you allow him to make love to you it won't end well. We're comfortable here. Our rooms are warm, we have good food, all three of us are earning. Once people arrive with Mr Hughes I'll be able to add the rent from our house to our savings. Start something with the master and when the mistress appears we'll be thrown out without a roof to crawl under or a kopek...'

'The way the count threw you out of the Beletsky mansion when he put Pyotr in your belly. No wonder Father took to drink.'

'I did what I thought best at the time. Not for me but for all of us.'

'Spare me the plea for understanding, Mama. You did what you wanted to.'

'You think I wanted to sleep with the count? I hated him. I still hate him. But he caught your father poaching. You know how often deer from the count's land ended up on Alexandrovka's tables. A charge like that with the count as magistrate, your father would have been sent to Siberia – and then how would have lived?'

'I've heard it all before, Mama.'

'I don't want to have to hear it again with you – not me – as the suffering one. Think of Pyotr. He's strong but he has the mind of a child. He needs looking after. This house is good, Praskovia, good for all of us. We can look to a secure future. I beg you, don't spoil it by throwing yourself at the master. If you do it will end in tears.'

'Nothing's happened between me and the master.'

'Yet, because you haven't any time together. Remember, when a man's peace and comfort are threatened he'll chose his wife over his mistress every time. It's not as though you're undamaged goods. You were brazen with Ivan. Everyone in Alexandrovka knew what you two were up to. Then there's all this talk about you and Alexei when there's nothing going on. What's that about?'

'That's my business and Alexei's,' Praskovia snapped.

'As my grandmother used to say, there's only one thing a fallen woman can do, and that's keep falling.'

'Not you, Mama.' Praskovia left the table. 'With Alexei's help and recommendation for this job I stopped you falling any lower.'

'Praskovia...' Yelena was talking to the door.

There was no night she regretted more than the one she'd privately christened 'her night of shame' when the count had entered the nursery. She'd been employed as wet nurse to one of his daughters. Afraid of waking the children and subjecting them to sights they shouldn't see, especially Alexei who'd been five at the time, she'd been too afraid to make a sound.

The count had laughed at her pathetic efforts to fight him off. It had been the first rape of many. He'd even waylaid her on her journeys to see her children in Alexandrovka. The count's threat to prosecute Pavlo for poaching and tell her husband she'd been willing had prevented her for confiding in her husband. She'd been too ashamed to tell anyone else what the count had done and was doing to her.

Nicholas Beletsky hadn't been able to resist boasting about his conquest. As a result the man she'd loved most – her Pavlo – had dulled his pain at her shame in vodka. She hoped Praskovia was right and this master was a good man but the master, like the count, had a wife...

She crossed herself, fell to her knees, reached for her prayer rope, and began telling off the knots.

'Please, blessed holy mother of God, let Praskovia see sense and please don't let us be forced from this house or our jobs. Please, blessed holy mother...'

Glyn Edwards' house, Hughesovka
September 1870

Peter found Sarah updating her journal in bed.

'Is the mattress comfortable?'

'Very.' She tucked her pencil inside the book and closed it before patting the spot next to her. 'See for yourself.'

'I will as soon as I've undressed. I walked around the garden. It's difficult to see much in the dark, but the country is so flat our first priority has to be to check the water table relative to the cesspits that have already been dug.'

'You used the outside thunder box?'

'Yes. You?'

'I did.'

'It needs cleaning out.'

'I could smell that much.'

'If it's indicative of the standards here, given the expected population explosion, we'd better brace ourselves for an outbreak of disease unless we can organise better sanitation.' He sat on the end of the bed and unlaced his shoes.

'I thought you'd discussed sanitation and rubbish disposal with Mr Hughes.'

'Discussed in the abstract. From what Glyn and Mr Hughes said, I assumed the intention was to build a town on an empty steppe, although common sense should have told me any people already here would have made arrangements to dispose of their rubbish, albeit unsuitable ones. It's going to take time to build incinerators and organise collection points.'

'There's nothing we can do about it tonight.'

'There isn't, sweetheart.' He placed his shoes under a chair, shrugged off his jacket, and hung it on the back.

'Perhaps we should look at what the Russians have been doing before we implement improvements. There hasn't been an outbreak of disease here recently. Has there?'

'None that Glyn's mentioned. It's a good idea of yours to ask the locals if they've made arrangements other than pits. As usual, my wife is providing the voice of common sense.'

'Flattery will get you everything you desire.'

'That's my intention.' He hung his waistcoat over his jacket, pulled his tie loose, unbuttoned his collar and shirt, and unclipped his braces. 'What do you think of this house?'

'It's a palace. I never thought I'd live in anything so grand. Can your brother afford it?'

'Courtesy of the mortgages Mr Hughes has arranged for all senior managers, he can. Our Glyn's gone up the world and we're climbing alongside him.' He leaned over the bed and kissed her.

'Glyn's lucky to have Praskovia. She might be young but she's an excellent housekeeper.'

'Alexei knew what he was doing when he recommended her for the job.'

'Is Alexei's father right? Is there something going on between Praskovia and Alexei?'

'You know as much as me, sweetheart.'

'Glyn hasn't said anything?'

'Unlike women, men don't gossip.'

'That, darling, is not true but if you want to delude yourself, go ahead.' She rearranged her pillows and dropped two to the floor.

He draped his shirt, tie, and braces on top of his waistcoat. 'What do you think men gossip about?'

'Women.'

'If you're fishing for information about Glyn and Betty, all I know is Glyn doesn't seem bothered by Betty's decision to stay in Merthyr. He did say he wished they'd formally separated shortly after their marriage.' He pulled his long sleeved vest over his head and unclipped his sock suspenders.

'I'm fond of your brother. He's a kind man who cares about people. He probably told you he wished he and Betty had separated to save face. I'll write to her...'

'No!' Peter broke in. 'Absolutely, definitely no. Whatever's between Betty and Glyn or not – is personal to them and should remain that way.' He pulled off his long drawers and padded naked across the room. Folding back the bedclothes he slipped in beside her. 'What are we lying under?' He lifted the bedcover. 'It doesn't feel like blankets.'

'It's not. I asked Praskovia when she showed me to the room. It's a featherbed – a sort of overlay eiderdown. All the beds have them here. They're lighter and warmer than blankets – or so she said.'

'You'd prefer blankets?'

'I'm used to lying under the weight of wool.'

'Are you cold?'

'No.'

'Then you don't need your nightgown?'

She unbuttoned her bodice before sitting up

and pulling her nightdress over her head.

He moved towards her.

'Ow! Your feet are cold,' she complained.

'Yours are warm. I call that the perfect combination.' He lifted aside the plait she'd knotted her hair into and caressed her breasts.

'I have something to tell you,' she whispered.

'You're pregnant.'

She failed to keep the disappointment from her voice. 'You know?'

'I'm a qualified doctor, sweetheart. At least, I've been given a certificate that says so. I love you and enjoy looking at you. You're pale in the morning – so pale you're bordering on green – your beautiful breasts,' he stroked her nipples tenderly, 'are larger, and there's a faraway look in your eyes that has to be down to more than being married to an incredibly handsome, clever man.'

'Why didn't you say something?'

'Isn't it a wife's prerogative to tell a husband he's about to become a father?' He kissed her. 'A father,' he repeated, as the import of the words sank in. 'A new life, a new baby, and when Huw and Glyn have the builders and bricks to spare, a new house for us and our son.'

'Our son could be a daughter.'

He pulled her even closer. 'No, it's a boy. Thomas Edward Edwards.'

'After your eldest brother and father?' From the way all three brothers spoke about Tom and their father Sarah knew how close they'd been.

'I wish you'd met them. My parents would have loved you, they adored children. They wanted grandchildren so much. It was a disappointment when Edward's wife and Betty didn't have any.'

'I think Thomas Edward Edwards should have at least two more names. John should be one as Mr Hughes is responsible for us being here.'

'And the other?'

'Something Russian. Ivan or Boris or Vladimir ... stop tickling me,' she shrieked.

'I'm not. I'm reaching for the lamp.' He turned down the wick, plunging the room into darkness. 'We've a busy day tomorrow, Mrs Dr Edwards.' He returned to his side of the bed, but not for long.

'I love you,' she whispered into the darkness when he entered her.

'I love you too. Both of you.'

Hotel Hughesovka
September 1870

Madam Koshka had transformed the rooms at the back of the newly built hotel into a replica of her elegant apartment in fashionable Tverskaya Ultitsa Street in Moscow. Within easy distance of the university, military headquarters, theatres, churches, and monasteries, the location had been perfect for her business. Glyn wondered at her motives for moving from the city to the steppe.

Unlike most 'madams' he and Mr Hughes had encountered in the European capitals, Koshka plied her trade subtly. Operating a 'salon'; treating the ladies who entertained her male clientele as much-loved 'nieces' she'd invited to amuse her 'guests'.

Her girls' dresses were fashioned from expensive fabrics but designed to leave little to masculine imagination. They exhibited more of their charms, particularly their breasts and legs, than any respectable female, but their demeanour was as demure as Queen Victoria's ladies-in-waiting.

The first Koshka girl Glyn had become acquainted with, confided that 'Madam' demanded bawdiness be kept from the salon and confined to the privacy of the bedroom. It was a wise decision on Madam's part. Her elegant rooms attracted men from the upper echelons of the Russian Empire as well as visiting dignitaries, and the quality of her services was reflected in her prices.

The hotel vestibule had smelled of paint and wet plaster, Madam Koshka's rooms of cologne and dried rose petals. They'd been decorated French Empire style, in cream, gilt, and red plush. Glyn recognised a few pieces from Koshka's Moscow apartment. The linen tablecloths were as pristine as they'd been in the capital. The wine, served in Koshka's Venetian glass goblets, light and delicately flavoured. The canapés, cakes, and miniature sandwiches arranged on Madam's Meissen porcelain could have come from a Moscow confectioner. Koshka had succeeded in recreating her salon in Hughesovka, even down to the ambience.

Huw was in his element, dancing attendance on a buxom, blonde Bohemian. Glyn watched them sidle out, Huw's hand clamped on the girl's buttocks.

'Glyn, my dear, dear, Glyn. You look bored. You were never that fond of wine.' Koshka took his glass from him and clicked her fingers. 'Brandy for Mr Edwards, Lily.'

A brunette appeared at Glyn's elbow with a brandy balloon and decanter.

'I'm exhausted, not bored, Koshka.' Glyn allowed the girl to fill the brandy balloon. 'I only arrived a few hours ago.'

'I hear you travelled with your brother, the doctor.'

'And Mr Hughes, all the workers we've recruited, a regiment of Cossacks, and three of their women.'

'Soldiers' women,' Koshka dismissed. 'I trust you'll bring your brother to the opening of my new house on Saturday. I'd like to make his acquaintance.'

'So he can meet his new patients?'

'Doctors need patients. My girls need medical attention, and he's your brother. If he's anything like you, he'll be good looking and – how do you say it in English – "a ladies' man".'

'He has a wife.'

'So does practically every man in this room.'

'Here, in his bed.'

'He's in love with her?'

'Very much.'

'In that case I will propose only a business arrangement.'

'Probably best.'

'It's crowded here. I have an office where we can talk in private.'

'I have a busy day tomorrow.'

'Brandy should never be rushed.' She led him to a curtained alcove and opened a door hidden behind the drapes.

Koshka's 'office' was small, exquisitely furnished with a desk, captain's chair, two comfortably upholstered chairs that flanked a tiled Dutch stove and a long, wide sofa that could accommodate three people lying side by side. As Glyn had discovered.

Koshka sat on one of the upholstered chairs, Glyn took the other.

'So when is Mr Hughes arriving – and how many people are travelling with him?'

'For people I take it you mean men. Tomorrow and several hundred including Mujiks.'

'Immigrants?' she questioned.

'About a hundred. What on earth possessed you to forsake Moscow for the outskirts of the empty beyond?'

'You and Mr Hughes informing everyone in Moscow that the hive of industry you will build here will be the new centre of Europe. Russia's capital of enterprise where the bold will make untold riches.'

'Koshka, you were making a fortune in Moscow. Something catastrophic must have happened for you to give that up.'

Koshka opened a gold and enamelled box and offered it to him. 'Cigar?'

He took one and reached for the cigar lamp. A silver-plated German model that resembled an Aladdin's lamp perched on a column. He lit Koshka's cigar then his own. She drew on the cigar, removed it from her mouth, and studied the stem.

'Do you remember Lucia?'

'Small, dark, pretty girl with one brown and

one blue eye.'

'That was her.'

'Was?'

'She was carved up by a customer. She died slowly and horribly.'

'You notified the authorities.'

'I had more sense. I ordered the man who killed her to stay away from my salon and tried to keep Lucia's murder quiet. It proved impossible. All the girls knew who'd killed her and he was aware they knew. He persisted in visiting us. The girls were terrified. None of them would go with him, no matter how much money he offered. Frightened people turn to anyone they believe trustworthy. My girls begged their patrons to help them get away from Moscow. Once the rumours started they spread like dandelion seeds.'

'Lucia's murderer is influential?'

'And rich, more than anyone as sick in the head as he is has the right to be. He wanted me and my girls dead or in Siberia. Fortunately, I possess a few friends. They managed to convince him that our mass murder, forced exile, or disappearance would give rise to gossip that might point in his direction. When I couldn't stand the strain of his visits any longer, I called him into my office and suggested he allow us to leave the city. He agreed. The girls and I signed confidentiality agreements promising never to speak of the reason behind our flight, and for your own safety I shouldn't have told you this much.'

'I'm more sorry than I can say about Lucia. My condolences to you and your girls, not only on the loss of Lucia, but on having to leave Moscow.'

'Thank you. I miss Lucia.' She forced a smile. 'But it's good to have a change of air and see you again. You'll come to my party?'

'Yes.'

'And bring your brother?'

'I'll answer for myself but not him. I can do no more than invite him.' Glyn kissed her cheek. 'I'm glad you're here, Koshka. You'll brighten my evenings and a great many men's nights.'

'Have you brought your wife with you?'

'No.'

'I have a new girl. She's very sweet, just your type.'

'Not tonight, but thank you.'

'You're waiting for the Cossacks' women?'

He smiled at her blatant fishing. 'Are you afraid of competition?'

'Not from girls who've been reduced to entertaining soldiers. See you soon, Glyn?'

'At your party. Thank you for the brandy and cigar.'

He returned to the salon. It was more crowded than when he'd left. Huw was nowhere to be seen. Deciding his friend could make his own way home, Glyn collected his coat and umbrella, walked down the stairs, and out of the front door of the hotel.

Glyn Edwards' house, Hughesovka
September 1870

Richard examined every inch of his room before he undressed for bed. Someone had unpacked his bag while he'd been at dinner and laid his damp clothes on the stove. He picked up his nightshirt. Warm, dry, just holding it felt comforting after the rain-sodden, wind-chafing days on the steppe. He laid it on the bed and began to stow away the rest of his belongings.

The wardrobe was massive. It would have filled half the basement house in Merthyr, if it could have been carried through the door. The new suit of clothes Edward Edwards had bought him as a going-away present looked forlorn when he hung it on a hook in its cavernous depths. His spare set of underclothes, socks, and shirts filled less than a quarter of one of the twelve drawers in the matching chest.

He put two books he'd borrowed from Glyn on his bedside table before sitting at the desk in front of the curtained window. It was a fine piece of furniture. A red-leather writing block was sunk in the centre of its brass inlaid surface. The eight drawers held stationery, bottles of ready-mixed ink, nibs, and pencils.

He imagined sitting there making notes Mr Edwards would find useful. Or writing letters to Morgan and Owen about his and Anna's new life, describing what was waiting for the boys when they joined them, but the more he looked around the more he felt like an interloper. A servant playing at being the master in a place he had no right to clean, much less visit. He wondered how he could begin to tell his brothers about the house. Then he realised Owen and Morgan may never set foot inside. He and Anna were "lodgers" in Mr Edwards' palace.

Mr Edwards had been born in a two-up-two-down terraced house in the Quarr. He knew because one of his fellow colliers had pointed it out to him. He remembered Mr Edwards' advice.

'Aim as high as you like, Richard, there'll be nothing to hold you back in Russia except the limit of your ambition.'

The only limit was his dreams and as his mother had said, he was good at building castles in the air. Would he – could he – ever buy himself a mansion like this?

He undressed, and pulled on his nightshirt. Loath to blow out the candle he continued to absorb his surroundings, the grand furniture, embroidered bedcover and curtains and gold-framed pictures. So different from anything he'd seen before, let alone been close enough to touch.

He moved the candle alongside the books, crawled between the thick linen sheets, arranged the eiderdown on top, and reached for Robert Hunt's *The Mineral Statistics of the United Kingdom of Great Britain and Ireland*.

The house closed around him, its atmosphere and smell very different from the stagnant taint of foul water that had hung over the court. The overwhelming scent was of honey with hints of Christmas spices.

Small noises reverberated outside his door, new, strange, yet comforting. Doors closing; footsteps on the stairs; whispers of conversation that brought the assurance he was among friends. He read until his eyelids grew heavy, made a note of the page number and closed the book. He was disturbed by a tap at the door.

'It's me, Anna. Can I come in, Richard?'

'Is something wrong?'

'No.' Anna entered in her nightgown, a woollen shawl Sarah had given her draped around her shoulders. 'When I peeked out and saw the light under your door, I knew you'd still be awake.'

'Everything here is so different from Merthyr it's no wonder you can't sleep.'

She sat on the bed. 'I'm glad you're here.'

'Homesick?'

'Not for Merthyr, but Mam, and the boys.'

'Those days, like our old home, have gone, Anna. We won't forget Mam but there's no going back. Just as there was no going back to Dad or our house in Treforest. As for the boys, we'll send for them as soon as we've earned enough to rent a house of our own. We might even earn enough to go back and fetch them...'

'No!'

'If you're thinking about the Paskeys, whether they're in gaol or not, they're a thousand miles away. We won't see them again.'

She shuddered. 'We would if we went back.'

He held out his arm and she leaned against his chest.

'Here, you're freezing, get under this eiderdown.' He lifted it over her, so she was lying on top of the sheet he was under but beneath the bedcover. 'Do you want to talk?'

She shook her head. 'Can I stay? Just a little while? Please?'

'Having a room to yourself takes some getting used to after sharing a sleeping shelf, doesn't it?'

'My room's even bigger.'

'You'll soon take it for granted, just as we did living in the court when we moved from Pontypridd to Merthyr.'

'I don't think so. This house is a mansion. Mam would have loved it.'

'Mam would have been too terrified of breaking something to move in it.'

'I never thought I'd be lucky enough to work as a maid in a place like this, let alone live in one of the best rooms.'

'Thanks to Mr Edwards this is our chance to make something of ourselves, Anna. In a year or two you could be a nurse and I might be a foreman on my way to being a manager. Between us, we could even earn enough to buy, not rent our own house.'

Her eyes rounded. 'You think so?'

'It wouldn't be anything as grand as this,' he qualified, as if he were already earning, 'because it will take me years to reach a position as high as Mr Edwards, but hopefully I can get something comfortable and big enough for the four of us.'

'It wouldn't have to be grand, just ours.'

'I'd rather it was grand than damp like the court.' Sensing she wanted to tell him something he waited for her to speak.

'I'm going to the hospital tomorrow with Dr and Mrs Edwards.'

'From what Mr Thomas said, the builders haven't made much progress, so don't go expecting too much.'

'I'm worried, Richard. What if I'm not clever enough to become a nurse?'

'You're clever enough. I lost count of the number of times Mrs Edwards told Mam she couldn't manage the kitchen of the Boot without you. You've proved you can turn your hand to anything. Face it, Mam wasn't well for years and it was you who did most of the work in the house.'

'Housework isn't like nursing. Proper nursing.'

'You know a lot about caring for people and looking after them when they're ill. It was you, not Mam, who nursed Owen and Morgan through the cholera.'

'I tried to look after the others...'

Richard hated talking about the brothers and sister they'd lost. 'You'll have Mrs Edwards to teach you,' he interrupted. 'She and Dr Edwards like you. They wouldn't have brought us here if they didn't.'

'I hope I don't disappoint them. It would be too awful if they regretted bringing me.'

A clock began to strike downstairs. Richard counted off the chimes. Anna joined him, as she used to when they were children and stood before the town clock in Merthyr.

'1 – 2 – 3 – 4 – 5 – 6 – 7 – 8 – 9 – 10 – 11 – midnight. Mr Edwards wants to make an early start. We should have been asleep hours ago.'

'Can I stay with you? Just for tonight?' she begged. 'I'll sleep in my room tomorrow.'

'Have you left the light burning in your room?'

'I brought my candle with me, it's next to yours.'

'Blow them out.'

She did as he asked and settled next to him, keeping her hand in his.

He lay quietly, hoping she'd begin talking about whatever was bothering her. But she didn't, and as her breathing steadied into the soft regular rhythm of sleep, he allowed his thoughts to drift.

Could either of them ever forget the Paskeys? He suspected they'd done more to Anna than beat her. But he was too afraid of the anguish in her eyes every time their name was mentioned to question her.

Then there was Alice. He was determined their separation was temporary. He loved her and no one – not her father, and certainly not the Paskeys – would stop him from marrying her.

He imagined himself helping to build the ironworks, sink collieries, and sending Alice a ticket that would enable her to leave Merthyr and come to him. He pictured their reunion – the expression on Alice's face when he showed her the house he'd bought.

It was preferable to trying to cope with thoughts of the Paskeys and the destruction they'd wrought in his and Anna's life.

Chapter Seventeen

Hughesovka and Glyn Edwards' house
September 1870

The rain had stopped, the sky was clear. The Mujiks had been right. The dark clouds had blown over, but not before they'd created havoc in Hughes's expedition.

Glyn had told Koshka he was exhausted. He

knew he should be. But the fresh air had woken his senses, his skin tingled, and he felt restless as he walked the short distance from the hotel to his house. A rough track spattered with puddles cut a swathe through the half-built wood and brick buildings that lined the settlement. Walking was slippery work but the street was crowded. Despite the hour, groups of workmen squatted around oil lanterns on piles of bricks and wood, sharing vodka pails, plates of bread, salt, and dried mushrooms.

In the space of a few yards he heard Russian, French, German, Dutch, Polish, and Ukrainian, along with a few dialects he didn't recognise. A Cossack played a violin, dancers slid in the mud around him and when one fell, the others laughed.

The street was relatively quiet around his house and he paused outside the wooden palisade that enclosed the substantial grounds of his new home. The balcony that ran the full length and width of the upper storey offered a vantage point that would give a bird's eye view of the comings and goings of the town – when Mr Hughes finished building it. He imagined himself relaxing there in a chair on a warm evening, a glass of iced wine at his elbow, a book on his lap.

He opened the gate and walked up the drive. A lane to the right led to the back of the house, the banya, and the stables. He turned left and walked to the front door.

The rain had beaten down a few low-growing bushes at the front of the house. Should he employ a gardener? Was it worth trying to grow flowers and vegetables when soon – hopefully very soon –

the ground would be affected by pollution from the works?

Lamps burned low inside the porch but the rest of the house was in darkness. Glyn assumed the servants slept at the back and everyone else was asleep. He suppressed yet another pang of envy for his brother and his close, loving relationship with Sarah. He tried to quantify his feelings. Hopefully he and Betty would live for years, but what would they make of their allotted time, separated as they were by estrangement as well as distance?

He had enough to occupy him: collieries to sink, ironworks and a town to build, a house to organise to his ideas of comfort and décor. He'd be busy, but would he, could he, be happy without a wife at his side? And Betty? Would she be happy in the Boot Inn? Would she be lonely? Would she be tempted to take a lover?

To his surprise, when he considered the idea, the more he saw it as a possible and welcome result of their separation. He'd rather think of Betty happy as not. He was hardly in a position to take the moral high ground when he recalled how many brothels he'd patronised since he'd begun working for Mr Hughes.

Hotels were lonely and impersonal. The best 'houses' created an illusion of domesticity, comfort, and the loving care of a woman until the money ran out. Would he find a new favourite among Koshka's current crop? A pretty, obliging girl who'd keep a few hours a week just for him?

Glyn tried the door. It was locked, as it should be at that time of night. It was only then he remembered he'd left the house without giving a thought to Praskovia or the discussion about extra staff.

He rang the bell. A shadow moved behind the door. It opened. Pyotr swayed in front of him, half-asleep, dishevelled in crumpled shirt and trousers.

'I'm sorry, I should have taken a key,' Glyn apologised.

Pyotr smiled but it was obvious he hadn't understood a word. He waited for Glyn to enter, closed and locked the door, and retreated to a small windowless room off the inner porch. He returned, carrying a candle in a hurricane lamp. Bowing, he handed it to Glyn.

Glyn glanced into the room. There was a chair, a bed and a table. He hadn't even asked Praskovia what arrangements she'd made to man the doors or secure the house at night. Carrying the lamp, he entered the drawing room. He looked at the brandy and whisky decanters and decided he'd drunk enough for one evening. If sleep eluded him he'd use the time productively. He'd relax in the banya and collect his thoughts.

The side door that led to the outside and the bath house was open. Given the number of drunks in the street the lack of security disturbed him. Anyone could walk up the path, enter, steal the household goods and murder them in their beds.

He took the key from the inside of the door and locked it behind him. A strip of light showed beneath the ill-fitting door of the banya. He pushed it open. A candle flickered in a glass bowl on a shelf above the hooks. He undressed and carried the lamp Pyotr had given him into the washing room. Rinsing himself off, he stepped into the steam room.

A haze of misty light shone high in the corner illuminating a pale, naked body on the topmost shelf. He recognised Praskovia. She made no attempt to cover herself when she sat up.

'I'm sorry, sir. I thought you wouldn't visit the banya again this evening. As everyone else in the house is in bed I presumed it would be empty.'

He couldn't stop staring at her or contrasting her figure with those of Koshka's girls, who were waifs in comparison. Praskovia's breasts were rounded and full, her waist slender. Her skin so white her body could have been carved from marble. In contrast, her long auburn hair rippled a reddish-gold waterfall over her back and arms.

Her eyes gazed, bright, piercing into his.

He stammered the first thing that came into his head. 'You're beautiful.'

'Thank you, sir. I won't use the banya again.'

'You must. You live in this house.'

'It's your house. You'll want privacy.'

'There's no need.' He realised his words could be misconstrued. The last thing he wanted was for his housekeeper to consider him lecherous, although from the way he'd been staring he suspected that's exactly what she thought of him. 'You were here first. I'm the one who should go. Please, stay.' Acutely aware of his body reacting to the sight of hers, he retreated to the washing room and grabbed a towel to conceal his burgeoning erection.

She followed. He looked away when she took a

towel from the shelf and wrapped it around herself.

'Feel free to use the banya any time convenient to you, Praskovia.'

'It wouldn't be proper, sir. With your permission I'll continue to use it late at night, but only when I'm certain everyone is in bed. Good night, master. Sleep well.'

'You'll need the key to the side door. It's on the shelf that holds the lanterns. I locked it behind me. There are a lot of people in the street, some drunk. We need to discuss security.'

'Yes, master.'

'Not now, tomorrow.'

'Yes, master.' She closed the door behind her.

He listened to her moving around the entrance room. She was a beautiful girl. If he were free...

He drove an image of Praskovia naked in his bed from his mind. Praskovia was his housekeeper – his employee. He had a duty to protect, not exploit her.

But duty didn't prevent him from wishing she worked for Koshka, not him.

Glyn Edwards' house, Hughesovka
September 1870

Praskovia tied on her wrap. The master might be older, wealthier, and more experienced in the ways of the world than Ivan but she knew from the way he'd looked at her, that naked, she'd had the same effect on him.

She considered what her mother had said.

Before the master's arrival, she'd hoped once he'd seen her capabilities as housekeeper, and sampled her mother's cooking, he'd appreciate the level of service they could provide. But now…

After Ivan had been killed she'd never expected to be attracted to another man. The moment the master had stepped into the hall and they'd looked at one another something happened. Her mother had recognised it, but her mother boasted that she'd inherited the "second sight" that had passed down the female line of their family.

She recalled one of her father's stories. She missed him, not the drunk he'd been the last years of his life, but the mentor and teacher who'd known so many magical tales.

'The prince was dressed as a swineherd ... he lived among swineherds ... he'd been brought up by swineherds ... he thought it was his fate to be a swineherd, but the moment he lifted his eyes to the princess he saw his future in her eyes. His tomorrows and hers entwined as they lived happily ever after in a glittering world of castles, jewels, golden coaches, royal blood...'

There would be no royal blood, jewels, golden coaches, or castles in her life; of that much she was certain. But had she seen her future in the master's eyes? Did a mysterious magical spirit exist? Had some essence emanated back from the life she and the master would one day share?

Her mother had never listened to her father's stories, or looked for more than Alexandrovka could give. Had Yelena been right when she'd scolded Pavlo for trying to escape from reality? She, like her father, wanted to believe in a world where dragons, fairies, snow maidens, and fire-birds existed alongside princes and princesses.

She entered the house, wondering if she should heed her mother's warnings or follow her own instincts. Her bedroom was next to the pantry where the china and silverware was stored. There, she sat in front of the mirror, brushed her hair, splashed on a little of the cologne Alexei had brought her from his travels in Germany, and gazed at herself.

Satisfied with her appearance, she picked up the spare set of keys she'd intended to give the master earlier, left her room, opened the door that connected to the main house, and slipped into the study. She set the keys on the desk next to the brandy decanter she'd carried in earlier, blew out the candle she'd brought, curled up in one of the chairs, and waited.

Glyn Edwards' house, Hughesovka
September 1870

Dressed only in a robe he'd taken from the banya, Glyn entered his room. He opened the drapes that curtained the bedroom alcove and dropped his clothes on a chair.

'Can I get you anything, sir? A drink, something to eat?'

Startled, Glyn turned to see Praskovia. 'Nothing, thank you.'

'I left the keys to the house next to the lamp. They're all on the ring. The front and back door, the wine cellar, silver vault, and one to a safe set behind that picture.' She pointed to a frame on the wall. Darkened by the patina of age and smoke from the stove, the canvas resembled a slice of coal waste.

'You could have waited until morning to give me the keys.' He was embarrassed by her presence in the intimacy of his bedroom when he was almost undressed. It didn't help that he was acutely aware of her body and exactly how she looked naked.

'If you need me in the night, sir, tap at the door set in the back wall. My room is just beyond it.'

Other than assuming they were at the back of the house, Glyn hadn't given a thought to the location of the servants' rooms in relation to his. He saw the door set discreetly in the wooden panelling and found it disturbing that Praskovia would be sleeping the other side of it.

'If you're worried about security, sir, there are locks on both doors to this room.' She moved gracefully to the door that opened into to the hall, and turned the key.

'It's late. We both have to be up early.'

'Are you sure I can't get you anything, sir?'

He couldn't stop mentally undressing her. His skin burned as he recalled her marble pallor, the gentle swell of her rose-tipped breasts, the inward curve of her stomach... 'I'll see you in the morning, Praskovia.'

She made no effort to leave.

'You and Alexei...' He fell silent.

'Sir?'

'Nothing. Sleep well.'

She walked to the back door, opened it, and closed it behind her. He followed and turned the key in the lock. He hoped loud enough for her to hear.

John Hughes was an exacting taskmaster. Tomorrow would be a long day, but Glyn also knew that after seeing Praskovia naked he wouldn't sleep. Unless... He grabbed his clothes.

Koshka said she had a girl who was his type. He hoped she was right.

Dower House, Beletsky Estate
September 1870

Sonya climbed the narrow staircase that led to the attics of Catherine's house. Alexei was looking through the telescope that had been his grandfather's.

'One day it will serve you right if a star falls out of the heavens and lands on you, squashing you into sauce.'

'I like looking at the sky.'

'I suppose it's more interesting than your other hobby.'

'What other hobby?' He prepared an argument in defence of his interest in engineering.

'Quarrelling with your father. It's all you've done since you returned from Allenstein.'

'He quarrels with me, not the other way round.'

'He quarrels with you because you disregard everything he tells you.'

'Where've you been?'

'Talking to the girls, Ruth, Miriam, and Rivka.'

'The girls are here?'

'They were. You would have seen them if you

hadn't hidden up here. Aunt Catherine arranged for them to meet Miss Smith so she could tell them about English customs. It took the governess an hour to explain that the English don't serve sugar lumps separately but stir them into their tea.'

'That must have been fun.'

'I've never been so bored. Miss Smith looked terrified, as though she expected the girls to attack her. She practically ran out of the servants' dining room when the hour she promised Aunt Catherine was up. The girls stayed longer. I think they were hoping to see you.'

'More like they stayed to sample my grandmother's marzipan and drink her cherry wine.'

'The cook was worried the quality wasn't up to the usual standard.'

'You lie so well. Do you have anything for me?'

'Yes, but I warned her if your father tracked you down you'd be back under lock and key in the Beletsky house.' She handed him a folded piece of paper.

He kissed it before opening it.

'If you marry you'll have to move. Her people won't accept you any more than ours.'

He was too busy reading his note to listen to her.

'All the girls send their good wishes. Yulia promised to light a candle in the church and pray for peace between you and your father.'

He finished reading the note and tucked it into his shirt pocket over his heart. 'Has Yulia any influence with God?'

'I doubt it, she likes playing naughty games with the boys too much. I talked to Aunt Catherine before she went to bed. Do you think she'll persuade your father to allow you to keep working for Mr Hughes's company?'

'I hope so.'

'If she doesn't?'

'She's offered to send me to university in Berlin or Vienna. It's generous of her but I don't want to study abroad when I could learn so much more from Mr Hughes and Mr Edwards here.'

'This place would be horrid without you. Yulia said Misha had written to his mother to tell her he's travelling with Mr Hughes.'

'I saw him.'

'Why didn't you tell me?'

'Because this is the first time I've seen you since I returned from Taganrog.'

'You could have sent a note with one of the maids.' She stared at him. 'You quarrelled with him, didn't you?'

'How do you know?'

'The look on your face. How could you? He's been away for three years...'

'You should have heard what he said about the Jews.'

'Misha's an officer in a Cossack regiment. What did you expect?'

'Him to say nothing against the people he grew up with.' Alexei reached for the telescope's dust cover.

'Did he look well?'

'And more handsome than when he left. Taller, broader, with a moustache. He's learned to dazzle the ladies with his captain's uniform. You should have seen the girls flocking round him in

Taganrog. He was preening like a lapdog at a tea party.'

'He was always happiest surrounded by women.'

'Which annoyed you because you were in love with him.'

'It was a schoolgirl crush. I was thirteen.'

'It didn't stop you crying enough tears to fill a vodka pail when he left.'

'I've grown up.'

'I hope so, for your sake.'

'This argument between you and Misha was serious?'

'You know my views on anti-Semitism.'

'Misha was one of your closest friends. The world isn't going to accept the Jews just because you've fallen in love with one, Alexei.'

He stepped down from the narrow platform that housed the telescope and sat on the top stair. 'I despair of the stupidity of hating someone because of the way they look or because their beliefs are different.'

'Spoken like a disciple of Father Grigor and Pavlo Razin.' She sat beside him. 'We both fell in love three years ago. I grew out of my childish passion, don't you think it's time you relinquished yours?'

'It's a not a childhood passion. And don't ever say anything like that in front of my father or grandmother.'

'Aunt Catherine isn't stupid.'

'You haven't told her?'

'I haven't said a word. But unlike your father I don't think she's swallowed the story that you're in love with Praskovia. One day, she and your father will see through the lies you've been spinning. If their suspicions settle on the real love of your life there'll be fireworks enough to set the steppe aflame.'

'If they don't believe I'm in love with Praskovia I could always pretend to be in love with you.'

'You know what your father thinks of me. I'm illegitimate which makes me unholy, barely one step up from a servant, as well as connected to you by blood.'

'A second or third cousin once or twice removed.'

'Cousins breed idiots.'

'Not distant cousins.'

'The threat of marriage to me might be enough make your father change his mind about Praskovia and see her as a daughter-in-law with better breeding potential. What would you do, Alexei, if your father ordered you to marry the girl you've been pretending to be in love with for the past two years?'

'I won't be old enough to marry until I'm twenty-one. A lot can happen in a couple of years.'

'For me too.'

'Grandmother will never allow you to become a governess.' He rose from the step.

'I can't live off Aunt Catherine all my life.'

'You're not living off her, you're her companion.'

'You and I both know she doesn't need one. I'm her charity.'

'You're well educated.'

'Which makes me a suitable governess. Aunt Catherine has been wonderful. I'm happy here but

I've seen the way governesses are treated. Exiled to no man's land between stairs, eating their meals off trays, because they're not allowed in the drawing or dining room to sit with the family, and are unwelcome in the servants' quarters. But it's either that or marriage to some boring, low ranking, little official who's prepared to overlook my illegitimacy in return for "career advancement" favours from your family.'

'There's a third alternative. Work. There are a lot of things you could do now the town is on the verge of being built.'

'Join Madam Koshka.'

'That's not funny.'

'Honestly, Alexei, from the expression on your face, you'd think you'd never heard the word whore.'

'It's not one a girl of good family should know.'

'There are times when you sound like your father.'

'Take that back.'

'Not when it's true. I've seen Koshka's girls going in and out of the hotel. They're well-dressed and fed and appear happy enough.'

'Think what they have to do every night.'

'Spread their favours among several grateful men as opposed to one grumpy husband.'

'You've been talking to Lyudmila again.'

'She should know. She's buried four husbands.'

'I spoke to Mr Hughes on the journey. He plans to open both an English and Russian school. You could teach the little ones English, or Russian to the English children, or music and drawing to both. You have the talent.'

'You think Mr Hughes would employ me?'

'I'll ask him.'

'No. He'll be living in this house. I'll ask him myself. Thank you for suggesting it, Alexei. Did you only just think of it?'

'The threat of marriage to a "boring little official" prompted it. Time we went downstairs.'

'Yulia, Ruth, and Miriam said they were going to the hospital tomorrow to see if they can train as nurses.'

'I suggested they try to Ruth. You know how hard life is in the shtetl. The hospital might be an idea for you too, if you can't get work in one of the schools straight away. Dr and Mrs Edwards said they wanted to recruit local girls to train as nurses, and men as porters. They'll also need a secretary to keep notes on the patients.'

'That could be interesting.'

'So you see, already Mr Hughes is creating opportunities for everyone. Women as well as men.' He brushed the dust from the back of his trousers.

'You have to face your father in the morning.'

He frowned. 'I have to stop him hauling me home like a sack of potatoes every time he finds me talking to someone he doesn't like.'

'How do you propose doing that?'

'Put poison mushrooms in his soup.'

'Don't joke about such a thing, Alexei. You'd feel terrible if something happened to him.'

'You're right, no one should wish their father ill; but that won't stop me from wanting him the Mongolian side of the steppe.'

He led the way down the stairs that led to the

kitchens and outside yard.

'Alexei...' she lowered her voice. 'If you should get caught meeting one another...'

'Fortune favours the bold.'

'As shouted by Turnus before he was destroyed by the Trojans. I studied the Aeneid alongside you and your sisters before you went to school – remember?'

He kissed her cheek, opened the yard door, and disappeared into the night.

Glyn Edwards' house, Hughesovka
Before dawn, September 1870

Glyn groped to consciousness. His head hurt before he opened his eyes and his shoulder muscles ached unbearably. He looked around the gloomy unfamiliar alcove before remembering he was at journey's end. He recalled the events of the previous day – and night – including his second visit to Koshka.

The throb in his head made sense. Energetic, loveless sex followed by too much brandy was a certain recipe for hangover. He reached for his pocket watch. It was too dark to see the face. He folded back the bedclothes, opened the drapes that separated the sleeping area from his study, and shivered. He grabbed his robe and slipped it on.

'Enter,' he shouted in response to a knock. It was followed by a second knock and he remembered Praskovia turning the key the night before. He opened the door. Praskovia struggled in with a loaded tray. She closed the door with her hip.

'Good morning, sir. I trust you slept well.' She set the tray of tea, vodka, and glass on the table in the study area, lifted a large enamel jug of hot water from the tray, and carried it to the wash-stand.

'Praskovia?'

'Sir?' She placed the jug on the marble top.

'About last night. You're right it makes sense to have separate bathing times. I'll ask everyone in the house not to use the banya between 10.00 p.m. and midnight. You can allot those two hours among your family and the other servants when you hire them.'

'This is your house, master. It is for you to make the rules.'

'If I work late it may suit me, Richard, and my brother to use the banya after midnight.'

'I'll tell the servants they can only use the banya between ten and midnight. Would you like me to pour your tea and vodka?'

'Tea please. I'm not used to spirits first thing. You won't be inconvenienced by time restrictions on the banya?'

'As I said, master. This is your house. It is for you to make the rules. Breakfast will be served in twenty minutes. Will that be all?'

He wondered if he'd dreamed he'd seen her naked or if the vision had merely been wishful thinking.

'Can I bring you anything else, sir?' she reiterated.

'No, thank you. I'll be in the dining room shortly.'

She left the room by the door to the hall. He went to the washstand, poured hot water into the bowl and his shaving mug, slid his cut-throat razor from its case, tested the blade against his thumb, dipped his brush into the mug, and lathered it.

He conjured an image of Praskovia naked. Would it have come so readily to mind if he hadn't seen her? Restless, aroused, resolving to drink less and keep a clear head in future, he started shaving. If he was going to do any useful work, he'd have to concentrate on more mundane things than his housekeeper. Naked or clothed.

Abandoned monastery on the banks of the Kalmius River
September 1870

Alexei lay in the centre of a copse of low growing trees and shrubs. He'd tethered his horse inside the broken walls, removed the saddle and blanket, and was dozing on an improvised bed he'd made of both.

He woke with a start. The stars were fading. The sky had lightened from deep rich navy to a lighter washed out tone. Dawn was about to break

Shivering, he sat up and rubbed his arms. He hadn't dreamed the sound. A dove's coo. He waited until it died away before sounding an answering cry. A few minutes later Ruth Kharber tiptoed through the remains of a doorway.

He clambered to his feet. 'I thought you'd never come.'

'Have you been here all night?'

'It's good to spend a night outdoors once in a while.'

'Ssh, not so loud. It's not good to sleep out when the ground's damp. You'll catch pneumonia.'

'I missed you every step of the way to Taganrog, all the time I was there, and every step back.' He folded his arms around her.

'I'm sorry. I couldn't get away sooner. It's been difficult since Nathan returned. He sleeps in my uncle's workshop downstairs, stays up half the night reading and even when he does sleep he wakes at the slightest sound.'

'He hasn't tried to stop you from seeing me.'

'No, but when we're alone he foretells tragedy for us. Every time he suspects I'm leaving the house to meet you, he looks disapprovingly at me.' She glanced over her shoulder. 'Rivka and Miriam are behind me. We're taking the laundry down to the river. I told them I wanted to visit my parent's grave. I dare not stay more than a few minutes or they'll look for me in the cemetery.'

'A few minutes are better than none.' He kissed her.

'Sonya said you've quarrelled with your father again and might have to leave.'

'If I do, it will only be for two or three years. I promise you, we'll be together one day.'

'So you keep saying. It's impossible, Alexei. A count, and a Jewess...'

'I'm not a count.'

'You will be.'

'Not if it means losing you.'

They froze when they heard the sound of laughter.

'Nothing's impossible, Ruth. Remember that. You're going to the hospital to ask for a job?'

'Yes, but I doubt I'll get one...'

He silenced her with a last kiss. 'You will, and then there'll be more opportunities for us to meet. Head straight for the river, it's not the quickest route to the cemetery but tell the girls you wanted to see dawn break over the water. I'll ride north and circle round.' He picked up the blanket and saddle and tacked up Agripin. Ruth waited until he'd mounted.

'Go please,' he whispered. 'We can't be seen together. Tonight?'

'I'll try.' She reached for his hand. He held it.

She didn't release him until he spurred Agripin on. The warmth stayed in her fingers. She closed her fist. She knew from experience it would stay with her all day.

Chapter Eighteen

Dower House, Beletsky Estate
September 1870

Nicholas Beletsky stalked into Catherine Ignatova's dining room to find John and four strange men sitting at the table with his mother-in-law and her lawyer, Dmitri. Nonplussed, he remained in the doorway.

'Good morning, Nicholas.' Amused by her son-in-law's uncharacteristic diffidence, Catherine took control of the conversation. 'As you see, Mr Hughes has arrived with the equipment and workers he needs to finish his plant. Mr Dmitri, you've met my son-in-law, Nicholas Beletsky. Gentlemen,' she turned to Mr Hughes's managers, 'may I introduce my son-in-law...' she monopolised the introductions, preventing Nicholas from edging a word in. 'Please, join us for breakfast, Nicholas.' She indicated a vacant chair halfway down the table.

Furious with his mother-in-law for surprising him with her guests, ignoring etiquette and introducing people of a lower caste to him as opposed to vice-versa, Nicholas snubbed her invitation.

'I came, as arranged, to talk to my son.'

'Regrettably, Alexei went riding before dawn. Young men and their energy,' Catherine shrugged. 'Forgive his absence, gentlemen. As you no doubt know from your own families, youth has no compunction in soliciting the indulgence of its elders.' Catherine was aware Alexei had been out all night, but she wasn't about to give Nicholas the satisfaction of another reason to be angry with his son.

'Good morning, Aunt Catherine, Mr Hughes, gentlemen, Uncle Nicholas.' Sonya curtsied to Nicholas, her aunt, and the men who rose at her entrance before taking her place at the opposite end of the table to Catherine. 'Thank you.' She took the plate of rolls a footman handed her.

'If you won't join us, Nicholas, perhaps you'll take tea in the library?' Catherine was aware that Nicholas's silence had stifled conversation.

'As I have to wait for Alexei, I may as well have

coffee here.' Nicholas nodded to John and took the chair he'd spurned earlier.

Catherine sensed Nicholas had recalled that not all the leases he'd negotiated with the Welshman had been signed. 'How is Olga this morning?'

'I've no idea. She rarely rises before noon these days.'

'My daughter is in poor health,' Catherine explained.

'I'm sorry to hear that,' John sympathised. 'We have an excellent doctor and nurse travelling with us. In fact they arrived last night and are staying with Glyn Edwards in the house you prepared for our use. Dr Peter Edwards is Glyn's brother; Peter's wife, Sarah, a nurse. They'll take over the management of the hospital when it opens.'

'Could I impose on Dr Edwards and his wife to call on my daughter, Mr Hughes?'

'I'm certain they'd be delighted to be of service, Madam.'

'Not necessary,' Nicholas interposed. 'Dr Meyer makes monthly visits. He's taken care of Olga through all her confinements. When he saw her two weeks ago he pronounced her healthy.'

'Dr Meyer isn't due to visit for another two weeks.' Catherine took three sugar lumps and placed them in the saucer of her tea cup.

'He said there was no need for concern.'

'You said Olga rarely rises before noon. That isn't normal, Nicholas. It will take Dr Meyer several days to reach here from Taganrog, especially after the recent rain, whereas Dr Edwards can visit Olga today.'

'Dr Edwards will be tired after his journey.'

'Knowing Dr Edwards, I've no doubt he's inspecting the hospital this minute.' John helped himself to grapes.

'I don't want to annoy Meyer by seeking a second opinion.'

Nicholas's blunt refusal gave rise to a constrained silence. To Catherine's surprise, it was Sonya who broke it.

'I thought I'd go along to the hospital this morning, Aunt Catherine, introduce myself to the doctor and his wife, and see if I can be of use as an interpreter or secretary.'

'How very public-spirited of you.' There was acid in Nicholas's voice.

'It is.' John chose to ignore Nicholas's tone. 'Language is going to be a problem until we master Russian.'

'Or the Russians master English,' Nicholas suggested.

'It would be arrogant of us to expect the locals to learn our tongue, which is why I'm grateful for the expertise of bilingual speakers willing to interpret, like your son and Miss Sonya, Count Beletsky. Thank you, Miss Sonya, on the company's behalf and that of my workers,' John lifted his teacup in a salute to Sonya.

'I approve, Sonya, order a carriage to take you.' Catherine left her chair. 'Please, gentlemen, enjoy the rest of your breakfast. I have matters to discuss with my son-in-law before my grandson returns. Nicholas, accompany me to the library, please?'

Nicholas hesitated but a glint in Catherine's eyes told him she would brook no procrastination. He followed her.

Hospital, Hughesovka
September 1870

Peter picked his way across the road from Glyn's house and studied the single storey building swarming with workmen. 'This is perfect. One floor, so no energy-draining stairs to haul patients up and down, tiled roof, stone walls and floors, easy to keep clean...'

'And bare,' Sarah interrupted when she and Anna caught up with him. 'Not a door, window, bed, or chair to be seen.'

'It will soon be finished, sweetheart. All it requires is a little imagination.' Peter slipped his arm around her shoulders.

'Plus hard work. Don't you think so, Anna?' Sarah asked.

'We can't start cleaning until the builders have finished,' Anna observed.

Peter watched the men working on the shell of the building. Not one gave him, Sarah, or Anna as much as a glance as they continued to shout at one another in Russian. 'I wish Glyn were here.'

'He has his troubles, we have ours. We can't rely on him to sort out the hospital or do our job for us, darling.' Sarah addressed the tradesmen more in hope than expectation. 'Do any of you speak English?'

'Yes, madam.' A labourer dressed in a long shabby black coat and wide brimmed black hat dropped a stack of wooden planks and joined them.

Peter held out his hand. 'I'm Dr Peter Edwards. This is my wife, Sarah.'

'Good day to you, sir.' The man brushed his hands off on the front of his coat before taking Peter's. 'Madam, miss.' He lifted his hat to reveal a skull cap.

Sarah's smiled faltered. Possibly it was her imagination, or antipathy to the man's sardonic appearance, but she read hostility in his eyes. He was thin, painfully so, six inches taller than the tallest of his fellow labourers, stooped and slight compared to the rest of the square-built, thickset, muscular builders. He made no attempt to introduce himself.

'How long will it take to fit the doors and windows and make this building habitable?' Peter asked.

The man spoke to a fellow worker. After a short exchange, Peter had his answer, but not the one he wanted.

'The overseer hopes to have stoves fitted in all the rooms by this time next week, Your Excellency. The doors and windows will take another two weeks. Possibly three.'

'It's a large building.' Sarah couldn't conceal her disappointment. After Huw had told them workmen had been burned in the brick factory she'd planned to spend the day making up beds and ministering to her first patients.

'Where are people being treated now?' Peter checked.

'Father Grigor's house, Your Excellency.'

'I'll never get used to "Your Excellency". Please call me Dr Edwards. Could you give me directions to Father Grigor's house?' Peter had never worked so hard to elicit so little information.

'It's outside the Cossack village of Alexandrovka on the road to the shtetl.'

'Is it far?'

'About two versts.'

'If we go to the office, we can ask Huw to find someone to take us there,' Sarah suggested.

'Has a caretaker been appointed for the hospital?' Peter hadn't yet given up on the conversation.

'I know nothing about positions within the hospital, Dr Edwards; I'm only a common labourer.'

The overseer spoke in Russian.

'He asked me to tell you girls came looking for work in the hospital this morning. They're waiting in the building where the materials are stored.'

'They're nurses?' Sarah asked.

'They're hoping to work as maids. You won't find a trained nurse within a hundred versts. The nearest hospital is in Taganrog.'

'Do any of them speak English, Mr...?' Sarah waited for him to give his name.

'A few have been to English lessons, Mrs Edwards. I can't answer for their fluency.'

'Your English is excellent, Mr...' Peter suddenly realised that the man could prove invaluable.

'Kharber,' Nathan replied reluctantly.

'Would you be interested in working in the hospital as an interpreter?'

'I have a job. If you'll excuse me, I must get on with it before I'm fired for wasting my employer's time.'

'Strange man,' Sarah followed Peter and Anna

to a wooden shed.

Anna glanced back at him. 'He looks sad.'

'He doesn't look strong enough for physical work.' Peter stood in front of the open doors of the warehouse. 'Well, you wanted ward maids and nurses, sweetheart. Looks like you have a week's work sorting out which ones you'll be employing.'

Sarah gazed at the scores of girls standing patiently inside the hut. 'I hope at least one of them understands English.'

'I'll take a walk to the office and check if Huw has employed any staff for the hospital.'

'Coward,' Sarah called after him when a tidal wave of girls threatened to overwhelm her.

Dower House, Beletsky Estate
September 1870

'How is Olga, really, Nicholas?' Catherine demanded after the footman closed the library door.

'You've seen her.' He sat in an armchair.

'Not for two days. You said she was too tired to receive me last night.'

'She was sleeping.'

'When I last saw her, she could hardly keep her eyes open.'

'Olga has always tired easily. Meyer's given her a tonic. It doesn't appear to be working.'

'You haven't seen her this morning?'

'Would you rather I disturbed her?'

'I'd rather my daughter wasn't worn down by constant pregnancies.' Catherine sat on a chair that faced his. 'This has to be the last child, Nicholas.'

'Olga is my wife...'

'Your wife. Not a brood mare. You're killing her.'

'Pregnancy is a natural state for a woman.'

'Not nineteen times in nineteen years, it isn't.'

'Only twelve children have survived.'

'You intend to impregnate Olga again after your thirteenth has been born?'

'I intend to welcome as many children into my family as God chooses to send. Olga has a capable housekeeper, conscientious servants, a governess to teach the girls, and nursery maids to care for the younger children. My steward makes all decisions relevant to the estate in my absence. There's nothing for Olga to do. She's bored and as a consequence imagines pregnancy as an illness. Your constant fussing over her doesn't help.'

Catherine pulled the bell pull. The butler entered. 'Has my grandson returned?'

'Five minutes ago, my lady. He's talking to Mr Hughes in the dining room.'

'Ask him and Mr Dmitri to join us. I'd like you and four footmen to remain in this room for the duration of our discussions. Order one of the maids to bring a tray of coffee and rolls. Alexei won't have eaten.'

'Yes, my lady.'

'Is it necessary for us to discuss family matters in front of the servants, Catherine?'

'Given your behaviour in Mr Edwards' house last night, Nicholas, I believe it is.'

'As you weren't present you're not in a position

to comment.'

'Alexei is a reliable witness.'

Nicholas left his chair, walked to the window, and looked out at the rain-ravaged gardens. 'Do you intend to entertain Mr Hughes and his entourage every mealtime?'

'They arrived at dawn. I considered it hospitable to offer them breakfast while their servants unpacked.'

'Mr Hughes will be running his own establishment?'

'As I told you.'

'Someone has to say this, Catherine; as head of the family it falls to me. You are a widow and a widow cannot be too careful of her reputation.'

Catherine began to laugh.

'I fail to see anything humorous in the situation.'

'Your concern for my reputation is touching, Nicholas, but unwarranted given my age.'

'Age is no excuse to flout convention. Mr Hughes is married and living apart from his wife.'

'Careful what you infer, Nicholas. Mr Hughes's domestic arrangements are none of your concern.'

'He may be a decade younger than you but I've no doubt the gossips would find that salacious. Older wealthy woman – younger man...'

'Who is considerably wealthier than me. Enough, Nicholas!' Catherine was relieved when Alexei walked in with Dmitri. The butler followed with the footmen and led them to the back of the library, within sight but out of earshot, provided voices remained low.

The maid brought in a tray of coffee, cups, and

rolls and set it on a side table but Alexei made no move towards it. He faced his father.

'Good morning, sir.'

'Have you an apology for me?' Nicholas demanded.

'For what, sir?'

'Leaving my house after I ordered you to remain in your room.'

'You locked me in my bedroom. I had no wish to remain a prisoner.'

'You still intend to work in your infernal modern industry?'

'I do, sir.'

'Although you know it contravenes all the plans I've made for you?'

'Yes, sir.'

'Why do you remain obdurate in defying me?'

'I have my own ambitions, sir.'

'I too have ambitions for my eldest son and heir.'

'I have no wish to live the empty life of a country-based aristocrat, Father.'

'I gave you a choice. You could go to the court at St Petersburg.'

'Or to become a courtier and lackey, sir.'

Nicholas's colour heightened to a rich burgundy. 'You're determined to follow a life of industry and engineering?'

Alexei paled in contrast to his father. 'Mr Thomas has found my assistance helpful. I wish to continue working for him and Mr Hughes despite my lack of relevant education.'

'Then I wash my hands of you.' Nicholas reached into his coat pocket, extracted a coin and flung it at Alexei. It stung his son's cheek before it fell to the floor. Alexei made no move to pick it up.

'That is the last kopek you will receive from me. From this moment my house is barred to you.'

'Mama...'

'I forbid you to visit your mother, sisters, or brothers when they return for the holidays. Or attempt to remove any item from the room that was yours. Should you defy me I will denounce you to my fellow magistrates as a trespasser and thief.'

'That is ridiculous, Nicholas,' Catherine intervened.

'You wanted your grandson, Catherine. You have him. He's no son of mine. You are all the family he has from this moment on.'

'And me?' Catherine enquired. 'Do you intend to stop me from visiting my daughter and grandchildren? Or prevent them from visiting this house?'

'If I discover you've carried any messages from that ... ingrate,' he pointed at Alexei, 'to Olga, or my children or servants, I will bar you from my house as well. That is my final word.'

Tight-lipped, Alexei continued to stand to attention. 'May I take leave of Mama, my sisters and brothers?'

'You may not.'

Alexei remained bolt upright, as if he were on a parade ground. 'May I trouble you to put that in writing?'

'Put what in writing?'

'That you disown me and have no further

interest in me or what I do. There is pen, ink, and paper on the desk.'

Nicholas went to the desk, scribbled a note, blotted it, and handed it to Alexei on his way to the door.

'Goodbye, Father.'

Nicholas neither turned nor answered Alexei. The butler opened the door and accompanied Nicholas into the hall. The front door opened and closed. The sound of carriage wheels turning on gravel resounded outside.

'Alexei?'

'I'm fine, Grandmother.'

A pulse throbbing at Alexei's jawline suggested otherwise, but Catherine didn't contradict him. 'That went better than I hoped. Dmitri, are the papers I asked you to draw up in order?'

'They are, Madam.'

'Alexei, you've turned your back on your father's fortune, you will, however, inherit mine with the exception of an annuity I've left to Sonya.'

'Of the two estates, your grandmother's is of more value,' Dmitri informed Alexei.

'How can that be, when Nicholas inherited half my late husband's assets in addition to the Beletsky fortune?'

'Your estate is mortgage-free, Madam.'

'Nicholas has mortgaged the house?'

'The entire estate, along with the Moscow and St Petersburg houses and dachas.'

'The money he inherited? Surely it hasn't all gone?'

'I'm not your son-in-law's lawyer, Madam, but people talk within the profession. There are rumours the count is having difficulty meeting his obligations.'

'Who holds the mortgages?'

'Would you like me to make enquiries?'

'Please.'

Dmitri laid a sheaf of papers on the table. 'Would you be so kind as to send for two of the gentlemen in the dining room, Madam, so they can witness your signature on these documents?'

Hospital, Hughesovka
September 1870

'Your English is good.' Sarah complimented Miriam, Ruth, and Yulia. 'If you're prepared to start as ward maids, I'll give you the opportunity to train as nurses. But it will be a long and arduous course. Ruth, do you know the other girls here?'

'Some of them, madam.'

'Please address me as "Matron", not "madam".' Sarah was taken aback by how easily the title had slipped from her tongue. If she'd remained in London she wouldn't have been allowed to continue nursing after her marriage. If she'd opted for a career instead of marriage, she probably wouldn't have reached the exalted state of matron until after her fiftieth birthday.

'I need another twelve ward maids besides you, Yulia, and Miriam, Ruth. Would you help me interview the girls so I can choose those most suitable? The first question I need to ask is: are they prepared to learn English.'

'There's something I need to tell you, madam

… Matron. About Miriam and me.' Ruth blurted. 'We're Jews, Matron.'

'Yes.'

'You knew, Matron?'

'Given your names I assumed you were. I'm British.'

'Some people might object to our working in the hospital.'

'Why?'

'The Russians tolerate Jews, Matron. They use the services of our craftsmen, but they expect us to live apart. They won't like being looked after by us.'

'Are you telling me a Russian would refuse to be nursed by a Jew?'

'Yes, Matron.'

'If a Russian finds him or herself in need of the services of the hospital they will either accept the staff we employ or go elsewhere for treatment.'

'Then you'll still employ Miriam and me, Matron?'

'As I said. Now, let's find twelve girls I can train alongside you.'

HQ of the New Russia Company
Hughesovka, September 1870

Peter made his way along the muddy track and headed for an enormous, roughly built wooden shed. He smiled when he saw the amateurishly painted Cyrillic lettering over the door alongside the English sign. *HEADQUARTERS OF THE NEW RUSSIA COMPANY*. It sounded grand, but the building didn't look as though it would afford any more shelter than the makeshift market stalls Eastern European immigrants threw up in Whitechapel back in London.

A queue of men, women, and children, most with bare feet, all in rags, snaked around the building. They stared at him curiously when he pushed open the rickety front door. It stuck on the uneven floor and he had to thump it to close it. Glyn and Richard were leaning on a chest-high wooden counter that separated the public from the office area. Huw was on the working side, rifling through stacks of maps. The sound of Russian conversation echoed through from a planking wall behind him.

'Lost your wife already?' Glyn asked.

'She's interviewing hordes of girls who've turned up at the hospital hoping to find work.'

'You exaggerate.' Huw's eyelids drooped from lack of sleep. 'There aren't hordes of girls within walking distance of this place. However, there's hardly any work for women. I've heard that that half the girls in Alexandrovka and three-quarters of the girls in the shtetl are hoping to find jobs in the hospital.'

'It looked like hordes. We met a man who spoke English. He told us the hospital may not be finished for weeks.'

'Regrettably he's right. Was he Nathan Kharber?' Huw handed Glyn a map.

'That's the name he gave us. He said the bricklayers who'd been burned are being looked after in a priest's house.'

'Father Grigor's just outside Alexandrovka,'

Huw confirmed. 'You'll like Father Grigor, he's the sort of priest who digs an old woman's garden when she's not well enough to plant her own potatoes. Nathan Kharber's recently returned from Paris. Alexei suggested he could be useful to us as he speaks French and German as well as English and Russian.'

'I doubt we'll need French and German,' Peter observed.

'You might not need French and German in the hospital, but once the furnaces are operational we'll have a lot of vacancies, metallurgists, laboratory assistants, and the ilk. Mr Hughes will be more interested in the quality of a man's work than the language he speaks. Have you all the maps you need, Glyn?' Huw asked.

'If I don't we're going to get lost out there. Ready, Richard?' Glyn rolled up the maps and inserted them into a cardboard tube.

'I will be when the carriage arrives and Mr Thomas gives me a compass.'

'I forgot. Sorry, I'll get one for you now.' Huw disappeared into a back cupboard.

'You need maps?' Peter asked Glyn.

'Richard's going to help me check the mines Mr Hughes has leased. He's been studying the geologist's reports. I've been looking at the output. We need to close the smaller, less viable operations and concentrate on the most productive pits. Ironworks eat coal. We'll need a stockpile before we begin production.'

'And the Edwards brothers colliery?'

'I won't have time to think about that until I have the New Russia Company's mines running at full capacity.'

Huw returned with the compass. 'How can I help you, Dr Edwards?'

'Sarah and I would like to drive out to Father Grigor's. We hoped you had a vehicle and driver to spare.'

Huw shouted to his assistant in Russian. The man left his desk, lifted a flap in the counter, and went out by the front door.

'It will be here as soon as the horses have been harnessed,' Huw said. 'None of our drivers speak English and I can't spare an interpreter. I've put them all on site so the workers who arrived with Mr Hughes can communicate with the builders.'

'We'll be fine as long as you tell the driver where to go.'

Huw tore a piece of paper from a pad and scribbled a name in Cyrillic letters. 'What am I thinking? Hardly anyone around here can read. Repeat after me...'

'My tongue will break. You sound as though you're trying to strangle yourself,' Peter complained.

'Huw only said "Father Grigor" in Russian,' Glyn laughed. 'Speak slowly. The locals will think you're an idiot, but they already assume you're not right in the head for wanting to live here.'

Peter tried again.

'Better,' Glyn complimented. 'As for you, young man,' he turned to Richard. 'No one has the right to laugh at anyone's efforts unless they can do better.'

Richard repeated exactly what Huw had said, syllable for syllable.

'A month and you'll be working as my interpreter,' Glyn predicted.

'Alexei coached me in the pronunciation of Russian on the journey.'

'You're a quick learner,' Huw complimented, 'and a credit to the New Russia Company.'

'I've been meaning to ask,' Peter looked at Glyn. 'Why the New Russia Company? Was there an old one?'

'In the sixteenth century a Russia Company was created with a view to exploring trade routes. A Captain Willoughby led the initial expedition. He froze to death along with his entire crew. His ship full of corpses was discovered the following spring by Russian fishermen.'

'That's a jolly tale.' Peter looked through a crack in the door. A carriage was drawing up outside.

'We're hoping for a more auspicious outcome for this venture,' Glyn said drily. 'That's our carriage, Richard.'

'If Alexei comes in...'

'I'll send him to the Old Man Snoring pit. I'd love to know how it acquired that name,' Huw cleared the surplus maps from the counter.

'Let's hope the "snores" weren't falls or explosions. Time we were off.' Glyn gave Richard a playful tap with his tube of maps. 'See you tonight, Peter. Good luck with your interviewing.'

'Sarah needs the luck, not me. Alexei not around?' Peter asked Huw after Glyn and Richard left.

'Not as yet. I hope his father hasn't sent him to Siberia. The boy's been a godsend when it comes to dealing with prickly locals.'

'He certainly made things easier for us on the journey here.' The unseen voices on the other side of the flimsy partition rose sharply. 'Why are people queuing at the back door?'

'They want jobs.'

'Even women and children?'

'Some of the women, but anyone who signs up is entitled to a food parcel to tide them over until their wages come in. The size of the parcel is determined by the number of people dependent on the worker's wage.'

'Mr Hughes certainly thinks of his workers.'

'Which is why people fight to work for him. Alexei, good to see you. Are you here to work?' Huw asked when he walked in.

'If you haven't sacked me for being late.'

'You're too useful to sack. You're not thinking of handing in your notice, I hope?'

'Not if you give me a pay rise.'

'That's something you discuss with Mr Hughes, not me,' Huw pointed to the troika that had pulled up at the door. 'Dr Edwards wants to go out to Father Grigor's to see his patients; would you show him the way?'

'My pleasure.'

'We need to pick up my wife and Anna first,' Peter warned. 'I left them interviewing girls at the hospital.'

'They were talking to them when I rode past. We'd better check that Mrs Edwards has chosen the best ones before we drive out to Alexandrovka.'

'By the best, you mean the prettiest, Alexei?'

Huw commented.

'Of course.' Alexei didn't return Huw's smile. 'Shall we go, Dr Edwards?'

Chapter Nineteen

Hughesovka
September 1870

'There's so many people, so many stalls. It's busier than Spitalfields on a Saturday.' Sarah leaned over the side of the troika to take a closer look at the crowds thronging the open-air bazaar that had sprung up next to the furnace foundations. There were a few primitive trestles but most traders – Mongols from the Eastern Steppe as well as locals and judging by the accents, natives from the Black Sea regions – had arranged their wares on tarpaulins on the ground. Most essentials were on offer; pyramids of swedes, beets, cabbages, and potatoes had been built next to slabs of meat, loaves of bread, mounds of boots, and assorted cooking pots.

'Now you know where to do your shopping, although it might be better to tell Praskovia what you want. She's an expert at haggling a good price.' Alexei had to shout as they passed a blacksmith's shop where men, stripped to the waist, were hammering metal rings onto carriage wheels.

'I was expecting Hughesovka to be smaller with fewer people,' Peter said.

‘Once word spread that a new town was being built which needed workers, people flooded in.’

‘There’s Mr Hughes, can you ask the driver to stop please, Alexei.’ Peter asked.

‘Mrs Edwards, Anna, Alexei,’ John walked over to greet them. ‘I was sorry to hear from Mrs Ignatova that the hospital isn’t finished, hopefully it shouldn’t take long. A month or so.’

‘More the “or so” from what we saw, sir,’ Peter commented. ‘We’re on our way to visit Father Grigor. He’s organised a makeshift hospital in his house until we can open ours.’

‘Offer whatever help he needs in the way of labour, medicines, and equipment, Dr Edwards, courtesy of the company.’

‘Hughesovka is larger and more advanced than I expected, sir,’ Sarah complimented.

‘Give me another six months, Mrs Edwards, and you won’t recognise the place. Please excuse me, I have labourers to galvanise.’ He joined a group of workers. Within minutes he was spreading cement on a brick and instructing them in the finer points of bricklaying.

‘Is there anything Mr Hughes doesn’t know about construction or industry?’ Alexei asked when they set off again.

‘I doubt it. Perhaps when he’s finished setting those bricklayers to rights he could visit the hospital and do the same there,’ Sarah suggested.

‘Glyn’s inviting him to dinner this week, you can bring it up then, sweetheart.’

‘Double coward.’ Sarah took his Peter’s arm and snuggled closer to him.

Alexandrovka
September 1870

'Dear God,' Sarah watched as a barefoot, ragged woman surrounded by a cluster of barefoot semi-naked children climbed out of a hole. 'People live underground here, like animals.'

'Only the Mujiks, and the poor among them have lived like that for centuries, Mrs Edwards,' Alexei helped Sarah from the troika and shook hands with Father Grigor who was leaning on his garden gate, waiting to greet them. 'Dr and Mrs Edwards: Father Grigor, our local saint.'

'Hardly, Alexei,' the priest demurred.

'There are those who venerate you as Alexander the Blessed.'

'If I was Alexander the Blessed I would be ninety-three, Alexei. There may be mornings when I feel that old, but I assure you before God I haven't been on this earth that long. I'm very glad to meet you, Dr Edwards, Mrs Edwards, and...'

'Anna, sir, a relative.' Sarah introduced Anna.

'Who's Alexander the Blessed?' Peter asked.

Alexei explained. 'Tsar Alexander I died suddenly of typhus in Taganrog in 1825. He was only forty-eight. Some say he didn't die, but disappeared to live the life of a holy man among the poor of Russia. When Father Grigor turned up here in 1855–'

'When I was forty years old.'

'Forgive me, Father, but you looked older,' Alexei continued, 'some Cossacks and Mujiks believed the saintly Alexander had come to live among us. It didn't help that Father Grigor could read, write, and speak French, English, and German as well as Russian, as only educated aristocrats can. He also owned books and scientific instruments. You may think you're not the blessed Alexander, Father, but the pious want to believe otherwise. They also know that even if you're not Alexander you are a saint for putting up with the natives here.'

'We'll continue this discussion later, Alexei. Please come into my house, you are most welcome.' The priest opened his door.

Father Grigor's house, outskirts of Alexandrovka
September 1870

Peter and Sarah were impressed with the makeshift hospital Father Grigor had set up in his living room. Although the injured lay on straw-filled pallets on the floor, their bedding was spotless, as was everything else in sight. The patients were being cared for by volunteers under the direction of the priest's housekeeper, Brin, a fierce, unsmiling harridan with a moustache a soldier would have been proud of.

Peter lifted a dressing on a leg wound to find it and the surrounding skin stained bright green. 'What are you using to treat this?'

Alexei peered at it. 'Moss.'

'It is has something in it that promotes healing,' Father Grigor explained.

Peter lifted his eyebrows. 'Really?'

'You're the first doctor to come here, Dr

Edwards. Until now the sick have had to rely on folk remedies that have been handed down through generations of Babki – the peasant faith healers. Most Babki are skilled herbalists. Some of their remedies work, there are others I suspect of doing more harm than good, but I've seen spectacular results when coal has been used to treat food and alcohol poisoning, and mustard flour, garlic, and various plants can cure some skin, stomach, kidney, and liver ailments.'

'There's not much difference between covering a wound with moss and the oatmeal, salt, and honey compound the midwives in Merthyr use to pack the miners' leg ulcers,' Sarah pointed out. 'You have to admit, the midwives' concoction works better than the mercury salts the hospitals use, and with less pain to the patient.'

'I bow to your philosophy of learning from the locals, sweetheart.'

'I believe most of our patients are doing as well as can be expected, Dr Edwards,' the priest said.

'I'm beginning to understand why you don't need a doctor here.'

'Believe me, we need one, Dr Edwards, particularly now the town is growing faster than mushrooms on the steppe. Please come into my study. Brin will bring us refreshments.' They followed him into a book-lined room, resplendent with Cossack embroideries; the gifts of his parishioners, as he explained to Sarah when she admired them.

The floor was covered with embroidered sacking, and the furniture had been carved by the priest himself. Brin brought in trays of homemade biscuits and set them around a steaming samovar. The priest invited her to join them but she answered in a torrent of Russian. Alexei translated.

'She would like nothing better than to sit and drink tea but she has to oversee the idle women who visit every day and plague the life out of the priest and patients rather than help.'

Peter and the priest plunged into a discussion about the best way to set broken bones, while Anna admired carved wooden angels and animals arranged in front of the books. Disturbed by the living conditions of the priest's neighbours, Sarah carried her tea to the window and looked out at the steppe. It was spattered with makeshift roofs of rough wooden planks and slabs of turf balanced over holes in the ground.

Alexei joined her.

'Those people might be used to living underground, Alexei, but they can't be left,' Sarah protested. 'Glyn said it often snows in October.'

'I'd say usually, not often. But every roof has a chimney. They have stoves they can use for cooking and heating, probably built from bricks they've filched from Mr Hughes's stockpiles.'

'I can't abide the thought of living in the palace Glyn's buying from your grandmother while women, children, and babies cower in the ground like animals.'

'The Tsar only freed the serfs nine years ago,' Father Grigor reminded her. 'They have nothing except their new-found freedom to walk as far from their previous masters as their legs will carry them. For them, that freedom is paramount. For the first time in their lives they can live where they choose and sell their labour to the highest bidder. Consider where they've come from, Mrs Edwards. If it was better than Hughesovka, they wouldn't have walked here.'

'I suppose you're right,' Sarah allowed reluctantly.

'You want to help them?'

'Anyone with a scrap of human compassion would.'

'Don't give them money. If you do, the men will use it to buy vodka. If you must give them anything, give the women food, blankets, and warm clothing for themselves and their children. Better still, give your donations to me or Brin.'

'You look after them?'

'We try. Brin knows which families are in greatest need and which are likely to sell what they're given to buy drink. I leave the distribution of donated goods to her because she's expert at sorting the deserving from the scrounging. Unfortunately some are more likely to beg at the doors of those they consider wealthy than work. Once word gets out your brother-in-law's house is occupied they'll be at your door.'

'I'll talk to Praskovia about them.'

'I heard she was your housekeeper. A wise choice, Mrs Edwards. Like Brin, Praskovia will know who really needs help.'

Hughesovka
Autumn 1870

The first few days in Hughesovka were difficult for all the emigrants. But as days became weeks and weeks months, they learned the rudiments of the language and how to cope. First with the cold, then the snow that covered the steppe.

Richard had never worked harder. When he wasn't underground with Glyn examining seams and talking to the miners at the coalface, he was pouring over geometry textbooks and designing new and improved methods of shoring.

Anna spent her days being instructed in the practical side of nursing by Sarah, alongside Yulia, Ruth, Miriam, and Rivka in Father Grigor's house, and her evenings studying Sarah's nursing text books.

Glyn spent most evenings with Huw and John, checking furnace plans and fretting at the delays caused by the weather. Alexei tried to make himself useful to whoever he felt needed him most. Peter fell into a routine of spending his mornings in Father Grigor's hospital, his afternoons making home visits to patients, and any spare time haunting the hospital, which despite all the builders' promises was only marginally nearer completion three months after their arrival than when he'd first seen it.

Even when Peter extracted a completion date of the first of January from the foreman of the hospital site, he remained unconvinced they'd be able to move in that soon.

John did his best to boost morale by organising

social evenings and hunting trips. Alexei instructed everyone, including Sarah and Anna, in the care and use of the guns in his grandmother's extensive arsenal. Catherine organised dinners and musical concerts with Sonya's piano playing as the main attraction but after she glanced around her reception room in the middle of one of Sonya's recitals to see more than half of her guests asleep, she confronted John and suggested he was working his people too hard.

His reply was a single raised eyebrow, which she had learned meant, 'I hear you, but Hughesovka's needs take precedence over those of its inhabitants.'

Glyn Edwards' house, Hughesovka
December 1870

A week before Christmas Sarah woke to the sound of the maids carrying trays up the stairs. She left the bed, opened the door, took the tray from the girl, set it on the washstand, and carried her tea to the window. She opened the curtains and looked out over the balcony veranda.

'It's snowing again.'

'I need you to come back to bed, not give me a weather report.' Peter snuggled further beneath the bedclothes.

'It's bad enough getting up once a day when you're six months pregnant, twice would be too much. I can't believe we've been here nearly four months.'

'You would believe it if we'd had any free time

since we arrived to look at our watches.'

'We'll have even less time when we move into the hospital.'

'*If* we move into the hospital. In retrospect I think it would have been easier to have shipped an entire hospital, bricks, beds, operating tables, instruments, porters, nurses, and all, from Britain than build one here.'

'Grumble, grumble, grumble.' She finished her tea went to the bed and kissed the top of his head. 'Think of next week. That should put a smile on your face.'

'Why?'

'Christmas is coming, your wife is getting fat...'

'This,' he reached out from under the eiderdown and stroked her burgeoning waistline, 'not Christmas, will put a smile on my face. Although if we're lucky we might get a whole day off provided no one breaks a leg or gets lethally drunk. Please come back to bed.'

'Absolutely, definitely not.' She went to the washstand, tipped hot water in to the bowl, stripped off her nightgown, and sponged herself down. 'You going to the hospital this morning?'

'The office first to see if the Baker-Brown-type cautery clamps we ordered have arrived, then the hospital. I want to check the flooring in the operating theatre. I'm afraid if I'm not there to oversee it, they'll put down a wooden instead of a tiled floor. We need to be able to disinfect the place.'

'You're talking to a nurse, darling.' She dried herself and began to dress.

He propped himself up on the pillows. 'That

Cossack smock suits you.'

'Which is as well as I've let out my stays to the limit.' She sat on a chair, rolled on a pair of thick woollen stockings, and fastened them with garters before pulling down her combiknickers. She slipped on her shoes, laced them and returned to the window. 'It's beautiful out there.'

'I've no doubt it is but don't you dare open the window and let out all the warm air.'

'I won't if you get out of bed and look. It's like a fairy tale. Everything is so white and clean...'

'And nobbling.'

'Trust you to be prosaic. Even the street looks spotless coated in snow.'

'It was white yesterday morning and the one before that. In a few hours it will turn filthy again once people have walked on it.'

She brushed out her hair, twisted it into a knot, and pinned it into a chignon. 'I'm ready and I'm going to have first choice of pancakes at breakfast.'

'Tell Praskovia I'll have eggs and ham, please.' He left the bed and moved towards her.

'Smile, Peter. We're one day closer to moving into the hospital.'

'I suspect there will be too many days before moving in day, for one to matter.' He pulled her close and kissed her. 'The bed's still warm.'

'I'm dressed.'

'I'm not.'

She pushed him back on the bed and slipped her hand between his thighs.

'I'd rather I wasn't the only naked one. But if this is all you're prepared to give, I'll exact full

payment tonight.'
'With interest?'
'You can bet on it.'

Beletsky Mansion, Hughesovka
December 1870

The butler knocked softly at the count's study door.

'Enter!' Nicholas looked up from the journal he was reading. 'If there's a household problem, solve it.'

'The mistress is ill, Your Excellency.'

'The countess is always ill.'

'Not this ill, Your Excellency. Miss Smith is with her as well as her maid and the housekeeper.'

Irritated, Nicholas went upstairs. The door to his wife's room was open. His wife's maid was standing beside the bed alongside Miss Smith.

He clamped his handkerchief over his nose and stepped in but didn't venture as far as the bed. His wife's skin was damp and grey. Her pillow was soaked in foul-smelling thin grey fluid which she was vomiting.

'What is the problem?' He addressed the housekeeper.

'Her ladyship's pulse is weak, Your Excellency. As you see, she has severe stomach pains and diarrhoea...'

'Send the groom to Mr Hughes's office to fetch the company doctor. I want him here immediately.'

Glyn Edwards' house, Hughesovka
December 1870

'You're late this morning, sir,' Praskovia commented when Peter appeared at the breakfast table.

Peter looked at the cleared places. 'Richard and Glyn have left?'

'They went to the office before dawn.'

'Sarah and Anna have gone to Father Grigor's?'

'Half an hour ago with Vlad in the hospital sleigh. Mrs Edwards told me to remind you Brin is making pancakes with meat sauce for lunch.'

'Good as Brin is, she's not as good a cook as your mother.'

'I'll be sure not to tell my mother that or her head will swell too big for her to walk through the door, sir. I'll fetch your ham and eggs.'

'Only if they're ready and it's no trouble.'

'They're ready, sir.'

Hughesovka
December 1870

Peter finished breakfast, wrapped himself in his overcoat, muffler, gloves, and fur-lined boots and tramped through the snow to the office. Richard, Glyn, and Huw were huddled around the stove.

'Good morning, have the medical supplies I ordered been delivered, Huw?'

'Nothing today, Peter. But now the storms have died down I'm expecting more deliveries to come through from Taganrog.'

'Good to see you all drinking hard instead of working.' Peter nodded to a clay jug on the counter. He'd been shocked the first morning in Hughesovka when Praskovia had set a bottle of vodka alongside the samovar and coffee pot on the breakfast table, but it hadn't reappeared at breakfast since. He presumed Glyn had told their housekeeper the British didn't begin the day with alcohol.

Huw raised his beaker. 'We are working hard, planning out work schedules.'

'You expect me to believe that?'

Huw avoided the question. 'The drink is alcohol-free and refreshing. Help yourself.'

Peter filled a beaker. 'It's good, what is it?'

'Cherry cordial from Count Beletsky's store,' Huw revealed. 'The first of last summer's brewing to be opened. The cook sent the pitcher down this morning. The recipe is secret; as well as cherries, it includes lemons and honey.'

'The Beletskys' cook chasing you, Huw?' Glyn suggested. 'Hasn't she heard about your evenings in Koshka's with the little blonde Bohemian?'

Huw didn't like humour that bordered on personal. 'The cook is being neighbourly and the cordial is a thank you after I sent her up a couple of boxes of English tea. Mrs Ignatova told me the countess is fond of it and they'd run out. According to the Beletskys' housekeeper the countess hardly leaves her bed.'

'I'm not surprised,' Peter said. 'Mrs Ignatova told me the countess is expecting her thirteenth child in the spring, although her last isn't out of nappies. I sent a message offering to attend her but the count has yet to take me up on it.'

'Is he home?' Glyn checked.

'Returned from St Petersburg two weeks ago,' Huw answered.

'We may not have a Hughesovka newspaper, but we have the next best thing: the gossip circle around Huw's stove,' Glyn joked. 'Now we've finished assessing the Company's collieries we can start surveying the first of the Edwards' brothers' pits. Ready, Richard?'

Huw glanced out of the window. 'Your sleigh hasn't arrived from the stable.'

'Then we'll just have to sit here warming our toes and drinking cherry cordial for a while longer.'

A man dressed in the outdoor livery of the Beletsky Estate galloped up as if he were charging on a battlefield. He reined in his horse, jumped from the saddle, barged through the open door, and shouted to Huw.

Huw listened to him before turning to Peter. 'Apparently the count did note your offer to visit the countess, Peter. She's ill and the count has sent for you, but by the sound of the invitation only because you're closer than the doctors in Taganrog.'

'That's my sleigh pulling up, take it, Peter. I'll use yours when it comes,' Glyn offered.

'Thank you. Ask the driver to drive past Father's Grigor's please, Huw? I need to pick up Sarah and my bag.'

Huw briefed the driver. 'Good luck.' He went to the door and watched Peter climb into the sleigh. 'Cure the countess and you'll have every aristocrat within three days journey queuing to join your practice.'

Beletsky Mansion, Hughesovka
December 1870

Count Beletsky was pacing up and down beneath the portico. 'I expected you sooner.'

'I'm sorry…'

The count cut Peter's apologies short. 'My wife is very ill.'

Peter grabbed his doctor's bag and jumped from the sleigh. 'Her symptoms?'

'Vomiting, diarrhoea...'

'Her temperature?'

'According to her maid her skin is cold and damp.'

Peter looked at Sarah. They'd seen hundreds if not thousands of people with those symptoms during a pandemic in London in 1866. The final death toll had stood at over four thousand in the East End alone. He entered the house.

'Upstairs,' Nicholas informed him.

Peter ran up the staircase.

A crowd of women, some wailing, their faces buried in their aprons had gathered outside a door on the gallery. Peter pushed through. A stern-faced woman dressed in black was hovering at the foot of an enormous bed.

'I'm Dr Edwards.' Peter turned. His host was nowhere in sight. 'Does anyone here speak English?'

'Yes.' The woman in black answered. 'I am the count's governess. Miss Smith.'

Sarah went to the bed. The countess was lying on a damp sheet. Two women in maids' uniforms were sponging her face, neck, and arms. Their sponges dripped, soaking the bed, but the countess lay staring at the ceiling, apparently oblivious to discomfort.

One of the women spoke in Russian.

'The children's nurse is asking if you wish to have a hot bath prepared or if you intend to apply electrical stimuli, Dr Edwards.'

'Neither until I've examined my patient. Ask the countess if she's in pain?'

Miss Smith clamped her handkerchief over her nose before stepping closer to the bed. The countess drew up her knees and screamed.

Sarah picked up Olga's hand and checked her pulse. 'Weak and thready.' She ran her hands over the sheet that covered the countess's abdomen. 'Five, maybe six months pregnant.'

Peter examined the countess's eyes and felt her skin. 'Is anyone else ill in the house?'

'Five of the count's daughters,' Miss Smith volunteered.

'They have the same symptoms?'

'All have been vomiting but not as violently as the countess. The youngest, a baby, is well.'

'Sarah, prepare a hypodermic of morphine and pass my bag.' Sarah gave the bag to him and Peter removed his stethoscope.

Sarah saw to the syringe. 'Miss Smith, order all the water used for cooking, drinking, and washing in the house to be boiled. That applies to the water used for washing vegetables and fruit as well as clothes and personal use. Take me to the count's daughters. I'll need salt...'

Miss Smith glared at her. 'And you are?'

'Mrs Edwards, Dr Edwards' wife. Matron of the hospital when it's finished.'

'You need hot water for baths?'

'I need every drop of water used in this house to be boiled,' Sarah reiterated. 'Please make a list of everything that needs to be done so nothing is forgotten. Is there anyone else in the house who speaks English?'

'The count.'

'Could I speak to him please?'

'I have no idea where he is.'

'Find him.'

'I'm not in the habit of enquiring after my employer's whereabouts.'

Sarah barely managed to keep her exasperation in check as Miss Smith led the way along the gallery.

'You wanted to see the count's daughters, Mrs Edwards. This is their bedroom.' She opened the door.

Maids were sponging down the girls. They curtsied when they saw Sarah and the governess.

'This struck suddenly. The girls and the countess were quite well at breakfast. Do you know what it is, Mrs Edwards?' Miss Smith remained outside the door.

'Yes. The children's nurse who asked about electrical stimulus and hot baths recognised it. It's cholera. It's vital we track down the source of the infection before anyone else succumbs. Pass on the directive about boiling all the water in the house immediately.'

'Cholera!' Nicholas looked up at Peter from behind his desk. 'That's impossible unless...'

'You were about to say, sir?' Peter had been surprised to find the count reading in his study. He recognised the cover of his book. Pornographic novels had littered the medical students' common rooms in London.

'The Jews. They've killed Christians for centuries, especially aristocrats. They've obviously broken into the house and poisoned the water supply.'

'I've made enquiries, sir. The water used in this house is drawn from an outside well behind the kitchen. Everyone has drunk from it, yet the only people exhibiting symptoms are your wife, five oldest daughters, and your cook. You, your baby daughter, and the rest of your servants appear to be unaffected. The only way of contracting cholera is by ingesting contaminated water or food. It's imperative we find the source.'

'The Jews. You may not have come across them in Britain but everyone in Russia knows that they carry disease and delight in spreading it.'

Peter was tempted to tell the count his mother had been a Sephardi Jew, but saw no point in inflaming him more than he already was. 'Have any Jews visited in the last twenty-four hours?'

'They wouldn't come here openly. They know I'd order the servants to set the dogs on them.'

'Then how could they poison your water supply?'

'By sneaking into the kitchen yard when everyone's in bed.'

'But not everyone in the house is ill.'

Catherine sailed into the room. She'd tied a servants' apron over her silk gown and rolled up her lace-trimmed sleeves.

'About to scrub the kitchen floor, Catherine?' Nicholas baited.

Catherine ignored him. 'Dr Edwards, your wife needs you. My daughter's worse.'

'Thank you, Mrs Ignatova.'

'Please, call me Catherine. Is there anything I can do? I feel useless. Seeing your wife ministering to my daughter and granddaughters makes me wish I'd taken up nursing instead of embroidery.'

'How about detective work?' Peter felt odd. One moment he was hot, the next cold. He was having difficulty focusing. Nicholas and Catherine appeared to be at the end of an elastic rope, pinging backwards and forwards ... backwards and forwards

'Are you all right, Dr Edwards?'

Peter heard Catherine but didn't answer her. 'I'm trying to track the source of the infection.' He quoted from a textbook. 'Cholera is waterborne and can only be contracted by drinking from an infected supply or eating fresh food that's been washed in contaminated water.'

'You think the water supply in the house is poisoned?'

'If it was, everyone would be ill.' Peter knew he was slurring. 'Please question the servants and the patients who can talk. We need to isolate...'

He put one foot in front of the other and staggered.

Catherine steadied him. 'Sit down, Dr Edwards?'

'I'm tired, that's all.' He stumbled and fell.

'Dr Edwards...'

'Fetch my wife, Catherine, please.'

Chapter Twenty

Beletsky Mansion, Hughesovka
December 1870

'I'm sorry, Catherine. I've been ordering you about as if you're a ward maid.' Emotionally and physically drained, Sarah sank down on a stool beside Olga's bed. The five Beletsky girls had been moved into the adjoining dressing room. She could hear one raving in delirium.

'Don't trouble yourself about my feelings, my dear.' Catherine patted Sarah's hand. 'I'm grateful there's someone in the house who knows what has to be done. The butler's moving Dr Edwards into a guest room in this corridor so we can keep all the patients in one wing of the house. Tell me what I can do?'

Sarah went through the mental check list she'd made. 'Miss Smith is ensuring that all the water in the house is being boiled. The assistant cook is making salt poultices, a parlour maid is mixing laudanum and starch for enemas, another combining turpentine and mustard to bind over the abdomen for counter-irritation.' She reached down for Peter's doctor's bag, opened it, and checked the morphine phials. 'We need to send someone to the Company Office to find more medication. Is there anyone here who can mix ammonia in brandy? Four drops to half a glass. It will help alleviate the patients' cramps.'

'Olga will have ammonia and brandy in the house. I'll give orders for the mix to be made.'

Catherine watched Olga draw her knees up to her chest.

'She can have half a glass of brandy and ammonia. I dare not give her any more morphine for four hours.'

The door slammed back on its hinges and the count materialised in the doorway. 'Catherine, I demand an explanation.'

'Quiet, Nicholas. Olga and the girls need rest.'

'You're giving *my* servants orders as if you're the mistress of this house.'

'Someone has to take control, Nicholas.'

'You've turned my home into a hospital.'

'It makes sense to nurse the patients in one place. You have rooms, servants, and Miss Smith is on hand to interpret Mrs Edwards' orders.'

Nicholas glared at Sarah. 'You're in charge of doctoring the patients?'

'I'm a nurse, not a doctor, Count Beletsky.' Sarah hadn't felt so inadequate since she'd begun her training.

'Quite! Yet you've set everyone in my household charging around as if there are half a dozen bears loose.'

'There's worse, Nicholas, there's cholera,' Catherine countered. 'Mrs Edwards has experience of treating the disease, which is more than anyone else.'

'I wish we could call on a doctor, Count Beletsky, but Peter's in no condition to give advice.' Sarah felt the count's criticism of her professional capability justified.

Alexei, dressed in a fur-lined cape and mud-stained riding boots appeared. He was risking more than inciting his father's wrath at his presence. Dirty boots worn indoors were a cardinal sin in the count's eyes.

'Alexei, I forbade you this house. You're filthy...'

'My apologies, sir. I hadn't time to change. Mr Hughes sent me to fetch Dr Edwards. Mr Edwards, Mr Thomas, Richard Parry, and two of the clerks are ill.'

'Sweats, vomiting, stomach cramps?' Sarah asked.

'Violent vomiting and flux.'

'Peter can't attend them, he has the same symptoms.'

'Where are they?' Catherine asked.

'The Company Office.'

'Tell Mr Hughes to convey them here.'

'Do that, Catherine, and I'll move into the hotel,' Nicholas threatened.

'Excellent idea, Nicholas. Then the servants can concentrate on caring for the patients instead of looking after you. Alexei, send for Nathan Kharber.'

'I'll have no Jew under my roof,' Nicholas thundered.

'As you won't be here, it won't make the slightest difference to you whether Nathan Kharber is here or not. Alexei, fetch him.'

'The builder?' Sarah asked Catherine.

'He studied medicine in Paris. He's a qualified doctor,' Alexei explained.

'Are there any nurses?' The countess, her daughters, Peter, Huw, Glyn, Richard, the clerks... How many more would be struck down? 'We need trained nurses.'

'If any of the women in the shtetl are even half-way trained, bring them, Alexei.' Catherine wrung out the cloth she'd been using to sponge her daughter's face, handed it to Sarah and said, 'I'll see to that brandy and ammonia.'

Sarah crouched over Peter, monitoring his breathing. Alexei had ordered the servants to move more beds into the room and Glyn, Huw, and Richard lay alongside Peter. All four were desperately ill, but the last time she'd checked, Huw's pulse was the weakest.

'Any change, Mrs Edwards?' Nathan Kharber had entered and she'd been too concerned by Peter's condition to notice.

'Not since the last time you examined the patients, Dr Kharber.' She wondered if it was her imagination or if Nathan had smiled when she'd addressed him as 'doctor.'

'Have you had much experience of cholera?'

'I nursed through the 1866 pandemic in London. Everyone in the hospital worked twenty-hour shifts. Despite our best efforts, more than three-quarters of our patients died.'

'You've had more experience of the disease than me.' He leaned against the wall.

'You haven't seen many cases?'

'A dozen mariners in Paris who sailed up the Seine on a boat stocked with infected water barrels, and fifteen cases in Vienna who drank from a contaminated well. I've studied the available papers but theory can never match experience. In your opinion what's the most successful treatment?'

'I'm a nurse, not a doctor, Dr Kharber.'

'A nurse who's treated more cases than anyone within a hundred miles. I need help, Mrs Edwards. I've already been accused of killing one man who was at death's door before I reached him. If the locals hear of more deaths they can blame me for, they'll burn me at the stake.'

'That's a poor joke, Dr Kharber.'

'It's not a joke, Mrs Edwards. There was an outbreak of cholera in Russia in 1852. A million died and over a hundred Jewish doctors were murdered for not saving their patients. The doctors favoured the aperient method of purging the patients to rid them of the poison, but doctors in Vienna believe the astringent method aimed at stopping vomiting and the flux, and conserving the body's fluids, to be best. The latest thought suggests that the hot bath, injection of saline solution, and morphine and chalk can give relief.'

'We tried everything in London; injections of saline solution, hot baths, electric shock, opium and chalk mixtures, brandy and ammonia. We kept records but found the application of different treatments had little effect on the death toll. As many patients died who'd been given laxatives as morphine and chalk. Some died within hours of exhibiting symptoms, some days after they appeared to make a full recovery. That was the hardest. Facing parents who'd seen their child responding to treatment, and believed they were out of danger.'

Peter moved restlessly. Sarah wrapped her hands around his.

Alexei stole in.

'Your sisters?' Sarah didn't relinquish her hold on Peter's hands.

'Ruth, Miriam, and Anna are with them. There's no change.'

'Your mother?' Nathan moved away from the wall.

'My grandmother is with her. I think it's possible the infection originated in the cherry cordial the cook made last summer. She opened the first of the bottles this morning. The kitchen maid said the cook put a pitcher of the cordial on my sisters' breakfast table. A glass was taken up to my mother on her breakfast tray. The maid couldn't say how many of the servants drank it, other than the cook and the girl who served breakfast and she's just collapsed.'

'That doesn't explain Peter, Glyn, Huw, Richard, and the clerks.' Sarah turned to Huw. He looked so close to death she watched until she could be certain she'd seen his chest move.

'The cook sent a pitcher to the company office this morning as a thank you to Mr Thomas for the gift of a box of English tea for my mother. I'm guessing Mr Thomas shared it with the others.'

'Wouldn't the cook have made the cordial with water from the well in the kitchen yard? We know that's not contaminated,' Sarah said.

'She would have also used cherries and lemons. I remember an argument in the spring between the head gardener and one of his assistants after the man used human waste to fertilize the fruit trees in the hot houses. The man was dismissed. The head gardener ordered the trees to be potted in clean earth. It's possible some weren't.'

'That could be the source,' Nathan agreed, 'we know outbreaks can be caused by contaminated fruit and vegetables as well as water. Thank you, Alexei.'

'What about the remaining bottles of cordial?' Sarah asked.

'I've asked the servants to stockpile all the wine and cordials the cook brewed last summer in one of the pantries. Is there some way of testing the contents for cholera?'

'Not that I'm aware of. The bottles will have to be disposed of well away from the water table and river. Until we can be certain the cordial is the source, tell Miss Smith to be vigilant and insist the servants continue boiling all the water until they're ordered not to,' Sarah reminded.

'I will, Mrs Edwards. Mr Hughes is downstairs. He's unpacking the morphine and medical supplies we brought.'

'Where's the maid who's been taken ill?' Nathan asked.

'In the cook's room. Mr Thomas's clerks are next door to them.'

'I'll look at her before I check your mother and

sisters.' Nathan went to the door. Alf Mahoney was hovering, cap in hand outside.

'Excuse me, sir...'

Sarah heard his voice. 'Alf?'

'I brought Praskovia here, Mrs Edwards. She wants to help. I heard Dr Edwards, Mr Edwards, and Mr Thomas are ill.'

'If you've come to help, you're very welcome, Mr?'

'Mahoney. Alf Mahoney.' Alf saw the stethoscope and added, 'Dr, sir.'

'I'll be back after I've checked on our new patient, Mrs Edwards.' Nathan left.

'You didn't go to the office this morning, Alf?' Sarah asked.

'No, Ma'am, I haven't been to the office in weeks. We've been that busy in Mr Edwards' colliery...'

'You haven't drunk any cordial?' Alexei questioned.

'Cordial? No, sir, only beer and that white stuff that looks like water but blows your head off.'

'You're not feeling ill, Alf?' Sarah persisted.

'No, Ma'am.'

'If you want to help, take an apron from that pile. The beds will need changing soon.'

'And me, Mrs Edwards?'

'Check with Dr Kharber and Mr Hughes, Alexei. If they don't need you I can find a million and one things for you to do.' She looked at the clock on the wall. 'It's time to monitor the patients' vital signs.'

Sarah busied herself for the next few hours, giving

orders, taking care when delegating responsibility not to entrust any of her untrained helpers with tasks beyond their capabilities. But, no matter which patient she was tending, she couldn't stop thinking about Peter or gravitating to his side every spare moment, although John and Alf had taken it upon themselves to watch over the men's room.

She was sitting next to Peter's bed at three in the morning when Alexei came looking for her.

'Nathan needs you. Mr Thomas's clerk is having trouble breathing.'

'Any change, Mr Hughes, please send Alf to fetch me or Dr Kharber.' Sarah followed Alexei down the landing to a door set discreetly behind a curtain. The servants' quarters were very different from those of the family, with narrow grey passageways and plain deal doors. There were no pictures on the walls to brighten the Spartan atmosphere. Alexei led her to an open door. Nathan was checking the pulse at a patient's neck. Sarah took one look and knew they were about to record the first death.

She waited until Nathan covered the man's face with the sheet. 'Did you know him, Alexei?'

'He was German. Mr Thomas took him on six months ago. His name was Horst Mulder.'

A footman was sitting next to the second patient in the room. Nathan checked the man's pulse and spoke to the servant in Russian before joining Sarah and Alexei.

'Alexei, Mr Mulder needs to be buried quickly, in high ground away from the water table.'

'I'll ask Mr Hughes if he's made plans for a

cemetery for his workers.' Alexei left.

'How are Dr Edwards and the other men?' Nathan enquired.

Sarah rubbed her eyes. They felt gritty and ached from lack of sleep. 'I'm concerned about Huw.'

'I'm concerned about all of them.' Nathan led the way back to the guest wing. 'Our first death.'

'I would like to believe it will be our last, but experience suggests that would be optimistic.'

'Four of the countess's daughters are very ill.'

'You don't think they'll recover?' Sarah's blood ran cold. As a nurse she was accustomed to death but she always found it difficult to accept the untimely curtailment of young lives.

'Their fate is in God's hands more than ours.' Nathan entered the men's room.

Alf was sitting beside Huw's bed. 'Mr Hughes went downstairs with Alexei to check maps.'

Sarah went to Peter, picked up his hand, and automatically checked his pulse.

'It's a nurse's lot to check someone's vital signs before talking to them,' Nathan commented.

'Especially when a doctor is watching.'

'Mr Hughes made an excellent choice when he appointed you matron of his hospital. You're not only a capable nurse but have first-class organisational skills. The two don't always go together.'

'Why didn't you tell Peter you were a doctor?'

'After a few months back in the shtetl I'd almost forgotten my qualifications.'

'No doctor would consider working as a builder in England. It would be regarded as a waste of his studies.'

'Even if he was Jewish?'

'As I said to the girls when I offered them positions as ward maids, what difference does religion make?'

'My sister said she found it difficult to explain to you what being a Jew in Russia entails.'

'Your sister?'

'Ruth.'

'She told me she was a Jew, but I fail to see the importance of someone's religion when it comes to working in a hospital.'

'You will if you stay in Russia.'

She glanced at the clock on the wall. 'Almost four.'

'The witching hour when the devil leaves his lair and hunts for souls to reap. Or so a nun in Vienna informed me.'

'I've noticed most deaths occur during the darkest hours.'

'And most births.' He smiled at her and she realised that behind the forbidding exterior was a warm, humane man. 'It's been nice talking to you, Mrs Edwards. Let's pray the devil doesn't walk abroad to harvest any more souls this night. Stay with your husband. I'll check the ladies.'

'Matron... Matron... Mrs Edwards... Mrs Edwards...' Sarah could hear someone calling her but the pull of sleep was too great. She didn't want to surface. The heavily accented voice persisted. She forced open her eyes. She was lying, slumped forward, her head resting on her arms on Peter's bed.

She looked anxiously at him. His skin was cold,

damp with perspiration. His face grey.

'Matron?'

Ruth was standing over her. 'Mrs Ignatova needs help in the countess's room. Miriam is fetching Nathan.'

Sarah leapt to her feet and ran. Praskovia and Catherine were hovering at Olga's bedside. The countess's face was pinched, her mouth slack. Her eyes glazed.

'Ruth, Praskovia, look after the countess's daughters. Mrs Ignatova and I can manage here.' She folded back the sheet and laid her hand on Olga's chest.

'Will she lose the child?' Catherine asked.

'I'm more concerned about the mother than the child,' Nathan walked in with Alexei.

'Mother...'

'Alexei, please go and sit with Alf,' Sarah ordered. 'If there's any change in the men's condition, fetch me.'

Sarah and Nathan both knew it would only be a matter of time before Olga Beletsky breathed her last, and as the child she was carrying was too small to survive outside of her womb it would die with her.

Sarah washed Olga, dressed her in a clean nightgown, and helped Catherine change the bed linen. When Olga looked as presentable as they could make her, Sarah pulled the sheet up to her chin.

'Time for my son-in-law and grandson to say their goodbyes?' Catherine was dry eyed but her voice was hoarse.

'Would you like me to fetch them?' Sarah asked.

'My grandson, please. Send a servant to the hotel. Count Beletsky should be informed. It will be his choice whether he attends Olga's deathbed or not.'

Alexei was at the door of the men's room. 'I sent a footman to the hotel. He's already returned. My father said he'll come in the morning.'

'He'll be too late.'

'My mother?'

'I'm sorry, Alexei. It won't be long.' She watched him walk down the corridor.

'Mr Thomas and Richard both look very ill,' Alf said after Alexei left.

'They can't have another dose of morphine for an hour. Please, keep sponging them down, Alf. That's all we can do for them at the moment.' Sarah returned to the countess's room. After a whispered conversation, Nathan picked up Peter's doctor's bag and went to the men's room.

Alexei sat next to his grandmother. Olga tossed and turned, occasionally moaning and crying out. Catherine closed the connecting door to the girls' room and warned Ruth to use the door that opened into the corridor lest the girls see their mother in pain.

When Olga finally fell quiet Sarah watched the life ebb from her body. It was sight she'd witnessed many times but always found hard to bear.

Catherine leaned close to her daughter watching every breath grow more laboured, until eventually they ceased.

Alexei released his hold on his mother's hand.

'I'll get Nathan.'

'He won't be able to do anything, Alexei, sit with your mother and say your goodbyes. I'll be back to help you lay your daughter out, Catherine.' Sarah went outside and bowed her head lest anyone see just how close she was to tears.

'Can I get you a cup of tea, Mrs Edwards?'

Alf was in front of her. 'That would be kind of you. Do you know where to go?'

'I'll ask Praskovia.'

'She's busy in the girls' room. If you go downstairs the night porter sitting by the door will show where the kitchens are. Take a cup to show him what you want.' She lifted one from a tray that had been left on a side table.

Sarah entered the men's room. Nathan had covered Huw's face.

Three deaths! She turned to Peter.

'No!'

Her scream was silent. She fell to her knees and fumbled blindly for Peter's hand. It was warm.

She knew the temperature of cholera patients rose before death and that their corpses continued warm, sometimes for hours. But that didn't stop her from hoping Peter would breathe again. Turn and smile at her, sick as he was, to let her know he was alive and would continue to live.

Something tore within her. A sharp pain felled her to her knees. When she looked down and saw bright red blood coating her shoes and legs she screamed.

She'd not only lost Peter, but the last vestige of him. Their child.

Chapter Twenty-one

Beletsky Mansion, Hughesovka
December 1870

'A little girl, a perfect little girl. Just too small to live or draw breath. God bless and keep her.' Yelena made the sign of the cross before taking the tiny body from the bowl of water and wrapping it in a towel.

'Please, let me see her.' Sarah begged. It was standard medical practice to remove stillborn babies and miscarriages from the mother as soon as possible 'for the mother's sake' but she desperately wanted to see her and Peter's child.

Nathan took the tiny bundle from Yelena, uncovered the baby's face, and placed it gently in Sarah's outstretched arms. Oblivious to the tears falling from her eyes, she cradled the corpse.

Unable to bear the sight of Sarah's grief Yelena picked up the bowl and carried it out.

'Would you like your daughter to be buried in the same coffin as your husband?' Nathan asked.

Sarah didn't look away from the child's face. 'Could you ... would you arrange it, please. I know it's illogical but I can't bear the thought of her lying alone and abandoned in unconsecrated ground.'

'If those are your wishes, Mrs Edwards, I'm certain Father Grigor will do his best to accommodate them.' Nathan took a loaded syringe from the side table.

'Morphine?' Sarah asked.

'You need rest.'

'I need to bury my dead.'

'For that you need strength.' He gave her the injection.

Yelena returned and busied herself bundling the soiled linen together. He spoke to her in Russian. 'After you've carried that out, please sit with Mrs Edwards. Call me if there's any change in her condition.'

Yelena watched Sarah's eyelids drop and her body relax in drug-induced torpor. 'The child?'

Nathan eased the tiny bundle from Sarah's limp arms and covered the baby's face again. 'I'll take it to her husband. Alexei and Mr Hughes are making arrangements for the funerals.'

'I knew it. I knew there'd be deaths this morning when a bird perched on the kitchen windowsill of Mr Edwards' house. Not content to sit there, it tapped the window with its beak. You know what that means?'

'The bird wanted whoever had been feeding it to put out crumbs?' The shtetl was as rife with superstition as Alexandrovka, and Nathan abhorred old wives' tales.

'No one had been feeding it,' Yelena retorted. 'I won't allow anyone to put out food for the birds. They are harbingers of death. As soon as the wretched creature tapped the glass I knew someone in the house would be laid in their coffin before the next sun dawned. But I didn't expect it to be two people and an unborn child.' She shook her head. 'People should stay where God put them. They have no right to travel. These foreigners should never have come to Mother Russia. They are not wanted here. This is just the beginning. They will all die for breaking God's laws ... you wait and see...'

'That's complete nonsense, Mother Razin.' Unequal to dealing with Yelena's irrational beliefs as well as the unfolding tragedy, Nathan carried the dead child to the door. He collided with a slight figure in the corridor.

'I'm Anna, Dr Kharber.'

'I know who you are, Anna. You work alongside my sister, Ruth.'

'You wouldn't let me sit with my brother Richard. Please, can I stay with Mrs Edwards?'

Nathan looked at the girl's white pinched face and recalled ordering her out of the men's room. He sympathised with her. Her only relative in Russia, her brother, could die at any moment. Two of the men who lived in the same house as her were already dead. The nurse who was training her had lost her child. Could there be something in Cossack superstition after all? Were the newcomers cursed?

He pushed the thought from his mind. Exhaustion had driven him to the borders of sanity. If he wasn't careful he'd find himself on the lunatic side. 'You can stay with Mrs Edwards, Anna. Find me when she wakes.'

Anna crept past him into the room.

He watched her sit beside the bed and reach for Sarah's hand. Sarah had lost everything but still had her life. He couldn't help feeling the remaining patients in his care might not be as fortunate.

Alexei found John studying maps in the drawing room.

'I've sent two grooms to Alexandrovka and the shtetl and asked them to bring carpenters back to measure the dead for their coffins, sir. I also asked them to bring any ready-made coffins they have. I doubt either carpenter will have more than one or two in stock.'

John sat back in his chair. 'It's been a long night for all of us, but especially you. My sympathies and condolences, Alexei.'

'Thank you, sir, but I can't think about my mother and sisters now. There's too much to be done.'

John recognised Alexei's need to delay his mourning. He knew from painful experience the loss of a loved one rarely registered until after the observance of funeral rituals.

A maid knocked the door and brought in a tray of coffee and sweet rolls.

'Four cups?'

'I asked my grandmother and Dr Kharber to come down. They're exhausted and all the patients are sleeping. There are enough people upstairs to watch over them and fetch Dr Kharber if he's needed.' Alexei went to the window and opened the drapes. The gardens were bathed in the icy clear grey light of dawn.

'You feel dawn shouldn't break?'

Alexei turned. 'How do you know?'

'I've experienced loss. Not as much as you in one night. But I know what it feels like to lose your parents, sisters – and your children.'

'I can't believe my mother and four of my sisters have gone. I keep expecting the maid to walk into my bedroom with my morning tea to wake me.'

'How is your grandmother?'

'Since Mrs Edwards collapsed she's taken it upon herself to help Nathan.'

'As soon as the sun's risen I'll check the sites we've marked as possible company cemeteries. It'll be with a heavy heart. I didn't think I'd need to look so soon.'

'I'll go with you after I've spoken to the carpenters.'

'You don't have to, Alexei.'

Alexei's eyes burned bright. 'I can't think of anything else I should be doing, Mr Hughes.'

John poured the coffee. He handed Alexei a cup. 'I'll order my driver to bring round the carriage. We'll leave as soon as we've seen the carpenters.'

Beletsky family graveyard, Hughesovka
December 1870

Two days after the death of Countess Olga Beletsky and four of her daughters, Catherine, Alexei, Sonya, John, Father Grigor, Mr Dmitri, and Nicholas attended their private funeral. The ceremony was 'invitation only' at Nicholas's insistence, although he hadn't been able to prevent the Cossacks, caps doffed in respect, from lining the road between the house and the cemetery.

After the last coffin had been lowered into the vault and Father Grigor had said the final 'Amen',

Nicholas walked to the gate. He shook hands with the priest, without removing his gloves, studiously ignored Alexei, and waylaid Catherine.

'I have pressing business in St Petersburg.'

She inclined her head to show that she'd heard him.

'From there I will travel to East Prussia and Allenstein to see the boys. I don't want them to find out about the death of their mother and sisters from a letter.'

'Your surviving daughters, Katya and Kira? Do you intend to visit them before you leave?' Catherine enquired.

'Katya's contagious and Kira's a baby. There's no point in my seeing them. As soon as the house is free from patients and has been disinfected, I've ordered my lawyer to find tenants for it. Perhaps you could suggest its suitability as a home to Mr Hughes?'

'You want me to discuss renting out Olga's home at her funeral?' Catherine's voice was brittle.

'Obviously not now or I would have spoken to him myself.'

'Katya and Kira?'

'Are your granddaughters. I trust you will offer them a home.' He didn't wait for her to reply. 'This is not the funeral I would have wanted for my wife and daughters. It seems wrong to bury the dead so quickly.'

'Not when they died of cholera.'

'The manager of the hotel told me there hasn't been a new case for twenty-four hours. Does that mean the epidemic is over?'

'I'm not a medical expert, Nicholas. You'd have

to ask Dr Kharber that question.'

'*Dr* Kharber...'

'Is a qualified practitioner.'

'Qualified ... he killed Olga, the girls, the English doctor, and the others, as well as Pavlo Razin...'

'I've no time to listen to your anti-Semitic ranting, Nicholas, when I've just buried my daughter and four of my granddaughters. I wish to mourn in peace. Alexei?'

'Grandmother?'

'Escort me and Sonya to our carriage, please.' She walked past Nicholas. Alexei handed her and Sonya into the carriage, and climbed in beside them.

'Your father...'

'I heard everything, Grandmother.'

'We're better off with him in St Petersburg. Don't let him upset you.'

'My father hasn't upset me. I'm worried about Katya, Mr Edwards, and the others.'

'We're all worried about them, Alexei, but everything that can be done for them is being done. Katya was sitting up in a chair this morning. She looked well. Pray God the worst is over.' Catherine grasped his hand, lifted it to her lips, and kissed it.

'I hope so.' He looked out of the window. 'I really hope so,' he echoed.

Beletsky Mansion, Hughesovka
December 1870

'John told me about Peter and the baby. You

shouldn't be here, Sarah,' Glyn protested when she sank down, pale and gaunt on a chair beside his bed.

'I had to see you.' She clasped his hand.

'You shouldn't touch me...'

'I'm a nurse. We're immune to infection.'

'Sarah, I'm so sorry.'

'I'm sorry for us both, Glyn. I know how close you and Peter were.'

'Not always.'

'It was only physical distance that separated you. Peter felt he'd really come to know and appreciate you on the journey here.'

'I should never have talked you into coming to Russia.'

'If you hadn't, Peter could have died in an epidemic in London, or Merthyr. Dr Kharber told me you blamed yourself for Peter's death. Please don't. Peter knew the risks of the profession when he chose to become a doctor.'

'The risks of the profession don't include travelling to Russia and drinking contaminated cordial.'

'There's as much contaminated water and fruit in Wales and England.' Sarah's eyes were dry, dead, her voice devoid of emotion. 'Concentrate on getting well. Mr Hughes needs you. We all do.'

'That's if Mr Hughes intends to continue with his plans to build a works here.'

'You said the New Russia Company couldn't afford to fail.'

'It can't, but I can't bear the thought of carrying on...'

She cut him short, 'Only because you're sick and weak. When you recover you'll feel differently. Things can never be the same for you, or me, Glyn, but we have to think how Peter would feel. This was his dream of a better life for every working man and his family.'

'A dream that's in tatters.'

'Only for Peter and us, Glyn.' She glanced across to the bed where Richard was sleeping. 'We owe it to Peter and Huw to do all we can to keep the dream alive for Mr Hughes and those who'll follow us.'

'What are you doing out of bed, Mrs Edwards?' Nathan strode in.

'Checking your patients are receiving the correct nursing care, Dr Kharber.' She squeezed Glyn's hand before relinquishing it. 'Please let Anna know when Richard wakes, Dr Kharber. She's worried about him.'

'He needs sleep.'

'So does Anna. She's asleep now. If she hadn't been I wouldn't have been able to leave my bed. How are the other patients?'

'All seem to be recovering.'

The 'seem to' burned in Sarah's mind when she returned to her room. As she'd told Nathan, the deaths of the patients she'd lost when they appeared to be making a full recovery had been the hardest to bear.

Catherine walked through the front door of the Beletsky mansion ahead of the mourners, entered the hall, and took the letters from the tray the butler handed her. 'Have you laid out refreshments?'

'Cold meat, cake, and salads in the dining

room, Madam.'

'Thank you.' She slit the envelope open with an ornamental dagger. It didn't take her long to read the single sheet of paper. She saw Alexei watching her. 'A condolence note.'

'That one is from my father's solicitor.' Alexei recognised his clerk's writing.

Catherine opened it. 'It's a formal eviction notice asking everyone residing in this house to leave within four weeks so arrangement can be made to disinfect the place before advertising for a tenant.'

'What about Kira, and what if Katya, Mr Edwards, and the others are still sick?'

'Your father will expect them to pay rent.'

'Miss Smith and the servants?'

'The solicitor makes no mention of them. Make enquiries for me please, Alexei. Ask if they've received payment in lieu of wages or been given notice.'

'I will. What about a plaque commemorating my mother and sisters on the family vault?'

'There's no mention of a monument. I trust your father won't interfere in any arrangements you and I make.'

The butler showed John, Father Grigor, and Mr Dmitri into the hall.

Catherine greeted them. 'Thank you so much for your support in our time of sorrow. It is much appreciated.'

John handed the butler his coat before kissing Catherine's hand. 'The least we can do, Mrs Ignatova.'

'My son-in-law wants to do business today of

all days, Mr Hughes. He wishes you to know that he intends to rent out this house.'

'I've no doubt the company will be able to make use of it when the next influx of workers arrive.'

'If you gentlemen will excuse me, I must enquire after our patients. Alexei, please take the mourners into the dining room and see everyone has everything they need. Sonya, please come with me.'

Alexei was talking to Father Grigor when Sonya came looking for him.

'I'm sorry, Alexei. It's Katya. There's nothing Nathan Kharber or Mrs Edwards can do for her. Your grandmother is with her. She sent me to get you.'

Chapter Twenty-two

British cemetery, Hughesovka
January 1871

John ordered the driver to stop his sleigh outside the gate of the company cemetery. Sarah sat on the bench seat opposite him, swathed in Olga Beletsky's sable cloak. Catherine had given the furs to her, insisting Sarah would do her the favour by taking them, as the Beletsky mansion had to be emptied before it could be rented and she couldn't bear to throw out her daughter and granddaughters' clothes, or store them at the

Dower House.

Catherine had used the same excuse when she'd passed Katya's furs and clothes on to Anna, but it had taken all of Sarah and the older woman's powers of persuasion to overcome the reluctance Mary had instilled in Anna to accept 'charity'.

Sarah was grateful for the sable. It was the first time she'd ventured out of doors since she'd lost her child. The air temperature was fifteen degrees below freezing and the snow that lay three feet thick was frosted by ice.

'You don't have to leave the carriage, Mrs Edwards. I can put those flowers on Peter's grave for you,' John offered.

Sarah picked up the bouquet of white roses Alexei had cut for her in his grandmother's hothouse.

'You're very kind, Mr Hughes, but as I wasn't well enough to attend their funeral I need to do it.'

The driver opened the door. John left the sleigh and handed Sarah out. He allowed her to walk ahead of him.

Hay had been scattered on a path that had been dug to a row of simple wooden crosses in a corner of the field. Each bore a name. Sarah stopped in front of the one carved with *Dr Peter Alfred Edwards 1842–1870 and daughter*. She brushed a layer of crystallised snow from the top and arms of the cross, knelt beside it, and set the roses on the mound of snow.

She pictured what would never be. A family life in a house that was hers and Peter's; meal and play times with the daughter they would never know. She felt cheated, angry, mourning as much for the future she'd lost, as her husband and child.

'It's too cold to stay here, Mrs Edwards, especially on your knees.' John offered her his hand. She took it and rose stiffly. The cold had already permeated her joints.

'Thank you for putting "and daughter". Until it happened to my child, I never realised how cruel it was to deny the stillborn a grave.'

'Had you chosen a name for her?'

'We'd discussed boys' names. Peter was insistent she was a boy, but he was teasing me. He'd have been delighted with a girl.' Her smile didn't reach her eyes. 'He would have been a wonderful father.'

'He would.' John led her back to the carriage. 'The crosses are temporary. I'll call in a stonemason after the thaw, have the ground compacted, and arrange for permanent monuments to be erected. Would you like to choose one?'

'Please, I'd like something plain with Peter's name and dates and a mention of our child.'

'And a line of text from the Bible?' he suggested.

'I'll need time to find something suitable.'

'You'll have plenty of that, Mrs Edwards. It's going to be a long, cold, hard winter. I've been warned that sometimes the snow doesn't melt here until the middle of May.'

'I used to love the spring.' She walked through the gate. 'Blossom on the trees in the London parks, snowdrops, then daffodils and tulips pushing through the flowerbeds. I sound like an old woman.'

'I wanted to talk to you before now, Mrs Edwards, but you – we – there didn't seem to be an appropriate time.'

'I can't believe five weeks have passed since Peter died.'

'Words aren't sufficient to express my feelings on a loss that has sorely affected us all.' John folded his hand over the gloved fingers she'd hooked into his elbow. 'Friendship aside, I had complete confidence in Peter, his medical ability, and the way he – and you – would have run the hospital.'

'Thank you. It's comforting to know you thought highly of him.' She looked back at the graves.

A picture so real filled her mind that she shuddered. She saw Peter's tall, perfect body lying shrouded in white silk and lace in his coffin six feet below the ground. His face marble white, ice cold in death. After five weeks in the earth in these temperatures his corpse would be frozen solid as would that of the child lying on his breast. But the warmth of spring would bring decay. Dark spots would appear and rot his white, fraying, fragile skin. His hair and nails would work loose

She hated herself for thinking that way. For not remembering Peter as he'd been, striding through life, vital, alive, loving – would she have been able to recall him and the times they'd shared differently if she wasn't a nurse and hadn't seen so much death?

She realized John was still talking.

'...It's ironic that now, when Peter is no longer with us, the workmen have finally made progress. Alexei tells me they expect to have the hospital ready for use in a day or two.'

'You will appoint Nathan Kharber director, won't you, Mr Hughes? He's an excellent doctor and has worked tirelessly in the Beletsky House. I know some people here don't approve of the Jews...'

'I trust you're thinking of the count, not me,' John said.

'The count, the Cossacks, the Mujiks ... Nathan and Ruth told me none of them like Jews.'

'It runs deeper than dislike.' John helped her into the carriage. 'There've been problems for centuries that have culminated in massacres and pogroms. It's not just the ignorant who are anti-Semitic. The count is educated, yet Mrs Ignatova told me he blames the Jews for introducing cholera into his house.'

'That's ridiculous.'

'You, I, Mrs Ignatova, Alexei, and common sense know that. But it's not only the peasants who are superstitious in this part of the world.'

'As a nurse I can honestly say no one could have saved those who died. The death rate from cholera has always been high. If it weren't for Dr Kharber, Glyn, Richard, and the Beletskys' servants would be lying in the cemetery alongside Peter, Huw, and the others.'

'Nathan told me Glyn and Richard are out of danger. Is he being optimistic?'

'No. They'll be well enough to return to Glyn's

house tomorrow.'

'Mrs Ignatova said you intend to work in the hospital as soon as it's ready. Are you sure you're not putting your own health at risk in doing so, Mrs Edwards?'

'I need something to keep me occupied, Mr Hughes.'

'You look pale.'

'It's the cold. This is the first time I've been out of doors since ... since...' Her voice broke.

The driver closed the door of the sleigh and climbed into his seat. They moved off.

'I hate bringing this up, but I have to say it, Mrs Edwards. If you want to leave Hughesovka, I'll understand and arrange passage for you on the first ship bound for Britain out of Taganrog after the spring thaw.'

'Leave ... you don't want me to be matron now Peter's gone?'

'I assumed without Peter you wouldn't want to stay.'

She turned her head and looked back, as much as to conceal her tears as take a last look at the cemetery. 'I couldn't leave Peter and our child, Mr Hughes.'

'They are with God, not in that Russian earth, Mrs Edwards. If you're worried about their grave being neglected, please don't trouble yourself. I'll arrange for the upkeep of any memorial you want placed there.'

'I hoped you'd allow me to stay.'

'I would be delighted but I was thinking of you. You must have parents, brothers, sisters, people who care for you.'

'No, Mr Hughes.' She pushed her gloved fingers deeper into the muff Catherine had given her. 'I have no one, and nowhere else to go.'

'It wouldn't upset you to see Nathan Kharber work in the hospital?'

'After the way he cared for his patients during the cholera epidemic, he deserves the post.' Nathan had proved his worth to her when he'd asked her advice. She hadn't worked with any doctor other than Peter who'd been prepared to admit that a nurse could contribute knowledge that could aid treatment. 'Nathan Kharber is a dedicated doctor who's received a thorough training. He speaks English, Russian, and, according to Alexei, several other languages. He's sympathetic, kind, and gentle, and conversant with the latest medical theories on the treatment of disease. You couldn't find a more dedicated or suitable man, Mr Hughes.'

'Could you work with him?'

'You mean if he took Peter's place?'

'That's exactly what I mean.'

'Yes, Mr Hughes, I could work with him. You see,' she looked up and met his steady gaze. 'All I have left is my profession.'

'Then you'll remain in Hughesovka as matron of my hospital.'

'If you'll have me, Mr Hughes.'

'I count myself blessed to have your expertise, Mrs Edwards.'

Glyn Edwards' house, Hughesovka
January 1871

Glyn was surprised when Sarah joined him at the breakfast table. 'Good morning, shouldn't you be in bed?'

'I could ask you the same question.' She looked him over with a professional eye. He'd lost a great deal of weight and appeared frail, a shadow of the man he'd been only a few short weeks before.

'Now we've determined we both look dreadful, let's change the subject. Do you know Alexei's moving in?'

'He told me before we left the mansion.'

'If you'd rather not stay in your room, you could take one of the others...'

'Praskovia told me you'd warned her I might want to exchange my room with the one Alexei's taken. I'd rather stay where I am, Glyn, but thank you for the thought.'

'If there's anything I can do to make you more comfortable...'

'I'm fine, Glyn, please don't treat me as an invalid. Peter's absence isn't going to be easy for either of us. I never had a brother but I look on you as one. I hope you don't mind me staying in your house.'

'I'm glad you want to continue living here. When Mr Hughes said he was going to offer you the opportunity to return to London, I hoped you'd turn him down.'

'Why didn't you say something to me before Mr Hughes took me to the cemetery yesterday?'

'I didn't want you to feel you had to stay in

Hughesovka on my account.'

'You know my history, Glyn. You know I have nowhere else to go. Especially now when the two people I loved the most are buried here.'

'I can't believe Peter's gone.' Glyn stared at the door as though he expected him to walk through it.

'Thank you for saying his name. It's good to know other people remember him.'

'It doesn't hurt you to talk about him?'

'It hurts more when people try to pretend he never existed. I want to concentrate on what I had with Peter, not what I've lost.' She checked the nurse's watch pinned to the top corner of her apron. 'I must go. I promised the girls I would look round the hospital this morning and make a list of what needs to be done before we can move patients into the wards.'

'We didn't celebrate Christmas or New Year this year, Sarah, but I want you to have this.' He handed her a small package.

'Peter bought something for you...'

'Keep it for next year and open that when you're alone.'

She couldn't bring herself to wish him a 'Happy New Year' when she knew it would be anything but for both of them. 'God be with you this coming year, Glyn.' She thrust the package into her apron pocket and left.

Glyn Edwards' house, Hughesovka
January 1871

Duster in hand, Praskovia left the drawing room when she heard the front door open. Alexei was hauling his bags into the house.

'Mr Edwards said you were moving out of the mansion today and into Mr Thomas's old room. I thought you'd return to your grandmother's.'

'All my grandmother and I do when we see one another is cry. Besides, I work so closely with Mr Edwards and Richard we decided it would be better for us to live as well as work together. As for sleep, I doubt any of us are going to do much of that until the furnaces are operational.'

'The room is ready for you.'

'Thank you.' He kissed her cheek.

'Can I talk to you?'

'That sounds serious.'

'It is. Pyotr, take Mr Beletsky's bags upstairs to the front bedroom, please.'

'Mr Thomas's old room,' Pyotr grinned at Alexei.

'It's Mr Beletsky's room now.'

'What's this "Mr Beletsky"? I'm the same old Alexei, Pyotr,' Alexei called after him.

'You're a guest of the master.'

'A paying guest. "Mr" me again and I'll tickle you until you scream. Vlad is bringing my trunk. Mr Hughes has offered him a job in the hospital. Between them Mr Hughes and Grandmother have taken on all my father's former servants. The Beletsky Mansion will be empty of people this time tomorrow.'

'What does your father intend to do with it?'

'He can burn it down for all I care.'

'It's your childhood home, sir...'

'I mean it, Praskovia. Call me Alexei, not "Mr" and certainly not "sir",' he ordered. 'I called in the office on the way here. Mr Edwards told me to tell you, he and Richard will be on time for dinner. As I will.'

'Neither the master nor Richard should be working.'

'They haven't recovered,' Alexei agreed, 'but I wouldn't like to try to stop them from doing what they feel has to be done.'

'Tea and cold snacks are set out in the dining room. With Mr Edwards, Richard, and Mr Mahoney in and out at all hours, Mrs Edwards getting the hospital ready for its opening although she looks as though she's knocking on death's door, and Miss Anna doing what she can to help Mrs Edwards, I never know who'll be in for meals and who won't.'

'I could eat.'

'You can always eat.' She avoided calling him anything.

They went into the dining room where he helped himself to a plate of savouries and a glass of tea from the samovar.

'What's this serious talk about?' he asked.

'You and me.'

'You and me?' he repeated, mystified.

'You and me being you and me no longer.'

He understood. 'You've met someone? That's marvellous.'

'Not when he won't come near me because he

thinks I'm in love with you.'

'Now my father's disowned me there's no point in us continuing to pretend. It's time I told my grandmother the truth.'

'And everyone else?'

'Grandmother's the only one who matters. Once she knows, I'll write a declaration that we are not in love, never have been, never will be, and nail it to the church door in Alexandrovka.'

'Save yourself the trouble and just tell Lyudmila. She'll broadcast it from Taganrog to St Petersburg.'

'I'll need time to talk to Ruth and Nathan as well as Grandmother. Can you wait a week?'

'It doesn't have to be that quick.'

'It does. With my father in St Petersburg, there's no reason for Ruth and me to wait to be married.'

'You won't be twenty-one for two years.'

'One year and four months,' he corrected, 'but if Father Grigor and Nathan agree we could marry sooner. Thank you, Praskovia; you've given me a reason to act. I'll go and see Ruth now.' He winked at her. 'Good luck with your paramour. Am I allowed to know his identity?'

'Not until I know whether he loves me back.'

'Tell him from me he's a lucky man.' He picked up a plate of sweet blinis stuffed with apple and cherry preserves. 'The girls cleaning the hospital will be hungry.'

'If they are, how many of those will they see?' Praskovia demanded.

'The wolf share.'

'I'll ask Anna how many you delivered.'

'I promise not to eat more than three.'

'I don't believe you.'

'No more than six,' he amended as he went out of the front door.

Hospital, Hughesovka
January 1871

Alexei found Ruth scrubbing the brick floor in the ward kitchen. It had windows on both sides. One looked out onto a patch of ground and beyond it the separate single-storey building that housed staff, the other the inside corridor that led to the wards. Aware they could be seen and the place was full of builders as well as Ruth's fellow maids who were cleaning under Sarah's supervision, they stood at opposite ends of the room.

He began by telling her about his and Praskovia's conversation. '...So, rather than ruin Praskovia's chance of romance, I've decided to tell Grandmother about us. What do you think?'

'I, like you, have had enough of sneaking around pretending we're only friends.'

He misunderstood her. 'Are you saying you want to stop seeing me?'

'I don't want to see less of you, Alexei, I want to see more. In fact,' she hesitated. 'I want us to make love.'

The room fell so quiet he could hear his pocket watch ticking in his waistcoat. 'If you get pregnant?'

'Nathan would have to allow us to marry.'

'That's not the way I want to marry you.'

'You're the one who says this is a new age. Mrs Edwards has shown all of us girls things that can be used to prevent pregnancy. French letters men can wear and shields women can put inside them to prevent conception...'

'Mrs Edwards has been talking to you about sex!'

'Nurses need to be aware of all problems related to health. We may have to advise women on how to avoid unwanted pregnancies so they don't have to resort to abortions that can kill both mother and child. The best way to do that is to give women aids that can prevent pregnancy.'

'If the church finds out...'

'Mrs Edwards says lovemaking is nothing to do with religion. It's personal and wonderful between a man and woman and of no concern to anyone else. She also said it should be enjoyable and it won't be for women until they have the threat of unwanted pregnancies lifted.'

'The church would disagree, and although I don't know for sure, I suspect your rabbi would too.'

'Rabbi Goldberg and Father Grigor are old men. They've no right to tell you and me how to live our lives outside of the church and synagogue. If God didn't want you and me to lie together he wouldn't have allowed us to fall in love.'

Alexei was shocked by the thought of Ruth discussing sex with Sarah, but then he remembered his mother and how she'd been worn down by successive pregnancies. Of the arguments between his father and grandmother over his father's determination to father as many children as he could. Would his mother have found the strength to fight cholera if she hadn't been pregnant and weakened by constant childbearing?

'Alexei...'

'Have you told Mrs Edwards about us?'

'No, because there's nothing to tell. I wish there was. Does it shock you that I want to make love with you? I thought after what had happened to your mother and sisters you'd feel the same way. Life is precious and uncertain. I don't want to go to my grave a virgin, Alexei. Not feeling the way I do about you.'

'If Mrs Edwards starts telling women how to avoid having children or distributing French letters to the women in the shtetl and Alexandrovka she'll have husbands as well as priests...'

Ruth interrupted in a loud voice. 'Alexei, thank your grandmother for the Hanukkah gifts of food and warm clothing she sent to the shtetl.'

Alexei glanced through the window and saw Anna and Yulia in the corridor. 'I will.'

'I'll walk you out.'

'Anna, Yulia, I brought you some of Praskovia's blinis,' Alexei gave them the plate.

'Thank you for not eating all of them, although from the smears of preserves there were a lot more,' Yulia observed.

'Ruth ate them. I couldn't stop her.'

'You expect us to believe that when she eats like a bird?'

'Lovely to see you looking so pretty, Yulia,' Alexei changed the subject.

'In this uniform? But then I've seen you flirt

with my grandmother.'

'See you at dinner, Anna. I've moved into Mr Edwards' house.'

'I heard.' Anna was still wary of every man except Richard but she gave Alexei a cautious smile. 'Thank you for the blinis.'

'Now I'm living across the road, I'll bring more when Yelena's made them.'

'I love your generosity with other people's efforts.' Ruth walked him to the door. She glanced over her shoulder to make sure no one could overhear. 'I'll find an excuse to visit you in Mr Edwards' house.'

'Not before I've talked to Nathan about us.'

'I can always visit Anna.'

They were still alone, but he wouldn't risk more than kissing his forefinger and placing it on her lips.

Hospital, Hughesovka
January 1871

'No new scarlet fever cases in the shtetl or Alexandrovka for two days. I wish I knew why some people become infected in a family and others don't.' Nathan entered the hospital office where Sarah was organising the stationery cupboards.

'The eternal question of the physician – why. Could it be the disease was swiftly contained because of your insistence on disinfecting all the linen that had come into contact with the victims?' Sarah filled a drawer with envelopes.

'Thank you, I'm learning to appreciate praise.'

He sat on the visitor's chair. 'I've noticed the disease spread more among Cossack families who share a single bed.'

'Perhaps you should write a paper on hygiene and the use of disinfectant in treating scarlet fever.'

'I'd need to do more research, and frankly I'd rather I didn't have the opportunity to accumulate it.'

'You didn't have to come in here today,' Sarah closed the drawer on a cabinet. 'What needs to done before we accept patients is being done.'

'I know you have everything under control but I wanted to thank you. Mr Hughes wouldn't have offered me the directorship of the hospital if you hadn't recommended me.'

'You've taken it?'

'I have.'

'I'm glad for you and the hospital. We need a qualified doctor. Not to decry your capability but there isn't another for a hundred miles, and doctors shouldn't work as builders. It ruins the hands for surgery.'

'It can't be easy for you to see me take you husband's place.'

'No one could possibly take Peter's place.' She softened her remark by adding, 'you're very different men, with very different approaches to medicine.'

'Not too different, I trust.'

'I didn't mean the way you treat your patients but your training. British doctors are encouraged to be arrogant, especially towards nurses. Peter was different with me because I was his wife. I don't know of any other British doctor who would ask a nurse's opinion on patients' treatment.'

'My first job in Paris was in the mortuary. From there I graduated to cleaning wards. It took me two years to earn enough money to pay the fees for my first year in medical school.'

'That couldn't have been easy.'

'I survived and qualified. The experience gave me valuable insight into what it is to be the lowest of the low in the medical hierarchy.'

'Perhaps it's something all trainee doctors should go through as part of their training.'

'Unless they're desperately short of money you'd never persuade them to agree.'

'You look like you'd welcome a cup of tea.'

'I would, it's cold out there. I'll ask the girls to make us one.'

'They're busy, I'll do it.' Sarah went into the kitchen, filled the kettle, and set it on the stove to boil. She looked at the biscuits Praskovia had sent over, laid a few on a plate for Nathan, and put cups and saucers on a tray. She felt something in her pocket. It was the package Glyn had given her that morning that she'd been reluctant to open because of his advice.

'*Open that when you're alone.*'

She untied the ribbon and unfolded the brown paper wrapping.

It was a silver photograph frame, the kind that folded over like a book. It held two photographs.

One she recalled Glyn taking in the garden of her and Peter's rented house in Merthyr. They were standing side by side in the kitchen doorway, smiling directly at the camera. The second had been snapped on the boat.

Unaware of Glyn's camera, she and Peter were leaning on the ship's rail. Her husband was smiling down at her, love etched in his eyes. In that instant, the image of Peter's corpse that she'd carried since she'd visited the cemetery faded. The photograph blurred, as emotions came flooding back. The tears she'd held in check for so long finally fell.

She kissed the damp glass and whispered, 'Thank you, Glyn, for giving him back to me.'

Chapter Twenty-three

Hotel Hughesovka
March 1871

A closed sleigh, blinds drawn, pulled up at the side door of the Hotel Hughesovka. Given the unsullied paintwork, it was obvious it hadn't travelled far. Catherine's butler, Boris, left the hallway and opened the door before the driver had time to climb from his seat. He helped a heavily veiled lady across the icy path into the building.

'Her ladyship and the lawyer are in a private room on the first floor, Madam. There's no one else. Your meeting will be private as you requested.'

The lady inclined her head and mounted the stairs. Boris followed. A liveried valet stood aside to allow them to pass. He stared at the woman but she was so shrouded in black silk and robed in furs it was impossible to make out her features.

Boris knocked and opened a door. She entered the room. Boris closed the door behind her and stationed himself in front of it.

'Someone important?' the valet fished.

'Not as important as your master, Mr Levsky,' Boris answered. Everyone in Hughesovka knew Levsky had rented the Beletsky Manor so he could be on hand to compile and forward unfavourable reports to the anti-progress faction in Moscow opposed to John Hughes and Tsar Alexander II's plans to industrialise Russia.

The valet took the hint and continued his journey down the stairs.

Private room, Hotel Hughesovka
March 1871

Catherine and Dmitri rose when their guest entered. Dmitri approached the lady and divested her of her furs. Catherine embraced her.

'It's good of you to see me,' the visitor lifted her veil.

'It's wonderful to meet again after so many years. I only wish you'd come to the house.'

'It wouldn't have been proper.'

'No woman my age needs to be concerned with "proper". Please, take a seat.' Catherine indicated a chair. 'We've ordered wine, tea, coffee, cake and savoury canapés.'

'Coffee would be lovely, thank you, Mrs Ignatova.'

'You used to call me Catherine. Dmitri, this is Madam...'

Koshka interrupted Catherine. 'Koshka.'

Dmitri's colour heightened 'We're acquainted.'

'Then we're all friends.' Catherine poured three coffees from the hotel's silver pot. 'Please, help yourself to food. As you asked for this meeting, S...' Catherine almost used the name Koshka had been christened. 'Madam Koshka, please begin.'

'I wish to lodge my will with your lawyer and set up an account for Sonya...'

'Tsetovna,' Catherine supplied. 'Although illegitimate, my brother formerly adopted her as his heir. Unfortunately, he doesn't have anything other than good wishes to leave her.'

'At present,' Koshka agreed, 'and possibly never, which is why I want to make provision for Sonya.' She pushed a large envelope towards Dmitri. 'I'd be grateful if you would look over these papers, Mr Dmitri, and action them.'

'It would be my pleasure, Madam Koshka. Do you mind if I read them now, ladies? Then we can discuss any alterations that may be needed before we leave?'

'Good idea, Dmitri.' Catherine handed him his coffee.

Dmitri carried the cup and envelope over to a desk.

Catherine picked up a tray and plate and offered both to Koshka. 'The smoked salmon canapés are delicious. I've already eaten three.'

'How can I refuse when you put it that way?' Koshka set one on the plate. 'I've seen Sonya.'

'And spoken to her?'

'Of course not. She's very beautiful.'

'You don't have to look at her from a distance. When I answered your letter I told you that you're welcome to call on me and Sonya anytime convenient to you.'

'As I replied, that would leave you and Sonya open to gossip. Aristocratic ladies do not allow brothel-keeping madams into their homes, nor do they visit them.'

'You are Sonya's mother. She has a right to know you.'

'I hope she never does nor finds out what I have become.'

Catherine spooned cream into her coffee. 'I've always admired and envied you.'

'You – envied me!'

'You had the courage to leave a brutal husband who made your life unbearable to live openly with my brother.'

'Which, given Sergei's fecklessness was not the most sensible move, but he made me laugh and I was in love.'

'Laughter and love excuses everything. When my brother ran through his inheritance and became a hopeless drunk, you attracted a more sensible patron.'

'Which I wouldn't have been free to do if you hadn't taken in my daughter.'

'My husband had just died. I welcomed the companionship.'

'Your son-in-law was opposed to your benevolence.'

'My son-in-law is an ass. Please don't spoil a pleasant morning by mentioning his name. You said you've seen Sonya?'

'Walking in and out of the hospital. She's very beautiful, a golden girl, as you were when you were young – and Olga.'

'And charismatic. Sonya's inherited Sergei's talent for making and keeping friends. People adore her.'

'Does she intend to become a nurse?'

'No. She's helping in the hospital office. Mr Hughes has offered her a position in either the Russian or English schools when they're built, possibly as a music teacher.'

'You spared no expense in her education.'

'Given Sonya's talent and diligence, tutors were queuing at my gate.'

'I'd forgotten your generosity of spirit, Catherine. That last time we met in St Petersburg you knew what my salon was, yet you never made me feel less than you.'

'You're a great deal more. A woman who's made her own living and way in the world. What have I done? I was kept as a pet by my father who believed no female should study anything beyond embroidery and the supervision of servants. After my marriage, which I can take no credit for, as it was arranged by my father and father-in-law, I became my husband's pet. His ideas were even more archaic than my father's. His only ambition for Olga was that she contract a good marriage. Not marriage to a good man. That I could have understood, but marriage to an old and aristocratic name, even if the bearer was a dunderhead.'

'I was devastated to hear of your daughter and

granddaughters' deaths.'

'God sends us all crosses to bear.' The loss of Olga and her granddaughters was too raw for Catherine to dwell on.

'Madam Koshka.' Dmitri joined them. 'Who drew up these documents for you?'

'A lawyer in Moscow. Is there a problem with them?'

'No, provided you stand by the intentions you've outlined. You want to open an account in Sonya Tsetovna's name?'

'Yes.'

'An account in which you intend to deposit two million roubles?'

'Yes.'

'Two million roubles...' Catherine was stunned.

'You wish Sonya Tsetovna to be aware how much money there is in this account, although she is only seventeen years of age?'

'I do, but I also stipulated the size of the annuity she is to receive.'

'Which is extremely generous, possibly overly so.'

'She's been brought up by Madam Ignatova who values money. Sonya will have to live within her income which is less than the annual interest accrued from the deposits in her bank account. Hopefully, they will ensure she never becomes destitute like her father. I know annuities can be sold. I trust Sonya will never have cause to. Also, I've made certain she can only access the funds outside of her annuity with the consent of her trustees, and even then only for a major purchase such as a house or estate.'

'I still counsel caution, Madam Koshka. Two million roubles is an enormous sum to give a young girl with no experience of the world.'

'I don't want Sonya to feel she has to take a position she doesn't want, or marry someone she doesn't love in order to survive in this world.'

'You mention trustees but you've only appointed one. A person of high standing and impeccable credentials.'

'An old friend I trust implicitly. He suggested there should be at least three. I was hoping I could impose on Madam Ignatova as she is Sonya's legal guardian.'

'I'd be happy to,' Catherine agreed.

'The third?'

'Would you consider the position, Mr Dmitri?'

'My firm would be honoured to take the responsibility, Madam Koshka. To move on to your will. On your death Sonya will inherit your entire estate apart from the house you've built in Hughesovka which is to be left jointly between whatever staff are employed there by you at the time of your death?'

'That is correct.'

'May I suggest you keep an up-to-date list of staff, and send any changes to my office? The wording says "present members of staff". That phrase could lead to arguments as to who exactly was working for you at the time of your death.'

'Excellent point Mr Dmitri, I will do as you ask.'

'You want Sonya Tsetovna's annuity to be paid from today?'

'Yes and I want Sonya to be informed it is a family inheritance. If she questions it, she's to be told it's from her father.'

'She has a right to know her mother,' Catherine pleaded.

'Please, Catherine, respect my wishes in this matter.'

Catherine reached for Koshka's hand. 'When do you want me to tell her that she is an heiress?'

'As soon as possible. Tell her ... no, there's no need. You'll warn her to be sensible with her good fortune.'

'I promise.' Catherine rose as Koshka left her seat.

'Thank you, both of you.' Koshka lowered her veil.

'I'll see you again soon? If not in my house then here?'

'That wouldn't be proper, Catherine.'

'Not even if I had important news of Sonya and needed your advice?'

'What advice could a woman in my profession give a wealthy independent, young woman like Sonya Tsetovna? Thank you for the refreshments, Catherine, and for your expertise and kindness Mr Dmitri.' She stood while he draped her furs around her shoulders then tapped the door.

Boris opened it. Koshka turned briefly, but her veil obscured her features. A few seconds later she was gone.

Glyn Edwards' house, Hughesovka
March 1871

'Richard, stop complaining about the cold. If

you're shivering run up and down the stairs until you're warm. No one likes what Mr Mahoney calls a "misery guts".' Freshly bathed, dressed in high-collared woollen Russian shirts with shoulder fastenings, black trousers, and leather boots, Alexei and Richard entered the dining room where they joined Glyn, Sarah, and Anna at the table.

Anna, who tried to be of use whenever she could, took Alexei and Richard's soup bowls and ladled out helpings of mushroom borsch with prunes.

'I'm not a misery guts, Alexei,' Richard countered, 'I'm exhausted. Fourteen hours on the freezing steppe is enough to drain anyone's energy.'

'I bet you rode in a sleigh for most of that time.' Anna passed Alexei the bread. 'Try running up and down the length of the hospital all day, caring for irritable patients and soothing their hysterical relatives.'

'You're getting cheeky, sis.'

'Not cheeky, confident,' Sarah corrected. 'I couldn't manage without her.'

'Your sister has a point, Richard,' Alexei interposed. 'The work we did today was hardly backbreaking. Mapping out mine locations, measuring distances for new roads, and looking for sites to stockpile mining waste.'

'It may not have been backbreaking but the sleigh was open.'

'So you continue to be a misery.' Alexei broke off a chunk of bread and crumbled it on top of his soup, 'Wrapped up in a sleigh is better than trudging over the steppe.'

'We might have been warm if we'd trudged.'

'In that case, you can run behind the sleigh tomorrow while I ride,' Alexei teased.

Praskovia entered with a maid. She set an enormous iron casserole dish in the centre of the table while the maid waited to clear away the soup bowls.

Alexei sniffed. 'Georgian chanakhi?'

'I don't know how you do it, sir, but you're right,' Praskovia replied.

'Call me sir again, Praskovia, and I'll start calling you madam.'

Praskovia lifted the lid on the dish a second maid brought in. 'Potato cakes with mushrooms and vegetable golubtsy. If you need anything else...'

'We'll ring the bell,' Glyn interrupted.

Surprised at his terseness, Sarah turned to him.

He gave her an apologetic look. 'As Alexei said, it's been a long day and I still have work to do.'

'You're driving yourself too hard, Glyn. You need to rest until you recover your strength,' Sarah warned. 'If you don't, you could find yourself back in bed.'

'The riggers have begun drilling in two new spots, and the miners are tunnelling three new seams in the old mines.' Alexei finished his soup and handed his bowl to the maid. 'What more can you do tonight that can't wait until morning, Mr Edwards?'

'List the possible sites for new pits in order of viability.' Glyn frowned. 'What are you doing here? Isn't this your night for eating at your grandmother's?'

'She sent a note telling me she has "private things to discuss" with Sonya and her lawyer.'

'Like how to cope with an annoying grandson and cousin?' Richard suggested.

'My grandmother doesn't find me annoying; she adores me, as does Sonya. It's probably something to do with the fund Father Grigor and Sonya are helping my grandmother set up for the widows and orphans of the cholera and scarlet-fever epidemics. My father's cook left four young children and the maid was supporting her widowed mother.' Alexei looked into the casserole dish. 'This chanakhi looks good. I don't know what Yelena does to lamb but it tastes so much better than at my grandmother's house.'

'Don't let Lyudmila overhear you say that,' Anna warned.

'If she knew, she'd ask Yelena for her recipe.' He piled his plate high. 'A beer house opened down the street today. Anyone want to visit it for a quick drink after dinner?'

'As long as it is quick one, I'm behind with my reading.' Richard helped himself to a potato pancake.

'Mr Edwards?' Alexei looked at him.

'I really do have to work.'

'Don't ask me,' Sarah pre-empted an invitation from Alexei. 'I doubt ladies will be welcome there and I have a book, glass of wine, and fire waiting in the drawing room.'

'I have to study. Ruth and Miriam have been coached by Nathan and they know much more than me.' Anna made room on the table for the dessert tray. 'Blackcurrant kisel?'

'My mother made it especially for you, Miss Anna,' Praskovia said. 'She knows how much you like it.'

A maid set a bowl of whipped cream on the table and gathered the last of the empty goulash bowls.

'Come on, Richard, eat up.' Alexei urged.

'You can't wait to get at the beer, can you?' Richard helped himself to more meat.

'Not the beer, to see the beer house. We've never had one here. Mr Hughes hasn't just given this place a name, he's brought civilization here.'

Glyn caught the look of incredulity in Sarah's eye and burst out laughing.

'What's funny?' Alexei demanded.

'You,' Glyn wiped his eyes with his handkerchief. 'You believe a beer house is a sign of civilization.'

It was only after they left the table that Sarah realized it had been the first time laughter had been heard in the house since Peter and Huw had died.

Dower House, Beletsky Estate
March 1871

Sonya's eyes rounded in disbelief. 'I'm rich?'

'Very,' Catherine confirmed.

'All the times Count Beletsky told me to apply for position as a governess or companion, you never said a word.'

'Because I didn't know about this bequest until Mr Dmitri confirmed it this morning.'

'The money has been given to me by my father?'

Mr Dmitri intervened. 'Perhaps I should explain the situation to Miss Sonya, Mrs Ignatova. As you know, Miss Sonya, your father is an invalid and not expected to leave the hospital in St Petersburg...'

Catherine blessed her lawyer's tact and ability to lie. Her brother was a dipsomaniac she'd been forced to confine to an institution for his own protection.

'...The money is family money, Miss Sonya, which is now yours. Should you need advice on your bank account or investments I would be happy to oblige or introduce you to a more qualified person than myself. Although, after looking at the arrangements already made, they appear sound. Is there anything you don't understand about the annuity or how it is to be paid?'

'No, Mr Dmitri. Thank you for explaining everything.' Sonya turned to Catherine. 'Does this mean I have to move out?'

'Don't be silly, Sonya.' They were both sitting on the sofa so Catherine hugged her. 'All it means is that you have your own money, and can buy whatever you want.'

'But you've just bought me a new mourning gown.' Catherine and Mr Dmitri exchanged glances.

'You can buy a great deal more than a new gown, or even jewels, if you wish, Miss Sonya, but you've plenty of time to decide what you want to do with your money.'

'I could invest it in one of Mr Hughes's enterprises.'

'You could,' Catherine agreed.

‘Or one of the coal mines Alexei and Richard are talking about sinking.’

‘My advice to you, Miss Sonya, is don’t do anything in a hurry. Become accustomed to your wealth before spending it.’ Dmitri finished his burgundy and allowed Boris to refill his glass. ‘Once word gets out, and it always does no matter how hard people try to keep financial matters confidential, you’ll have suitors flooding to the door.’

‘There’s plenty of time for suitors and marriage,’ Catherine countered.

Sonya’s thought turned to the only suitor she wanted. Her “secret” love. So secret not even he knew how she felt about him. She suspected that he wouldn’t be swayed by her sudden fortune. She had a peculiar feeling that her money may even make her unattractive in his eyes.

‘Can we keep my inheritance a secret?’ she asked, ‘just for a while. I’ll tell Alexei of course, he’s family, but no one else.’

‘A good idea, child,’ Catherine endorsed. ‘I’m pleased with the way you’ve taken this news, but I admit, after the way I’ve brought you up I didn’t expect you to react any differently. More wine, Dmitri?’

Glyn Edwards’ house, Hughesovka
March 1871

Sarah was curled in a corner of the enormous sofa, lost deep in her book when Richard gusted in, red faced on a draught of freezing air.

Sarah marked her page with an envelope. 'How was the beer house?'

'Bit like the pubs in Merthyr. If anything even more rough and ready.' He rubbed his hands and examined them. 'If you visit, take care with the tables and chairs lest you pick up a splinter. The surroundings are what Mr Edward Edwards would have called "primitive".'

'And the beer?'

'The fermented bread beer, kvass, is too sweet and weak for my taste and the German beer too strong.'

'There's wine in the carafe and brandy, whisky, and vodka in the decanters if you want a drink.'

'No, thank you, I have to be up early and in what Alexei calls "a happy mood". I left him talking to a couple of Cossack Officers who'd been ordered to look around the town and report back to the colonel with a list of bars willing to welcome soldiers. It's the first time any of the regiment have been given leave since they arrived. Their colonel was so concerned about the cholera and scarlet fever he quarantined the garrison.' He pulled a chair close to the fire.

'A wise precaution on the colonel's part.'

'Is the scarlet fever epidemic over?'

'It's too soon to tell.' She picked up her wine glass.

'And the cholera?'

'Dr Kharber thinks they may be a recurrence in the spring and I agree with him. Anna said your brothers and sisters died of the disease in Merthyr.'

'They did.' Wanting to change the subject

Richard looked around and saw the chess board Glyn had left set up on a side table. 'Would you like a game of chess, Mrs Edwards?'

'You play?'

'Mr Edward Edwards taught me the moves. I watched Dr Edwards and Mr Edwards play. They were incredible. I'll never be as good.'

'Dr Edwards used to say all you need to play well is practice. I'm not sure he was right. I practised a lot but never beat him,' Sarah admitted. 'But as for playing a game now, it's been a long day.'

'Is Anna in bed?'

'Fast asleep with a book open in her hands when I took her up some warm milk an hour ago; I turned down her lamp.'

'She's happier than I've ever seen her since she's been working with you.'

'And you?' Sarah asked seriously.

'Glad to be alive after the cholera. Missing Mr Thomas and Dr Edwards. The house doesn't seem the same without them.'

'No it doesn't, Richard.' She looked at him thoughtfully. 'Would you tell me the truth if I asked you a question that concerned Mr Edwards and Mr Hughes?'

'If I can. Anna and I owe you and Mr Edwards everything.'

'Are Mr Hughes and Mr Edwards hard task-masters?'

'You've been listening to some of the colliers' griping.'

'Three of them came in with minor injuries this afternoon, just cuts and bruises and a wrenched thumb, but they behaved as if they were on their deathbeds. They told me they'll return to Merthyr as soon as the thaw comes and the port opens.'

'They're idiots. Mr Hughes and Edwards don't work anyone harder than themselves. Yes, the work isn't easy, but there's more opportunity here than Merthyr. I can't wait to bring my brothers over.'

'You love it here, don't you?'

'Anna and I have never lived so well. It's not just the house, the clothes, and the food, Mrs Edwards. It's having all the books I can read and more to hand, listening to Mr Edwards, your, and Alexei's conversation. Visiting Mrs Ignatova and hearing Sonya play the piano. Everything is so different from Merthyr, so much better and...' He suddenly realised he was being disloyal to the way his mother had brought him up.

'I know what you mean about the books and music. I didn't have access to either when I was growing up.'

'I'm glad you understand. It's like I'm being shown a whole new world.'

He looked so young, so eager, so happy, so childlike she couldn't help but return his smile. She felt the need to give him something – if only a sop. 'About that game of chess...'

'I'd love one, thank you Mrs Edwards.' He pushed the table with the board closer to the sofa she was sitting on.

It was then the thought came to her that if she and Peter's child had been a boy, she'd have wanted him to be just like Richard.

Hughesovka and Dower House, Hughesovka
March 1871

Alexei saw Mr Dmitri pass in his sleigh when he left the beer house. He checked his pocket watch. It wasn't quite ten o'clock. He knew his grandmother rarely retired before eleven so he returned to Glyn's house, saddled Agripin, and rode to the Dower House. He'd steeled himself to tell his grandmother that he'd never loved Praskovia, and although she'd cancelled his dinner invitation he didn't want to wait a moment longer than necessary to inform her he loved Ruth.

What he hadn't expected was to find Sonya with news that was more important than his.

'So my little cousin is going to be hugely wealthy and will have to beat off suitors with sticks.' Alexei was amazed and pleased. 'That's wonderful, Sonya.'

'Thank you, but I haven't begun to accept my good fortune yet. You're not to tell a soul.'

'I promise.'

'No one must know other than you, me, Mr Dmitri, and Aunt Catherine.'

'No one will find out from me, but I'd love to be there when my father hears about it.'

'Were you so curious as to why I put you off dining with us this evening that you had to call at this hour, Alexei?' Catherine asked.

'I have news of my own.'

'About Praskovia?' Catherine guessed.

'Sort of.'

Sonya left her chair. 'I'll have an early night.'

'What's going on?' Catherine grasped Sonya's hand as she passed her chair.

'Ask Alexei, Aunt Catherine.' Sonya kissed both of them and left the room.

'I take it Sonya knows what you want to talk about and is being tactful.'

'More like getting out the firing line,' Alexei amended.

'So what is this "sort of" about you and Praskovia? We all know you love her.'

'I don't and never have.'

Catherine recalled all the times she'd seen Alexei and Praskovia huddled together laughing, whispering ... there'd always been at least one other person hovering in the background and it hadn't always been Sonya.

'I've been a fool. It's Ruth Kharber you love, not Praskovia, isn't it?'

'Sonya told you?'

'No, the only wonder is, I didn't see it earlier.'

'You're angry with me?'

'I'm worried for you, Alexei. Being born a Jew is very different to being born a Russian. The Jewish religion is not just a way of worshipping God; it's a rulebook that lays down how every part of life should be lived. There are laws on what can and can't be eaten. How to dress, worship, communicate with people – even light candles. Has Ruth told her family about you?'

'Nathan knows.'

'And?' She waited for a reply that was slow in coming.

'He doesn't approve.'

'Nathan is talking to you?' she queried.

'Not about Ruth.'

'How often do you see her?'

'You're wondering if it's the thrill of forbidden fruit I'm in love with, not Ruth.'

'To be frank, yes.'

'I've loved her since I was thirteen years old, Grandmother.'

'Men grow out of their childish passions.'

'What I feel for Ruth is not a childish passion.'

'How often do you see her?' she reiterated.

'When I was in school in East Prussia, hardly ever, but we wrote to one another under cover of Sonya's letters. Since my return, not as frequently as we wished but when she nursed the cholera patients in the Beletsky Mansion, it was every day. Now with Sonya and Mrs Edwards working in the hospital I have an excuse to call in there but Nathan takes care to ensure Ruth's rarely alone.'

'If you saw so little of Ruth before the cholera outbreak, I have to wonder how serious you are. Does she want to marry you?'

'She's worried about her family and the people in the shtetl, but she loves me. She wants to marry me. She just doesn't believe it's possible.'

'I share her concern. You're both very young. You're nineteen, she's what? Sixteen?'

'Seventeen, and I'm almost twenty. Age has nothing to do with love, Grandmother.'

'As I used to say to your poor mother, you were born old. Even as a baby you knew what you wanted and did everything in your power to get it. This time I believe you've overreached yourself. However, if Nathan is prepared to talk to you we must invite him and Ruth here. I would say for dinner but I know they have rules about eating in Christian houses. If they come for afternoon tea or supper I'll order wine, sandwiches, fruit, and cake to be served. No pork or ham, but I think they can eat chicken.'

'I thought you'd be angry.'

'I'm not your father, Alexei. I don't anger easily. You're absolutely sure of your feelings for Ruth?'

'I wouldn't have spoken to you if I wasn't.'

'You're not just excited by the knowledge that you'll be shocking both your families not to mention every, Jew, Christian, and Cossack for miles?'

'I love Ruth, Grandmother, more than anyone else in this world.'

'I hope you do, because if you marry, you'll have to be everything to one another. The Russians will never receive her. The Cossacks will hate both of you for what they'll see as your betrayal as a Russian. The aristocrats will believe you've sullied your class and the Jews will cast Ruth out, unless...' she looked at him. 'You're not thinking of converting?'

'I considered it, but Ruth said the community would never accept me.'

'You'd have had to be circumcised.'

He made a wry face. 'I know.'

'At least Ruth is being realistic about her people's reaction.'

'We're not asking for acceptance. We know we won't get it outside of Mr Hughes's employees. But I'm earning enough to support a wife and her religion won't make any difference to the way my colleagues will think of her or me. Mr Hughes intends to build houses for his managers. As soon as he does, I'll borrow money from the company to buy one and we'll marry.'

'You're forgetting your age.'

'Father's disowned me, I don't need anyone's formal consent. Ruth is over sixteen. She would like her brother's blessing, I would like yours, but if we have to, we'll do without.' Alexei moved to a chair. 'I talked to Father Grigor in confidence after mass last week. He said if you and Nathan agree and attend the ceremony he'll marry us.'

'If we don't?'

'I'll try to persuade Father Grigor to reconsider his stipulation that you and Nathan be present.'

'Ruth was brought up by her uncle and aunt after her parents' death, wasn't she?'

'Yes, but first I think we should just invite Nathan and Ruth here.'

'And hope that their visit will open a discussion between both families.'

'I can imagine what the discussion would be if my father were here.'

'The least said about him, the better.' Catherine glanced at the clock. 'Have you talked to Sonya about Ruth?'

'She knows we want to marry.'

'Has she seen Misha?'

'I don't think so. The Cossacks have been confined to barracks since the cholera and scarlet fever outbreaks. Why do you ask?'

'Something Sonya said about you and Misha.'

'If she told you we quarrelled about the Cossacks attitude towards the Jews, we did.'

'You can't fight centuries of prejudice by arguing

with a childhood friend, Alexei,' she warned. 'That's another reason for you to reconsider your relationship with Ruth.'

'Believe me, I've done all the considering that needs to be done, Grandmother.'

Chapter Twenty-four

Hospital complex, Hughesovka
March 1871

Alexei crouched low below the beams of the oil lamps as he turned the corner to face the staff apartments behind the main building. He crawled to the last window on the left and made a dove call. When there was no response, he reached up and tapped the glass.

'If you want to see my sister, Alexei, I suggest you visit during daylight hours.' Nathan was standing over him.

Feeling foolish Alexei rose to his feet and brushed the snow from his boots and trousers. 'I told my grandmother tonight that I love Ruth and will marry her as soon as possible.'

'Was she overjoyed?'

Alexei stepped into a yellow circle of light that turned his skin white. 'As overjoyed as you.'

'That happy?' Nathan's breath was foggy in the artificial light.

Ruth opened her window, saw Alexei, and smiled until Nathan stepped between them.

'Grandmother asked me to invite you both to supper or afternoon tea,' Alexei blurted.

'And you decided to deliver the message at...' Nathan pulled out his watch and squinted at the face. '...ten minutes to midnight.'

'I was passing.'

'As you live opposite the hospital, you do that every day. Couldn't it wait until morning?'

'Will you accept my grandmother's invitation?'

'What would be the point in such a meeting, Alexei?'

'You and Ruth could sample my grandmother's cook's baking, which is excellent. My grandmother and you could discuss Ruth and me and agree we're both insane and Ruth and I can spend time together.'

'Put like that, how can I possibly refuse? I will look at the duty rotas and write to your grandmother to let her know when Ruth and I are able to visit.'

'Thank you, Nathan.'

'In the meantime I expect you to behave like a gentleman, Alexei, and you, Ruth, to behave like a lady. Go to bed and close your curtains.'

Ruth slammed her window shut and pulled the drapes.

'Behaving like a gentleman, Alexei, means no visits to Ruth's bedroom, at any hour.'

'I am outside your front door, not in her bedroom.'

'If I hadn't been here, how long would have stayed outside?'

When Alexei didn't answer Nathan continued. 'I want your word that you will respect Ruth.'

Alexei sensed Ruth listening at her window.

'Alexei?' Nathan repeated.

'You have my word.'

Sunday 10th April 1871
Easter Day in Gregorian Calendar, fourteen days before Easter in the old Julian Calendar used in Russia

'What are you doing here?' Nathan asked Sarah when he walked into the office to find her and Sonya working on the supply ledgers. 'I thought you were dining at Mrs Ignatova's today to celebrate the British Easter.'

'We're not going until this evening,' Sarah explained. 'When Sonya called in to see Anna this morning she mentioned she was concerned that we were about to run out of chloroform, belladonna, mercury salts, and sulphur.'

'Are we?'

'Not if the last order we sent to Taganrog is delivered this week, but given the storm that blew up yesterday, I doubt it will. I hope whoever's bringing the delivery wasn't caught on the steppe. If he was, he'll have frozen to death.'

'There were warning signs. The delivery drivers are adept at finding shelter.'

'You've finished the ward round?' Sarah checked.

'I have.'

'Everything quiet?' she asked.

'You heard Cossack soldiers came into town last night, drank the beer shop and hotel dry, and caused trouble?'

'I couldn't help but hear them myself. They spent half the night singing in the street below my balcony. I hoped the snow would drive them indoors but it didn't seem to have much effect.'

'Nothing does when it comes to drunks. More officers came in from the garrison this morning. They rounded up the wounded from the ward, and the stragglers from the town. They sent them back under guard and stayed on only to carry on drinking where their comrades left off.'

'You're expecting more trouble?' she questioned.

'I think we should make the most of this peaceful interlude. The officers are celebrating their first leave for months and celebrating for the Cossacks means a prodigious consumption of vodka. That usually leads to frayed tempers and fights. If I were a gambling man I'd put every spare rouble on us having a few more broken heads and fists through the door before morning.'

Sarah closed the ledger she'd been working on and handed it to Sonya.

'Shall I make tea?' Sonya replaced the ledger on the shelf.

'Yes, please,' Nathan replied.

'Me too, please,' Sarah added. 'If you've finished your round, I should check on the patients.'

'You've trained the girls so well there's nothing for you to do. Ruth, Rivka, and Miriam have every man in the place washed, shaved, fed, and tucked up so tight he dare not turn in his bed or lift his head from the pillow for fear of creasing the linen.'

She winced. It was the sort of teasing remark

Peter used to make.

'So go dress for Mrs Ignatova's dinner.'

Sarah made sure Sonya wasn't in the corridor within hearing distance before replying. 'I'd rather stay here. I'd only look around Mrs Ignatova's table and think of all the people who should be there but aren't.'

'I feel the same way on our festival days when I look at the chairs my father and mother used to occupy and they both died years, not months ago.' He glanced through the window.

'So you'll tell Sonya you need me?'

'I may have to. I'm a fortune teller. A casualty is about to walk in. It looks like he needs stitches and possibly chloroform.'

Sarah joined him at the window. Two lieutenants were half-carrying, half-hauling a third under the direction of a captain.

'As you foretold, a broken head,' Sarah noted the blood trickling down the man's cheek from a scalp wound.

'I can see they're drunk from the way they're walking. Leave me to deal with them.'

Sarah ignored him and stepped out. 'Take him into the treatment room,' she ordered the captain in Russian.

'You're the English nurse?'

'She is.' Nathan moved beside her.

'I want you to see to my friend.' The captain jabbed his finger at Sarah and ignored Nathan. 'Not a Jew boy.'

'You'll do as you're told in here, Misha Razin, or get out.' Vlad, who'd been appointed head porter appeared from the back room where the porters were eating their midday meal.

'He...' one of the soldiers aimed a wavering finger at Nathan, 'is a...'

'Doctor, and lucky for you he's here.' Vlad drew himself up to his full height. 'All of you leave your friend so he can be attended to.' Vlad eyed the casualty. 'That's Yulia's brother, Kirill, isn't it?'

'It is,' Misha slurred.

'Take my advice, get yourself and your lieutenants back to the barracks to sleep it off, Misha, before your mother sees you.'

To Nathan and Sarah's amazement, all three officers walked out without a murmur.

'Prepare the operating theatre please, Matron. The sooner we stitch up this idiot the sooner he'll stop bleeding.'

'Yes, Dr Kharber.' She wondered if she'd imagined the wink or if he'd really lowered his eyelid.

Dower House, Beletsky Estate
British Easter Day, April 1871

Catherine raised her glass and looked down the table at her guests. She couldn't bear to mention her daughter or granddaughters but neither could she ignore the losses they'd all suffered. 'Absent friends,' she toasted.

Glyn and John touched their glasses to hers. Although Glyn had lost weight, and his face was pale and drawn, it was his eyes that affected Catherine the most. They were cold, without a spark of light.

Richard and Anna were at the opposite end of the table with Sonya and Alexei. She'd hoped the young people would create a lively atmosphere but they'd sat through the meal as solemn and silent as monks and nuns in retreat.

'Thank you, Catherine, for a superb meal. A real Russian Easter.'

'An early Ukrainian Easter, Mr Hughes,' Alexei corrected. 'The shynka – that's the ham – lamb, and veal are traditional Ukrainian fare.'

'I stand corrected. A real Ukrainian Easter. You couldn't have felt much like celebrating,' John acknowledged.

'As everyone keeps reminding me, life continues whether we want to partake or not. Besides, our Easter is two weeks away and I intend to spend that day in silent prayer for my dead and contemplation of Christ arisen.' Catherine sipped her wine. 'How is Sarah? I've scarcely seen her since we left the Beletsky manor.'

'Throwing herself into work. Stitching drunken Cossacks back together and hoping the outbreak of scarlet fever that's kept her and her trainees busy is over,' Glyn answered.

'I trust it is. I don't need anything else to delay the building of the furnaces,' John added.

'More labour is coming in every day.' Alexei took one of the cigars the butler was handing out. 'I've delegated the housing of the incomers to the hetman in Alexandrovka. As the newcomers will be their neighbours I thought the Cossacks should have a say in where they live. He's had bachelor pits, with dormitories of fifty bunks to a room, dug, with communal kitchens.'

'I've seen entire families come in,' Glyn observed.

'The hetman is allowing them to dig their own pits within boundaries he's laid out.'

'It must be cold, living in a hole in the ground at this time of year.' John watched sparks fly up the chimney after a footman threw an extra log on the fire. 'I know Mrs Edwards is concerned about the conditions. I wish we had more houses at the company's disposal so every worker and his family could have one, but it will take years to build that many.'

'The Mujiks have lived in holes for centuries, and people wouldn't have travelled here if they had better where they'd come from.' Alexei repeated Father Grigor's observation.

'They're no different from the Irish who flocked to the ironworks and collieries in Wales during the famine, sir,' Glyn said philosophically.

'People brought low by hunger are enslaved by their desire to live. I hoped for better conditions for my workers.' John finished his wine.

'You're upset about what was said in the Duma about the wages your company pay your Russian workers,' Catherine guessed. 'Anyone with a modicum of intelligence would realise the reason behind the disparity. It's logical for a skilled man to be paid a higher rate than an unskilled worker.'

'Fifty kopeks a day is more than twice what my father paid his workers who lived out of the main house and they were paid in goods, not money.' Alexei glanced out of the window. The twilight had thickened. Night was drawing in.

'So the English Easter day ends. Thank you, all

of you, for making it pass. Shall we ignore convention and instead of separating ladies from gentlemen retire to the drawing room for tea, coffee, wine, and brandy?' Catherine suggested.

'I'll take a bottle of cherry wine to the hospital, Grandmother.' Alexei held Catherine's chair while she rose. 'Mrs Edwards, Dr Kharber, and the girls might appreciate some cheer.'

'Take some of Lyudmila's Easter biscuits. What the girls don't want they can pass on to the patients.'

'You want to come with me, Sonya, Richard, Anna?'

'Please,' they chorused. The meal had been excellent, Catherine's hospitality faultless, but none of them wanted to stay in an atmosphere so redolent of loss.

'Thank you for today, sirs,' Alexei said to John and Glyn. 'My grandmother, Sonya, and I weren't looking forward to this English holy day.'

'None of us were, and I doubt you would have celebrated it if we British hadn't been here.' Glyn moved so the butler could clear his glass.

Alexei held the door open for Sonya and Anna.

'You returning here?' Catherine asked.

'No thank you, Grandmother, I have to work in the morning.'

'I hoped we could persuade you and Miss Sonya to dine at my house next Sunday,' Glyn invited. 'If so, perhaps we could prevail on Sarah and possibly Nathan and Ruth to join us as well.'

'I'd be delighted.' Catherine looked at Sonya.

'So would I, Aunt Catherine.'

Catherine took John's arm. Alexei and the

young people shouted their goodbyes. Before the footman drew the drapes, Catherine saw Richard and Alexei tossing snowballs at one another as they raced down the drive.

'It takes longer for boys to grow up than girls.' Glyn watched Sonya and Anna link arms and walk sedately behind the boys.

'That depends on the boy, Mr Edwards. Draw your chairs up to the fire, gentlemen. Boris, leave my guests to serve themselves and enjoy your evening meal in the servants' quarters.'

'Thank you, Madam.' Boris closed the door behind him.

Catherine took the glass Glyn gave her. 'You're not allowing the Moscow press to upset you, are you Mr Hughes?'

'Press?' Glyn asked.

John slipped his hand into the inside pocket of his jacket and removed a folded page of newspaper.

Glyn opened it to reveal a cartoon. A caricature of John on top of a hill; coins spilling from a bulging sack slung over his shoulder as he stood beneath a sign pointing to "England" in Russian.

Uncertain how much Russian Glyn had acquired, John explained, 'the sign says England. The coins are silver roubles.'

'I gathered the gist of it, sir. You may have enemies but you also have friends. Didn't Grand Duke Konstantin promise to visit as soon as we're operational?'

'He did.'

'Here's to becoming operational soon. A toast to the works and Hughesovka iron.' Glyn held up his glass.

'If we're going to have this many toasts we should open another bottle of wine,' Catherine suggested. 'This brandy is going to my head.'

'We can afford to relax today,' John returned the newspaper cutting to his pocket. 'Tomorrow we'll be so busy there'll be no time to laze in front of a roaring fire.'

'You're happy with the way Praskovia and her mother are running your house, Mr Edwards?' Catherine enquired.

'Very.'

'Sarah too?'

'She's so busy in the hospital she's only too delighted to hand over the domesticity to Praskovia.'

Catherine finally broached the subject she'd been leading up to. 'Sarah's also happy to be working with Nathan, his sister, and the girls from the shtetl?'

'Why shouldn't she be?'

'Their religion makes no difference to her or you?'

'Absolutely not,' Glyn and John concurred.

'Alexei told me that you and your British workers hold no prejudice against the Jews. I find that difficult to believe.'

'Everyone knows how you stood up to your son-in-law when he tried to ban Nathan from his house,' John reminded.

'Nicholas was being idiotic, ordering the only doctor for miles out of his house in a cholera epidemic.'

'Why are you asking about our attitude to

Nathan? There've been no complaints about him or the hospital, have there?' John asked.

'None I know of.' Catherine decided there was no point in trying to conceal what Alexei would soon be announcing to the world. 'Alexei wants to marry Nathan's sister Ruth.'

'Alexei wants to marry Ruth Kharber! Are you sure?' Glyn was astounded.

'I was amazed as you, Mr Edwards, but I don't need to explain why he's concealed his love for Ruth given the hostility towards the Jews.'

'But Praskovia...'

'She and Sonya helped with the deception. They were friends as children and they're still close. My grandson's subterfuge has shocked you, Mr Edwards? Or is it his choice bride?'

'Neither, Mrs Ignatova.' Glyn splashed brandy into all three glasses. 'It's wonderful news. We must toast the health of the future bride and groom.'

Hospital, Hughesovka
British Easter Day 1871

Ruth pulled the dressing trolley up to Kirill's bed and drew the curtains that separated him from his neighbours. She'd discovered the strongest man could be transformed into a whimpering child when it came to pain, and the worse a nurse could do was to expose him to ridicule by allowing others to witness his tears.

'How are you feeling, soldier?' She lifted Kirill's hand and placed her fingers on his pulse.

'What do you care, Jew whore?' He opened one eye and glared at her.

Ignoring his retort, she lifted the dressing from his scalp and checked the stitches Nathan had used to close the wound. As she leaned over Kirill, he threw back the bedclothes, lifted his hospital nightshirt, grabbed her hand, and pressed it against his erection.

She dropped the dressing, balled her right hand into a fist, and brought it down hard on the base of his penis as Sarah had taught her.

Kirill yelped. 'Jewish bitch! I'll get you for that.'

'Trouble, Nurse Kharber?' Sarah opened the curtain. She took in the situation. 'Amend this patient's notes please, nurse. Curtains are not to be pulled around his bed under any circumstances.'

'Yes, Matron.'

'Take your break. Ask the head porter to come here please.'

Ruth pulled back the drapes. Sarah moved close to the bed. 'Shall we say you were drunk, concussed, and not in possession of your faculties, soldier?'

'That Jewish...'

'Disagree with me and you'll be the last Cossack soldier to be treated in this hospital. It's snowing again. Would you like to leave, right now, this minute, and dress outside? Your clothes are in the locker at the side of your bed.'

'It must be the vodka,' he muttered.

'A full apology that includes the word sorry, an assurance you will treat my staff with respect, won't cause any more trouble and I may – may–'

she emphasised, 'allow you to stay.'

Kirill continued to glare at Sarah but he complied with her demands. Vlad appeared. He too assessed the situation without being told.

'You'd like me to station a porter at this man's bedside, Matron?'

'Please, Vlad, one of the strongest.'

'Leave it to me, Matron.'

Hughesovka
Evening, British Easter Day 1871

Misha dismounted, secured his horse's reins to the hitching post, and looked at the hospital. The oil lamps had been lit but the blinds hadn't been drawn. To the right of the door was an office full of people. He saw Alexei and Richard, and recognised Richard's sister Anna from the journey out of Taganrog. Sonya moved among them like a golden glittering angel. She was pouring wine and talking to Ruth, Miriam, and Nathan. He balled his fists. The last people he wanted Sonya to talk to were Nathan and Ruth.

A hand clamped on his shoulder. Startled, he whirled around.

Vlad looked down at him. 'You sober now?'

'I am.'

'Your mother lives across the road.'

'I know.'

'What brings you here and not there, Misha?'

'I wanted to ask after the man I brought in earlier.'

'He's in better condition than a drunk with a

broken head has a right to be. You Cossack soldiers never learn.'

'You're a Cossack.'

'But not a soldier any more, thank God and Christ.' Vlad made the sign of the cross. 'Your man needs rest but no one will object if you go into the office to ask after him.'

'They're having a party. I don't want to disturb them.'

'How can you disturb people you grew up with?'

The last person Misha wanted to see was Alexei, especially in company with Nathan and Ruth. He took a package from his pocket. 'Do me a favour, Vlad? Ask Sonya to come out. Tell her an old friend wants to see her.' He held up the parcel. 'I'd like to give her this.'

Vlad smiled, showing twin rows of brown, broken teeth. 'So it's like that between you two, is it?'

'It's not like anything, Vlad. I haven't seen her in years.'

'It's freezing out here. Come into the nurses' kitchen.'

'Who's in there?'

'No one. All but two porters have left for the night and they're in the office.'

Hospital, Hughesovka
Evening, British Easter Day 1871

'Someone in the nurses' kitchen to see you,' Vlad whispered to Sonya as she carried a tray of glasses out of the office. He pushed open the door to the kitchen and retreated.

Sonya saw Misha sitting there. Alexei was right. He was taller, broader, and even better looking than she remembered.

'Hello, Misha. Come to see your officer?'

'I came to see you.' He thrust the package at her. 'I would have been here sooner but the day we arrived we were confined to barracks so we could build, repair, and clean our quarters in between drills and weapon practice. As soon as everything was to the Colonel's liking we were quarantined because of the cholera. Then there was scarlet fever. This is the first leave I've had since my return.'

'Shouldn't you be spending it with your mother and Praskovia?'

'I'll visit them later. Will you come with me?'

'I can't. I promised my aunt I'd spend the evening with her.'

He took the tray from her. 'Open your present.'

Sonya was reluctant to take the box because she sensed what was in it.

'You remember what I promised to give you the next time I saw you?'

'We were children, Misha.'

He set the tray down and wrenched the box open. Inside was a three-banded wedding ring, one in yellow, one in rose, and one in white gold. 'It's from a Moscow jeweller,' he said proudly. 'The best. He promised this ring will last a lifetime. The gold is real, top quality. I'm a captain, Sonya. We can marry...' Sonya heard Alexei call her name. She retreated into the doorway.

Misha grasped her wrist. 'Sonya?'

The look on Misha's face was heartbreaking. The last thing she wanted to do was hurt him. But he left her no choice.

'I'm sorry, Misha. I can't marry you.' She wrenched her arm free and fled.

Glyn Edwards' house, Hughesovka
Evening, British Easter Day, 1871

'Misha, my son!' Yelena smothered him in an embrace. 'God heard my prayers and brought you back to me.' Gripping his forearms, she pushed him momentarily from her so she could study him. 'So tall, so handsome in uniform. A captain. We had your last letter.'

'It's good to see you too, Mama.' He disentangled himself from her arms.

'I hope your colonel will allow you to spend more than five minutes with us.'

'Mama, let the boy into the warm.' Praskovia looked up from the cake she was slicing.

'What do you think I'm doing, girl.' Yelena locked her arm around Misha's waist and pulled him into the kitchen.

'I hope you're hungry, Misha,' Praskovia smiled.

'I ate at the barracks.' He succeeded in freeing himself from Yelena and kissed his sister's cheek.

'You'll have a glass of cherry wine and a bliny?' Yelena pressed.

'I'd prefer vodka.'

'What time do you have to be back?'

'Mama, the boy has just come through the door.'

'I can stay an hour or so.' Misha took the vodka pail and glass Praskovia gave him. He filled the glass, raised it, and toasted, 'to our family.'

Praskovia filled three glasses with cherry wine and handed one to her mother. 'Our family.'

'Where's Pyotr?' Misha asked.

'Seeing to the fires and stoves.' Yelena left and reappeared with an embroidered bag and Pyotr in tow. 'We have presents for you, Misha. We bought them at Christmas.' She emptied the bag on the table while Misha hugged his brother.

'This is from me.' Praskovia pushed two pails of vodka towards him.

'You know me so well, little sister.'

'They're not for you alone but to share with your fellow officers.'

Misha raised his eyebrows. 'Perhaps, if they're good.'

'From me.' Pyotr handed him a box of cigars.

'Thank you little brother, they're expensive.'

'Mr Edwards is paying me to live here and the work isn't hard,' Pyotr confided.

'In that case, I'll enjoy them and think of you.'

Yelena presented him with a package wrapped in tissue paper. 'This is from me. Every stitch made with love.'

Misha unwrapped a hand-knitted sweater. He embraced his mother, turning his head aside so she, Pyotr, and Praskovia wouldn't see his tears. 'I've missed you, my family.'

'Well, you don't have to miss us any longer,' Praskovia bustled around to conceal her mounting emotion. 'Now your barracks are in order you'll be getting regular leaves.'

'Who told you they're in order?'

'Cossack soldiers visiting family and friends in Alexandrovka. It's all over the village that your colonel couldn't manage without you and you'll be made a major before spring.'

'I wish I knew as much, but I've been busy. Life's easier for the lower ranks than officers. All they have to do is obey orders. We don't have such an easy time. We have to check the men's work, chastise them for not doing it properly...'

'Chastise?' It was Praskovia's turn to raise her eyebrows.

'Punish those who fail to carry out their orders efficiently and arrange for the work they left incomplete to be finished to the required standard.'

'You sound like a rule book,' Praskovia teased.

'I've read it. As a regiment we've made progress. Our new quarters are finally at the required standard and provided they stay that way I should have more time to visit you.'

'Alexei is living here.' Pyotr was excited at being able to give his brother news.

'I may not have been able to leave the barracks but I do know a little of what has been going on in the outside world. Are you happy working for this Welshman?' Misha asked Yelena.

'Very happy, Misha, although I can't understand a word he says.'

'Mr Edwards is making more of an effort to learn Russian than you are to learn English, Mama,' Praskovia chided.

'It's enough that you can talk to him. We told him about you, Misha. He said you can stay here whenever you want. There are spare bedrooms in the servants' quarters although we've taken on more people to help us run the house.' Yelena pointed to the food on the table. 'We live and eat like aristocrats. The master never complains about the cost of housekeeping or the amount of wood we use on the fires and we dine on the same meats and vegetables as him and his guests.'

'You may live like aristocrats, but thanks to your hard work he lives likes a Tsar.'

'He pays us as well, Misha,' Yelena said.

'How much?'

'More than Mama, Pyotr, and I would earn if we were carting coal or working in Efim's fields.' Praskovia took her brother's question as a reproach for the way she was caring for the family.

'If Alexei is living here, I suppose you're looking after him as well.'

'Why wouldn't we?' she demanded. 'He's paying the master rent.'

'Stop it, you two.' Yelena stepped between them. 'Sometimes I think you've never grown up. Misha, why spoil for a fight when we haven't seen you in years? Sit, finish your vodka, and eat. I've been baking, not just for the master but for you.'

Misha sat at the table. He emptied his pockets and set three small parcels on the table. 'These are for you.' He pushed a package towards Pyotr.

'For me?'

'For you,' Misha smiled at his brother's reaction to the pocket watch he'd won at cards.

'They're beautiful, Misha. Could you afford them?' Yelena held up a pair of amber earrings.

'No, but I did. I thanked you for your vodka.

Aren't you going to open your present?' he asked Praskovia.

She opened the box and removed a small silver and amber spider.

'It seemed appropriate. You used to spend all your spare time crocheting.'

'Thank you.' She pinned it to her smock.

The door opened. Misha rose.

Glyn walked in. 'Please, sit down, the last thing I want is to disrupt your private celebrations.'

'You're not, sir,' Praskovia answered. 'My brother has arrived from the barracks for a visit.'

Glyn extended to his hand. 'Hello again, Captain Razin. We met on the journey from Taganrog.'

After what his mother had said, Misha was surprised by the fluency of Glyn's Russian. 'We did indeed, sir.'

'Please, feel free to visit your family here any time. It is their home as well as mine. I trust your mother told you there is a room for you whenever you choose to stay.'

'She did, sir. Thank you.'

'Praskovia, I'm expecting guests next Sunday for dinner. I'll leave the menu to you. Nothing fancy. Just soup and one of your mother's regular meals.'

'Of course, sir. Will there be many guests?'

'No more than twelve including the people who live in the house.'

'I will have everything ready, sir.'

'I will have everything ready, sir,' Misha mocked after Glyn left.

'That's enough from you, Misha,' Yelena snapped. 'The master is a good man.'

‘If it was up to you, Misha, Mama, Pyotr, and I would have starved to death after Papa was killed.’ Praskovia regretted her outburst when she saw Misha’s reaction but it was too late. The words had been spoken.

‘I’ll leave you in peace to serve your master.’ Misha opened the back door.

Yelena picked up the sweater, cigars, and vodka and thrust them at him. ‘You’ll come again soon?’ she begged.

‘Given sister’s welcome, I’ll take you to tea in the hotel next time, Mama. The waitresses there might give me a smile.’ He took the sweater and cigars from her slammed the door and walked down the path.

The lamps were still lit in the hospital. They illuminated the office. Sonya was standing between Nathan and Ruth. She was looking up at Nathan, eyes shining, a smile curving her lips. He clenched his fists.

‘One day, Jew,’ he muttered. ‘One day…’

Chapter Twenty-five

Glyn Edwards’ house, Hughesovka,
Evening, British Easter Day 1871

Sarah changed out of her uniform as soon as she returned to Glyn’s house. She picked up a copy of *Moll Flanders* from her bedside table, went down to the drawing room, poured a glass of wine, and curled on the sofa. She was lost, deep in Moll's criminal activities in the London of the last century, when Glyn came in with two plates he'd filled at the cold supper buffet Praskovia had laid out in the dining room.

'I thought you'd be too tired to move after tending to a troublesome officer.'

'You heard?'

'Vlad called into Catherine's kitchen and the news percolated up from the servants' quarters. The gossip grapevine in Hughesovka is almost as good as the one in Merthyr.' He handed her one of the plates.

'Smoked salmon, potato salad, piroshky, caviar, pate, and Yelena's home-made bread, all my favourites, thank you.'

'You were missed at Catherine's dinner.'

'As it happened I was needed at the hospital, but to be honest I couldn't face the empty chairs.'

'There weren't any, Mrs Ignatova ordered her servants to carry them out of the room. We all experienced loss in that cholera epidemic, Sarah, and we're all concerned about you and want to help, if you'll let us.' He sat next to the open hearth and stretched his legs in front of the fire.

'I'm grateful to all of you for your concern, especially you. I haven't thanked you properly for the photographs you gave me, but there always seems to be someone else around. Whenever I look at it, I...' tears started in her eyes and she faltered.

'I'm sorry...'

'Please, don't be, Glyn. I love the frame and the

photographs. They're wonderful, the best gift I've ever received apart from the ones Peter gave me. For a while after Peter died the only image I carried of him was his corpse. Now I only have to look at the photograph you took on the boat to see Peter as he was. It's as if you've given him back to me to live again, at least in my memory.'

'I did debate whether to keep the photograph for year or two. In the end I decided it would upset you whenever I gave it to you.'

'Those pictures are a beautiful reminder of Peter and what we had together.' She set her book aside.

'I knew the one I took on the ship was special as soon as I developed it. Whenever I look at it, I almost believe Peter's in the room with me. You made him so happy, Sarah. If I'm ever fortunate enough to have a tenth of what you two had, I'll die content.'

'Please, no talk of dying. Did you have a good time at Mrs Ignatova's?'

'The afternoon passed quickly. Did you know that Sonya and a few of your ward maids and porters came here afterwards with Richard, Anna, and Alexei?'

'We walked here together.'

'They're holding an impromptu party in the dining room but I thought it would be more peaceful for us mature people in here. I told Praskovia we'd serve ourselves until it's time to clear the table. Before I forget, I've invited Mr Hughes, Catherine, and Sonya to dine here next Sunday. You won't be working in the evening, will you?'

'Barring another epidemic I should finish by

seven, which gives me plenty of time to come back here and change.'

'Would you invite Nathan and Ruth to dine with us as well?'

'You know how reluctant Nathan is to accept invitations.'

'It might help if you ask him for a list of things they can eat in Christian households so Praskovia can plan a menu to suit them. Mrs Ignatova told me Alexei wants to marry Ruth.'

'Ruth Kharber!' Sarah's eyes rounded in astonishment.

Glyn explained Alexei's subterfuge and Catherine's concern at his choice of bride.

'I understand Catherine's unease.'

'Nathan knew about Alexei and Ruth. He hasn't mentioned it to you?'

'We're too busy to discuss anything other than hospital business. Besides, it's a personal matter that only involves his family – and Alexei.'

'And Praskovia,' Glyn added.

'Poor girl.'

'Why "poor girl"?'

'If she was in love with Alexei...'

'According to Mrs Ignatova, she never was. It was a ruse to divert attention away from Alexei and Ruth. You know what Alexei's father is like.'

'Unfortunately,' she concurred. 'How unselfish of Praskovia to risk her reputation to help Alexei.'

'As her brother's called in, perhaps we should invite her and her family to have a drink with us. They could join us in the dining room before the servants clear the table. I'll ask them.'

Before Sarah could remind Glyn that Praskovia

was determined to keep a distance between the residents and servants in the house, he'd left the room.

'No, sir,' Praskovia refused. 'Servants do not mix with their masters and my brother has left. Should you require more food I would be happy to serve you.'

'We won't need more food. You've laid out enough for a regiment.'

She continued to block the doorway. Behind her, he caught a glimpse of the footman playing a violin and Pyotr whistling down a pipe. The table that dominated the room had been moved to make space and two of the housemaids were dancing. They appeared to be having so much fun he had to stifle the urge to sweep Praskovia off her feet, carry her back in to the kitchen, and set her on his knee so they could both enjoy the spectacle.

'Will that be all, sir?'

'Yes, thank you, Praskovia.'

'Let me know when you want the table cleared, sir.'

'I will, thank you.' He retraced his steps, wondering if it was the loss of Peter that had made him so conscious of his lack of family.

'Thank you for a lovely evening, Mr Edwards.' Sonya stood on tiptoe and kissed his cheek.

'I'm glad you enjoyed it, Sonya, and thank you for forgiving me for leaving you young people to your own devices. Are you sure you don't want me to ask Pyotr to harness the sleigh?'

'Please don't disturb him, Mr Edwards. I'll enjoy the fresh air.'

'I'll saddle Agripin and the mare and escort Sonya to the Dower House.' Alexei set his fur hat on his head.

'It'll take you an hour there and back and you have to be up early,' Sonya protested.

'Drunken Cossacks are abroad,' Alexei warned.

Suspecting Alexei's offer had more to do with snatching a quick visit to the Kharbers' quarters than concern for Sonya's safety, Glyn conceded defeat over the sleigh and closed the front door.

'May we clear the table now, sir?' Praskovia asked.

'Of course. I hope we didn't keep you up.'

'No sir. It's only half past nine.'

'In that case I'll make a quick visit to the bath house; I'll be out by ten if anyone wants to use it, Praskovia. Goodnight everyone.' Glyn headed for the back door.

Sarah, Richard, and Anna helped Praskovia and Yelena load the trays for the kitchen. After the maids had carried them away Sarah hugged Anna.

'You look exhausted and you're on afternoon shift tomorrow. You know the rules.'

'Look after yourself or you won't be able to look after the patients,' Anna chanted.

Sarah dropped a kiss on the top of Anna's head. 'See you at breakfast, darling.'

Anna kissed Richard goodnight before running up the stairs. Sarah returned to the drawing room.

Richard followed. 'I don't feel tired.'

'Neither do I although I know I should. Shall

we be devils and have one more glass of wine?'

While Sarah poured the wine, Richard moved the chess board. 'Do you fancy playing another game with me, Mrs Edwards?'

'Why not.'

'If it upsets you...'

'Why would playing chess upset me?'

'You said that you used to play with Dr Edwards.'

'I like doing things I used to do with him. It's an affirmation of life. A way of remembering him and the good times.' She suddenly saw the truth that lay behind the trite phrases people used at times of unbearable sorrow. 'He would have wanted me to carry on living. He wouldn't have wanted me to waste my life in mourning.'

She moved her chair closer to the table, picked up two pawns, hid them in her hands, and held them out. 'Choose and find out if you have black or white?'

He tapped her right hand. She unfolded her fingers to reveal a white pawn. 'You're in luck, you have the edge.'

Their fingers touched as he took the piece from her hand. She glanced up to see him watching her. For the first time she caught a glimpse of the man emerging from the boy, and for some reason she couldn't quite quantify, found it disturbing.

Wrapped in his robe, Glyn shivered when he exchanged the heat of the banya for the ice of the night. He ran into the house and made his way to his room. A log fire was blazing in the hearth and the brandy decanter and a glass were on the table next to his favourite chair.

He poured himself a drink, revelled in the luxury of warmth, and tried to think through the implication of the news that Alexei was in love with Ruth.

An image of Praskovia filled his mind. Tall, statuesque, decked out in a gold-embroidered scarlet gown she'd worn when she, Yelena, and Pyotr had left the house to attend a Cossack wed-ding.

She didn't love Alexei! He smiled at the thought that she was free before remembering he wasn't. He opened his watch and gazed at a photograph of his wife. Betty's dark eyes stared back at him.

Days – weeks passed without him sparing her a single thought. The only time he remembered he had a wife was when he received one of her infrequent letters. Even then he often left it unopened for the best part of a day, or even days. Waking or sleeping, his dreams were of Praskovia, not Betty, but much as he wanted Praskovia he knew all he could offer her was loss of reputation and respectability.

'Sir?' Praskovia had to call him a second time before he realised she'd entered his room through the hall door.

'Sorry, my mind was elsewhere.'

'I did knock, sir. The servants are going to bed. Can I get you anything?'

'No, thank you and thank your mother for preparing such a splendid cold supper.'

'I will, sir.' She picked up the empty plate.

'Praskovia.'

'Sir?'

He recalled the night they'd met, the glimpse of

her naked body that haunted his sleeping and waking moments. 'Why didn't you tell me you didn't love Alexei?'

'It was Alexei's secret, not mine.'

'Do you always do what Alexei asks?'

'I loved Ivan Kalmykov. After he was killed it didn't matter what anyone thought of me. Alexei and Ruth are my friends. They needed help. I offered.'

He had to ask. 'Is there a young man who's been waiting for Alexei to reveal the truth so he can court you?'

'No, sir, but it's a relief the lying is over. My mother will be pleased. She suspected there was something odd about me and Alexei.'

'I thought you'd have told her.'

'She was tired after my brother's visit. I'll tell her tomorrow.'

He couldn't stop looking at her. She was close, so close; all he had to do was reach out to touch her.

She stepped away from him. Instead of opening the door, she set the plate she was holding aside and turned the key in the lock.

'Praskovia...'

'Sir?'

'I'm married.'

'Without a wife.'

'She may not be here but all I can offer you is a position as my mistress. I respect you too much for that.'

She slipped the buttons from the loops on the front of her gown and allowed it to fall to the floor. She wasn't wearing anything beneath it.

His breath caught in his throat. The feelings that had taken him by storm the first time he'd seen her naked, overwhelmed him. The tide of emotion washed away all sense, caution, logic...

Moments later, his robe lay next to hers on the floor and they were on his bed. She explored his body with her fingertips, lips, and teeth. Caressing his mouth, nipples, torso, and genitals with her tongue.

He buried his hands in her hair, and when he couldn't stand the torment of her touch a moment longer, he lifted her on top of him and pierced her body with his own.

He'd had sex with more women in brothels than he could recall. He'd been allowed 'his rights' with Betty, but he'd never made erotic, unselfish love with anyone the way he did that night with Praskovia.

She anticipated his needs before he knew them. She kissed, fondled, and embraced his body with every inch of her own until he felt they'd fused into a single being. At the climax, he only existed as an extension of their combined pleasure.

Afterwards, there was no shame as there would have been with Betty. No grabbing of clothes to cover nakedness. Praskovia lay in his arms, basking in the warmth from his body and the heat from the fire, her breasts on his chest, one hand resting between his thighs, the other caressing his face.

'I knew this would happen the first time I saw you. My grandmother had second sight. I must have inherited it. Did you know we'd become lovers?'

‘I thought it was a wishful dream.’

‘I love you, master.’

Her eyelids were drooping, heavy with sleep. ‘No more master.’ He kissed her forehead. ‘From now on it will be...’

Will be what? Restless, he shifted on to his back, moved her head on to his shoulder, and breathed in her scent, a beguiling mix of cinnamon, cloves, orange, lemon, and rose water that reminded him of childhood Christmases.

When sleep came he dreamed of Betty. They were lying in their bed in the Boot Inn and it was cold, so cold there was ice on the window pane. His wife moved close and whispered, ‘I’ve lifted my nightdress. You can take your rights.’

Praskovia was lying the other side of him, naked and unashamed. He didn’t hesitate. He turned his back on Betty and opened his arms to Praskovia.

Praskovia opened her eyes. The lamp wick had burned down and the room was in darkness, but she knew instinctively that morning wasn’t far away. She lifted Glyn’s hands away from her and waited.

He rolled towards her. She moved to the edge of the bed. After a long – very long minute, his breathing settled back into the rhythm of sleep.

She left the bed and found her gown. She slipped it on and made her way to the back door. She turned the key and stepped into the corridor. The door to her room was ajar. A lamp burned on the dresser. Her mother was slumped, snoring on a chair next to the bed. When she walked in Yelena sat up, blinked and stared blindly at her before focusing.

'You have your own room.' Praskovia threw back the bedcover and stepped into the bed.

'As do you, but you don't use it. What do you think you're doing?' She gave Praskovia no time to answer. 'The master is married. Have you given a thought as to what will happen to you – to us – when the mistress arrives?'

'She won't.'

'How do you know?'

'She's not here.'

'She could take it into her head to turn up. It's her right to live in her husband's house. The master's a good-looking man. He's rich. His wife could be missing him and his money. If she arrives and sniffs out what's gone on between you two, you'll be thrown out and Pyotr and me after you.'

'She's not coming and he won't be throwing us out.'

'That's what Pyotr's father said before he opened my legs.'

Praskovia snuggled into her pillow. 'Mr Edwards is not the count. He's a good man.'

'You're not a good woman and the master's not your first.'

'I told him about Ivan. Even if I hadn't, he would have guessed.' Praskovia glared at her mother daring her to say more. 'It's good between us, Mama. In every way.'

'You're risking everything. Not just our work but our future.'

'I'll make sure there's no gossip about the master and me.'

'Have you considered what will happen if you have a child? He'll have to throw you out then...'

'Not another word, Mama! I have to rise in an hour. I want to sleep.'

Yelena relinquished the chair.

'I know what I'm doing.'

'I hope you do, my girl, because I've never had it as comfortable as I have here. I'll never find anywhere else as good and neither will you – or Pyotr. You know how difficult it will be to find a home that offers work and food on the table for him.'

Glyn woke with a start and smiled when he recalled the events of the night. He reached out. The sheet alongside him was empty and cold. He climbed out of bed, opened the drapes that separated the sleeping area from his study, picked up his robe from the floor and shrugged it on.

'Enter,' he shouted at a knock at the back door. He hadn't opened it since he'd locked it the night he'd arrived in Hughesovka. When Praskovia walked through he realised she must have unlocked it when she'd left that morning.

'Good morning, sir. I trust you slept well.'

'"Sir"? Praskovia...' He tried to take the tray from her but she held it fast.

'If there are to be more nights like last night, sir, we must maintain our master and servant relationship.'

'No...'

'If we didn't it would leave you – and me – open to gossip, master. My reputation would be ruined.'

'After what happened between us last night I

can't treat you like a servant.'

'You don't have to when I share your bed, master. But you pay my wages. I am your housekeeper. We can't afford to excite suspicion that I am taking advantage of your kindness, or you my dependent position. If anyone should suspect we're lovers, my mother and brothers would never be able to hold their heads up in Alexandrovka again.'

A door closed somewhere in the house and they heard voices.

'Shall I pour your tea, sir?'

He didn't answer but she poured it. He looked at her mutely. 'It can't be any other way, sir. If you want me in the night leave the back door unlocked.'

He glanced at both doors to check they were closed before pulling her close to him and kissing her.

She stepped back, straightened her clothes, and said, 'Breakfast will be served in twenty minutes, master.' She left by the back door.

He realised the logic in what she'd said. If she was to keep her reputation it was the only way they could live. But it wasn't what he wanted – not after what they'd shared and what he'd hoped their future would be.

Hospital, Hughesovka
April 1871

'I'm sorry, Dr Kharber.' Sonya handed Nathan a patient's notes. He slipped them into a file and marked it with a black tab.

'It's always hard to lose a patient.' Nathan turned his back on Sarah and Anna who were disinfecting the tarpaulin-covered mattress and iron frame of a bed at the end of the ward. The Cossack miner had been in the final stage of lung disease when he'd been brought in, but knowing there'd been no hope hadn't stopped him from wishing for a miracle.

'Can I get you a cup of tea?'

'That's the kindest thing that's been said to me today since Ruth asked what I'd like for breakfast.' He went into the office and sat at the large desk that faced the room. Sonya's desk was positioned close to the doorway that opened into the hall so she could monitor the comings and goings of staff, patients, and visitors.

Sonya brought in a tray. On it were two cups of tea and a plate of biscuits and cake. 'Given the orgy of baking that's going on in every house in Hughesovka in preparation for the Russian Easter we're going to be eating rich, spiced confectionery for months.' She set a cup and plate on Nathan's desk.

'Better too much than too little. Will you leave the hospital when the school opens?'

'You've heard Mr Hughes has offered me a teaching post?'

'Hughesovka is getting to be like the shtetl. No one can keep a secret from the neighbours for long.'

'What are we put on this earth for if not to amuse our neighbours?'

'Have you been talking to my aunt?' Nathan

smiled. 'That's one of her favourite sayings.'

'Then the shtetl has the same philosophy as Alexandrovka. It's a foolish person who thinks they can keep their affairs secret from gossips.' She returned to her desk. Every moment she spent in Nathan's company only served to reinforce her love for him. She recalled something Yulia had said about not being able to understand why Alexei spent so much time talking to Ruth because Ruth 'wasn't pretty'. Ruth wasn't pretty in the conventional sense, any more than Nathan was handsome. But she was bewitched by his dark, sardonic features, his gentle manner, and the kindness he showed to patients, their families, and the staff. Every time she saw the hint of a smile animating his eyes or lifting the corners of his mouth it sent her pulse racing.

Nathan was the reason she'd sent Misha away although the doctor had never treated her differently from any of the ward maids...

'...did you hear what I said, Sonya?'

'Sorry, my mind was elsewhere.' She hoped her thoughts hadn't been written on her face.

'I said I'd be sorry to lose you. You keep this hospital running smoothly. Not an easy task.'

'Thank you.'

'The shelves are stocked with supplies. The laundry picked up and returned. The place is clean...'

'That's down to Danil and his wife. They were grateful Mr Hughes gave them work after Danil was injured in the mine.'

'It's you who ensures that everyone does what they're supposed to.'

Sarah came to the door. 'You're needed on the ward, Nathan.'

Nathan reached for his spectacles. 'Yuri?'

'I think you're right. His heart is affected by the scarlet fever.'

Nathan picked up his stethoscope. He laid his hand over Sonya's when he passed her desk. She looked up and realised he knew she loved him.

There was something else in his look, but it wasn't until he'd left the office that she realised. He loved her back.

Glyn Edwards' house, Hughesovka,
Russian Good Friday, April 1871

'The Cossacks are out in force this morning.' Richard looked through the window at the column of men riding slowly past the gate.

'They on military exercises, Praskovia?' Glyn asked.

'How should I know, master?'

'Your brother is at their head.'

'He's a captain, that's where a captain rides, at the head of his men. Can I get your anything else?'

'No thank you.' Glyn and Richard chorused.

Alexei looked at Praskovia but she turned away. He knew the ways of the Cossacks as well as she did. Misha was exercising his men all right; displaying the full might of his company where he wanted to, outside Nathan Kharber's office window.

Hughesovka might be John Hughes's town but

Misha Razin was showing the Jews who had the most strength. Not that the Jews needed showing. They fed their families by farming and using their artisan skills. It wasn't in their nature to fight or even hunt, and he knew of none that owned a gun. If ever a race was born without an aggressive bone in their bodies it was the Jews. Or possibly submission had been beaten into them throughout history by pogroms and attacks.

The Jews knew who had the upper hand on the steppe. But Alexei was worried. He had a shrewd suspicion his erstwhile friend's tactic was about more than belittling the Jews. He'd seen the way Sonya looked at Nathan. He also knew from what Vlad had told him that Sonya had sent Misha packing when he'd called on her. Knowing Misha, he suspected the show of force outside the hospital so close to the Christian Easter – a time frequently used by Cossacks to attack the race they called "Christ killers" – had something to do with Sonya sharing an office with Nathan Kharber.

Was he the only Russian who'd fallen in love outside of his race? Could Hughesovka survive two mixed marriages?

Chapter Twenty-six

Offices of New Russia Company, Hughesovka
Good Friday in Russian Julian Calendar, April 8th 1871

Glyn, Richard, and Alexei walked into the company office to find John ensconced in the room he'd furnished as his private work space but rarely occupied. Usually he was out harrying the builders, the colliers, or working with the engineers in a building he'd had erected for them close to the furnaces.

'I didn't expect you three to breeze in here this morning. I thought you'd be out looking at the collieries the Cossacks are trying to sell you, Glyn?'

'I will be after we've talked, sir.'

'Pull up some chairs. Alexei, tell Igor to bring in coffee and pastries for four.'

Alexei closed the door after he'd spoken to John's clerk.

Glyn had never kept bad news from John. 'Alexei believes the Cossacks are planning to attack the Jews.'

'A pogrom? Here in Hughesovka?' If John was surprised he gave no indication of it.

Alexei nodded. 'I can't prove it, sir but the way Misha Razin was exercising his men outside Nathan Kharber's office window this morning was tantamount to a declaration of war.'

Alexei had proved an accurate and useful barometer of local opinion. The boy had been right about too many things since he'd been in the company's employ for John to dismiss his suspicions. 'Would just the Cossack regiment be involved or the villagers as well?'

'I believe just the regiment, sir, although if the soldiers raid the shtetl I've no doubt civilians will join in.'

'Any idea when this is likely to happen?'

'If I was planning an offensive on the shtetl I would set out after dark this evening. Anti-Semites call Jews "Christ killers". Good Friday – the day Jesus died on the cross – is one of the holiest days in the Christian calendar. The Cossacks regard the date as a just one on which to punish Jews. Sunset on Friday also marks the beginning of the Jewish Sabbath. Early this evening every Jew in the shtetl will make their way to the synagogue. At sunset they'll all be together.'

'A neat target for any group.' John pressed his fingertips together. 'Have there been other attacks on the shtetl?'

'Three incidents over the last ten years, sir. One on the Jewish Passover which falls in March, one at Yom Kippur in September seven years ago, and the last on Good Friday three years ago. On each occasion shtetl houses were burned, shops looted and smashed, and Jews who tried to defend their property killed. Six died altogether, one a fourteen-year-old girl. As I was away at school at the time I don't know the details, but my grandmother can tell you more.'

'We can't allow anything like that to happen again.' John lit a cigar and offered the box around.

Alexei shook his head when the box reached him. 'We have to do something in the next few hours, sir.'

John thought for a moment. 'Alexei, you and Richard visit all the Welsh, German, French, Dutch, Scandinavian, and English foremen and managers. Tell them to come here and pick up weapons from the gun cabinets. There won't be enough to go round but after all the hunting rifles and guns have been distributed to the best shots, and tell the foremen to make sure they do go to the best shots, order them to arm their remaining men with staves. Only the nationalities I've mentioned. No Russians are to be armed, not even with a pea shooter or catapult. Is that clear?'

'Yes, sir.' Richard left his chair.

Alexei hesitated. 'I haven't warned the Jews, sir. Do you want me to talk to the rabbi?'

'You're friendly with Nathan Kharber?'

'I talk to him, sir.'

'Suggest he advises the rabbi to postpone prayers in the synagogue until later this evening, or better still tomorrow morning.'

'With respect, sir, you don't know the rabbi, Nathan, or the Jews. They'd as soon think of dancing around the town naked as flouting the laws of their Sabbath.'

'Then tell Nathan to warn the rabbi to bar the doors of the synagogue.'

'If they did that, the Cossacks would fire the building with the congregation inside and shoot anyone who tried to escape.'

'They'd burn people alive?' Glyn was as shocked by Alexei's pronouncement as John and Richard.

'It wouldn't be the first time, sir. There are centuries of bad blood between the Russians and Jews. Because Jews dress and wear their hair differently and observe different traditions they're an easy target to blame for anything that goes wrong. From natural disasters, outbreaks of disease, floods and fires, to any and everyone's personal tragedies. It doesn't help that even some priests call them Christ killers.'

'I've never heard Father Grigor use that term,' John commented.

'He doesn't, Mr Hughes. He and my grandmother do what they can to make the Mujiks and the Cossacks accept the Jews as neighbours, but they don't always succeed.'

'I'm beginning to understand how brave you and your young lady are to contemplate marriage, Alexei. All right, warn Nathan there might be trouble, but tell him I trust him to keep the information to himself and not start a panic. Assure him I'll do everything in my power to protect him and his people and he can rely on me to provide armed men to patrol the shtetl.'

'I can tell you what his answer will be, sir. He'd rather trust in God. The rabbi will never allow armed men, especially Christians, into the settlement. Some Christians regard Jews as heathens. I believe all Jews regard the Christians as just that.'

'In my experience God is too busy to help those who don't help themselves but you don't have to tell Nathan or the rabbi that. Go and see the managers and foremen and tell them to arm themselves. Not you, Glyn. We have people to visit. We'll stop off at the hotel first.'

Hotel Hughesovka
April 1871

'One hundred and fifty pails of vodka, sir?' Gunther Bronski eyed John as if he'd taken leave of his senses.

'You have that much in your cellars?'

'Yes, but if I sell it to you it will leave me short. The officers and men from the regiment drink here.'

'I'm buying it for them. I'll be paying the same price they would, and they can only drink so much.'

'When it comes to Cossack soldiers and officers I wouldn't be too sure of that, sir. They have gullets that would swallow the Don if it ran with vodka and still complain they were thirsty.'

'Name your price.' John took out his wallet. It was stuffed with high-value rouble bills.

'One hundred and fifty pails?'

'One hundred and fifty pails,' John reiterated.

Gunther named a figure. John didn't haggle. He counted out the required number of notes and handed them over. 'Can you deliver the pails to the garrison?'

'Yes, sir.'

'By this afternoon?'

'I'll send the cart out immediately, sir.'

'Thank you. I'll be visiting Colonel Zonov shortly. I hope to see the pails there.'

'You will, Mr Hughes.'

'I knew I could rely on you, Gunther. I'll be in for dinner this week as usual with my managers. Would you care to join us as my guest and share a bottle or two of your good wine?'

'It would be my pleasure, sir.'

John and Glyn left Gunther calling for the cellar man and walked outside to John's sleigh.

'Father Grigor's,' John ordered as they climbed in. 'As soon as we've picked him up we'll go on the garrison.'

'You're hoping to persuade Colonel Zonov to ground the regiment and dole out the vodka as a sweetener?'

'More anaesthetic than sweetener. You know how Cossacks drink.'

'It's a tall order to expect even a Cossack's hang-over to last from Friday to Monday morning.'

'I'll ask the colonel to lock the garrison down for two nights and a day and limit leave from Sunday morning to half a dozen men at a time for a week or two. A pogrom needs a mob. Half a dozen wouldn't be enough given the number of able-bodied men we can call on to assist the Jews. Hopefully the Cossacks will realise that and the vodka will help them to get over any disappointment.'

'I hope your plan works, sir.'

'If the colonel allows me to send in food and a couple of Koshka's girls for the officers as well as the vodka, it might. I'm hoping he'll extend an invitation to us.'

'Us and a couple of men?'

'Just us. We can't afford to exacerbate any suspicions the officers may have about our motives. I've a couple of revolvers we can take. We shouldn't need them but you know me, always over-cautious.'

'Not always, sir. A cautious man wouldn't have come to Russia.'

Hospital, Hughesovka
Good Friday, April 1871

Nathan listened to Alexei. When Alexei finished he left his desk and opened the office door. 'Excuse me, but someone might need me. If they see the door closed they'll assume I'm examining a patient and leave without knocking.'

Exasperated, Alexei looked to Richard who shook his head slightly in a gesture of commiseration. 'Didn't you hear a word I said, Nathan?'

'I heard.'

'You saw Misha parading up and down outside the hospital with his men this morning?'

'Given the commands Misha was shouting, the rattle of sabres, and the sound of the horses' hooves, I couldn't fail to hear. I went to the window to look. They appeared to be on manoeuvres.' Nathan returned to his chair.

'You know what Misha's like...'

'No, I don't,' Nathan interrupted. 'I only know what he was like as a child before I left for Paris. In those days, he was an annoying small boy who thought he knew it all, just like you.'

'Now he's an even more annoying captain in the Cossack regiment who's embraced every prejudice of his race and rank.'

Nathan picked up his white coat from a hook on the wall behind his desk and slipped it over his worn black suit. 'You really believe he's organising an attack on the shtetl?'

'Yes,' Alexei replied.

'Yet you keep telling me that times are changing and miracles are possible in Mr Hughes's new modern industrial town. That all races, including the sons and daughters of Abraham, will be allowed to live in peace alongside Russians and Cossacks and even marry them.'

'I said times are changing, not that they've changed, Nathan. I've warned you what Misha's capable of, but you're not going to do anything about it, are you?'

'What can I do to stop Misha ordering his men to attack the shtetl? If he wants to, he will. All I can do is go about my business and hope he'll change his mind.'

'You can talk to the rabbi and elders so they can take precautions.'

'What precautions? We're not soldiers, we don't fight.'

'Not even when you're threatened?'

'You want to marry my sister knowing so little about us?'

Sensing the atmosphere cooling between Alexei and Nathan, Richard said, 'Surely Misha wouldn't be so stupid as to attack the shtetl knowing he could hurt the only doctor for miles?'

'Misha is stupid enough to do just that.' Sonya was standing in the doorway and none of the men had noticed her.

Nathan walked out. 'Gentlemen, if you'll excuse me, it's time for patient rounds. Sonya, will you take the files to the ward please?'

Sonya entered the office and sorted through the papers on her desk.

'Can you talk sense into him, Sonya?' Alexei pleaded.

'What makes you think I've any influence with Nathan?'

'The same reason I've a little – very little – influence with Ruth.'

She picked up a stack of files. 'I'll try because you asked me, Alexei, but it will be a pointless exercise.'

'Have you talked to Misha lately?'

'Not recently.'

'When was the last time you spoke to him?'

'After Aunt Catherine's dinner party on the British Easter day.'

'Is this personal between you and Misha?'

'I don't know what you mean.'

'Yes, you do,' Alexei contradicted.

'I have no control over Misha.'

Sonya's snapped declaration confirmed what Alexei had suspected. That Misha had nurtured hopes of marrying Sonya which she'd dashed. 'Pity. Perhaps I should talk to Praskovia.'

'Misha hasn't spoken to Praskovia since they quarrelled the last time he called on his family a couple of weeks ago.'

'What did they quarrel about?'

'How should I know?'

'You and Misha...'

'You're seeing romance where there is none,

Alexei. I'm no more in love with Misha than you were with Praskovia.'

'Then I'll try talking to Yelena. Misha must have some regard for his mother.'

'If I were you I wouldn't bother. Cossacks take more notice of and advice from their horses than their women.' Sonya followed Nathan out of the office door.

'Where to now? Across the street to talk to Yelena?' Richard asked after they left the hospital and he and Alexei climbed on their horses.

'No, we take these guns to the steppe to get in some target practice before tonight, and make sure there are a few handguns in the hospital in case they're needed.'

Father Grigor's house, Hughesovka
Good Friday, April 1871

'You want me to accompany you to the garrison?' Father Grigor asked John.

'I know it's Good Friday and you have masses to conduct but we'd appreciate your help in persuading Colonel Zonov to order a curfew.'

'If he agrees, you think the vodka you've sent will be enough to keep the Cossacks within the barracks.'

'I hope so.'

'If it's not?' the priest queried.

'I've armed all the non-Russians in my employ.'

The priest nodded. 'Where will you station them?'

'The shtetl seems the obvious place.'

'The rabbi would never allow them within the walls, but you could station some of your employees here. The upstairs rooms have a view of the road to the shtetl and my housekeeper makes a delicious salt herring salad, just what's needed on Good Friday. As for the rest of your men, the shtetl cemetery isn't a good place to spend a night but the wall affords some shelter. It's also a vantage point that gives a good view of the entire perimeter of the Jewish settlement, but they'll have to sneak in when the Jews aren't looking. After sunset when the Jews will be in the synagogue might be a good time.'

'You've obviously spent time thinking this out. Were you expecting trouble tonight?' John probed.

The priest shrugged his wide shoulders. 'I hear rumours.'

'Like Alexei?'

'We Russians keep our ears to the ground. I'll get my hat and call on Colonel Zonov with you.' He glanced at the clock on the wall. 'There's enough time for me to get back for evening mass.'

'If you and Father Grigor don't need me at the garrison, sir, I could borrow one of the priest's horses, return to Hughesovka, and brief the men. Father Grigor's suggestion makes sense. If we split the armed men into two groups, Alexei could take the half that hide in the shtetl cemetery. Being a local he'll be better placed to placate anyone who'll take exception to them being there.'

'He's very young,' John observed.

'He's not a hothead.'

'He isn't, Glyn, but tell him not to move in

until after dark when there's less risk of being seen, and to keep a low profile. From what Alexei said, the Jews won't be on the lookout for trouble but the Cossacks might. Vlad also has a cool head, tell him to stay with Alexei.'

'Wouldn't he be better left in the hospital, sir, in case there's trouble there because of Nathan, Ruth and the other girls?'

'You're right, leave Vlad in the hospital. Make sure he's armed and warn him what might happen.'

'You did say "no Russian should be armed",' Glyn went to the window and looked at their coachman who was waiting in the carriage.

'Vlad's a company man before he's a Russian. Alf can come here with Richard and help him organise the second group.'

'And us?'

'If I manage to wangle invitations from the colonel for you, me, and the good father we might be able to prevent trouble leaking out from the garrison in the first place.'

Cossack Garrison, Hughesovka
April 1871

Colonel Zonov poured three measures of vodka and handed two to John and Father Grigor. 'The door's closed, we can't be overheard. Let's be clear so there's no misunderstanding. You've sent 150 pails of vodka here as a bribe to keep my officers and men inside the garrison tonight?'

'*All* your officers and men for two nights and a

day starting at sunset,' John confirmed. 'I thought the pails might soften the curfew.'

'You believe if I allow my men to patrol as usual, there'll be trouble in the shtetl?'

John didn't hesitate. 'Yes.'

'I've heard rumblings,' the colonel admitted.

'The Russian communication system never fails to amaze me. It's even faster than the Welsh.'

'Carried by crows across the steppe, or so my grandmother used to say. I think an officers' dinner is called for tonight. Don't concern yourself with providing food, John. We have excellent cooks. And forget Koshka's girls. Given the amount of vodka you've supplied, we'll free the officers from social constraints and make the dinner "gentlemen only". Then they can curse, tell filthy stories, and behave as coarsely as they like. I'll tell my wife to organise something in my private quarters for the officers' ladies. I'll have to leave a dozen officers on duty within the garrison to ensure the men behave but a pail of vodka apiece payable when they're relieved should keep them happy. Have you an excuse for your largesse that I can deliver to allay suspicions the command has been manipulated? Not that the more intelligent won't realise exactly what you've done and your motives for doing it.'

'"The management of The New Russia Company wishes to reward the Cossack Regiment for their hard work in policing Hughesovka and keeping the town ... relatively trouble-free. The gift of vodka is the first instance of an annual tradition during which responsibility for policing the town for forty-eight hours falls on the New Russia

Company staff so the regiment can take a well-earned rest."'

'This annual tradition to take place at the same time every year?'

'It wouldn't become an annual tradition if it didn't,' John said.

The colonel topped up his guests' glasses before his own. 'Next you'll be telling me this new tradition of the New Russia Company has nothing to do with the celebration of Christ Arisen.'

'Pure coincidence,' John concurred.

'I'll make the announcement, cancel all leave, and order all officers and men to be within the walls of the garrison two hours before sunset this evening. Officers to dine at nine o'clock. You will join us, Father, Mr Hughes?'

'After midnight mass, I'd be delighted,' Father Grigor said.

'I'll send an escort to accompany you from the church.'

'No need. No Cossack would attack a priest. I'll make my own way here.'

'As you wish,' the colonel nodded.

'I, together with my associate, Mr Edwards, will be delighted to accept your kind invitation, Colonel Zonov.'

The colonel made a wry face. 'On behalf of my officers and men, thank you for the vodka, Mr Hughes. I'll try to ensure it is enjoyed in the spirit it was given.'

Hospital, Hughesovka
April 1871

'Mr Hughes appointed me director of this hospital. I refuse to allow guns on the premises. This is a place of healing, not killing, Alexei.' Nathan was unequivocal.

'Just one in the office,' Alexei pleaded. 'That way should staff be threatened it could be used as a deterrent.'

'I've never held a gun and I have no intention of doing so now.'

'Sonya knows how to use one.' Alexei looked at her. She ignored him and continued to sit, silent and expressionless at her desk. 'As does Mrs Edwards and Anna. I could leave it...'

'Absolutely not, Alexei.'

'The Cossacks have guns.'

'I'm not a Cossack. If you'll excuse me, a mother has just brought her sick child in from Alexandrovka. I need to examine the boy.' Nathan left, crossed the corridor entered the examination room, and closed the door behind him.

Alexei looked at Richard in despair.

'Leave it with me, sir.' Vlad stepped in from the hall where he'd overheard the altercation. He was carrying the canvas bag that held his prized Berdan rifle. 'Dr Kharber doesn't go into the porters' dining room, and we often bring our guns in so we can go straight out on to the steppe to hunt when we finish our shifts.'

'You'll be going out hunting after your next shift, Vlad?' Alexei asked.

'I won't be free until tomorrow morning, sir. If

I'm tired I may rest and delay my hunting trip, but I like to keep my rifle close in case I have a sudden burst of energy.' He winked at Alexei before disappearing.

'Does Nathan go into your desk, Sonya?' Alexei asked.

She glanced at the open door before shaking her head.

Alexei stood in front of the door, blocking the view of the office from the corridor. He handed Sonya a pistol. She placed it at the back of the top drawer behind a stack of envelopes.

'You'll tell the others it's there?' Alexei whispered.

Sonya nodded.

Glyn Edwards' house, Hughesovka
April 1871

Praskovia picked up Glyn's tie and handed it to him. 'You look very handsome in a dinner suit. Good enough to eat.'

'I hope not. The last thing I want is a load of Cossacks chewing on me.' He pulled at his collar. 'I can't breathe with anything this tight around my neck.'

'The Cossacks say if you complain about a tight collar it means you were hung in a previous life.'

'I didn't know Cossacks believe in reincarnation.'

'We don't. It's just a saying.'

'This waistcoat has shrunk.' He failed to bring the buttons and buttonholes together.

'That fabric doesn't shrink. It's time you took a trip to the shtetl and asked Mr Blumberg to either let out your clothes or make you a new evening suit and waistcoat.'

'I will, when I find the time.' He turned to face her so she could tie his bow tie. 'It's your fault my clothes are tight. The meals you serve are enormous.'

'My mother prepares them. If you're concerned about putting on weight take smaller helpings.'

'I would if everything didn't taste so good.'

'There, finished. The perfect Welsh gentleman.' She gave his tie a final tweak.

He checked his reflection in the cheval mirror. 'Has Misha said anything to you about the Jews or the shtetl?'

'No, but I told you, Misha hasn't spoken to me since we argued two weeks ago.'

'What I can't understand is why he's planning trouble now. That's if Alexei's right and Misha's plotting to attack the shtetl tonight.'

'Has Alexei said Misha's behind it?'

'Alexei said he was concerned when he saw Misha exercising his men in front of the hospital this morning.'

'You men aren't very bright. Misha's not angry with the Jews – at least not all of them. He's in love with Sonya and Sonya...'

'Sonya's what?' Glyn was confused.

'It's not my place to say.'

'She's not in love with Misha.'

'She isn't.'

'She's in love with someone else?'

'I think so.'

'Who?'

'That's her business.'

'As she works in the hospital, I can guess.'

'You won't say anything to her, will you?' Praskovia pleaded.

'No.' He poured two glasses of French burgundy and handed her one. 'You're trembling. Not working too hard, are you?'

'I could tell you I have an evil master who whips his servants and makes them work day and night but you know I'd be lying. Go. Enjoy your men's dinner.'

'And you?'

'I'll pray Mr Hughes's plan works.'

'What plan?'

'It's no secret you and Mr Hughes are trying to stop a pogrom by getting Colonel Zonov to impose a curfew on a drunken garrison.'

'Who else knows?'

'It would easier to tell you who didn't in Hughesovka.'

'Do you think the Cossacks in the village will cause trouble?'

'I think they'll remember who pays their wages and stay home this evening.'

'I hope you're right.' He finished his wine.

'You will take care of yourself?'

'Surely that isn't a tear?' He took a handkerchief from his pocket and blotted her cheek.

'I'll have to get you a clean one.' She turned aside so he couldn't see her face, opened a drawer, and handed him another.

He frowned. 'You need to rest. You'll go to bed early tonight?'

'I was going to wait up for you.'

'We won't leave the garrison before dawn unless...'

'There's trouble.' She said what he couldn't bring himself to say.

'There won't be,' he said with more assurance than he felt. He took his watch from his waistcoat. 'Mr Hughes will be here any moment. 'See you in the morning, my love.' He kissed her. Praskovia's concern for him was touching and frightening. Frightening because he could no more bear the thought of anything happening to her than she could him, and after Peter's untimely death, he was all too aware of the fragility of life.

Garrison, Hughesovka
April 1871

At first light a corporal marched to the door of the duty office next to the gate and rapped on it with his knuckles. He waited for permission to enter before opening the door.

'Colonel Zonov has sent for you, Captain Razin.'

'Thank you, corporal, dismissed.'

'Sir.' The corporal snapped to attention and marched off.

Misha turned, 'Kirill, fetch Isay. You both know what to do?'

'Yes, sir.'

'Hughes first. Then the Jew. You have your passes?'

'Yes, sir.' Kirill handed them to him.

Misha checked the barely decipherable signature. He'd tricked the officer who'd taken delivery of John Hughes's vodka into signing the documents after he'd sampled more of a pail than was good for his senses.

He returned the passes to Kirill. 'Your horses are saddled?'

'Sir.'

'Go.'

Misha waited until he'd heard the gates open and close, so he could truthfully say he hadn't seen Kirill or Isay leave the garrison He straightened his tunic, fastened his top button and left the office.

'Man the doors until you're relieved,' he ordered the sentries. 'No one leaves without a pass.'

The sentries snapped to attention.

John stood between Glyn and Colonel Zonov at the window of the officers' mess. The officers who hadn't stumbled to their beds were slumped over the table snoring in an unmelodic chorus. Father Grigor had taken leave an hour ago after promising to pass messages on to Alexei and Richard, telling them to stand their men down.

'Dawn?' Glyn said as light began to creep up from the shadowy parade ground below them.

'It always seems a miracle we're not sentenced to live in perpetual darkness. Little wonder primitive man worshipped the sun. Well, gentlemen, aside from a few bruised heads and frayed tempers among the men and a couple of black eyes among the officers, so ends an uneventful night.' Colonel Zonov lifted his glass to John. 'Congratulations.'

'There's still a day and a night to go,' John reminded.

'The state the parade ground and I've no doubt the barracks are in, it'll take forty-eight hours to return to the garrison to a military standard of cleanliness and that's without allowing the injured time to lick their wounds.'

'If you'll excuse us, Colonel Zonov, we'll return to the town. Thank you for a wonderful meal and memorable hospitality.'

'My pleasure. I'll order your sleigh.'

John and Glyn waited by the window until they saw one of the company's junior employees drive John's sleigh across the yard.

'He looks lively,' Glyn observed, 'I wonder where he hid out last night?'

'A hay loft judging by the wisps stuck to his back. From the look in his eyes I'd say he managed a few hours' sleep, which is remarkable considering the racket the soldiers were making.'

'I've never seen a man ride in a saddle on his head before.'

'We must invite you to our annual open day, Mr Edwards, Mr Hughes.' The colonel returned with two officers. Glyn recognised Praskovia's brother.

'We've met,' he held out his hand. 'Captain Razin, isn't it?'

'It is, sir.'

'Help those of your brother officers who are unable to walk to their beds, captain, lieutenant,' Colonel Zonov ordered. 'I want this room cleared in ten minutes.'

'Sir.' Misha snapped to attention.

'Was that your housekeeper's brother?' John

asked Glyn as they followed the colonel down the stairs.

'It was.'

'He doesn't look happy.'

'I doubt any of the officers on duty last night will be smiling,' the colonel said. 'But they have tonight and pails of vodka to look forward to.'

John stretched as he looked up at the sky. 'I've a feeling not much work is going to be done on the company sites today.'

'None would be done at all if your workers had to clear up after a pogrom in the shtetl, Mr Hughes,' Colonel Zonov replied.

Chapter Twenty-seven

Cemetery outside the Shtetl, Hughesovka
April 1871

Alexei hung back with Father Grigor as the last of the Company men left the shtetl cemetery. Rifles slung over their shoulders, they walked through the gate, their silhouettes blending with the soft grey light of dawn as they headed for the copse that concealed their sleighs. After the first vehicle moved out and headed west towards Hughesovka, Alexei and the priest mounted their horses.

'It's a fine thing Mr Hughes did this night,' Father Grigor declared.

'It would be a finer thing, Father, if the Cossacks and Mujiks learned to live peaceably with the Jews.'

'It would, Alexei. But what chance is there for different races to live peacefully side by side when there is frequently discord under the same roof.'

'If you're thinking of me and my father I can't argue with you, Father.'

'But today at least there will be quiet in the shtetl. Would you breakfast with me? I happen to know Brin's baked more Easter bread than my household can eat.'

As it would take him half an hour to ride to town, Alexei accepted. 'Thank you.'

'Looks like the rest of Mr Hughes's men are leaving my house now.'

Alexei rose in his stirrups to take a closer look. The men who'd spent the night in the priest's house were climbing into sleighs ranged up in front of the door. He spotted Richard mounting his horse.

'If you'll excuse me, Father, I'll ride ahead and persuade Richard to stay for breakfast as well so we can ride into town together.'

'Brin would like nothing better than to have two good-looking young men at my table.'

Alexei waved to Richard but his friend was staring north, over the steppe. Alexei looked in the direction Richard was studying. A company sleigh, bearing the unmistakeable fur-coated figures of John and Glyn was heading from the garrison towards Hughesovka. A shot rang out, whistling loud and ominous over the snow-blanketed waste.

One man in the sleigh jerked backwards, the other grabbed him to stop him from falling from the open sided vehicle. Alexei watched Richard rein in his horse and lift his rifle to his shoulder. He spurred Agripin on as a second shot echoed across the steppe.

The steppe outside the Shtetl, Hughesovka
April 1871

The uniformed Cossack swayed in the saddle. Slowly, infinitely slowly, he slumped on his horse's neck before tumbling headlong to the ground. Richard was aware of hoof beats thundering behind him, but he urged his horse into a gallop.

'Mr Edwards...'

'I'm all right, Richard.' Glyn was holding his right shoulder. Blood poured from a bullet hole, soaking his fur overcoat.

'Mr Hughes?'

'I'm fine, Richard, thanks to you, and Glyn who took the bullet intended for me. We'd better see if our assailant needs help.'

Richard turned his horse. The Cossack was lying on the snow in front of his mount. A pool of iced blood soaked the left hand side of his jacket but his eyes were open. He was holding a standard issue, single shot Berdan rifle. Knowing there'd been no time for the soldier to reload, Richard dismounted, grabbed the barrel, and threw it aside as a third shot rang out, scattering the birds from the skeletal branches of a nearby tree.

John's driver ducked instinctively as he reined in the horses.

Richard looked around. Alexei was galloping

towards them, brandishing his rifle. There was no sign of his target. The sleigh drew to a halt. John made Glyn remove his coat so he could check his wound.

'A flesh wound,' John helped Glyn fasten his coat.

'You could have taken my word for it, sir,' Glyn grumbled.

'Just making sure you're not being a hero.' John left the sleigh and walked over to Richard.

'A Cossack. Wounded but alive, sir.' Richard informed John.

Alexei charged up in a thunder of hooves and flurry of snow. 'A Cossack we don't have to worry about, unlike the one I missed who rode away. You all right, Mr Edwards?' He looked anxiously at Glyn who'd remained in the sleigh.

'Fine, Alexei, no bones broken, just a nick.'

'If you're going to get shot, it's as well to wear a thick coat that can absorb the impact.'

'Did you recognise the second Cossack?' John asked.

'He was too far away for me to make out his features.' Alexei dismounted and walked over to the man on the ground. 'But I know this one. He's Yulia's brother, Kirill.' Alexei crouched beside him. 'Why did you shoot Mr Edwards?' Alexei jerked his head sideways to avoid the gob of spittle Kirill aimed at him.

'Get him to my house, so Brin can tend to him. You too, Mr Edwards.' Father Grigor caught up with them on his ancient mare.

'Thank you, Father. But as Glyn's not seriously hurt and this creature doesn't look as though he's in imminent danger of dying, I'd rather go to the hospital in Hughesovka, and keep an eye out for that second Cossack on the way.' John picked up the Cossack's rifle that Richard had kicked aside.

'Someone should ride over to the garrison and tell Colonel Zonov about this.' Glyn took the clean handkerchief Father Grigor handed him and used it to plug his wound.

'I agree. I'd rather hand over this man to the colonel for punishment after his wounds have been treated than deal with him. Richard, you and Alexei go to the garrison, but keep a sharp look out in case that Cossack is lying in wait,' John ordered. 'The last thing we need is more bloodshed. Help me get this scoundrel into the sleigh first.'

Richard and Alexei pulled Kirill to his feet. John's driver produced a length of leather whipping that Alexei used to fasten Kirill's wrists behind his back. Father Grigor helped manhandle him into the sleigh.

'If you're not too tired, Father, we'd be glad of your company,' John said. 'I hate to impose but I would like to know how many people want me dead and this man may be less likely to lie to a man of God than me.'

'I can try to persuade Kirill to entertain us with conversation on the journey. Mr Hughes.'

'We'll take your horse back to your house, Father,' Alexei took the reins from the priest before mounting Agripin.

'Remember what I said about keeping a sharp look out,' John shouted as they rode off.

The steppe and Hughesovka
April 1871

Isay saw Kirill's bullet hit one of the men in John Hughes's sleigh. He'd also seen Kirill fall to the ground. As a Cossack would rather die than be unhorsed, he presumed his companion was either dead or mortally wounded. He recalled Misha's warning. If John Hughes wasn't stopped, the Jews would take over Hughesovka. It had been Kirill's job to kill John Hughes, his to kill the Jewish doctor. If Kirill hadn't succeeded, that was Captain Razin's problem. There was no way he was going to fail in the task his captain had entrusted to him. He turned his horse towards Hughesovka.

He stopped when he reached the sheds used to store building materials on the outskirts of town. They were locked, and from the noise emanating from the beer house most workers were already celebrating Christ Arisen. He knocked the lock from a door with the hilt of his sword, walked his horse inside, and tethered it to a hook on the wall. Buckets of water were ranged next to stacks of concrete bricks and bags of cement. He tasted the water to make sure it was clean before placing one of the buckets within reach of his horse.

A worker's jacket lay on a stack of bricks. He pulled it on over his uniform. It hid his tunic but not the red stripes down his trousers. He slit open a bag of cement with his sword and rubbed the grey dust into his trousers. He left the shed and glanced around. Men armed with hunting rifles were patrolling in front of the hospital. He walked away from them, before circling around to the back of the building.

Kirill had told him that the Jewish doctor lived in a separate block behind the hospital and Kirill should know after spending time there as a patient. All he had to do was lie in wait. If he used his sword there'd be no noise.

No noise at all.

Hospital, Hughesovka
April 1871

'I'll leave you in Matron's capable hands, Glyn,' John flattened himself against the wall as two porters carried Kirill, thrashing and cursing, into the treatment room. 'The sooner I return to the office, the sooner I can get more men out on patrol around the town. I'm worried about that second Cossack.'

'That second Cossack will be halfway to Taganrog by now,' Father Grigor prophesied.

'I'll post more men outside, Vlad. If you need more send to the office.' John said.

'Don't concern yourself, sir. I'll patrol the inside of the building myself and leave two men on duty in the hall and corridor, although I think Father Grigor is right. That Cossack is long gone.'

'You'll send word to the office on Glyn's condition – and Kirill's?' John asked.

'Of course, Mr Hughes.' Sarah waited until John and Father Grigor left before turning to Glyn who was slumped, white faced on a chair in the corridor. 'As Nathan's in the treatment room, we'll use the dressing station, Glyn.'

'I'm fine, Sarah. Stop fussing and tend to your other patient.'

'I can see how fine you are, Glyn,' Sarah snapped, concern for him making her terse. 'As for our other patient, Nathan is seeing to him, although after the idiot took a pot shot at you, don't think he deserves medical care.'

'You'd leave him outside to freeze to death?'

'It would have solved a number of problems if Richard had taken better aim.'

'Given the distance, I'm amazed Richard hit him, and coming from you that's vicious. You can't really want the man dead?'

'The beast shot you, I feel anything but magnanimous towards him.'

'He has a bullet in him.'

'Which is good. Now behave like an adult, go into the dressing station, and let me see to your wound.'

Glyn finally allowed her to lead him into the tiny room.

'Sit.' She pointed to an examination couch.

He jumped on the high seat, removed his coat, and looked ruefully at his dinner jacket. 'Damned man ... sorry for the language. But he's ruined a perfectly good fur coat, evening suit, and shirt.'

'I'll ask Praskovia to take them to the tailor in the shtetl. If he can't repair them he can use them as a pattern so you can replace them.'

'I suppose the jacket and shirt were tight.'

She helped him take off his evening jacket and collar. Dried blood had glued his vest and shirt to his skin. She soaked the fabric and peeled it gently away before studying the wound, and probing it gently with her fingertips. 'You're right, no bones are broken.' She filled a bowl with water and antiseptic. 'This will sting.'

'You mean it will be agonising.'

'Didn't Peter tell you all doctors and nurses love to inflict pain?'

'I watched him kill the ants in our mother's pantry with boiling water when he was four or five years old. He had a gleeful look on his face.'

'Peter the ant murderer. That's something he never told me.'

'I wonder if all medical personnel have something of the sadist in them.' He winced when she irrigated the wound and swabbed it with cotton wool and gauze.

'First lesson new staff are given is how to ignore people who complain.' She probed the area around the entry and exit holes to make sure there was no residue left inside. 'There, all done apart from the bandaging. I'll give you something for the pain. Then you go home, put your feet up, or better still go to bed. I'll look in on you when I finish my shift.'

'Forget the pills. I'll ask Praskovia to bring me a brandy.'

'One, maybe two, no more,' she lectured. 'You've had a shock.'

'I've survived worse.'

'No doubt. But if you've any sense you'll stay out of rifle range in future.'

'I'll take an umbrella with me the next time it rains bullets.'

'I'm serious, Glyn. A lot of people depend on

you ... need you ... love you...'

'Hey,' he grabbed her hand. 'I'm indestructible.'

She was about to say Peter thought he was too, when Nathan knocked and opened the door.

'What's the prognosis?'

'A flesh wound, cleaned and bandaged, although he moaned a lot,' Sarah answered.

'My commiserations, Glyn. She can be brutal.'

'Glyn knows how brutal I am. I was about to send him on his way.'

'Good. I need you to help me operate on Kirill. The bullet's lodged in a rib. It's shattered the bone and there are splinters in his lung. Rivka and Ruth are preparing the theatre now. I've asked Rivka to assist. She needs more theatre practice.'

'As soon as I've found someone to clear up here I'll be with you.'

'Ruth can do it when she's finished in the theatre. Anna and Miriam are on the ward. I thought it best to send Yulia home.'

'Will her brother live?' Glyn asked.

'There's no clinical reason why Kirill shouldn't survive the operation and live until he's ninety. However I won't answer for his chances if he persists in shooting innocent people.'

'Hopefully Colonel Zonov will cure him of that tendency after we hand him back.' Glyn jumped down from the examination couch. Faint, he grabbed the door handle.

'I'll get one of the porters to take you home.'

Weak, irritable, Glyn snapped, 'For pity's sake, Sarah, it's across the road.'

'A slippery, snow- and ice-covered road that's busy with traffic.'

'It's useless to argue with her,' Nathan advised.

'So I see.' Glyn put his coat on over the bandages and picked up the bundle Sarah had made of his bloodied clothes. 'All right, Matron, call a porter, and thank you for putting me back together,' he added by way of an apology for his outburst.

'I'll see you when I get home. Don't forget...'

'Rest,' Glyn finished. 'I will as soon as I've helped Mr Hughes dig the foundations for the church he's building and finished erecting the furnaces and...'

'You must be feeling better if you can tease me.' She kissed his cheek.

Sarah watched the porter help Glyn to his front door, before checking the ward. She called in on Ruth who was cleaning the treatment room and reminded her to sterilize the dressing station. Finally she went into the office. Sonya had compiled the lists of supplies they needed and was putting on her coat ready to take them down to company headquarters.

'One of the porters can do that,' Sarah said.

'I heard Lyudmila's finished making her Easter bread. I thought I'd bring some back for the porters.'

'Then take a porter with you.'

'You think that Cossack is in Hughesovka?'

'Take one with you, just in case,' Sarah repeated.

Nathan called to Sarah.

'Save me and Nathan some Easter bread, please, Ruth,' Sarah said. 'We'll need it after we've finished operating. Bone fragments in lungs are always tricky.'

Glyn Edwards' house, Hughesovka
April 1871

Praskovia ran to meet Glyn as soon as he walked through the door. 'Mrs Edwards sent a message to say you weren't badly hurt but you'd need to rest, master. Your bed's ready. Pyotr's stoked the fire. Are you hungry, thirsty? Here, let me take that from you.' She took his bundle of clothes and handed it to a maid.

'I'm in need of rest from fussing females. I don't know who's worse, you or Sarah.' Glyn opened the door to his room. As usual, a fire was burning in the hearth, the brandy decanter and glass set out.

'Can I get you...'

'Nothing, Praskovia,' he said in a softer tone after she'd closed the door. 'I really am all right. If I need you I'll call you.'

'Yes, master.'

He poured himself a brandy, took a cigar from the presentation box John had given him for Christmas, and sat down.

Even when the bullet hit home, all he'd thought about was Praskovia. Her correct, subservient, and distant manner, so appropriate in a servant, so infuriating in a lover and so different from the way she behaved when she visited him at night. He was obsessed, entranced, and bewitched to the point where he could think of nothing and no one else.

The back door that connected to the servants'

quarters opened and Praskovia stood, framed in the doorway.

'Ask if you can get me anything and I'll ... I'll...' He couldn't even shout at her lest one of the other servants overhear.

'You'll what, master?'

He wondered if it was his imagination or if she was laughing at him. 'Given the way you behave towards me in the day I wonder if our nights are a dream.'

'If they are, I dream them too, master.'

'I'm not your bloody master.'

'Not here in this room at night you're not.' She locked the door behind her.

'What are you doing?'

'The door was open; I thought you'd need...'

'Something?'

'Me.'

'After the way you treat me. Curtseying, waiting on my every whim.'

'I'm your housekeeper, Glyn.'

It was the first time she'd spoken his name and he loved the way she said it. 'You're my lover.'

'In private.'

'I'd prefer you to drop the housekeeper and settle for being my lover.'

'You were the one who reminded me that you're married and all you can offer me is the loss of my reputation unless we keep our relationship secret.'

'I'm not sure I can keep it secret.'

'If you don't, I'd be in trouble. I don't know what it's like in your country but here people like to gossip and condemn the way their neighbours live.'

'In my experience people think and behave the same the world over. Only languages are different. Our nights...'

'Are wonderful.'

'We agree on something.' He returned her smile.

'You know I check the back door to this room every evening before I go to bed. You might not know there is a door in the passage beyond my room. It also has a lock. I told my mother and the other servants I keep it secured except at meal times to safeguard the china and silver cupboards. No servant knows where I spend my nights, other than my mother, who guessed, but only because she saw the way I look at you.'

'And every morning you leave my bed before the rest of household rises and spend your days serving me and curtsying...'

'Because that way no one will suspect I'm anything more than your housekeeper.' She curled up on the floor beside his chair and rested her head on his knee. 'I've told the servants you're sleeping and I'm working on the household accounts in my room and not to be disturbed.'

'So we have an hour or two to ourselves.' He stroked her hair. 'You look tired.'

'I couldn't sleep last night for worrying about you and the others.'

'The bed is over there.'

'I hoped you'd say that.'

'I'm not fit for much other than sleep.'

'Neither am I, but it would be good to sleep together.' She rose and held out her hand.

Hospital, Hughesovka
April 1871

Ruth finished cleaning the treatment room and dressing station and lifted out the enamel bin that held the soiled gauze and cotton wool. She called the porters and told them to empty it. After scrubbing her hands in the sink of the treatment room, she went to the ward. The patients had finished their midday meal. Miriam had cleared away the trays and Anna was settling them down for their afternoon naps.

'Tea?' Ruth asked.

'Please,' Anna replied.

'I'll bring it in so we can update the patient charts while we drink it.' Ruth went into the kitchen, picked up the kettle from the stove, and realised from its weight there wasn't enough water to make three cups of tea. She filled it at the pump over the sink before setting it on the stove.

She found a tin of Easter biscuits a grateful patient's family had sent in and arranged a selection on a plate. She was setting out cups and saucers on a tray when she glanced through the window that overlooked the back of the building. Vlad was outside the staff quarters talking to the porters she'd asked to empty the bin. The reflection of a man was staring back at her. She realised he was standing behind her and whirled round. Before she could scream, the man pushed his hand into her mouth, lifted her off her feet and away from the window. He rammed her against a low cupboard.

'I know you. You're the Jew doctor's sister. Time

for some fun.' He thrust his hand up her skirt.

'Ruth's slow with the tea,' Miriam said to Anna.

'Stove's probably playing up. It went out twice yesterday. I'll see if I can help.' Anna left the ward and walked down the corridor. She looked through the glass window into the kitchen and saw a man, his back turned to her, pushing Ruth down over a cupboard.

Ruth's eyes, enormous terrified, stared blindly over his shoulder.

Anna was instantly transported back to the court in Merthyr. She smelled the stench of stagnant water. Shuddered with the same fear that had paralysed her when Ianto and Mervyn Paskey had carried her down the steps into Jenny Swine's kitchen. Tasted again the metallic tang of sheer terror when she'd found herself alone, isolated, and powerless in the face of the Paskeys' brutal savagery. Relived the shame of being stripped, the humiliation of the indignities they heaped on her...

She'd been helpless then but she wasn't now. And she wouldn't allow anyone to do to Ruth what the Paskeys had done to her.

She ran into the office, wrenched open the top drawer of Sonya's desk, took the gun and charged back to the corridor.

Anna remembered what Alexei had taught her. She faced the glass window.

'*Balance – take aim – squeeze the trigger.*'

She pointed the barrel at the centre of the man's back and fired ... once ... twice ... three times.

She kicked the kitchen door open after he'd crumpled to the floor and fired again. Four ...

five ... six...

She could hear Alexei's voice echoing in her head. '*Most hand guns hold six bullets. These Smith & Wesson models hold seven. They're the first firearm to use metal-cased cartridges. Your target won't move again if you hit it.*'

Seven...

The man on the floor stopped moving. She was aware of Ruth sobbing. Of Vlad and another porter running towards her. Of Sarah, bloody from the theatre, hugging her.

'He was hurting Ruth. I'm not sorry. I'll never be sorry. He was hurting Ruth...'

'I know, darling. You were brave...' Sarah's tears, harsh salt mingled with hers.

Anna lifted her face defiantly. 'I'm not sorry. I'll never be sorry.'

Chapter Twenty-eight

Hospital Complex, Hughesovka
April 1871

Nathan glanced out of the window of his private quarters at midnight to see Vlad sharing a flask with Alexei and Richard. All three were standing at the back of the hospital a few feet from his front door. He put on his coat and joined them.

'How's Ruth?' Alexei asked.

'Sleeping in her room with Anna and Mrs Edwards.'

'No, I'm not, Nathan.' Barefoot, a wool shawl draped around her nightgown, Ruth stepped on to the veranda. Alexei went to her. She wrapped her arms around him, buried her face in his shoulder, and hugged him.

Embarrassed at witnessing such an intimate scene, Richard and Vlad moved into the shadows.

'You all right?' Alexei asked Ruth.

'Thanks to Anna. She and Sarah are staying with me.'

'Nathan told me.'

'Tell your grandmother I received her letter, Alexei, and Ruth and I would be pleased to accept her invitation to drink tea with her the first Sunday of next month.'

Ruth lifted her head and looked at her brother. 'You mean it, Nathan?'

'I mean it. Go back to bed before you catch pneumonia.'

Ruth hugged him before disappearing inside.

'I will look after Ruth, Nathan,' Alexei promised.

'I don't doubt it, Alexei. After today, I've had to accept she needs more looking after than I have time to give her.'

'I have a spare revolver. I can teach you how to use it.'

'No. Thank you, but no, Alexei. That's Vlad's job. I'll see you on Sunday. Goodnight, Richard, Vlad.' Nathan followed Ruth into the house.

Glyn Edwards' house, Hughesovka
Russian Easter Day 1871

Richard left the breakfast table when he saw Anna walk in. He took her bag from her. 'Let me carry that upstairs for you.' He ran up, opened her bedroom door, and dropped it inside.

'Thank you.' She walked up behind him.

'How's Ruth and how are you?'

'Ruth's recovering and I'm fine. Why wouldn't I be?'

'Because you shot a man yesterday.'

'I killed a man yesterday,' she corrected. 'And I'd do it again. No man has the right to put his hand up a woman's skirt.'

He was struck by her vehemence. His suspicions as to what exactly the Paskey brothers had done to her surfaced – again. 'Look, Anna…'

'What?' She confronted him.

'I'm your brother. I love you. I'm proud of you. Everyone is. That brute could have killed Ruth.'

Tight-lipped, she nodded.

'We're so busy, me with Mr Edwards, you in the hospital, we never have time to talk. I want you to know I'm here if you should need me for anything. Anything at all.'

'I know, Richard, and I'm grateful, but I don't want to go over what happened yesterday again. That's all I've done since I fired the gun.' Her eyes were bright, burning.

'Love you,' he repeated impotently.

'Love you too.' She went into her room and closed the door.

'Don't try and make her talk before she's ready,

Richard.' Sarah was on the top stair behind him. 'Anna will talk to you when the time's right for her. She knows you love her.'

He nodded. She took his hand. He squeezed it gently before running back down the stairs.

Dower House, Beletsky Estate
Russian Easter Day, April 1871

Boris opened the door to Alexei, who'd been invited to join Catherine and Sonya at the family lunch Catherine had asked Lyudmila to prepare.

'Good wishes on Christ Arisen to you and all the servants, Boris. For the servants.' Alexei handed him a selection of the chocolate eggs John had ordered from Moscow.

'Thank you, sir. Greetings on Christ Arisen to you.' Boris showed him into the drawing room. Sonya was sitting on the rug in front of the hearth playing with his baby sister. Kira smiled and clapped her hands when she saw him.

'She recognises her big brother,' Sonya moved to make room for Alexei. 'You can take over building brick towers for her to knock down.'

'I have something better than wooden bricks.' Alexei took a parcel from his pocket and gave it to Kira. She dropped it. He unwrapped it.

'Alexei, that's beautiful.' Sonya examined the jointed wooden doll. 'The clothes are exquisitely made and the face beautifully painted. If I didn't know better I'd say it was made by Papa Pavlo.'

'Yelena made the clothes. Praskovia painted the face, Pyotr carved the doll.'

'Looks like Mr Edwards doesn't keep his servants too busy. Thank you for coming, Alexei,' Catherine poured coffee. 'How are Ruth and Anna?'

'Shocked, shaken, but recovering. Neither is hurt but you must have heard that.'

'Mrs Edwards sent a note in reply to mine enquiring after the girls. She said Anna will need time to come to terms with killing a man.'

'She has the consolation that the brute deserved it.'

'Amen to that,' Catherine agreed. 'I also see you didn't waste any time giving Nathan and Ruth the invitation we discussed.'

'You've had a reply?'

'This morning. Nathan said he'd be happy to bring his sister here the first Sunday afternoon in May.'

'Our Sabbath is not the Jewish day of prayer.'

'I know.'

'You will be here when they come won't you, Sonya?' Alexei checked.

'I promised Anna and Richard I'd visit that day.'

'When did you promise?' Alexei challenged.

'It was a promise made in advance.'

'In other words you've just made it up.'

'Alexei, I love you like a brother and Ruth is a wonderful friend. I hope it works out for both of you, but I'd rather not be around during the working out.' What Sonya didn't say was she didn't want to hear Nathan outline all the arguments against inter-religious marriage.

'I'm a grown-up; I can stand a tongue-lashing

from Grandmother and Nathan without your support.' Alexei picked up the coffee his grandmother had poured him.

'Thinking ahead, Alexei, if you marry Ruth...'

'When I marry Ruth,' Alexei contradicted his grandmother.

'When you marry Ruth,' she corrected to appease him, 'it might be as well you do so with as little fuss as possible. No formal engagement, no announcement, just a simple wedding that takes everyone by surprise. How many people have you told already?'

'You, Sonya, Nathan, and Ruth, and none of them is likely to broadcast the news.'

'I told Mr Hughes and Mr Edwards when they came for lunch two weeks ago,' Catherine confessed.

'How did they react?'

'They toasted you and Ruth and wished you well. As you said, Mr Hughes and Mr Edwards pay no credence to differences of race or religion. Will Ruth move into Glyn Edwards' house with you after you're married?'

'She could.' Alexei considered his grandmother's suggestion. 'I was hoping to buy or rent a house of our own but there's plenty of room in Mr Edwards'. My bedroom is enormous, and has a sitting and study area. Should Ruth want to carry on working in the hospital it's only across the road and with Anna, Mrs Edwards, Richard, and Mr Edwards in the house she'd be living among friends. Thank you for the suggestion, Grandmother.'

'I'm not sure I meant to give it to you.'

'But you're right; we should marry sooner rather than later.'

'Don't make too many plans, Alexei,' Catherine warned. 'Your father may have washed his hands of you but Nathan and his Uncle Asher are still Ruth's guardians. Don't do anything to annoy them.'

'As if I would, but do you have any reason in particular for saying that?' Alexei sat next to Kira and lifted her on to his lap.

'I won't say more than Mr Hughes is considering making a few changes.'

'Ones that will affect the Cossacks and the Jews?'

'He told me that after what happened with Isay and Kirill, he's anxious to ensure there's no more trouble.'

'There won't be if Colonel Zonov succeeds in controlling his troops in general, and one officer in particular.'

'You don't know for certain Misha ordered Isay and Kirill to attack Mr Hughes and Ruth,' Sonya protested.

'I'm certain he didn't, but I'm quite sure he ordered them to attack Mr Hughes and Nathan. I think the assault on Ruth was a spontaneous decision on the part of Isay when he saw her alone in the kitchen.'

'Has Kirill implicated Misha?'

'Kirill's refusing to say a word. Colonel Zonov believes the passes Kirill and Isay used to leave the garrison were forged. The officer who signed them has no memory of doing so, but like most of the garrison he was drunk when they left. No knows how Kirill and Isay acquired them, as all unsigned passes are kept locked in a cupboard that only officers have access to.'

'Have you heard what's going to happen to Kirill?' Sonya asked.

'Colonel Zonov met Mr Edwards and Mr Hughes in the Hotel this morning to discuss the matter.'

'You were there?'

'Richard and I were present. Kirill will be posted to a punishment battalion in Siberia as soon as he's well enough to travel. Until then, he'll remain under guard in the hospital and, when he can be moved, the garrison. Isay's body is being returned to his family.'

'Yulia?' Sonya questioned.

'Wants to carry on working in the hospital and Nathan and Sarah are happy for her to continue her training.'

'There's no reason why she should be punished for what her brother did,' Catherine observed. 'So, the guilty have been killed and punished and the incident is history?'

'And Misha free to drip his anti-Semitic poison into the head of any idiot prepared to listen.'

'You have no proof...' Sonya began.

'I don't need it, Sonya, and if you were honest with yourself, you wouldn't either,' Alexei cut in.

Sonya fell silent. She didn't want to believe Misha capable of instigating murder but Alexei's anger was understandable in the face of what Ruth and Anna had suffered.

Glyn Edwards' house, Hughesovka
May 1871

Glyn lay on the bedcover, watching the flames lick around the logs Pyotr had piled on the fire. His head was on a feather pillow, his arm wrapped around Praskovia. The firelight danced over both of them, painting gold highlights in her red hair.

'I'd love a photograph of you like this.' Half-asleep, he'd spoken his thoughts aloud.

'Like what?'

'Naked like one of Titian's Venuses.'

'What would you do with such a photograph?'

'Lock it away from prying eyes, bring it out, study it – and remember you when you weren't around.'

'You can take one if you promise not to show it anyone.'

He opened his eyes. 'Do you mean that?'

'We're lovers, I'd enjoy the time before – and after – the posing. But there is a condition.'

Wary of her smile, he asked, 'What?'

'I want a photograph of you naked.'

'No one wants a photograph of a naked man.'

She rolled on to her stomach and looked up at him. 'I do.'

'Then I'll take one of me naked too.'

'With an enormous erection.' She slid her hand downwards.

'Give me five minutes. You're wearing me out.'

'It's a man's job to satisfy a woman.'

'I will, in five minutes. Do you realise I know hardly anything about you?'

'There's nothing to know.' Mischief glittered in her green eyes.

'There's a great deal to know. Let's start at the beginning, what were you like as a child?'

'Happy.' She ran her fingers through the hair on his chest. 'It was fun growing up in Alexandrovka. There were horses to ride and dogs and cats to play with. My father was a wonderful storyteller. He used to entertain all the children, not just me and my brothers. He also used to take us all hunting. At the time I thought my life would never change and my father would always be there. When he started drinking and stopped hunting we had no food so Mrs Ignatova found my mother a job as a wet nurse to her granddaughter. That's when our family's problems began and my childhood ended.'

She told him how her father had changed after the count had raped Yelena, and blackmailed her into having sex with him whenever he wanted, in return for refraining to prosecute her father for poaching.

Glyn was horrified. 'I knew the count was a vain and worthless man but I never thought he'd do something so low. Your poor mother. I'm so sorry.'

'As my mother says, everyone has to carry the crosses God sends them. My father hated knowing it was my mother, not him who put bread on our table. But when my mother could stand the count's pawing no longer, she left the mansion. It was then that my father stopped drinking and began to work in the mine. The rest you know.'

'Your name, Praskovia, it's beautiful.'

'Praskovia is a popular name among the poor in Russia because of Praskovia Kovalyov. She was born a serf in Yaroslavl. Her master, Count Sheremetev, was the richest man in Russia. He had her schooled as a singer, actress, and dancer, and when she grew up, he fell in love with her. In the days of serfs and masters, as now in the days of peasants and aristocrats, it wasn't done for a count to marry beneath him, but he married her in secret. When she bore him a son, Dmitri, he petitioned the Tsar to recognize their marriage. The Tsar granted his request, but pregnancy and childbirth had destroyed Praskovia's health and she died a few weeks later in the Sheremetev palace in St Petersburg. When news of their marriage became known, society was scandalized. Devastated by grief, Nikolai Sheremetev built an almshouse for the sick, poor, and orphaned in Moscow in Praskovia's memory. Ever since, almost every peasant family has named one of their daughters Praskovia in the hope she will lift her entire family out of poverty as Praskovia did when she married her count.'

'Girls no longer have to make their fortunes through marriage. They can work as you, Mrs Edwards, Ruth, Anna, and the others are doing.'

'Things haven't changed that much, Glyn. You only have to look at Alexei and Ruth to see women are still enslaved by their families, who tell them who they can and can't marry.'

'Ruth and Alexei have religious as well as social inequality to contend with. Believe me, the days of arranged marriages, princes, and peasants are over.'

'There is more to Praskovia's story which has become part of the history of Russia. Her son, Dmitri, inherited his father's wealth. In 1861 when he was walking with the Tsar, he told him the story of his mother. Affected by Praskovia's story, the Tsar freed all the serfs. Now they can travel wherever they want in Mother Russia, but it seems to me that most are travelling here to Hughesovka.'

'Thankfully for Mr Hughes, me, and the New Russia Company. We need all the labour we can get. Speaking of freedom, if I were free I would marry you tomorrow.'

'All I want from you, Glyn, is what you've already given me. If we can spend our nights together it's enough.' Careful to avoid touching the wound in his shoulder she moved on top of him and there was no more time for thought.

Afterwards, when they lay quietly in the firelight again, he thought of Betty and considered talking over his dilemma with John. There was always divorce but he'd heard enough gossip over the years to know that the first thing a wife loses after divorce is her reputation. If her husband strayed into another woman's bed, it was "because she didn't look after him." If she was the one to stray she was a "whore". On those grounds he doubted Betty would agree to formalize their separation.

As for talking over the problem with John, hadn't his boss solved his own domestic problems by leaving them in Greenwich while he travelled a thousand miles across inhospitable country to build a town where he could finally be himself?

Dower House, Beletsky Estate
May 1871

'My uncle and I are Ruth's joint guardians, Mrs Ignatova,' Nathan said. 'So any decisions will have to be made as much by him as me. The only firm promise I can give is that I will return and discuss this matter with you, Ruth, and Alexei again after Ruth's eighteenth birthday in six months' time.'

'I do hope you and Ruth will visit me often before then, Dr Kharber.' Catherine handed him a glass of tea.

'You hope Alexei and I will change our minds about wanting to marry during the six months, Nathan?' Ruth confronted her brother.

'Frankly, yes.'

'We won't.'

Catherine admired Ruth's spirit. She knew enough about the Jewish way of life to understand how much courage it had taken Ruth to question her older brother. 'So, Ruth, you want to marry Alexei as much as he wants to marry you?'

'Yes, Mrs Ignatova. Although I admit, until now I didn't believe it would be possible.'

'What's changed to make you believe it's possible now?' Nathan interrupted.

'Mrs Ignatova inviting us to drink tea, so we could talk about Alexei and me marrying,' Ruth said.

'I like ambitious young women who are prepared to work outside their homes, as you are in the hospital, Ruth. I'm also glad you haven't been put off by that dreadful incident with the Cossack soldier.'

'He frightened me but not enough to stop me from working. If I allowed him to do that he would have succeeded in his aim of ruining my life.'

'You and Anna were very brave.'

'Anna, not me, Mrs Ignatova. I'm not sure I would have been able to kill a man.'

Feeling a change of subject necessary, Catherine picked up a plate of cakes and offered them to Nathan. 'I admire your spirit in accepting Alexei's proposal of marriage, Ruth. Too many young girls – and boys – allow their elders to make their important decisions for them.'

'Surely you can't approve of Alexei and Ruth marrying, Mrs Ignatova?' Nathan set down his tea.

'It's occurred to me that if you added up your, Ruth's and Alexei's years, you'd still be a few short of mine, Nathan. May I call you Nathan or would you prefer Dr Kharber?'

'I would be honoured if you'd address me as Nathan. It would imply friendship.'

'I hope we will become friends, Nathan. Good friends.' She leaned against the back of her chair. 'My age doesn't make me wiser than you, but I've had time to see more of the world and people's follies as well as their generosity. I've also seen how much misery has been generated in this small corner of Russia among all classes, aristocrats, Mujiks, Cossacks, and Jews, when young people have been prevented from marrying the person of their choice.'

'Are you saying you will give Ruth and Alexei your blessing?' Nathan asked.

'If they want to marry in six months.'

'Knowing the opposition they'll face?'

'Every morning, winter and summer, I walk out on the balcony in front of my bedroom. For all but one of the years I've lived in the Dower House, the view has been the same, but when Mr Hughes started building his ironworks the countryside changed out of all recognition. In another year it will have changed even more. He's transformed a rural backwater into a frontier of industry. Where hundreds of people lived, we now have thousands, and I suspect in a year or two we will have tens of thousands. Any opposition to Ruth and Alexei's marriage that comes from the shtetl or Alexandrovka will be insignificant compared to the acceptance of them as a married couple by the employees of the New Russia Company. You don't have to look any further than yourself, Nathan. A year ago, few people outside of the shtetl would have accepted a Jewish doctor. Now you're running a hospital, and from what I've heard running it extremely well.'

'You flatter me.'

'My intention is to convince you that times are changing and there is room for a married couple in Mr Hughes's Hughesovka who were born an aristocrat and a Jew.' Catherine looked at Alexei and Ruth. They shared a sofa but, mindful of Nathan, were sitting at opposite ends.

'I take your point, Mrs Ignatova.'

'Catherine, please, Nathan. I have a suggestion. Why don't we meet every Sunday at six o'clock?

I often have lunch guests but I keep the evening free for family. That way, Alexei and Ruth could meet under your supervision and we could get to know one another better.'

'With a view to us becoming one family?'

'That is up to the young people, but after meeting Ruth and knowing Alexei as I do, I have no doubt that if we deny them our blessing they'll simply marry and do without.'

'I'll call into your room in Mr Edwards' house tomorrow,' Ruth whispered to Alexei as they hung back in the drawing room at the end of her and Nathan's visit.

'No...'

'I want to belong to you in every way...'

'And I need to be able to look your brother in the eye.' Hearing his grandmother and Nathan still talking to Boris in the hall, Alexei pulled Ruth behind the door and kissed her, long and lovingly.

'Ruth?' Nathan called from the hall.

'I must go.' She moved reluctantly away from him.

'Six months will soon pass, and until then there'll be lots of stolen kisses.'

She fingered her lips before running from the room.

Dower House, Hughesovka,
May 1871

John and Glyn entered Nathan's house behind

the hospital, took skull caps from the tray Ruth offered, and placed them on their heads. Ruth bobbed a curtsey before disappearing into the kitchen. A babble of feminine voices rose and fell when she opened and closed the door.

Nathan greeted John and Glyn in the tiny hall and ushered them into his crowded living room. Rabbi Goldberg, Nathan's Uncle Asher, and six elders from the shtetl were seated, waiting for their arrival. John and Glyn were amazed at the similarities between the furnishings of the Jewish house and those of the Cossacks. The same wall hanging, plethora of hand-made lace, and embroidered cloths and carved furniture furnished both. Only the Menorah – the Jewish seven-armed candlestick – and a leather-bound copy of the Torah wrapped in a fine lace cloth marked Nathan's house as that of a Jew.

A side table held beakers, plates, jugs of wine and water, cinnamon rolls, honey cake, and almond biscuits.

'You are most welcome, Mr Hughes, Mr Edwards, please, sit down.' Nathan indicated a bench set below the window.

'Thank you for agreeing to meet me, Rabbi Goldberg, elders.' John shook the rabbi and all the elders' hands before taking a seat.

'Nathan insisted we should, Mr Hughes, although I am mystified as to what purpose our meeting will serve,' the rabbi countered suspiciously.

'We should talk over what happened last month, Rabbi.'

'When the Cossacks shot Mr Edwards and

attacked Ruth Kharber in the hospital.'

'Yes.'

'Cossacks can be violent. We are sorry Mr Edwards was hurt. Usually they only chose victims from our race. We are used to it.'

'I am not used to it, Rabbi Goldberg. And if I can, I'll not allow anything like those attacks to occur in my town again,' John stated unequivocally.

'We know you've sent more men to guard the hospital and for that I thank you. Nathan Kharber is one of us.'

'Every man who lives in Hughesovka is "one of us", Rabbi.'

'A citizen of your town?'

'Precisely, and one who deserves equal treatment along with every other citizen, no matter what his or her race.'

'For us, Mr Hughes, that is a dream. We have always lived apart from our neighbours.'

'That is what I would like to talk to you about. I would like you to consider leaving your shtetl.'

'You want us to leave our homes?' The rabbi's face darkened.

'No, Rabbi Goldberg, I want you to move your homes, your shops, and your businesses into the town.'

Asher Kharber rose to his feet. 'I've heard enough. Not even the Cossacks wanted to drive us from our shtetl.'

'Please, Uncle Asher,' Nathan pleaded, 'listen to Mr Hughes.'

'What I'd like you to do, gentlemen, is move your homes to an area I've outlined solely for your use.' John nodded to Glyn who produced a map case and opened it on a table.

'This is the town as it stands. This section at the lower end of the street below the hospital could be yours. I know Jews have to live within walking distance of the synagogue, and you could build a fine brick or stone one here. There is an abundance of land so the rabbi could also build his house and a school if you want a separate one for your children.'

'We have a synagogue and school in the shtetl, we have lived there for generations,' Asher protested. 'So why should we move to suit you and your plans, Mr Hughes?'

'First, if you lived in the town, you would receive the benefit of the protection of the company's officers who patrol the streets. Here, on the boundary between the lower end of the main street and the area you could occupy, I intend to build a fire station which will be manned by company employees. It will be their job to keep the town secure as well as douse any fires.'

'And the shtetl?' Rabbi Goldberg asked.

'I would purchase the land the shtetl stands on from you, so you in your turn could purchase land in the town. You have my word that no one will be out of pocket and all your people will make enough money to either move your existing wooden houses or build new brick ones. The company would also make a substantial contribution to the building of the new synagogue and school.'

'What would you want for this largesse, Mr Hughes?' the rabbi asked.

'I would like you to move your businesses into

the town. Every day more and more people flock into Hughesovka. They need bakers, butchers, tailors, shoemakers. You have the expertise and the businesses. But the shtetl is too far from the town for most people to walk there after a day's work. If you move into the town, Hughesovka would have a business and commercial sector worthy of the name. Your tradesmen would benefit and so would my employees.'

The elders looked at one another.

'You really want my people to live in your town, Mr Hughes?' Rabbi Goldberg checked.

'I do, Rabbi Goldberg.'

'As the equal of every other citizen,' Nathan added.

'This needs to be discussed at a full meeting of the elders in the shtetl.'

'Thank you for listening to me, Rabbi Goldberg.'

'When would you like us to move, Mr Hughes?' the rabbi asked.

'That is for you and your people to decide, Rabbi. I have no timetable in mind but, ever the optimist, I've set money aside to finance the transfer of your people which can be accessed immediately.'

'What would you do with the land the shtetl stands on?' Asher demanded.

'Use it to expand the company. We haven't decided on a definite location for the railway station as yet, but the land could be utilised for warehousing, a goods yard, or even factories, after it's cleared of course.'

'And the shtetl cemetery?' the rabbi asked.

'Will be treated with the respect it deserves. It's no further from the town than it is from the shtetl. Your present synagogue and school are made of wood. We can either move those buildings into the town or erect temporary new ones until brick replacements can be constructed. I'll not deny there'll be problems relocating a community the size of yours, but I've yet to encounter a situation that can't be solved by throwing money at it. As the company and the town will benefit as much as the people in the shtetl from this plan, it's only fair the company contribute to the cost of the move. Good day to you.' First John then Glyn shook hands with everyone again before they left.

'That went well, don't you think, Glyn?' John said when they were on the street and out of earshot.

'I'll let you know when the first family moves into town, sir,' Glyn said cautiously.

Asher Kharber's House, Shtetl
June 1871

'We've been waiting for you to start the Shavuot feast,' Asher complained to Nathan when he entered his uncle's house.

'I'm sorry. I had business with Levi and Abraham Goldberg.' Nathan removed his hat and coat, hung them on a hook at the back of the door, took his skull cap from his trouser pocket, and placed it on his head,

'The elders have agreed to the move. The first buildings will be transported into the town next week, so what did you have to discuss with Levi and Abraham Goldberg?' Asher asked.

'I can guess.' Leah beamed. 'You and Levi have set the date for Abraham's wedding to Ruth?'

Ruth trembled as she tried to concentrate on laying the table. 'There won't be a wedding between Abraham and Ruth,' Nathan faced his uncle.

Leah turned on her niece. 'You stupid, ungrateful girl...'

'Please sit down, Aunt Leah, Uncle Asher. We must talk before we eat.'

'The food...'

'Please, Aunt Leah,' Nathan pleaded. 'This won't take long. All the decisions that need to be made have been. All that remains is to tell you about them.'

'You made decisions without consulting your uncle. Decisions about Ruth, when we brought her up, treated her as if she were our own daughter. Do we need to remind you your uncle is head of this family, Nathan?'

'The boy is of age, Leah. It could be argued he is in charge of his own small family now my brother is dead,' Asher said.

'We were good enough to take care of Ruth all the years Nathan was away having a fine time in Paris but now we're not good enough to advise her.' Leah sat on the bench next to Ruth.

'Abraham Goldberg is highly respected among our people,' Asher said to Nathan.

'I know, Uncle Asher.'

'He's as learned as his uncle, the rabbi, and it never hurts to have a rabbi in the family. He'll be as wealthy as his father one day. Perhaps wealthier.

Butchery is a good trade. Once married to Abraham you'll never starve, Ruth. There'd be no need for you to continue working at the hospital.'

Ruth kept her eyes downcast. She'd been dreading Nathan approaching her uncle and aunt as much as she'd been looking forward to marrying Alexei.

'No one makes Ruth work in the hospital, Aunt Leah,' Nathan protested. 'She wants to earn her own living.'

'Caring for sick and naked men is not a suitable occupation for a young girl. There's no point in a woman learning anything other than how to cook, clean, and run a house. When Ruth is married to Abraham...'

'Please, Aunt Leah, may I speak?'

'Let the boy have his say, Leah. I have a feeling we're not going to like it but better he tell us the worst, than someone outside of the family,' Asher laid his hand over his wife's.

'I met Catherine Ignatova and Alexei Beletsky after the Cossack attacked Ruth. Alexei loves Ruth, she loves him, and Catherine and I agreed that if they both felt the same way about one another in six months we would allow them to marry. Those six months will be up in September...'

'Love!' Leah broke in. 'What do children know about love? Ruth is seventeen. Alexei Beletsky not much older.'

'She'll be eighteen next month, Alexei is twenty, and didn't you just say that Abraham Goldberg would make a suitable husband for Ruth – so you must consider her ready for marriage?'

'Abraham Goldberg is of our faith. A sensible man. A wealthy man, an older man who can guide Ruth in the ways of the world.'

'Ruth doesn't want to marry him, Aunt Leah.'

'It's not for young girls to decide who they do and don't want to marry. I never heard such non-sense. Love comes after marriage. I didn't set eyes on your uncle until our wedding day and we have been together forty-two happy years. We accepted the wisdom of the matchmaker, our parents, and the rabbi. They knew what was best for us. Ruth should follow our example and allow her elders to guide her. Whoever heard of a young girl choosing her own husband? Or a marriage between a Russian Orthodox aristocrat and a Jew?'

'Aunt Leah, I gave Catherine Ignatova my word that if Ruth still wanted to marry Alexei in six months, she could. They'll marry in September.'

'I never thought I'd live to see the day when you'd allow your sister to marry outside of our faith, Nathan.' Asher's softly spoken reprimand was harder for Nathan and Ruth to bear than their Aunt's shouting.

'It's either that, or lose her, Uncle Asher.'

'Better you lose her than allow her to turn her back on God. From this moment you are both dead to me and your aunt. You are no longer welcome in my house.'

Ruth kept her eyes averted from her uncle and aunt as she went to the door and retrieved her shawl.

'Ruth will be marrying out of our faith but...'

'It's not enough that you work with Christians. Now you refuse to go from my house when I order you.' Asher stepped towards Nathan.

'There is one more piece of news you must hear before we go. I will not be marrying out of our faith. My wedding to Levi's daughter, Vasya, will take place in the synagogue next Thursday evening. I would be honoured if you and Aunt Leah would attend and give us your blessing.'

'Nathan ... no.' Ruth turned to him with tears in her eyes.

'Vasya is a good woman.' Nathan took Ruth's hand.

'What of your children, Nathan?' Leah demanded. 'You're twenty-seven; she's more than ten years older. A dried-up spinster who never found a man...'

'That's enough, Aunt Leah. She is to become my wife. The wedding will be at seven o'clock. Afterwards Levi has invited everyone from the shtetl to his house to celebrate with food and drink.'

'Does he know about Ruth and Alexei?' Asher demanded.

'He knows and he, Vasya, and Abraham have invited Ruth to the wedding. Come, Ruth.' Nathan opened the door and ushered his sister outside. He'd left the hospital troika in his uncle's yard. The horses pawed restlessly while he helped Ruth into it and pulled a rug over her knees.

'You're only marrying Vasya because I refused to marry Abraham. You're saving face for the Goldbergs...'

'I'm not as brave as you, Ruth. My faith is the foundation of my life. I cannot forsake the God of our fathers.'

'But Sonya...'

'I made no promises to Sonya, nor she to me.'

'You've seen the way she looks at you when you're in the same room. I've seen the way you look at her...'

'It was never possible, Ruth.'

'Alexei and...'

'You and Alexei are different. Please, not a word to anyone in Hughesovka about my marriage to Vasya. I will tell those who need to know.'

'I can't bear my happiness to be at the expense of yours.'

'It won't be. I'm looking forward to being married. Vasya is the old-fashioned kind who'll spend her days cooking and taking care of me. Just what a busy doctor needs.' He shouted at the horses and they quickened their pace. He drove straight into the wind, knowing it would carry away their voices and any chance of conversation. Just as he intended.

Chapter Twenty-nine

Hospital, Hughesovka
June 1871

Nathan spoke to Sonya as soon as she arrived in the office the next morning. He'd had a sleepless night, most of which he'd spent rehearsing speeches he intended to make to her. The more he reflected, the more he realised it wasn't a question of what he'd said, rather a question of what he'd wanted to say and had never found the courage to put into words.

Knowing Sarah and the girls were busy waking the patients and giving them breakfast, he closed the office door.

She smiled at him. 'Would you like tea?'

'No, thank you, Sonya, but I would like to talk to you. I've something to tell you that I want you to hear before anyone else in the hospital.'

She felt as though a chill wind had blown into the room.

Now the moment had arrived Nathan couldn't recall a single one of his carefully rehearsed sentences. 'I'm getting married next week.'

'Married...' She tried to recall if he'd ever mentioned a girl ... a woman he visited. Until that moment he'd never said anything of a remotely personal nature. Had she built a future for herself on the basis of a few smiles and kind words?

She considered their relationship – if she could even call it that – and realised he'd never given her more than a passing glance. One that she'd obviously read far more into than he'd intended.

Her lips ached from the strain of smiling. 'Congratulations, Dr Kharber. Do I know the fortunate girl?'

'I doubt it, she lives quietly. It's Vasya Goldberg, the butcher's daughter from the shtetl.'

Tears pricked, burning the back of her eyes. She knew Vasya; a withered old spinster with thin hair and a wrinkled complexion, who occasionally accompanied the seamstress who visited her aunt's house to repair the drapes and soft furnishings.

He began to speak quickly, barely aware of what he was saying, talking simply to fill the void that had opened between them.

'It may seem sudden to you and most people in Hughesovka, but this is the way my people arrange marriages. The father of the bride or groom approaches the other family and suggests a match. If the proposal is acceptable to both parties there's no point in wasting time.'

'I recall Ruth telling me that your aunt and uncle wanted her to marry Abraham Goldberg.'

'The families have been friends for years. Levi, Abraham's father, was my father's best friend.'

'I see.' It was a pitiful comment but she couldn't think of a better one.

'You know, Ruth is to marry Alexei in September.'

She couldn't resist saying, 'So you're to take Ruth's place in this union between your two families and marry Levi's daughter.'

'It's not a sacrifice, Sonya. It's a marriage between two Jews.'

She turned to the filing cabinet and opened a drawer because it gave her an excuse to look away from him. 'I hope you'll both be very happy.'

'Thank you.' He hesitated before realising there was nothing else he could say.

No declarations of love or even friendship had been made by either of them. How could he possibly begin to explain a look that had meant more to him than anything else in the world?

Steppe outside of Alexandrovka
June 1871

The transition from winter through a spring that lasted only a few days, to summer, was swift. One day the snow lay metres thick on the steppe, the next it melted away. Rain followed, green shoots of rough grass sprouted, and the unmade roads and tracks in Hughesovka dissolved into mud canals.

Embryonic crops of vegetables appeared in rich black earth the farmers tilled until it looked as though it could be turned over with a teaspoon, and when the rain blew over, warm welcoming sun shone, inviting people to forsake their houses for the outdoors.

The employees of the New Russia Company who'd believed nothing more could be squeezed into their waking hours when the days were short and the nights long, discovered summer brought a flurry of activity that left even fewer hours for sleep. None were busier than John and Glyn.

Blinking hard to adjust to sunlight after the black of the pit shafts, John, Glyn, and Richard climbed out of a primitive cage at the head of the latest Cossack mine John had acquired, to see Alexei engulfed by a sea of bleak-faced men.

'What do you think?' John asked. 'Do we drill down and widen this shaft in the hope of finding richer seams than those we've discovered, or should we sink a new pit on one of the new sites the geologist pinpointed?'

'Either way we need to drill out seams wide and deep enough for men to stand in, sir. The conditions in Merthyr weren't good but in this pit they're so cramped they're dangerous.' Richard had learned that John was prepared to listen to advice when it came to sinking pits, even from his youngest employees.

Glyn nodded. 'I agree with Richard, sir. The only wonder is more men haven't been killed or injured here.'

'I know you acquired the lease of this pit as a going concern, sir...'

'Going concern or not,' John cut Richard short, 'the last thing I'm prepared to be reckless with is men's lives.' He joined the miners. 'How do you see this pit's future?' he asked in Russian.

No one answered.

'Speak your minds, the truth can't sting that much.'

'Most who work here say the seams are giving out, Your Excellency,' one ventured, 'but they're afraid to talk in case they lose their jobs.'

'Let me make one thing clear: no one, absolutely no one,' John emphasised, 'will lose their job. Go underground and tell the men down there we're closing this pit. Ask them to clear out the tools and bring everything useful to the surface by the end of the day. Everyone should report to the main office first thing tomorrow. The sooner we assign them to another mine the sooner we can get quality pits into production. In the meantime, we'll go,' he opened his leather map case. 'There.' He took a pencil from his pocket, and circled a spot before handing the case to Alexei. 'Ride to the office and tell them to make arrangements to cap this mine, clear the surface buildings, and move the drilling rigs to this location. The conditions there are no better than here, but the geologist found three new seams off the main shaft that warrant a closer look. Mr Edwards, Richard, and I will go there now.'

'After I've been to the office, sir?' Alexei asked.

'You re-join us.'

Alexei beamed. 'Thank you, sir.' He whistled for Agripin.

'The quicker we decide which pits to develop, the sooner I can concentrate on getting the furnaces into production. If the builders ever finish them.'

'The way the German and Polish foremen are working the men, they'll be commissioned before you know it, sir,' Glyn assured John.

'I doubt that, Glyn. Nothing in this town is happening rapidly enough for me.' John strode towards his carriage.

Hospital, Hughesovka
June 1871

When Praskovia knocked the door of the office, Sarah was helping Sonya update patients' files. It was a task that Nathan usually claimed, but for the last few days he'd spent so much time in his consulting room Sarah wondered if he was researching treatments or simply trying to avoid Sonya.

'That's what I call timing, Praskovia, we were just about to take a break and make tea for the staff. Join us?' she invited.

'Thank you, but I was hoping to talk to you if you're not too busy.'

'Professionally?' Sarah questioned.

'If you've time.'

'I can always find time for you, Praskovia, especially when I consider all the things you do for us. Come into the examination room.' Sarah opened the door. 'Please, sit down. Are you ill?' she asked when they were alone.

'I think I'm going to have a baby.' Praskovia blurted. 'If you're shocked...'

'I'm not shocked. The first thing we have to do is check that you really are pregnant, and if that's the case, both you and the baby are doing well. Undress and lie on the couch please.'

Sarah examined Praskovia gently and carefully. When she felt her abdomen she said, 'How long have you suspected that you're pregnant?'

'About two months.'

'Are you nauseous?'

'Most of the time.'

'Do you actually vomit?'

'Most mornings.'

'That should wear off soon. Try four drops of this in half a glass of water three times a day after meals.' Sarah took a bottle of peppermint essence from a cabinet and gave it to Praskovia.

'It won't hurt the baby?'

'No. I promise it won't. I took it myself when I was pregnant. I'd say you're about ten to twelve weeks, which means you won't be able to keep your condition a secret for more than another month or two, even in the flowing smocks you wear. Does the baby's father know?'

'No.' Praskovia reached for her clothes.

'Will you tell him?'

'When I'm ready.'

'Have you thought about your and the baby's future?'

'I haven't made any firm decisions.'

Sarah felt selfish for asking but she persisted. 'Will you continue running the house for us?'

'I hope to, but that might prove difficult with a baby to look after. If the master wants me to leave I'll go.'

Sarah had no idea how Glyn would react to the news that his housekeeper was carrying a bastard, but she felt the need to reassure Praskovia. 'I can't see Glyn throwing you out.'

'I hope not.'

'If you marry the father...'

'I won't be marrying anyone.' Praskovia slipped her smock over her head and fastened the buttons.

Sarah didn't press her. 'What about your mother?'

'She won't be pleased.'

Sarah sensed from Praskovia's reply that her response was an understatement. 'Would you like me to tell Glyn?'

'No, please don't. I'll speak to him myself. Will you keep this a secret for a few weeks until I decide what I'm going to do?'

'Of course. I'll do everything I can to help you and ensure that you keep your job. You're not just our housekeeper, you're our friend, Praskovia. I mean all of us, not only me. Glyn, Richard, Anna – none of us could have survived without you. We arrived without having a clue about the country or the customs. You took care of us through a horrible time of loss when we weren't capable of looking after ourselves. None of us will ever forget that.'

'Thank you, you're very kind, Mrs Edwards.'

'How many times do I have to ask you to call me Sarah?' Sarah hugged the girl. 'I'd regard it as a privilege if you allow me to help you in any way I can.'

'Thank you for the offer of tea, but I've been away from the kitchens for too long as it is. It's baking day.'

'I'll see you tonight, Praskovia.' Sarah walked her to the door and watched her cross the road.

Sonya joined her. 'Is Praskovia ill?'

'No.' Sarah didn't want to think about the prejudice and gossip the young girl would face. From Praskovia's reaction to her question about Yelena she had the feeling unmarried mothers were subjected to the same narrow-minded bigotry in Cossack society that they were in Britain. As for Glyn, the more she tried to anticipate his response to Praskovia's news, the less she was able to hazard a guess as to how her brother-in-law might react.

Glyn Edwards' house,
Hughesovka June 1871

Yelena was kneading bread dough when Praskovia walked into the kitchen.

'You've been to see Mrs Edwards?' she asked without looking up from the table.

'I told you where I was going.' Praskovia sat on a stool and lifted a glass under the tap on the samovar. She took a slice of lemon from a bowl and dropped it into the tea she'd poured.

'Why did you bother to see Mrs Edwards when you already knew you'd disgraced yourself and your family?'

'I wanted something that would stop me from vomiting every morning.'

'I told you, chew on a lump of coal.'

'It didn't work, Mama.' Praskovia took the bottle Sarah had given her from her pocket, uncorked the top and sniffed the contents.

'When are you going to tell the master?' Yelena demanded.

'In a time of my own choosing. You're not to say a word to anyone. Do you hear me?'

'I hear you.'

'Especially Misha. Is that clear?'

'As clear as Don water.' Yelena slammed a dough ball on to a baking tray. 'If you're expecting the master...'

'I'm not expecting anything of the master.'

'If he throws you out? And me and Pyotr after you? Then what? We don't even have a house to go to now there are Welsh miners in our home...'

Praskovia took her tea and left the kitchen. She went to the corridor that opened into her room and Glyn's, unlocked, closed, and relocked the door that separated it from the servants' quarters. Bypassing the door to her room, she walked into Glyn's.

She sat in the chair that faced the fire, stared into the flames and tried to imagine what Glyn would say when she told him he was about to become a father.

How angry would he be? Would he try to buy

her off? Give her money to go far from him and Hughesovka? The brave face she'd adopted when she was with Yelena crumpled. She sank her face into her hands.

She was no better than her mother. Just like the woman who'd borne her, she'd allowed a man to make love to her outside marriage and she'd no choice but to pay the price for her sin.

Three Firs Mine, steppe outside of Alexandrovka
June 1871

'How are we doing down there?' John asked Glyn when he came up in the cage.

'It looks good, sir.' Glyn brushed the sweat from his brow with his arm. It was hot and airless underground. 'We've hit a broad seam of anthracite over six feet high and twice as wide. Shoring's going to be a problem. The Cossacks have been cutting corners. There's nowhere near enough timber down there to bolster the shaft. I'd say we need about ten times as much as that just to secure the entry chamber.' He pointed to a stack of timber at the pithead. 'Richard and Alf are calculating what we'll need for every yard of seam we cut.'

'Given our transport problems it's anyone's guess how long it's going to take to haul timber up here. The sooner the iron works gets into production the sooner we'll have rail tracks.' John was growing more impatient with every delay. 'I'll take a look at the seam myself.'

Alexei returned in time to hear the end of the

conversation. 'We won't get iron for rail tracks without coal to fuel the furnaces, sir.'

'Thank you for that reminder, Alexei.'

John's scowl couldn't dispel Alexei's good humour. 'Just pointing out we need to start mining coal as soon as possible, sir.'

'If you know any storks or witches on brooms that can fly in the materials we need, now's the time to contact them, Alexei.' Glyn followed John to the hut where his boss picked out a miner's helmet and Davy lamp. John checked the oil well on the lamp was full before striking a Lucifer.

'Want me to come down and write notes for you, sir?' Alexei needed to prove he was capable of working underground. He'd reacted badly the first time he went down in a cage. Unnerved, terrified by the foul-smelling, claustrophobic blackness, he'd fainted. His excuse that he'd found the atmosphere airless hadn't rung true, even to his own ears.

'You're better off up here annoying the surface workers...'

A thunderous din blasted up the shaft. A rumble shook the ground. Seconds later a plume of dust shot up darkening the air. It fell on the bare earth around the shaft, speckling it with ragged, darker blotches.

Glyn held his breath, dreading yet half expecting the sound of collapse to be followed by an explosion of firedamp.

John was the first to speak. 'Only a fall.' He ran and jumped into the cage. Glyn followed.

'No.' John forestalled Alexei when he tried to join them. 'Richard...' Alexei cried. He couldn't bear to think of his closest friend injured ... or worse.

'Someone has to stay up top and direct operations. Send for the doctor. We'll need transport for the injured and...' John couldn't bring himself to say 'dead' until he'd seen bodies. He called out to the man operating the cage. 'Down!'

He and Glyn pulled up their mufflers and tied them over their noses and mouth as the cage was lowered. Soon the air was so thick it took all their strength just to draw breath into their lungs.

Hospital, Hughesovka
June 1871

Sarah carried a glass of tea into Nathan's consulting room. She set it on his desk. 'Congratulations on your marriage.'

'Thank you. I suppose it was too much to expect word not to get out when Vasya's brother moved her trunk into my apartments this morning.'

'Don't blame Ruth for letting it slip, but she mentioned you were getting married tonight when she left to move in with Alexei's grandmother half an hour ago.'

'Vasya and I wanted Ruth to stay with us until she marries, but Ruth thought she'd be in the way. Not that she would have been.'

'Weddings are wonderful occasions.'

'Mine will be simple but that's how I want it.'

'Mine to Peter was hardly elaborate as we were both working in the hospital that night, but I think Mrs Ignatova is as excited as Ruth and Alexei about theirs. Although Alexei insists he wants a quiet ceremony, I doubt Hughesovka will allow it to be.'

'It's difficult to organise a celebration when you work in a place that has to be kept open, like the hospital, but once Vasya has settled in, she'll invite you and some of the staff to our home for a meal.'

'I'll look forward to it and I'm sure the others will. Don't worry about the hospital this evening or tomorrow. Enjoy your wedding. I'm on night shift and I'll stay here until you get back. My very best wishes, Nathan, to you and your bride.'

She kissed his cheek and left the office. She felt there was something odd about Nathan's marriage. He hadn't even smiled when he'd mentioned Vasya's name. Ruth had told her arranged marriages were common in the shtetl and for most Jews, love came after, not before the wedding. Was she so addicted to romance that she'd seen love between Nathan and Sonya where there was only friendship?

Underground, Three Firs Mine
June 1871

Richard was in a daze. The world seemed strangely muffled and intensely black. His mouth and nose were packed with dry, suffocating dust. He coughed in an effort to expel it. Faint, dizzy, the darkness gradually became tinged with red as he lay limp and helpless on what felt like a bed of rubble.

Strong hands hauled him upright. A shower of rocks and small coal clattered around him. Someone thumped him hard between his shoulder blades, forcing thick, dense air into his lungs.

'Don't go dying on me, boy.'

'Alf?' He'd meant to say the name out loud but couldn't hear his voice. He sensed movement. Lights flickering. A lamp swung in front of his eyes.

'Dear God and all that's holy!' Alf exclaimed.

A solid cliff of coal loomed over them. A minute passed before Richard realised he was no longer deaf.

Cage, underground, Three Firs Mine
June 1871

Halfway down the shaft the cage began to judder and shake violently. John held up his lamp but the beam failed to penetrate the swirling particles that clogged the atmosphere. A thud that sent him and Glyn reeling against the wooden bars of the cage suggested they'd hit the bottom of the shaft, although the cage was perched sideways.

Glyn lifted the bar. 'Step carefully, sir; we're on a pile of slag, not firm ground.'

John clambered over a heap of debris and blocks of coal. He lost his balance and slithered helplessly on to his back when he hit a river of slippery dust. He heard stones rattle and realized Glyn had fallen behind him.

'Sirs! Look to your right.'

John recognised Alf's voice. Lights wavered

dimly, almost obscured by dust.

'Boss... Boss...'

Miners surged forward heading for him and Glyn. Desperately trying to gain a purchase on the scree, John struggled to his knees.

'Looks like the seam I was telling you about collapsed, sir.' Glyn spoke low close to John's ear but his voice was distorted as if they were under water. John saw a silhouette he recognised as Richard holding out a lamp and inching towards the fall. Glyn scrambled alongside him. The Russian miners gathered around them.

'Your Excellencies,' Yuri, the foreman Glyn had appointed on Praskovia's recommendation, hailed them. 'I've done a head count. Twelve men are this side of the fall, four hurt.'

'Badly?' John asked.

'They have broken bones. They're all conscious. Two men are dead and twenty missing.'

'Under the fall or on the other side?' Glyn asked.

'That's for us to find out, sir.' Alf cleared a flat area and set down his lamp. 'I need tools and all the able-bodied men capable of digging.'

'Yuri, take two men and begin loading the cage with the injured. Get them to the surface. Two injured and one able-bodied man to a cage,' John ordered.

'Yes, Your Excellency.' Yuri ran.

Hospital, Hughesovka
June 1871

'How many are injured?' Sarah asked the miner

Alexei had sent to the hospital.

'I don't know, Matron. All I know is Mr Alexei Beletsky told me to come here and ask the doctor to go to the mine with as many troikas as can be spared.'

'Richard...'

'I don't know anything except what I've told you, Matron.' Nathan overheard him. 'Go to Madam Ignatova's in the Dower House. You know the Dower House?'

'Yes, Your Excellency.'

'Tell Madam Ignatova to send as many carriages as she can spare to the Three Firs mine. Then go to the company offices and tell them to get messages to all the pits. Mr Hughes may need help if men are trapped and they should prepare teams of miners in case they're needed. Go, as quickly as you can. Lives may depend on your speed.'

'Yes, Your Excellency.' Bursting with self-importance the man ran out of the door.

'You stay here,' Nathan said to Sarah. 'I'll go to the pithead with Miriam and Rivka. The way you've trained the girls, they're almost as good as you, and that will leave you with enough staff to prepare the operating theatre and make up extra beds. You'd better send to the Dower House and ask Ruth to return.'

'She was on night shift. I'll wait until we need her.'

'You're right, it may take some time to get the men out.'

Anna charged towards them. 'Richard...'

Sarah grasped her shoulders. 'No one knows

anything as yet. It might be better if Anna goes with you, Rivka, and Miriam,' she suggested.

'Richard could be involved.'

'If he is, Anna is professional enough to treat him as she would any other patient,' Sarah interceded, knowing Anna would be no use whatsoever in the hospital if she was worrying about Richard. 'But the hospital...'

'Is as safe in your hands as mine, Matron.'

'What if there's an emergency?'

'You'll deal with it and admirably.' He went to the office to fetch his bag. When he emerged, he said, 'Send a messenger to the Goldbergs in the shtetl, please. Tell him to give the Goldbergs my apologies and explain that under the circumstances I'll have to delay the wedding.'

Three Firs Mine
June 1871

Alexei ran over to the cage as soon as it surfaced. 'Mr Richard Parry? Mr Hughes, Mr Edwards?' he demanded of the miner Yuri had put in charge of the injured men.

'Are unhurt, Your Excellency, thanks be to Christ. They're trying to rescue the men who are trapped.'

'Carry these men into the shed – carefully,' Alexei added, when a surface worker grabbed one of the men's shoulders roughly.

Vlad drove up in the hospital troika. Anna, Rivka, and Miriam were wedged in the back, surrounded by packages. Nathan was sitting alongside Vlad in the front. As soon as Vlad reined in the horses, Nathan lifted out his bag and climbed from the carriage.

Anna ran to Alexei. 'Richard...'

'Alive, and directing operations below ground with Mr Hughes and Mr Edwards,' he assured her.

Nathan looked into the shed. 'Lay a sheet on the floor in here,' he called to Anna. 'Set the injured on it,' he ordered Alexei who followed Anna in.

'We need boiling water.' Anna looked around.

'There's a pan on the stove in the corner,' Alexei informed her.

'It's rough down there. I need to get back. My brother...' one of the injured miners struggled to sit up.

'You're not going anywhere, Artur.' Nathan checked him over. 'Your right arm and leg are broken. Anna, prepare the bandages. You'll have to bind the limbs as soon as I've set them. Miriam, Rivka, all the patients need to be washed before we can treat them.'

'We'll bring water as soon as it's boiled, Dr Kharber.' Anna unfolded a bundle of sheets to reveal two metal bowls, one filled with medical instruments, the other soap, disinfectant, antiseptic, and scrubbing brushes.

'What's it like down there?' Alexei crouched on his heels beside Artur.

'Blacker than the devil's arsehole.'

'We have ladies present,' Alexei reprimanded.

'Sorry to the ladies, but it is.'

'When did you last see the devil's arsehole,

Artur?' Vlad walked in.

'When he farted so loud in the pit he brought the walls down.' Artur looked groggily up at Alexei. 'Two dead. Twenty missing. The Welshmen are tunnelling through the fall to try to reach them.'

'How many injured?' Nathan asked.

Artur' s eyes closed.

'Is he...' Alexei stared down at him.

'Fainted, probably from the pain,' Nathan diagnosed. 'This would be a good time to set his bones. Hold him up while I pull his trousers off, will you?'

A shout came from the pithead. 'Two more injured.'

'Get the ones who are breathing in here, Alexei. As for the dead...'

'I'll deal with them,' Alexei went to the door.

'You'll need sheets, Alexei.'

Alexei looked at Anna in confusion.

She lowered her voice. 'For shrouds. Make sure the bodies are taken to the hospital mortuary so we can wash them and lay them out properly before the families see them. Have you notified Father Grigor? The Cossacks will want the last rites, and send someone to the carpenter in Alexandrovka. We'll need coffins to carry the bodies from the mortuary to the village. Write down the measurements of the dead and give them to the messenger in case the carpenter has something suitable in stock. Let me know the minute you have news about Richard.'

Alexei was dumbfounded. Anna wouldn't be fourteen for a month but she sounded as authoritative and confident as Sarah Edwards. Then he remembered the soldier she'd shot and killed.

'Here.' She thrust a pair of sheets at him. 'Sorry Miriam and I are too busy to help you, but the injured take precedence over the dead. Lay the body diagonally in the centre of the sheet and bring the corners forward over the head and feet. That way you can cover the entire body ready for transport. Rigor will set in soon in this warm weather, get the corpses to the hospital as quickly as possible.'

'I'll try.'

'You being sarcastic?'

'I wouldn't dream of it in the face of such efficiency.' Alexei left the hut.

'The Matron's transformed those girls into wise angels.' Vlad offered Alexei a flask. Alexei looked back through the open door to where Anna, Rivka, and Miriam were washing the coal-encrusted limbs of the injured. He lifted the flask to his lips and drank a mouthful of rough vodka. 'If they're angels, they're bossy, not wise ones.'

Underground, Three Firs Mine
June 1871

Richard looked to the miner who'd crawled to the foot of the fall. 'Try again – and SILENCE, the rest of you.'

The miner tapped a rock at his feet three times in quick succession. Silence reigned, claustrophobic in a gloom pierced by the inadequate light of the miners' lamps. After what seemed like an eternity, three faint but definite answering taps echoed from the behind the fall.

'Someone's alive,' Glyn breathed.

'We need the rods, Mr Edwards,' Alf shouted. 'I'll push them through as far as I can. With luck there'll be air pockets we can use to open a tunnel through the debris.'

'Rods,' John ordered Yuri who'd returned from the cage where he'd delegated the task of moving the injured to the surface.

Richard motioned the miner with the pick to retreat as he inched his way forward alongside Alf.

'Who made you two chief rescuers?' Glyn questioned.

'If anyone's had more experience than me and this boy, we'd be glad to hand over the responsibility, sir,' Alf replied.

'All our nerves are at breaking point, Glyn, but it looks to me as if those two are doing all that can be done,' John declared.

'I couldn't do better and I wouldn't do different. It's just seeing that boy put himself in harm's way...' Glyn emphasised his concern by lifting his lamp beam on to an overhang of coal that projected down from the ceiling of the shaft. 'That looks as though it could crash on Richard and Alf at any minute.'

'The whole lot could go,' John agreed. 'I wish I could light a cigar.'

'Do it, sir, and we'll all be knocking on St Peter's Gate.'

'The rods are going through and there's a crack that looks wide enough for me to get through.'

Richard highlighted a narrow gap close to the floor of the shaft.

'It's too narrow, Richard. You'll never squeeze through that,' Glyn warned.

'I crawled through narrower back in Merthyr. Here, hold this for me please, and pass me those ropes.' Richard handed Alf his lamp. 'Keep the beam trained on that spot. Keep a tight grip on these ropes, as soon as I reach the trapped miners, I'll hand over the other ends. That way, even if we can't get the men out straight away we'll be able to send through water and food.'

'The boy's the wiriest here,' Alf assured Glyn. 'If you or me tried to force our way through with our broad shoulders, we'd bring the roof down.'

'As no one has a better idea, go ahead, Richard.' John sat upright, too wary of starting another fall to lean against anything.

Minutes crawled past while Richard continued to gain ground inch by painful inch. He dislodged a lump of coal and pushed it behind him. It rolled, gathered momentum and crashed, splintering in a mess of small coal and dust.

'For Christ's sake, boy, be careful,' Alf cried.

'I am being careful,' came the muted reply.

'That boy has the courage of a dozen men,' Alf muttered.

'That boy is foolhardy. Is that the cage?' Glyn asked.

'My brother Viktor has brought down food, water, and more oil for the lamps sir,' Yuri informed John.

'The injured we sent up?' Glyn kept his eyes

focused on the studded soles of Richard's boots.

'The doctor's setting their broken bones before sending them to the hospital.'

'Is he leaving with them?'

'No, we told him we can hear the trapped men. He said he'll stay until you get them out.'

'Until–' Glyn kept the thought to himself that 'in case' might be more appropriate.

Richard shouted. Seconds later another fall of rock, slag, and coal tumbled into the shaft.

The Cossacks, Glyn, John, and Alf closed their eyes and covered their heads with their arms.

Chapter Thirty

Surface, Three Firs Mine
June 1871

Alexei waved off Miriam and two of the injured miners and entered the hut. Nathan was setting the leg bones of one of the injured, Anna was bandaging his handiwork, and Rivka was washing another patient.

A deep rumble resounded from beneath the ground. They all froze.

'Was that a fall?' Anna demanded.

Alexei charged back to the cage. He returned moments that seemed like hours later. 'I don't know anything,' he pre-empted Anna and Nathan's questions, 'other than it shook the miners who were coming up in the cage.'

'They reached the surface?' Nathan asked.

'Safely, but the cage operator is refusing to send anyone else down until he hears from below.'

'Are there more injured?' Nathan checked.

'None on the surface, but Mr Edwards has sent up some miners who appear to be suffering from shock. Should I give them vodka?'

'In moderation, no more than a shot or two each. Send them back to the hospital, Sarah will treat them. How many are still down there?'

'Nine we know are alive including Glyn, Richard, and Alf,' Alexei divulged. 'From what the miners who've come up are saying, they're doing all they can to rescue the missing men. They can hear them, but the fall was heavy and there's no way to get at them except through the debris. I offered to go down after the last lot came up but Mr Hughes sent a message telling me to stay up here.'

'Mr Hughes needs trained colliers underground, not well-meaning amateurs, Alexei. Untrained men are a hazard and a nuisance in a disaster,' Anna declared.

It was one remark too many from a girl six years younger than him. 'What would you know about a coal mine, missy?'

'I worked in a drift mine in Merthyr for five years as a trapper. I saw three falls in that time.'

'You're a child.'

'I was a child then.'

'Stop arguing about things you know nothing of, and get the bodies and shocked miners back to Hughesovka, Alexei.' Nathan reached into his bag for a phial of morphine.

'Has anyone mentioned Richard?' Anna questioned. The only indication of strain was in her eyes.

'No one's said anything about him, other than he's working to get the men out and he's a hero,' Alexei replied. 'I'm sure he'll be fine, he's...'

'Organise transport for these two injured men,' Anna interrupted, unable to bear Alexei's well-meaning but irritating platitudes. 'They need to get to the hospital as soon as the troika returns. Have you sent the corpses to the hospital?'

'I was about to.'

'Do it.'

Underground, Three Firs Mine
June 1871

Richard covered his nose and mouth with his scarf, held his breath, and waited until the avalanche subsided. When the only sounds were those of the men behind him struggling to breathe, he called out. 'Everyone all right?'

'In one piece and better placed than you, boy. Get back here,' John replied.

'It's worth my carrying on for a few more minutes, sir.' Richard tightened his grip on his short-handled pick and wriggled forward on his stomach. After a tense five minutes of hard scrabbling and pushing at the new fall, he halted and shouted.

Several voices yelled back in unison from behind the debris.

'They're close. Keep them talking, Mr Edwards,'

Richard cried out, 'so I can aim at the sound.'

'Call out your names. Yuri take note,' Glyn ordered.

Alf turned his head.

'There's a gap to the left of Richard, sir,' Alf breathed heavily. 'Look, there's light shining through from the other side.'

Glyn blinked hard and blinked again. Alf was right. A flickering but unmistakeable light was shining at the head of the hole Richard was crawling through. 'Any sign of fire damp?' he demanded of Yuri.

Yuri shouted to the Cossacks who'd been monitoring Richard's progress from the perimeter of the fall.

They answered.

'No sign of gas, sir.'

'That hole looks large enough to haul a man through.' Glyn hoped the uncertain light wasn't playing tricks on him.

Alf grinned, his teeth showing white in the gloom. 'Shall we give it a try, sir?'

Richard's trousers were torn through. He knew because he lost more skin from his knees every time he crept forward. His shirt and jacket were thick, but like his moleskin trousers, not thick enough to resist tearing or cushion his body. He gritted his teeth and continued to shuffle towards the light, inch by painful inch, until his elbows and knees felt raw. Every time another shower of dust rained on him he froze and thought about the tons of coal above his head – and the miners he'd worked with who'd been entombed in shafts because Management had balked at the expense of recovering their bodies.

The light drew closer ... and closer ... shadowy figures reached out to him.

'Your Excellency...'

Hands grasped his shoulders and pulled him forward. He pushed the ends of the ropes he carried through to the trapped men and smiled at a face that grinned back at him. 'Hold on to this and tie them together so we can set up a pulley. Time to widen the hole and get you out.'

Men both sides of the fall cheered, precipitating another shower of dust.

'Pull me through and get the smallest man up here so he can be pushed out of this hole.'

A young boy was bundled towards him. Richard fastened him firmly to the rope and tugged it.

'First one, coming through.'

John Hughes answered. 'That's music to my ears, boy. Don't waste time, get the next one ready. No heroics, I want everyone out here safe and sound and in one piece.'

'How many alive and how many injured?' Glyn shouted in Russian.

'Five injured, fifteen alive. Next one coming through is injured. I'm guessing multiple breaks in his legs,' Richard answered in Russian.

Yuri helped Alf retrieve the first boy. 'Thanks be to God.'

'Thanks be to Richard and Alf.' Glyn felt another tug on the rope. A young man momentarily blocked the light before he was pulled and pushed towards Alf.

Above ground, Three Firs Mine
June 1871

Alexei finished wrapping a corpse and lifted it into a troika with the help of a miner. They set it alongside a body Vlad had covered.

'These two dead weights are as much as I can take in the back, sir, without risking overturning,' Vlad warned.

'Take one of the fitter miners with you in the front seat, Vlad.'

'I thought you'd be coming back to the town with me, sir.'

'There's too much to do here. Send the troika back even if you don't bring it yourself. If Mr Edwards gets those twenty miners out we're going to need transport to get them to the hospital quickly.' Alexei watched Vlad drive off before returning to the pithead. The cage was moving up again. He ran over in time to help lift out a man.

'His legs are crushed, sir.'

'I thought all the injured were up.'

The miner grinned. 'This is the first of the men from behind the fall, sir. One of the Welshmen crawled in and made a hole big enough to get them all out.'

'Mr Edwards?'

'No, sir, Mr Parry. He must be a good man to risk his own life to save Russians.'

Alexei fought the emotion rising in his throat but his voice was still hoarse. 'Yes, he is. A very good man.'

Hospital, Hughesovka
June 1871

'You should have seen Richard, Mrs Edwards,' Alf said as Sarah bandaged his hand. 'The way he took control and snapped orders. He wasn't afraid of anything or anybody. Only concerned with getting those miners out alive. I didn't know the boy had it in him.'

'An emergency can bring out the best in people, and no can foretell how anyone will react until it happens. Stretch your fingers for me, Alf. The bandage isn't too tight, is it?'

'No, but it's too big considering I only have a scratch.'

'A scratch from underground left to fester can turn septic and poison the body in no time.'

'I suppose so. Thank you, Mrs Edwards, although I'm sure you have a lot worse than me to look after.'

'Not until the next batch of injured arrive from the mine. Frankly after hearing what happened and seeing the broken and crushed arms and legs I'm surprised only two died.'

'They were killed in the first fall before Mr Hughes and Mr Edwards went down. All the others owe their lives to them and Richard.'

'And you, Alf, I've mastered enough Russian to recognise praise from the Cossacks. They said once Richard forged a path through to the men who were trapped you worked like a demon until you freed every one.'

'They exaggerated. If you've finished, Mrs Edwards, I'll go off now and see if my supper's cooked.'

'They looking after you in the bachelor dormitory?' Richard and Anna had been disappointed when Alf had moved out of the house but she could understand him wanting to move in with his fellow colliers and away from Glyn who was his boss.

'The cooks are looking after all of us, Tonia's a nice girl.'

Sarah suppressed a smile. She'd heard rumours that Alf had found a woman. 'Rest that hand. Don't try using it until you come back here the day after tomorrow so I can check the wound and dress it again.'

'Thank you.'

'Matron!'

'Must go. Take care.'

'You too, Matron.'

Nathan was in the main entrance. 'The last three patients are outside waiting to be unloaded. How have you coped?'

'Fine, the broken limbs are all comfortable and resting. I sent for Ruth and put her in charge of them while I've been dressing wounds.'

'Two more miners in this convoy have crushed legs. I hope I won't have to amputate but I won't know until I operate. Can you assist?'

'Yes. The theatre's ready.'

'Richard and Glyn are with me. Their hands are skinned. Tell the girls to see to them while we're in surgery.'

Glyn Edwards' house, Hughesovka
June 1871

Sarah didn't leave the hospital until all the patients had been treated and were sleeping, including the man who'd had both his legs amputated. She entrusted the ward to Ruth, Yulia, and two of the Cossack girls, after giving them instructions to sleep in four-hour shifts and call her in an emergency. Concerned about the amputee, Nathan had stretched out on a couch in the office in case he should be needed and she wondered if he'd sent a second message of apology to Vasya.

When she crossed the road, she glimpsed a shadow that looked suspiciously like Alexei flitting around the corner of the hospital. She decided he was probably hoping to steal some time with Ruth but she was too tired to investigate what wasn't her business.

After washing in the banya she wrapped herself in a robe and carried her clothes into the house. The hall clock struck three when she climbed the stairs. Only three hours and she'd have to rise again.

A light shone under Richard's door. She tapped it quietly and whispered his name. When there was no reply, she opened the door.

Richard was lying in bed, grimacing in pain.

'Is it your hands? Nathan said you'd skinned them.'

Richard shook his head. 'My chest.'

'Coal dust?'

'No.' He folded back the eiderdown and unbuttoned his pyjama jacket.

'Dear Lord, Richard, did the girls see this?'
'I thought it was a scratch.'
'You miners and your scratches.' She opened his jacket and examined the shredded skin that curled over an angry expanse of raw flesh blackened by coal dust.
'I tried to clean it in the bath house.'
'By the look of it, all you succeeded in doing was getting dirt ingrained in the wound. Don't move. I'll get the medical box.'
Sarah returned with the box and a jug of hot water. She turned up the lamp and set to work. It took half a painful hour – for Richard – to irrigate and clean the wound, and twenty minutes to bandage him.
'I didn't hurt you too much, did I?' Sarah asked as she fastened the last of the bandages around Richard's chest and pinned it in place.
'No more than you did when the Paskeys floored me.'
'Is that the last of the "scratches"? Or should I look for more.' She untied the string on his pyjama bottoms and checked his lower abdomen. The skin was clean, unblemished but her light, gently probing touch had the same effect as when she'd nursed him in Merthyr after the Paskeys had beaten him.
He looked up at her, reached out, pulled her head down to his, and kissed her. A long, lingering kiss that carried sharp painful memories of Peter and the exquisite erotic relationship they'd shared. The way his lips had felt when they'd touched hers ... the touch of his hands on her bare skin ... the expression in his eyes when he'd gazed at her...

The intense loneliness that had crippled her since Peter's death seemed more agonising than ever. Could it ... would it be so wrong of her to seek solace with a boy who suddenly seemed a man?

She untied her robe and slid into the bed beside him.

Richard was terrified of the passion Sarah engendered in him, of losing control, but most of all, of failing her. She'd taken the initiative and it felt right. If he'd been capable of rational thought he might have reflected she was the one who'd been married. She'd made love before; she knew what she was doing. But lost, aroused, overwhelmed, all he was certain of was that he was a quivering, confused novice.

Slowly, surely, she moved over him, careful to avoid his wounds as she straddled his thighs. She guided him inside her, moving her body closer and closer to his, tantalizing yet holding back until he climaxed.

Afterwards he felt spent, exhausted, yet he wanted to stay locked within her for ever. When she finally lifted herself away from him, he felt bereft. He reached out and caught her by the waist to prevent her from leaving his bed. Ignoring his pain he pulled her towards him until he was nestling into her back, his head buried in her lavender-scented hair.

'Please, don't go,' he whispered.

'I have to. That was insanity, Richard. You're a child...'

'I'm a man, and if that was insanity I hope I

never regain my senses.' He kissed her shoulder, her neck, caressed her breasts. She turned to face him. He kissed her lips and that kiss led to another – and another – until the urgent need they generated in one another left no time for protests – or even thought.

That time he took the lead; keeping pace with her until they both sank back before plunging headlong into sleep.

'Are you in pain?' Praskovia sat up when Glyn left the bed.

In the subdued light of the open fire she looked like a Renaissance Madonna with her long red hair flowing over her shoulders and naked breasts, her eyes drowsy, seductive, beautiful, desirable – and she was his. That was the problem, but he didn't want to talk about the questions it raised until he'd found a solution.

'I didn't mean to disturb you, please go back to sleep.' He picked up his robe and slipped it on.

'Are you in pain?' she reiterated.

'No.' He held up his bandaged hands. 'I can't even feel the cuts and bruises. Ruth did a good job of cleaning them and Nathan gave me something to dull the pain.'

'Then what?' She moved close to him as he sank down on the edge of the bed.

'Today, underground...' he began. 'Have you ever been in a mine?'

'Once with my father. Misha and I were curious. When we asked questions about what it was like he took us down, but only as far as the entry chamber. I was so petrified I couldn't stop shaking. It was just how my father described the evil world of witches and goblins in his fairy tales. Everything dark, horrid, damp, stinking, and dirty. It was easy to imagine fearful things lurking in the shadows beyond the lamplight.'

'I've never considered a pit frightening, but then I've never been caught in a fall before today. I grew up on tales of mining tragedies – explosions, pit props that shattered, and splintered coal faces. It was impossible not to when you worked in the industry in Wales. I can even recite the number of casualties in any given year. One hundred and forty miners killed in Risca in 1860, one hundred and seventy-eight in Ferndale in 1867, fifty-three in Ferndale last year. To me they seemed like someone else's tragedy. Firedamp, explosions, falls, and dead miners left to rot in abandoned seams because it was deemed too expensive to bring them up for a Christian burial – none of it seemed relevant to me. Until now the pits I went down were simply places to work. I never thought I'd end up entombed in one.'

She wrapped her arms around him. 'You won't.'

'I wish I could be as certain as you.'

'Everyone said the twenty miners who were trapped would have died if it hadn't been for you and Richard.'

'Richard, not me. He was the one who risked his life to wriggle through a dangerously small hole to reach the trapped men without sparing a thought as to what would happen to him if there was another collapse. It was pure luck the second fall didn't kill someone. But despite Richard and Alf's best efforts and my poor ones, two men are dead, three out of the twenty who were trapped are so severely injured they might not recover, and there's injured besides...'

'The deaths and injuries aren't your fault, Glyn. Mr Hughes has only just bought that mine from my people. Cossacks have always been reckless when it comes to safety. They think it's manly to laugh at danger. You only have to consider the way my father died. One of the miners told me the pit prop that collapsed and brought the rocks down on his head had been cracked for weeks yet no one bothered to repair it.'

'That's no excuse. I should have checked that mine the minute Mr Hughes bought it.'

'When you had so many others to assess? You and Mr Hughes never stop working. Look in the mirror. You haven't regained the strength you lost when you had cholera. You asked Alf and Richard to examine the mine today. If they'd declared it unsafe you would have closed it. Remember, no one forced those men to go underground. Every one of them knows mining's a dangerous business.'

'Hunger doesn't give a man a choice where he works,'

'Men work where they can and close to where they live. Here it's always been the mines. We've had worse disasters but we've never had anyone as brave as Mr Hughes, you, Richard, and Alf prepared to risk their lives to save others. Even Alexei did what he could up top, sending for the doctor, organising transport...'

'You know a lot about what happened.'

'I went to the hospital this afternoon to see if I

could help. When the first miners arrived they told us how you'd insisted they go up top to safety so you could concentrate on rescuing the men who were trapped.'

'How did they know Richard risked his life?'

'They didn't, but people came to the kitchen door later to tell us.' Careful to avoid his hands she wrapped her arms around him. 'Are you coming back to bed?'

'I should. I probably won't be able to keep my eyes open in the morning.'

'Morning is almost here.'

He picked up his pocket watch from the table, opened it, and peered at its face in the firelight. 'At best we'll have another hour or two in bed. I didn't thank you for refraining from bombarding me with questions when I came home.'

'You may have been on your feet but you were sleeping.'

'I was exhausted.' Wanting to check on the injured as well as have his hands seen to, Glyn had stayed in the hospital until two o'clock. He recalled returning to the house, hugging Praskovia, and falling into bed. She was right, he might have been upright, but he'd been sleepwalking. His last memory was of her tugging off his boots as he lay face down on the bedcover.

'Have you slept at all?' she asked.

'A little. I think I'm thirsty.'

'The brandy decanter's on the table.'

'In my present state that would finish me off. I'd prefer kvass, or even better, water.'

Praskovia slipped on her robe, left the room by the back door, and reappeared a few minutes later with a tray of cheese, ham, bread, a jug of water and another of kvass.

'I didn't ask for a midnight feast.' He noticed there were two plates and glasses.

'We're both awake.'

After she set the tray on the table he lifted her onto his lap. 'When I was underground watching an overhang of rock that looked as though it could come crashing down at any minute...'

'On you?'

'Me, Mr Hughes, Richard, Alf, the miners who were helping us – all I could think of was you and this room. I couldn't bear the thought of never seeing you again, never touching you, never kissing you...' He broached the concern that had been keeping him awake. 'If anything should happen to me, Praskovia...'

'It didn't and it won't.' She laid her fingers over his mouth. 'Never mention such a thing again, Glyn. Never talk or even think about it because if you do, it will happen and I will lose you.'

'Superstitious nonsense.'

'It's true.'

He picked up a slice of ham. 'I see you have old wives' tales in Russia as well as Wales.'

'Old wives know about life, especially when it comes to giving advice to young girls on how to look after their men.' She buried her fingers in the thick hair at the nape of his neck and massaged his taut muscles.

'I'm serious.'

She thought of the secret she had to tell him. If he'd noticed she'd put on weight he hadn't mentioned it. But it could only be a matter of time.

And then ... it was easier to put it from her mind and enjoy the moment. 'I don't want to think about anything except you and making love.' She fed him another slice of ham before linking her arms around his neck, snuggling close, and kissing him.

Realising he would get no sense from her while she remained in her present mood he lifted her from his lap. 'We need to sleep. I've arranged to meet Mr Hughes in his house after breakfast.'

'You're coming to bed?'

'In a few minutes. Warm the sheets for me.' He watched her climb back beneath the eiderdown.

'Glyn...'

'I'm coming.'

Her eyes closed. A few minutes later her breath steadied into the rhythm of sleep. He reached for his box of cigars and matches, lit one, sat back, and stared at the fire. His priority had to be making provision for Praskovia if anything untoward happened to him.

He'd amassed considerable savings since he'd begun working for John Hughes. Because the company paid all his travelling and living expenses he'd been able to bank practically all his wages except for the allowance he paid Betty. After a particularly bad Channel crossing early in his career he'd taken out a life insurance policy payable both as an annuity and lump sum to his wife on his death.

Betty would be able to live in comfort for the rest of her days, but now there was Praskovia. He couldn't bear to think what could have happened to her if he'd been killed in that fall.

Would Sarah and Richard have stayed on in the house and continued to employ her, Yelena, and Pyotr? The house was mortgaged to the company. Would the company have taken possession and sold the property evicting not only his lodgers but his servants?

He had to check his savings...

Praskovia opened her eyes. 'Glyn, you said you need to sleep.'

'I'm coming, my love.'

'My love'! How easily that phrase had come to him. He climbed into bed, wrapped his arm around her, and was mentally listing his assets when sleep washed over him. A deep sleep in which he was aware of nothing except Praskovia lying next to him.

Sarah woke with a start. The room was dark. Then she heard the sound that had woken her. Footsteps running lightly over the landing and down the stairs. They were followed minutes later by a slightly heavier more masculine tread. Anna and Alexei.

She moved and felt the warmth of a body lying alongside her own. Her spirits soared. Peter…

She opened her eyes, stared into the shadows until her eyes burned and remembered. Memories came flooding back of the previous day and – night. Ashamed, embarrassed by the thought that she'd seduced Richard, a child over a decade younger than her, she grabbed the white splash of robe lying on the floor, slipped it on, and tied it at her waist.

'What time is it?' Richard mumbled groggily

from the bed.

'I've no idea,' she whispered. 'I can't see a thing but I heard Alexei and Anna go downstairs.'

Richard sat up and fumbled with the matches and lamp on his bedside table. He lit the lamp at the second attempt, replaced the shade and read the clock on the wall.

'Twenty past six. I have to get moving if I'm going to talk to Mr Edwards over breakfast.'

'As long as it is just talk. You can't work with those hands...'

'They're not that bad.'

'You've had hardly any sleep.'

'I had as much as you.'

She felt colour flooding into her cheeks and looked away from him. 'The first thing every nurse learns is how to live without sleep.'

'Sarah...'

'I have to get back into my own room without anyone seeing me.'

Richard lifted the bedcover, scrabbled for his pyjama trousers, which he found in a crumpled heap at the foot of the mattress, and pulled them on. The bandages on his chest were already stained by blood. He went to the French windows, opened the drapes, and looked out at the balcony. 'There's no one in the street, but there's a sprinkling of rain, you'll need your shoes.'

'I have them.' She found her leather slippers under the bed.

'Is your window open?'

'I never lock it.'

'Good, I'll come in that way tonight.'

She glared at him. 'You will not...'

'We need to talk.'

'Last night...'

'Was a mistake?' he challenged. 'I don't think so, Sarah.'

'"Sarah"! I'm still Mrs Edwards, Richard.'

'As soon as I'm free I'll visit the hospital.'

'With the number of patients we admitted yesterday I'll be busy all day.'

'Then I'll sit and wait until you're free.'

'Richard – last night was–'

'Wonderful.'

Speechless, all she could do was look at him.

'Can you honestly say any different?'

'This is not the time to argue. Is the street still empty?'

'Yes. Go. I'll follow and mess up the puddles on the balcony so the maids won't see your tracks.'

Sarah slipped out through the door, letting in a draught of fresh morning air. Richard picked up his robe, thrust his feet into his slippers, and followed her. He saw her prints in the pools of water and trod in them, walking up and down, covering the steps she'd taken with his own. He glanced occasionally at the window of her room but the curtains remained resolutely closed.

'Sir?' A maid peeked out of the French windows to his room. 'Shall I close the door?'

'No, thank you. I'm coming in now. I wanted some air.' He continued scuffing the pools of water with the damp toes of his wool work slippers as he made his way inside.

'I brought your warm water and tea, sir.'

'Thank you.'

The girl bobbed a curtsey and left.

He realised how quickly he'd become accustomed to being waited on. If his mother could see him she wouldn't be proud of one of her children ordering other people around.

He poured water into the bowl on the washstand, and managed to ignore the pain in his skinned hands long enough to wash his hands and face. He lathered his shaving brush but he couldn't concentrate on the simplest task because his thoughts kept returning to the events of the night. He even caught himself smiling at his reflection.

After his initial fumblings, what had happened between him and Sarah – he'd never be able to think of her as Mrs Edwards again – had been so natural, exhilarating, and passionate that he couldn't wait to repeat the experience – and the only way he could think of ensuring that was to marry her.

Lost in imaginings of his future married life he didn't give a single thought to Alice or her existence until he finished dressing.

Mr Edward Edwards had been right in advising him to forget Alice. It had been nothing more than a childish infatuation on both his and Alice's parts. It had probably only lasted as long as it had because of her father's opposition.

Whereas Sarah was now his entire world.

Chapter Thirty-one

Glyn Edwards' house, Hughesovka
June 1871

'You will be careful today?' Praskovia handed Glyn a freshly laundered shirt.

'I'll have no choice until my hands heal. I can't fasten a button, let alone pick up a shovel, drive a carriage, or operate machinery.'

She waited until Glyn pushed his arms through the sleeves of the shirt and buttoned it for him. 'You look tired. You should have stayed in bed.'

'I have to see Mr Hughes. Decisions have to be made about the pits.'

'Surely there's nothing that can't wait.'

'If the company's ever going to manufacture iron we haven't a minute to spare. We were hoping to run the initial production tests early next year. At this rate we'll be lucky to run them ten years from now.'

'You and Mr Hughes are going to drive yourselves into the ground.'

'Rubbish. We thrive on hard work.' He snapped without intending to.

'I suppose that means you're going to go underground again today, although with your hands the way they are if you trip you won't even be able to stop yourself from falling.'

Glyn heard a tremor in her voice. 'I'll be fine.'

'You say that but...'

'I'll be home early, Praskovia. I promise. I'll find an excuse so we can have supper here, alone together.' He wiped a tear from her eye.

'I must check that the girls have laid the breakfast table properly.'

'I'm sure they have. Praskovia...'

'We'll talk when you come back early.'

He wondered if she'd intended to sound sceptical.

'Richard. We weren't expecting to see you until late afternoon.' Glyn entered the dining room to find Richard and Alexei already at the table.

'I want to take a closer look at the mine,' Richard said. 'That fall brought down a wide section of seam. There's quite a few tons of coal just lying there, ripe to be picked up and hauled to the surface.'

'Before we do anything about the coal we need to make the entry shaft and the area around it that leads to the seams secure.' Glyn managed to grasp up a fork in his heavily bandaged hand and spear a piece of bread.

'I'll go down with Alf and examine the props.'

'No work and no digging until those hands heal,' Glyn ordered. 'Good morning, Sarah. You're another one I didn't expect to see until afternoon, the time you went to bed last night or should I say, early this morning.'

'Patients can't look after themselves, Glyn.' She reached for the coffee pot and filled her cup.

'Aren't you going to sit down?' Richard asked.

'No time. Look after your hands and chest.'

She avoided his gaze.

'Chest?' Glyn asked.

'He skinned it yesterday but didn't tell the girls in the hospital. I dressed it last night but it needs to be looked at again today.'

'I'll visit the hospital this afternoon,' Richard said.

She remembered the fresh blood staining his bandages. 'Make your visit this morning.'

'You're not eating?' Glyn asked.

'I'll grab something in the hospital. See you later.' Sarah left her cup on the table and almost ran out.

Immersed in his thoughts Glyn didn't notice she'd gone until after she'd left, but Alexei did.

'Like your sister, Sarah's in a hurry to get at the patients this morning.'

'Some of those miners are badly injured,' Richard reminded Alexei.

'I was there, I saw them.'

'Sorry, too tired to think properly.'

'In which case you're definitely not going underground today, Richard.' Glyn looked up as Praskovia entered with a tray.

'Fried and boiled eggs, ham, and blinis. Thank you, Praskovia.' Alexei helped himself to fried eggs.

'If you tell me what you want I'll put it on your plate to save your hands, master.'

'Ham and boiled eggs please. Thank you,' Glyn gave Praskovia a conciliatory smile. It wasn't reciprocated.

Hospital, Hughesovka
June 1871

Sarah used the excuse of the influx of patients to remain in the hospital until late evening. She ate sandwiches in the office with Nathan rather than cross the road to share the evening meal with Glyn, Anna, and the one person she didn't want to face – Richard.

It was Nathan who demanded she go home. 'What is it you tell your nurses when they work until they fall asleep on their feet? I believe it's something about "being no use to themselves or their patients".' He looked up from a copy of *The Lancet*; one of several Peter had packed, 'in case they proved useful'.

'I'm concerned about the double amputee.'

'We all are, which is why I've made a bed up for myself on the sofa in here again. As I'm staying here, you won't be needed tonight, Sarah, but you will be tomorrow, especially if the girls call me in the early hours.'

'I'm going.' She left Sonya's desk where she'd been making out the ward maids' rotas for July and August.

'There's no need for you to hurry over in the morning. Catch up on some sleep. In fact, you could do with a few days' break, just don't take it until all the miners are well enough to be discharged.'

'And you? You have a wedding to go to, remember?' She lifted her cape and hat from the back of the door.

'The rabbi has postponed it until next Thursday.'

'Let's hope we don't get any more patients between now and then.'

'I've no doubt Vasya has sent up a prayer. Goodnight, Sarah.'

Sarah shouted 'Good night' but she couldn't resist making a last visit to the ward. Yulia was sitting at the nurse's desk that had a vantage point of all the beds. The patients were all sleeping, either naturally or as a result of the soporifics Nathan had prescribed.

She waved to the porters in their room, went out, and crossed the road. Pyotr opened the front door of Glyn's house as she reached the gate.

'Mrs Edwards, I've been waiting for you.' Praskovia came to meet her. 'We've cleared the dining room but I can lay the table again, or make you up a tray.'

'Neither, but thank you, Praskovia. I should have sent a message. I ate in the hospital.'

'My mother made poppy seed cake, and fresh coffee is brewing.'

Sarah smiled. 'You know how to tempt me. I'll have it in the drawing room, please.' She hung up her cape and walked in to find John Hughes sitting with Glyn, Alexei, Anna, and Richard around the fire.

'How are the invalids?' John asked.

'All the patients are resting, but some are better than others.' She avoided Richard's eye as she took the comfortable chair Glyn pulled close to the fire for her.

'You sound like a hospital bulletin board,' Glyn poured her a glass of wine. 'What about the man whose legs were amputated?'

'He isn't doing as well as we'd like. Nathan's sleeping in the office in case he's needed.'

'You were right about Dr Kharber, Mrs Edwards,' John said. 'He's proving to be an excellent medical director.'

'I've worked with many doctors, but few as dedicated as him. We're lucky to have him.'

'We were just talking about the Cossacks – the regiment not the people. Colonel Zonov has invited us all to go hunting with the officers after church on Sunday,' Glyn updated her on the conversation.

'Hunting what?' Sarah asked.

'Hares, deer, wild boar, wolves if we find any.' Alexei took the cigar Glyn offered him.

'Thank you,' Sarah took the coffee and cake Praskovia brought in for her.

'Every woman living on the steppe should learn to hunt, lest they become the prey. Venture out alone and you could be stalked and attacked by a bear, boar, or...' Alexei lowered his voice to a booming and, he hoped, frightening baritone, and howled in a fair imitation of a wolf.

'Women stand more chance of being attacked by a two-legged drunk in this town than a four-legged animal.' Praskovia cleared their empty plates and glasses.

'Surely not.' Glyn was instantly concerned for her safety.

'We're used to looking out for ourselves. But Alexei's right,' Praskovia conceded, 'women should learn to hunt. As my father used to say, every cookpot needs filling.'

'Not with wolf, I hope,' Glyn commented.

'Some venison or wild boar wouldn't go amiss. But whether we succeed in filling the cookpots or not, hunting's good, healthy exercise, and a day in the fresh air might do us all some good. That's if Richard and Glyn's hands are up to holding reins. If they're not they can ride in a troika.' John rose. 'Time I left if I'm going to put in a day's work tomorrow. See you in the office first thing, Glyn, Richard, Alexei. Goodnight, everyone.'

'I'll tell your coachman you're leaving, sir.' Praskovia headed for the kitchen where she knew she'd find the man flirting with the parlour maid.

'I'll walk you to the door, sir.' Glyn went out with John.

'Do you think our new riding habits will be ready by Sunday?' Anna asked Sarah.

'I'll ask Miriam to call in the shtetl tailor's tomorrow. If they are, he can send them down.' Sarah sipped her coffee. 'Will your grandmother allow us to borrow her horses again, Alexei?'

'She'll be glad to have them exercised.'

'That's what I love most about your grandmother. She always makes her generosity appear as if the recipient is doing her the favour.'

'It's a gift she has,' Alexei acknowledged.

'If it wasn't for her I'd never have learned to ride,' Anna said. 'Her horses are so well-schooled compared to the hired mounts I've seen people taking out of the public stables.'

'As the Cossacks buy up every decent foal on the steppe, the only ones left for hire are either broken down nags or wild.' Alexei stretched his arms above his head. 'After yesterday I need an early night.'

'I should go up, too. I have a textbook to finish.'

'You need sleep, Anna, not study, or if you must read, do so for pleasure.' Sarah kissed the cheek Anna offered her. 'Sleep tight.'

'Goodnight, Alexei, Mrs Edwards.' Richard, who'd been unnaturally silent since Sarah had entered the room, followed his sister out.

Glyn returned as the boys left. 'Would you like me to visit Peter and your daughter's grave with you tomorrow, Sarah?'

'It would be good to have company. Neither of us need Peter's birthday to remember him but I'd like to mark the day.'

'You are happy here, aren't you?' Glyn asked seriously. 'We're all so busy there's never much time for talking. I still feel guilty for dragging you and Peter here.'

'I told you when Peter died, it was our choice to come here and it was a marvellous opportunity. If we'd stayed in London, or even Merthyr, we wouldn't have had the freedom to run our own medical facility until we'd reached old age.'

'An old age Peter never saw,' he said soberly. 'And you're alone...'

'I have my career and I wouldn't have more if I returned to Britain. Here, I not only have my work but the gratification of training the girls. Giving them the means to live independently means a great deal to me.'

'I suspect more to them. From what I saw when I first came here with Mr Hughes the only work open to women was domestic or in the fields. There won't be many opportunities for women once the furnaces are built, other than a few positions in the offices and laboratories.'

Sarah forced a smile. 'So, will you accept that although happiness went with Peter and our child I'm content here?'

'I will. We're almost a family with Richard, Anna, and Alexei. A sort of proxy uncle and aunt.' He reached for the brandy decanter. 'Although they make me feel a hundred years old on occasions.'

'I never thought of myself as a middle-aged aunt, but you're quite right, Glyn. That's exactly what I am.'

Glyn wondered if he'd imagined the bitterness in Sarah's voice. 'Drink?' he held up the decanter.

'No, thank you. Not with a full ward to minister to in the morning. Sleep well.'

Sarah undressed, climbed into bed, and read until she realised she hadn't absorbed a word. She turned down the lamp, lay back on her pillows, and listened to the sound of horses' hooves accompanied by conversations as men rode beneath her window towards Madam Koshka's and the hotel.

She turned over and was staring at the shadows that loomed above the stove when the French doors that led to the balcony opened and closed.

She sat up.

'It's only me.'

'Go back to your room,' she ordered Richard.

'We need to talk.' He tripped over a chair.

'Quiet!' She fumbled for the matches next to the lamp and lit it. 'Last night was a huge mistake.'

'No it wasn't. Please,' he held up his hand. 'If I crept in there beside you I guarantee in less than a minute there'd be no more arguing.'

'Richard, can't you see this isn't as it should be.' She was determined to be honest no matter how much it hurt her – and Richard. 'I'm twice your age...'

'If you were twice my age you'd be nearly forty.'

'I'm thirty, and since Peter died unbearably lonely. I'm using you...'

'Use away.'

'It's not right. You're young, your hormones are raging, and I'm...'

He covered her mouth with his and untied his robe. His touch was more assured than it had been the night before. Afterwards he held her close as they lay together in her bed.

Restlessness forgotten, Sarah closed her eyes and gripped Richard's hand. Too exhausted and beset by guilt to sleep, she felt like an adulteress who'd betrayed both Peter and their love for one another. But guilt didn't prevent her from taking comfort from the warmth of Richard's presence in her bed.

Experience had taught her that infatuation, unlike love, couldn't last. And Richard was only infatuated with her; of that much she was certain. But even knowing what she shared with the boy would be fleeting, she still silently blessed him for being there.

Hughesovka
August 1871

Sarah's visit to Peter's grave was brief, and she missed the hunting trip because the miner who'd had both his legs amputated succumbed to septicaemia. It spread to one of the other injured patients in the ward and despite Nathan's efforts both died.

The day after Nathan married Vasya and his bride moved into his house, a young boy who lived in one of the "pit" dormitories was brought to the hospital suffering from a high fever. When Nathan saw rose-coloured spots on the boy's lower chest and abdomen, he diagnosed typhoid.

Nathan, John, and Glyn immediately set about trying to improve sanitation, hygiene, and waste disposal in what the locals had christened the "hole houses" but it took over two months of work by both the company and hospital staff, during which wells were sunk and fresh cesspits dug, to contain the outbreak.

Like Nathan, Sarah rarely managed more than four hours sleep a night while the epidemic raged, but they were hours she shared with Richard simply because he was in her room when she reached it. Too tired to argue, glad of his company, she gradually began to accept his presence in her bed and her life without protest.

On Glyn's birthday, Sarah left Yulia and Miriam instructions to fetch her if any of the typhoid patients' conditions worsened in the night, and crossed the road. She bathed in the banya before changing into her mourning evening gown in honour of the occasion, and for the first time in two months joined the others for dinner, albeit late.

John was at the table with Glyn, Richard, Anna, Alexei, Catherine, Sonya, Ruth, and, surprisingly, Alf. Their claret glasses were full, as were the vodka glasses alongside them. The men rose to their feet when she entered, and she realised from their heightened colour they'd been celebrating for some time.

'I've had an unexpected birthday present.' Glyn handed her an envelope.

She took it from him and studied the crest. 'A double-headed eagle. This can't be from...'

'The Tsar? Yes, it is.' Richard couldn't contain the momentous news a moment longer. 'It's the Romanov coat of arms. I've had one as well as Mr Edwards and Alf.'

'Richard, Glyn, and Alf are to be given gold medals by the Tsar for saving the miners.' John filled Sarah's glass as one of the maids brought in a bowl of reheated soup for her.

'We've all received invitations to a reception in the Winter Palace in St Petersburg,' Richard continued.

'When are you going?'

'Tomorrow,' John replied, 'and Mrs Ignatova, Ruth, and Sonya are coming with us.'

'Ruth needs wedding clothes,' Catherine explained, 'and as I'm chaperoning her and Sonya, I'd like to take Anna as well, with your permission, Sarah.'

'Of course, Anna can go with you. It'll be a marvellous opportunity for her to see more of the countryside as well as the city.'

'Not to mention the Tsar and Tsarina,' Alexei enthused.

'If we go tomorrow we should be back in good time for Alexei and Ruth's wedding,' Glyn handed Sarah the bread basket.

'When the Tsar extends an invitation it's not

done to keep him waiting, especially when the New Russia Company is dependent on him for his good will,' John added.

'How long will you be gone?'

'No more than two or three weeks,' John declared. 'We'll go North by rail from Moscow to St Petersburg and we'll take carriages to where the railway starts this side of Moscow.'

'Come with us, Mrs Edwards?' Richard pressed. 'You'd have a wonderful time.'

'I'm sure I would but I dare not leave the hospital at present with so many patients seriously ill.'

'Are you sure the hospital can manage without me, Mrs Edwards?' Anna asked.

'We haven't had a new case of typhoid fever for four days, Anna, and you're not indispensable yet. Besides, you should go. It's the chance of a lifetime to visit St Petersburg. Will you actually see the Tsar?' Sarah asked.

'According to the invitations. They all say "and party" which means those receiving medals can bring guests,' John confirmed.

'Take lots of photographs, Glyn, so you can show them to me when you return.'

'I doubt I'll be allowed to take one of the Tsar, Sarah, but I promise to take as many as I can of everything that's worth seeing so you'll know where to go when you visit the city.'

'Mr Hughes has telegraphed the Hotel Angleterre and made reservations for us,' Richard handed the maid his dirty plate. 'Imagine me staying in a hotel. Do your remember us talking about it in the court in Merthyr, Anna?'

'And you saying we'll never find out what it

feels like.'

'But you won't be staying in the hotel, Anna. The girls will be staying with me in my town house,' Catherine informed Sarah, 'and we really would love to have you accompany us.'

'Please, come with us, Mrs Edwards,' Richard coaxed.

'Please, Mrs Edwards,' Ruth, Sonya, and Anna added their pleas to Richard's.

'I really can't leave the hospital at the moment, but perhaps next time you go I'll be able to travel with you.'

Alexei raised his vodka glass. 'To my brave friends, and the Tsar, who recognises their worth.'

Sarah hadn't eaten all day and the vodka went straight to her head. She was pleased for Glyn, Richard, and Alf, but the thought of a couple of weeks without Richard was suddenly and unexpectedly hard to bear. Until she remembered that shortly she'd have to learn to live without him for a lot longer than a few weeks.

The party broke up when Catherine, Ruth, and Sonya left, escorted by John and Alf. As Glyn had invited everyone to a six-o'clock breakfast before they set off the following morning, Richard prepared for the journey before bed. He went to his room, packed all the clean clothes he could find, and checked the wallet he'd bought in the company shop when he'd last been paid. He still counted his wealth in pounds, shillings, and pence. He had over ten pounds in roubles but he had more in savings deposited in the company bank, although he sent a third of his wages to his brothers in Merthyr every month.

He'd intended to buy a new winter coat for himself before the cold weather set in, and wondered if they'd be any cheaper in St Petersburg. He deposited his travelling bag next to the door, laid out his clothes for the morning, undressed, wrapped himself in a robe he'd taken from the bath house, and stole on to the balcony.

As he'd hoped, Sarah had left her window open. He slipped inside.

'Are you asleep?' he whispered.

'If I was, I'm not now.' She folded back the bedclothes. He climbed in beside her.

'I'm going to miss you. Will you miss me?'

'I won't miss being woken by you as soon as I've gone to sleep,' she teased.

'Sorry, but I always wait to make sure everyone else in the house is asleep or at least in their rooms.' He wrapped his arm around her waist.

'This medal is an honour for you. One that you, Alf and Gly deserve,' she murmured.

'I wish…'

'What?'

'That my mother had known.'

'If you believe in an afterlife, she does.'

'Do you believe in an afterlife?' he asked seriously.

'I try not to think about it too often, but I'd like to believe that Peter and our baby are alive somewhere. I have days when they seem close. But I also have days when the idea of heaven and an afterlife seems impossible.'

'If there's no such thing, it gives us an excuse to make the most of the here and now.'

'It does.'

He reached out to her. He'd come a long way since they'd first made love. Now he was neither timid nor faltering. He'd learned exactly how to please her, and she'd always known how to please him.

Glyn checked the dining and drawing rooms; turned off the lamps to save Pyotr the trouble, and went to his room. As usual, the brandy decanter and a glass were on the table next to his chair and a plate of tiny delicate sandwiches next to it. But there was no sign of Praskovia. He went to the door and checked it was open. It was.

Normally he was in his room if not in bed by ten thirty. It was after eleven. He didn't want to disturb Praskovia if she was sleeping but as she'd overheard the conversation at the dinner table he wanted to talk to her.

The door in the passage was locked so he risked tapping her bedroom door. When there was no answer he tried it. It opened. Praskovia was sitting in front of the mirror brushing her hair. Her eyes were heavy and there were tear stains on her cheeks.

He moved behind her chair and looked at her face in the mirror. 'I missed you.'

'You're going away.'

'Only for a few weeks. Is something the matter?'

Tears fell from her eyes but she made no sound.

He sat on the bed opposite her. 'Whatever's wrong?'

'I'm having a baby.'

'A baby! You're sure?'

'I saw Sarah a few weeks ago, she confirmed it. I didn't tell her that you were the father...'

'A baby,' Glyn repeated.

He'd wondered if there was something wrong not only with him, but his family. Edward's wife Judith had never become pregnant. Sarah had lost Peter's baby which was understandable in the circumstances, but even his brother Tom had died without fathering a child, although Mary had gone on to have a large family with her second husband.

'I'm sorry. If you want me to go...'

'Go – what on earth are you talking about? Where would you go with my child? This is wonderful news, Praskovia.'

'You want the child?'

'I want you and our child.' He took the hairbrush from her hand and lifted her on to his lap. 'I'm going to be a father. This calls for some changes. From now on you must behave like the mistress of this house, not the housekeeper. That means living with me, eating with me – you'll have to move into my room, we must be a family, Praskovia. A real family... I have so much to do, so much to think about. I must write to my wife and ask her for a divorce...'

'You're pleased?' She couldn't believe what he was saying.

'Pleased... Praskovia, you've given me so much, and now this. Pleased is not a big enough word. I'm delighted, ecstatic... I'm...'

'My mother said that you'd throw me, her, and Pyotr out of the house.'

'That's insane. Come into my room. It's warmer there, and we have to talk. I can't possibly go to St

Petersburg now.'

'You have to. The Tsar wants to see you so you must go.'

'It's more important that I make provision for you and our child should anything happen to me.'

'Please don't talk like that. You mean everything to me, Glyn. I never thought a man would be so kind to me.'

'Kind ... this is just the beginning.'

'I have to pack for you. You will go St Petersburg, won't you?'

'If I must,' he kissed her, 'but it will be a very long two weeks without you.'

Praskovia packed while Glyn wrote out a new will. He arranged for a transfer from his private bank account to pay off the mortgage on the house and the residue to be paid to Praskovia in the event of his death.

He placed all the relevant papers in an envelope so the company lawyer could look them over in the morning. He went to bed with Praskovia. She fell asleep after they made love but unable to close his eyes, his mind in turmoil with thoughts whirling around his head he went to his desk and wrote one last document. A letter to his wife Betty.

Hughesovka, August 1871

Dear Betty,

I am sorry to have to write this to you instead of telling you in person, but given the distance between us for some years, and I don't mean in miles, it can't be entirely unexpected.

I have met a girl in Hughesovka. I love her and she is going to have my child.

Please forgive me and please give me a divorce. I will continue to pay you the annuity I settled on you when we married. In addition, you will inherit the proceeds of my insurance policy on my death which should ensure that you will live in comfort for the rest of your days.

I regret that I have not been a better husband, Betty. Thank you for the good times. If you can find it in your heart to forgive me, I would be grateful.

Glyn Edwards.

Chapter Thirty-two

Glyn Edwards' house, Hughesovka
August 1871

Richard left Sarah's bed, lit the lamp, and checked the clock. The hands pointed to five. He palmed Sarah's ring box from the bedside table on his way to the washstand. After checking she was still asleep, he opened it. He'd never seen Sarah remove her wedding ring, but the box held a ring she wore in the evenings and on Sundays when she wasn't working. A simple gold band set with seed pearls arranged in a flower pattern. She'd told him Peter had given it to her when she'd agreed to marry him.

He took the ring from the box and slipped it over the little finger on his left hand. He couldn't push it further than the top of his knuckle.

'Time you were gone. Everyone will be up in a few minutes if they're not already.'

Startled he turned to the bed. Sarah's eyes were open.

'I was just about to leave.' Hoping she hadn't seen him with the ring, he surreptitiously returned it to the box and replaced the lid while ostentatiously pouring water into the china bowl and splashing his face.

'Go! You've a reception in a palace to attend, a Tsar and royalty to meet, and a hotel to visit. The way you were talking yesterday I'm not sure what you're looking forward to most. The hotel perhaps?' she teased.

'What I'm really looking forward to is returning to you.' He dried his hands and face, and under cover of returning the towel to its hook, pushed the ring box into a corner at the back of the wash stand.

'In order to return you have to leave.'

He knotted the belt on his robe and went to her. 'A kiss to keep me going for the next few weeks,' he begged. He leaned over the bed and kissed her on the lips, a loving kiss that ended abruptly when Alexei thundered down the stairs singing the Russian national anthem at the top of his voice.

She felt tears pricking at the back of her eyes. 'Have a wonderful time.'

'Not without you, I won't. Love you.' He opened the door to the balcony and slipped out.

Sarah was waylaid by Glyn outside the dining room. He led her into the drawing room and closed the door.

'Praskovia told me you know she's pregnant.'

'I also told her I wouldn't tell anyone her secret until it became obvious,' she hedged.

'The child is mine.'

Speechless, she stared at him.

'Please say something, even if it's "How could you seduce a girl fifteen years younger than you?"'

She sank down on to the nearest chair.

'I've written to Betty and asked her for a divorce. As soon as I'm free, I'll marry Praskovia. When we return from St Petersburg, she'll join us at the table and live with me, as my wife. In effect, she'll be mistress of this house even more than she already is. I'm sorry, Sarah. I can see that I've shocked you.'

'No, you haven't,' she smiled when she regained her composure. 'This is marvellous news, Glyn. For you and Praskovia. I've been worried about you, living for work, having no one closer to you than Mr Hughes, me, Richard, and Anna. You're a man who needs a wife. And a baby as well. It's wonderful, I'm so pleased for you – all three of you.' Sarah had no idea why she was crying at such good news but her cheeks were wet with tears.

'You'll stay on in this house?'

'Where else would I go? Where's Praskovia? I must give her my love.'

'You'll look after her when I'm in St Petersburg?'

'Not that she needs me to look after her,' she avoided his question.

They heard Pyotr opening the front door.

'Our breakfast guests,' Glyn said as voices resounded in the hall. 'You'll let me tell everyone in my own time. It's not that I'm ashamed or...'

'An early breakfast before a journey isn't the best time to make an important announcement.'

'No it isn't.' Glyn kissed her cheek. 'My brother was a lucky man.'

'I was a lucky woman.' Sarah dried her tears, opened the door and went out to greet John, Alf, Ruth, and Catherine.

'Sonya will be with us in a moment,' Catherine explained when they entered the dining room. 'She left her journal in her desk in the hospital office.'

Sarah glanced through the window. The blinds were open in the hospital office and she could see Sonya and Nathan facing one another across the room. Even if Sonya had left her journal in her desk she doubted Sonya wanted it as much as she'd wanted a private word with Nathan Kharber.

Hospital, Hughesovka
1871

'...So, as I've taken a position in Mr Hughes's offices as his personal assistant, I won't be resuming my duties here when we return from St Petersburg.' Unable to face Nathan's penetrating gaze, Sonya lowered her eyes.

'Thank you for telling me in person.'

Feeling the need to elaborate, Sonya continued, 'Mr Hughes has letters that need to be translated into several languages.'

'You're an expert linguist. I'm sure he'll find your skills invaluable.' Nathan couldn't stop looking at her.

'It's not as though I'm leaving you without anyone to run the office. I've spent the last couple of weeks training Rivka and Ruth to take over the ordering and updating of the files. Sarah has an overview of everyone's job...'

He couldn't bear to listen to any more of her excuses when they both knew exactly why she was leaving. 'You'll still be living in Hughesovka, won't you? What am I saying? If you're working for Mr Hughes, you'll have to live here. So we'll still see one another.'

'Probably.' Anxious to end the conversation, she held out her hand. 'I wish you and your wife my very best wishes, Nathan. If you'll excuse me, I must go.'

He took her hand but instead of shaking it as she'd intended, he clasped it. 'Good luck with your new position, not that you need it, and tell Mr Hughes from me he's a lucky man.'

'Thank you.'

He breathed in her scent, an intoxicating mixture of vanilla and orange, entwined her fingers into his and gripped them tightly.

She looked into his eyes and kissed him lightly on the cheek before walking away. Vasya was standing in the hall, holding a tray. Sonya nodded to her and carried on walking.

Hotel Angleterre, St Petersburg
September 1871

Richard answered John's knock at the suite he

was sharing with Alexei.

'Is the accommodation to your liking?' John asked.

'Very much, Mr Hughes, thank you for arranging it and paying the bill.'

'Least I could do for the New Russia Company's hero.'

'I had no idea a city could look like this. Golden, like something out of a picture book. The buildings are so large and yet they seem to float on the water when you look at them. This hotel is even bigger and more comfortable than Mr Edwards' house. Do you know we've two bedrooms? Alexei is unpacking in his. Do you want to see him?'

'No, I came to see you, Richard.' John noticed Richard's empty Gladstone bag. 'You've finished your unpacking already?'

'I didn't have that much to put away, sir. Alexei's taking me to his tailor's so I can buy new clothes for the Tsar's reception.'

'You may find this useful.' John handed Richard an envelope. 'Mr Edwards told me you're thinking of buying a new winter coat. Make it fur, preferably sable, and it will last a lifetime. I know Mrs Ignatova gave your sister furs so you don't have to buy her any, and don't go buying her any new gowns. As a thank you for the way all three girls worked in the hospital after the mine disaster I'm paying for their court clothes. Needless to say, Mrs Ignatova, not me, will be helping the girls to choose them. There should be enough there,' he indicated the envelope, 'for a new outfit for you to wear to the palace, as well as a fur coat and a few other things besides.'

Richard took the envelope John handed him and opened it. 'Mr Hughes...'

'It's a bonus, Richard. If those trapped miners had been killed the New Russia Company would have been finished before it started. I've never witnessed bravery like yours before. Forging a path through a fall with no thought whatsoever to your own safety, only the predicament of the men entombed behind it.'

'But, sir, this is a fortune.'

'No more than you deserve. You've earned it.' John opened the door. 'Enjoy your trip out with Alexei but don't lose track of time. We'll have to leave here at seven to dine with Mrs Ignatova and the girls.'

After John left Richard counted the notes inside the envelope three times, because he couldn't believe how many were there. Alexei emerged from his room.

'Who were you talking to?'

'Mr Hughes. He called in to remind us we have to leave here at seven to dine with Mrs Ignatova.'

'Ready to go to my tailor's?'

'I'm with you.' Richard reached for his suit jacket and buttoned the envelope securely into an inner pocket.

'Do you mind if we go to my jeweller's first? I wrote ahead and asked them to prepare two trays of rings. I have to buy Ruth a wedding and engagement ring and perhaps Christmas and birthday presents for the next few years because we may be too busy to leave Hughesovka again for some time.'

'I've never been in a jeweller's shop,' Richard

confessed as they left their suite and walked down a staircase large enough to accommodate a marching band.

'You may find a Christmas or birthday present for Anna.'

'I may.' Richard thought of the money in his pocket and smiled. He had enough money to buy something really special – and not just for Anna.

St Petersburg
September 1871

Alexei asked the doorman to hail a cab to take them to the fashionable shopping street of Bolshaia Morskaia. Just like Taganrog, Richard spent most of the short journey hanging out of the window absorbing the sights before the driver halted in front of the imposing marble façade of a four-storey building studded with stained-glass windows.

Alexei opened the door, left the cab, paid and tipped the driver.

'The shop's in the basement?' Richard asked in surprise as Alexei ran down a flight of steps.

'I've heard the proprietor intends to move into larger premises soon.'

The door opened before they reached it. An assistant in white shirt, tie, and black frock coat bowed before ushering them into a lustrous wonderland of gleaming glass and mirror-backed cases. The display shelves held jewellery and ornaments fashioned from glistening gold and silver, set with precious and semi-precious stones of every shape, size, and hue.

'Mr Beletsky, we have prepared the trays you asked to see. If you'd care to follow me?' A dark-haired salesman glided over the thick carpet to greet them.

They were shown to an alcove that held a round table inlaid with mother-of-pearl. The salesman clicked his fingers and two assistants produced comfortable chairs.

'Can I get your and your friend...'

'Mr Parry,' Alexei supplied.

'Mr Parry,' the salesman bowed to Richard, 'refreshments, coffee? Cognac perhaps?'

'Cognac might loosen my purse strings,' Alexei answered.

An ornate glass, silver, and enamelled decanter and two tumblers appeared, cognac was poured and handed out. Richard looked back into the main area as he sat down. The décor was impressive: gilt and white furniture and walls, green flooring with a pile so deep it almost covered his boots, and a mass of electric lights, their reflections glistening and glittering, dazzlingly bright against the proliferation of glass and mirrors.

'Wedding bands, Mr Beletsky.' The salesman donned white gloves to handle the tray he set down on the table before Alexei.

'These are in the right size?' Alexei checked.

'The size you stated in your letter, sir.'

Alexei studied the tray for a few minutes. 'A plain platinum band, I think.' He picked one up and examined it before handing it to the salesman. 'I'd like it engraved.'

'Of course, sir, and if I might say, an excellent choice.'

Taking advantage of Alexei's preoccupation with the salesman, Richard picked up a Russian three-banded wedding ring. He slipped it on to the little finger of his left hand. It would go no further than the top of his knuckle.

'You would like that ring, sir?' one of the junior assistants hovering behind his chair asked.

Richard checked Alexei was still busy with the senior salesman. 'How much is it?'

The salesman mentioned a price considerably less than Richard had expected and, after his unexpected windfall from John Hughes, one he could well afford. 'I would like to buy other things as well. Could you set it aside without my friend seeing it?'

'We offer discretion above all else, in Gustav Fabergé, sir.' The tray of wedding rings was whisked away and replaced with an array of engagement rings. Richard was bedazzled by the variation in stones and settings.

Alexei took more time selecting an engagement ring than he had done the wedding ring. As he had done with the wedding bands, Richard waited until Alexei was busy talking to the salesman before lifting a ring from its velvet bed. It was larger than any of the others, a knotted two-headed serpent with an intricately woven body. One head was set with a diamond 'eye', the other, a sapphire.

He slipped it on to his little finger. It was the same size as the Russian wedding ring – the right size for Sarah. There was nothing else that remotely resembled the design but it was so different from Sarah's rings he wondered if she'd like it.

'A very unusual ring, Mr Parry; it would serve either as a wedding or an engagement ring.'

Richard asked the price of the snake ring. The assistant named a figure that would take a quarter of what John Hughes had given him. 'I'll take it,' he said without hesitation. 'I'd also like to see a locket and earrings, something suitable for a young girl.'

'Our enamelled daisy range might suit your requirements, sir.'

Alexei saw Richard talking to the assistant. 'Are you thinking of buying something for Anna, or one of the girls?'

'Something for Anna that she can wear with her new dress to the Winter Palace.'

'Just Anna?' Alexei fished, as the assistant brought a tray of enamelled lockets, pendants, and earrings to the table. 'Are you sure you're not thinking of one of the others. Yulia, Rivka, Miriam or ... Praskovia...'

'You see to your shopping, Alexei, I'll see to mine.'

'Just asking.' Alexei turned back to the salesman.

Richard picked out a pretty enamelled locket and earrings in blue and white. He checked the price before handing them to the assistant to add to his other purchases.

Alexei finally settled on a platinum ring set with a bar that lay upright along the length of the finger. Set with three large diamonds and surrounded by sapphires, it was elegant, beautiful, and showy; an aristocrat's ring, not a nurse's.

Richard hadn't spent as much money as Alexei,

but he didn't have a generous independent allowance like the one Alexei's grandmother had bestowed on him. Only the hope that the gifts he'd chosen for Anna and Sarah would be accepted in the loving spirit he tendered them.

Tsar's reception, Winter Palace
September 1871

Richard stood to attention alongside Glyn and Alf in front of John, Catherine Ignatova, and the girls. He felt like a tailor's dummy in his stiff, high-necked collar, black bow tie and long-tailed frock coat. But that was hardly surprising. All he seemed to have done since they'd reached St Petersburg was stand tall and erect to be measured, first in Alexei's tailor's, then for the furrier John Hughes had recommended he visit to buy his sable coat and hat.

The first thing Mrs Ignatova did after their arrival was summon her dressmaker for a consultation. The result was simple white silk gowns with long sleeves and trains for the three girls, and a white embroidered green velvet gown, cut to the same elegant pattern for herself.

Richard had been astounded by the transformation of his sister from child to poised, elegant young woman. He barely recognised her when they gathered in the reception hall of the palace before entering St George's Hall, the throne room where the ceremony was to take place. At John's prompting he offered Anna his arm, and they walked in procession, John escorting Mrs Ignatova, then Glyn and Sonya, followed by himself and Anna, Alexei with Ruth, and Alf bringing up the rear like an overgrown pageboy.

He and Anna had never seen such an elegant well-dressed throng, or so many women dressed in silks, lace, velvet, and satin. Most of the stares aimed in their direction were for Sonya, Ruth, and Anna, and the majority came from men who weren't admiring the girls' gowns but the girls.

They were shown where to stand, and when the master of ceremonies called 'Richard Parry' it was as well John was able to nudge him in the back as he hadn't recognised the Russian pronunciation of his name.

He stepped forward, walked up to the Tsar, bowed deeply the way Mr Hughes and Glyn had coached him, and waited until the Tsar hung the medal around his neck before stepping to one side and waiting for the ceremony to be repeated with Alf, then Glyn. The MC continued to describe their heroic feats throughout the bestowing of the medals and afterwards the court applauded.

They returned to the position they'd been given and continued to watch further ceremonies for a further numbing two hours.

A slight but detectable murmur of relief rippled through the hall when the Tsar and Tsarina rose from their thrones and left the hall. After an interval of several minutes the courtiers began to disperse.

'You looked as though you were having teeth pulled, Richard,' Sonya commented as Anna and Ruth examined his gold medal.

'I was terrified.' Richard glanced around. 'What

happens now?'

'Mr Edwards and I have been invited to dine with the Tsar's brother, Grand Duke Konstantin, before the ball this evening. We're hoping he'll give his continued support to our ventures,' John said.

'I'm sure he will,' Catherine reassured.

'Another ball? We've been to three this week,' Richard complained.

'Anyone would think you want to rush back to work in Hughesovka,' John smiled.

'To be honest, Mr Hughes, I wouldn't mind. This standing around dressed in fine clothes is all right once in a while but it doesn't result in anything you can be proud of.'

'It doesn't.' Alexei spotted his father across the hall. Alexei stepped forward but Nicholas passed him as if he was invisible and went directly to Catherine. Nicholas inclined his head and Catherine curtsied.

Nicholas opened the conversation. 'I've heard Sonya's good news. I was amazed to discover that your brother hadn't squandered his entire inheritance.

'Who told you about Sonya?' Catherine enquired. There was ice in her voice.

'People talk.' Nicholas gazed at Sonya and the girls for so long all three inched closer to Richard, Glyn, John, and Alexei. Realising he'd been staring, Nicholas continued. 'Have you brought Sonya here for the season, Catherine?'

'No, we're returning to Hughesovka tomorrow. Mr Edwards, Mr Mahoney, and Mr Parry were summoned to receive medals from the tsar.'

'So I saw. Congratulations.'

'Thank you, Count Beletsky,' Glyn replied.

'Aren't you going to acknowledge your son?' Catherine asked.

Nicholas Beletsky walked away without another word.

Alexei watched him leave. 'So much for trying to build bridges with my father.'

'As we all look so splendid, I insist on buying everyone ices at the Hotel Angleterre, before we leave for the ball where I expect you young people to dance the night away,' John said.

'And tomorrow, at first light, we go home,' Richard suggested hopefully.

'Good!' Anna hooked her arm into her brother's and took another look at his medal.

'You don't like St Petersburg, Anna?' John asked.

'This city and this life is all very splendid, Mr Hughes, but...'

'But?' he prompted when she didn't continue.

'It's not real. As Richard said, all this dressing up in fine clothes and visiting palaces and eating in restaurants achieves nothing. It's like a perfect dream. And nothing real or interesting ever happens in perfect dreams.'

'I've never considered life in a city that way, but you're right, Anna.' Glyn thought of Praskovia and realised just how much he was missing her. 'St Petersburg is all very wonderful but it's simply not real.'

Hospital, Hughesovka
September 1871

'Did you sort out your business with Igor?' Nathan asked Sarah when she returned to the hospital from the company head office.

'Yes, thank you. Nathan, I did. I'm sorry, but I have to leave.'

'The hospital?'

'Hughesovka.'

He turned his chair around until he faced her. 'May I ask why?'

'I'm needed back in England. I have family problems.'

'You want to bring up your child in England?'

'How did you...' it was then she remembered that Peter knew she was pregnant before she'd told him. 'You doctors know far too much about the human condition.'

'Is Glyn the father?'

'Glyn?' She repeated in confusion.

'I try to avoid gossip, but people who should know better have been saying that it was a mistake for you and your brother-in-law to share a house after your husband's death. I know it's forbidden for a brother to marry his dead brother's wife in England so I assumed...'

'You assumed wrong, Nathan. No, Glyn is not the father of my child. My leaving is nothing to do with him. In fact I have to ask you to keep an eye on Praskovia. She's pregnant with Glyn's child. He told me in confidence before he left for St Petersburg. He's hoping his wife will divorce him so he can marry her.'

'Forgive me for being so wrong, but I'm only a simple doctor.'

'You're anything but,' she smiled at his pretence of humility. 'I want to leave before Glyn and the others return as they'd only try to persuade me to stay and I really do have to go. Vlad is travelling to Taganrog tomorrow to fetch supplies and he's agreed to take me with him.'

'And from there?'

'I'll take a ship to London.'

'You have sufficient money?'

She was touched by his concern. 'More than enough. Peter left me well provided for. As for the hospital, Anna and Ruth may be young, but both are qualified to take my place. I've taught them everything I know.'

'The girls are good but I'll be sorry to see you go, Sarah. It was your generosity that secured me this position when I never thought I'd work as a doctor in Russia.'

'We've worked well together, you and I, haven't we?'

'We have. The father of your child? Does he know...'

'I appreciate your concern, Nathan, and I know you're asking because you're worried about me. But the matter is personal and no one's business but mine.'

'My apologies. I know from something Ruth said that you've tutored the girls in methods of birth control, yet you didn't practise them yourself.'

'I didn't practise what I preached,' she agreed. 'But perhaps I wanted a baby more than I wanted my reputation, although it certainly wasn't a conscious decision.'

'I can understand any woman wanting a child after losing one. You intend to keep the baby?'

'Oh, yes. I intend to keep it.'

'I'm sorry. I didn't mean to pry, it's that Vasya and I ... we can't have a child.'

'Premature menopause?'

'You recognised the symptoms?'

'I'm sorry, Nathan.'

He shrugged. 'We would like to adopt a baby.'

'I hope you're successful.'

'Thank you. Good luck to you and your child, Sarah.'

'I hope Vasya will forgive me for sneaking a kiss.' She embraced him and kissed his cheek. 'Goodbye, Nathan.'

'You'll tell the girls that you are going?'

'If you don't mind, I'd rather not, but I will write letters to everyone.'

'When are you leaving?'

'Vlad is picking me up at four o'clock in the morning. Goodbye and thank you for everything.'

'I'll look after our hospital for you, Matron. If you should wish to return...'

'I won't, Dr Kharber. Thank you, it's been good knowing you.' She opened the door and walked out of his office and the front door.

Hughesovka, Glyn Edwards' house
September 1871

Sarah was dressed packed and ready to leave

Glyn's house at two thirty. Restless, impatient, she sat at her desk and flicked through the letters she'd written. To Praskovia, thanking her for her friendship and wishing her well with her baby and Glyn, and enclosing money to buy fabric to make baby clothes. Glyn for being a true brother. Anna, Ruth, Yulia, and all the girls she'd trained in the hospital for being conscientious and exemplary students. John Hughes for giving her and Peter the opportunity of a lifetime. Alexei and Ruth a letter congratulating them on their marriage and some roubles to buy a present.

The letter that had been the most difficult to write was in an unsealed envelope.

She opened and re-read it.

My dear, dear Richard,

I'm so sorry to leave you without saying goodbye but I know I wouldn't be able to do so without shedding tears.

My family need me in England. I have deliberately timed my departure before your return from St Petersburg because I know you would try to dissuade me and I'm afraid I would be weak enough to listen to you and in so doing so only succeed in upsetting both of us.

I love you and will always remember you fondly but it would never work between us. I will keep in touch with Anna so there's no need for you to write to me.

Thank you for showing me that there can be life – and love – after loss.

Your friend,
Sarah Edwards.

She replaced it in the envelope, sealed it, and placed it at the bottom of the pile.

Hughesovka
September 1871

The house was in darkness when Sarah stole outside. She carried her travelling bag. Vlad removed his boots to minimise the noise of his footsteps, went up to her room, and hauled out her trunk. She glanced across the road before climbing into the troika. Nathan was standing, holding a candle, at the window of his office. He smiled at her. She smiled back, waved, and sat in the troika.

A bitterly cold wind blew from the north, the precursor of winter. She was glad. It gave her an excuse to explain away the tears on her cheeks.

Chapter Thirty-three

Hughesovka, Glyn Edwards' house
September 1871

Pyotr opened the door the moment he saw Catherine Ignatova's carriage turn into the drive. Glyn was first out. He ran to Praskovia who was waiting for him in the porch, swung her from her feet, and hugged her.

Richard, Alexei, and Anna watched in astonishment.

He turned to them. 'I'll marry Praskovia the moment I'm free, but until then, she'll be the mistress of this house in every way, just as she would if we were legally married. And,' Glyn couldn't help himself, his smile broadened, 'we're having a baby.'

Dumbfounded, Alexei and Richard remained stock-still, but Anna kissed Praskovia on her way into the house. 'Congratulations, Mr Edwards, Praskovia.'

'I'm so pleased for you, both of you,' Richard followed her inside.

'Wonderful news,' Alexei kissed Praskovia's cheek.

'I have a meal ready in the dining room, soup and snacks, I thought you wouldn't want something heavy just before bed.'

'Perfect,' Glyn couldn't stop smiling or looking at Praskovia.

Richard looked around the hall. It was after ten but there was no sign of Sarah. Given the noise they were making he'd expected her to join them.

'Is Sarah working late?' he asked Praskovia when Glyn finally stopped talking long enough for him to edge a word in.

'She left a week ago, Mr Richard...'

'Richard.' Glyn corrected.

'Went? Where?' Richard was mystified.

'England. She left letters for everyone. In the one she wrote to me, she said she had to return to England for family reasons.'

'But she was brought up in a workhouse. She has no family in England, or anywhere for that matter, besides me and my brother,' Glyn said.

'Where's my letter?' Richard questioned urgently.

'In your room,' Praskovia answered.

'Richard!' Anna called after him as he rushed up the stairs.

Praskovia went to the tray on the hall stand, sorted through the mail that had arrived for Glyn and handed him the one Sarah had written. 'I put your letters in your rooms,' she explained to Anna and Alexei.

Glyn opened and read his letter. 'This reference Sarah makes to family doesn't make sense. Apart from a few friends, my brother and his wife in Merthyr, and the people Sarah worked with in the hospital in London, she has no one in England or Wales.'

Richard rushed back down the stairs. He was still wearing his coat and hat. He picked up the travelling bag Pyotr had just carried into the hall.

'We've only just got here. Where are you going at this time of night?' Alexei asked.

'To get the woman I love before she leaves the country.'

Glyn's eyes rounded in shock.

'You and Sarah ... I mean Mrs Edwards,' Alexei was only marginally less astounded than Glyn, but unlike Glyn he was capable of speech. 'And I thought Ruth and I were clever in concealing how we felt about one another.'

'I love Sarah and I will marry her if it's the last thing I do,' Richard emphasised.

'Hopefully it won't be,' Alexei observed.

'Can I borrow Agripin, Alexei?'

'No. You're not that good a rider. Besides, if you

want to catch up with Sarah ... how long ago did you say she left?' Alexei questioned Praskovia.

'A week. Vlad had to go to Taganrog to fetch supplies. She went with him, at four in the morning, or so Dr Kharber said.'

'In the hospital's troika?' Alexei said thoughtfully.

'Yes,' Praskovia confirmed.

'You need a carriage, Richard,' Alexei said. 'Pyotr, run to my grandmother's. Tell her we need to borrow the six-horse carriage that's just brought us here, but it needs to be harnessed with a fresh team. We also need Egor, he's my grandmother's most experienced driver,' he assured Richard. 'And his assistant Rurik if she can spare him.'

Pyotr left.

'With two experienced drivers and frequent changes of horses, and you can trust Egor to know which inns and private houses to approach, you may catch up with Mrs Edwards within three or four days of her reaching Taganrog. Just hope no ship was ready to set sail when she arrived.'

'Here, Richard, you'll need money.' Glyn recovered his senses enough to reach for his wallet. He opened it, took out all the large-denomination bills, and handed them over.

'I have your blessing, sir?' Richard asked.

'You have my blessing to try.'

'We wish you every success and happiness, Richard.' Praskovia looked up at Glyn. 'How could we do otherwise?'

Hughesovka
September 1871

'The only drawback will be the horses. Without frequent changes they'll tire and slow you down,' Alexei warned Richard as he saw him off. 'Egor and Rurik will take it in turns to drive, I've told them that you won't mind if the one who's resting rides inside the carriage with you.'

'Of course I won't mind.'

'Go get her, Richard. Hughesovka is getting to be a more interesting place every day.'

'You sure you won't come with me?'

'I'd only be in the way when you find her. I hope you won't have to go to England to do that.'

'So do I.' Richard meant it, because he knew that he wouldn't have a clue where to look for her in London, let alone an entire country.

Taganrog
September 1871

Sarah, wrapped in the furs Catherine Ignatova had given her, left the consulate after lunch to take her afternoon walk in the public garden of Taganrog. An ice-laden Arctic wind was blowing through the town and there'd been no let up for a month, or so the consul had told her. Even worse than the drop in temperature, it had prevented any ships leaving port for two weeks.

The consul and his wife had been kind, putting their largest and most comfortable guest room at her disposal, and insisting she share their meals and evening entertainments, but as she'd made the decision to leave Russia she couldn't wait to sail.

It didn't help that she hadn't formulated a plan as to what she'd do when she reached England, other than 'rent a house' until the baby was born. The life insurance Peter had taken out on their marriage would cover her and the baby's living costs but after Glyn's house she suspected she would find an existence without friends somewhat lonely.

She could hardly return to Merthyr in her condition, as Peter's brother Edward and the friends they'd made in the town before they'd left for Russia would know the baby wasn't Peter's. And, as she'd discovered before Peter had entered her life, London could be a lonely place. It also wasn't the healthiest place to bring up a child.

Thoughts whirled in her mind like the dead leaves at her feet as she strolled down an avenue of trees. She came to a seat. Tired, she sank down on the bench, grateful for the protection the trees offered from the weather.

She tried to banish images of the lonely life she suspected she and her child would lead in Britain with no uncles and aunts to visit. Would they make friends – good friends as she'd done in Hughesovka?

'I warn you, no matter how far or fast you travel, I'll track you down. We're meant to be together.'

She looked up. Richard was in front of her, barely recognisable in a sable coat and hat that somehow made him appear older and sterner than his years.

She rubbed her eyes, as much to wipe away a

tear as to make sure he wasn't a mirage. 'How did you find me?'

'I went to the consulate. The doorman told me you often walked here after lunch.'

'I left you a letter.'

'I read it.'

'You, me ... it's impossible, Richard.'

'Glyn and Praskovia will marry when he's free and he's nearly fifteen years older than her.'

'It's different when the man is older.'

'Why?'

'Because that's the way it is. I have to go back to England...'

'For family reasons, or so you said in your letter. Glyn told me you have no family other than Peter's.'

'I don't.'

Richard sat beside her on the bench. 'I spoke to the consul. There's an Anglican Church and vicar in Taganrog. We could be married by special licence tomorrow because we'd qualify as travellers.'

'You're too young to know what you want from life...'

'I'm not. So you're older than me. No couple are ever perfectly suited. Alexei never thought he'd be allowed to marry Ruth because of their religious differences until Mr Hughes built a town on the steppe. Mr Edwards and Praskovia are living together as man and wife although he has a wife living in Merthyr. And no one in Hughesovka is horrified.'

'Hughesovka hasn't a chapel minister or vicar yet.'

'If they're easily shocked they won't last long in the town because Mr Hughes has made sure anything is possible in Hughesovka. Even us.'

It had been so easy to run from him when he'd been away. It wasn't possible when he kissed her and held her close.

She revelled in the warmth of his lips on hers, the feel of his arms wrapped around her shoulders, the comfort he offered.

'I have something for you.' He reached into his pocket and pulled out the box that held the snake ring. He opened it and the diamond and sapphire set in the heads winked up at her in the cold afternoon light.

'It's beautiful, Richard.'

'Do you mean that?'

'Yes.'

'You're not lying...'

'I promise you I am not lying now, nor will I ever lie to you, but there's a condition. If you ever tire of me...'

'I never will.'

She took her hand from her fur muff and laid it across his mouth. It lay warm on his lips.

'If you tire of me,' she repeated, 'you'll tell me, and allow me to walk away from you with dignity so we can both remember the happy times.'

'There'll only be happy times for us from now on, Sarah. I won't allow you to run from me again. That much I promise you.'

'There's something else you don't know.'

'What?'

She smiled. For once she would be able to surprise a man – and Richard was a man. The boy she'd seduced had grown up. 'You won't be the only person in my life or my family for much longer, Richard. There'll soon be another.'

Epilogue

Owen Parry's ironworker's cottage
Broadway, Treforest, Pontypridd. Evening, 1956

My pillows are soft, the temptation to lay back on them too great. So much happened in 1871 and with the benefit of hindsight I can see that year was a turning point. The year the ironworks were finished, although not capable of production.

It was the year John and Glyn began to turn a profit from their respective mines. The year Alexei married his childhood sweetheart, and Sarah fled Hughesovka and I took her place for a few weeks, as Matron of the hospital at the untried age of fifteen.

I picked up the file of letters and flicked through them until I found the ones I wanted.

Boot Inn
High Street
Merthyr Tydfil

August 4th 1871

Dear Glyn,

I have sad news. My father breathed his last four

days ago. He was laid to rest beside my mother this morning. He left everything he owned to me. I received a good offer for the Boot the day after he died and took it. So, there is nothing to keep me in Merthyr and that brings me to my next piece of news.

Morgan and Owen Parry have been nagging me for some time to allow them to go to Russia to join their brother and sister. Given their age I thought it best to accompany them.

Edward hasn't been the same since Judith died last month – he said he was going to write to you about his loss – if he hasn't, I'm sorry. I didn't want to be the one to tell you but thinking about it, it's only right you should know. When Edward heard me and the boys making plans he decided to join us.

Edward asked if he could live with us, as he is your brother I told him he could. I know from Richard and Anna's letters to Owen and Morgan that they are living with you. Would you find another house for all four Parrys so we can live in private as a family for the first time in our married life?

Try not to be angry, Glyn, but I have to confess that I've kept a secret from you. Don't blame Edward or anyone else for not writing to you about it. I begged Edward and others to keep silent because I wanted to do what was best for my father.

You have a daughter, Glyn. I named her Harriet Maud after my mother and grandmother. She was born nearly eight months after you left Merthyr, at six o'clock in the morning on Sunday February 5th 1871. There is nothing of me in her. As Edward says, and poor Judith used to say, 'she is all Edwards.'

She has your dark eyes and hair, doesn't know what it is to be still or quiet, and is a healthy child. I have spent as much time with her as I could. The maids looked after her when I was busy in the inn and I've been careful to only leave her with the better-spoken, better-behaved girls.

She knows you are her father as I show her your photograph every night when I tuck her into bed.

As I've written, I've been busy looking after the Parry boys but most of all helping my father. The reason I didn't tell you about Harriet is I knew you'd want me to take her to Russia.

I couldn't do that because the first thing Dad said to me after she was born was, 'I suppose you'll be taking her away from me to Glyn in Russia now.' He couldn't bear the thought of not being able to see his only grand-child growing up. Now he's gone there's nothing to keep me here, or us apart any longer. Owen and Morgan are excited about seeing Richard and Anna again. They've showed me the letters they've received from them.

I couldn't believe what I was reading. Fancy Richard Parry, little runny-nosed Richard Parry, working as your assistant, and Anna the kitchen skivvy, a nurse. I would never have thought it possible. Not even in a land of heathens.

Enough of my ramblings and more of the plans Edward has made. All of us, that's Owen and Morgan as well as Edward, me, and Harriet, have decided to travel to Russia with a view to staying permanently.

The photographs you sent of your house suggest it could be made comfortable once it's been refurnished and decorated. I was relieved to hear you've found a good English-speaking housekeeper as well as a cook and servants. I know the town is still being built. I hope it will be a fitting place to bring up Harriet.

We'll be leaving Merthyr early next week and taking

a train to Southampton. Edward says we'll be following the same route you took and we'll be travelling with other collier and ironworker immigrants bound for Hughesovka.

Richard will have a surprise too. Don't say anything to him but I know Alice, that was Perkins, and is Wilkins now, has written to him. Her husband died a month ago. He left half his money to his children and half to her. It's a tidy sum and she wants to escape from her father and the gossips and go to Richard. At least now he'll be able to marry the girl of his choice.

That's all for now, Glyn.

There'll be no point in me writing when we're travelling as I'll reach you before any more of my letters.

Edward tells me he hopes we'll reach Taganrog by September or early October at the latest, which he said will be before the really cold weather sets in. It would be nice if you could come to meet us, but if not, Edward says he will arrange transport for us.

With fondest regards,

Your wife Betty and daughter Harriet

I didn't have to imagine the look on Glyn Edwards' face when he read Betty's letter. I saw it myself when I walked into the drawing room minutes after he'd opened the envelope. But I had to imagine the look on Richard's face when he read his letter from Alice because I was working in the hospital when he returned from Taganrog and went through his mail.

I presume he read it several times because it had more creases than any of the others in the box.

High View
High Street
Merthyr Tydfil

August 4th 1871

Dear Richard,

Are you shocked to hear from me after all this time? I think of you and the promises we made one another often. I still love you as I know you love me. You must have heard even in Russia that my father forced me to marry Josiah Wilkins after he caught us on the mountain together. He threatened me with all sorts if I didn't. I had no choice. Josiah died a month ago. I don't want to write what it was like being married to such a horrid old man but I will say that I never stopped loving or thinking of you.

I can't wait to leave Merthyr. You know what people are like here and how they point fingers. After you left there was nothing but gossip, about the way your mother dropped dead when she saw how the Paskeys had beaten you, and how the Paskeys raped Anna. But you know all that. Anyway I thought we'd be better off making our lives in Russia rather than you come back here.

Betty Edwards said that you write to Owen and Morgan and that you and Anna are living in Mr Glyn Edwards' house. Well, that'll have to change, Richard. I want my own house and I'd rather not have your brothers living with us, or Anna. Not after what the Paskeys did to her. I'd feel dirty every time she came near me. It might be as well if you look for a house for us as soon as you get this. Betty says her husband has found servants that can speak English;

I hope you can do the same. Betty also said the shops won't be as good as the ones in Cardiff or even Merthyr but she said that Mr Glyn Edwards wrote that he can order most things to be delivered. Please don't order any major items of furniture before I get there. I'd like to organise our first home together.

There's no point in answering this letter. By the time you get it I will almost be there.

Looking forward to our life together.

Love Alice.

There was another letter written the same day from Merthyr to Hughesovka. It was more of a note from Edward to Glyn.

Cartref
High Street
Merthyr Tydfil

August 4th 1871

Dear Glyn,

I know Betty has written to you and Alice to Richard.

I hope you can forgive me for not telling you about your daughter. I felt guilty about it from the beginning but Betty was adamant that she wanted to stay to care for her father and your letters were so full of the difficulties you were encountering in setting up the works and the collieries while grieving for Peter I thought it best to go along with what she wanted.

We should reach Taganrog in September or October at the latest. if I can arrange transport to Hughesovka I will.

Like Betty there's one piece of news I hoped to keep not only from you but Anna and Richard as well, but I'm afraid I can't, not any longer. The Paskeys were tried for raping Anna but the case collapsed because there were no witnesses to the actual assault. The judge even told Jenny Swine she was lucky not to find herself in the dock for causing grievous bodily harm to Ianto.

Deputy Perkins fired the Paskeys and they haven't found regular work since. Both have signed up as ironworkers with Mr Hughes's agents. They travelled out a month ago, which is why I booked passage for Betty, Alice, and the boys so late. I didn't want to be on the same boat as them.

I hope this reaches you before the Paskeys so you can be prepared

If you can put a word in with Mr Hughes for me I'd be grateful. I'm not expecting the same job or wages I had in the drift mine in Merthyr but frankly Merthyr is such a lonely place without Judith I'd welcome anything.

Your brother, Edward.

I replaced all three letters in the files, closed my eyes and drifted once more through my memories. This time one I'd only heard about.

September 1871 – the year Sarah Edwards and my brother Richard married in a simple ceremony in the Anglican Church in Taganrog, two days before they came face to face on the Taganrog quayside with Edward Edwards, Betty Edwards, Alice Wilkins, and my brothers Morgan and Owen...

The publishers hope that this book has given you enjoyable reading. Large Print Books are especially designed to be as easy to see and hold as possible. If you wish a complete list of our books please ask at your local library or write directly to:

Magna Large Print Books
Magna House, Long Preston,
Skipton, North Yorkshire.
BD23 4ND

This Large Print Book for the partially sighted, who cannot read normal print, is published under the auspices of

THE ULVERSCROFT FOUNDATION

THE ULVERSCROFT FOUNDATION

... we hope that you have enjoyed this Large Print Book. Please think for a moment about those people who have worse eyesight problems than you ... and are unable to even read or enjoy Large Print, without great difficulty.

You can help them by sending a donation, large or small to:

The Ulverscroft Foundation,
1, The Green, Bradgate Road,
Anstey, Leicestershire, LE7 7FU,
England.
or request a copy of our brochure for more details.

The Foundation will use all your help to assist those people who are handicapped by various sight problems and need special attention.

Thank you very much for your help.